Aviation Chicago Timeline

MICHAEL HAUPT

EAA # 585747

AVIATION CHICAGO PRESS

Aviation Chicago Timeline

By Michael Haupt

Edition 1, Revision 0
Aviation Chicago Press • Mt. Prospect, IL
Aviation-Chicago.com

Publisher's Cataloging-in-Publication Data provided by Five Rainbows Cataloging Services

NAMES	Haupt, Michael, 1947, Author.
TITLE	Aviation Chicago Timeline / Michael Haupt.
DESCRIPTION	Edition 1. • Mount Prospect, IL : Aviation Chicago Press, 2018. Includes bibliographical references and index.
IDENTIFIERS	LCCN 2018911629 • ISBN 978-1-7327990-1-1 (hardcover) ISBN 978-1-7327990-0-4 (pbk.) • ISBN 978-1-7327990-2-8 (ebook)
SUBJECTS	LCSH: Aeronautics—Illinois—Chicago—History • Aeronautics—Exhibitions. Air mail service—History • Chicago (Ill.)—History • BISAC: TRANSPORTATION / Aviation / History. • HISTORY / United States / State & Local / Midwest (IA, IL, IN, KS, MI, MN, MO, ND, NE, OH, SD, WI)
CLASSIFICATION	LCC TL522.I4 H37 2018 (print) • LCC TL522.I4 (ebook) DDC 629.13/0977311—dc23.

Proudly Produced in the United States of America.
Printed on archival paper.

EDITOR	Cynthia Clampitt	worldplate.com
COVER & OVERALL DESIGN	M Hurley	teknigram.com
DETAIL DESIGN & TYPESETTING	Linda Shew Wolf	networktype.com
FINAL QUALITY CONTROL	Alexandra Uth	loomisandlyman.com
AUTHOR PHOTOGRAPH	Peter Wagner	peterwagnercreative.com

About the Book

A viation Chicago Timeline traces the pivotal role that Chicago played in the development of aviation in the United States. Long before the Wright Brothers took to the air, Chicago had an active balloon community, and Octave Chanute was providing the latest aviation research to scores of experimenters. In the 1910s, the city was bustling with flight schools, airplane manufacturers, air shows, and aviation developers. By the 1920s, Chicago was the core of the U.S. air mail system and easily transitioned into a major air passenger hub. Throughout its history, Chicago has produced leaders who shaped U.S. aviation policy, including Benjamin Lipsner (the first Superintendent of Aerial Mail of the Post Office Dept.), Daniel McCracken (major designer of the Air Commerce Act of 1926 and the the first Assistant Secretary of Commerce for Aviation), and Samuel Skinner (Secretary of Transportation under Pres. George H.W. Bush).

Aviation Chicago Timeline offers a fascinating account of more than a thousand events documenting the development of aviation in Chicago and the surrounding region. The author, Michael Haupt, provides a series of accessibly written stories that portray Chicago's gripping aviation history in an inviting and interesting fashion. Haupt's meticulous research, attention to detail, and exhaustive notes make this book an essential tool for everyone interested in the history of aviation in the U.S., but especially in Chicago.

TABLE OF CONTENTS

FOREWORD

In the year 2018, aviation in the Chicago area is still relatively new, compared to other modes of transportation, like trains, a technology developed in the early 19th century, and maritime travel, which goes back thousands of years.

And even after the Wright brothers proved the possibility of three-axis control of an aircraft in 1903, on the sands of Kitty Hawk, NC, in the Chicago area it would still be several years before anyone could claim to see a heavier-than-air aircraft ascend into the heavens. In that time, this advanced technology was more like a rumor. Unless one saw it for themselves, it was hard to believe that such a thing was possible.

When I first read through Michael Haupt's book in manuscript form, I thought I knew a lot about Chicago Aviation. Mike's attention to the facts showed me I did not. What it did demonstrate was that I had forgotten much of what I thought I knew, and Mike's presentation nudged me into remembering.

And then there were the pleasant surprises, like my grandfather Pierce "Scotty" O'Carroll, making an appearance as the operator of Monarch Air Service back in the 1930s, when Midway Airport was named "Municipal" and a pilot trying to make a go of it during the Great Depression was free to starve at his chosen profession.

Mike Haupt has missed nothing. When reading along I would think, "I bet he won't write about the Gordon Bennett Races." Nope. Or the Gray Goose Fire? Not a chance. The *Graf Zeppelin* arrival over Chicago's skyline? He got that one too!

That's what is so valuable about Michael Haupt's book, his great attention to detail. It reminds me of an Ansel Adams photograph of Yosemite—one sees the great bulk of Half Dome, but also the details of the rock, crevices, and foliage, crystal clear on the photographer's negative.

This compelling book will no doubt become required reading for those interested in Chicago Aviation history.

Christopher Lynch, 2018 • Aviation historian and author of:
Chicago's Midway Airport: The First Seventy-Five Years

Introduction

Chicago, the Aviation Capital

Most people today consider Chicago to be an "aviation capital" only in its demonstrated ability to thoroughly disrupt air travel throughout the nation. Many who are older or have an interest in Chicago history realize that Municipal/Midway Airport was the nation's aviation crossroads for decades.

Is there any city showing a wider interest in aviation than Chicago?

When one thinks of U.S. aviation centers, cities such as Dayton, OH, Hammondsport, NY, Seattle, WA, and Wichita, KS come to mind, not Chicago. But in fact, Chicago arguably surpassed all these cities in the early decades of the 20th century. As an article about aviation in the September 18, 1910, issue of the *Chicago Tribune* proclaimed:

> It is doubtful if there is any city on the continent which can show a greater activity and a wider growth of interest in aviation than Chicago. It is the outcropping in a new field of the same old celebrated "Chicago spirit" which thrives, as it does under no other conditions, when encountering opposition and obstacle.[1]

To support this bold claim, we have only to look at the facts:

- In 1910, dozens of companies were building and selling airplanes around Chicago, plus a hundred amateurs were building their own aircraft of all sorts of designs.

- In 1911, Chicago hosted the largest air show of that era. To this day, it remains the largest air show held in the center of a major city.

- In 1911, the E.B. Heath Aerial Vehicle Co., known nationwide as Heath's Airplane Trading Post, operated a catalog supply company

providing barnstormers and amateur builders with hard-to-get parts
for any and all airplanes.

- In 1912, Chicago's first permanent airport, Cicero Field, became the
busiest airport in the country.

- In the late 1910s, the U.S. Post Office Dept.[a] conducted numerous air
mail tests in Chicago. After the Postal Service initiated regular air
mail service, Chicago was the hub for numerous routes as well as the
site for the Air Mail Service's maintenance and repair facility.

- In the 1920s, when the Commerce Dept. initiated the reorganized
Contract Air Mail (CAM) Service, Chicago was the origin for 9 out of
34 CAM routes.

Chicago's influence spread far beyond the city.

- Chicago authors and editors produced the earliest books on aviation.
Even before the Wright Brothers, Octave Chanute published *Progress
of Flying Machines* in 1894. In 1909, the first aviation books in the
country were *First Lessons in Aeronautics* by M.K. Kasmar and
*Vehicles of the Air: A Popular Exposition of Modern Aeronautics with
Working Drawings* by Victor Loughhead. In 1912, *Aerial Age* became
the nation's first aviation periodical.

- Many of the country's major airplane manufacturers were founded by
aviators rooted in Chicago, including: Edward Heath, Benny Howard,
Emil "Matty" Laird, Bill Lear, Allan Loughhead (of Lockheed), James
McDonnell, Glenn L. Martin, Eddie Stinson, Bill Stout (Ford
Tri-Motor), Chauncy "Chance" Vought, "Buck" Weaver (of WACO)
and others.

- Aviation corporations and organizations started or based in Chicago
include: Air Line Pilots Organization, American Airlines, Challenger
Air Pilots Assn., Early Birds of Aviation, Underwriters Laboratories,
and United Air Lines.

- Practically all professional aviators in the first half of the 20th
Century spent a lot of time flying in and around Chicago.

Chicago's aviation impact is undeniable and it was not all hype
when in 1929, this aviation school ad described Chicago as one of the
school's advantages:

---

a   The Post Office Dept. reorganized as the U.S. Postal Service in 1971.

Only Greer Students have the advantage that Chicago, "the Air Capital of the United States," can give them—the world-famous Municipal Airport about which are grouped the hangars of every famous transport company East and Midwest—endless varieties of industries are here both in the field of Aviation and out of it. Here, if anywhere, are the greatest opportunities for the graduate.[2]

Aviation Chicago Timeline

The *Aviation Chicago Timeline (ACT)*, as its title implies, is a chronology of aviation milestones in the greater Chicago region. It provides a unique perspective of Chicago as the major center of aviation in this country, if not the world.

Why another book? Especially when there is such an abundance of well-written works?

ACT does not attempt to provide a comprehensive narrative of the development of the area's aerial activities, as is excellently done in David Young's *Chicago Aviation: An Illustrated History* or Howard Scamehorne's *Balloons to Jets, A Century of Aeronautics in Illinois 1855–1955*. This volume does not present an abundantly illustrated and thorough examination of one aspect of Chicago aviation as does Chris Lynch's *Chicago's Midway Airport: The First Seventy-Five Years*, David Kent's *Images of Aviation: Midway Airport*, and Michael Branigan's *A History of Chicago's O'Hare Airport*. *ACT* is not a collection of marvelously fascinating anecdotes and oral histories (hangar stories) such as are found in Nick Selig's *Lost Airports of Chicago* and *Forgotten Chicago Airfields*. Nor does *ACT* contain the wonderful verbal descriptions of a popular institution such as those contained in Gerry and Janet Souter's *Chicago Air and Water Show: A History of Wings Above the Waves* or Gary Krist's meticulously researched and documented yet wonderfully readable *City of Scoundrels*.

Why another book? Especially when there is such an abundance of well-written works? *ACT* arises from my experience while reading these and other sources and having difficulty fitting things together. Chicago has such an abundance of aviation activity that no one book can tell the whole story. While reading about some event, I'd have vague recollections of having read something different about it or something similar, but would have little luck in finding the details. *ACT* strives to address this complexity by making it easier to fit the pieces together.

Why a timeline? As any viewer of detective shows knows, the best way to unravel a mystery is to draw a timeline and fit the pieces into it. Our goal is to piece together the rich tapestry of Chicago's aviation history.

ACT is, by definition, Chicago-centric. This definitely presents a distorted view. The brief bios of individuals often omit many life accomplishments or summarize them in a single sentence. The purpose of this volume is to offer an overview to demonstrate the quantity and breadth of aviation activity in the Chicago area rather than provide a comprehensive look at every individual and topic.

However, no topic is an island.[a] Chicago's aviation did not take place apart from everything else. To provide context, there are short entries about other aviation activity outside Chicago as well as non-aviation events both in Chicago and in the rest of the world.

Because this book is focused on the Chicago area, all cities and towns mentioned are in Illinois unless otherwise specified. Likewise, except where specified, streets and other locations are in Cook County.

A Note about Notes

ACT incorporates both footnotes and endnotes. The few footnotes included are for the reader's convenience, pointing out ancillary information about the topic without the need to turn to the back of the book. Often these notes identify conflicts of differing dates for an event or of the spelling of names.

Even a casual perusal of *ACT* reveals a copious number of endnotes. Traditionally, notes perform two important purposes: to give proper credit to others and to demonstrate a basis for the statements being made. This work is no exception. Its compilation would not have been possible were it not for countless hours invested by scores of others referenced here. Also, in this age of "alternative facts," it is sadly necessary to demonstrate that the facts presented here do not come from my imagination but reflect real people and events.

However, it is my hope that for some readers, the notes will provide a gateway to more information. As I stated at the beginning, *ACT* does not tell a story. But stories are essential to understanding what happened. After reading a brief writeup in one of the entries, check out one of the references for a fuller description of what happened. Your investment will be rewarded.

---

a   Apologies to John Donne.

All of the newer works are available at a library. If you find yourself wanting more information, consider purchasing a copy. Many, if not most, of the older works are available online in digital versions, many for free or for a minimal charge.

Take some time and check out documents of the period. Look at the *Chicago Tribune* account of Gen. Balbo's flight into the Century of Progress Exposition. It doesn't just tell you how many planes landed when, but gives a feel for what the reception was like. And while you probably don't want to read Chanute's 1894 *Progress of Flying Machines* from cover to cover, it's well worth spending a few minutes perusing the digital book to get a sense of aerial activity before the Wrights flew.

If You See Something … Say Something

As an ardent lover of facts, I must make a confession to you: This book is wrong. Not very wrong … just not completely precise or absolutely complete in some cases.

Despite my best efforts and countless hours of research plus several very thorough technical reviews, exhaustive copy editing, and detailed proofreading, it is inevitable that some errors will creep in and need to be eliminated. Primarily this is because of incomplete, or even conflicting, information. Unfortunately, sources don't always cooperate by providing all the information that I would like. Often an event is described without stating when it took place. Other times dates are given as "in 1927 or 1928" or "in the early 1930s." Details about people, companies, and airports are often vague and names vary.

Finally, there are numerous omissions, ones that I'm aware of and others that I'm not. Limitation of time and space prevent the book from ever being *complete*. As an author, I'm forced to choose what to include and what to omit. But to make an intelligent choice, I need to know what I don't know.

That's where you come in. Some of you will catch errors in the text or will have more detailed information than is presented. Others will wonder "Why didn't he include…?"

If you see something, *say something*. Don't just grumble and keep your thoughts to yourself. Let me know.

It's my intent to release future editions, in which I can correct errors and elaborate on the current content. But corrections can't wait until the next edition is printed. The site, *Aviation-Chicago.com,* has a section devoted to *ACT* and will include corrected and expanded entries as the information becomes available.

The *AviationChicago.com* site also has provisions for you to contribute content or simply to comment on the book itself. Or you can email me at *content@Aviation-Chicago.com*. I can't guarantee how quickly the suggestions will be incorporated, but they will all be welcomed and considered.

Thank you all for your support, and Blue Skies Forever.

Pre-1900

1783   Montgolfiers' Balloon

In France, the Montgolfier brothers, Joseph Michel and Jacques Étienne, pioneered flights with hot air balloons. At Versailles on September 19, they conducted the first flight with living beings aboard—a rooster, a duck, and a sheep. Two tethered manned ascents were made on October 15. The first free flight on November 21 reached an altitude of 3,000 ft. and traveled about 5.5 mi.

A little over a year later, on January 7, 1785, Jean-Pierre Blanchard and Dr. John Jeffries made the first flight across the English Channel, from Dover to Calais, using a Montgolfier balloon.[3]

1800/05/07   First European Leaves Chicago

Jean Baptiste Point du Sable[a] sold his trading post to Jean La Lime and moved further west to St. Charles, MO.

Born in Haiti, du Sable had been trading furs with the French in the Great Lakes region since the 1770s. By 1790, he had a well-established trading post at the mouth of the north bank of the Chicago River near the current Chicago Tribune building.

Du Sable's trading post was on 800 acres of land and included a barn, mill, smokehouse, workshop, and other small buildings. It became a major provisioning post for other traders throughout the region.

Four years after du Sable's departure, La Lime sold the duSable settlement to John Kinzie, who has often, mistakenly, been called the "Father of Chicago."[4]

---

a   Pacyga and other sources refer to "de Sable."

1837/03/04   Chicago Becomes Chicago

The State of Illinois granted Chicago its City Charter.[5]

1847/06/10   *Chicago Tribune* Goes to Press

The first issue of the *Chicago Daily Tribune* was published on June 10, 1847. The founders, John E. Wheeler, K.C. Forrest, and James Kelly produced 400 copies of the four-page newspaper.[6]

Joseph Medill became a co-owner and editor of the newspaper in 1855, making it a strong voice for abolition and the Republican Party.[7]

1848/04/10   I & M Canal Opens

Begun in 1836, the Illinois and Michigan Canal connected the Chicago River at Bridgeport with the Illinois River 96 miles away at LaSalle. When opened in 1848 it became possible to travel or ship goods by water from the Atlantic Ocean at New York through the Erie Canal and Great Lakes to Chicago then through the I&M Canal to the Mississippi River, ending at New Orleans and the Gulf of Mexico.

The I&M Canal became the lynchpin for transportation throughout the Midwest. It was natural, therefore, that railroads would similarly center in Chicago to take advantage of existing water connections. Later, airlines would follow the same pattern by connecting to the railroads.[8]

1848/11/20   Rails Reach Chicago

Chicago took the first steps toward becoming the transportation hub of the nation when William Ogden's Galena and Chicago Union Railroad began operation.[9]

1853   First Manned Glider

The first manned flight was made in a glider created by Sir George Cayley in England. Cayley, regarded as the "Father of Aeronautics," established the principles of flying machines with fixed wings, a pilot in a fuselage, and a combined tail of vertical fin and rudder. Cayley also pioneered the idea of lift coming from a shaped wing.[10]

1855/07/04   First Illinois Balloon Ascension

Silas M. Brooks, a pioneering American balloonist, made the first balloon ascension in Illinois when he launched the *Eclipse* from a vacant lot at Randolph and Peoria streets on July 4, 1855. From New England, Brooks traveled the country prior to the Civil War, amazing people with the ability to go as high as birds.[11]

1855/12/31   Chicago Pulls Itself Out of the Mud

During 1856 and 1857, Chicago buildings were raised up to six feet by jacks and new foundations were laid below. George Pullman, who later produced railway cars, developed a system for lifting very large buildings slowly and without damage. Pullman's company raised the city's prestigious Tremont House while it was occupied and without cracking the plaster or breaking a glass.

Sanitation in Chicago was horrendous, resulting in regular outbreaks of cholera and other diseases. An estimated 5% of the population died in 1854 from the unhealthy conditions. The city needed a sewer system. Because the streets were nearly level with the river and lake, it was impossible to bury pipes with sufficient slope to drain.

The solution was to build the sewer above the current street level by raising all the streets and adjacent buildings above the pipes. Chicago created the Board of Sewerage Commission to implement the solution.[12]

1861/07/21   First Military Observation Balloon

The first use of a balloon for military observation was at the First Battle of Bull Run during the Civil War.[13]

1865/12/25   Stockyards Open

On Christmas Day 1865, the first livestock arrived at the newly constructed Union Stock Yard & Transit Co. on the South Side of Chicago. For over a century, the stockyards were a primary hub of meat distribution throughout the country.[14]

1867/06/08   Frank Lloyd Wright Is Born

The best-known, and arguably the most-influential, architect associated with Chicago was born in rural Wisconsin. Although Frank Lloyd Wright spent only a small portion of his career in the Chicago area, it was his formative period during which he developed the Prairie Style.[15]

1868/05/22   Grant Nominated for President

A resident of Galena, IL, Ulysses S. Grant became a hero as the Commanding General of all Union armies who led the North to victory during the Civil War. At their convention in Chicago, the Republicans nominated Grant as their candidate for President. He served two terms as President between 1869 and 1877.[16]

1871/10/08   Great Chicago Fire

A fire broke out on DeKoven St. on Chicago's South Side on the evening of October 8, 1871. The inferno raged for 36 hours, destroying over 3 square miles of the heart of Chicago.[17]

1872/04   First Mail-Order Store

Aaron Montgomery Ward established the first general-purpose mail-order store capitalizing on the abundant rail transportation in Chicago. He started the business the previous summer but everything was destroyed in the Great Fire. Although there had been some earlier mail-order businesses, they specialized in very narrow product lines. Ward was the first to offer a wide and ever-increasing range of products.[18]

1886/05/04   Protests at Haymarket Square

During a labor rally for better working conditions being held at Haymarket Square on May 4, 1886, an unknown person threw a bomb. The bomb was thrown as police tried to break up the otherwise peaceful protest. Seven police and one civilian were killed during the resulting riot. In the aftermath, eight anarchists, including some who were not even present at the rally, were arrested and convicted. Four were hanged.[19]

1887   Orchard Becomes a Place

In 1887, Elvin Scott donated an acre of his farmland to the Wisconsin Central Railroad in exchange for construction of a depot. The railroad named the stop Orchard Place.[20]

1889/09/18   Hull House Opens

Hull House opened its doors on September 18, 1889, to serve the poor and immigrant communities by providing language and other classes. The leadership of founders Jane Addams and Ellen Gates Starr made Hull House the best-known settlement house in the country.[21]

1890   U of C Opens

University of Chicago opens with William Rainey Harper as President.[22]

1891   Chanute Publishes Aviation Information

In order to foster manned flight, Octave Chanute published experimentally based articles about flight in *The Railroad and Engineering Journal*,[a] of which he was the editor. Chanute, a Chicago resident, devoted himself to disseminating information about aviation as widely as possible. He maintained contact and corresponded voluminously with individuals worldwide who were pursuing aviation.

Chanute's publications and correspondence were helpful to the Wright brothers in their early days.[23]

1892   Field's Opens New Store

In 1856, when he arrived in Chicago, Marshall Field became active selling dry goods. He jointly owned a series of stores including a collaboration with the aging retailer and developer Potter Palmer. Following the destruction of his store in the Great Chicago Fire, Field rebuilt. In 1881, he began retailing under the Marshall Field and Co. banner.

In 1892, Field commissioned architect Daniel Burnham to build a stunning retail store on his State St. property as a showcase to impress those attending the World's Columbian Exposition the following year. Burnham's store was modified and expanded until the current 1.3 million sq. ft. structure was completed in 1914. Occupying an entire square block, Field's State St. store was the largest retail store in the world.

In 2005, Field's became Macy's when Marshall Field's sold the building, along with the remainder of their retail business, to New York retailer Federated Department Store (originally R.H. Macy and Co.).[24]

1892/06/06   First Chicago "L"

Chicago's first elevated train began operation between Congress Pkwy. and Wabash Ave. going south to State St. and 39th St. (Pershing Rd.). By the following year, the line extended to Jackson Park for the World's Columbian Exposition. Part of this line has been incorporated into the current Green Line.[25]

---

a   Various sources interchangeably associate Chanute with a variety of publications. *The American Railroad Journal* and *Van Nostrand's Engineering Magazine* are often referred to with shortened versions of their name. The two publications merged to become *The Railroad and Engineering Journal* which was later called *The American Engineer and Railroad Journal*.

1893   Baseball Popularity Soars

The National League introduced the Sunday ball game which for the first time permitted those working six-day weeks in factories and offices to attend ballgames.[26]

1893/05/01–10/30   World's Columbian Exposition

Organized to commemorate the 400th anniversary of Columbus's arrival in the New World, the World's Columbian Exposition (the Chicago World's Fair of 1893) ran from May 1 through October 30, 1893. This world's fair showcased Chicago's rebound from the fire twenty years earlier. The Main Fairgrounds presented new technologies and offered cultural exchange while the Midway provided a plethora of entertainment options.[27]

1893/06/07   Balloon Rides at the World's Fair

Starting June 7, 1893, attendees at the the World's Columbian Exposition could ascend to 1500 ft. in the *Chicago*, for an astronomical $2.00. The tethered balloon was inflated with 100,000 cu. ft. of hydrogen

The *Chicago* was short-lived, however, because on July 10 a storm tore the silk to shreds spreading it over a half mile.[28]

Also in the area was a Balloon Park at 35th St. and Cottage Grove Ave. which also offered tethered ascensions from 10 a.m. to 10 p.m.[29]

1893/07/06   First Open Heart Surgery

The world's first open heart surgery took place at Provident Hospital on July 6, 1893. The surgeon, Dr. Daniel Hale Williams, an African American, was one of the founders of the interracial Provident Hospital. The patient had been stabbed in the heart and was bleeding internally. Dr. Williams opened his chest and stitched the gash in the heart. The patient survived and was discharged 50 days later.[30]

1893/08/01–04   Third International Conference on Aerial Navigation

At the suggestion of Albert Zahm, a professor of physics and mathematics at Notre Dame University, Octave Chanute organized the Third International Conference on Aerial Navigation to be held in conjunction with the World's Columbian Exposition.

Chanute organized and chaired the Conference attended by over a hundred delegates assembled from around the world the first week of

August 1893. Sessions were held in the World Congress Art Hall in Lake Front Park at Adams St., in the building now known as the Art Institute.[a]

Nearly 50 speakers presented their findings on balloons, kites, gliders, engines, and theoretical aspects of flight.

The following year, Chanute published the Conference Proceedings. Also in 1894, he published *Progress on Flying Machines*, a compilation of aviation articles he had previously published in *The Railroad and Engineering Journal*.[31]

1896/05/06   Langley's Model Flights

Samuel Pierpoint Langley, who was Secretary of the Smithsonian Institution between 1887 and 1906, was an avid aviation experimenter. He designed and built a number of model flying machines that used different wing configurations.

Langley's models, which started small with rubber band-powered versions, culminated with large ones powered by a steam engine and launched by a catapult. During experiments in May 1896, his Aerodromes #5 and #6 flew approximately 3300 ft., but they lacked three-axis control. Later experiments with a full-size Aerodrome failed.[32]

1896/06/07   Chanute Glider Flights

In the summer of 1896, Octave Chanute conducted hundreds of flights in kites and gliders of many different configurations. Chanute, who was already in his mid-60s, flew the gliders at Miller Beach on the Indiana Dunes along with his associate, August Herring. Always an engineer, Chanute made meticulous notes about the performance of the various configurations in differing conditions. Chanute's biplane glider stayed aloft 14 sec. and traveled 359 ft.

Chanute's work, including his detailed notes and his methodology, proved helpful to the Wright brothers efforts.[33]

1896/08/10   Lilienthal Dies in Glider Crash

German aviation pioneer Otto Lilienthal was seriously injured when a glider he was testing stalled and crashed on August 9, 1896. The 48-year-old died the next day in a Berlin hospital.

---

a   The Chicago Academy of Fine Arts was founded in 1879 and changed its name to the Art Institute of Chicago in 1882. The Art Institute moved into the World Congress building after the end of the Columbian Exposition.

Starting in 1891, the German experimenter conducted about 2,000 manned and countless unmanned glider flights. He carefully recorded the results of various configurations of airfoils and wing shapes. Lilienthal was the first person to plot lift and drag values for varying angles of attack, although the accuracy of his results was severely limited by his instrumentation.

Lilienthal extensively communicated with Octave Chanute who, in turn, conducted his own glider experiments and data collection.[34]

1897   The "L" Loop Completed

Chicago's initial elevated train lines stopped outside downtown, which was served by cable cars in a square area known as the "Loop." Chicago businessman Charles Yerkes began building elevated tracks to connect various separately-owned elevated train lines together. In 1897, a train completed the first complete circle of the elevated Loop.[35]

1897   Chicago's Public Library Opens

Built on the last available parcel from Fort Dearborn, the building, which today is the Chicago Cultural Center, was shared by two organizations: the Chicago Public Library and the Grand Army of the Republic memorial.

The south entrance on Washington St. led to the Chicago Public Library, which had a collection that included 12,000 books donated by Britain after the Great Fire. At the top of a grand staircase was Preston Bradley Hall, the main circulation and reading room, which contained the world's largest Tiffany Dome.

Entering from Randolph St. on the north led to a memorial for the Grand Army of the Republic, an organization of veterans of the Civil War.[36]

1898   First Santos-Dumont Dirigible

A Brazilian living in France, Alberto Santos-Dumont built the first of 14 powered dirigibles and flew around Paris in 1898. On October 19, 1901, he won 100,000 francs by flying his airship No. 6 in a circuit around the Eiffel Tower.[37]

1898   Chicago Starts Loop Tunnel Project

In an effort to alleviate street congestion, the City of Chicago authorized Illinois Telephone & Telegraph Co. to construct a series of tunnels under the downtown area. A small, electric railroad was installed primarily to deliver coal and remove ashes from scores of buildings. The tunnels were also used to transport mail and freight.

In 1959, the Chicago Tunnel Company went out of business. Some tunnels were later used to house cables but they were mostly ignored and forgotten until the 1990s.[38]

1899   First Zeppelin Flight

Ferdinand von Zeppelin's first dirigible, LZ-1, made its first flight in Germany.[39]

1900–1904

1900/01/02   Chicago River Flows Backwards

The 28-mile Sanitary and Ship Canal opened on January 2, 1900, connecting the Chicago River with the Des Plaines River and ultimately the Gulf of Mexico. The opening of the canal reversed the flow of the Chicago River diverting sewage from Lake Michigan toward the Mississippi River.[40]

1900/10/22   First Wright Trip to Kitty Hawk

The Wright brothers made the first of their annual trips to Kitty Hawk, chosen as a test site for their glider experiments because of its strong winds.[41]

1901/08/18   Wilbur Wright Addresses Conference

In Chicago, Wilbur Wright addressed the Western Society of Engineers. His presentation included lantern slides of their gliders at Kill Devil Hills and information on their aerodynamic experiences.

Wright's presentation came at the request of the society's President, Octave Chanute. The Wright brothers began corresponding with Chanute in May 1900 and developed a close relationship. The elderly Chanute even visited the Wrights at Kill Devil Hills during their glider experiments.

The presentation was well-timed in that it stimulated Wilbur, whose enthusiasm and optimism had been waning with their lack of success. Following the presentation, Wilbur prepared the 10,000-word paper "Some Aeronautical Experiments," which was published in the society's journal.[42]

1902/05/24   First of the Chicago-Style Bridges Opens

The Courtland Street (formerly Clybourn Place) bridge over the Chicago River was Chicago's first double-leaf fixed-trunnion bascule bridge.[a] The design, in which each side of the bridge is counterbalanced by a large weight that reduces the effort to raise and lower it, became popular worldwide as the Chicago-Style Bridge.[43]

---

a   Despite the common claim that this was the first bridge of this type in the U.S., the Grand Ave. bridge in Milwaukee opened three months earlier.

1903   White City Amusement Park Establishes Balloon Base

Horace B. Wild, a Chicago aeronaut, established a balloon base at White City Amusement Park on the South Side not far from the 1893 World's Fair site.

Wild flew both tethered and free-flight balloons as well as powered dirigibles of his own design. White City visitors could watch demonstrations or take sightseeing flights in lighter-than-air craft.[44]

1903/03/23   Wright Brothers File Patent

Nine months prior to the successful flight at Kitty Hawk, the Wright brothers file an application for a "Flying Machine." The application is based on lateral control during flight rather than powered flight.[45]

1903/12/17   Wright's First Flight

Orville Wright made the first flight of a controllable, heavier-than-air vehicle. That flight lasted 12 sec. and covered a distance of 120 ft. with a maximum altitude of 10 ft.

Over the next couple of days, the Wrights made three additional flights, the longest of which lasted nearly a minute and covered more than 850 ft. On their fifth flight, a wind gust caught the plane destroying it in a crash.[46]

1903/12/30   Iroquois Theater Fire

A little more than a month after it opened, the Iroquois Theater was packed with 1,900 people. Nearly 600 people died when a fire broke out and the patrons found many of the exits locked.[47]

1904   Riverview Park Opens

Chicago's iconic Riverview Amusement Park opened in 1904 on the bank of the North Branch of the Chicago River, by Belmont and Western avenues.[48]

1905–1909

1905   Aero Club of America Formed

New York aviation enthusiasts (primarily balloonists) formed the Aero Club of America in New York City in 1905.[a] Its purpose was to promote aviation as was being done by the Aero Club of France, although the structure was similar to the existing Automobile Club of America.

The Aero Club of America became the major aviation body in the U.S., issuing pilot licenses, sponsoring events, and supporting similar local groups such as the Aero Club of Illinois.[49]

1905/01   Wrights Begin Sales Demos

After a year of perfecting their airplane in relative secrecy in Dayton, the Wright brothers contacted their Congressman offering to sell their airplane to the U.S. military.

The Congressman referred the request to the War Department's Bureau of Ordinance and Fortification. This agency had recently invested $50,000 in Samuel Langley's Aerodrome which was a spectacular—and public— failure. Not inclined to be humiliated again, the War Department sent the Wrights a stock rejection letter.

Almost concurrently, the Wrights approached the British government. Although the British had previously shown interest in the Wrights' accomplishments, nothing ever came from the negotiations.[50]

1905/05/05   *Chicago Defender* First Published

With a first press run of 300 copies, Robert Sengstacke Abbott published the first issue of a weekly newspaper for Chicago's African American community. By WWI, the *Chicago Defender*, distributed via the railroads, was the most influential black newspaper in the country, with over two-thirds of its readers outside Chicago.[51]

---

a   Some sources place the founding at 1902 based on photographs stamped with the words "Aero Club." However, since this was prior to the Wright flight, it may be a different balloon association.

1906   Original Sears Tower Opens

Ten years after its 1894 founding, Sears, Roebuck & Co. purchased land for a new complex in the Homan Square area on the West Side. The first buildings that opened in 1906 included the first Sears Tower, a 250 ft., 14-story structure that provided offices for the distribution complex.

For a while, part of the Tower housed radio station WLS, which stood for "World's Largest Store." In 1974, Sears moved the management offices to a new and much larger tower in the Loop. The Homan Square facility remained a distribution center until it closed in 1987.

Now called the Nichols Tower, the original Sears Tower completed a $15 million restoration in 2016. It is listed on the National Register of Historic Places.[52]

1906/01   Kodak Ordinance Passed

In order to combat the "evil of the Kodak fiend," the Chicago City Council passed an ordinance stating that "no person shall take photographs in the streets or public grounds of any person or persons without his or their consent."[53]

1906/02/26   Stockyard Conditions Exposed

On February 26, 1906, Upton Sinclair's novel, *The Jungle* was published. The book sensationalized the unsanitary conditions at the Union Stockyards as well as the exploitation of the workers. A strike by the workers on July 12, 1904, focused local attention to the situation, but quickly faded from the public eye. Sinclair's work had a longer-lasting impact across the nation, primarily in legislation concerning food handling.[54]

1906/05/22   Wright Patent Issued

The U.S. Patent Office issued patent 821,393 "for a Flying Machine" to Orville and Wilbur Wright.[55]

1906/10   Chicago Cross-Town World Series

An all-Chicago World Series pitted the Chicago Cubs, who played at the West Side Grounds, against the Chicago White Sox, playing at South Side Park. The Sox bested the Cubs in a six game series that included snow flurries during the first two games.[56]

1906/10/23   First Official European Flight

After making short hops for over a month, Brazilian Albert Santos-Dumont made the first officially observed European flight on October 23, 1906, when he flew 197 ft. On November 12, he flew the 14-bis for 772 ft. and received the French Aero Club's prize for the first European flight over 100 meters (328 ft.). Resembling a box-kite, the 14-bis was unable to perform either sustained or controlled flight.[57]

1907   First Monoplane

The Bleriot V, the first somewhat successful monoplane, was designed by Louis Bleriot and Gabriel Voisin. The Bleriot V crashed but after several enhancements during the year, the successful Bleriot VII established the general pattern for later Bleriot planes.[58]

1907/07   Aeronautique Club of Chicago Commences

In July, 1907,[a] aviation enthusiasts chartered the Aeronautique Club of Chicago primarily to serve the large community of balloonists. The Aeronautique Club was affiliated with the Federation of American Aero Clubs and elected Charles A. Coey its president. Octave Chanute and Horace B. Wild were among the 140 members.[59]

1907/11/13   First Helicopter Flight

Paul Cornu makes first free flight in a helicopter at Lisieux, France.[60]

1908/02/08   Army Signal Corps Orders First Plane

The U.S. government placed an order with the Wright Corp. for a Model A airplane, the first of many aircraft the U.S. military would acquire over the next century.[61]

1908/05/21   Glenn Curtiss First Flight

Aviation pioneer Glenn Curtiss makes his first flight in the *White Wing*, an airplane designed by his colleague, Alexander Graham Bell. The *White Wing* had wheeled landing gear and was controlled using ailerons rather than wing warping. The following month, Curtiss designed and flew an airplane of his own design, the *June Bug*.

Curtiss and Bell were part of the Aerial Experiment Assn. (AEA) of Hammondsport, NY, a group dedicated to experimentation with various

a   Souter places the formation in February, 1908.

designs for flying machines. All AEA planes used ailerons rather than wing warping to maintain control. Since Curtiss did not seek patent protection for ailerons, they were widely copied over the next few years and have become the standard to control wing position.[62]

1908/07/04   First International Aerial Race

In February 1908, the Aeronautique Club of Chicago hosted representatives from other Aeronautique Clubs around the country. Their goal was to adopt rules for aerial contests as well as to promote and educate the public about aviation. [63]

One of the Chicago club's first activities was to sponsor the First International Aerial Race from Chicago to Canada. The club contracted to construct two balloons, one 77,000 and the other 67,000 cu. ft. Aeronautique Club President Charles Coey entered his own *Coey's Chicago*, the first American balloon of 110,000 cu. ft.[64]

On Independence Day 1908, an estimated 150,000 people gathered at the two launch sites: White City Amusement Park and Washington Park. The event drew nine participants, including international figures Horace B. Wild, Charles Coey, Alberto Santos-Dumont, and Lincoln Beachey. The race winner travelled 895 mi. to Sheffield, Quebec.[65]

1908/08/08   Wrights Fly in Europe

The Wrights traveled to Europe in January in an attempt to interest purchasers. On August 8, they made their first public flight in Europe. Unlike previous flights by French experimenters, the Wrights amazed the audience with their ability to bank and turn with ease. The following summer, they established a flight school at Pau, France.[66]

1908/08/18–19   Patent Wars Begin

On August 18, 1908, the Wright Brothers filed a lawsuit against the Herring-Curtiss Co. demanding royalties on their sale of an airplane two months earlier. The following day, they sued the Aeronautique Society of New York, the purchasers of the Curtiss airplane, to prevent any use of the airplane because it infringed their patents.[67]

1908/09/17   First Airplane Fatality

While flying with Orville Wright, Army Lt. Thomas Selfridge became aviation's first fatality in a crash that also injured Orville.[68]

1908/12   First Chicago-Made Airplane Flies

Iowa-native Carl S. Bates attended Armour Institute[a] in Chicago, where he was taught by Octave Chanute, among others.

Bates started building a plane of his own, a smaller version of Curtiss's plane. While trying to build airplanes, Bates discovered the need for reliable, lightweight engines so he built his own. He formed the Bates Aero Motor Co. which produced high-quality air- and water-cooled engines.

In December1908, Bates completed the first aircraft built in Chicago using his own 10 hp engine. He took his plane to Washington Park Golf Course, where he made a few short hops

Later that month, the owner of White City Amusement Park, which already had an existing balloon and dirigible port, cleared some land to make a landing strip for Bates to use as he improved his airplane designs.

A year after building a scaled-down Curtiss plane, he expanded his business. Bates produced aircraft of his own design, although most were modifications of other aircraft. Nevertheless, his planes and reliable, lightweight engines became popular throughout the area.[69]

By the time of the Aviation Meet in the summer of 1911, Bates had designed a monoplane combining the best features of many planes. The body was similar to the Nieuport while the wing was an improved version of the Morane plane with wing-warping and a "pigeon-tail empennage." It used the Bates-Heinemann motor.[70]

1909   First *Jane's Aircraft* Published

In London, Fred T. Jane published the first edition of a compendium that came to be known as *Jane's All the World's Aircraft*. Except for brief periods during the two world wars, the book has been published annually.[71]

1909   First Aviation Books Published in Chicago

The first two of many aviation books to be published in Chicago on powered flight went to press in 1909.

An early Chicago aviation enthusiast, M.K. Kasmar wrote *First Lessons in Aeronautics,* which was published by the American Aeronautical Society. The following year, Kasmar would found the city's first aeronautical school, the Chicago School of Aviation.[72]

Victor Loughhead (pronounced "Lockheed") began working as a mechanic for James Plew's White Steam Automobile and Curtiss Airplane

---

a   Armour Institute later became the Illinois Institute of Technology.

dealership. He was soon joined by his brother Allan. Both learned to fly and became members of the Aero Club of Illinois.

Victor became so enthusiastic about aviation that he wrote *Vehicles of the Air.* It was an extensive (500-page) work covering all aspects of aerodynamics as well as describing some of the early aircraft. Later, Victor and Allan had a falling out and Allan returned to California, where he changed the spelling of his name and founded what would become Lockheed Aircraft Corp.[73]

1909   Jimmie Ward Learns to Fly

At 15, James "Jimmie" Ward ran away from his Minnesota home and moved to Chicago. Loving speed and thrills, Ward got into automotive work both as a mechanic and as a driver competing in numerous speed contests for various manufacturers or dealers.

Ward's proclivity for adventure naturally drew him to flying. About 1909, he taught himself to fly using a plane manufactured by Carl Bates. Soon thereafter James Plew, who had just started a Curtiss dealership, hired Ward to be one of his pilots.

The next year, 1910, during one of his exhibitions in Chicago, Glenn Curtiss met Ward and hired him to be part of the Curtiss Exhibition Team. As part of the Curtiss team, Ward flew a 24-hp Curtiss airplane named *Shooting Star* all around the country.[74]

1909/06/10   Wrights Awarded Gold Medals

A joint resolution of Congress conferred gold medals on the Wright brothers in recognition of their flight achievements. On June 10, 1909, President Taft bestowed the medals on the Wrights in the East Room of the White House.[75]

1909/06/26   Curtiss Sells First Airplane

Glenn Curtiss made the first U.S. commercial sale of an airplane, the *Gold Bug.*[a] Curtiss believed his design did not infringe on the Wright patent and refused to pay royalties.[76]

1909/07/04   Plan of Chicago Published

Daniel Burnham published his *Plan of Chicago,* laying out a plan for development of Chicago's lakefront and city. The plan was sponsored by the Commercial Club of Chicago as a guide for what would now be called urban

a   Also called the *Golden Flyer* or Curtiss No. 1.

planning. While the plan presents a grand ideal that was never fully realized, elements of the plan have shaped Chicago's development.[77]

1909/07/19   Latham Falls in the English Channel

Hubert Latham built one of the early successful monoplanes, the Antoinette. A rival of Bleriot, Latham took off the morning of July 19, 1909, and flew toward Dover. Unfortunately, his plane did not make it and Latham was fished out of the English Channel unharmed.[78]

1909/07/25   Bleriot Crosses the English Channel

Louis Bleriot crossed the English Channel in the Bleriot XI, beating his rival Hubert Latham to the distinction on July 25, 1909.

Earlier in the year, Bleriot's XI became the world's first mass-produced airplane. Bleriot made the 22-mi. trip from Calais to Dover in 40 min. at an average speed of 46 mph. His arrival created confusion for custom's officials who only process entries from the sea, so they identified Bleriot as a Ship's Master and his aircraft as a yacht. [79]

1909/08/22–29   Rheims Holds First Major Air Show

The first great air show was held in Rheims France drawing 250,000 spectators. The show included at least 22 flying machines from Curtiss, Bleriot, Henri Farman, and others. The Wrights did not attend personally but sent six of their planes. Glenn Curtiss beat Bleriot for the fastest plane, winning the Gordon Bennett[a] Cup. Curtiss also won the most prizes, taking the International Cup.[80]

1909/10/15–17   First Public Airplane Flights in Chicago

Hawthorne Race Track became the site of the first public airplane flights in the Chicago area[b] when Glenn Curtiss flew on October 16 and 17, 1909. His exhibition followed his winning the Gordon Bennett Cup earlier that year.

The night before the exhibition, civic leaders, including Harold McCormick and Charles Dickinson, hosted a dinner for Curtiss. Discussions at the meeting led to the formation of the Aero Club of Illinois.

---

a   James Gordon Bennett Jr., the publisher of the *New York Herald,* lived a lavish lifestyle in the U.S. and Europe. Having an adventurous nature, Bennett sponsored espeditions and races. He established a separate Gordon Bennett Cup for winners of international races for yachts, automobiles, balloons, and airplanes.

b   According to Young (p. 40), Horace B. Wild, the famous Chicago balloonist, claimed to have built and flown his own plane as early as 1907, but there seems to be no substantiation for the flights.

On the first day, winds limited the performance to a single flight of the Curtiss Pusher. It was brief, only about 40 sec. long and covering a quarter of a mi. at an altitude of about 10 ft. Nevertheless, it was impressive to those who had never seen an airplane.[81]

Thomas Scott Baldwin, a nationally renowned balloonist and parachutist, was able to give an excellent demonstration of his powered airship.[82]

1909/11   Wright Brothers Form Corporation

Wright Brothers filed incorporation papers in New York. Financial backing was provided by notables of the period including Cornelius Vanderbilt. Wilbur served as President and Orville as Vice President.[83] The Wrights had previously formed sales companies in both France and Germany.[84]

1909/12   Chicago's First Airplane Dealer and Airport

James Plew was one of those impressed with the Glen Curtiss demonstrations at Hawthorne Race Track in the fall of 1909. Plew, who was a White Steam Motor Car dealer, also started selling Curtiss airplanes. He dedicated an entire floor of his four-story building to his aeronautic department.

Plew and another pilot, Otto Brodie, demonstrated his planes from a tent hangar in a farm pasture in the Clearing District, which became Clearing Field. Plew sent Rudolph William "Shorty" Schroeder, who worked for him, to the Curtiss School to become a mechanic.

Clearing Field became the nation's first permanent full-time airport; however its location is uncertain, since it seems to have had two locations during its existence. Probably the Clearing Field's first location[a] was south of the big rail yards between 69th and 71st streets, and between Central and Menard (58th) avenues. Other sources, probably later, place it north of the rail yards at 65th St. and Major Ave. The former location was remote and ideal for those wishing to develop machines in secret while the latter was somewhat more convenient to the public for exhibitions.[85]

---

a A *Chicago Tribune* article September 18, 1910, (quoted in *Chicagology*) gives the location of the first airport as "the vicinity of Berwyn," which is well north of the two Clearing locations.

1910–1914

1910   First Airplane Noise Complaint

First noise complaint came from British military officers on Salisbury Plain who complained about the aeroplanes "unnecessarily frightening the cavalry's horses." As a result, the British army did not use aircraft for several years.[86]

1910   First Landing Field in Rock River Valley

Flying came to the Rock River Valley in 1910[a] in a pasture called Franing Field, which was selected as a landing site on the first coast-to-coast flight.[87]

Later that year, the first airport in Whiteside County opened near Rock Falls at McCue's Corner, now the intersection of McCue Rd. and Route 2. The landing field soon closed and became a race track.[88]

1910   First Aviation School Opens

In early 1910,[b] M.K. Kasmar and J.W. Curzon opened the Chicago School of Aviation, the first formal aviation school in the country. Originally located at W. 118th and S. Morgan streets in West Pullman, the school later moved to Hawthorne Aerodrome, as Hawthorne Race Track was sometimes called.

Kasmar was an early Chicago aviator who wrote *First Lessons in Aeronautics* in 1909. Curzon was credited with bringing the first Farman airplane from France to the U.S.

Soon after starting their flight school, they expanded their operation to become the American Aeroplane Manufacturing Co. and Chicago School of Aviation. Students at the School of Aviation could both learn to fly and build their own airplanes of three designs: the Curzon #1 (small biplane with a box-kite elevator), the Curzon #2 (biplane with a single-plane elevator), or the Curzon #3 (monoplane similar to the Farman).

By 1913, the Curzon and Kasmar enterprises had disappeared from the public eye.[89]

---

a   Some sources give the date as 1919 instead of 1910.
b   Young dates the school's opening to April 1911.

1910   Chicago Area's First Airplane Factory

After a successful career manufacturing "wire rope," Coal City's Mayor, William "Billy" Sommerville, turned his attention to aeronautics in 1910. He developed both a monoplane and biplane, which he produced in the Illinois Aero Construction Co. factory in Coal City.

In December 1912, Sommerville's factory burned to the ground, taking with it a number of planes under construction along with all his plans and records. He tried but was unable to revive the company.

Somerville didn't abandon aviation totally. In 1913 he acquired a crashed French Morane-Borel monoplane. After rebuilding that plane, which joined the exhibition circuit, he produced copies that were sold by the William Somerville I.A.C. company.[90]

1910/01/10–20   Los Angeles Air Show

The first major American air show was held at Dominguez Field in Los Angeles.[91]

1910/02/10   Aero Club of IL Created

After Glenn Curtiss made demonstration flights in 1909 at Hawthorne Race Track, civic leaders became enthusiastic about aviation.

On February 2, 1910, a group of Chicago's business and civic leaders formed the Aero Club of Illinois, which they modeled after the Aero Club of America. An article in the *Chicago Tribune,* February 13, 1910, described the purpose of the club:

> The principal aim of our big project is to bring Chicago to the forefront of aeronautics in the United States. Chicago belongs there, and it is shameful that she has not that preeminence right at this moment … If the right start is made Chicago will take the same lead in aviation in the middle west as it does already in automobiling.

The ACI named Octave Chanute the President. Chanute's health was failing and he was primarily a figurehead the few months until his death. James Plew succeeded Chanute as President.

Early and enthusiastic members included: Harold F. McCormick, a son of Cyrus McCormick; James Plew, a White Steam Automobile dealer who had already become a dealer for Curtiss airplanes; Charles "Pop" Dickinson, owner of Dickinson Seed Company; Judge Charles S. Cutting of the Probate Court; Joseph H. Defrees, President of the Chicago Bar Association; Milton J. Foreman, Chicago Alderman; and James Deering, V.P. of International Harvester.[92]

1910/07/12   First British Air Fatality

Charles Stewart Rolls (of Rolls-Royce fame) crashed his Wright Flyer at the Bournemith Air Week. becoming the first Englishman to be killed in a plane crash. Rolls was a co-founder of the Royal Aero Club and the first person to make a two-way crossing of the English Channel.[93]

1910/07/02–05   Curtiss Demonstration at Hawthorne

Half a dozen members of the Curtiss exhibition team returned to Hawthorne Race Track for another exhibition. Organized by the Colonial Aero Club of Chicago, the meet gathered many of the country's top aviators. In addition to Curtiss, 32 aviators had expressed their intention to perform, including Chicagoan J.C. "Bud" Mars and nationally recognized Charles K. Hamilton, as they competed for a $10,000 purse. Among the highlights were flights by Eugene Ely in the *Herring-Curtiss No. 9.*

Besides the aerial exhibition, there were automobile races organized by the famous driver Barney Oldfield.[94]

1910/07/05–07   Wright Exhibition in Aurora

Arthur L. Walsh flew three exhibition flights for the Wright Co. during celebrations at the opening of the Aurora and DeKalb Electric Railway.[95]

1910/09/12   Heath's First Flight

Not long after graduating Lane Technical High School, Chicagoan Edward Bayard Heath moved to Amsterdam, NY, where he began constructing a copy of the Bleriot XI from plans that were readily available. On the evening of September 12, 1910, Heath took his plane to a nearby golf course for its first flight. Just prior to takeoff, a wing support failed. The failure spurred Heath to improve airplane construction for the rest of his life.[96]

1910/09/16   First American Woman Solos

At Hempstead Plains, NY, on September 16, 1910, Bessica Medlar Raiche took off in a plane that she and her husband, Francois Raiche, built.

The Aeronautical Club of America credits her with being the first woman to solo[a] in the U.S. By the end of the day, after several successful flights, she also became the first woman in the country to crash a plane.

---

a   Early Birds of America credits Blanche Scott with having soloed 10 days earlier, September 6, 1910, while learning to fly with Glenn Curtiss in Hammondsport NY. Scott joined the Curtiss Exhibition Team and made her debut performance October 24 of the same year.

Originally from Beloit, WI, Bessica became enamored with flying in France where she saw the Wrights fly. The Raiches eventually moved to Chicago where they both became instructors at the Standard School of Aviation.[a] While there, Bessica organized the first class exclusively for women.

The Raiche's interest in aviation was short-lived. By 1920, the Raiches had moved to southern California, where Bessica was an obstetrician and her husband a lawyer.[97]

1910/09/18 *Tribune* Sees Chicago as Aviation Center

An article in the *Chicago Tribune* claimed that Chicago had become a "Vast Testing Ground for Amateur Aviators." To support its claim, the paper reported that:

- More than 100 amateurs building airplanes within the city, identifying over 30 of them
- Two aviation schools—one led by M.K. Kasmar and J.W. Curzon and another led by E.W. Morey of the Chicago Technical College
- "Two aviators of world fame with the aviation game"—John B. Moisant and J.C. "Bud" Mars
- Three aviation societies—the Aeronautical Society of Chicago,[b] the Aero Club of Illinois, and the Illinois Aeroplane Club
- The first permanent aviation field in the country, with a photo showing several tent hangars (probably Clearing Field which has that distinction although the *Tribune* article places it "in the vicinity of Berwyn" significantly west of Clearing Field)
- Two locally published aviation books— *First Lessons in Aeronautics* by M.K. Kasmar and *Vehicles of the Air: A Popular Exposition of Modern Aeronautics with Working Drawings* by Victor Loughhead

The *Tribune* article concludes with a proud refutation of comments made earlier by Glenn Curtiss.

> It will be remembered that Glenn H. Curtiss, one of the foremost of American aviators, declared on a recent visit to Chicago, following a series of short flights here after long baffling by obstreperous winds, that Chicago is the most unfavorable of all cities in the country in which, or rather over which, to fly, as its location made it subject to the most freakish and

a   Apparently Raiche never formally got her pilot's license, which was not required at the time.
b   The article claims it was the first aviation organization in the country. It had a nationwide membership over 10,000 with M.K. Kasmar as the secretary. The society was primarily interested in lighter-than-air dirigibles and balloons.

unexpected weather manifestations. He said that it was as dangerous and treacherous serially as its lake was to the mariner, and Lake Michigan's character is admittedly the famous sky rider. It is doubtful if there is any city on the continent which can show a greater activity and a wider growth of interest in aviation than Chicago. It is the outcropping in a new field of the same old celebrated "Chicago spirit" which thrives, as it does under no other conditioned, when encountering opposition and obstacle.[98]

1910/09/27–29   Brookins Flights Thrill Chicago

Walter Brookins made the first airplane flights over the Loop and city instead of the suburban Hawthorne Race Track or Aurora. His flights over the city on September 27 and 28, 1910, were in preparation for a cross-country flight to Springfield on the 29th.

Flying his Wright Model A, Brookins made a total of six flights over the two days. Taking off from Randolph St. near the lakefront at noon and 5:00 in the evening both days, Brookins flights covered the downtown area. He circled around the Ward's Tower, the Illinois Central Railroad Station, and the Post Office, reaching heights of 2,500 ft. and speeds of 56 mph. An estimated 250–300,000 people watched the flights each day. A passenger accompanied him on some of the flights.[99]

On September 29, Brookins made a flight from Chicago to Springfield to claim a $10,000 prize offered by the *Chicago Record Herald*. Brookins made the 187-mi. trip in 5 hr. 49 min., including two 30-min. fuel stops. A train that accompanied the flight carrying reporters and dignitaries took ten minutes longer.[100]

A Dayton native, Brookins attended school where Katherine Wright, the sister of the Wright brothers, taught. There he picked up an interest in aviation. He was the first civilian pilot trained by the Wrights and became their first instructor and assisted with the formation of the Wright Exhibition Team.[101]

1910/10/02–08   Exhibition Week and New York Race

Several individuals and publications put up a $25,000 purse for the winner of a race from Chicago to New York City. Although the race was to start on October 8, 1910, the rules specified that the pilots and planes must make prior flights in Chicago to demonstrate their capability.

Sponsors organized Exhibition Week, October 2–7, at Hawthorne Race Track as a way both for pilots to complete their qualifying flights and to

generate some income to offset their expenses. Pilots delighted up to
25,000 spectators daily with their flying. Glenn Curtiss himself joined them
flying in the first couple of days of the show. On the final day, Charles F.
Willard flew a five-mi. race against an automobile around the track.

Initially, pilots from both the Wright and Curtiss teams planned to
enter. Gradually, they realized that they would be risking their lives and
planes flying over previously uncharted territory (at least from the air).

The pilots chose Eugene Ely as the only pilot to make the journey. He
set out on the morning of October 9, but had mechanical problems before
he left Chicago. After repairing the problems, he was on his way again, but
had engine failure and crashed near East Chicago, IN, ending the race.[102]

1910/11/10   Teddy Roosevelt's First Flight
A year after he left office as President, Teddy Roosevelt was campaigning for
Republican candidates in St. Louis. At the Kinloch Airport, Roosevelt met
Arch Hoxsey, one of the Wright exhibition pilots. Always up for a new
adventure, Roosevelt accepted Hoxsey's offer of a flight.[103]

1910/11/10   Chanute Dies in Chicago
On November 10, 1910, Octave Chanute died of pneumonia in Chicago at
the age of 78.

Chanute acquired the title of the "Father of Aviation" primarily after a
long and successful career as an engineer designing bridges and other
structures for the railroads. In later life, Chanute applied his passion and
precision toward the goal of enabling man to fly.

Unlike many early experimenters in aviation, Chanute was not secretive
or possessive of his work. Chanute served as an unofficial clearing house of
aviation experimentation. He corresponded with many experimenters,
freely sharing his information and encouraging the efforts of others.

The Wright brothers first became aware of Chanute when the
Smithsonian Institution recommended Chanute's *Progress on Flying
Machines* to them. On May 13, 1900, Wilbur Wright wrote Chanute for
some information. Over the years, they exchanged 435 letters and tele-
grams. Chanute made two trips to visit the Wrights at Kill Devil Hills in
1901 and 1902.[104]

Following the Wrights' successful flights, there was a falling out
between them and Chanute. Chanute felt the Wrights were too secretive
and restrictive of other aviation endeavors. The Wrights believed Chanute
was too loose-lipped with what they deemed proprietary information and

were offended at Chanute's criticism of their practices. Some sources indicate there was a thawing of the hostilities before Chanute died, but the best sources are unable to support that claim.[105]

Despite whatever hostilities had existed, Wilbur Wright did attend Chanute's funeral. He also published a glowing tribute in *Aeronautics*.

> If he had not lived, the entire history of progress in flying would have been other than it has been, for he encouraged not only the Wright Brothers to persevere in their experiments … His writings were so lucid as to provide an intelligent understanding of the nature of the problems of flight to a vast number of persons who would probably never have given the matter study otherwise, and not only by published articles, but by personal correspondence and visitation, he inspired and encouraged to the limits of his ability all who were devoted to the work. His private correspondence with experimenters in all parts of the world was of great volume. No one was too humble to receive a share of his time. In patience and goodness of heart he has rarely been surpassed. Few men were more universally respected and loved.[106]

1910/11/14   First American Plane Takes Off from Ship

Eugene Burton Ely took the first flight off a temporary wooden deck constructed on the USS *Birmingham* on November 14, 1910. Ely flew his Curtiss flying boat for two miles before landing on a beach. Two months later, on January 18, 1911, Ely landed his plane on a platform built on the deck of the USS *Pennsylvania* using wires attached to sandbags as arresting gear. He then took off from that platform.[107]

Although he learned to fly elsewhere, Ely tested for and received his license at Clearing Field in Chicago on October 5, 1910, receiving License #17.[108]

1910/12/22–23   Deadly Stock Yards Fire

At 4 a.m. on December 22, 1910, a watchman discovered fire in a warehouse at the Chicago Union Stock Yards. The inferno, which wasn't struck until 6 a.m. the following morning, resulted in an estimated $1 million damage.

However, the costliest part of the fire was borne by the Chicago Fire Department. A wall collapsed on a crew, killing 23 firefighters including Fire Chief James Horan. The fire remains the deadliest ever for the Chicago Fire Department.[109]

1911   Heath Starts Aircraft Supply Company

In 1911 or early 1912,[a] after a short sojourn in upstate New York, Edward Heath returned to Chicago and started the E.B. Heath Aerial Vehicle Co. Heath's company was based on his plane-building experiences in which he found it difficult to obtain the parts needed to build a plane. He focused on selling parts and accessories including paint, propellers, turnbuckles, and wheels for a wide variety of popular aircraft types.

Heath used the business model pioneered by Montgomery Ward and Sears, Roebuck & Co. He distributed catalogs listing hundreds and eventually thousands of parts required to build and repair planes of all types. Everyone from first-timers building a plane in their barn to barnstormers needing repairs on the circuit would send Heath a telegram or letter. In just a few days the exact parts they needed arrived at the train station nearest them.

Heath's business boomed. Soon, his company became known informally as Heath's Airplane Trading Post.[110]

1911   Kiddy Karr Takes to the Air

Harold "Kiddy" Karr began flying in 1911. A 15-year old student at Crane Technical High School, Karr flew a glider towed into the air by a car. Later Karr became the Navy's first licensed pilot.[111]

1911/02   Brodie Starts Airplane Company

In February 1911, Otto Brodie, along with partners James R. Sollitt and Joseph W. Latimer, formed the Franco-American Aviation Co. of Chicago.

They purchased a Farman airplane from France with a Gnome engine. The Farman had two seats that enabled it to be used for sightseeing and flight training. Shorty Schroeder came to work as Brodie's mechanic.[112]

Otto Brodie started out as a balloonist and parachute jumper who received flight lessons from Glenn Curtiss. In December 1909, James Plew hired Brodie as a pilot for his new Curtiss dealership, which used a field that would become Clearing Field.[113]

---

a   There is some confusion about the early part of Heath's involvement with aviation. Young (p. 126) and Scamehorn (p. 69) state that Heath was in Chicago fabricating parts for machinery in 1909. Heath himself reiterated this claim in each of his catalogs by stating that he was in business "since 1909." However, Peek's book (p. 1–3) cites newspaper accounts of his 1910 flight in upstate New York and his brief employment with Glenn Curtiss's motorcycle manufacturing facility before returning to Chicago.

In May 1911, Brodie was the first tenant to move to the new Cicero Flying Field. There he gave flights to well-known passengers including Katherine Stinson, Charles Coey, and many others.[114]

1911/04/14   Wrights Demand Royalties

While planning an aviation meet for the summer of 1911, the Wrights contacted the Aero Club of Illinois demanding a $10,000 royalty.

On April 14, 1911, Harold McCormick and John McCutcheon went to Dayton to meet with the Wrights. The Wrights remained firm on their demand and clearly stated they had three goals. First, they didn't want foreign aviators to fly in America. Second, they wanted to get as much money from the meet as possible. Third, they wanted to support their patents.

The ACI formed a separate nonprofit company, the International Aviation Meet Association, to actually sponsor and organize the meet. The dispute gained national attention among the aviation community. Harold McCormick and the ACI resisted the Wright demands and went on with the meet.

In the end, an unofficial deal was reached. Alfred Lawson,who saw himself as a key figure in the aviation community claimed credit for brokering the agreement between the Wrights and the ACI. The Wrights did file suit but didn't pursue it. Many of the pilots individually paid a royalty to the Wrights for their participation.[115]

1911/05   Chicago's First Full-Time Public Airport

Cicero Field, Chicago's first full-time, public airport,[a] began in early 1911 when Harold McCormick loaned 180 acres to the Aero Club of Illinois for five years. Cicero Field was located between 16th and 22nd streets and 42nd and 48th avenues.[116]

Flying started at Cicero in May 1911, soon after the lease was signed. One of the first users of Cicero Field, even before its official opening, was the Franco-American Aviation Co. owned by Otto Brodie, who sold Farman biplanes.

During the first few months after opening, Cicero Field was cleared and leveled using a 5-ton steam roller and a fence erected around the perime-ter.[117] ACI hired Horace B. Wild as the full-time Field Director or Field Captain for Cicero Field soon after it opened.

---

a   Clearing Field, which was in use by September 1910, appears to have been an on-again, off-again operation in several locations.

In his role as Field Director, Wild oversaw all flight operations. He inspected and ensured that planes and pilots were safe for flight. He had the authority to ground planes or pilots he considered unsafe. Each day, he filed an activity report with the ACI which owned and operated the field.

Wild was a noted aeronaut who previously flew balloons and powered dirigibles at White City. Wild claimed to have built a powered airplane in 1907, but there is no substantiation and his description sounded somewhat far-fetched for the technology at the time. He did have a plane by 1910 which he planned to use for exhibitions, but it was damaged before his first public performance.[118]

1911/05   Yet Another Aviation Company

The International Aeroplane Co. was founded in May 1911. The firm manufactured airplanes at a factory in downtown Chicago. It also ran a flight school at Cicero Field. Allan Loughhead was one of its early graduates. International Aeroplane flew frequent exhibitions at Cicero and around the Midwest.

After about seven months, International Aeroplane Co. was succeeded by National Aeroplane Manufacturing Co.[a] National Aeroplane carried on the previous activities plus it added the French Nieuport with the Anzani engine to its product line. National hired Billy Robinson from Max Lillie's school to fly the Nieuport in exhibitions.

Most of the company's activity was outside Illinois, but there weren't enough sales to sustain it. National Aeroplane went out of business around 1913.[119]

1911/06   Mills Brothers Aviation Enterprises

Brothers George P. and James R. Mills started Mills Aviators in June 1911. They sold a biplane of their own design as well as plans of other planes including Bleriot, Curtiss, and Farman.

By 1912 they also formed an aviation booking agency: Mills and Mills Aviation Exchange. Operating out of offices in Medinah Temple, they handled some of the biggest exhibition flyers of the period, including Art "Smash Up" Smith.

Also in 1912, George Mills designed a hydroaeroplane which the company actively marketed. Competition in the early years was fierce and the Mills brothers went out of business around 1914.[120]

---

a   National Aeroplane Manufacturing Co. had no relationship to the National Aeroplane Fund formed in 1915 by the Aero Club of America.

1911/07/04   Cicero Field's Grand Opening

More than 5,000 people attended the grand opening of Chicago's first
full-time, public airport, Cicero Flying Field. Horace B. Wild presided over
the official opening day ceremonies on the Fourth of July 1911.

Cicero Field was ideally located between 16th and 22nd streets and
42nd and 48th avenues. People could easily access the field by the Metropolitan Douglas Park elevated railway or two adjacent streetcar lines.[121]

Airplanes of a variety of designs were available for the public to see both
on the ground and in the air. Some pilots, such as Otto Brodie with his
Farman, took spectators on brief flights. A balloon launch also thrilled
the crowd.[122]

Harold McCormick and other Aero Club members lavished money on
the airport, providing it with the best equipment and materials available.
World-class flyers and builders used Cicero as their base of operation
drawing aviation people from around the country to take advantage of their
services and facilities. Chicago's central location and rail network made it
the center from which exhibition teams shipped their equipment.

Frequent air shows and performances at Cicero gave flyers an opportunity to perform and hone their skills. The performances also exposed many
non-flyers to aviation, creating the next generation of enthusiasts.

Cicero was distinctive, if not unique, among the approximately 40
public, full-time airports around the country prior to WWI. It had a clearly
defined perimeter along with a groomed surface for flight operations. It
was home to multiple companies and individuals providing flight training,
aircraft manufacture and repair, sightseeing and other services. A
full-time Field Director was always available controlling operations and
ensuring safety.[123]

1911/07/13   First Chicago Aviation Fatality

On July 13, 1911, Dan Kreamer was qualifying for his pilot's license when
he went into a spin and crashed. He left behind a widow and two children.

Kreamer was flying one of the Curtiss aircraft from James Plew's
dealership and flight school. His death disturbed Plew so much that he left
the aviation business.

An early aviation supporter, Plew was a founder of the Aero Club of
Illinois and became president after Octave Chanute's death. Plew opened
his Curtiss dealership in Chicago the end of 1909.

During his short sojourn in aviation, Plew attracted some of the top talent. His pilots, Jimmie Ward and Otto Brodie both went on to illustrious aviation careers. His mechanics included Rudolph "Shorty" Schroeder, as well as half-brothers Victor and Allan Loughhead.[124]

1911/08   Reimers-Mair Biplane Becomes Standard

In November 1910, the Reimers-Mair Biplane Co. was incorporated in Chicago. The three principals were F.C. Reimers, J.E. Mair and A.P. McArthur.[125] They operated a flying school at Avondale Field.

In the summer of 1911, Reimers-Mair changed the name to Standard Aviation[a] Co.[126] and was often called the Standard Biplane Co.[127] The flying school became the Standard School of Aviation. Both companies had offices in the Manhattan Building in downtown Chicago.

In August 1911, Standard shifted its flight operations from Avondale to the larger Clearing Field.[128]

1911/08/02   Harriet Quimby Is First American Woman Licensed

A Michigan native, Harriet Quimby was the first female to receive a pilot license from the Aero Club of America on August 2, 1911. Only one other licensed woman in the world was Marie-Louise Draincourt of France, who had qualified in a biplane. Quimby qualified in a monoplane at Moisant's Garden City, NY,[b] flying school, becoming the first in the world to do so. A few days later, she also flew and landed at night, becoming the first woman to accomplish that feat.

Quimby was the drama critic for *Leslie's Illustrated Weekly*, a weekly literary and news journal of the highest caliber that was published in New York City. She took an interest in flying at the 1910 air meet in Boston, where she met French-born aviator John Moisant.

Following the death of Cal Rogers, Quimby became the spokesperson for the *Vin Fiz* beverage.[129]

---

a   According to the Wikipedia article on *Standard Aero Corporation (c. 1911)*, Standard Aviation Co. of Chicago is unrelated to the Standard Aircraft Co. which was formed in 1916 and produced thousands of planes during and after WWI until it ceased operating in 1931 as the New Standard Aircraft Co. The currently operating StandardAero is unrelated to both previous Standard companies. Based in Arizona with dozens of offices worldwide, StandardAero began in 1911 in Manitoba as Standard Machine Works.
b   The Garden City landing strip later became known as Roosevelt Field, site of many aviation events including Lindbergh's departure point.

1911/08/12–20   First Chicago International Aviation Meet

The Aero Club of Illinois organized the First International Aviation Meet from August 12–20, 1911. The previous year, there were major meets in Los Angeles, Boston, and New York's Belmont Park, but the Grant Park air show was the first held in the center of a city and remains so today.[130]

The meet offered $80,000 in prizes, much coming directly from the pockets of Harold McCormick. The overriding goal was the betterment of aviation as evidenced by the statement that "prizes offered are not for flimsy performances of the spectacular, but for straight flying of the kind that means something. Such inducements will tend to bring out the real merits of aeroplanes and motors, and the best sort of ability in individuals."[131]

A total of 35 planes participated in the meet of which 10 were Wright, 6 were Curtiss, and a variety of other domestic and foreign aircraft. Glenn Curtiss personally attended, presenting his recently developed flying boat. Orville Wright also attended but was concerned with collecting royalties and did not fly.[132]

The Aviation Meet drew large crowds. Grandstands along Michigan Ave. seated 80,000 spectators. Organizers constructed 15 substantial hangars with steel girders, windows, and hefty wood doors. The press booth had telegraph and telephone wires as well as a wireless station.[133] Up to 400,000 people attended on the peak day of August 20 and were backed up to State St. An estimated 90% of the spectators had never seen a heavier-than-air vehicle fly before this meet.[134]

1911/08/14   Aviation Meet Results

Monday, August 14, 1911, was a busy day at the International Aviation Meet. Earle Ovington's Bleriot won the 12-mi. speed race for monoplanes. Also flying a Bleriot, Tom Sopwith won the 14-mi. over-water race flying laps around an intake crib in the lake. In the speed contests Sopwith had 7 first-place, 2 second-place and 1 third-place prize. He was the meet's top winner with $14,020 in prize money.

One of the crowd favorites was Lincoln Beachey's signature piece, a series of "death-dips," or the "Dive of Death." Beachey would put his Curtiss into a steep vertical climb until the plane stalled. Then he would push the nose over into a number of scoops culminating in a power dive straight toward the ground pulling out at the last minute. Beachey finished second with $11,667 in prize money.

Calbraith Perry Rodgers of the Wright team won the endurance prizes. Out of the potential 31.5 hr. during the 9-day event, Rodgers was aloft 27 hr. 16 sec. His longest flight was 2 hr. 55 min. 33 sec. Overall Rodgers received $11, 285, third in the winner totals.[135]

Jimmie Ward was a local favorite having started flying in Chicago before becoming part of the Curtiss exhibition team. In the meet, Ward won $2,900, placing 10th out of the 21 prize winners. As a local flyer, he received a lot of newspaper publicity. After one of his flights, he was met by several policemen who escorted him to a local police station. Ward's two wives had recognized him in the newspapers and had him arrested for bigamy.[136]

1911/08/14   Atwood Flies from St. Louis to Grant Park

At 6:30 p.m. on August 14, Harry Atwood landed in Grant Park after departing that morning from Forest Park in St. Louis. Atwood's Burgess-Wright plane made the 286-mi. journey in 9 hr. 54 min., including a two-hour stop both in Springfield and Pontiac. At times Atwood averaged the unheard-of speed of a mile-a-minute as he followed the Chicago and Alton Railroad, waving to crowds at every town along the way.

This was the first leg of Atwood's trip to New York and ultimately Boston.[137] He finally reached New York on August 25, making the 1,256-mi. trip in 28.5 hr. with 11 stops.[138]

1911/08/14   First Air-Sea Rescue Accomplished

Probably the world's first air-sea rescue took place on August 14, 1911, in Lake Michigan during the First Air Meet. Rene Simon was flying his Moisant over the lake when the engine failed and he glided into the lake. At the time Hugh A. Robinson was airborne in his Curtis hydro-aeroplane and witnessed the crash. Robinson landed and picked up Simon, remaining by his plane until it could be towed to shore. [139]

The situation happened again on Wednesday, August 16, when Arthur Stone's plane, a Queen, went down in the lake. This time, it was James E. Pugh who completed the rescue using his own Disturber II hydro-aeroplane.[140]

1911/08/15   Fatalities at Aviation Meet

There were two fatalities during the International Aviation Meet, both on Tuesday, August 15, 1911.

William "Billy" Badger attempted to duplicate Lincoln Beachey's stunt the "Dive of Death" in his Baldwin biplane. After making the steep dive, he

pulled up but the steel tubes in the wings were unable to handle the
g-forces and the plane plummeted to the ground.

Later that day, St. Croix Johnstone, who lived on Chicago's South Side,
flew his Moisant monoplane with a rotary engine for hours without incident.
Suddenly the plane dove from 3,500 ft. into the lake, killing Johnstone.[141]

1911/08/18   Over-Water Distance Race at Meet

On the Friday of the Aviation Meet, August 18, Tom Sopwith won the
over-water race. He flew a Bleriot the 16 miles from Grant Park to South
Shore Country Club and back. Sopwith's 80 hp plane also won two other
speed events the same day.[142]

1911/08/19 Endurance Record With Passenger Set

On August 19, George Beatty, a relatively new pilot, set an endurance
record carrying a passenger in his Wright for 3 hr. 43 mins., 22.5 sec. The
passenger was a *Chicago Tribune* photographer who carried two dozen
plates for aerial photographs.[143]

1911/08/20 Beachey Sets Altitude Record

The last day of the Aviation Meet hit the heights in several ways. The meet
saw the largest crowds ever.

Lincoln Beachey's Curtiss soared above the altitude record set only a
few days earlier by P.O. Parmlee in his Wright plane. Beachey climbed his
aircraft at the optimum angle of attack reaching 11,642 ft. before his fuel
was exhausted. Then he volplaned, gliding down in a slow spiral, until he
landed where he started in Grant Park. Beachey's record went unbroken for
three years.[144]

1911/08/21   Aviation Fundraiser

On August 21, the day after the meet closed, several of the pilots took to
the sky despite a storm with 30 mph winds. The pilots flew an exhibition to
raise money for St. Croix Johnstone's widow, following his tragic death
earlier in the week. They raised over $10,000 for her and her family.[145]

1911/08/27   Dickinson Takes to the Air

Charles "Pop" Dickinson's first documented flight followed the Air Meet on
August 27, 1911, when he paid Cal Rodgers $150 for rides for himself and
some friends including his chauffeur. However, it is likely that Dickinson
was in the air long before that. Reports indicate that starting in 1910,

Dickinson frequented Cicero Field where he wasn't afraid to get his hands dirty, a rarity for gentlemen of the privileged class. Another report claimed Dickinson had a flight with Claude Grahame-White in his Farman at New York's Belmont Park International Aviation Meet in October 1910.

Dickinson became interested in aviation around 1910, about the time his wife Marie died. Dickinson had the unusual combination of disliking automobiles but loving airplanes. Dickinson along with Harold McCormick, was one of the original founders and supporters of ACI.[146]

The *Chicago Tribune* quoted Dickinson in his later life saying "… my only wish is to see Chicago become the center of American flying." That attitude pervaded everything Dickinson did.[147]

Like McCormick, Dickinson was a major financial supporter of Chicago aviation. While McCormick gave lots of money providing facilities and prizes, Dickinson took a more personal approach. He supported struggling aviators and their families by providing funds, food, and transportation when it was needed most.

Dickinson's father owned a grain and seed company as well as warehouse storage along the river, although they were consumed in the 1871 fire. Charles eventually took over the grain and seed business. His business success spread and he opened offices in Minneapolis and Lansing, MI, and held positions as director and/or officer in several companies in Minnesota and New Jersey. Several lengthy business trips throughout Europe further extended his influence. Dickinson was a very generous person, who provided employee benefits unusual for the period, including an employee cafeteria.[148]

1911/09   Cicero Field Expands

Following the the International Aviation Meet, in September 1911, the Aero Club moved all the hangars and other facilities they had erected in Grant Park to Cicero Field.

They also provided an office where the Field Manager could work and also kept a supply of parts needed to and maintain the airplanes. By the end of 1911, more than 20 planes were based at Cicero.[149]

1911/09/23–10/21   First Air Mail Trials in NY

The first trial air mail flights consisted of delivery of mail from Garden City to Mineola, NY. The pilot, Earle Ovington, flew his Bleriot and dropped a mail pouch in a Mineola field from which it was retrieved and taken to the local post office.[150]

1911/10/08   *Vin Fiz* Visits Chicago

Cal Rodgers and his *Vin Fiz* visited Chicago as a stop on his coast-to-coast flight in October 1911 in his pursuit of the Hearst prize. William Randolph Hearst offered a $50,000 prize for the first airplane to fly coast-to-coast in less than 30 days.

Rodgers had participated in Chicago's International Aviation Meet a couple of months earlier as a member of the Wright team. He used his Chicago connection to convince Armour and Co. of Chicago to sponsor his flight. Armour emblazoned the name of their new grape drink, Vin Fiz, on Rodger's new Wright EX. Armour also provided a special three-car train to accompany the flight.

Rogers and the *Vin Fiz* departed Sheepshead on Long Island the afternoon of September 17, 1911. He expected to reach Chicago in four days; however, a crash delayed him three weeks. Eventually he arrived in Grant Park. On October 8, Rodgers took the *Vin Fiz* back into the air and departed Chicago for five additional stops in Illinois.

The *Vin Fiz* continued to be beset by adverse weather conditions, mechanical difficulties, and 16 crashes. Rodgers refused to quit, even when it became clear that time to win the Hearst Prize had elapsed. Although 19 days late for the challenge, 15–20,000 people showed up to greet him when he arrived in Pasadena on November 5. During the 49-day trip, Rodgers had flown 4,321 mi. in 82 hr. 2 min. at an average speed of 52 mph.[151]

1911/10/22   First Airplane in Combat

The first airplane used in combat was a Bleriot which made a reconnaissance flight in North Africa for the Italian Army.[152]

1912   First Airplane Designed to Carry Passengers

In Germany, Siegfried Hoffman designed the first aircraft for carrying passengers (4 plus the pilot).[153]

1912   First Women's Flight Class

Bessica Raiche, a flight instructor at the Standard School of Aviation in Chicago, organized the first flight instruction class exclusively for women.[154]

1912   First Aviation Periodical Goes to Press

The Aero Club of Illinois started publishing the first aviation periodical in the country, *Aerial Age*.[a] William Bushnell "Bill" Stout was the editor and chief publisher of the short-lived publication.[155]

As a youth, Stout moved around the Midwest eventually settling in Minneapolis for college. He had a strong technical background and interest but became a journalist, writing how-to articles using the pseudonym Jack Kneiff (Jack Knife). In the early 1900s, Stout began building and selling vehicles in Minneapolis, including motorcycles and trucks, under a variety of working arrangements.

Stout became interested in aviation. He constantly read about the early aviators and built model airplanes. In June 1910, Stout, as Jack Kneiff, was in charge of a model airplane contest held in conjunction with an air show at the State Fairgrounds in St. Paul. There he met such notables as Glenn Curtiss and Lincoln Beachey. When Eugene Ely's plane crashed, Stout was hired for a day as a mechanic to assist in getting the plane ready for the next day's performance.[156]

Stout's attention to aviation increased. His newspaper columns in the Twin Cities gained attention in Chicago. He moved to Chicago, where he became the automobile and transportation editor of the *Chicago Tribune* still using the pseudonym Jack Kneiff. In that role, he covered the 1911 Aviation Meet for the Tribune. After the meet, Otto Brodie, who had started business with a Farman airplane, gave Stout his first ride in hopes of getting some publicity.[157]

1912   Cicero Becomes Busiest Airport

By the end of 1912's flying season, Cicero Field had been the site of 2,265 flights which made it the busiest airport in the country before WWI. The official flying season started on Decoration Day (now Memorial Day) weekend and continued through Labor Day.

At the time, there were only 40 flying fields in the whole country and Cicero was among the best. Not only did it have a full-time Field Director, Andrew Drew, who had replaced Horace Wild, but Cicero was the only aerodrome where the director was actually a licensed pilot.

As Field Director, Drew established strict safety rules about which pilots and planes could fly. Only licensed pilots could carry passengers and

---

a   This was unrelated to *Aerial Age Weekly,* which began publication in New York City in March 1915.

there were restrictions on trick flying. All planes had to pass a regular safety inspection conducted by two aeronautical engineers, Chance Vought and Sidney James.

The 160-acre omni-directional field had been rolled as smooth as parade grounds. Twenty steel-trussed hangars held planes and equipment. During the summer flying season, additional tent hangars were available. By the end of the 1912 season, the Field Director had a separate office building instead of using a portion of a hangar.

During Chicago's winters, many pilots went south to give lessons and exhibitions in the warmer climate. Others just hunkered down at the field and worked on their planes. A few even lived in their hangars. Sometimes they would fly, testing their planes as early as March and continue into late October. Although the airport wasn't totally deserted during the off-season, pilots had to do without the usual level of support available at the airport.[158]

1912   Heath Buys Bates

Edward Heath expanded his aircraft supply business by purchasing the Bates Areo Motor Co. from Carl S. Bates. Heath sold planes of Bates' design along with those of his own.

Heath's philosophy was to make aviation available to as many people as possible. He kept his planes small, light, and inexpensive. Besides keeping prices low, Heath provided his customers purchasing options, making planes available as ready-to-fly, fully assembled without an engine, a set of all necessary parts, or the blueprints to build the plane from scratch.[159]

1912/01/10   Curtiss Tests First Flying Boat

The *Flying Fish*, a Model F flying boat designed and built by Glenn Curtiss, was successfully flown at Lake Keuka in New York. Hydroaeroplanes, as they were called, were popular because of the abundance of lakes and rivers that could be used as landing sites.[160]

1912/01/23 Model Aero Club Forms

The Illinois Model Aero Club[a] was founded in January 1912 as a subsidiary of the Aero Club of Illinois. Bill Stout and R. Robbins formed the club "to popularize and study the science and art of aviation through model aeroplanes."[161]

One of the first model aero clubs in the nation, it pushed to attract students. On January 23, the ACI sent letters to area high schools inviting

a   Some sources give the name as Model Aero Club of Illinois.

teachers to the first meeting in January 1912. ACI members worked with and through the schools directly with students interested in flying. The club was very successful in bringing youth into aviation. Matty Laird attributed his start in aviation to the Model Club.[162] James McDonnell, later founder of McDonnell Aviation in St. Louis, was also a member.[163]

The Model Club held meets at Cicero Field and drew enough spectators that crowd control became an issue.

Founder Bill Stout had gained experience previously with model airplanes while living in Minneapolis. In June 1910, Stout was in charge of a model airplane contest at the Minnesota State Fair. He went on to have a long, distinguished career designing motorcycles and automobiles as well as airplanes for a variety of companies.

Working with the Aircraft Production Board (later the Aircraft Board) during WWI, Stout did extensive research at McCook Field in Dayton using their wind tunnel. His work furthered efforts to reduce drag by using a single-wing rather than bi-wing design, implementing cantilever wings to eliminate external wires and supports, and reducing the size and weight of engines.

After the war, Stout settled near Detroit where he developed the Stout Air Pullman, 2-AT, a two-engine cabin plane of corrugated metal. He added a third engine, creating the 4-AT and eventually 5-AT Ford Tri-Motors. Henry and Edsel Ford heavily invested in Stout, eventually making his company a division of Ford.[164]

1912/03   Lillie Starts Flying School

Max Lillie, born in Sweden as Maximillian Liljenstrand opened the Lillie Flying School in March 1912. Flying Wright airplanes at Cicero Field, Lillie gained a national reputation, drawing students from around the country, including Katherine Stinson, DeLloyd Thompson, and many others. Lillie also hired Chance Vought as an instructor and aeronautical engineer.[165]

1912/04/16   Quimby Flies the Channel

On April 16, 1912, Harriet Quimby became the first woman to fly across the English Channel, departing destined for Calais. At the time her trip was mostly overlooked because of the coverage given the *Titanic*.

Less than three months later, on July 1, Quimby died in an accident at the Boston Aviation Meet. While flying her Bleriot XI, the plane pitched forward throwing Quimby and her passenger to their deaths.[166]

1912/05   Aviators Arrested in Parks

On May 17, 1912, Farnum Fish, flying with a female passenger, landed in Grant Park. He was promptly arrested, based on a recent Chicago law banning the common practice of using parks and boulevards as flying fields. In court he claimed engine problems and avoided a fine.[167]

Later that month, Max Lillie was a guest at a luncheon at the Columbia Yacht Club at the foot of Randolph St. Upon landing to attend the event, Lillie was promptly arrested, but intervention by Commodore James Pugh of the Pistakee Yacht Club got him released.

Following the luncheon, Lillie took Commodore Pugh for a flight to review the fleet. When they landed fifteen minutes later, they were both arrested and taken to the police station, where Lillie was released on bond.

At the trial, Lillie's attorney explained the landing was an emergency due to a broken strut. He also presented a letter to the judge from Mayor Carter Harrison Jr., who had attended the luncheon with Lillie. The judge was not moved and fined Lillie $10.[168]

1912/05/25   First Advertising by Airplane

In one of the first commercial uses of aviation, Farnum Fish flew from Chicago to Milwaukee. Sponsored by the *Milwaukee Journal*, Fish made the 93-mi. flight in his Wright B Flyer on May 25, 1912, over the lake but never out of sight of the shore. He dropped 7,500 handbills advertising Wisconsin's Boston Store before he delivered four bolts of cloth and an "unofficial" mail delivery.

A Los Angeles native, Fish learned to fly in Dayton, receiving some instruction from Orville Wright. In 1911, he became the world's youngest licensed pilot at age 15. The same year, Fish bought a Wright Model B and competed in Chicago's Aviation Meet where he came in 7th of the 20 winning cash prizes.[169]

1912/05/30   Wilbur Wright Dies

Wilbur Wright contracted typhoid fever and died on May 30, 1912. Stricken by grief, Orville lost a lot of his enthusiasm for the aviation business.[170]

1912/05/30–06/02   Triple City Aviation Meet

Chicago aviators kicked off the 1912 flying season in a big way with the four-day Triple City Aviaton Meet starting on Decoration Day (May 30).

Activities were held in Elmhurst and Wheaton as well as Cicero, where most of the flying activity was centered.

Among the many Chicago aviators who gave demonstration flights, some carrying passengers, were: Max Lillie, Otto Brodie, Farnum Fish, DeLloyd Thompson, Andrew Drew, Marcel Tournier, George Mestach, and Paul Studensky.[171]

1912/05/30–06/02   First Chicago Air Mail Demonstration

The Post Office Dept. conducted a formal air mail trial[a] in Chicago between May 30 and June 2, 1912, in conjunction with the Triple City Aviation Meet.

Postmasters of Cicero, Elmhurst, Wheaton, and Chicago established branch offices near landing fields. Chicago's Grant Park and the Elmhurst Golf Club were two of the sites used. Max Lillie and several other pilots who were officially authorized to fly mail carried it from the outlying airports to Grant Park, from which it was driven to the Chicago Post Office. Over 450 lbs. of mail were transported during the four-day demonstration.[172]

1912/05/30–06/02   Unique Plane Designs Shown at Cicero

Visitors to Cicero Field could inspect 14 experimental airplanes with unique designs, including two of Harold McCormick's pet projects, during the Triple City Aviation Meet starting May 30, 1912.

An enthusiastic aviation supporter, Harold McCormick chaffed at what he saw as negative effects of the Wrights' patent battles. McCormick funded several "eccentric" designs attempting to circumvent the Wright patent. In his quest, he hired some of the top aviation design talents.

While living in New York, William Romme won a design contest to produce a successful airplane that did not violate the Wright patents. Romme's plans for the *Cycloplane* placed the pilot in the middle of a large, circular, spoked wing with bracing wires above and below. A Gnome engine was mounted in front. Its overall appearance gave it the nickname *Umbrella Plane*.

In September 1910, Harold McCormick and John D. Rockefeller, Jr. began supporting Romme's development of his design. Romme's work proceeded with little progress first in New York and then Texas. A crash during testing left the craft unusable. When Cicero Flying Field opened in 1911, McCormick had Romme bring his plane to Chicago, where it became known as the *McCormick-Romme Cycloplane*.

a   During 1912, the Postal Service conducted 31 such trials around the country.

McCormick recognized the need for greater talent, so he hired Chauncy Milton "Chance" Vought, an engineer from the University of Pennsylvania who had been working at McCormick Harvesting Machine Co. Vought learned to fly at Max Lillie's Flying School[a] at Cicero Field, where he received License #156 from the Aero Club of America.

With Vought's assistance, the *Cycloplane* made its first "successful" flight on August 23, 1911, reaching an altitude of 15 ft. More modifications throughout 1912 and into 1913 gave it the ability to circle the field. Despite Vought's best efforts, the overall design was fatally flawed and doomed to failure. When the *Cycloplane* was damaged on May 22, 1913, Lillie salvaged whatever parts were usable and dumped the rest in Lake Michigan.

In a 1913 newspaper interview, Vought referred to the plane as a "freak." Throughout its life the *Umbrella Plane* had at least seven major design modifications, yet performed pathetically at best. After the project was scrapped, Vought went to work for Lillie as both a pilot and an engineer. In 1914, Vought also became editor of *Aero and Hydro*, the influential aviation weekly publication.

Another of McCormick's aviation hires was Sidney James. An engineering graduate of Armour Institute, James was hired by McCormick in 1911. James worked a little on the *Umbrella Plane* but primarily on another of McCormick's pet projects, the *Longitudinal Monoplane*.

The *Longitudinal Monoplane* was so-named because it had a a single high wing that extended longitudinally from the front to the back of the plane instead of horizontally to the sides. The plane was commonly called the *Mustard Plaster* because of its yellowish color. Like the *Umbrella Plane,* the *Mustard Plaster* was an abysmal failure.[173]

Other unusual planes included:

- John W. Smith's *Smith Monoplane* was a torpedo-shaped, all-metal aircraft with similarities to a Bleriot.[174]
- Henry S. Keller's *Keller Multiplane* with seven staggered wings and a Bates engine was also called "Steps to Heaven." [175]
- Thomas Preston Brooke, a bandmaster turned aviator, made the *Brookes Tractor Biplane* which used a non-gyro engine of his own design. The plane was advertised as having the ability to be flown "hands-off." [176]

---

a   Vought's eulogy at Vought.org states he took his lessons at the Wright School in Dayton
    rather than with Max Lillie, who was a Wright-trained instructor.

- R.D. Dwight and James B. Lund created the massive *Dwight-Lund Quadraplane* which had eight tandem wing surfaces with over 800 sq. ft. of surface. The 1700-lb. plane was over 18 ft. tall and 33 ft. long. They created a variable-pitch propeller that was nearly 12 ft. in diameter. Powered by only a 50 hp engine, the plane never got off the ground and was eventually scrapped.[177]
- Grover Sexton's *Sexton Monoplane* featuring a 100 hp engine and a low-center of gravity. [178]
- D. Kaiser's *Tandem Biplane* featured tricycle landing gear, tilting fore and aft wing cells, and a metal-covered fuselage.[179]

1912/07   Aero Club of Illinois Issues Licenses

In July 1912, the Aero Club of America authorized the Aero Club of Illinois to issue pilot licenses in conjunction with the Federation Aeronautique Internationale (FAI). The ACI named Harold McCormick, James Plew, Francis X. Mudd, and Grover F. Sexton as licensing representatives.

ACI's requirements for a license exceeded those required by the FAI. A pilot had to complete two flights of 50 m altitude and 5 km in length over a closed course that consisted of left and right turns, figure eights, and landing within 50 m of a designated point.

An expert license additionally required a cross-country round trip of 50 mi. The pilot also had to climb to 2,500 ft. then cut the engine and glide down to land within 100 m of a designated point. Immediately, nine Cicero pilots qualified for their expert license including Max Lillie, Otto Brodie, and Glenn Martin. [180]

1912/07/14   Katherine Stinson Licensed

On July 14, 1912,[a] Katherine Stinson became the 4th woman pilot (Federation Aeronautique Internationale License #148) in the U.S. after training at Max Lillie's Flying School. Her flight test required flying figure-eights and climbing to an altitude of 500 ft. At the time of her licensing, Stinson was the only woman pilot in the country. Harriet Quimby and Julia Clark had both died and Mathilda Moisant had retired from flying.

Stinson also persuaded Lillie to teach her stunt flying so she could do demonstration flights. She purchased her first plane from Lillie, a well-

---

a   Scamehorn places the date in March but that is dubious because it was outside Cicero's official "flying season."

used Wright Model B and immediately flew exhibitions around the Midwest. Only 21 years old, Stinson continually amazed seasoned aviators as well as spectators. Since she was just 5 ft. tall and weighed 100 lbs., many doubted she could control her Wright airplane, which had a reputation for being difficult to handle in Chicago's weather. From her youth and frail look, she became known as the "Flying Schoolgirl."

Unlike most exhibition pilots, however, instead of flying with an exhibition team, she remained independent, incorporating herself as the Stinson Aviation Co. Throughout her career, Stinson was known as a meticulous mechanic, starting with her first plane. Before the exhibition season, Stinson took her plane apart, thoroughly cleaning it and replacing any parts that showed the slightest wear. She also pioneered the preflight walk-around, thoroughly inspecting her aircraft before each takeoff. Not surprisingly, Stinson's exhibition aircraft were free from many mechanical problems that plagued less conscientious flyers.[181]

1912/07/12   First Model Aero Meet

On July 12, 1912, the Illinois Model Aero Club held its first meet at Cicero Field. High-school-age members designed and constructed model airplanes using rubber-band powered engines. In the process, they learned the fundamentals of aerodynamics and design techniques. The winner, breaking all previous records, was Arthur E. Nealy, whose plane flew for 56 sec. traveling a distance of 1,500 ft.[182]

1912/09/09   Gordon Bennett Aviation Race

The Aero Club of Illinois sponsored the Gordon Bennett Race on September 9, 1912, in conjunction with the Second International Aviation Meet.[183]

The Gordon Bennett Race consisted of entries representing participating countries vying for the fastest time flying around an oval course. The country winning the race would become host for the following year's race. Following a win by an American in 1911, Chicago was chosen as the U.S. host city.

The race consisted of 30 laps around six pylons on a 4.14 mi. course for a total of 124.8 mi. Race planes with fast landing speeds and no brakes needed a large open space to land, which was not available at Grant Park. The race was held at Clearing Field, between 69th and 71st streets, and Central and Menard (58th) avenues, which wasn't heavily built up. Only about 1,500 spectators watched the Gordon Bennett Races, primarily due to difficulties getting to the remote Clearing Field.[184]

Hosting the race also meant that Chicago had to provide an entry to represent the U.S. Charles Dickinson encountered difficulty raising funds for the race, so he personally put up approximately $25,000 of his own money for the race and built the American entry.

Dickinson had Norman Prince design a fast plane, the *Chicago Cup Defender,*[a] for the race. Unfortunately, it was difficult to design and build such an advanced plane on short notice. Delivered shortly before the race, there were questions over its airworthiness, so Dickinson withdrew it from the competition. The plane never flew and ultimately was stored with old cars outside Dickinson's feed company.[185]

The French entry, the Deperdussin Monocoque, won the race flying at an average speed of 105.5 mph.[186] For comparison, the contemporary automobile speed record in 1914 was 124 mph.[187]

1912/09/12–15   Aero Club Sponsors Second Meet

The Aero Club of Illinois sponsored the Second International Aviation Meet held September 12–15, 1912. Like the first meet, most of the activities were held in Grant Park, but Cicero Flying Field was also the site of some events.

The event attracted fewer national names, but the nation's most famous aviator, Lincoln Beachey, returned to thrill the crowds with his flying. Chicago's winds were particularly nasty and caused flying to be suspended one day. The meet was marred with accidents, including several that happened over the lake and required that the pilots be rescued. A mid-air collision during a practice at Cicero Field took the life of Howard Gill, a Baltimore pilot.

Although the meet was a success, it was far less so than the first meet and has been largely overlooked. Because the first meet lost money, it was more difficult to find investors so much of the expense was borne by Aero Club leaders. Prize money was about a third of the 1911 meet, drawing fewer competitors. By then, aviation was no longer a novelty in Chicago. The second meet received less publicity and drew far smaller crowds, with attendance estimated at only 100,000 people.[188]

After the disappointing financial return from their two Aviation Meets, the ACI decided to forgo similar events in the future and change their direction. Future events were intended to expand the realm of aviation.[189]

---

a   In some sources, the plane is called the *American Defender.*

The Post Office Dept. conducted another air mail demonstration, which took place in Grant Park following the Second Intrernational Meet between September 19–22, 1912.[190]

1912/09/14   Lillie Receives Expert License

Notable Chicago aviator Max Lillie received the Aero Club of America's Expert Aviator License #1 on September 14, 1912. An April 1913 ad emphasized that Lillie's school was the only flying school in the country where all the instructors held Expert Aviator Certificates. Students could choose either an "over-land" or "over-water" course for $300.[191]

1912/09/16   Lady Parachute Jump

During additional performances in Grant Park following the Second International Meet, Tiny Broadwick made at least two parachute jumps out of Glenn Martin's plane on September 16, 1912, becoming the first woman to free-fall parachute from an airplane. Broadwick, whose real name was Georgia Ann Thompson, was nicknamed "Tiny" because she was 5 ft. tall and weighed only 85 lbs.[192]

1913   Knabenshue Builds First Passenger Dirigible

Roy Knabenshue built the *White City,* the first dirigible for carrying passengers. Knabenshue was an early pilot of steerable balloons and dirigibles. Starting in 1913, Knabenshue thrilled sightseers with breathtaking aerial views from his base at White City Amusement Park.[193]

1913   Partridge and Keller Mean Business

Two Chicagoans, Elmer Partridge and Henry S. "Pop" Keller, started the P-K Flying School at Cicero Field in 1913. Soon they expanded into manufacturing and opened the Partridge-Keller Co.

Partridge-Keller built planes of their own design at Cicero Field. When Cicero closed in 1915, they moved their factory to their own Partridge Keller Aviation Field at 87th St. and Pulaski Rd. They were known for outstanding custom-built aircraft. They closed their own airfield and moved their manufacturing operation to Ashburn Field shortly after it opened.

Katherine Stinson, who also flew out of Cicero Field, was impressed by their workmanship. In 1914 she had them build a custom-designed biplane, *Looper*, which she used in her exhibition flights throughout the U.S. and Asia.

After a hiatus during WWI, Partridge and Keller specialized in converting surplus military aircraft to civilian use.[194]

1913   Lawrence-Lewis Aeroplane Co.

George R. Lawrence and Harry S. Lewis ran an aircraft company in Chicago between approximately 1913 and 1919. Lawrence was the aviator and Lewis an investor. Additional investments came from a Wisconsin engine manufacturer, Purcell,[a] who supplied the engines.

Lawrence-Lewis built somewhere between three and five aircraft of two different models. Each plane had a fully-enclosed cabin, among the first to provide that feature. Their patent applications also show air brakes and a pilot-ejection system with a parachute, although neither of these were actually incorporated in real airplanes. Ailerons were placed between the biplane's wings.

Some of the planes, outfitted with floats, were flown from Lake Calumet. When the Lawrence-Lewis B-model crashed during testing at Fox Lake, the company was out of funds and closed its doors.[195]

1913/02   Filming an Air Mail Demonstration

The Essanay Film News Company filmed Otto Brodie landing at Clearing Field carrying mail delivery from Argo. The film was processed and shown to audiences at the Orpheum Theater.[196]

1913/04   Cicero Field Gets Wind Tunnel

Cicero Field was already well-equipped but in April 1913, Harold McCormick installed a wind tunnel. He paid Sidney V. James, one of the engineers at Cicero Field, $25,000 to design and build the device. The 4 ft. wind tunnel had equipment that generated a wind speed of 80 mph. At the time, wind tunnels were only used by some of the larger design and manufacturing companies and were unheard of at an airport.[197]

1913/04/16   First Schneider Trophy Awarded

Awarded for the fastest seaplane or float plane, the initial race for the Schneider Trophy was won in Monaco by a Deperdussin Monocoque on floats flying nearly 46 mph.[198]

1913/04/19   Brodie Dies in Crash

On April 19, 1913 the tail of Otto Brodie's Farman came off during a flight. Brodie died in the crash and was buried in Chicago's Montrose Cemetery.

---

a   Possibly Putnam and Purcell of Madison.

After founding the Franco-American Aviation Co., Brodie took over the Standard School of Aviation. Previously the Standard School had developed a poor reputation for both safety and instruction and had been characterized as "fraudulent" in the press. Brodie used his skill and reputation to turn the school around. However, without Brodie, the Standard school foundered and soon declared bankruptcy.[199]

1913/07   McCormick Buys Hydroaeroplane

Never one to be left out, in July 1913 Harold McCormick joined the flurry of flying boat activity by purchasing a Curtiss flying boat that he named *Edith* after his wife, Edith Rockefeller. McCormick's plane was a Model F that had been enlarged to accommodate five people.

A Curtiss pilot stayed with McCormick for a couple of months to teach him to fly and McCormick permanently hired a mechanic to take care of the plane and act as an aerial chauffeur. Soon after purchasing the Curtiss, McCormick showed off his new plane at a party in which his pilot and Glenn Martin, who also owned an airboat, took guests on sightseeing flights. The three women who flew were, according to the *Chicago Tribune,* the first women to fly in an airboat.[200]

1913/07/01   First Flight Across Lake Michigan

Although Farnum Fish had flown over waer en route to Milwaukee in May 1912, he hugged the shore and never lost sight of land. On July 1, 1913, Logan Archibald "Happy Jack" Vilas flew his new Curtiss hydroaeroplane over open water from Silver Beach in St. Joseph, MI to Chicago in 94 min. Mist over the lake made navigation difficult, especially since he had no compass on board.

Vilas was born and raised in Chicago, and, as an adult, was a neighbor and friend of Harold McCormick. Along with McCormick, he developed an interest in flying boats. Vilas spent a month at the Curtiss School and received Hydro-License #6 along with the Curtiss F-Boat he purchased. With only five hours of flying experience he flew his new plane from Hammondsport, NY back to Chicago.[201]

1913/07/02–8   Great Lakes Flying Boat Cruise

In 1913, the ACI sponsored the International Great Lakes Flying Boat Cruise. The event reflected the Club's disappointment with the two previous money-losing International Aviation Meets. In addition, many ACI members including Harold McCormick and Jack Vilas, had a newfound fascination in hydroaeroplanes.

Two events were planned. First was an "efficiency" contest, which was a race over a closed circuit, starting at Grant Park. Unfortunately, winds were high, so most flights didn't take off. At least one plane, flown by Glenn Martin, crashed and was damaged.

The second event was a long-distance race starting in Grant Park on July 8. Planes would skirt the coastline to the other side of the lake, then fly across the state to Detroit. Storms also dogged this event, causing flyers to delay their flights and causing damage to their planes. Beckwith Havens finally won the 886-mi. race when he arrived on July 18, ten days after his departure with 15.5 hr. in the air.[202]

1913/09/01   First Loop Performed

French pilot Adolphe Pegoud made the first voluntary loop-the-loop in a Bleriot monoplane.[203]

1913/09/15   Laird's First Airplane Takes Off

In 1913 at age 17, Emil "Matty" Laird taught himself to fly at Cicero Field. Earlier that year, he had built the plane at his house, then had it trucked to Cicero Field for testing. The plane was simple, even primitive. There was no throttle, only a button to turn the engine on and off.

Having spent all his money building the plane, Laird couldn't afford flight lessons, so he taught himself. On September 15, 1913, while taxiing the plane around, it took off a few feet into the air but had some minor damage on landing. Gradually Laird's skill improved and soon he was making circuits around the field.

Laird grew up in Chicago where, after graduating eighth grade, he went to work at a bank in the Loop. In September 1910, when he was 14, Laird looked out the bank window and marveled at Walter Brookins flying his Wright airplane through the skies. He was instantly hooked on aviation. The International Aviation Meet the following year further stoked Laird's aviation fire.

Right after the meet, he built a 36 in. scale model of an airplane from memory. The next year, Laird became a charter member of the Model Aero Club of IL, a youth program of the ACI. He began making rubber-band powered model airplanes. Laird's models were well-made and he began selling them. He received $5 for each model, which was more than the $4.50 he earned each week at the bank.

Laird used the proceeds to fund construction of a real airplane. He hung around Cicero Field, where he found scrap parts and got to know the big names in aviation. Many of them, including his mentor Pop Dickinson, liked Laird's enthusiasm and supported him with their advice and "deals" on parts he needed, including a 12 hp engine. Laird's design was similar to the *Chicago Cup Defender*, a monoplane Dickenson had acquired for the Gordon Bennett Race of 1912, although the plane never flew.[204]

1913/09/15   Max Lillie Killed in Crash

Max Lillie, one of Chicago's top aviators, was killed in a crash while flying an exhibition in Galesburg, IL, on September 15, 1913. Lillie was flying at about 150 ft. high when his Wright plane experienced mechanical problems. With his plane headed for the grandstand, Lillie pulled the nose up and put the plane into a sharp turn, snapping the wing. Lillie succeeded in avoiding the spectators but hit the ground and was crushed by the Wright's pusher engine as the plane crashed on top of him.

Lillie had opened the Lillie Flying School in March 1912 and trained many notable aviators using Wright airplanes at Cicero Field. He had an Expert Pilot License and was widely known as a skilled pilot with highest regards for standards. He had made over 4,000 flights, 1,700 carrying a passenger.

Earlier in 1913, Lillie and two partners formed the Weckler-Armstrong-Lillie Co. to produce flying boats. Lillie opened a branch of his flying school at the Columbia Yacht Club in Grant Park to provide instruction in flying boats.

However, Lillie's high standards may not have extended to his equipment. Grover Loening, an engineer who worked for the Wright Company, inspected the wreckage and concluded they showed poor maintenance and inferior parts. Unfortunately, Lillie's school and other enterprises did not have sufficient momentum to survive without him.[205]

1913/10/31   Lincoln Highway Created

The Lincoln Highway, America's first transcontinental highway, was dedicated on October 31, 1913. Stretching from Times Square in New York to Lincoln Park in San Francisco, the highway was conceived by Indiana automotive pioneer Carl G. Fisher. The highway was mainly funded by civic minded executives in the automotive and highway construction industries as a way to show the public the benefits of automobiles for long-distance transportation.

The original route of 3,389 mi. was mostly patchwork of existing roads designated as part of the Lincoln Highway. The route changed numerous times over the years but roughly followed the routes later taken by US 30 and I-80.[206]

1913/12/11   Sikorsky Builds First 4-Engine Airplane

In Russia, Igor Sikorsky's four-engined S-21 The Grand first flew on December 11, 1913.[a] The Grand was a truly luxurious airplane with a glass-enclosed passenger compartment containing four seats, a table, and a washroom. The design was later modified into a bomber, the S-22 Ilya Muromets which served in combat against the Germans in 1915.[207]

1914   Goldblatt's Opens Its Doors

Simon and Hannah Goldblatt opened a neighborhood grocery store in 1914. By 1928, Goldblatt's had grown into a five-story department store. Subsequent years saw it expand to a regional chain with more than 35 stores. Goldblatt's was a retail innovator, allowing customers access to merchandise in the open rather than keeping it behind counters, as was the practice elsewhere.

Over the years the retail landscape changed. Goldblatt's gradually closed stores and finally filed for bankruptcy in 1981.[208]

1914   Buck Weaver Takes to the Sky

Chicago native George Erastus "Buck" Weaver[b] learned to fly with the ACI[c] in 1914 and spent a lot of time around Cicero Field with the other avia-tors.[209] In November 1917, Weaver and Pop Keller became civilian flight instructors at the Army Air Corps' Rich Field in Waco, TX.[210]

After the war, Weaver partnered with several other aviators, forming Weaver Aircraft Co. (WACO) in Lorain, OH. On the first test flight of WACO's initial plane, Weaver crash-landed, badly damaging the plane and suffering extensive injuries. Shortly after, Weaver left WACO for a period. The partners changed the corporate name to Advance Aircraft Company but retained the WACO brand for their airplanes.[211]

---

a   Some sources place the date of The Grand's first flight on May 12, 1913.
b   George "Buck" Weaver is not to be confused with Carl "Buck" Weaver, who was the mechanic on the *Wingfoot Express*.
c   Post states that Weaver learned to fly at Wright Field instead of Chicago.

1914/01/01   First Airline Starts Operation

The St. Petersburg-Tampa Airboat Line is usually cited as the country's first airline offering scheduled flights. Flying the Benoist XIV flying boat, the airline operated for only three months before shutting down.[212]

However there are reports that in 1913, Silas Christofferson operated a passenger shuttle service between San Francisco and Oakland.[213]

1914/02   Army Demands Tractors

The U.S. Army adopted standards in February 1914 that required that all airplanes acquired in the future would use a tractor engine.

Since the initial Wright Flyer, many aircraft designs, particularly in the U.S., used a pusher engine to the rear of the pilot instead of a tractor engine at the front of the plane. Experience with many crashes led experts to conclude that the tractor design was safer for pilots, since it was better for a pilot to fall on top of the propeller and engine rather than be under them.

Despite the Army's demands, the Wright Co. insisted on producing pusher-engine airplanes.[214]

1914/05   Lake Shore Airline Formed

In May 1914, several ACI members started Lake Shore Airlines with regularly scheduled flights between Lake Forest, Grant Park, and the South Shore Country Club.

Harold McCormick and Jack Vilas both owned flying boats, which they had been using to commute between their North Shore homes and their downtown offices. They saw the airline as a way to provide the service to their friends and neighbors.

Scheduled flights of Lake Shore Airline started on June 10 for a cost $10. Weather frequently disrupted operations, and the airline ceased operation before year's end.[215]

1914/05/16–18   Aero Club Air Meet at Grant Park

The ACI sponsored another aviation meet May 16–18, 1914. Smaller than the previous Aero Club events, the meet wasn't billed as an "International Aviation Meet," as were the previous ones. Air shows were becoming commonplace and no more than 100,000 people attended. Lincoln Beachey made his last Chicago appearance before he crashed in San Francisco almost exactly a year later.[216]

1914/06/14   City of Chicago's First Aviation Facility

The first permanent aviation facility under city management was the Cornelia St. Hydroaeroplane Harbor that opened on June 14, 1914, in Lincoln Park. The Park Commissioner set aside an area for flying boats at the north end of the park at the foot of Cornelia St.

To celebrate the opening aviation activity took place all over the city. At the new hydroaeeoplane port, Harold McCormick and Jack Vilas gave sightseeing flights around the harbor out of their new lakefront hangar.

Roy Knabenshue took passengers sightseeing on his airship *White City* from its port at White City Amusement Park.

In Grant Park, Katherine Stinson made three flights for several thousand spectators. Stinson's flights were an exhibit for the Exposition and Congress of Women's Achievements that was being held at the Coliseum.[217]

1914/07/28   War Explodes in Europe

During his visit to Serbia, an assassin killed Austrian Archduke Ferdinand in Sarajevo on June 28, 1914.

A month later, on July 28, Austria-Hungary declared war on Serbia. Over the next few weeks, due to treaties and long-standing rivalries, the other European countries aligned themselves with one or the other in what became one of the bloodiest and most protracted conflicts in history.[218]

1914/08/29   Stinson Suffragettes

The two Stinson sisters, Katherine and Marjorie, flew their Wright biplanes as part of a Suffrage Field Day in Chicago. Each plane towed a big yellow banner proclaiming "Votes for Women." After their air show, they helped the suffragette campaign raise $50,000.[219]

Although not as closely linked to Chicago as her older sister, Marjorie was no stranger to the aviation community here. Her suffragette flight was made less than three weeks after she earned her license (#303) from the Wright School in Dayton on August 12. At age 18, she was the ninth and youngest woman pilot in America. Marjorie later earned the moniker "Flying Schoolmarm" for training over 100 pilots by the time the Stinson flight school in San Antonio closed in 1917 because of the war.[220]

1914/10/20   Chicago's First Long-Distance Mail Delivery

On October 20, 1914, William C. "Billy" Robinson, Sr. arrived at Cicero
Field with mail from Des Moines and Grinnell, IA, making Chicago's first
long-distance mail delivery

Robinson's journey actually began three days earlier, on October 17,
1914, when he left Des Moines in his self-designed *Grinnell-Robinson
Scout*. Approaching Chicago, he encountered dense clouds and feared
overflying his destination and landing in the lake. Instead, he diverted and
flew to Kentland, IN. Robinson made the nonstop 332-mi. trip in 4 hr.
40 min., establishing a new U.S. record.

A tinkerer and bicycle repairman, Robinson grew up in Grinnell, IA. He
developed an interest in flying and constructed his own plane around 1910.
In 1911, Robinson met Max Lillie and wintered with him at his flying
school in Florida, where he took formal flying lessons. Robinson spent the
summer of 1912 in Chicago working as a mechanic and instructor at Lillie
Flying School at Cicero Field. Later that year, he began doing exhibitions
for the National Aeroplane Manufacturing Co. flying their Anzani-powered
Nieuports. He eventually returned to Grinnell, where he formed his own
aircraft manufacturing company. [221]

1914/11   Cook County Creates the Forest Preserve District

Jens Jensen, a landscape architect, and Dwight Perkins, an architect,
spearheaded a movement to create space where those living in the city
would have access to natural areas to enrich their lives. Thanks to their
efforts, Cook County created the Forest Preserve District. [222]

1914/12/21–25   First German Bombing Raids on England

As a perverse Christmas present, German airplanes made the first of many
bombing raids on England on December 21–25, 1914. On May 31, 1915,
the first German Zeppelin bombed London. [223]

1915–1919

1915   Dickinson Heads ACI

In 1915, Charles "Pop" Dickinson, owner of a seed company, became president of ACI, holding the post for twenty years. As its primary sponsor, Dickinson supported many of the ACI activities, including Ashburn Airport, from his personal funds.[224]

1915   National Aeroplane Fund Formed

With war looming, in the Spring of 1915, the Aero Club of America, with support from the ACI and other groups, formed the National Aeroplane Fund[a] to draw attention to America's aviation unpreparedness. The fund lobbied legislators and military leaders to improve the aviation arsenal. Individuals and groups donated airplanes to state reserve units.[225]

An active supporter of the fund, the ACI raised $20,000 to improve Ashburn Field so it could handle an Aviation Reserve Squadron and Training Center.[226]

1915   ACI Member Forms Lafayette Escadrille

Fluent in French, ACI member Norman Prince sailed to France in 1915, where he was instrumental in convincing the French to form the "Escadrille Americaine," otherwise known as the Lafayette Escadrille.

Prince was raised in a traditional and privileged Massachusetts home and attended Harvard and Harvard Law School. Prince wanted to fly despite his father's disapproval so he went to Atlanta under an assumed name and received his pilot's license in August 1911.

Prince's father didn't react positively. As a member of the Board of Armour and Co., the elder Prince "banished" his wayward son to work at a Chicago law firm. Contrary to his father's expectations, Prince quickly became active with the ACI. He submitted the winning design for the *Chicago Cup Defender*, the U.S. entry in the 1912 Gordon Bennett Race, although the plane didn't actually compete.[227]

---

a   The fund is totally unrelated to the National Aeroplane Manufacturing Co., a Chicago airplane
     builder that went out of business about 1913.

1915/03/03   Pres. Wilson Creates NACA

President Woodrow Wilson created the National Advisory Committee on Aeronautics on March 3, 1915. The creation of a small group of unpaid advisors was an amendment to a naval appropriations bill. With an initial budget of only $5,000, the group's purpose was to "direct and conduct research and experimentation in aeronautics, with a view to their practical solution."

NACA was instrumental in coordinating and encouraging aviation organizations to support aviation research and promotion. NACA assisted organization such as the Manufacturers Aircraft Assn. and the Bureau of Aeronautics in the Commerce Dept. It also spurred on the Weather Bureau's efforts to develop information that would benefit aviation.[228]

1915/03/09   Aero Club's Final Grant Park Air Show

The Aero Club held its final air show in Grant Park on March 9, 1915. Following the recent crash and death of Lincoln Beachey, the ACI substituted the young Art "Smash-Up" Smith.

Born in Fort Wayne, IN, Smith was an exhibition pilot for Mills Aviators flying their planes out of Cicero Field. Smith was a real crowd pleaser, flying an amazing 32 continuous loop-the-loops.

That night, Smith flew the first recorded night air show. After attaching fireworks to the trailing edges of his wood and fabric wings, he flew a variety of stunts, including rolls and loops. Later that summer, Smith's spectacle thrilled crowds nightly at the San Francisco Panama-Pacific International Exposition.[229]

1915/04/15   Hassell Gets Nickname "Fish"

Bruce "Bert" Raymond John was flying solo over Lake Michigan on April 15, 1915.[a] About a mile and a half from shore, he encountered turbulent air that knocked him into the lake. Hassell clung to the wreckage as Harold McCormick's gardener rowed out to rescue him. His ordeal earned him the nickname "Fish" which stuck with him the rest of his life.

Hassell, a Wisconsin native, learned to fly at Glenn Curtiss's school where he soloed on June 15, 1914, and received Pilot's License #20. On and off throughout his career, Hassell would barnstorm, performing exhibitions

---

a   According to the Early Aviator website, this incident took place over Reed Lake near Grand Rapids, MI.

to support himself. He moved to Chicago and purchased a Curtiss Flying Boat from McCormick.[230]

1915/06/29   Vilas Pioneers Fire Spotting

At his summer home in northern Wisconsin, Lake Forest resident and aviator Jack Vilas took the *Chief Forester* on a flight on June 29, 1915.

Vilas demonstrated the plane's utility in spotting forest fires, impressing the chief forester. Vilas was appointed a flying fire warden and flew patrols throughout the summer. That fall, an article in *American Forestry* magazine ran an article on the program and it was quickly copied around the country.[231]

1915/07/24   *Eastland* Disaster

The *Eastland*, a Lake Michigan excursion ship, capsized in the Chicago River while loading passengers on July 24, 1915. More than 825 people died, making it the largest loss of life on the Great Lakes. Afterward, the ship was salvaged and converted into a navy training ship, the USS *Wilmette*.[232]

1915/07/18–19   Katherine Stinson First Woman to Perform Loop

At Cicero Field, Katherine Stinson was the first woman to loop-the-loop on July 18, 1915.[a] She went on to do it more than 500 times in her career.

Earlier that year, working with Elmer Partridge and Pop Keller, Stinson sketched out requirements for a closed-cockpit exhibition plane. The Partridge-Keller Bi-Plane, also known as the *Looper*, became Stinson's prime exhibition plane, with a Laird biplane as her backup.

During one performance at Cicero, Stinson looped-the-loop three consecutive times and was attempting a fourth. At 4,000 ft., the stress ruptured a gasoline valve causing the engine to quit. The plane went into a nose-first dive, plunging over 3,000 ft. before she was able to right it and land safely.

In December of 1915, Stinson became the first woman to fly a night exhibition using magnesium flares on the trailing edge of the wing.[233]

1915/08   Partridge & Keller Start Their Airport

In response to the closing of Cicero Flying Field, Elmer Partridge and Henry "Pop" Keller rented some land nearby for P-K Field at 87th St. and

---

a   Ruth Law also claimed to have been the first woman to loop-the-loop, according to Scamehorn p. 72.

Pulaski Rd. The two men moved their businesses, the Partridge-Keller airplane manufacturer and the P-K Flying School, from Cicero to their new airport. Several other Cicero residents also joined them.

When Pop Dickinson established Ashburn Field for the ACI in 1916, Partridge and Keller abandoned their own field and transferred all operations to Ashburn.[234]

1915/08/02–07   Market Week Demonstrations

The Chicago Chamber of Commerce sponsored a week of aviation demonstrations in Grant Park August 2–7, 1915, to celebrate Market Week.

Each day was highlighted by Katherine Stinson looping-the-loop. Two days featured competitions by the Model Aero Club of Illinois.[235]

1915/09/09   Laird's First Paid Performance

Matty Laird made his first paid exhibition performance in Sebring, OH, on September 9, 1915, receiving $350 for his performance.

Laird's performance came as result of his association with Katherine Stinson. They both flew out of Cicero Flying Field, where the young Laird impressed Stinson with both his flying skills and the airplane he built, *Baby Biplane.*

Stinson arranged for Laird to fly some unpaid demonstration flights during the Market Week celebration in Grant Park that August. Chicagoan Bill Pickens, booking agent for both Stinson and Lincoln Beachey, immediately recognized Laird's potential and signed him for the rest of the flying season. Laird had launched a new career.[236]

1915/10/13   Wright Sells Company

Orville Wright sold his interest in the Wright Corp. Essentially, Wright was becaming inactive in the aviation industry although, as the recognized "Father of Flight," he continued to receive various honors and served on advisory boards.

The Wright Corp. was purchased for $500,000 by a syndicate comprised of William B. Thompson (a mining engineer and financier), Albert H. Wiggin (Chase National Bank president), and T. Frank Manville (of the H.W. Johns-Manville asbestos manufacturer). They introduced Models K and L, both to lackluster reception.[237]

1915/11/05   Navy Uses Catapult

On November 5, 1915, the U.S. Navy first used a catapult to launch a Curtiss plane off the USS *North Carolina*. Naval aviator Henry C. Mustin was at the controls.[238]

1916   Chicago Gets Its Big Shoulders

Chicago Poems was published to critical acclaim in 1916 by Carl Sandburg. The poem *Chicago*, which contains the memorable line, "City of the Big Shoulders," first appeared in the March 1914 issue of *Poetry*.

Early in his career, poetry income was not enough to sustain the Maywood resident's family. To provide regular income, Sandburg, a Socialist, was a journalist for the *Chicago Daily News* where he specialized in labor issues.[239]

1916   Earhart Finishes High School

After a troubled childhood, Amelia Earhart spent several years in Chicago, where she graduated from Hyde Park High School in 1916.

Her family chose to send Earhart to Hyde Park HS because it had a better science program than her nearby school. Despite the change, Earhart's high school experience was marginal at best. Although she had yet to develop her interest in flying, Earhart was drawn to male-dominated professions, including law, engineering, and film direction.[240]

1916/01   Curtiss Sells Company

Glenn Curtiss sold all of his aviation companies to a New York investment group headed by William Morris Imbrie. Curtiss received $5 million in cash and another $3.5 million in stock of the new company: Curtiss Aeroplane and Motor Company. Curtiss continued his close association with the company as a member of the board of directors, as well as being in charge of day-to-day operations.[241]

1916/04/15   Cicero Field Sold to Developers

When the Aero Club of Illinois' five-year lease for Cicero Flying Field expired, Harold McCormick decided not to renew it and the airport was sold to developers on April 15, 1916.

Due to McCormick's early enthusiasm, his airport had the two distinctions of being Chicago's first full-time, public airport and being the first of many Chicago area airports to fall to developers. Harold McCormick's interest in aviation waned over the years as he dealt with a divorce and moved to Switzerland.[242]

1916/04/16   Dickenson Purchases Ashburn Field

The day after Harold McCormick sold Cicero Field to developers, on April 16, 1916, Charles Dickinson purchased 640 acres to provide the Aero Club with a new flying field.

The new Ashburn Field was between 79th and 85th streets and 40th (Crawford/Pulaski) and 48th (Cicero) avenues, although most of the activity centered around 83rd St. and Cicero Ave. It was named Ashburn because the general area had been the dumping grounds for Chicago's ashes.

Unlike Cicero Field, which McCormick intended primarily for use by ACI members, Ashburn was open to the general public. Ashburn was a few miles farther south than Cicero, located near the Ashburn station on the Wabash Railroad. Although not as accessible to the city as Cicero Field, it was nevertheless easier to reach than Clearing Field.[243]

Although McCormick sold the land, he donated all the Cicero Field buildings and equipment to ACI, moving them to Ashburn.[a] The first three hangars were used by Laird Aviation, Partridge-Keller Aviation, and Katherine Stinson.[244]

1916/06/29   First Boeing Airplane Flies

Near Seattle on June 29, 1916, the first Boeing airplane, the *B&W*, took to the air.[245]

1916/06/29   Volunteers Trained for War

The ACI and the Army Signal Corps created the U.S. Central Aviation Reserve to train volunteers to fly, so they would be prepared in event of a war. They raised funds and accepted applications from volunteers. However, the program was dismantled later that year when the War Department established its own aviation school for the reserves.[246]

1916/07/04   Municipal Pier Opens

With great fanfare, the $4.5 million Municipal Pier opened on Chicago's lakefront on Independence Day 1916. The 3,000-ft. pier served both freight and passenger shipping. During both world wars, the U.S. Navy used the pier for a variety of functions. In 1927, the city renamed it Navy Pier.[247]

---

a   Since the same buildings appear in photographs at both airports, some photos have the location misidentified.

1916/08/07   Wright Merges with Martin

The syndicate owning the Wright Corp. sold the company to Glenn L. Martin Co., and was reorganized as the Wright Martin Aircraft Co. Orville Wright retained the title of Chief Consultant Engineer, but was inactive.[248]

1916/10/12   Chicago Ace Killed in Action

After flying a bombing escort mission on October 12, 1916, Norman Prince's wheels struck wires during his landing. His plane flipped over with Prince beneath it. He died of his injuries.

Norman Prince, a practicing Chicago lawyer, had been one of founders of the Lafayette Escadrille. While in France, he flew 122 missions and was credited with 5 victories, making him Chicago's first ace.[249]

1916/10/28   Ashburn Field Officially Opens

Ashburn Field officially opened on October 28, 1916, when it was occupied by an Army Signal Corps unit with five pilots, making it one of three Army aviation schools in the country.[250]

The ACI held an air show to rally support both for the new field and for the Army's presence.

At first, the field was primitive with tents and rudimentary equipment, but it developed quickly as buildings were moved from Cicero Field. Dickinson further developed the airport adding runways, hangars, access roads, a bunkhouse, and water well for the Aero Club. Other facilities included a building with a wind tunnel and other aeronautical test apparatus. Later, the field added a 50-ft. tower for observation and traffic control using hand signals instead of radios—probably the first control tower in the country.

The Signal Corps quickly discovered that the equipment of the period was not compatible with flying in the Chicago winter. In February of 1917, they temporarily relocated the training unit to Memphis.[251]

1916/11/02–03   Sunrise-to-Sunset Flight Between Chicago & NY

The *New York Times* issued a challenge for a sunrise-to-sunset flight from Chicago to New York City carrying a limited amount of mail as a feasibility demonstration.

On November 2, 1916, Victor Carlstrom, an instructor for Curtiss in Newport News, departed Ashburn Field carrying about 1,000 letters for New York. Although he was flying the latest Curtiss Model R biplane, not coincidentally named *New York Times*, the plane developed a gas leak which forced a landing in Erie, PA. However, he had established a distance record of 452 mi. After repairing the leak, he made another stop in Hammondsport, NY. He completed the final leg to Governor's Island the next day establishing the cross-country speed record of 134 mph. Carlstrom made the 850 mi. journey in 8 hr. 26 min. of flying time.[252]

1916/11/04   Laird's Election Night Reporting

Minnesota's main newspaper, the *Saint Paul Pioneer and Dispatch,* contracted with Matty Laird to announce the results of the Presidential election by igniting a flare, white for a victory by Woodrow Wilson and red for Charles E. Hughes. Laird flew is *Boneshaker* in a night sky laced with snow and rain. At 11 p.m., he fired the red flares as he had been instructed. However, with the precipitation the red flares appeared as white on the ground, correctly reflecting Wilson's victory.[253]

1916/11/19   Ruth Law Sets Distance Record

Ruth Bancroft Law[a] took off from Grant Park on November 19, 1916, landing 509 mi. away, breaking Victor Carlstrom's recently established distance record.

Headwinds had forced Law to land about 10 mi. short of her first planned stop in Hornell, NY, on her sunrise-to-sunset Chicago to New York flight. She refueled and ontinued to Binghamton, NY, where darkness forced her to stop. Law arrived at Governor's Island the next morning after 8 hr. 55 min. of flight time.

Law's total flight time was only about a half hour longer than Carlstrom's, which is remarkable considering the difference in the capabilities of the planes they flew.

Carlstrom, a Curtiss instructor, flew Model R, the latest of the Curtiss military biplanes, with a 200 hp engine. Law had tried to purchase a new airplane, but Curtiss refused to sell her one saying "it was too much for a girl to handle." Instead Law used her obsolete Curtiss Pusher biplane with a 100 hp engine.

Law's plane was primitive in several ways. The pilot sat at the front of the plane with no protection from the wind or elements. The throttle was controlled by her foot but the other flight controls were two levers that required constant handling, making it difficult for her to look at her

a   She later married becoming known as Ruth Law Oliver.

compass and maps and perform other necessary tasks. For protection from the cold, she wore two woolen suits and two leather suits with a full face mask, which further impeded her movements.[254]

1916/12   Katherine Stinson's Asia Trip

In December 1916, Katherine Stinson joined a troupe of flyers on an Asian tour. She used the Partridge-Keller *Looper* and Matty Laird's *Boneshaker* throughout her trip through Japan and China. In Tokyo, 25,000 people watched her perform, and throughout the two countries she became known as "Air Queen." The tour concluded with a return to the U.S. in May 1917.[255]

1917   Planes at Rockford's Camp Grant

Only months after the U.S. declared war on Germany, in June 1917, the Army established Camp Grant on the banks of the Rock River in Rockford. Camp Grant thrived and served the needs of the Army through both world wars.

At various times, a portion of Camp Grant's parade grounds were used as a landing field. During the 1920s, the Camp was host to both temporary summer aviation encampments and a small permanent contingent for short periods.[256]

1917/03/08–12   Russian Revolution Begins

Revolutionaries took to the streets on March 8, 1917,[a] eventually forcing Tsar Nicholas II to abdicate and dissolve the Russian Empire on March 12. He was replaced by a Provisional Assembly dominated by capitalists and nobles.

The Bolsheviks under Vladimir Lenin staged a nearly bloodless coup on November 6–7, replacing the Provisional Assembly with local soviets consisting of soldiers, workers, and peasants.[257]

1917/04/16   U.S. Declares War on Germany

Congress declared war on Germany and Austria-Hungary on April 16, 1917. The U.S. committed to providing the Allies with 4,500 airplanes, 5,000 pilots, and 50,000 mechanics within a year. At the time, the U.S. had only about 100 airplanes and 1,000 pilots.[258]

1917/05   Aircraft Production Board Created

With the Army having a little over 200 airplanes to use in the war, Congress created the Aircraft Production Board to function in an advisory role,

---

a   At the time, Russia used the Julian calendar, which identifies the dates as February 23–27 and October 24–25 respectively.

selecting designs and recommending production techniques. Detroit businessman Howard E. Coffin was appointed chair. On October 1, the board was reorganized with additional military representatives and renamed the Aircraft Board.

Following the war, the decisions and actions of the board were the focus of public dispute and it became the subject of four separate investigations including one led by former Supreme Court Justice Charles Evans Hughes.[259]

1917/05/09   Boeing Airplane Company Created

In Seattle, William Boeing changed the name of Pacific Aero Products to Boeing Airplane Co.[260]

1917/06   Great Lakes Forms Air Squadron

As commander of the Great Lakes Naval Training Center, Capt. William Moffett formed an aviation training squadron in June 1917. Moffett's attitude on the importance of aviation was greatly influenced by his North Shore neighbors and ACI members, particularly William Wrigley Jr., Jack Vilas, and Pop Dickinson.

Using equipment donated by various ACI members, the new training unit used three flying boats to instruct both pilots and mechanics. Wrigley's son Philip was the first ensign put in charge of the flight school. Other privileged young men who joined the squadron included Joseph Pulitzer and Logan Vilas.

It quickly became obvious that winter in Chicago was not the best time for flight instruction in open cockpit hydroaeroplanes on Lake Michigan. In October 1917, Moffett transferred flight training to Pensacola, but Great Lakes continued training mechanics and support personnel, graduating 2,100 by the end of WWI.

After Moffett left Great Lakes, the Navy promoted him to Rear Admiral in 1921 and placed him in charge of organizing the Navy's Bureau of Aeronautics. Moffett is unofficially known as the "Father of Naval Aviation."[261]

1917/07   Aviation Patent Pool Formed

With U.S. entry into the European war looming, the military experienced difficulty obtaining airplanes because manufacturers were afraid of infringing on Wright and other patents. In 1917, Congress appropriated $1 million to "to secure by purchase, condemnation, donation, or otherwise" any patents that were necessary to manufacture or develop aircraft.

The Manufacturer's Aircraft Association (MAA) was established to hold all the aviation patents in a pool. It charged a small, agreed-upon royalty to those using the patents and made payments as appropriate to the patent holders.[262]

1917/07/16   Chanute Field Becomes Operational

Chanute Field became operational when the Army Signal Corps transferred its squadron from Ashburn Field on July 16, 1917. The mass movement of 23 airplanes was the largest conducted up to that time.

Chanute Field was constructed despite the efforts of Charles Dickinson and the Aero Club to convince the War Department to expand Chicago's Ashburn Field into a military base. However, the War Dept. found land and associated costs were prohibitive for major expansion, plus fierce Chicago winters limited flying. The found that farmland in Rantoul, IL far less expensive and it was near the University of Illinois, which had been chosen to give ground school-type training.

The War Dept. commissioned Chanute Field on May 21, 1917 and began construction. It was to be one of 32 Air Service Camps nationwide. Initially called Rantoul Aviation Field, the name changed prior to the arrival of the squadron to honor the Chicago Aviation pioneer, Octave Chanute. During the war Chanute Field provided training in both pilots and mechanics with a new class graduating every six to eight weeks.[263]

1917/08/02   First Carrier Landing

On August 2, 1917, British Squadron Commander E.F. Dunning landed his Sopwith Pup on the deck of the HMS *Furious*. This was the first landing made on a ship contructed as an aircraft carrier, instead of another type of ship with a makeshift deck attached as an afterthought.

The following July, the *Furious* launched seven Pups, which destroyed two Zeppelins moored on the ground.[264]

1918   Heath Changes Name and Opens School

Around 1918, Edward Heath changed E.B. Heath Aerial Vehicle Co. to the Heath Aircraft Co. and added a school he called Heath University to train pilots and mechanics.

Heath's entrepeneural ventures were always interrelated, with the ultimate goal of making aviation accessible to as many people as possible. Heath viewed flight training as essential for new pilots purchasing his planes, believing that pilots trained in his planes would be more likely to purchase them.

Heath kept the tuition for his training substantially lower than other schools of the time, attracting a larger pool of students. To make training even more affordable, students could exchange work for training. For a token tuition, the student would work in the factory for a week and receive a half-hour lesson on the week-end. At the end of three months, the student could be a pilot. Students could continue working in the factory, using their wages to buy a kit to take home and build with the knowledge they had acquired.

Trading work for lessons was not unique to Heath and had broad benefits. The most obvious was the double benefit that the student could learn to fly inexpensively and that Heath had a low-cost and enthusiastic labor source. An added benefit was it spread Heath's reputation nationally. Following WWI, people experienced increased interest in events outside their local area and had increased mobility. A person who spent months living in Chicago, became a pilot, and was building a plane of his or her own, would become a minor celebrity back home.[265]

1918/02   First U.S. Combat Aircraft Production

The British de Havilland bomber DH-4 became the first combat plane to be manufactured in the U.S. Boeing Airplane Co., Dayton-Wright Airplane Co., Fisher Body Co., and Standard Airplane Co. all produced the DH-4 using the 12-cylinder Liberty engine. After the war, production continued with modified versions that were used by the U.S. Army as well as the Mail Service.[266]

1918/04/01   Britain Founds RAF

On April 1, 1918, the British military merged the Royal Flying Corps and the Royal Naval Air Service to create the Royal Air Force.[267]

1918/04/21   Red Baron Shot Down

After 80 combat victories, WWI's top ace, "Red Baron" Manfred von Richthofen, was killed when his Fokker Dr. 1 triplane was shot down.[268]

1918/05/08   Top Illinois Ace Makes First Kill

In a dogfight on his first combat flight, May 8, 1918, Reed Landis, flying his SE.5a, downed his first enemy plane.

Landis enlisted in the U.S. Army in 1916 and learned to fly at Chanute Field. In August 1917, he was assigned to the British Air Service. His combat victories with the British continued on August 8, 1918, when Landis shot down two German fighters and the observation balloon they were guarding.

The next month, September 1918, Landis was assigned to the American Army where his record continued. By the end of the war, Landis was Illinois' top-ranking ace with either 12 or 10 kills, depending on British or American counting methods. In all, Landis was credited with one observation balloon and eight airplanes destroyed, plus three planes driven "down out of control." For his service, Maj. Landis received the British Distinguished Flying Cross and the American Distinguished Service Cross.

Landis was the son of Chicago federal judge Kenesaw Mountain Landis who was also the first Commissioner of Baseball.[269]

1918/05/15   U.S. Regular Air Mail Service Begins

The Postal Office Dept. initiated regular air mail service between New York City and Washington.[270]

1918/05/20   Army Air Corps Is Born

Less than a week after passing in Congress, President Wilson signed the Overman Act officially creating the Army Air Corps as its own command, no longer a part of the Signal Corps.[271]

1918/05/23   Katherine Stinson Sets New Records

On May 23, 1918, Katherine Stinson departed Chicago carrying mail for New York City but ran out of fuel in Binghamton, NY. Her 783-mi. trip set the distance record and her 11-hr. 12-min. flight established a new endurance record.[272]

1918/07/18   Lipsner Heads Aerial Mail

On July 18, 1918, Benjamin Lipsner became the first Superintendent of Aerial Mail of the Post Office Dept. Although he had no direct aviation experience, Lipsner's enthusiasm for the field coupled with his professional and organizational skills made him perfect for the position. During his brief term, air mail flights went from being sporadic demonstrations to being a regular, reliable cross-country service.

A Chicago native, Lipsner studied mechanical engineering at the Armour Institute. About 1910, he became enamoured with aviation at Clearing Field. Although he never learned to fly, he hung around the airport talking with pilots and mechanics, particularly pilot Otto Brodie

and the mechanic Shorty Schroeder who worked for James Plew's
Curtiss dealership.

Lipsner served as a Captain in the Army Signal Corps during WWI.
As a nonpilot, his role was to support the Army planes flying some air mail
domestically under Maj. Reuben Fleet.[273]

1918/07/27   First Unattached Parachute

Floyd Smith filed a patent for the first unattached parachute on July 27,
1918. Born in Chicago, James Floyd Smith[a] and his wife, Hilder, worked as
trapeze performers in a circus on the West Coast.[274] He built an airplane
and in June 1912 received License #207.

In April 1914, Glenn Martin needed a girl parachutist for two jumps in an
exhibition. At the time, parachutes had a static-line attached to the aircraft
which dragged the parachute out immediately after the jump. Floyd and
Hilder agreed to do the jumps for Martin but Floyd decided he needed to
make some jumps before Hilder. Her two jumps were successful, but problems on the second jump got Floyd thinking about improving parachuting.

During WWI, Smith served with the U.S. Army in Dayton. As the war
was ending, Smith served in parachute development, working with static-
line chutes, when he came up with an alternative.

Smith filed a patent on July 27, 1918, for the Floyd Smith Life Pack.
Smith's parachute was the first that was entirely self-contained in a pack on
the aviator's back. He or she was free to jump from either side of the aircraft
and could free-fall until pulling the ripcord. The free-fall capability made this
design extremely popular for barnstorming exhibitions and was an essential
element for using the parachute in combat. The Smith Life Pack became the
basis for the design of the Army Type A parachute in early 1919.

In 1919, Smith left the army and formed the Floyd Smith Aerial
Equipment Co. with offices on Adams St. in Chicago. His parachute patent
was granted on May 18, 1920.[275]

1918/08   Laird Forms His First Chicago Company

In August 1918, Matty Laird formed the E.M. Laird Co of Chicago and
designed the Laird Model S Sport Planes. The OX5-powered planes carried
two passengers in front of the pilot. By the time the Armistice was signed,
ending WWI, Laird had begun constructing the five planes of his
new venture.

---

a   The National Air & Space Museum site gives his name as Floyd Kenton Smith.

Laird had become an airplane manufacturer as a result of a plane crash. While wintering in Texas in March 1917, Laird was testing a plane of another designer when it went into a flat spin, severely injuring one of Laird's arm and both his legs.

When released from the hospital, Laird returned to Chicago and made a few exhibition flights, until the U.S. banned all civilian flying for the duration of WWI. Laird took time for much more surgery and rehab to address his leg and arm problems. During his extended recovery, Laird looked at his future realizing he could not be as great an exhibition performer as he had once hoped. Instead, he decided the future needed planes that could carry passengers and he would build them.

He exhibited the Model S at a static air show held in the Auditorium Building in December 1919.[276]

1918/09/04–06   NY-Chicago Air Mail Demonstration

Following the success of the New York City to Washington air mail service, Benjamin Lipsner endeavored to demonstrate the feasibility of a longer route between the country's two largest cities, New York and Chicago, which required 24 hr. by train. Lipsner organized a series of pilots and planes to make the trip.

On the morning of September 5, 1918, two planes took off from Belmont Field Racetrack in Queens with the goal of reaching Chicago by sunset. Weather and mechanical problems caused delays and the first pilot, Max Miller landed his Curtiss R-4 in Grant Park at 7 p.m. on September 6. His delivery of 480 lbs. of mail was sufficient to convince officials that the service was feasible.[277]

1918/11/11   WWI Armistice

The Armistice brought a cessation to the fighting in WWI. Since the U.S. entered the war, the Army Aviation Corps expanded from 52 officers, 1,100 men, and 200 civilian employees to 20,000 officers and 150,000 men (nearly half in Europe). Thousands of pilots and surplus military airplanes returned to the U.S. where they engaged in all sorts of activities from exhibition flying the mail to transporting mail.[278]

1918/12/6   Lipsner Leaves Post Office

Less than six months after accepting the position, Benjamin Lipsner resigned as head of the Post Office Dept.'s Air Mail Service on December 6,

1918. During that brief period, Lipsner inaugurated regular air mail service between the nation's two largest cities, New York and Chicago.

There are various accounts surrounding the resignation. One version describes constant clashes between Lipsner and his superior in the Post Office, Otto Praeger. Lipsner resisted what he considered unwise and unsafe decisions, including that a pilot had been fired for refusing to fly in dense fog.

Another version places the conflict between the Post Office and the Army, which was actually flying the mail. The planes and pilots were under the command of Maj. Reuben Fleet, who had been Lipsner's commander while he was in the Army. Fleet rankled at the idea of taking orders from a previous underling who was then a civilian and sought to undermine him at every turn.

Yet another version suggests Lipsner had unspecified expense account irregularities. No matter which version or combination of versions was true, Lipsner's brief tenure was a major influence in the development of air mail. After leaving the Post Office Dept., Lipsner went on to a long and successful career during which he consulted with a number of aviation and oil companies.[279]

1919   Black Sox Scandal

Eight members of the Chicago White Sox were accused of throwing the World Series, after which the press labeled them as the "Black Sox."[280]

1919   International Air Traffic Association Formed (IATA)

Formed in The Hague, Netherlands, the original IATA (International Air **Traffic** Assn.) was created to establish standards for airlines and ticketing in the infancy of scheduled air travel. Toward the end of WWII, the IATA would be reorganized into the International Air **Transport** Assn. on April 19, 1945 in a meeting in Havana Cuba. Initially the 1945 iteration of IATA had 57 members representing 31 nations.[281]

1919   Monmouth Field Is Planted

In 1919, the Post Office Dept. established an emergency landing field in Monmouth, IL that was described as "80 acres near the Country Club."[282]

In 1921, some Monmouth businessmen convinced Curtiss-Iowa Corp., an airline proving passenger service between Des Moines and Ft. Dodge, IA, to make Monmouth a destination as well. On December 8, 1921, the businessmen received a state charter for the Monmouth Aero Club, which operated the airport.

As of 2018, Monmouth is the oldest, continuously-operating airport in Illinois.[283]

1919   Laird's Wichita Sojourn

After recovering from injuries sustained in a plane crash, formed the E.M. Laird Co. of Chicago and started building the Laird Model S Sport Plane.

The potential of the Model S was quickly recognized by Billy Burke of Oklahoma and Jacob M. "Jake" Mollendick of Wichita. They convinced Laird to move to Wichita to build his plane. In 1919, Laird moved to Wichita and started the E.M. Laird Co. of Wichita as a three-way partnership with Burke and Mollendick. Burke and Mollendick put up cash and Laird contributed his plans for the Model S in a three-way partnership. Like many deals in "oil-country," it was bound only by a gentlemen's handshake.

Instead of building a few planes at a time, the group established the country's first completely commercal aviation venture in which airplanes were mass produced without any government or military subsidy. They introduced the Swallow based on Laird's Model S.

The Swallow, which sold for $650, was a three-place biplane that soared in popularity. The Swallow was similar in design to the Curtiss Jenny trainer, which was abundant in the surplus market. The Swallow, however, had several advantages over the Jenny, making it appealing both to barnstormers and operators of flight schools. With a a shortened wingspan, the Swallow was more maneuverable for both exhibition flying and instruction. The widened front seat accommodated two passengers, doubling the income potential from sightseeing flights.[284]

1919/01/08   Chicago Stops

For five full minutes, at 1:45 p.m., January 8, 1919, the city of Chicago came to a standstill. "Street cars and elevated trains shut down; schools and factories suspended operation; crowds gathered on street corners for a moment of silence" as the city paid its respects to former President Theodore Roosevelt at the hour of his funeral.[285]

1919/04/19   First Nonstop Chicago to NYC Air Mail

The first nonstop air mail flight between Chicago and New York was flown on April 19, 1919. Capt. Earl E. White flew a modified DH-4 from Ashburn Field to Hazelhurst, Long Island in 6 hr. 50 min.[286]

1919/05/15   Regular Chicago to NYC Air Mail Service Begins

The Post Office Dept. began regular air mail service between Chicago and New York using a combination of planes and trains. An airplane would fly the mail during the day from Chicago to Cleveland, OH, where it would be transferred to a train for the remainder of the journey.[287]

It quickly became obvious that the de Havilland DH-4 aircraft were not rugged enough for the rigors of the air mail service. The planes were substantially modified by strengthening the landing gear, moving the axle forward to prevent nose-overs, sheathing longerons in nickel-steel and placing the pilots in the rear seat. The modifications were so successful the U.S. Army began making them for their aircraft as well.

The modified planes began entering service on May 15, 1919, the first anniversary of air mail service. The first 24 planes went into service in Chicago at Grant Park for service flying on the Chicago-Cleveland and Chicago-New York routes.

While the DH-4s were adequate for most air mail routes, by the end of 1919 the air mail service began to replace them on the Chicago-New York route. Glenn Martin manufactured the largest planes in service. A civilian modification of the MB-1 bomber, the planes could carry up to 1,500 lbs. of mail at 100 mph for more than 500 mi. The planes only stopped in Cleveland during the trip and were able to reduce the operating costs by approximately 50%. With a closed cockpit, the Martins had an excellent record of operating in inclement weather.[288]

1919/06   First Scheduled European Passenger Service

The first scheduled passenger service began between London and Paris operated by Handley Page Transport Co. They used modified Handley Page O/400 bombers that had been modified into passenger planes that carried 14 passengers in what was considered luxury for air travel of the day.[289]

1919/06/03   Air Delivery to Clothing Stores

After WWI, Society Brand Clothes, the brand of Alfred Decker and Abraham Cohn, invested $50,000 to establish air delivery to its stores in Danville, Kankakee, Champagne, Valparaiso, and South Bend. They developed Checkerboard Field on 40 acres in Maywood at 12th St. (Roosevelt Rd.) and 1st Ave. On June 3, 1919, the field opened with a ceremony presided over by the president of the Chicago Chamber of Commerce.

Society Brand built a hangar but didn't see the need to prepare a runway, preparing the field as an all-direction airport. Initially called Society Brand Field, it quickly became known as Checkerboard Field, because of the checkerboard design painted on the wings of the company's Jennies.[290]

Society Brand hired David L. Behncke as their chief pilot and airport manager. A Wisconsin native, Behncke had enlisted in the Army at 16 and served in Gen. Pershing's Mexico campaign. During WWI, he trained pilots and tested aircraft at Chanute Field. Following the war, Behncke performed on the barnstorming circuit as Behncke's Flying Circus.[291]

1919/07/21   Blimp *Wingfoot* Crashes

Goodyear's first commercial blimp, the *Wingfoot Express* made its maiden voyage on July 21, 1919, flying over the Loop at about 1200 ft. The pilot, John Boertner, felt heat and looked back to see the tail on fire. Within seconds the entire ship was engulfed in flames.

As soon as he saw the fire, the pilot ordered everybody to use their parachutes. The passengers, presumably less familiar with using chutes, didn't survive. The crew made it over the side and two survived. The flaming *Wingfoot* crashed through the skylight of the Illinois Trust and Savings Bank.[a] The bank was closed but employees were still closing out the day's transactions. Flaming gasoline and debris filled the main floor. Twenty-eight bank employees were injured and ten killed. Along with the three deaths from the airship, the death toll of 13 made this the worst aviation disaster in U.S. history.

Following WWI, Goodyear had decided to build commercial blimps similar to those it had built for the Navy during the war. Goodyear's blimp components were constructed in Akron and assembled in a large hangar at White City Amusement Park on Chicago's South Side. The $100,000 *Wingfoot Express* was named after the Goodyear logo.

Goodyear's blimps, like all airships of the time, used hydrogen for lift. Hydrogen's flammability was well known but the recently isolated helium was prohibitively expensive. At the time, 1,000 cu. yd. of hydrogen cost $5 whereas the same amount of helium cost $125. Since helium provided 92% of the lift of hydrogen, more helium was required to lift the same weight.

Earlier that day, the *Wingfoot* flew up the lakeshore from White City to Grant Park, where the public marveled at the massive airship. Later, it flew

---

a   Located on the corner of LaSalle Street and Jackson Blvd., later became the site of the Continental Bank which was acquired in 1994 by BankAmerica.

on a three-hour test flight north along the lake and returned without any trouble.

Just before ending for the night, *Wingfoot* took a couple of passengers, including a publicist and a newspaper photographer, on a brief jaunt over the Loop. That is when the fire broke out. *Wingfoot's* pilot was arrested at the scene, as were 16 other Goodyear employees. They were never brought to trial since there was no evidence of any criminal act.

The city reacted quickly. Only six hours after the crash, the City Council pass a resolution to draft an ordinance giving Chicago control of all airplanes and airships flying within the city limits. In December, the City Coucil passed an ordinance that banned all flying over the Loop and thickly populated areas without a permit.

The *Wingfoot* disaster also triggered a response from the insurance industry. Through their underwriting and premiums, insurance companies exerted more regulatory pressure on aviation than did the government. Pressure from numerous insurers led Underwriters' Laboratories to commence licensing of both airplanes and pilots in 1921.

Investigators were unable to establish a specific cause of the fire. The two main suspects were static electricity or either sparks or hot oil thrown off from the engine. As a result, the U.S. began using helium in all its airships. Helium was considered a critical resource and the U.S. refused to export it, so hydrogen remained in use throughout the rest of the world.[292]

1919/08   Wrigley Uses Airplane Sales Promotion

In a sales promotion, William Wrigley used charter airplanes to deliver Spearmint gum to cities nationwide.[293]

1919/08   Martin Bomber "Rim" Tour Stops in Chicago

Created during WWI, the MB-1 Martin bomber was new when the war ended. In order to test the endurance of the plane and to increase public support for the Air Service, the Army sent the bomber on the Around-the-Rim tour. The plane left Washington, DC, on July 24 with two pilots and six repair people. They flew north to Maine then west to Seattle, stopping briefly in Chicago. After flying down the Pacific Coast, the MB-1 turned east and flew to Florida, then up the coast and back to DC. The plane covered 9,823 mi. during the 108-day trip with total flying time of 114 hr. and 25 min.[294]

1919/08/31   Lawson Airlines Maiden Flight

Alfred W. Lawson, of Milwaukee, built America's first commercial large-cabin transport. It made its first flight August 31, 1919. Charles Dickinson provided Lawson with financial backing both to develop the plane and to establish passenger service between Ashburn Field and New York.

Lawson was a self-taught aeronautical engineer. His plane which carried 24-passengers, weighed seven tons and was powered by two 400 hp Liberty engines. Lawson's huge plane was extremely underpowered. During its maiden flight on August 31, 1919, the plane experienced many difficulties and delays, but fortunately there were no injuries. In May 1921 Lawson built an even bigger plane, but it crashed on its first flight.[295]

1919/10   Wright-Martin Reorganized

Barely a year after merging with the Wright Co., becoming Wright-Martin, Glenn Martin had resigned and formed the Glenn L. Martin Aircraft Co. in September 1917. With Martin gone, in October 1919, Wright-Martin changed its name to the Wright Aeronautical Corp. The new Wright enterprise gradually migrated from aircraft to engine production.[296]

1919/10/13   Convention for the Regulation of Air Navigation

A subcommission of the Paris Peace Conference, the International Commission on Aerial Navigation, signed the Convention for the Regulation of Air Navigation, also known as the Paris Convention of 1919. The Convention established standards for international flights.[297]

Although the U.S. signed the Convention, it never ratified it because of its association with the League of Nations, which the U.S. avoided.[298]

1919/12   England to Australia Flight Completed

In 1919, a prize of £10,000 drew six planes into a competition to link the farthest reaches of the British Empire. The London to Sydney race of 12,000 mi. had to be completed within 30 days. The winners were two Australian brothers, Keith and Ross Smith, who had flown with the British during WWI. Their surplus Vickers Vimy was a twin-engine, open-cockpit biplane that had been used as a heavy bomber during the war.

This 1919 epic journey was recreated with races in 1934, 1969, and 2001. Also, in 1994, on the 75th anniversary, a replica of the Vickers Vimy followed the original route.[299]

1920–1924

1920/01/08–15   Chicago Aeronautical Expo

The Manufacturers Aircraft Assn. sponsored the first commercial exposition displaying aircraft. Chicago was the first of three national venues to showcase aeronautical products in a manner similar to the popular car show. The Auditorium was filled with airplanes and blimps, as well as engines and accessories, showcasing them to thousands of visitors.[300]

1920/01/17   Volstead Act Takes Effect

The 18th Amendment to the U.S. Constitution was ratified by 46 states and became law on January 17, 1920. The Amendment, which passed Congress in 1917, banned the manufacture, transportation, or sale of alcohol.[301]

As written, the Amendment was vague, particularly in the area of enforcement. The National Prohibition Act (the Volstead Act) passed Congress in October 1919. President Wilson vetoed the bill, but Congress overrode his veto the following day, providing enforcement capabilities when the Amendment went into effect.[302]

Almost immediately, some people sought to circumvent the law, and airplanes became a preferred tool. One Detroit reporter quoted a smuggler, "Airplanes cost less than a good speedboat. Fly loads right to Chicago..."[303]

1920/01/22   Chicago Air Mail Operations at Checkerboard

All Chicago air mail operations shifted from Grant Park to Checkerboard Field in Maywood on January 22, 1920.

The Grant Park location had fallen into disfavor because its north-south runway frequently forced cross-wind take-offs and landings. In addition, following the crash of the *Wingfoot Express,* the City Council and other officials were wary of air activity over the city.

Checkerboard was selected despite the fact that the airport was small and required immediate expansion to accommodate all the operations. However, the main alternative, Ashburn Field, was too remote to be convenient.

Checkerboard Field was owned and operated by David Behncke, who had purchased the field and planes after Society Brand Clothes quit the air delivery service. Until the arrival of the air mail service, he struggled to make ends meet by doing flight training, sightseeing, aerial photography, and delivery service. On weekends, he gave aerial exhibitions which drew people to the airport.

As soon as Behncke completed cinder runways at Checkerboard, the Post Office Dept. transferred the air mail service to the facility. The Post Office also constructed several new hangars and made Checkerboard the main repair center for the entire air mail service.

The Air Service Maintenance Facility didn't simply perform operational maintenance but did extensive modifications on planes entering service. The de Havilland DH-4 bombers they used were not designed to be reliable enough for the rigorous schedule and were unable to accommodate heavy mail loads. The Maintenance Facility totally rebuilt 100 DH-4s that the Post Office had acquired from the Army.[304]

1920/06   Republican Convention Gets Newspapers

The *New York Times* astonished members at the Republican Convention in Chicago by delivering several hundred copies of the paper by air, arriving on the same day they were printed. Normally trains brought the newspapers into town on the following day.

Airplanes were already widely used to get photographs from events back to newspapers prior to going to press, but this was a significant advancement in the rapid delivery of news to the readers.[305]

1920/06/11   NACA Gets Wind Tunnel

Five years after its formation, the National Advisory Committee on Aeronautics formally dedicated the Langley Memorial Aeronautical Laboratory on June 11, 1920. A key element of the research facility was the first of many wind tunnels to study aerodynamics.

Later, NACA added specialized wind tunnels to research specific aerodynamic areas. The Propellor Wind Tunnel, which went into service in 1927, was 20 ft. in diameter and was the largest at the time. In 1928, they built the Cowling Wind Tunnel that focused specifically on drag over the engine. Their research resulted in cowling designs to increase efficiency by smoothing the airflow over the front portion of the plane.[306]

1920/07/27   Taxi War Escalates

Competition between Chicago taxi companies was fierce, often marked with fistfights and occasional fires in offices and garages. The early morning of July 27, 1920, the war escalated as shots rang out. Lines of Yellow Taxis drove at high speed past the Checker Cab office as gunshots peppered the building. Checker drivers responded in kind, attacking Yellow Taxis and facilities. Fortunately, no one was killed.

The Yellow Cab Co., which introduced taxi meters to Chicago, was started in 1907 by John Hertz and William S. Shaw. In 1915 Yellow Taxi began manufacturing their own automobile, which flooded the streets and discounted fares. By 1920, all competitors had been driven out of business except one, Checker Cab.

In June 1921, a Yellow Taxi driver was shot by an occupant of a Checker Cab. Battles between the rivals waxed and waned over the following years as competition took various turns. At one point, the Chicago City Council threatened to revoke the licenses of both companies and arrest all of their drivers in the city.

Hertz grew his taxi company into a real empire. By 1925 he was president of at least nine companies including Yellow Taxi, several coach companies, a couple of truck and coach manufacturing companies, a motor fuel company, and a car rental company.[307]

1920/09/28   First Retractable Landing Gear

The first practical landing gear was used on the Dayton-Wright RB-1 Racer for competition in the Gordon Bennett Cup. [308]

1921   UL Certifies Aircraft

Starting in 1921, Chicago-based Underwriters' Laboratories (UL) embarked on a program to register aircraft and pilots. The effort was an alternative to the jumble of varying standards designated by the various licensing agencies, such as the Aero Clubs.

Major proponents for this standardization were insurance companies, who wanted a reliable method to set rates, and local governments concerned about safety in their jurisdiction but without the expertise and funds to do it themselves.

Registration was based in part on the standards established by the Convention for the Regulation of Air Navigation. The U.S., which was suspect of everything associated with the League of Nations, refused to ratify the Convention and to establish a Federal Agency to provide establish its own standards. Therefore, UL envisioned its role as an interim agency provided much-needed regulations until eventually be replaced by some yet unplanned federal agency.

Chicago aviator Shorty Schroeder joined UL as an aviation engineer to develop their inspection and registration standards.[309] UL assigned registration numbers with the country prefix ("N" for the U.S.) followed by four letters, usually (but not always) issued sequentially, starting with ABCA, ABCB and so on.

To promote aircraft registration, Schroeder took a Laird Swallow (the second plane registered, N-ABCB), on a nationwide tour in the summer of 1921.[310] Schroeder was also noted for being instrumental in the adoption of the freefall parachute, developed by his fellow-Chicagoan Floyd Smith. He wore and promoted the Floyd Smith Life Pack throughout his tour.[311]

1921   Fire Destroys Checkerboard Field

In late 1921, fire destroyed many of Checkerboard Field's buildings. The government acquired land across the street from Checkerboard, on the west side of 1st Ave., and the Post Office Dept. established its own field, Maywood Air Mail Field, to handle all flights and the maintenance facility. Without air mail revenue, business at Checkerboard faltered.[312]

By 1921, Chicago was the hub of the national air mail system. Flights from Checkerboard and later Maywood Field extended to New York, Minneapolis, St. Louis, and Omaha.[313]

1921/04   Nimmo Black's Air Service

In April 1921, Nimmo Black established Nimmo Black's Flying Field at Peterson Ave. and Lincoln Ave. to support his flight operations. Black constructed hangars and other buildings to support planes used by his own pilots as well as other aviators.

A Chicago native, Nimmo Black had become a Reserve Military Aviator in April 1918. He flew for various Chicago companies for a few years before starting Nimmo Black's Air Service.

Black's Air Service primarily delivered film to Chicago newspapers, including from events such as the Kentucky Derby, the Dempsey-Firpo boxing match and President Harding's funeral. Airport workers would build bonfires beside the runway to enable night landings.

Ed Heath of the Heath Aviation Co. used Black's Flying Field to test and demonstrate airplanes he built in his factory near Lincoln Park. His activity there became so common that the airport was often referred to as Heath Flying Field #1.[314]

1921/06/15   Bessie Coleman Gets Her License

On June 15, 1921, Bessie Coleman became the world's first licensed African American pilot and the first American of any race or gender to be licensed directly by the Federation Aeronautique Internationale (FAI) when it awarded her International License #18,310.[a]

A Texas transplant, Coleman came to Chicago in 1915, where she worked various jobs in offices and beauty salons. As a manicurist for men, she heard from veterans about flying and the respect Europeans gave black pilots. She saved her money until she had enough to learn to fly. However, none of the American schools would accept African Americans, so she traveled to France and studied at the Ecole d'Aviation des Freres Caudron et Le Crotoy.

She returned to the states a celebrity in the African American community where she was known as "Queen Bess." She intended to open a flight school but was unable to raise sufficient funds to purchase a plane. She went back to Europe to study stunt flying so she could become a barnstormer. Coleman made her first exhibition flight over Labor Day weekend 1922 in Garden City, NY. The next month, Coleman first performed in Chicago at the Checkerboard Aerodrome.[315]

1921/07/21   Mitchell Sinks Battleship

In a well-publicized demonstration, Brig. Gen. Billy Mitchell demonstrated that airplanes are able to sink capital ships.[316]

1921/09/05   Chicago Air Derby

Chicago's first air race in ten years was held over a 50-mi. course starting at Ashburn Field. David L. Behncke won the event with a time of 44 min. 35 sec. Daniel Kiser and Price Hollingsworth placed second and third respectively, less than 30 sec. after Behncke.[317]

1921/11/12   First Aerial Refueling Stunt

The first mid-air refueling was accomplished on November 11, 1921, with a wing walker climbing from one plane to another carrying a can of gasoline. Wesley May strapped a five-gallon can of gasoline on his back and took off in a Lincoln Standard flown by Frank Hawks. At an altitude of about 1,000 ft., they met up with a Curtiss Jenny piloted by Earl Daugherty.

---

a   Licensing, at this time, was optional for pilots. Military pilots were not officially "licensed," which was a civilian function.

May climbed from the Standard's wing to the Jenny's and poured gas into the tank, then became a passenger in the Jenny for the remainder of the trip.[318]

1922   Aero Club of America Changes Name

The Aero Club of America incorporated and changed its name to the National Aeronautic Assn.[319]

1922   Mayor Thompson Proposes Airport on Island in Lake

Chicago Mayor William Hale Thompson attended an aeronautic conference in Detroit and returned with a plan to spend $10 million to create an airport on an island in Lake Michigan linked to shore by a tunnel that would be built near the Field Museum. Thompson's plan died in City Council. [320]

1922   Wilson Airport Started

The precursor to Wilson Airport took root in 1922. A former German flyer, Max Schusin, and American aviator Stanley Wallace opened an airport at Lawrence Ave. and River Rd. along the Des Plaines River.[321]

1922   Heath Introduces the Favorite

After changing his company name from E.B. Heath Aerial Vehicle Co. to the Heath Aircraft Co. around 1918, the company began introducing popular airplane models. In 1922, Heath introduced the Favorite.

All of Heath's designs were for "flyvver" airplanes, what today would be considered Light Sport Aircraft. This was in keeping with his goal of enabling everyone to fly. Flyvver planes were easy and inexpensive to build, and small and easy to store or transport.

The first of his popular airplanes, the Feather, came in 1918. The single-seat biplane weighed 325 lbs. including the engine. To keep expenses down, Heath used modified motorcycle engines and a propeller of his own design.

The Favorite, introduced in 1922, was another biplane. The Favorite was essentially a converted Jenny with improvements attractive for commercial users. For example, Heath would install electric lights on the lower wing, enabling the Favorite to be used for night advertising.[322]

1922/01/01   Aeronautical Chamber of Commerce Formed

The Aeronautical Chamber of Commerce of America was formed to foster and promote aviation. It had more than a hundred founding or charter members. Its headquarters were in the New York City offices of the Manufacturers Aircraft Assn., which the Chamber supplemented but did not replace.[323]

1922/10/01   Kemp Dedicates His Flying Field

On October 1, 1922, Col. Philip Kemp dedicated Col. Kemp's Flying Field (Air Strip) with a single runway and two taxiways. For his aerodrome, Kemp leased farmland from the Stickney Board of Education located between Cicero (48th St.) and LaVergne avenues and between 59th and 61st streets.

Kemp had been a flier in WWI before coming to Chicago, where in 1922, he became commander of the Chicago Group Unit of the Air Service Reserve Officers.[324]

Kemp's air strip was also known as the Chicago Air Park after the name of Kemp's main tenant, the Chicago Air Park Co., which operated five planes for aerial photography and mapping in addition to offering flight instruction and charter flights. Pilots from other airports such as Ashburn and Checkerboard also used the landing strip as a practice field.

Only a few years later, Kemp's Flying Field became a part of the city's Chicago Municipal Airport.[325]

1922/04   Stinson Airline Between Detroit and Chicago

In April 1922, Eddie Stinson began passenger flights between Ashburn Field and Detroit with plans to add another route to Kansas City. He disbanded operations shortly, however, having made only three flights by June 5th.

Stinson flew the six-passenger Junkers-Larson JL-6, probably the earliest metal airplane in the world. Junkers introduced this plane in Germany as the F.13 in 1919. Later, it was brought to the U.S. as an air mail plane by John Larsen.[326]

1922/11   Franing Field Formed

Several years after Franing Field had been used on a coast-to-coast flight, three Moline, IL, residents made Franing Field an operating airport starting in November 1922. Gustaf De Schepper, Floyd Ketner, and Dr. C.C. Sloan expanded the 30-acre pasture to 120-acre flying field. They also constructed hangars, bought a Laird Swallow, and made other improvements such as constructing a well, installating an electric generator, and the paving of a state road for access.

In June 1925, five Martin Bombers on tour from Langley Field visited Franing Field.[327]

Air mail service came to Franing Field in 1926, and the following year Boeing Air Transport made Moline a stop between New York and San Francisco (CAM-18).[328]

1923   Yackey Buys Checkerboard

In late 1923, Wilfred Alonzo "Tony" Yackey purchased Checkerboard Field from David Behncke after the Air Mail Service shifted operations to Maywood Airport.

Originally from St. Louis, Yackey became an ace with the Italian military in WWI. When the U.S. entered the war, he transferred and flew with American forces.

Following the war, Yackey settled in Chicago and flew air mail with Lindbergh on the St. Louis to Chicago route (CAM-2). During this time, he developed his association with Checkerboard Field. Leaving the Air Mail Service, Yackey began a business at Checkerboard doing flight training as well as participating in exhibitions and races around the country.

In 1922, he formed Yackey Aircraft Co. at Checkerboard. Yackey modified French Breguet 14 bombers into the Breguet 14T.bis, a cabin aircraft for transport that could carry up to four passengers. The company also modified Thomas-Morse airplanes, primarily the S-4 Scout, into the Yackey Sport, a very popular plane for racing and endurance flights.[329]

1923   Elmhurst Gets an Airport

In 1923, Elmhurst resident Fred Bouchard and Chicago pilot Joe James started Eagle Flying Field. When James moved on in 1929, Eagle Field continued operating as Elmhurst Airport, sometimes known as Elmhurst-East.[330]

1923/01   Maywood Gets Mail

A fire in January 1923 destroyed the Post Office Dept.'s repair hangar at Checkerboard Field. The Air Mail Service had already outgrown Checkerboard and was searching for a new location and quickly completed new facilities and shifted operations to Maywood Field.

The Municipality of Maywood had constructed an airport across the street from Checkerboard Field on the west side of 1st Ave. and Cermak Rd. in the early 1920s. Maywood was able to provide the Air Mail Service with necessary facilities on short notice.

Like Checkerboard, Maywood quickly became the primary site as the Air Mail Service Maintenance Facility. The Maintenance Facility rebuilt DH-4s for Air Mail Service as well as repairing planes that were worn or damaged operationally.

The move to Maywood began a trend of the Air Mail Service to use publicly-owned rather than privately-owned airports. [331]

1923/05/02–03   First Transcontinental Nonstop Flight

The first transcontinental nonstop flight was made May 2–3, 1923 by Lts. Macready and Kelly who flew 2,625 mi. in a Fokker T-2 from Mitchell Field in NY to Rockwell Field in San Diego in 26 hr. 50 min.[332]

1923/06/27   First Practical Mid-Air Refueling

The first demonstration of a practical technique for air-to-air refueling took place at Rockwell Field on June 27, 1923. An Army DH-4 took off from the San Diego Field and lowered a 50 ft. hose, which passed gasoline to another DH-4.

In previous refueling flights, a person carried a fuel can to the receiving plane, where he would complete the flight. Since this was a one-time ocurrance, it was not a practical technique to substantially extend an aircraft's flight time. Within a few years, refueling via a hose enabled planes to remain in the air for days at a time.

Alexander Seversky first proposed refueling via hose in 1917 while in the Russian military. After emigrating to the U.S., Seversky received the first patent for air-to-air refueling in 1921.[333]

1923/07/26   Dickinson Starts Airline

On July 26, 1923, a new and yet unnamed airline started by Charles "Pop" Dickinson's made a demonstration flight from Chicago to New York. After the first World War, Dickinson envisioned airlines that would fly passengers between destinations. Despite an earlier failure with Alfred Lawson, Dickinson tried again, this time making overnight flights between Chicago and New York City.

Eddie Stinson and Art Gray piloted the single-engine Junkers that departed Ashburn Field at 11 p.m. and arrived at Curtiss Field in Garden City, NY at 8:30 the next morning. Dickinson, the sole passenger on the flight, which demonstrated the feasibility of night flying and the potential of passenger service.[334]

Almost a year after the July, 1923 demonstration flight, Dickinson's still-unnamed airline started service on May 2, 1924 using a Yackey-modified Breguet bomber. Again, Dickinson made the first flight which lasted a little over eight hours including a meal break in Cleveland.

Air travel at that time was loud and uncomfortable and only for the hardiest people with a keen interest in flying. Most people preferred the comfort of the train, and Dickinson's airline was unsustainable. Although Dickinson's airline never took off, the flight was instrumental in the Post Office decision to fly mail day and night.[335]

1923/09/08   Boston Dedicates Airport

The City of Boston transformed a muddy area of East Boston called Commonwealth Flats into one of the country's first municipally owned airports.[336]

1923/09/27   Laird Leaves Wichita

Following a long-standing dispute, Matty Laird and Jake Mollendick dissolved their business relationship on September 27, 1923.

Initially, sales had been brisk after the 1919 introduction of Laird's Swallow. Optimistically, Laird produced a new twin-engine plane, while Mollendick hired additional staff and built a new factory.

Not only had Laird established himself as a major airplane designer and manufacturer, but like Johnny Appleseed, he produced an abundant crop of other aircraft designers and manufacturers.[337] Laird hired Lloyd and Waverly Stearman and Walter Beech, all of whom would later become major aircraft manufacturers on their own.[338] Clyde Cessna had built a few planes but had gotten out of the business by the time Laird arrived. However, Cessna's purchase of a Swallow rekindled his aviation interest. Later, after Laird was back in Chicago, Cessna partnered with Beech, and Stearman to form the Travel Air Co. in Wichita.[339]

A long-time friend of Laird, George "Buck" Weaver joined with some partners in Troy, OH, founding Weaver Aircraft Co., which produced WACO airplanes. Weaver temporarily left his own company in 1921 and spent a year working with Laird in Wichita before returning to WACO.[340]

An economic downturn dried up sales and created hard times for Laird's Wichita company. Laird and Mollendick clashed over running the company. In Laird's opinion, Mollendick had squandered corporate funds as he relied on other income sources for his wealth.

After dissolving their partnership, Laird returned to Chicago. Mollendick changed the Wichita company's name to Swallow Airplane Co. and produced a slightly modified variation of Laird's design called the New Swallow.[341]

1924   Nimmo Black Shutters His Flying Field

By 1924, Nimmo Black's interests had shifted into other areas of flying so he closed his Air Service and sold the Flying Field that he opened in 1921. Black did allow Heath Aircraft Co. to continue using the field until Heath could establish a field of his own.[342]

1924   Chester Teaches Wilhelmi to Fly

Art Chester was an Illinois pilot who went on to fame as an air racer. In the early 1920s, Chester leased some land on the Wilhelmi family farm south of Joliet, on Route 66 (currently IL-53 near Laraway Rd.). Chester established a flight school and charter service.

In 1924, the farmer's 16-year-old son, Herman Wilhelmi, soloed. The younger Wilhelmi loved flying and took over running the airport when Chester moved on to other endeavors. Wilhelmi flew for Eastern Airlines for 30 years, commuting in his small plane between his own airport and the Eastern base.[343]

1924   Laird Opens Chicago Factory

Following a painful business experience in Wichita, Matty Laird resolved never again to rely on outside investors to produce his designs. Over the next few months, Laird built up some capital by participating in exhibitions and ferrying news reporters to various events such as the Kentucky Derby and Indy 500.

In 1924, Laird started the E.M. Laird Airplane Co. in some rented storefronts at 23rd St. and Archer Ave. He began building his new line of planes, the Laird Commercial (LC-). Without outside financing, planes had to be custom built to order rather than being produced in quantity.

Laird Commercial planes were some of the first with metal tubular frame construction. They were intended for long-distance flying of mail and/or passengers. But they also offered the superior performance and handling that made them ideal for air racing. At the Dayton Air Races, Perry Hutton flew the LC and handily beat the New Swallow and other competitors.

By 1925, Laird had left the storefronts for factory space at Ashburn Field. His LC planes were a hot commodity, spurred by the Kelly Act that established the Contract Air Mail (CAM) system which encouraged use of newer, higher performance airplanes. The LCs were powerful, making them popular despite their $4500 price tag. Costs of competitor's planes at the time were: Travel Air 2000-$3500, Super Swallow-$2750, and the WACO 9-$2200.

Lindbergh's transatlantic crossing fanned the flamesof public interest in aviation. Flyers were as famous as sports heroes. A whole variety of races and competitions were held across the country into the mid-1930s, when the Depression became too deep and the public became sated with aviation news.

Laird was at the center of this flurry. Pilots who sought out Laird for a plane included Speed Holman, Ervin Ballough, Jimmy Doolittle, and Roscoe Turner. Laird race planes like the *Whirlwind*, *Speedwing*, and *Super Solution* consistently finished at or near the top of the races.[344]

1924/07/01   NY-SF Air Mail

The Post Office Dept. began a 30-day trial of air mail service between New York City and San Francisco, all passing through Chicago.

Pilots flew around-the-clock relying for navigation on a chain of gas-powered beacons built by the federal government every 25 miles along the route. The government also rented land for a series of emergency landing fields along the route. The trial was so successful that the service became permanent.[345]

1924/07/19   Buck Weaver Flies West

Chicago aviator and manufacturer of WACO airplanes George "Buck" Weaver took ill and died on July 19, 1924. The cause of his death isn't recorded but there is speculation that it resulted from internal injuries caused by the crash during a test flight several years earlier.

In 1923 and 1924, Weaver had done stunt flying for several movies including *Blind Virtue* and *Enemies of Youth* made by Atlas Educational Film Co. of Oak Park, IL.

Pop Dickinson, Matty Laird, Eddie Stinson, and Shorty Schroeder flew over his funeral, dropping wreaths in tribute.[346]

1924/09/28   World Cruisers Complete Flight

Three specially-designed Douglas World Cruisers (DWC) completed an around-the-world flight by landing at their departure point in Seattle on September 28, 1924. On April 6, 1924, the flight of four Army aircraft began the 27,553-mi. trip that took 371 hr. of flying time. Only one of the four planes encountered difficulty and was unable to complete the journey.

Nearing the end of their adventure, the planes made an overnight stop at Maywood Air Mail Field on September 15, and the pilots were honored at a banquet. One of the DWCs, the *Chicago*, is currently displayed at the National Air and Space Museum.[347]

1925–1929

1925   Chicago Flying Club Field Formed

The Western Airplane Corp. of Chicago established the Chicago Flying Club Field in 1925 at Irving Park Rd. and Cumberland Ave.[348] The field, also known as Cook County Airport #1, survived until the mid-1960s.[349]

1925   Gauthier's Flying Field

Starting in 1919, itinerant barnstormer Roy Gauthier[a] made regular visits to an area near Dam #1 on the Des Plaines River. By 1925, the area was informally known as Gauthier's Flying Field.[350]

1925   Heath Starts Suburban Flying Field

In 1925, Edward Heath established his own airport at River Rd. and Touhy Ave. to conduct flight testing of the planes he manufactured in a factory on Broadway on the north side of Chicago. With no landing field near his factory, Heath designed his planes to be easily disassembled, simplifying transportation as well as storage.

Initially, Heath flew out of the old Nimmo Black Flying Field (sometimes called Heath Flying Field #1) at Peterson and Lincoln avenues until Black closed his operation. Heath's new airport was known as Heath Flying Field #2.[351]

1925/02/02   Air Mail Act Goes Into Effect

The Air Mail Act, commonly known as the Kelly Act, went into effect on February 2, 1925.

Under the Kelly Act, air mail was flown by private companies rather than the Post Office Dept. This Contract Air Mail (CAM) system established a number of routes, each awarded exclusively to a company. Carrier compensation was calculated as a percentage of the postage on the mail carried. This complicated system was simplified by a June 6, 1926, amendment that changed compensation to a weight basis.[352]

---

a   Various sources state his first name was either Roy or Ray and his last name was spelled Guthier or Gauthier.

The air mail business developed precursors to major air carriers, including United and American. The mail planes also carried passengers— if they were willing to pay to sit on top of mail bags in an open cockpit.[353]

Maywood Field became the hub for the CAM routes to both coasts as well as throughout the Midwest. Charles Lindbergh was a regular visitor flying CAM-2 to St. Louis for Robertson Aircraft.[354]

1925/04/01   Chicago Leases Land for Airport

The Chicago City Council approved an ordinance on April 1, 1925, to lease land for a municipal landing field.

The City Council became interested the year before when the Post Office Dept. started around-the-clock transcontinental service through Chicago. The effort was spearheaded by Alderman Dorsey Crowe who observed the number of routes serving Chicago as well as the number of small airfields around the city. He introduced resolutions to get the City more involved in aviation.

In early 1925, Mayor William E. Dever appointed Philip Kemp as the head of the Chicago Municipal Aero Commission under the Bureau of Parks, Playgrounds and Beaches. In that role, Kemp, who had operated his own airport along Cicero Avenue for several years, was a key figure in developing Chicago's role civil aviation.

Also early in 1925, Matty Laird grew frustrated with his factory's location and the conditions at Ashburn Field. He approached the Stickney Board of Education to lease some land near Kemp's landing field on Cicero Ave.

Laird's request came as the City Council's interest in aviation intensified as the Kelly Bill was becoming law. Under the Kelly Bill, transportation of air mail would be done by private companies and not the Post Office Dept. Council members believed the new structure would increase air mail activity in Chicago.

The Board of Education discussed Laird's proposal with Kemp, who wanted the land for the City. He negotiated a 25-year lease on a 300-acre parcel that was a half-mile on each side. The new area at 63rd St. and Cicero Ave. that encompassed Kemp's existing field was named Chicago Municipal Aviation Field.

Alderman Crowe introduced an ordinance to lease the property recommended by Kemp. The City Council passed it in less than a week. The following year the Council appropriated additional funds to improve the field.

Kemp's vision for the new airport was that it would become a major commercial aviation center. He believed that manufacturing and testing aircraft would interfere with commercial operations and denied Laird's request. Laird remained at Ashburn Field, but moved his factory to a new location at the northern side along 83rd St.[355]

1925/04/15   Ford Begins Air Freight Service

On April 25, 1925, Ford Air Transport Service became the world's first scheduled cargo airline when it began service between Ford Airport in Dearborn, MI, and Ford Field in Lansing, IL.

The Ford family started the airline to ferry supplies between Ford's Dearborn operation and its factory in Hegewisch. In 1923, they purchased 1,400 acres of farmland near the Indiana border at Lansing and Burhnam roads for the landing field. The airline flew the Stout 2-AT, an all-metal single-engine plane in which the Ford family had invested.[356]

1925/05/21   National Air Transport Begins

Incorporated on May 21, 1925, National Air Transport (NAT) began operating with $10 million in capital. NAT was the brainchild of Clement M. Keys, a New York financier who had purchased Curtiss Aeroplane & Motor Co. in 1920.

NAT was unique among aviation companies in that the board of directors had no aviators or designers. Only financiers, including Chicagoans Marshall Field, Philip Wrigley, Lester Armour, Philip Swift, and others, held positions on the board.[357]

To run the daily operations, Keys hired Paul Henderson as VP and General Manager. Previously, Henderson had served as the Second Assistant Postmaster General in charge of air mail operations.[358]

1925/09/28–10/04   Ford National Reliability Air Tour

In order to promote public acceptance of and confidence in air travel, the Fords sponsored annual air tours, officially known as "The National Air Tour for the Edsel B. Ford Reliability Trophy," but were commonly called the "Ford Reliability Air Tours." Tours were held annually from 1925 through 1931, when the Depression took its toll.

The air tours featured an assortment of aircraft, but always showcased one of the Stout AT Pullman planes. To attract the interest of aviators, the tour was structured as an efficiency contest with points given not just for speed, but also for the reliability of the aircraft.

Each year's tour took a different route. The first tour in 1925 visited only ten cities around the upper Midwest with the distance totaling 1,900 miles. In 1928, the tour flew all the way to Seattle and down the West Coast before completing the circuit. Tours always started and ended at Ford Airport in Dearborn. Chicago was inevitably an early stop. The first tour stopped at Maywood Field. Subsequent tours visited Municipal Field and even Sky Harbor.[359]

1925/10/26   Doolittle Wins Schneider Trophy

Jimmy Doolittle won the Schneider Trophy for fastest seaplane, setting a new world speed record of 245 mph in his Curtiss R3C-2 floatplane.[360]

1926   Behncke Becomes Northwest's First Pilot

David Behncke was hired as the first pilot for Northwest Airways, regularly flying the Chicago to Minneapolis route (CAM-9). Later Behncke moved from Northwest to Boeing Air Transport, which later merged into United.[361]

1926   Burnidge Airport Begins

Burnidge Field, the first airport in the Elgin area, started in 1926 as a part of the Hornbeck farm, west of McLean Blvd.

Burnidge was the home of Elgin Airways, a dealer for the Laird-designed Swallow airplanes made in Wichita. For a short time in 1928, Burnidge was the test field for airplanes manufactured by Ta Ho Ma Aircraft and Motor Co. factory in Elgin.

In 1930, fire destroyed a hangar containing two airplanes and a repair shed. Burnidge closed, but there was another landing field northeast of Elgin at Trout Park.[362]

1926/02/15   First Contract Air Mail Service to Chicago

Ford Air Transport Service was the first carrier to operate in Chicago under the new Kelly Act. Mail between Chicago and Detroit (CAM-7) began arriving on February 15, 1926, several months before Robertson Aircraft or National Air Transport began mail service.

Flying the Stout-designed, all-metal, single-engine planes, Ford Air Transport had experience carrying freight and passengers on a schedule giving them a head start on the other carriers.[363]

1926/03/16   First Liquid-Fuel Rocket Launch

Robert Goddard launches the world's first liquid-fueled rocket at Auburn, MA.[364]

1926/04/15   Robertson Begins Mail Service

Charles Lindbergh, chief pilot for Robertson Aircraft (later American Airlines), departed Maywood Field, making the first mail/passenger flight between St. Louis and Maywood Field (CAM-2) on April 15, 1926.[365]

1926/04/30   Bessie Coleman Dies in Accident

Bessie Coleman, the first licensed African American pilot died on April 30, 1926, at Paxon Field in Jacksonville, FL while preparing for a show.

At Paxon Field, Coleman and her mechanic were doing an orientation flight over the area. She turned the controls over to her mechanic and unfastened her seat belt so she could look over the side. Abruptly the Jenny lurched into a spin and Coleman went over the side falling to her death.

Her body was returned to Chicago, where funeral services were held at Pilgrim Baptist Church. Coleman was buried at Lincoln Cemetery in Alsip.[366]

1926/05/08   Chicago Dedicates Municipal Field

Chicago informally dedicated an unfinished 120-acre Municipal Airport at Cicero Ave. and 63rd St. on May 8, 1926. During the ceremony, four homing pigeons were released, each destined for a member of the President's Cabinet. The only air traffic that day was a single plane that took off for Maywood. The event was described as a "great deal of hoopla but very little business."[367]

From the beginning, Municipal was saddled with obstacles that stymied its development. Running across the north end of the airport were the Chicago and Western Indiana Railroad's (Belt Line) tracks leading to one of the country's busiest switching yards. Later, when the airport expanded, the tracks cut through the middle of the airport, resulting in numerous air traffic delays as the trains had the right-of-way.

In the fall of 1926, the Chicago Board of Education opened Nathan Hale Elementary School at 63rd St. and Central Ave. on land not leased by the airport. Initially, the small planes of the period didn't interfere with class-room learning. Later, as planes grew more powerful and the airport ex-panded, school activity was disrupted by the noise and airport activity was impeded, since the airport closed one runway during the school day.[368]

1926/05/12   NAT Begins Air Mail Service

National Air Transport began service on the Chicago to Dallas air mail route (CAM-3) on May 12, 1926. NAT flew ten Curtiss Carrier Pigeons, which were then built by North American Aviation, another company owned by Clement

Keys. A year later, April 2, 1927, NAT was awarded the Chicago to New York route (CAM-17).[369] That year, NAT flew only 168 passengers, because the Carrier Pigeon could only carry a single passenger along with the mail.

Paul Henderson, VP and General Manger of NAT, was a big proponent of night flights. NAT led the way in round-the-clock flying, often cutting a full business day from delivery time.

Unlike most other air mail carriers, NAT phased out passenger service, especially on the Chicago-New York route, because Keys was pushing passenger service between St. Louis and New York by another of his ventures, Transcontinental Air Transport (TAT).[370]

1926/05/20   Air Commerce Act Takes Effect

President Coolidge signed the Air Commerce Act into law on May 20, 1926. The Act was drafted at Coolidge's request by Chicago attorney William P. MacCracken Jr. because of his extensive legal and aviation experience.

MacCracken received both his PhD and JD from Northwestern University. He learned to fly in the Army and served as an instructor during WWI, developing a continuing interest in aviation.

Returning to his law practice after the war, MacCracken became active in Cook County and Illinois politics. Always active with the American Bar Association, he served as the ABA Secretary for nearly ten years and also served on its committee on Aeronautical Law. MacCracken also served on the Board of Governors of the National Aeronautic Assn. In 1925, he helped organize National Air Transport and, as its general counsel, helped it acquire mail contracts.

Modeled after the maritime industry, the Air Commerce Act made the Federal government responsible for aircraft, airmen, navigational facilities, and air traffic regulations. This included licensing of both airplanes and pilots. However, the government was specifically prohibited from supporting ground ports, which were to be provided by local communities, with private industry suppling everything else.[371]

1926/06/01   Wheeling Farmers Start Swallow Airplane Field (Pal-Waukee)

In June 1926, brothers Frank and Pete Barchard dedicated 40 acres of their farm to become a permanent airport at the intersection of Palatine Rd. and Milwaukee Ave. The Barchard's owned a farm near Dam #1 on the Des Plaines River. Barnstormer Roy Gauthier freequently flew in the area which came to be known informally as Gauthier's Flying Field. However, the brothers had the foresight to see aviation's long-term potential, not just momentary entertainment.

The brothers were not content simply to let transient pilots use a corner of their farm as a landing field. The Barchards invested in the airport, building a hangar and other improvements. They hired pilot Wynn Bradford to run the operation. The Barchards sent Bradford to Wichita to purchase an OX-5 Swallow. Initially the airport took on the name of the airplane based there, Swallow Airplane Field.

Bradford used the Swallow for sightseeing rides, flight instruction, aerial advertising, and other commercial uses. At first, the airport used a war surplus tent hangar. By the time the Barchards sold the airport two years later, they had erected two permanent hangars housing twenty airplanes.[372]

One of the owners, Frank Barchard, became the exclusive distributor of "New Swallow" aircraft in the area. He also opened a service station, what would today be considered a Fixed Base Operator (FBO), at the intersection of Palatine and Milwaukee. The new station, which he named Pal-Waukee Air Port and Service Station, gassed and serviced both cars and airplanes. The name "Pal-Waukee Air Port" quickly supplanted "Swallow Airplane Field" as the airport's name.[373]

1926/06/07   Dickinson's First Air Mail Venture

Following several unsuccessful passenger airline ventures, Charles "Pop" Dickinson formed another airline, this time to transport air mail. CD Air Express underbid National Air Transport to be awarded the air mail route. He purchased some Laird Commercial LC-B biplanes from Matty Laird, whom he had mentored in the Aero Club's high school program.

Dickinson also recruited top-notch pilots, many from Chicago, with his friend David Behncke his first hire. Other initial pilots included Nimmo Black, William S. Brock, Daniel Kiser, Pop Keller, Matty Laird and Elmer Partridge.

The airline encountered problems from the beginning. The first day was a disaster. Worst of all, shortly after departing Minneapolis, Partridge died when his plane crashed in Mendota, MN. Two other pilots were forced to make off-airport landings. Kiser came down near Milwaukee and Keller landed not far from LaCrosse, WI. Only Black actually completed the route.

In addition to the losses he experienced, Dickinson had bid the contract too low to cover his operating costs. In August, Dickinson asked for the contract to be cancelled. On October 1, 1926, the Chicago to

Minneapolis route (CAM-9) was taken over by the recently incorporated
Northwest Airways.[374]

1926/06/11   Ford Tri-Motor Makes Debut Flight

The Ford 4-AT Tri-Motor made its first flight on June 11, 1926, at Ford
Field in Dearborn, MI. Designed by Bill Stout, the 4-AT shared many
characteristics with his earlier single-engine design the 1-AT Pullman. A
single cantilever wing minimized drag and weight and the corrugated
metal skin was durable. The Ford Tri-Motor was America's first truly
successful passenger plane.[375]

1926/08/11   MacCracken Becomes Head of Aeronautics

Prominent Chicago aviation attorney William MacCracken was instrumen-
tal in developing the Air Commerce Act that took effect in May, 1926. On
August 11, then Secretary of Commerce Herbert Hoover appointed
McCracken the first Assistant Secretary of Commerce for Aviation.[376]

1926/09/04–13   Heath Starts Winning Air Races

Always seeking a cost-effective way to promote his brand, Ed Heath
decided to enter the air racing circuit. At the time, the National Air Races
(NAR) were as popular as NASCAR is today and were covered in the
national newspapers.

Unlike Matty Laird's and Benny Howard's high-performance aircraft,
Heath's planes competed in events for planes with limited engine size. At
the 1923 and 1924 National Air Races, he entered modified versions of his
Favorite and Feather respectively. Neither performed very well in the races.

For the 1925 NAR, Heath entered his specially designed *Humming
Bird*. It was a streamlined all-wood plane with an open cockpit and enclosed
engine. The fully-cantilevered high wing with no braces or wires, had a 26
ft. wingspan. The Humming Bird was an improvement over his earlier
entries, but still fell short of the winner's circle.

At the NAR in Philadelphia in September 4–13, 1926, Heath entered the
Tomboy, which was the *Humming Bird* with a larger engine. The *Tomboy*
won each of the seven races it was entered in, yielding $2,250 in prize money.

For the remainder of his life, Heath had at least one plane competing in
the NARs annually and won most, if not all, of the events in which his
planes were entered. The Cleveland NAR in 1931 was held about six months
after Heath's death. Three Heath planes were in the competition, but only
one won.

Heath's air racing program had been an advertising success. Besides the newspaper coverage, Heath's catalogs and advertising prominently featured his race trophies and recognitions. Customers sought his planes and attended his school in order to be part of the winning image. But with Heath out of the picture, the company did not continue air racing.[377]

1926/09/05–06   Cook County Fair at Swallow Airplane Field (Pal-Waukee)

Only a few months after the Barchard brothers opened the Swallow Airplane Field, the Cook County Fair Assn. selected it as the site of the annual county fair.

The two-day event, held on Sunday and Monday, September 5–6, 1926, had all the traditional events for the still largely agricultural county. That year it added an "air circus" featuring William "Bill" Bollinger, who had been an air mail pilot both in the U.S. and in Honduras, performing dare-devil stunts in a Swallow brilliantly finished in black and gold. Wing walking and a parachute drop were included in the show. Tickets for plane rides ($5 for 10 min.) went on sale a month in advance.

Sunday of the fair was the "political rally day" during which candidates for mayor, judgeships, and the county board, including Board President A.J. Cermak, conducted a meet-and-greet with their constituents.[378]

1926/09/16   Lindbergh Bails Out

While flying air mail for Robertson Aircraft between St. Louis and Maywood Field, Lindbergh abandoned his airplane on more than one occasion.

The night of September 16, 1926, is probably the most retold and memorable of Lindbergh's jumps. After running out of gas, Lindbergh jumped out of his DH-4. As he parachuted down, the plane's nose dropped enabling remnants of gas in the tank to revive the engine. Power from the engine raised the nose and cut off the gas again. The cycle continued four or five times as the plane spiraled around Lindbergh descending at about the same rate. Fortunately, Lindbergh guided his chute away from the plane and landed safely.[379]

1926/12/07   First Aeronautics Airway Beacon Operational

The first airway light beacon erected by the Aeronautics Branch was located 15 mi. NE of Moline, on the Chicago-Dallas air mail route. Previously the Post Office Dept. had erected beacons to light 2,041 mi. of airways.[380]

1926/12/31   First Air Commerce Regulations Go Into Effect

The first regulations drafted subsequent to the Air Commerce Act took effect. Directed by William MacCracken, the new regulations drastically changed aviation in this country, putting the Federal government in charge, rather than a hodge-podge of state and local regulations.

Under the new regulations, aircraft engaged in interstate or foreign commerce were required to be licensed and marked with an identification number. Pilots of licensed aircraft were required to hold Private or Commercial Licenses. Unlicensed pilots were permitted to fly unlicensed aircraft that weren't engaged in interstate commerce, such as flight instruction. Commercial pilots were classed as either Transport or Industrial. Mechanics engaged in air commerce were required to secure either Engine or Airplane Mechanic Licenses or both. Air traffic rules controlled the airspace for all users whether civilian or military, commercial or not, within a state as well as those crossing state boundaries.

Under the new regulations, individuals had until May 1, 1927, to file their applications for appropriate licenses. Failure to comply met with a $500 fine.[381]

1927   Lowell Thomas Tours Europe By Air

In 1927, the same summer that Lindbergh reached Paris and U.S. airlines had passengers riding on top of mail sacks, journalist and traveler Lowell Thomas and his wife Frances embarked on a tour of Europe with the goal of using only commercial airlines without any trains or ships.

Starting in London, the Thomases visited all the capitals in Europe including Paris, Basel, Constantinople, Berlin, and Moscow. By the time they concluded their 1927 journey, they had traveled 25,000 mi. Lowell Thomas chronicled their adventures in a book, *European Skyways.* By comparison, Lindbergh's tour of 80 U.S. cities later that summer took him a mere 22,000 mi.[382]

1927   Route 66 Created

In 1927, Route 66 signs were posted along a variety of existing roadways creating a highway that extended from the Great Lakes to Los Angeles. The northern terminus was Grant Park at Michigan Ave.[a] and at Jackson Blvd.[383]

---

a   In 1933, the terminus was moved to Lake Shore Dr. from Michigan Ave.

1927   Spokane to New York Air Derby

After his unsuccessful airline attempts, in 1927 Charles "Pop" Dickinson developed an interest in air racing. He purchased two Laird Commercials and entered them in the Spokane to New York Air Derby. They were flown by two pilots from Dickinson's short-lived air mail route. Charles "Speed" Holman won the race followed by Ervin Ballough, who carried Dickinson as a passenger.[384]

1927   First Radio Navigation Aids Enable Instrument Flying

In 1927, Eugene S. Donovan, a Ford engineer, patented the first electronic aerial navigation facility, the Low-Frequency Radio Range (LFR)[a] system. Under the direction of the Ford Motor Co., Donovan pursued work begun before WWI by the German company Lorenz.

LFR systems located a waypoint at the center of four quadrants, with a low-frequency transmitter in the center of each quadrant. Two diagonal quadrants broadcast a continuous "A" (dit-dah) and the other two broadcast an "N" (dah-dit). The pilot would adjust a loop-type antenna on the plane for the strongest reception in the direction he was traveling.

Staying on course, the plane would fly along the overlap area between the towers, and the pilot would hear a continuous sound. Drifting to one side or the other would cause either the "A" or "N" pattern to dominate. To determine whether flying toward or away from the waypoint, the pilot would adjust the volume until the tone was barely audible. If the tone disappeared, he was flying away and if it got louder he was flying toward the goal.

A transmitter in the center of the range would periodically broadcast the three-letter identifier of the range. Following a series of LFR ranges would enable a pilot to navigate between designated destinations. Using LFR, a pilot could navigate cross-country in instrument conditions in a plane with only an aural receiver.

As soon as it was developed, Ford Air Transport equipped its planes with receivers and established LFR ranges at Dearborn, MI, and Ford Field in Lansing, IL. LFR proved successful in improving Ford's cargo deliveries in all weather conditions.[385]

---

a   The technology was also called the Four-Course Radio Range, the A-N Radio Range, the Adcock Radio Range, or LF/MF (Low Frequency/Medium Frequency) Range.

1927   First Waukegan Airport Starts

In the summer of 1928, the Waukegan Chamber of Commerce created the original airport when they leased a site on part of the Burris Farm at Green Bay Rd. and Sunset Ave.

The Waukegan Chamber also started the National School of Aviation and purchased a Swallow for flight instruction by Johnnie Miller and Edward Hedeen, both WWI pilots.

National School of Aviation failed within a year. The Chamber left the aviation field and sold its airplane. Linden Burris, son of the farmer who owned the land, became airport operator in 1928 and started the Waukegan Flying Club with Vernon Ramsey as instructor.

By the early 1930s, the 64-acre Burris Field was used as an emergency landing field by Northwest Airways on the Chicago-Milwaukee leg of the route to Minneapolis (CAM-9). Around 1934, a rotating beacon and a manned weather station were added to the steel hangar.

When Frederic Stripe managed the airport in 1936–37, Burris Field had expanded to include a garage and service station, office and living quarters, and a small restaurant.[386]

1927   Sterling Gets an Airport

More than fifteen years after the short-lived Whiteside County Airport at McCue's Corner, the county got another airport. The Sterling Airport opened in 1927 at the corner of IL-40 near Lynn Blvd.[387]

1927   First Aurora Airport Opens

In 1927, Midwest Airways Corp. of Monmouth formally opened an airport that became a commercial airport the following year. John Livingston was made airport manager. During the late 1920s and early 1930s, Livingston was also a regular winner on the air race circuit.

Between 1921 and 1923 a flying field, located along Route 31 beside the Fox River on the south side of Exposition Park, was used by Aurora Aviation Co. for giving sightseeing flights to the public.[388]

1927   Casey Begins Managing Municipal

Chicago native, John Casey became Superintendent of Operations for the new Municipal Airport in 1927. Casey remained in that position for for almost 40 years, until his retirement in March 1966. Casey's aviation experience dated back to 1919, when he became a mechanic for the Air Mail

Service when they were flying out of Grant Park. In 1925, he received his pilot's license. In 1929, Casey enlisted in the 108th Observation Squadron of the Illinois Air National Guard where he rose to the rank of Lt. Col.[389]

1927   Sporrer Becomes First Corporate Pilot

Alfred Sporrer became America's first corporate pilot in 1927 when he began flying for Charles Horton, chairman of the Chicago Bridge and Iron Co.

After learning to fly in the mid-1920s, Sporrer did some barnstorming around the Midwest. After flying for Horton, Sporrer became a corporate pilot for Chicago investment banker F.B. "Frank" Evans, who was a major investor in the G. Heileman and Berghoff breweries.[390]

1927   Legion Field Opens in Chicago Heights

August "Auggie" Maross, a barnstormer, settled down in 1927 and opened a flying field in Chicago Heights. Located at Ashland Ave. and Joe Orr Rd. (203rd St.) near Lincoln Highway (US 30), Legion Field was also known as Ashland Airport and Chicago Heights Airport.[391]

1927/01   Post Office Awards Boeing Contract

The Post Office Dept. awarded Boeing Airplane Co. the contract for air mail service between Chicago and San Francisco (CAM-18) on January 28, 1927. Later that year, Boeing formed Boeing Air Transport to fly mail and passengers using the Boeing Model 40A.[392]

1927/01   Ford Hangar Completed in Lansing

In early January 1927, Ford Air Transport opened its new hangar at Ford Field in Lansing, IL. Designed by architect Albert Kahn, the innovative hangar incorporated features unique at the time. Its cantilevered roof supported an open area that could hold three Ford Tri-Motors without any impediments. Full-length doors on two sides of the building were on wheeled tracks which allowed them to be opened by one person providing easy access for aircraft. The Ford Hangar was added to the National Register of Historic Places in 1985.[393]

1927/02/28   Heath Introduces Parasol

After a successful air racing season in 1926, Edward Heath decided to use his winnings to introduce a new flyvver airplane for less than $1,000. To keep the cost down, Heath designed the plane around a supply of surplus lower wings from the Thomas-Morse S-4C Scout. The 26-ft. wing was used as a parasol, supported by braces that allowed it to go unbroken above the one-man fuselage which was less than 17 ft. long. The Heath Parasol, introduced on February 28, 1927, weighed less than 300 lbs., cruised at 70 mph, and sold for $575 ready to fly.

Timing of the introduction was perfect. With Lindbergh's transatlantic flight and subsequent national tour, interest in aviation was stratospheric. An affordable airplane from a race-winning manufacturer brecame a hit.

Heath quickly ran through his supply of Scout wings and was forced to use a wing manufactured in-house. The Super Parasol, with the new wing, cost $975, up $400 from the earlier model.

Heath was very aware of his customers' budgets. Even before the Depression, $1,000 was a lot of money for the average working man to accumulate. As with his earlier planes, he offered options. For example, a complete ready-to-fly *Parasol* cost $975, or $690 without the engine. The customer could buy a complete set of parts for $199. The kits were available for welded frames, or for those with only hand tools, with bolted frames.

But even $199 was a big chunk of cash, so Heath divided the kit into individual groups, so customers could "buy as they built." For $12.47, the customer could purchase parts for the wing ribs. When he had finished the ribs, he would pay $13.08 for the wing frame, and so on. After 11 sections, the plane was complete, just waiting for the engine.

As with his other planes, Heath sold a complete set of plans for $5. But he went beyond that. Heath wrote a series of articles in *Popular Aviation* between December 1930 and July 1931. The articles included detailed instructions for building a plane, along with complete plans and parts list. Anyone with the passion and determination would be able to build their own Parasol.[394]

One of Heath's goals was to make his airplanes as convenient as possible for his customers. All of his planes were available on wheels, skis, or floats. Wings on all Heath planes were removable, reducing the space required for storage. Removable wings were also essential for Heath, whose factory on Chicago's North Side was miles away from the flying field he used for testing and demonstrations. All his planes were trucked or towed from the factory to the airport.[395]

Engines had always been the most expensive part of Heath's planes and he was constantly searching for low-cost alternatives. His catalogs offered many engine options, mostly from motorcycles but also from Ford's Model T engine.

With the Parasol, Heath introduced the Heath-Henderson B-4 engine. The B-4 was basically a four-cylinder, 25–30 hp engine from the Henderson motorcycle. Heath made numerous modifications to the engine to make it suitable for use in an airplane. As with his airplanes, customers could purchase a complete engine, a kit of parts to make the modifications, or plans to do it themselves if they had access to a machine shop.[396]

1927/03/22   Aeronautics Branch Becomes Fully Operational

By the middle of March 1927, the Commerce Dept.'s new Aeronautics Branch became fully operational under William MacCracken Jr.

One of MacCracken's first actions was to appoint Louis Hopewell Bauer as the Department's first Medical Director. On February 28, 1927, Bauer published the first list of what would later be called Aviation Medical Examiners (AME). The original list contained only 57 physicians nationally. By 1929, Chicago alone had three AMEs, including William P. MacCracken Sr.[397]

On March 22, the Aeronautics Branch issued major amendments to the Air Commerce Regulations that went into effect only three months earlier. A new Limited Commercial Pilot's license was added, allowing pilots to carry passengers up to 10 mi. from their base as they built up time for the Transport Pilot's License. The amendment also made changes to the aircraft identification numbers. The "N" was only required for aircraft involved in foreign commerce. Numbers could be prefixed by "C" (Commercial), "S" (State) or "X" (Experimental). The previously used "P" (Private) designation was eliminated. Aircraft Type Certificate #1 was issued on March 29 for a Buhl Airster C-A3.[398]

1927/04/06   Federal Government Issues First Licenses

The head of the Aeronautics Branch, William MacCracken, was issued U.S. Pilot License #1 on April 6, 1927. Previous licenses had been issued by various groups, such as the Aero Clubs, but now licensing and standards were controlled by the Aeronautics Branch. MacCracken had offered the honor of the first license to Orville Wright, but he declined because he didn't fly any longer. On July 1, the Aeronautics Branch issued the first Mechanic's License.[399]

1927/05/02   "City Within a City" Opens

James Stevens and his son Ernest[a] opened the Stevens Hotel (currently the Chicago Hilton), the world's largest hotel at that time. Prominently located on Michigan Ave., the Stevens was across Balbo Dr. from the already

renowned Blackstone Hotel. The first guest was U.S. Vice President Charles
G. Dawes, an Evanston resident.

The architectural firm of Holabird and Roche designed the Beaux-Arts
structure that cost $30 million (ten times the cost of Yankee Stadium, built
around the same time). The luxurious interior featured oil paintings on the
ceilings, crystal chandeliers, and bronze fittings.

The Stevens was one of the first Chicago structures designed for
mixed-use and was dubbed a "City Within a City."[b] In addition to 3,000
guest rooms, the Stevens boasted a 1,200-seat theater for talking pictures,
a hospital with two operating rooms, an 18-hole golf course on the roof,
and a candy factory. Retail outlets included an ice cream shop, jewelry
store, flower shop, children's toy/clothing store, 24-hour drugstore, 5-lane
bowling alley, and 25-seat barber shop.[400]

1927/05/21   Lindberg Lands in Paris

Charles Lindbergh made the first solo transatlantic flight from New York to
Paris. He departed in the early morning of May 20, 1927, from Roosevelt
Field on Long Island. After flying 33½ hours, he landed at Le Bourget Field
in Paris to throngs of well-wishers.

Not only did Lindbergh win the $25,000 Orteig prize, he became a
household hero around the world and a spokesman for aviation.[401]

1927/06/30   First Federal Aeronautical Chart

On June 30, 1927, the Aeronautics Branch issued the first aeronautical
chart. Unlike contemporary charts that cover an entire region, early ones
were airway strip maps that covered only the specific routes flown by air
mail pilots. The first available strip map covered the segment between
Moline and Kansas City, MO on the Chicago to Dallas route (CAM-3).[402]

1927/07/01   Post Office Transfers Control to Commerce Dept.

The transcontinental airway system used for flying air mail was transferred
from the Post Office Dept. to the Commerce Dept's Aeronautics Branch.
The New York to San Francisco airway was 2,612 mi. long of which 2,041
mi. were lighted. The transfer included 92 intermediate landing fields, 417
acetylene beacons, 101 electric beacons, and 17 radio stations[c].[403]

a   Ernest's son, John Paul Stevens, who was 7 years old when the hotel opened, went on to
    become a Justice on the U.S. Supreme Court.
b   Marina Towers and the John Hancock Center were later prominent mixed-use structures.
c   Probably Low Frequency Radio Ranges.

1927/07/01   IL Air National Guard Based at Municipal

After being demobilized following WWI, the 108th Observation Squadron
was reactivated on July 1, 1927, as part of the 33rd Aviation Div. of the IL
National Guard at Municipal Field, flying PT-1 trainers.[a]

The 108th Aero Squadron has proudly served our country since 1917,
albeit with a variety of designations. The 108th was originally formed as a
repair squadron on August 28, 1917, at Kelly Field, TX. In February 1918,
the designation was changed to the 802nd Aero Squadron while it served in
France. Upon returning to the states, the 802nd was demobilized.

In 1929, the Army stationed George Marshall (architect of the post-
WWII Marshall Plan) as the Unit Advisor for the 108th. Also in 1929, the
108th started parachute training using Harlem Airport since it was less
congested than Municipal. Practice sessions drew small crowds of spectators who enjoyed the free air show. A side benefit was that so many young
men became interested in joining the 108th, that they had a wait list
several years long.[404]

1927/07/01   Boeing Carries Mail and More to San Francisco

Boeing Air Transport (BAT) inaugurated service on the Chicago to San
Francisco route (CAM-18) on July 1, 1927. Previously the Post Office Dept.
flew that mail route itself.

Of the contract air mail companies, BAT was the one most interested in
passenger traffic. Accordingly, Boeing Aircraft designed the 40A specifically
for mail-passenger transport. Using an air-cooled P&W Wasp engine, rather
than a more common water-cooled engine, gave the 40A twice the payload
of competitive mail planes. Although it had an open cockpit for he pilot,
the mail and up to two passengers were carried in a closed cockpit.[405]

Within a month of beginning service, BAT flew its first passenger, a
woman reporter, from Chicago to Omaha. Ira Biffle, noted for being
Charles Lindbergh's flight instructor, was the pilot on that flight.[406]

1927/07/04   NW Airways Inaugural Flight

Less than a year after Charles Dickinson gave up the CAM-9 air mail route
between Chicago and Minneapolis, Northwest Airways made its inaugural
flight between the two cities.

---

a Lewis (p. 7) states that in 1927, the 108th was based at Camp Grant in Rockford where it used
   the parade grounds for a runway. There is no other reference to the unit being based there but
   Hill (p. 383) mentions that in August 1929 the 108th spent a two-week encampment at
   Camp Grant.

Northwest Airways was organized on October 1, 1926, by Col. L.H. Brittin and other Minneapolis businessmen to fill the void on the Minneapolis mail route.

Two of Dickinson's pilots became the first to fly for Northwest: Speed Holman, who became the chief pilot and operations manager for Northwest, and David Behncke.

Behncke had always been a very safety-conscious pilot in a period when many pilots could be considered reckless. He criticized Holman, who was a sportster, for often taking Northwest's Stinson Detroiter for aerobatics prior to passenger flights. One day in 1927, Behncke refused to fly a Detroiter after a Holman flight, because Behncke questioned its airworthiness. Northwest terminated Behncke for not making the flight.[407]

1927/07/08   Machesney Rockford Airport Opens

On July 8, 1927, Machesney "Rockford" Airport opened for business. The eventual 160-acre site extended west to the Rock River, with provisions for seaplane operations.

A former barnstormer, Fred Machesney had moved to Rockford in June 1926 and opened a landing field on a local farm. Within a year, the the facility proved too small, and Machesney moved about a half mile north to 8600 N. Second St. Machesney Field was extremely active during the late 1920s and early 1930s and Fred Machesney pushed development of the field.[408]

1927/07/30   Universal Aviation Corp Is Formed

The Universal Aviation Corp. (UAC), formed in Chicago on July 30, 1928, initially provided only passenger service between Chicago and Cleveland. UAC had substantial cash reserves and began a rapid string of acquisitions. By the end of the year UAC had purchased Robertson Aircraft, based in St. Louis, and Northern Air Lines, out of Minneapolis/St. Paul. Eventually, UAC had more than 4,000 mi. of routes.[409]

1927/08/13   Lindbergh Visits Chicago

While Municipal Airport was still under development, Charles Lindbergh visited there with the *Spirit of St. Louis* on August 13, 1927.

Lindbergh's selection of the unfinished Municipal Airport, rather than one of the area's other facilities, gave Municipal a big boost in recognition. Both area residents and the national press covering the tour saw Municipal as the latest and greatest of Chicago's airports.

The Chicago stop was part of Lindbergh's 80-city, 22,000-mi. tour that
visited all 48 states. During the course of his tour, more than 30 million
people turned out to see the national hero. Thousands of Chicagoans
greeted him at Municipal Airport and thousands more filled Soldier Field
for a huge rally. Lindbergh's promotion of aviation was credited with a
fourfold increase in the number of air passengers in the year following his
Paris flight.[410]

1927/08/28   Lindbergh's Tour Reaches Moline

Charles Lindbergh's national tour brought the *Spirit of St. Louis* to Moline.
More than 10,000 people turned out to welcome him to Franing Field on
August 28, 1927.[411]

1927/09/22   Soldier Field Witnesses the "Long Count"

Jack Dempsey, former heavyweight champion and considered by many to
be the country's greatest boxer, had a rematch at Soldier Field with Gene
Tunney, who had defeated Dempsey a year earlier. With nearly 105,000
people in attendance the gate was over $2 million, the largest in entertain-
ment to that time. Millions more tuned their radios to hear the fight live.

In the 7th round, Dempsey knocked Tunney down. The referee waited
until Dempsey was in a neutral corner before beginning the ten-second
count. Tunney struggled to his feet as the count ended, having been given
13–14 seconds instead of 10. In the end, Tunney won the fight based on the
judges' points.

Following the disputed fight, Dempsey retired from competitive
boxing, although he continued to do exhibition bouts.[412]

1927/10/10   Pan Am Begins Service

Pan American Airways began service on October 10, 1927, as an international carrier launching air mail flights between Key West and Havana.
Passenger service began on January 18 the following year.[413]

1927/10/04   Tony Yackey Crashes, Followed by Checkerboard

While making a test flight on October 4, 1927, Tony Yackey died in a crash.
An Italian WWI ace, Yackey had purchased Checkerboard Field as the home
for Yackey Aircraft Co. At first, Yackey modified WWI aircraft for the
civilian market but later added planes of his own design. The high-wing
Yackey Monoplane finished fifth in the 1927 National Air Race from New
York to Spokane.

Unable to continue without him, Yackey Aircraft Co. shuttered its doors. Checkerboard Field deteriorated and the newly-formed Civil Aviation Board declared it unsafe. Checkerboard Field was condemned in 1928.[414]

1927/12/08   Air Mail Shifts from Maywood to Municipal

A few days before Chicago Municipal Airport's official dedication, the Post Office Dept. shifted all air mail flights from Maywood Air Mail Field to Municipal, although air mail flights still continued at Lansing Air Mail Field. On December 8, a Boeing Air Transport plane, piloted by Ira Biffle, arrived from Omaha becoming the first commercial arrival after the opening.[415]

After the departure of air mail activity, Maywood Field continued operating but at a much lower level into the 1930s. Its name changed on charts and it was known as Veterans Auxiliary Field and then Hines Field. Sometime after 1937, the Maywood Field closed, although the runways were still visible in photographs for several years.[416]

1927/12/12   Municipal Officially Opens

Although Chicago Municipal Airport had an unofficial dedication in May 1926, the formal dedication came more than a year later on December 12, 1927.[a] During the ceremony, Mayor William Hale Thompson remarked that every 60 seconds, a train arrived in Chicago and foretold that the same would eventually be true for airplanes.[417]

During the first year after the official opening, Municipal was the base for over 100 airplanes. It became the world's busiest airport with 41,660 flight operations[b] and 15,498 passengers. It would be another two years before there were more passengers that flight operations. Municipal retained the title of world's busiest airport until 1960, when it relinquished it to O'Hare.[418]

1927/12/17   Embry-Riddle Begins Service to Chicago

Embry-Riddle began mail service on December 17, 1927,[c] between Chicago and Cincinnati (CAM-24) using Waco cabin airplanes. T. Higbee Embry and John Paul Riddle started the company that was based at Cincinnati's Lunken Airport.[419]

---

a   Hill dates the dedication to December 1, 1927.
b   An airport flight operation is either a takeoff or a landing.
c   *The Centennial of Flight* site places the date as the 17th, but Scamehorn dates it as December 7.

1928   Phoebie Omlie Sets Altitude Record

Phoebie Fairgrave was born in Iowa and learned to fly in 1920 in Moline. On June 30, 1927, she became the first woman issued a pilot's license (#199) by the Aeronautics Branch. She also received one of the early Aircraft and Engine licenses.

Phoebie married another pilot Vernon Omlie, then toured as the Phoebie Fairgrave Omlie Flying Circus. Phoebie was fearless, performing wing-walking and parachuting as well as aerobatics.

In the summer of 1928, Phoebie Omlie was flying for the Mono Aircraft Co. in Moline. Mono provided aircraft for her use, and she generated a great deal of publicity for them. Attempting to set an altitude record, she flew a 65 hp Monocoupe to 25,400 ft. As she continued her climb, the engine blew a spark plug and the main oil line was damaged. As blinding oil sprayed from the engine, she fumbled with her oxygen and was nearly unconscious as she landed the plane. Her flight established a new world altitude record for women and light aircraft.

Phoebie's flying career continued. She became interested in air racing and flew in the first Women's Air Derby in 1929, winning in the light plane category with her Monocoupe. Franklin Roosevelt called upon Phoebie and her Monocoupe to fly him around during the 1932 presidential campaign.[420]

1928   Wheeling Gets a Second Airport

In 1928, Charles Balling and Mel Larson rented a field from Frank Haben on Milwaukee Ave. just north of Deerfield Rd. Wheeling Airport was several miles north of the larger Pal-Waukee Air Port.

Balling and Larson flew passengers in their three-seat Lincoln-Page airplane. When their plane crashed, the men ended their flying careers and the airport closed.[421]

1928   Ravenswood Airport Begins

Ravenswood Airport started operating sometime around 1928, in unincorporated Cook County on Touhy Ave. two miles west of Mannheim Rd. According to a study by Cook County in 1929, it was one of five airports in the county determined to be safe for operations. William Turgeon did a brief stint as Ravenswood Airport Manager around 1930.[422]

1928   *Chicago Daily News* Flies Reporters

As early as 1928, the *Chicago Daily News* pioneered the use of airplanes by news organizations.

The *Blue Streak* was a Bellanca twin with tandem engines (both a tractor engine in front and a pusher engine in the rear) that was custom built for the newspaper. It was designed to carry a large load for long distances with instrumentation that allowed it to fly in all weather. The paper used the *Blue Streak* to fly reporters, photographers, drama critics, and the like to breaking news locations around the Midwest.[423]

The *Daily News* also operated a fleet of Bellanca CH-300 Pacemakers to deliver newspapers to their customers vacationing in Eagle River, Mackinac Island, and other locations in surrounding states. Over 108,000 pounds of newspapers were flown from Pal-Waukee in 1929.[424]

1928   Heath's Factory Burns

Fire destroyed the Heath Aircraft Co.'s Chicago factory at 2856 Broadway in Spring 1928. The fire destroyed Heath's supplies as well as a number of aircraft that were in the process of being built.

Fortunately, a building nearby became available and Heath moved into 1721–1727 Sedgwick, in the Lincoln Park area. The company remained at this location the duration of Heath's life.[425]

1928   Stout Buys Ford

Bill Stout started an air mail route in 1926 using the Ford Tri-Motor that he had designed. Stout Air Services provided scheduled passenger service as well as mail delivery between Detroit and Grand Rapids. In 1928, Stout Air Services purchased the air mail routes from Ford Air Transport Service and started serving the Chicago to Detroit route (CAM-7).

Stout Air Services was acquired in April 1929 by United Aircraft and Transport Corp. (UATC) but continued operating under its own name. [426]

1928   Roy and Mae Wilson Buy an Airport

Stanley Wallace and Max Schusin operated a small flying field along the Des Plaines River at Lawrence Ave. and River Rd. In 1926, they sold it to Ralph Wilson who renamed it Wilson Airport.

Ralph Wilson only kept the airport about a year, before selling it to Edwin Greer of Greer School of Aviation, which changed the name to Greer Airways Field (Airport) #2.

The airport changed hands again, about a year later when Roy and Mae Wilson[a] purchased the field from Greer and changed the name back to Wilson Airport.[427]

1928/01/31   First Reported Federal Noise Complaint

The *Domestic Air News*, a publication of the Aeronautics Branch, reported a complaint that airplane noise was disrupting egg production at the Crackle Corner Poultry Farm in Garrettsville, GA.[428]

1928/01/02   Lindy is "Man of the Year"

Time magazine began its tradition of naming a "Man of the Year"[b] in the January 2, 1929, issue, when it placed Charles Lindbergh on its cover.[429]

1928/03   Speed Holman Sets Loop Record

In March 1928, Charles W. "Speed" Holman, a Minnesotan who had close connections with Chicago, set a record by consecutively looping-the-loop 1,433 times. The following year he astonished crowds by flying a Tri-Motor plane inverted and looping it a number of times.

He flew the CAM-9 Air Mail Route between Chicago and Minneapolis, first for Pop Dickinson and then Northwest Airways.

However, Holman loved thrills in the air and developed a reputation as a daring, even hazardous, pilot. While flying for Northwest in 1927, one of the other pilots, David Behncke, was fired for questioning the airworthiness of a plane that Holman had just used for stunt flying.[430]

1928/03/20   Federal Radio Beacons Become Operational

Under William MacCracken's direction the Civil Aeronautics Authority conducted tests of radio navigation using the Low-Frequency Radio Range (LFR) system using three ranges between Newark and Cleveland.

The LFR system was based on the technology used successfully by Ford Motor Co. between Ford Field in Lansing, IL and Dearborn, MI. The Aeronautics Branch standardized the format and scaled it up for national use.

On March 20, the first part of the system became operational, with seven LFR ranges laying out a course from Newark to Omaha and from Key West to Havana. By the outbreak of WWII, 90 ranges marked more than 18,000 miles of airways in the U.S.[431]

---

a   There does not appear to be any connection between Ralph and Roy Wilson other than the fact that they owned the same airport a few years apart.
b   *Time* began bestowing the "Person of the Year" honor in 1999.

1928/05   First In-Flight Movie

During a flight of a Ford Tri-Motor over Los Angeles, passengers viewed the movie *Speedy* starring Harold Lloyd.[432]

1928/05/01   Eastern Air Transport Begins

Eastern Air Transport commenced operations along the Atlantic Coast as Pitcairn Aviation. In 1930, it began passenger service between New York and Washington, DC, as Eastern Air Transport. After acquiring a number of other airlines, the name changed to Eastern Air Lines in 1934.[433]

1928/05/16   Transcontinental Air Transport Starts Operating

Transcontinental Air Transport (TAT) was popularly known as the "Lindbergh Line" because of Charles Lindbergh's active involvement. Like other airlines of the period, TAT leadership included manufacturers and operating airlines along with financial backers. However, TAT was unique in that it gave preference to passengers over mail.[434]

1928/06/20   First Illinois Air Tour Begins

The first Illinois Air Tour left Municipal with 16 planes including a Ford Tri-Motor. The three-day tour visited 15 cities, flying as far south as Carbondale, with overnight stops in Monmouth and Springfield. Organized by the Aviation Committee of the Illinois Chamber of Commerce, the Illinois Air Tour was intended to promote aviation throughout the state. The Illinois Chamber intended to hold annual air tours similar to the national Ford Reliability Tours.

There was no tour in 1929. Then in 1930, the Chamber organized a tour to be held before the National Air Races (NAR) at Curtiss-Reynolds Field in Glenview. Merrill Meigs, Chairman of the Chicago Aero Commission, was the director of the four-day 1930 tour, which visited 23 cities around the state, promoting the NAR as well as aviation in general.

By the next year, the effects of the Depression were being felt. Trying to maintain the current level of aviation activity was difficult enough without attempting to generate more activity. The tours were discontinued.[435]

1928/06/30   Accident Investigation Board Created

The Aeronautics Branch created an Accident Investigation Board. The five-member panel was to investigate and analyze airplane crashes to determine and eliminate the causes. Although it had limited jurisdiction, the Investigation Board is the precursor to the current National Transportation Safety Board (NTSB).[436]

1928/07/01   Chicago Receives Weather Teletype

Chicago and three other locations were the first to install teletypes that received Commerce Dept. weather reports distributed from a central office in Washington.[437]

1928/08/16   Flying the Great Circle

The *Rockford Daily Republic* sponsored a flight to Stockholm to publicize Rockford. The flight would be financed by a group of Swedish-Americans from Chicago.

The trip would roughly follow Leif Ericson's path through Labrador, Greenland, and Iceland. This northern Great Circle route was a shorter path to Europe rather than the apparent "direct" route which appears shorter on flat maps.

In October 1927, Bert R.J. "Fish" Hassell was named the pilot and he selected Parker D. "Shorty" Cramer as his co-pilot. Hassell's friend Eddie Stinson customized a Detroiter for the long distance journey. *The Greater Rockford,* a name selected by means of a newspaper contest, was painted on the plane in the blue and yellow colors of the Swedish flag.

After a failed attempt on July 26th, the pair finally embarked on their journey on August 16' 1928. On the second leg of their journey, they went off-course during the 1,600-mile flight to Greenland. Running short of fuel, Hassell made the first successful landing on an icecap, leaving the plane undamaged.

The pair hiked for about two weeks toward the coast before some Eskimos contacted a research station which sent a rescue party. A few days later, on September 3rd, the research station closed for the season and they all boarded a sloop to leave. Unfortunately, the ship struck a reef and sank. No one was injured, but everyone was stranded for three days until a rescue ship arrived.

Eventually Hassell and Cramer made it back to the U.S. Treated as heroes, they received a ticker tape parade in New York and met President Coolidge in Washington, DC. Although their flight failed to reach its destination, it was instrumental in establishing the navigational advantage of the Great Circle Route.[438]

1928/09/26   Lear Gears Up in Chicago

William Powell Lear joined with Paul Galvin on September 26, 1928, becoming a one-third owner in Galvin Manufacturing Company, later renamed Motorola. While working with Galvin, Lear developed the first car radios.

Lear had two great passions: electronics and aviation. During WWI, Lear served as a wireless instructor at Great Lakes Training Center. After the war, he moved around servicing mail planes. In 1924, Lear returned to Chicago, where he was employed by several radio and electronics companies and credited with several inventions.

After leaving Galvin in the early 1930s, he started Lear Developments and opened a shop in a small portion of Hangar One at Curtiss-Reynolds Field. There, Lear developed a lightweight receiver for radio navigation beacons and other aviation electronics. However useful his inventions, during the Great Depression buyers were scarce and the company filed for bankruptcy.

Lear moved first to the East and later the West Coast, where he continued his ground-breaking work in radio electronics for aircraft. He introduced the Lear L-5 Autopilot in 1949 for which he won the Collier Trophy.

Starting a new venture in Wichita, Lear developed a small, private jet designed for corporate transportation. The Lear 23 was certificated by the FAA in August 1964. That same year, Lear developed the 8-track tape player technology. [439]

1928/11   Pal-Waukee Air Port Incorporates

Following Lindbergh's 1927 transatlantic flight, aviation caught the public eye. The public flocked to air shows and followed aviation events in the newspapers and on the radio. The rich and adventurous bought airplanes and hired instructors to teach them to fly.

Three of these "sportsmen" from Lake Forest, who all regularly appeared on newspaper society pages, sought a place near their homes to fly. In November 1928, they purchased the Barchards' airport, intending to make it the best-equipped airport for North Shore residents. At the time of the purchase, the airport housed twenty planes.

Owen Barton Jones, the prime mover of the project, became President. His friend, Jesse Lathrop Moss Jr., was the Vice President. Duncan Hodges, the son of Gen. Harry F. Hodges, became the Airport Manager. Cliff Condit replaced Wynn Bradford as the airport's chief pilot. [440]

An heir to a zinc empire, Jones and his wife had traveled extensively around the world. During one of their sojourns in Bermuda, Jones was bitten by the flying bug and learned to fly a seaplane.[a] In March 1928, he was severely injured in a crash and confined to the hospital for many weeks,[441] but his accident and injuries didn't dampen his aviation enthusiasm.[b]

In November 1928, Jones and the new owners officially incorporated the landing field as Pal-Waukee Air Port, Inc. Almost immediately they invested $30,000 in infrastructure to improve drainage and provide heating in the airport's largest hangar.[442]

1928/12   Stinson School Opens in Chicago

Another of the Stinson clan, Jack B. Stinson opened an aviation school in Chicago, becoming the fifth in the chain of the Stinson School of Aviation. The curriculum included: "History, Aerodynamics, Construction, Engines, Design, Meteorology, Navigation, Regulations, Photography, Airplane Sales, Airports & Airways, and 30 lessons in the air."[443]

1928/12   Interstate Airlines Begins Service

Interstate Airlines, a Chicago company, started flying the air mail route between Chicago and Atlanta (CAM-30) in December 1928. In 1930, Aviation Corp. of Delaware (AVCO) acquired Interstate, incorporating its routes into their national system.[444]

1928/12/01–09   First International Aeronautical Exposition

The Aeronautical Chamber of Commerce held the First International Aeronautical Exposition in Chicago, December 1–9, 1928. It was the first of several venues around the country that were timed to celebrate the 25th anniversary of the Wright brothers' flight.

The Exposition was a resounding success. Originally planned for the Chicago Coliseum, the number of exhibitors forced the addition of the First Regiment Armory. On display were 79 airplanes from 53 manufacturers, including everything from single-seat sport planes up to tri-motor transports. Also exhibiting were 25 engine and 131 accessory manufacturers.[445]

---

a   Wynn Bradford, Pal-Waukee airport manager and chief pilot during the Barchard years, claimed that he taught Jones to fly (McIntyre p. 143). Bradford may have instructed Jones to qualify for his U.S. licens

b   The crash did dampen the enthusiasm of Jones' wife. In 1930, she sued for divorce. A subheading in the *Chicago Daily Tribune* claims "His Flying Is Blamed." According to his wife, after being nearly killed in a crash, Jones didn't give up flying but became even more passionate about it. She viewed his obsession with aviation as insanity and desertion.

1928/12/12–14   First International Civil Aeronautics Conference

President Coolidge called for the First International Civil Aeronautics Conference to commemorate the Silver Anniversary of flight by addressing issues on international flying. More than 100 countries sent representatives to Washington, DC to address problems of flying between countries.

Prior to the opening of the Conference, 200 international delegates from 50 countries were flown to Chicago in a fleet of 14 transports to attend the International Aeronautical Exposition. Delegates were also treated to a formal banquet in Chicago by the Aeronautical Chamber of Commerce.[446]

1928/12/17   Early Birds of Aviation Forms

In conjunction with the International Aeronautical Exposition in Chicago, which commemorated the 25th Anniversary of the Wright brothers' first flight, a group of aviation pioneers formed the Early Birds of Aviation on December 17, 1928.

In order to recognize the feats of the earliest aviators, Early Birds limited membership to people who soloed on or before December 17, 1916. The 1916 cutoff was selected to eliminate the rapid influx of pilots with the U.S. entry into WWI. The exact date also recognized the Wright flight. For European members, the solo threshold was likewise placed at August 9, 1914, prior to their military surge. The Early Birds accepted 568 members and produced the newsletter *Chirp*.[447]

1929   Air Traffic Control at Municipal

By 1929, airplane ground traffic was so heavy that Municipal Airport needed a flagman at the end of the runway to control flight operations. Police were also needed, especially on weekends, to control crowds of spectators.[448]

Municipal had a somewhat unusual design for airports of the period. Given the weight and power of aircraft of the period, wind direction was crucial to safe operations. Many airports were an omnidirectional field, allowing planes to land in any direction depending on the wind. Other airports, where land was constrained, built only one or two runways aligned with the prevailing wind. Municipal, on the other hand, was one of the few that had eight hard-surface runways, two aligned with each of the four major compass directions, and was therefore able to accommodate any wind pattern.[449]

1929   Cook County Safety Report

A Cook County, IL Board report in 1929 analyzed conditions and practices at the many airports in Cook County and determined that only six could be considered safe: Curtiss Commercial Field (previously Curtiss-Reynolds Field), Curtiss School Field, Ford Field (Chicago Hammond) in Lansing, Pal-Waukee Air Port in Wheeling, Ravenswood Field in unincorporated Cook County, and Sky Harbor near Glencoe.

The two-month long study was made by Maj. Reed Landis of the Aero Commission, Prof. Fred Fagg of the Air Law Institute at Northwestern University, and the county coroner, Herman N. Bundeson.

At the majority of the airports, the study found unsafe flying conditions, such as the field being too small or too close to heavy automobile traffic, the use of planes that were not airworthy and often overloaded when flown, and activity by many unlicensed pilots.

The importance of pilot licensing was demonstrated by a two-year study by the coroner of 17 aviation fatalities in Cook County. Sixteen of the fatalities involved unlicensed pilots or planes. The 17th fatality was a licensed pilot flying a licensed plane who had the misfortune of having a mid-air collision in which neither the other pilot nor his plane were licensed.[450]

1929   Curtiss Flight School Comes to Chicago

In 1929, Curtiss Flying School added to their aviation chain by opening a school in Chicago for pilots and mechanics. When it opened, it was the only Chicago aviation school approved by the Commerce Dept. Later that year, the name changed to Curtiss-Wright Flying School, reflecting the merger of the two parent companies, Curtiss and Wright.

By 1933, the school had reorganized into the Curtiss-Wright Aeronautical University. The school occupied 3–4 floors of the seven-story building at 1338–1342 S. Michigan Ave.[a]

The school offered three separate pilot courses, as well as training in aviation administration, mechanics, and welding. Labs on the lower floors allowed hands-on practice for mechanics and welding. The upper floor held a variety of aircraft engines for students to work on. The flying portion of the program was conducted at Curtiss-Reynolds Field in Glenview.

The Master Mechanics Course cost $250. A Private Pilot License cost $50 for the ground school portion plus $600 for the flight portion. Flying for the Transport Pilot License was $4,000.

a   The building was listed on the National Register of Historic Places in 2013.

The Great Depression forced Curtiss-Wright to make drastic cutbacks, and in 1933, they sold both the Aeronautical University and Curtiss-Wright Field. The existing staff of the Aeronautical University continued conducting classes for a while, but without use of the airport, it was difficult to draw students.[451]

1929   Elgin Airport Starts

What was to become Elgin Airport started on Route 30 east of the city in 1929, when a Swallow dealer, Elgin Airways, leased part of the Kelly Farm in Dundee Township.

Later Northwest Airways included the airport as part of its proposed Chicago to Minneapolis (CAM-9) air mail route. The Elgin Association of Commerce raised money for improvements, including lights for night operations, and soon took over the airport. A local resident paid for the beacon that the Post Office required. It was erected along Route 20 on what came to be known as "Beacon Hill."[452]

1929   Schroeder Starts Elmhurst Airport

Eagle Flying Field was opened in 1923 in Elmhurst, at Church Rd. and Lake St. (Route 20), by Fred Bouchard and Joe James. It became Elmhurst Airport[a] in 1929, when the originators had moved on and Dan Schroeder leased the land.[453]

1929   Pal-Waukee Becomes a First-Class Airport

By 1929, Pal-Waukee had become one of the best airports in the Chicago area. In addition to the airport facilities, Pal-Waukee maintained offices in the Marquette Building in the Loop.

Within less than a year of purchasing the airport, Owen Jones and his partners had invested more than $60,000 in expanding and improving the facility. The airport footprint expanded from 40 to 52 acres. The owners also doubled the size of one of the two existing hangars to hold 15 planes and built a third hangar for another 15 planes.

The airport also purchased a new Stinson Detroiter, which had an enclosed six-passenger cabin, a great improvement over the Swallow's open cockpit with room for only three people. Pal-Waukee was a distributor for Bellanca, Swallow, and Whittelsey Avian (a U.S. version of the English Avro

---

a   Sometimes known as Elmhurst West Airport, to distinguish it from an airport across the
    street operated by Edwin Greer.

Avian) aircraft. It also operated an authorized Wright engine service center as well as a flight school and charter service.

Pal-Waukee developed a reputation as an airport with the best personnel and accommodations in the Chicago area. It was one of five airports determined to be safe according to a study by Cook County in 1929. The study emphasized the role of licensing of both pilots and planes to providing a safe environment, especially for passengers. As of the middle of 1930, Pal-Waukee had yet to have an accident at the airport.

The Commerce Department located Airway Beacon #2 near Pal-Waukee on the Chicago to Milwaukee segment of CAM-9 route to Minneapolis.

In 1930, Pal-Waukee introduced night flying with a five million candle-power[a] floodlight. They also equipped their Bellanca with two 500 candle-power lights for night sightseeing flights.

Pal-Waukee also constructed a large administration building costing $30,000. It provided offices for the airport as well as rooms and showers for pilots. The first floor also boasted a "first class restaurant with super service catering to the public which desires the best in luncheon and dinners."

Chicago's first Aviation Country Club started at Pal-Waukee when it rented the second floor of the administration building as a lounge for members. A dumbwaiter to the second floor provided food from the restaurant for Country Club patrons. Initially, 20 North Shore sportsmen each paid $120 each to join. The additions made Pal-Waukee second to Municipal Field in size and capabilities.[454]

1929   Greer School of Aviation Soars

In the late 1920s, Edwin Greer branched out from his auto mechanics training school and established the Greer School of Aviation. Greer offered a comprehensive program to compete with Curtiss-Wright Aeronautical University.

By 1929, Greer's offices at 2024 S. Wabash contained "12 floors of machinery, motors, classrooms, assembly shops and materials." Their training programs included an Aircraft Construction and Motor Mechanics Course, Pilot's Ground Course, Pre-Solo and Private Pilot's Course, Limited Commercial and Industrial Pilot's Course, and the Transport Pilot's Course.[455]

---

a   Candlepower measures the amount of light on a specific area as in a narrow beam and is generally an obsolete measurement. Lumens is a modern measurement that is more applicable to light over a large area. 1 candlepower = 12.57 lumens. Roughly a 70W incandescent light produces 100 candlepower.

Greer operated two or three airports simultaneously in the Chicago area. Greer had opened a flight school in Elmhurst. Greer had a dispute with then airport manager Dan Schroder and acquired land across the street on the west side of Church Rd. where he opened his own airport. The 1930 sectional also depicts the second airport as "Greer Elmhurst College" or Greer Field #1, which eventually came to be called Elmhurst-West to distinguish it from the original Elmhurst-East.[a] Eventually, the original Elmhurst (East) Airport closed and the former Greer facility became the official Elmhurst Airport.

As was true at many flight schools, Greer often held Sunday air shows featuring stunt flying by their instructors as a way to stir interest in their programs.[456]

In 1929, Greer also claimed in an ad to be the WACO dealer for the Chicago area. However, a full-page ad in the same magazine a week earlier indicated Chicago Aero Sales, with offices in the Pure Oil Building at Wacker and Wabash, was a dealer for "Waco Sport and Training Planes." It is unclear whether Waco changed their official dealer or both companies were dealers.[457]

1929/01/01   First Official Air Traffic Controller

At the St. Louis airport, Archie League was hired, becoming the first govern-mental air traffic controller. League, who was also a pilot and mechanic, waved flags on the field to control operations. In the early 1930s, a radio tower was constructed and League became the first radio air controller.[458]

1929/01   Lighted Beacons from New York to San Francisco

In January of 1929, the Aeronautics Branch installed their 25th lighted beacon, completing the final 20-mi. segment of the New York City to San Francisco airway.

The Post Office Dept. began the program of installing lighted beacons along the airways, and the program was expanded by the Aeronautics Branch under the Air Commerce Act of 1926.[459]

1929/02/01   United Aircraft and Transport Corp (UATC) Formed

William Boeing of Boeing Airplane Co. and Frederick Rentschler of Pratt & Whitney Co. combined their companies on February 1, 1929, to form United Aircraft and Transport Co. (UATC).

a   The sectional shows another Greer Airport northeast of the two Elmhurst ones. This location later became Wilson Airport.

Headquartered in Chicago, UATC, the first vertically integrated aviation company, immediately embarked on an acquisition program. In short order, the new company acquired numerous other aviation manufacturers including Chance Vought Co., Hamilton Standard Propellers, Sikorsky Aircraft, Stearman Aircraft, and Northrup Aircraft.[460]

1929/02/14   St. Valentine's Day Massacre
When members of Al Capone's organization gunned down seven members of a rival gang on February 14, 1929, the event quickly became known as the St. Valentine's Day Massacre.[461]

1929/03/03   Aviation Corp. of Delaware (AVCO) Formed
With the backing of Wall Street financiers W. Averell Harriman and Robert Lehman, Fairchild Aviation created a subsidiary, Aviation Corp. of Delaware (AVCO), on March 3, 1929.

Fairchild formed AVCO for the purpose of acquiring Embry-Riddle of Cincinnati. Embry-Riddle had been operating the Cincinnati and Chicago (CAM-24) air mail route, but discovered it was undercapitalized.

Fairchild had intended AVCO raising about $1 million to support Embry-Riddle and possibly acquire a few other small companies. Instead, AVCO's financiers raised $35 million and went on a buying spree. In addition to buying Embry-Riddle, AVCO bought out its parent, Fairchild. Within six months, AVCO acquired nine airlines including Chicago-based Universal Aviation Corp. (UAC), which itself was a conglomeration of smaller airlines. Several years later, AVCO became American Airlines.[462]

1929/06   Licensing of Aviation Schools
The Aeronautics Branch began issuing licenses for both flying and ground schools.[463] The first school licensed in Chicago was the Curtiss-Wright Aeronautical University. [464]

1929/06   Sky Harbor Dedicates Airport
More than 6,000 people turned out in June 1929 for the dedication of the ultra-modern Sky Harbor Airport and Aviation Country Club. The airport was located about four miles west of Glencoe on the north side of Dundee Rd. and Anthony Trl.[a] on 135 acres of what had previously been a swamp.[465]

---

a   In Selig's *Forgotten Chicago Airfields,* a list of old airports on page 73 states Sky Harbor was
    at Wheeling Road instead of Anthony Trail.

Universal Aviation Corp. (UAC) spent $500,000 to construct the airport for its subsidiary Gray[a] Goose Airlines. Another UAC subsidiary, North Shore Airport Co., handled the construction of the facility intended as the "Airport of Tomorrow," to serve Chicago's North Shore residents.[466]

Sky Harbor's design included both runways and an all-way turf landing area for pilots to use if the runways were busy. By 1937, there were four cinder runways, the longest of which was 2,500 ft. A 75-ft. rotating beacon and runway floodlights enabled night operations.[467]

Architects Alfred P. Allen and Maurice Webster designed a beautiful art deco terminal and a stylish hangar with an elaborate curved roof.[468] The airport offered three fine restaurants open to the public. They were popular not only with aviators but also with North Shore residents attending Ravinia or just wanting a nice night out. In addition, the top level of the terminal building featured the lavish Club Petrushka, which offered a fabulous view of the airport, along with dining and dancing. A membership fee was required for the club, which also had a location on Michigan Avenue.[469]

A safety study by Cook County in 1929 identified Sky Harbor as one of five airports in the county considered safe for flying.[470]

Not long after Sky Harbor's dedication, UAC sold the airport and Gray Goose Airlines along with the flight school and North Shore Airport Co. Sky Harbor's new owner, Chicago Air Service Inc., assumed all operations and management.[471]

Note there was no connection between Chicago's Gray Goose Airlines, which was operational before 1928, and Jonathan Caldwell's Grey Goose Airways (with an "e" in "Grey"). Caldwell incorporated the Airways in Nevada in 1928 and issued 10,000 shares of stock. He set about to develop a goose-like ornothopter with flapping wings attached to a motorcycle. Caldwell's Airways seems to have been active in Colorado, New York, and New Jersey, which charged the company with fraud. Caldwell reformed the company in Maryland and opened an office in Washington, DC as he tried to develop a circular-wing autogyro. None of Caldwell's inventions seem to have become airborne and the business finally folded in 1939.[472]

1929/06   Curtis Operates Amphibian Ramp at Grant Park

As early as 1913, there was a permanent public aero slip at the Chicago Yacht Club near Peck St. off Grant Park. Harold McCormick and others made frequent flights to the dock.[473]

---

a   Some sources, including a widely distributed poster, use the spelling "Grey." However, period photos of the aircraft logo show the airline spelled its name "Gray."

In June 1929, Curtiss Flying Services opened the Grant Park Ramp on Lake Michigan at the foot of 8th St. The ramp was home for Curtiss amphibians that were used for sightseeing as well as being part of a commuter and mail shuttle between Curtiss-Reynolds Field and Municipal Field. Maj. R.W. "Shorty" Schroeder was in charge of operations.[474]

1929/06/14   Chicago Tribune Plane Stuck in Ice

The *Chicago Tribune*'s amphibian *Untin' Bowler*, took off on June 14, 1929, attempting to fly from Chicago to Berlin via the northern route, over Greenland and Iceland.

At the controls of the twin-engine Sikorsky plane were Bob Gast and Parker "Shorty" Cramer. They were accompanied by Robert Wood, the *Tribune*'s aviation editor. The prior year, Cramer and Bert "Fish" Hassell attempted unsuccessfully a Great Circle flight from Rockford to Stockholm.

As with the previous flight, the *Untin' Bowler*'s trip ended abruptly when the plane got caught in an ice floe in the Hudson Straits and sank. The crew was unharmed and safely returned.[475]

1929/06/14   First Coast-to-Coast Air/Rail Passenger Service

On June 14, 1929, Universal Aviation Corp. (UAC) became the first company to offer coast-to-coast service, with a combination of air and rail. During the 67-hour journey between New York City and Los Angeles, passengers would fly during the day and ride a train overnight.[476]

Less than a month later, on July 7, Transcontinental Air Transport (TAT) inaugurated similar service between New York and Los Angeles.[a] Charles Lindbergh selected sites along the route and flew the first leg of the service of the inaugural flight. Unlike UAC, whose beginning and ending legs were via train, TAT started and ended with a flight. TAT's service was faster, taking only 48 hours.[477]

1929/06/17   Delta Makes Its First Flight

A crop dusting service Huff Daland Dusters, made its first passenger flight from Dallas to Monroe, LA as Delta Air Service. In 1945 the company would become Delta Air Lines.[478]

a   Some sources identify this as the first coast-to-coast air/rail trip.

1929/07   Mail Shuttles from Muny to Lakefront

An experimental program began in July 1929 shuttling air mail from
Chicago Municipal Airport by amphibian to the lakefront dock. The lakefront location was only five minutes from the Post Office, saving more than
a half-hour drive time from Municipal. The program appears to be short-
lived from a lack of other references.[479]

1929/07/05   Curtiss-Wright Corp. Formed

The once bitter rivals merged on July 5, 1929, forming the Curtiss-Wright
Corp. At the time of the merger, Orville Wright had nothing to do with the
business and Curtiss was only nominally involved for a short period.

In addition to the Curtiss and Wright companies, ten other aviation
companies merged into the Curtiss-Wright Corp., which was organized
into three manufacturing divisions producing airframes, engines, and
propellers. In addition, to have a national presence, they operated a chain
of upscale airports and prestigious flight schools. The company's main
presence in Chicago was Curtiss-Reynolds Field in Glenview and the
Curtiss-Wright Aeronautical University in the South Loop.[480]

1929/08/28   *Graf Zeppelin*'s Chicago Flyover

After making its maiden flight on September 19 of the previous year, in
1929, the *Graf Zeppelin* embarked on a 21-day voyage around-the-world to
showcase the German marvel. As part of the tour, it flew over Chicago on
August 28, but the city was not one of the three stops the airship made
during the trip. This was the first around-the-world flight since 1924, when
the Army Douglas World Cruisers flew.

Following the spectacular voyage, the airship conducted regular
passenger service between Europe and South America. Before its retirement in 1937, the rigid airship had flown more than a million miles. [481]

1929/09/24   First Instrument Only Flight

Using a hood to restrict his vision (and accompanied by a check pilot),
Jimmy Doolittle took off, flew a course, and landed entirely on instruments
as part of a research project. He relied on a Low Frequency Radio Range
using a sensitive altimeter, directional gyro, and artificial horizon.[482]

1929/10/20   Curtiss-Reynolds Dedicates Luxurious Airport

In the late 1920s, Curtiss Flying Service established a chain of upscale airports across the nation to provide a consistent high level of service and conditions for air travelers, with preference given to commercial carriers flying Curtiss airplanes.

Curtiss Flying Service established the luxury facilities in 12 major locations, plus another 35 facilities in smaller markets.[483] Chicago already had a large Curtiss presence with their Aeronautical University in the Loop that provided mechanics and ground school training. They also had a number of practice fields in the area, mostly on the North Side.

In early 1929, Fred Reynolds opened Reynolds Field on the north side of Lake St. Later that year, Reynolds partnered with Curtis Flying Service, which invested an additional $3 million in facilities at Curtiss-Reynolds Field. Shorty Schroeder, then VP of Midwest Operations for Curtiss supervised the construction to make the airport the finest in the chain.

More than 35,000 people, including many from Chicago's social register, attended a lavish dedication on October 20, 1929. A highlight of the festivities was the arrival of the National Air Tour, organized by Ford to demonstrate the reliability of air travel.

Hangar One was the best part of the airport facilities. Essentially, it was built as three separate hangars under a continuous roof about five times the size of the average hangar of the day. A concrete ramp for planes surrounded three sides of the hangar.

Passengers were pampered with a restaurant and lounge on the upper level. A promenade around the entire upper level had glassed in galleries where passengers could watch both plane activity outside and the mechanics working inside.[484] The promenade was said to hold more than 2,000 people.[485] To enable night operations, a single 1-billion-candlepower light was positioned at the north end of the field.[a]

Nine days after the exuberant dedication, the stock market crashed. The deteriorating economic situation rapidly siphoned off a major portion of the intended customer base.

Following the Curtiss and Wright merger earlier in the year, the airport experienced naming confusion as the various subsidiaries incorporated both names. At various times, the airport was referred to as Curtiss-

---

a   1 candlepower = 12.6 lumens. For comparison, a 75W light bulb, car headlight, and film projectors are roughly 1,000 lumens.

Reynolds, Curtiss-Wright-Reynolds, Curtiss-Wright, Curtiss-Chicago, and, often, just Curtiss Field.[486]

1929/10/29   Stock Market Crashes

A major stock market disruption on October 24, 1929, was followed by a major crash on the 29th that was considered the onset of the Great Depression.

Aviation was particularly hard hit. Lindbergh's fame had been a huge boon to the aviation business, with over $1.5 billion invested during 1928 and 1929. More than 60 passenger airlines were operating in 1929. Aviation stocks soared. Pan American alone had gone from $15 to $90 per share.

Following the crash, money dried up quickly. Private investment in airports dropped from $35 million in 1930 to only $1 million in 1933. Airlines ran at substantial losses, if they were able to continue operating at all.[487]

1929/11/02   99s Formed

The Ninety-Nines (99s), an international organization of women pilots, was founded by Amelia Earhart and 98 other women pilots at Curtiss Field in Valley Stream, NY.[488]

1929/11/28–29   First Flight Over South Pole

Richard Byrd was one of the first four people who flew in a Ford Tri-Motor over the South Pole, becoming the first people to fly over the Pole.[489]

1929/12/02   AIRINC Created

The not-for-profit Aeronautical Radio, Inc. was established by a group of fifteen air carriers. AIRINC's purpose was to aid the air transport industry by coordinating aerial communications with a network of ground stations.[490]

1930–1934

1930   Cleveland Airport Uses Radio to Control Airport Traffic
Cleveland became the first airport to establish radio control of airport traffic, setting an example for other cities.[491]

1930   Chicago Is Air Mail Center
By 1930, Chicago had become the major Air Mail hub, serving 9 of the 34 Contract Air Mail (CAM) routes.[492]

1930   Municipal Field Doubles in Size
In 1930, Chicago Municipal Field doubled in size from occupying a quarter of the square-mile plot to covering the southern half of the square-mile of Board of Education land. The airport used the new land to lengthen runways, allowing use by larger aircraft such as the Ford Tri-Motor.[493]

1930   Chicago Instrument Flying Demonstration
During a flight from Chicago Municipal to Detroit, pilot W.E. Larned demonstrated "blind flying" techniques. After takeoff, Larned placed cardboard over the windows and a curtain between him and the first officer. Larned flew to Detroit and when the instruments indicated he was over the airport, he removed the cardboard and landed.

Instrument landings were still in the future, but the ability to navigate cross-country through poor visibility was a boon to air travel.[494]

1930   Lindbergh Beacon Lights the Way
Named after the famous aviator, a nautical navigation beacon was placed on top of Chicago's Palmolive Building. With over 2 billion candlepower, the Lindbergh Beacon was the world's brightest light and visible to aviators 300 mi. away.

Following numerous complaints from occupants of high-rises built long after the beacon was installed, the light was partially shielded and then removed completely. In 2007, the building owners installed an 18,000 watt light that was much dimmer and directed over the lake without rotating.[495]

1930　Rose Creates Parrakeets

Jennings W. "Jack" Rose formed the Rose Aeroplane and Motor Co. on Armitage Ave. Rose manufactured the Parrakeet,[a] a single-place, open-cockpit biplane. Several years later, he began manufacturing his four-cylinder Tornado engine that produced 75 hp.

Rose was a colorful character who was first exposed to an airplane as a child in 1910. During WWI, he worked as a construction worker at Chanute Field in Rantoul. During his off-hours, Rose would sneak into the Officers' Club to read everything he could about aviation.

In 1923, Rose went into the Army, where he became a pilot. Later as a civilian, he eventually earned both his Transport License and a Mechanic's License. He did all sorts of flying including barnstorming and reportedly some bootlegging. As a Wheeling resident, Rose often used Pal-Waukee for testing and housing his aircraft.[496]

1930/01/16　Whittle Patents Turbojet Engine

A British engineer and RAF officer, Frank Whittle, received a patent on January 16, 1930, for the design of a turbojet engine. However, even an experimental version of the engine wasn't produced until 1936.[497]

1930/01/25　American Airways Formed

During its 1929 buying spree, Aviation Corp. of Delaware (AVCO) had acquired 90 aviation companies, from airlines to manufacturers and more. It was a massive company that was extremely disorganized with unrelated and often competing parts.

On January 25, 1930, AVCO reorganized itself, placing all airlines into a subsidiary American Airways. The new airline had a network of more than 6,200 mi. extending from New England to California.[498]

1930/03/07　Commercial Service Comes to Rockford

Mail service came to Rockford with a big celebration on March 7, 1930. Thousands of people turned out to Machesney's airport for an air show that was covered live on a local radio station.

North West Airways operated the mail service and soon after introduced passenger service to Rockford. The Great Depression seriously affected the operations and North West debated dropping service.

a　Rose always used the British spelling with a double instead of a single "r."

There was a proposal to convert the airport from private to municipal ownership to provide funding for continued service, but Rockford voters rejected the idea.

The Chamber of Commerce provided some financial support to maintain service, but not enough. North West finally discontinued service in July 1934.[499]

1930/03/26   Chicago Gets an Approved Repair Station

National Air Transport in Chicago received one of the first two Repair Station Certificates issued by the Aeronautics Branch.[500]

1930/03/31   First Transcontinental Service

Shareholders of National Air Transport ratified a takeover by Boeing's United Aircraft & Transport Co.(UATC) on March 31, 1930,[a] creating a coast-to-coast airline network.[501]

1930/04/30   Congress Passes the McNary-Watres Act

During Herbert Hoover's presidency, Congress passed the Airmail Act of 1930, also known as the McNary-Watres Act. The new law gave the Postmaster General, Walter Brown, the power to essentially restructure the air mail system.

The Act changed the payment structure for carrying mail. Rather than paying a flat rate per mile, the new structure was based on the per mile weight of the useful load carried by the aircraft (not the actual weight of the mail). Awards were made to the "lowest responsible bidder," giving preference to companies with larger and multi-engine planes, experience operating longer routes, and those with a longer history of carrying mail.

Postmaster Brown asked William MacCracken, who had left the Aeronautics Branch for private practice on October 1, 1929, to chair the selection meetings. The outcome of these "Spoils Conferences," as they came to be known, was that most routes were awarded to Boeing Air Transport, Transcontinental Air Transport, and Robertson Aircraft Corp.

The result of these changes transformed the U.S. aviation industry. Because payment was made for space available to carry mail rather than the actual weight of mail carried, the airlines purchased larger planes with available capacity for passengers as well as mail.[502]

---

a   Other sources date the acquisition as May 7, 1930.

1930/05   Coffey Becomes Student Pilot

Cornelius Coffey and John C. Robinson were African American transplants to Chicago. They became friends when they resided at the local YMCA because of their mutual passion for flying.[a]

In the late 1920s, Coffey worked as a mechanic for a Chevrolet dealership owned by Emil Mack. After meeting Robinson, Coffey convinced Mack to hire him as well.

Because of their race, the two men had difficulty finding someone to teach them to fly. Eventually, they found a helping hand at Akers Airport[b] in Elmwood Park. The owner offered them a room and gave them flight lessons in exchange for their doing mechanic work. They acquired a well-worn Waco #9, which they restored and learned to fly.[503]

Coffey was given his initial permit in 1928 and received his CAA Student Pilot Permit in May 1930. Although the exact dates are unknown, Robinson received his licenses at roughly the same time.[504]

1930/05   Jacoby Takes Over Sterling Airport

Eugene Jacoby, a Moline native, moved to Sterling in May 1930. Jacoby took over the Sterling Airport, which had opened in 1927. Under Jacoby's guidance, the airport grew and expanded. On May 19, 1938, the first air mail flight arrived at Sterling.[505]

1930/05/15   First Female Cabin Attendant Hired

Ellen Church, a nurse hired by Boeing Air Transport, made her first flight as a cabin attendant between San Francisco and Cheyenne.

Previously, some airlines had employed young men as stewards or attendants. Church convinced BAT that having a nurse on board would comfort skittish passengers. The practice spread quickly through other airlines.[506]

1930/05/15   Airline Certification Required

The Commerce Dept. required that airlines engaged to carry interstate passengers obtain a Certificate of Authority to operate.[507]

---

a   There are many sources that relate the early background of black aviation pioneers Cornelius Coffey and John Robinson. Many of the dates associated with their activities conflict with each other. In fact, sources seem to disagree on the sequence of events such as whether they learned to fly before or after receiving their aviation mechanics licenses. The sequence presented in this work is the author's best guess, but with a moderate degree of confidence.
b   Some sources spell it Ackers or Acres Airport.

1930/06/25   Hangar Fire at Municipal Destroys 27 Planes

On the night of June 25, 1930, an explosion and fire started at Municipal in Universal Airline's hangar, which housed planes of its subsidiary Stout Air Services. The fire quickly spread to an adjacent hangar used by Gray Goose Airlines. Both hangars and a total of 27 airplanes were destroyed in the blaze. The fire severed powerlines, plunging much of Municipal and the surrounding area into darkness. The airport brought emergency lighting to land planes that were circling. Fortunately, nobody was injured in the incident.[508]

Shortly after the fire, in September 1930, National Air Transport (NAT) acquired UATC and Stout ceased operating under its own name. The following year, 1931, United Air Lines acquired NAT.[509]

1930/06/27   Alleged Mob-Related Hangar Fires

At 2:45 a.m. Friday June 27, 1930, a night watchman discovered a fire in a hangar at Pal-Waukee Air Port. It destroyed one plane but quick action by the staff kept the fire from engulfing the hangar, unlike the Municipal fire a few days earlier.

Both fires started in planes owned by the Texas Oil Co. There were reports that the Capone gang had purchased several planes from Texas Oil to smuggle liquor from Canada, but Capone was dissatisfied with the planes. There were suspicions the fires were meant to express Capone's displeasure to Texas Oil.[510]

1930/06/10   Elgin Airport Dedication

Elgin Airport's formal dedication was held on June 10, 1930. There were 77 planes participating in the celebration, including 30 from the Army Air Corps under the command of H.H. "Hap" Arnold. Thousands of people turned out to watch stunt flying, parachute jumps, and to take sightseeing flights.

Airfields in Elgin dated back to 1926, starting with part of the Hoornbeck farm on the west side of McLean Blvd. In July 1929, Elgin Airways leased part of the former Todd farm, then owned by Earle Kelley. Elgin Airways was a Swallow dealer offering instruction and other flight services.

The Elgin Assn. of Commerce, along with some local businessmen, took over the lease from Elgin Airways and made improvements to the field, including lights for night operations. After months of preparation, Northwest Airways began mail and passenger operations at Elgin on March 8, 1930. The airport handled about four pounds of mail each day between the morning flight from Chicago and the evening flight from Madison, WI, via Rockford, IL, and Janesville, WI.[511]

1930/07/04   Hunter Brothers Set Flight Endurance Record

On the Fourth of July, 1930, two brothers from Sparta, IL set the flight endurance record while flying above Sky Harbor Airport in Glencoe. The Hunter Flying Circus consisted of four brothers from Sparta who barnstormed the Midwest. They were determined to establish the record for the longest flight. Their endeavor was truly a family affair.

On June 11, 1930, John and Kenneth Hunter took off from Sky Harbor Airport in a Stinson SM-1 Detroiter named the *City of Chicago*. They flew in a large circle, remaining in sight of the field.

Every six hours, brothers Walter and Albert took off in *Big Ben*, their supply plane. The planes matched speeds and flew in tight formation as they established mid-air contact to resupply the endurance plane. Each supply trip required wing walking by one of the pilots on the endurance plane.

A rope suspended from the supply plane delivered solid provisions (including oil, food, and clothing) to the endurance plane. Similarly, a rubber hose supplied gas from the provisioning plane to the gas tank on the endurance plane. Pilots on the endurance plane had to climb out in front of the cabin regularly to add engine oil.

On the ground, the men's mother and sister prepared meals, cleaned their clothes, and handled other necessities. The *City of Chicago* did not have a radio so written notes accompanying the provisions were the only form of communications between those in the air and their ground-support team.

After flying for about a week, the endurance plane's gas tank developed a leak. To continue the attempt to break the record, the Hunters were forced to double the frequency of supply flights, making a trip every three hours around the clock.

The afternoon of Sunday June 29, the Hunter Brothers broke the existing endurance record. An estimated crowd of 75,000 turned out to witness the event. The brothers continued flying as long as they could in order to establish a new record.

Eventually, the nonstop wear on the engine took its toll. The oil filter clogged and the engine no longer performed up to par. The *City of Chicago* landed on July 4, establishing a new record of 533 hr. (23 days, 1 hr.), 41 min., and 30 sec.

During that time, John and Kenneth flew approximately 38,000 mi. at about 70 mph. During more than 300 provisioning flights, made night and day regardless of weather, Walter and Albert transferred 8,405 gal. of fuel.

The Hunter brothers became celebrities and began making personal appearances and giving endorsements. Their share of the Sky Harbor gate was more than $3,000.[a] Curtiss-Wright donated a new 300 hp J-5 engine to replace the 220 hp J-6 that was worn out in the flight. They received another $7,000 from the sponsor of the radio broadcast of their flight, and Rockland Oil gave them $10,000 for using their products.

The Hunter brothers left Chicago for Hollywood, where they made more appearances both in person and in the movies.[512]

1930/08/23–9/01   National Air Races

From August 23 through September 1, 1930, the National Air Races were hosted by Curtiss-Reynolds Field. The best pilots competed for $150,000 in prizes. A grandstand seating 65,000 people was built in front of Hangar One and another 35,000 people could view the events from open areas around the runways.[513]

Speed Holman, from Northwest Airlines, was among the top winners in the 1930 NAR. A good friend and customer of Matty Laird, Holman flew the Laird Solution (LC-DW300) to win the Thompson Trophy with a speed of over 200 mph.[514]

1930/09/10   Taylor E-2 Cub Takes to the Air

Clarence Gilbert Taylor introduced the remarkably designed E-2 airplane that first took to the air on September 10, 1930, at Emery Airport, Bradford, PA.

Clarence, with his brother Gordon, had formed Taylor Brothers Aircraft Co. in September 1927 in Rochester, NY. After Gordon's death the following year, Gilbert had moved to Bradford where he continued enhancing his aircraft designs. The work resulted in the E-2.

Although the E-2 was remarkable, Taylor was pressed for cash and filed for bankruptcy in late 1930. A Bradford investor, William Piper, bought the company assests in bankruptcy for $761 but kept Taylor on as President and designer.[515]

1930/09/21   Pop Dickinson Gets License

After taking his first flight in 1910 or 1911, Charles "Pop" Dickinson didn't solo for another decade, which he did on February 13, 1921. It was nearly another ten years, September 21, 1930, before he finally obtained his license at age 72. The press labeled Dickinson as the "nation's oldest pilot." He is also one of the people who took the longest time to obtain a license.

---

a   There is no record of Sky Haven's share of the receipts.

Dickinson was one of Chicago's earliest aviation supporters. He was a founder and President of ACI, purchased Ashburn Field for the club's use, and contributed substantially to the city's early aviation meets.

In his waning years, Dickinson pursued another aviation-related hobby. He collected tickets by making the inaugural flight on new airlines in the rapidly expanding industry. He accumulated 13 tickets showing Number 1, indicating the airline's first flight.[516]

1930/10/15   All-Air Transcontinental Passenger Travel Available

Instead of air by day and rail by night, passengers could opt for continuous flights across the country. On October 15, 1930, American Airways began offering flights from Atlanta to Los Angeles.[517]

1930/10/25   TWA Develops

On July 13, 1930, Transcontinental Air Transport (TAT) acquired Western Airlines. Several months later, on October 25, TAT formed Transcontinental and Western Airways (TWA) as the operating company for its various airline subsidiaries.

The same day TWA came into existence, it introduced its first transcontinental route between Newark and Los Angeles through TWA's St. Louis center. [518]

1930/12/24   Fire in Pal-Waukee Hangar

On Christmas Eve, a hangar fire broke out in the furnace room roof of a hangar at Pal-Waukee Air Port. The blaze destroyed the hangar and 17 aircraft, including planes belonging to Fred Foote, business manager of *Life*, Col. Robert R. McCormick, publisher of the *Chicago Tribune*, and Forest Mars, of Mars Candy Co.[519]

1931   C-W Aeronautical University Graduates African Americans

The Curtiss-Wright Aeronautical University in the South Loop graduated the first African Americans, Cornelius Coffey and John Robinson. The achievement was not accomplished without a struggle.

Coffey and Robinson were auto mechanics with a passion for flying. They sought to become aircraft mechanics and applied to various schools. In 1929, they registered by mail and paid tuition to Curtiss-Wright Aeronautical University in downtown Chicago. However, when they arrived for class, they were turned away because of their race.

With the support of his employer, Emil Mack, who owned a Chevy dealership, Coffey threatened the school with a lawsuit.

Robinson persisted in a different way. He was hired by the school as a janitor. While working at the school, he picked up materials out of the trash, listened in on lectures, and examined the equipment when no one was around.

Robinson discovered information on the Heath Parasol, and the two men purchased a kit and modified a motorcycle engine to power it. One of the school's instructors took interest in their project and accompanied them to Washington Park for the plane's test flight. Impressed with their skill and perseverance, the instructor intervened with the school's administration on their behalf.

In exchange for dropping the lawsuit, the school agreed to offer a segregated night class for them, when few white students were on the premises. In 1931, Coffey and Robinson graduated as master aircraft mechanics, the first blacks to receive the Aircraft and Engine license. They delighted in bragging that Coffey graduated first in his class and Robinson second, usually omitting their inside joke that they were the only two students in the class.

The school found the experience better than expected and agreed when Coffey and Robinson urged them to open another class for African Americans. Curtiss-Wright established a separate night class with 35 non-white students to be taught by Coffey and Robinson. Some students who attended had come from China following the Japanese invasion of Manchuria. They went on to become the core of China's Royal Air Force.

Although the classes were successful, hostility from many white students forced the school to discontinue offering classes for blacks.[520]

1931 Robbins Airport Opens and Challenger Formed

John C. Robinson and Cornelius Coffey were pioneering African Americans who, after initial rejection, had received their Mechanics Licenses from Curtiss-Wright Aeronautical University and went on to teach additional classes for non-white students. Robinson and Coffey had learned to fly at Akers Airport, the only one in the area that wasn't concerned about their race. The two men were determined to accommodate without discrimination anybody who wanted to fly and formed the Brown Eagle Aero Club, primarily of their former CWAU students.

Around 1931, CWAU discontinued classes for non-whites due to the attitudes of the white students. About the same time, Akers Airport closed. Frustrated by the lack of aviation options for blacks, Robinson and Coffey acquired some land in Robbins, a predominately black township where they set up Robbins Airport.

The Brown Eagles Aero Club expanded into the Challenger Air Pilots Assn.,[a] to provide mechanic as well as flight training. They selected the name Challenger because of their affinity for the Curtiss Challenger engine.[521]

1931/03/23   Cord Starts Century Air Lines

On March 23, 1931, Errett Cord launched the passenger-only Century Air Lines. Radiating from its Chicago hub, Century intended to connect twenty states throughout the Midwest and South. With no air mail contract to subsidize operations, Cord drove volume up by cutting prices to match train fare with Pullman accommodations. This proved extremely popular and the January 1932 issue of *Forbes* reported that Century carried a third of all air passengers in the country. In September 1931, Century expanded its operations into a large hangar at Municipal Airport

Prior to starting airlines, E.L. Cord had had a career as an auto mechanic, race car driver, and car salesman which led to managing and controlling automobile companies. He was best known for designing the Auburn, Cord, and Duesenberg cars.

An interest in aviation led to him becoming a pilot. Cord became an early investor in National Air Transport (NAT) and later he acquired Stinson Aircraft Co. because he liked the design and features of their planes. In 1929, he formed the Cord Corp. as a holding company for more than 150 transportation companies, including many in aviation.[522]

1931/04/04   Navy Airship USS *Akron* Crashes

About an hour after leaving Lakehurst, NJ, the Navy dirigible USS *Akron* was caught in a thunderstorm over the Atlantic and crashed. All but 3 of the 73-man crew were lost, making this the worst aviation disaster to date.[523]

1931/04/29   Weather Maps Transmitted by Telegraph

Starting on April 29, 1931, Chicago was one of five cities participating in tests by the Aeronautics Branch of transmitting weather maps over special Teletype circuits that process pages rather than tapes. In December 1932,

a   The group was often referred to as Challenger Airmen's Assn.

the system went live transmitting national weather maps to more than 70 stations six times a day.[524]

1931/05/01   Chicago Connects to TWA's Transcontinental Route

TWA connected Chicago to its coast-to-coast service on May 1, 1931, when it inaugurated flights between St. Louis and Chicago. This made Chicago one of the few cities with two transcontinental choices, United and TWA.[525]

1931/05/17   Speed Holman Dies Performing Stunt

As his nickname suggests, Charles "Speed" Holman, the President of Northwest Airways, had a reputation as a daredevil flyer. Holman's signature move was to fly inverted and grab a handkerchief attached to a pylon or long pole, then roll back straight and level. While performing the stunt in Omaha on May 17, 1931, Holman fell from his plane and was killed.[526]

1931/05/21   600 Army Planes Fly in Review

A total of 600 Army planes staged a review in Chicago as part of an Army exercise in coordination and logistics. The planes arrived at four different airports around Chicago the evening of May 21, 1931. The following morning they rendezvoused at West Chicago, then proceeded to fly a circle around Chicagoland before returning to Dayton and Cleveland.[527]

1931/05/31   Rockne Killed in Plane Crash

Knute Rockne, Notre Dame's championship football coach, was one of eight people who died in a crash of TWA Flight #3 near Bazaar, KS. Rockne's national popularity resulted in the first full-scale crash investigation by the newly-formed Accident Investigation Board. The board made a series of incorrect determinations before identifying the actual cause as a problem with the glue on the wing spars of the Fokker F-10A.

The plane was taken out of service until the problem could be addressed. Design issues made inspection of the spars difficult. To avoid public distrust, airlines pulled Fokkers from their fleets. TAT's reaction was most extreme. It gathered its fleet of Fokkers and, having removed the engines, publicly burned the airframes. The national attention ruined Fokker's reputation in the U.S.[528]

1931/06/23–07/01   Wiley Post Flies Around the World

Departing from Roosevelt Field in New York, Wiley Post and his navigator, Harold Gatty, flew around the world in eight stops. However, because his flight near the Arctic Circle totaled only a little over 15,000 miles, it was not recognized by the Federation Aeronautique Internationale (FAI) .[529]

1931/07/01   United Air Lines Created

Several months after United Aircraft and Transport Co. acquired National Air Transport to form the first coast-to-coast airline, the company reorganized.

UATC created United Air Lines Transport Co. as a management company for the various airlines it owned and operated. UALTC operated as United Air Lines. Both the company's advertising and aircraft markings stressed their ability to travel across the country by air.[530]

1931/07/27   Airline Pilots Organize

On July 27, 1931, David Behncke and 24 trusted fellow pilots from various airlines met in Chicago's Morrison Hotel and formed the Air Line Pilots Assn. (ALPA), electing Behncke president. Retaliation against the union was swift. Those suspected of union affiliation were demoted to flying open-cockpit planes at night or shuttled among crew bases to impose hardships on their families.

Behncke had considerable experience in a variety of aviation roles, from being an Army flight instructor during WWI to barnstorming and flying air mail. For a time, Behncke owned and operated Checkerboard Field as the air mail maintenance center.

Always a cautious pilot, Behncke's safety concern had escalated while flying air mail. He had issues with hot-shot pilots who repeatedly took unnecessary risks. Behncke's main concern, however, was the prevailing corporate attitude that planes and pilots were expendable. Owners pushed pilots to fly in unsafe airplanes and weather conditions.

Behncke decided to form a pilots' union to stand up for safer conditions. Starting in 1930, he met with a handful of associates from United, American, and Northwest Airlines about organizing, and eventually formed ALPA.

Behncke retained his post as President of ALPA until 1951. Under his leadership, ALPA affiliated with the American Federation of Labor (AFL) and grew into the largest pilots' union.[531]

Throughout its history, ALPA has advocated with airlines for pilot rights and safer working conditions, as well as with the government over safety and regulatory issues. ALPA continues to consider Chicago as its headquarters with the main office located in Des Plaines.[532]

1931/08/31   Landis Heads Aero Commission

After WWI, in February 1919, Illinois top ace Maj. Reed Landis returned to Chicago and chose a business rather than a flying career.[533] In 1920, Landis even did a stint as a movie actor.[534] Most of his professional career was spent running the Reed G. Landis Advertising Co.[535]

Landis did not, however, lose his interest in either aviation or public service. He served as VP of Interallied Aircraft Corp. for a year in 1919. In 1920, Landis published a book, *The Business Future of Aviation.*[536]

In 1925, Landis testified for the defense in Gen. Billy Mitchell's court martial. By 1929, Landis had become an outspoken critic of the practice in Illinois of having air safety standards enforced by the county sheriff's staff, whether or not they had any aviation knowledge. That year, he was appointed to a special coroner's jury in Cook County investigating four deaths in a mid-air collision.

Landis's advocacy was officially heard and on August 31, 1931, Gov. Emmerson appointed him chairman of the Illinois Aeronautics Commission, where he was responsible for regulation of pilots and airports throughout the state.

In later life, Landis became a VP for American Airlines, organized New York City's civil defense under Mayor La Guardia, and served in the Army and Air Force during WWII and in Korea.[537]

1931/10/17   Capone Convicted

Notorious gangster Al Capone was convicted in Federal Court of tax evasion on October 17, 1931, for which he received a prison sentence of 11 years.[538]

Instrumental in Capone's conviction was Edward J. "Easy Eddie" O'Hare, the father of WWII ace Butch O'Hare. Eddie O'Hare was a businessman and lawyer who was a close confidant of Capone. He became disenchanted with Capone's operations and his cooperation with the authorities provided the government with needed evidence. Just before Capone's scheduled release from prison, two gunmen with shotguns greeted Eddie O'Hare soon after he left Sportsman's Park, the Cicero racetrack.[539]

1931/11/15   First Terminal at Municipal

In response to increased activity, in 1931 Municipal constructed a new, modern terminal designed by Paul Gerhardt Jr.[a] Municipal dedicated the

---

a   Paul Gerhardt Jr. was the City of Chicago's architect who designed many city buildings.

new $100,000 terminal on November 15, 1931, greatly improving the facilities for both the airlines and their passengers.

At the dedication ceremony, Reed G. Landis, head of the Illinois Aeronautics Commission, presented Municipal with the state's first airport license. Chicago dignitaries included Mayor Anton Cermak, Merrill Meigs (Chair of the Chicago Aero Commission), and Walter Wright (Chicago Superintendent of Parks and Aviation).

A highlight of the day was a demonstration of in-flight radio as a United Air Lines pilot broadcast a message that was played over the new terminal's public address system.[540]

1932   Post Office Cornerstone Laid

Though the cornerstone of the Chicago's Main Post Office, the world's largest, was laid in 1932, but the 2.5 million-square-foot structure wasn't completed for another two years. The massive building even provided for the Congress Expressway to pass through the lower levels. Serving mail order giants Sears, Spiegel, and Wards, the Chicago Post Office processed more parcel post traffic than the next five largest cities in the nation.[541]

1932   Airline Pilots Strike Century Airlines

E.L. Cord, best known as the designer of the Auburn, Cord and Dusenberg automobiles, had started Century Air Lines in March 1931. Because Century didn't have any air mail contracts to subsidize its operations it had to rely solely on passenger revenue.

To build passenger volume, Cord reduced ticket prices, forcing the company to implement extreme cost-cutting measures. Century slashed pilot salaries from $350/month to $150/month. As their flights landed at Municipal, security guards escorted each pilot into the office to sign a new contract at the lower salary. The pilots all refused.

Century's chief pilot sought assistance David Behncke, president of the Air Line Pilots Assn. (ALPA) less than a year after the union was formed.

Behncke led the pilots on strike with the assistance of the AFL. There was a long and ugly campaign. Both sides made heavy use of radio and newspaper ads as well as appealing to legislative bodies including the U.S. Congress. New York Mayor Fiorello La Guardia became a champion for the ALPA cause.

By late 1932, the tide turned against Cord and he sold Century Air Lines to Aviation Corp. of Delaware (AVCO).[542]

1932   AVCO and American Airways Restructuring

As part of the settlement of the pilot strike against Century Air Lines, E.L. Cord exchanged his controlling interest in Century for stock in Aviation Corp. of Delaware (AVCO) and a directorship on its subsidiary, American Airways.

Not long after the settlement, Cord initiated a successful proxy fight to get rid of Averell Harriman and Robert Lehman. Cord became chairman of AVCO and owned the controlling interest of American Airways.

Cord made a former VP for United Air Lines, Lester D. Seymour, head of American and moved its offices to Chicago.[543]

1932   Coffey Becomes Both Pilot and Mechanic

Cornelius Coffey had begun flying in 1928 at Akers Airport and in 1931 had graduated from Curtiss-Wright Aeronautical College with his Aircraft and Engine License. Coffey received his Private Pilot License in 1932, becoming the first African American to hold both a pilot's and mechanic's license.

Coffey went on to qualify for his Limited Commercial Pilot License in 1934, and in 1936, he received his Transport Pilot License.[544]

1932   Monarch Air Service Starts at Municipal

Pierce "Scotty" O'Carroll learned to fly at Ashburn Field in a JN-4 Jenny in the 1920s. By 1930, he was working as an instructor for the Illinois Flying School at Ashburn.

In 1932, O'Carroll started Monarch Air Service at Municipal Airport with sightseeing as the backbone of its business. O'Carroll saw his mission as giving ordinary people a chance to get into the air. For a mere $3.50, anyone could have a 20-minute flight, seeing Chicago's skyline and the lake. Others would charter Monarch's planes for vacations and hunting or fishing trips in surrounding states.

For decades, Monarch was a fixture at Municipal offering FBO, charter, and non-scheduled airline services.[545]

1932   Goodyear Builds Blimp Hangar at Pal-Waukee

In early 1932, Goodyear built an airship dock and hangar at Pal-Waukee and the blimp *Puritan* occupied it throughout the summer. In early 1933, Goodyear enlarged the hangar to accommodate a second blimp. The hangar was as long as a football field and as high as a seven-story building.

During the Century of Progress, the two Goodyear blimps, *Puritan* and *Reliance,* gave sightseeing rides to the public from a dock on Northerly Island near the Travel and Transport Building.[546]

The blimp hangar at Pal-Waukee was dismantled in June 1942, and the scrap given to the practical arts shops at Maine High School. Even after the hangar was dismantled, Pal-Waukee retained a mooring pole for decades, to accommodate blimps visiting the airport.[547]

1932   Darby Becomes Parachutist

African American Chicagoan Dorothy Darby, who billed herself as "the only professional female parachutist in the country," made her first jump in the summer of 1932.

Darby was a graduate of the Chicago Curtiss-Wright Aeronautical University and a good friend of John Robinson and Cornelius Coffey. Darby and Robinson were Willa Brown's instructors and they became close as part of the Challenger Air Pilots Assn.[548]

1932   Greer Airport Becomes Park Ridge Airport

Edwin Greer, owner of Greer School of Aviation, operated several airports in the Chicago area. Sometime after selling Greer Field #2 to Roy and Mae Wilson in 1928, he purchased more land north of Wilson Airport. The newer Greer Airport was located at the intersection of River Rd. and Touhy Ave.

By 1932, the airport had changed its name to Park Ridge Airport. Somewhere in the 1935–1937 timeframe, it was again renamed River Road Airport. Shortly after 1940, the airport closed.[549]

1932   Johnson Buys a Ford

Chicagoan Harold Johnson decided to become a barnstormer but knew he needed something unique to attract a crowd. Johnson reasoned that doing aerobatics with a 6-ton Tri-Motor would thrill audiences, so he purchased a Ford 4-AT Tri-Motor

Johnson formed National Air Shows and performed around the country in his Ford doing rolls, loops, and spins. He established the record of 17 consecutive loops in his Tri-Motor. Another of Johnson's signature acts was to scrape the plane's wingtips along the runway. Naturally the wingtips needed regular replacement so Johnson established a CAA-certified repair station in a truck that toured with the air show.

Johnson's aviation interest had developed early and he soloed while still a teenager. In 1927, he was instrumental in opening the airport in Tilton,

IL, where he established the Aerial Transit Co. as a dealership for WACO airplanes. He moved to Chicago where he served briefly as the chief instructor for Chicago Aeronautical Service before flying for the *Chicago Daily News*.[550]

1932/01/26   Eddie Stinson Hits Flagpole

While demonstrating a plane to prospective Chicago buyers on January 26, 1932, Edward Anderson "Eddie" Stinson Jr. was forced to make an emergency landing on a golf course in Jackson Park.[a] Stinson's plane struck a flagpole, severing the plane's wing. Stinson was killed in the crash but his passengers survived. Though only 38 at his death, Stinson had logged over 16,000 hrs, more than any other aviator at that time.[551]

Like his sisters Katherine and Marjorie, Eddie had close ties to Chicago. During the 1916 flying season, he bunked with Matty Laird and his crew in their hangar at Ashburn Field.

After March 14, 1917, when Laird crashed while testing a plane for the Stinsons, Stinson spent countless hours sitting with Laird in the hospital. Recovery techniques from a spin, the cause of Laird's crash, were the subject of much of their conversation. Later, Stinson enlisted in the Army and became an instructor in the Air Corps. He was considered the first person to teach spin recovery techniques to Army trainees.[552]

In April 1922, Stinson started a short-lived airline providing service between Ashburn Field and Detroit. The following July, he piloted the plane for Charles Dickinson's airline's early attempt at providing overnight flights between Chicago and New York.[553]

In 1920, Stinson started the Stinson Aircraft Co. in Dayton. After several reorganizations, name changes and relocations, the company wound up in Detroit. On January 26, 1926, the Stinson SM-1 Detroiter made its first flight. In September 1929, E.L. Cord acquired 60% of Stinson Aircraft. In 1930, the company marketed six different models from the small Junior up to the Stinson 6000 Tri-Motor. The Detroiter and the SR Reliant were Stinson's most popular aircraft.[554]

1932/05/21–22   Amelia Earhart Makes Solo Crossing of Atlantic

Amelia Earhart became the first woman to fly solo across the Atlantic. She made the flight in a Lockheed Vega from Harbor Grace, Newfoundland, to Londonderry, Northern Ireland.[555]

a   Scamehorn identifies the location as Washington Park.

1932/07/02   Roosevelt Flies Into Municipal

After the delegates at the Democratic Convention in Chicago nominated Franklin Roosevelt, he chartered a Ford Tri-Motor for a flight from Albany, NY, to Chicago to accept the nomination on July 2, 1932. A crowd of 25,000 supporters greeted Roosevelt at Municipal Airport.

Roosevelt's flight was doubly significant. Not only did Roosevelt become the first president or candidate to fly,[a] but this was also the first time a candidate appeared at a convention in person to accept the nomination.[556]

1932/09/11   Sky Harbor Air Meet

The American Legion sponsored a charity fundraiser at Sky Harbor Airport on September 11, 1932. Two dozen flyers from Chicago and around the Midwest performed in races and other exhibition flying as part of the largest air show of the period. More than 50,000 spectators enjoyed the aerial events.[557]

1933   Municipal Gets Radio

Municipal Field got a radio control tower to communicate with planes.[558]

1933   Janet Harmon Bragg Gets into Aviation

In 1933, a billboard kindled an aviation interest in African American nurse Janet Harmon Bragg. She enrolled in Curtiss-Wright Aeronautical University attending evening classes for non-white students taught by John Robinson and Cornelius Coffey. She was the only woman among 24 men in the class.

Born in Georgia, Janet Harmon found her way to Chicago, where she became a registered nurse and later pursued advanced nursing and public health degrees at Cook County School of Nursing, Loyola University, and the University of Chicago. She spent her working career in the health services field.

After finishing CWAU. Bragg became active in the Challenger Air Pilots Assn., which Robinson and Coffey founded. CWAU only provided ground school for pilots, so she purchased a plane that Robinson and Coffee used to provide flight instruction for her and others at Robbins Airport. She received her Pilot's License in 1934.

In the 1930s, as Janet Waterman (using her first husband's name), she wrote a column titled "Negro Aviation" in the *Chicago Defender*.[559]

a   After leaving office, Theodore Roosevelt became the first former President to take to the air.

1933   Robbins Gets Blown Away

Cornelius Coffey and John Robinson started Robbins Airport, the country's first airport intended primarily for African Americans in late 1931 or early 1932. Members of the Brown Eagles Aero Club, which Coffey and Robinson founded, volunteered to construct makeshift hangars and other facilities.

The do-it-yourself construction at Robbins was not rugged enough to accommodate Chicago weather. In 1933, about a year after it opened, a severe windstorm destroyed the airport. With their only hangar and most of their equipment destroyed, the Challenger Air Pilots Assn. (as Brown Eagles was then called) abandoned Robbins Airport.

William and his brother Fred Schumacher, who ran Harlem Airport in Oak Lawn at 87th St. and Harlem Ave., invited Coffey and Robinson to share their airport. Although Bill and Fred Schumacher were personally accepting of Challenger's integrated approach, many of their customers weren't as tolerant. The Schumachers and Challenger agreed that their operations should be at opposite ends of the field, so Challenger set up at the south end of Harlem.

In order to raise money to build a hangar and replace the planes that were destroyed, Challenger held frequent air shows, sightseeing rides, dances, dinners, and other fundraising functions.[560]

1933   Marmels Operate Ravenswood

By 1933, Abe and Shirley Marmel operated Ravenswood Airport. The 40-acre field had four runways with the longest being 1,800 ft.

Around 1940, Al Tufts and George Edgecumbe opened a Piper Dealership at Ravenswood.[a] Later, the Marmels maintained Ercoupes and had a large stockpile of parts. Twenty years after Ravenswood opened, Marmel's wife ran the airport. She was arrested on gambling charges in June 1953, when authorities alleged that Ravenswood, like other smaller airports, supplemented their income with slot machines.[561]

1933   Dacy Airport Opens

On Airport Road southwest of Harvard, IL, John Dacy started Dacy Airport in 1933 as a small landing strip for his plane. Dacy licensed it as a commercial airport in 1946 and expanded it to three turf runways. During the 1970s it was home to one of the largest Cessna dealers in the country.[562]

---

a   It is unclear whether this was prior to or concurrent with Tufts-Edgecumbe's operation at Pal-Waukee.

Currently, the airport is the base for Dacy Airshows, the longest, continually operating airshow company in the country, which is currently run by John Dacy's children. Dave and Susan perform aerobatics in their Stearman biplanes and are joined by other performers in a variety of aircraft. Another of John's sons, Phil Dacy, performs as an airshow announcer and Julia, Phil's wife, handles many administrative responsibilities.[563]

1933   Mae Wilson Takes Control

Wilson Airport was a very vibrant field until Roy died while teaching spins in 1933. His wife Mae assumed control of the airport. Although Roy had given Mae a few lessons, she wasn't enthusiastic about flying and didn't pursue her license.

Over the next few years she became increasingly dissatiffied with the marginal performance of pilots she hired. Mae took matters into her own hands and learned to fly. In order to impress people who were hesitant about hiring a woman instructor, she also learned aerobatics and stunt flying at shows to promote the airport. Soon she had enough business to keep herself and the airfield going.

After WWII, the suburbs were developing all around the airport. Mae sold Wilson Airport and moved her operation to Elmhurst Airport.[564]

1933/03/30   Boeing 247 Enters Service with United

United placed the first Boeing 247, the first modern passenger airplane, into service on March 30, 1933.The passenger airliner was an outgrowth of Boeing's 220 Monomail and its military B-9 bomber.

The twin-engine plane was the first modern airliner with stressed metal skin (semimonocoque construction), a fully cantilevered wing, partially retractable gear, and the ability to fly on one engine. Other advanced features included trim tabs, de-icing boots, and an early autopilot.

The sleek 247 carried 10 passengers at a cruising speed of 189 mph for 745 miles. That made it faster than the U.S. Army's main fighter, the open-cockpit Boeing P-12. The 247 was able to travel coast-to-coast in under 20 hr., almost 7 hr. faster than a Ford Tri-Motor. Boeing prominently displayed its 247 in the Travel and Transport Building at the Century of Progress World's Fair in Chicago.

Because of the close arrangement between Boeing and United, United ordered the 247 while it was still on the drawing board. They ordered 60 aircraft which were to be delivered to United prior to any other airlines.

This gave United exclusive rights for about a year, propelling it to become the largest carrier in the country.[565]

1933/05/27   Century of Progress Opens

The 1933–1934 World's Fair, the Century of Progress Exposition, opened on May 27, 1933. The exposition on Chicago's downtown lakefront featured the latest technological advances in a wide range of fields—including aviation.[566]

An open air pageant *Wings of a Century: the Romance of Transportation* was held on a large stage with Lake Michigan as a backdrop. Written by Erv Hungerford, the pageant showcased transportation progress from Native Americans on horseback to railroads, cars, and airplanes.

The popular Travel and Transport Building included a static display that showcased all types of aircraft. Taylor Brothers Aircraft displayed their E-2,[a] a modern high-wing, two-seat monoplane with an enclosed cockpit. The centerpiece of the building was a Boeing 247 suspended from the dome, showing the epitome of modern air travel. A variety of air racers of all types were also shown as well as some historic planes, including the *Vin Fiz*.[567]

Just prior to the opening of the Century of Progress, Municipal Airport's control tower added a two-way radio for enabling direct communication with radio-equipped airplanes. For the first time, many World's Fair attendees flew to the event. Transportation into the Loop was via car or streetcar with one transfer.[568]

1933/05/27   Northerly Island Flights Begin

A lakefront airport had long been a part of Chicago planning. Edward Bennet, the co-author of Burnham's Plan proposed such an airport in 1916. When Northerly Island was being constructed in the early 1920s, Mayor William Hale Thompson was advocating an airport there.[569] In 1929, Chicago began another planning effort for a lakefront airport to cost $10 million, but nothing came of the effort.[570]

Northerly Island became the flight center for fairgoers at the Century of Progress. Two Goodyear blimps, *Puritan* and *Reliance*, gave rides to the public from a dock on Northerly Island near the Travel and Transport Building. When not flying, the blimps were housed in a specially built hangar at Pal-Waukee.[571]

---

a   Piper later bought out Taylor Brothers and release a modified version of the E-2 as the J-3 Cub.

Fair attendees could take sightseeing flights in two Sikorsky S-38 amphibians. The ten-passenger planes were owned and operated by Pal-Waukee Air Port.[572]

When the Century of Progress ended in 1934, both the Illinois legislature and Chicago City Council authorized construction of a permanent airport on Northerly Island. However, between problems with the economy and political considerations, the project was delayed until 1946.[573]

1933/05/31   Elgin Airport Languishes

Elgin Airport began its rapid decline on May 31, 1933, when Northwest Airways stopped service to the airport. Improved aviation technology meant planes needed fewer intermediate stops. In addition, the economic effects of the Great Depression resulted in a major decline in both mail and passenger volume.

A tornado later that summer destroyed several hangars and planes. Unable to raise sufficient funds for repairs, the Elgin Assn. of Commerce turned its lease over to the city, allowing it to seek Federal funds. The funds never materialized and the the Kelley family closed the airport. For the remainder of the 1930s, Elgin flyers shifted back to Trout Park and Burnidge Field. By 1938, aerial photographs show an open grass field where the airport had been.

At the beginning of WWII, the Navy leased airport grounds for a satellite training field. One grass runway was covered by perforated steel planks, the same technology the Navy used for building airports in the South Pacific.[574]

1933/06/11   Sightseeing Seaplane Crashes

Only a couple of weeks after the opening of the Century of Progress on June 6, 1933, a crash marred the festivities when a sightseeing plane that took off from Northerly Island crashed.

Pal-Waukee Air Port operated a sightseeing concession giving sightseeing rides over Lake Michigan using a pair of Sikorsky S-38 amphibians. When an unexpected storm popped up, they immediately cancelled flights. As the final plane landed to discharge passengers, the pilot heard a loud crack and saw a wing pontoon had been broken by a wave.

Immediately, he took back to the sky and headed to Curtiss-Reynolds Airport in Glenview, which could handle the maintenance. About a mile from the airport, the wing failed and the plane crashed and burned, killing both crew members and a full load of eight passengers. The crack the pilot heard was not just the pontoon but the spar.

The crash was the worst aviation disaster in Chicago since the airship *Wingfoot Express* crashed in 1919. However, the incident did little to dampen the public's enthusiasm for flying. By the end of 1933, more than 17,000 people had flown on the S-38s. For about 70% of the passengers, it was their first time in the air.[575]

1933/07/01–05   American Air Races

The biggest Chicago aviation event in decades was the American Air Races (AAR) held July 1–5, 1933. Sponsored by the *Chicago Tribune*, the AAR were held in conjunction with the Century of Progress.

Most events were held at Municipal Airport, but some of the heats required longer distances, with planes flying between Municipal and Hawthorne Race Track, where additional pylons had been erected. The big AAR winners were John Livingston and Harold Neumann.[576]

In addition to the races, spectators were entertained with aerobatic performances. Two members of the Chicago Girls Flying Club, Margaret McCormick and Helen Colton, thrilled the crowd with low-level stunt flying. They performed so low that the Department of Commerce threatened to revoke their licenses if they continued.[577]

The Chicago Girls Flying Club was formed by Mae Wilson (of Wilson Airport) and others in the early 1930s.[578] The Club was unusual for the time in that it welcomed African American pilots. Willa Brown and Janet Bragg were both members in the early 1930s.[579]

The AAR were held concurrently with the National Air Races in Los Angeles and thus did not draw some of the biggest name performers. Since the National Aeronautic Assn. (NAA) and FAI did not sanction the American Air Races, some of the competitors lost their license to race for the remainder of the season.[580]

1933/07/04   Lakefront Air Show

On Independence Day, the Century of Progress held an air show at the lakefront that entertained 60–75,000 spectators. Performers included a Ford Tri-Motor doing a loop, an autogyro demonstration, a flight display of Naval aviation from Great Lakes, and a parachutist who descended while banging a sack of flour to show his position.[581]

Another parachutist made a jump that night with spotlights playing across him. Sadly, his chute malfunctioned and he plunged to his death in the lake.[582]

1933/07/15   Italian Flying Boats Visit Fair

At 5:45 p.m. on July 15, 1933, a formation of 24 Italian flying boats flew across Lake Michigan landing at the Century of Progress. General Italo Balbo and the contingent of Savoia-Marchetti SM.55X aircraft departed Orbetello, Italy on July 1, flying the entire trip in close formation.[583]

The city was so impressed with the feat that it named a nearby street, Balbo Dr. after the aviator. In response, Mussolini donated an ancient Roman column to Chicago commemorating Balbo's journey. The monument currently stands in Grant Park.[584]

1933/07/15   *Lituanica* Begins Its Flight

Attempting to set a nonstop distance record, two Lithuanian-born Americans, Steponas Darius and Stasys Giernas,[a] departed Floyd Bennett Field in New York at 6 a.m., July 15, 1933, in the *Lituanica* destined for Kaunas Lithuania, 4,350 miles away.

Darius and Giernas were pilots for the *Chicago Daily News* out of Pal-Waukee Air Port. To raise money for their venture, the pair flew exhibition flights and carried passengers. Lithuanian communities in Chicago and around the country held numerous fundraisers to support the trip.

They purchased a new Bellanca CH-300 Pacemaker, the same type of plane they flew for the *Daily News*. Matty Laird made the modifications necessary to make the long-distance flight. Laird gave the airplane a new higher-performing engine, longer wings and horizontal stabilizer, wheel farings, and larger fuel tanks. Due to weight considerations, the pilots opted to omit a radio and navigation instruments. The plane received a bright orange coat of paint with the name *Lituanica* boldly painted on both sides.

During the flight, weather was marginal, especially over the North Atlantic, forcing them to take a more northerly route over Scotland. They successfully crossed the Atlantic and were flying near Soldin, Germany (now Pszczelnik, Poland) when their plane crashed, killing both pilots. The *Lituanica* was only 400 miles from its destination. The cause of the crash has remained unclear.

Darius and Giernas were regarded as national heroes. The President of Lithuania declared a national day of mourning. More than 60,000 people attended their funeral in Kaunas, conducted by an Archbishop.

Today at the crash site, a monument marks the end of the *Lituanica's* flight. Its wreckage is on display in the Great War Museum in Kaunas. The

---

a   Some sources use their Americanized names: Stephan Darius and Stanley Giernas.

image of Darius[a] and Giernas adorn a Lithuanian stamp and the front of the 10 litas banknote, which bears the *Lituanica* on the reverse side.

In 1935, a large granite memorial to the flyers was erected in Marquette Park. In 1957 in Lituanica Square in Brooklyn, the community erected a granite flagstaff with the pilots in bas-relief.[585]

1933/07/22   First Solo Flight Around the World
Wiley Post made a second around-the-world flight, this time solo. A new Sperry autopilot and radio direction finder, both still in early development, aided his flight. Post's trip set a new record of 7 days, 18 hr., and 49 min., including stops for gas and repairs.[586]

1933/09/01–04   International Air Races at Curtiss-Reynolds
The Century of Progress held its second major air competition of 1933 hosting the International Air Race at Curtiss-Reynolds Field on September 1–4, 1933.[587] Many of the top names in aviation attended the IAR including Jimmy Doolittle, Charles and Anne Lindbergh, Wiley Post, and Eddie Rickenbacker.[588] As part of the IAR, Frank Hawks completed a significant cross-country trip from Chicago to Los Angeles to Seattle and back to Los Angeles. Hawks completed the 4,500-mile trip in under 24.5 hr.[589]

1933/09/02   Gordon Bennett Cup Balloon Races
The Century of Progress conducted a balloon race to award the Gordon Bennett Cup. On September 2, 1933, aeronauts from six countries, including the U.S., departed from Chicago. The Polish team came in first, flying more than 38.5 hr. and covering 845 mi. before landing in a wilderness in Quebec.[590]

1933/10/10   Chicago-Bound Plane Explodes
A United Boeing 247 departed Newark destined for Oakland, CA. During the flight from Cleveland to Chicago, the airplane exploded in the sky near Chesterton, IN. The first passenger plane explosion in American history killed three crew members and four passengers.

The FBI extensively investigated the explosion and determined a nitroglycerin bomb exploded in the cargo compartment near the tail. However, they were unable to identify either the bomber or the motive.[591]

a   The Darius portrait used on the banknote has an interesting Chicago connection. The patch on his hat contains "Palatine" written vertically and "Milwaukee" horizontally in recognition of the intersection of his beloved Pal-Waukee Air Port.

1933/10/26 *Graf Zeppelin* at World's Fair

The *Graf Zeppelin* made her second visit to Chicago as part of the Century of Progress and moored at Curtiss-Reynolds Field.[592].

In addition to flying over the fairgrounds, the ship flew in a large circle around the entire city for all to see the wonderful airship.[593] The Zeppelin's port (left) tail fin was adorned with a swastika and the starboard (right) fin with the black-white-red of the German flag. The Nazi symbol had created controversy, so when the Zeppelin's commander circled the city, he flew in a clockwise direction so the flag pattern would be visible to more people than the swastika.[594]

1934 Suicide Jones Earns Nickname

William "Willie" Jones was a stunt aviator and an active member of the Challenger Air Pilots Assn. Although he was a pilot and flew in some air shows, he was best known as the only African American wing-walker and parachutist. There are two versions of how he earned the nickname "Suicide," both from about 1934.

In one version, Jones's ripcord became entangled in his bootlaces. Plummeting to earth he managed to work the cord free and the chute opened at the last second. The pilot and others on the ground were sure he fell to earth and perished.[a]

The other took place during a night jump in Little Rock to allow the Coast Guard to test their searchlights. Jones accepted the jump after other parachutists had refused it as too dangerous. Jumping from 10,000 ft., Jones was blinded by the lights and, unable to judge his altitude, was forced to guess when to pull his ripcord.[595]

1934 Patterson Takes United's Controls

William Allan "Pat" Patterson first became involved with airlines as a loan officer at Wells Fargo Bank, working with Pacific Air Transport (PAT). He was instrumental in assisting in PAT's acquisition by Boeing Air Transport (BAT). Patterson's abilities impressed William Boeing, who hired Patterson as an assistant to Philip Johnson, BAT's President.

When BAT merged into United Aircraft and Transport Co. (UATC) in 1931, Patterson moved to Chicago as GM and was later promoted to VP.

---

a   Gubert places this incident in 1939 or 1940.

As a result of the Air Mail Scandal concerning the Spoils Conferences, the airlines were forced to reorganize. Patterson took over the helm of United Air Lines Transport Co. (UALTC), which operated as United Air Lines.[596]

1934/02/09   Air Mail Contracts Canceled

President Franklin Roosevelt's new Postmaster General James A. Farley reacted negatively to the way air mail contracts had been awarded by the Hoover administration and immediately canceled all air mail contracts immediately on February 9, 1934

Operating under the McNary-Watres Act of 1930, the previous Postmaster General Walter Brown met with various air mail carriers and decided on contracts to be awarded. Farley viewed this lack of competitive bidding under Postmaster General Brown as collusion between the Postmaster and the airlines. These meetings became known as the "Spoils Conferences."

The Senate conducted a hearing on the "Air Mail Scandal," during which William MacCracken, who had chaired the meetings, refused to turn over his documentation, citing attorney-client privilege. The Senate cited MacCracken for contempt and he served ten days in jail after the Supreme Court rejected his claim.

The Army Air Corps was called upon to fly the mail. This was an "emergency action" that gave the Army minimal time for preparation, organization, training, or selection of equipment. The lack of preparation resulted in 66 accidents with 12 fatalities within several months. The average operating cost rose to $2.21 per mile compared to $0.54 per mile of the previous operating companies.

By May, the Post Office began awarding limited three-month contracts to air mail carriers and by June, Army pilots were no longer needed for mail service.

The new Air Mail (AM-) route structure was very similar to the previous Contract Air Mail (CAM-) routes; however, the new fee structure severely impacted the airlines financially. For example, United, which made a profit of $175,000 in 1933, lost $300,000 a month during the cancellation period.

Eventually, it was discovered that claims of alleged "spoils" were false. Lawsuits were brought against the government for the cancellations and on February 4, 1935, the Appellate Court in Washington, DC ruled that government action was a breach of contract without due process. The lawsuits dragged on until the last one was settled in 1942. On July 14, 1941, the

Commissioner of the U.S. Court of Claims ruled that there was no fraud or collusion when the contracts were awarded under the 1930 Air Mail Act.[597]

1934/04/11   AVCO Divests American Airways

As part of the response to the Spoils Conferences scandal, proposed legislation prohibited airlines carrying mail and manufacturers from being part of the same company. In anticipation of the law's passage, on April 11, 1934, AVCO divested itself of the airline portion of its business and spun off American Airlines, giving it all of the previous American Airways routes, personnel, and equipment.

Later, E.L. Cord replaced Lester Seymour with C.R. Smith, who took the corporate reins as CEO of American Airlines on October 26, 1934. A native Texan, Smith had been a VP of another AVCO organization, Southern Air Transport. Except for a brief period during WWII, Smith served as American's CEO from 1934 to 1968 and again briefly in 1973 and 1974.[598]

American had the most southerly transcontinental route of the major carriers (UAL and TWA being the others). Flying from New York to Los Angeles, American flew through Cincinnati, St. Louis, Dallas, and Phoenix. A spur from St. Louis connected Chicago to their cross-country route.[599]

1934/04/13   Pat Patterson Heads United

William "Pat" Patterson became President of United Air Lines on April 13, 1934. He continued as President until 1963 when he became CEO and Chairman of the Board. He retired from United in 1966.[600]

1934/05/10   ALPA Successfully Limits Pilot's Flight Hours

Following the Air Line Pilots Assn. (ALPA)'s success in 1932 against E.L. Cord and Century Air Lines, the airlines formed their own organization. Participating airlines instituted a reduced pay scale coupled with longer hours that required pilots to fly 140 hours each month.

David Behncke and ALPA brought a grievance before the National Labor Relations Board (NLRB). On May 10, 1934, the NLRB made a ruling establishing a maximum of 85 flying hours per month as well as a framework for determining pilot pay. The NLRB ruling was incorporated into the Air Mail Act of 1934 and the Civil Aeronautics Act of 1938.[601]

1934/06   Challenger Plants Tuskegee Seeds

Cornelius Coffey and John Robinson were African Americans who became pilots and aviation mechanics. They envisioned a school similar to

Curtiss-Wright Aeronautical University that served people of all races and genders. Tuskegee Institute had an outstanding auto mechanic program from which Robinson had graduated. The two men believed that Tuskegee would be the perfect place for an aviation school.

They made an appointment with the President of Tuskegee Institute in June 1934. Coffey and Robinson, accompanied by Grover Nash, flew two planes from Chicago to Alabama as a demonstration of their aviation abilities. Their meeting failed to convince the Tuskegee President to start an aviation program. His reasons were never specifically stated, but there were many obstacles. During the Great Depression funds were certainly a limiting factor. Also, there may have been fear of a negative reaction from the white community to having African Americans flying over them.

However, Coffey and Robinson's efforts planted seeds that grew as war threatened. Tuskegee Institute was named a Civilian Pilot Training Program school. Some historians consider the meeting with Coffey and Robinson as the beginning stages of the Tuskegee Airmen program.[602]

1934/06/03   C&S Serves Chicago

An entrepreneur, Carleton Putnam, was awarded the Chicago to New Orleans route (AM-8) via Memphis and Jackson and began carrying mail on June 3, 1934, adding passenger service soon thereafter.

Putnam's first aviation venture was the Pacific Seaboard Airline, which he started in July 1933 to serve West Coast destinations. During the shakeup of the airline industry in the wake of the Spoils Conference scandal, Putnam bid on an air mail contract as Illinois, Pacific Air Transport. In 1935,[a] Pacific Seaboard Airline officially changed its name to Chicago and Southern Air Lines.[603]

1934/06/12   Air Mail Act of 1934 Signed into Law

Acting on unproven allegations of collusion the Air Mail Act of 1934. This Act dramatically changed the world of commercial aviation.

Long-term air mail contracts were allowed rather than the limited three-month interim contracts. However, air mail carriers were prohibited from having financial interest in any other aviation enterprise except airports. Since many mail carriers shared ownership with manufacturers, this Act resulted in the divestiture and reorganization of many companies.

---

a   Scamehorn indicates the new name was in use by July 1934.

The Interstate Commerce Commission (ICC) was mandated to determine compensation rates for each route based on miles and load. Together the ICC and Postmaster General were authorized to regulate the accounting practices of the carriers. The Secretary of Commerce established pilot regulations (hours and compensation) and airplane specifications (load, capacity, and safety equipment). The President appointed a five-member Federal Aviation Commission on July 11 to survey the broad policy of U.S. aviation.

In a related action, on June 19, an amendment to the Air Commerce Act of 1926 gave the Aeronautics Branch stronger authority to investigate accidents. The Branch was given the power to subpoena witnesses to testify or provide documentation about the cause of an accident. For all accidents involving a fatality or serious injury, the Branch Secretary was required to issue a statement about the cause.[604]

1934/07   Airline Renaming
One side effect of the Air Mail Act was the renaming of many companies since previous contract holders were either prohibited from or at a disadvantage when bidding on new contacts. Starting in July 1934, most major airline companies changed their names to comply with the new regulations. American Airways became American Airlines, Eastern Air Transport became Eastern Air Lines, Northwest Airways became Northwest Airlines, Transcontinental and Western Air became Transcontinental and Western Air, Inc. United Air Lines was the only major operating company that did not have a name change at this time.[605]

1934/07/01   Aeronautics Branch Renamed
The Dept. of Commerce changed the name of the Aeronautics Branch to the Bureau of Air Commerce.[606]

1934/07/09   American Airlines Sleeper Service
American Airlines offered the first sleeper service on its New York to Chicago route. The Curtiss T-32 Condor IIs were configured with 12 sleeper bunks instead of the normal 18 seats.[607]

1934/07/18   Baker Commission Report
Following the problems the Army had flying air mail, on April 18, 1934, the Secretary of War established the Baker Commission[a] to examine military

a   This was the 15th board or commission in 16 years to examine problems in the Army Air Corps.

aviation. The commission found that the U.S. aviation was generally superior to other nations. However, the Army Air Corps lagged behind U.S. commercial aviation primarily due to a lack of funds. The commission recommended that the military stop trying to compete with the commercial sector but rather take advantage of what was already available in the commercial market and improvements in the competitive bidding process. Major improvements in training, especially night flying, and a reorganization of the flying units were also conclusions of the commission that were put into place.[608]

1934/07/20   UATC Splits into Separate Companies

Pursuant to the Air Mail Act of 1934, prohibiting joint ownership, United Aircraft and Transport Co. (UATC) was forced to divest itself of some of its companies. Boeing and Stearman formed separate aircraft manufacturing companies. UATC continued to control the remaining manufacturing companies.

On July 20, United Air Lines Transport Corp (UALTC) was created as a management company for its air transportation subsidiaries. UALTC included Boeing Air Transport, National Air Transport, Pacific Air Transport, Stout Air Services, and Varney Airlines. The new UALTC operated as United Air Lines (UAL) promoting its transcontinental service from New York through Chicago to San Francisco with feeder routes to Dallas, Los Angeles and Seattle.

When the Post Office rebid air mail contracts, UAL retained all its routes except the Chicago to Dallas (CAM-3/AM-9) one, which was awarded to Braniff Airways.

However, UAL did not come out of the reorganization unscathed. William Paterson, the UAL President, challenged the government's cancellation of air mail contracts in court. The issue consumed UAL resources, holding UAL back for nearly a decade until 1942 when the U.S. Court of Claims ruled against UAL.[609]

1934/09/05   Post Discovers Jet Stream Using a Pressure Suit

Wiley Post was interested in exploring long-distance flight at a high altitude rather than brief altitude-record setting flights.

Because his airplane, the Lockheed Vega *Winnie Mae*, was structurally unable to be pressurized, Post and his backers developed a pressurized suit. After a couple of unsuccessful attempts, Post's team created a workable suit. The helmet resembled one worn by deep-sea divers and accommodated earphones and a throat microphone while maintaining the pressure of an altitude of 17,000 ft.

Flying above Chicago, Post set an altitude record of 40,000 ft. on September 5, 1934. He also noticed a drastic increase in his ground speed, discovering the jet stream. His flight later reached 50,000 ft. but was not recorded as an official record.

In March 1935, Post flew the *Winnie Mae* from Burbank to Cleveland taking advantage of the jet stream. The Vega, with a top speed of 179 mph, made the 2,035 mi. trip in 7 hr. 19 min. at an average ground speed of 279 mph.[610]

1934/12/31   First Woman Airline Pilot

On December 31, 1934, Helen Richey started flying a Ford Tri-Motor on the Washington to Detroit route for Central Airlines, a Pennsylvania-based air carrier that became part of United Air Lines. Richey's airline career was cut short when the all-male union created problems.[611]

1935–1939

1935   *House of Tomorrow* Moves to Indiana

The Century of Progress included the *Homes of Tomorrow Exhibition* to
highlight current designs, technologies, and building materials. About a
dozen showcase residences were built by different architects.

One of the most acclaimed and popular was the *House of Tomorrow,*
designed by Chicago architect George Frederick Keck. The twelve-sided
building had three stories of decreasing size like a wedding cake, the top
two with glass walls. The lower level included a hangar complete with a
small biplane.

After the fair in the winter of 1935, Robert Bartlett moved five of the
houses, including the Keck house, to his new development in Beverly Shores,
IN. On June 30, 1986, the National Register of Historic Places added the
houses as the Beverly Shores—Century of Progress Architectural District.[612]

1935   Moline Buys Franing Field

In 1935, the city of Moline, IL purchased Franing Field, making it a municipally owned facility called Moline Airport. Airport development required a
Works Progress Administration (WPA) project of more than $500,000, the
second-largest WPA project in Illinois.[a] By 1939, a new terminal serviced
five daily scheduled airline flights.[613]

1935   Municipal Doubles Again

After the Century of Progress closed, the Chicago Meadows Golf Course
north of Municipal went out of business. The city quickly leased the property, doubling the size of the airport. Municipal Airport now occupied a full
square mile in the heart of the city and the nation.

The airport relocated the golf course's clubhouse to 57th St. and
Central Ave. and modified it to become the home for John Casey, the
airport manager. The lack of a resident caretaker had been the only thing
that prevented Municipal from being designated as a first-class airport and
receiving Federal grant money.

---

a   Only Chicago Municipal Airport had a larger WPA project.

A $1 million WPA project funded the airport's much-needed expansion. By 1940, Municipal had nine runways, some sufficient to handle four-engine aircraft, including the B-17. Municipal became the aviation lynchpin of the nation. The busiest airport in the world connected the East, West, and southern coasts by air.[614]

However, the Belt Line train tracks, which previously ran along the northern edge of the airport now bisected the airport. The railroad had a perpetual right-of-way on the land.

These were not the typical railroad tracks over which a few trains passed each day. Belt Line tracks provided access for trains entering and leaving their massive switching yards, which assembled a large percentage of freight for destinations across the country. The numerous, full-loaded trains then passed through the middle of Municipal Airport.[615]

1935   Challenger Becomes Military Order of Guard Unit

Like many Americans, members of the Challenger Air Pilots Assn. foresaw the coming war and wanted to help the country prepare for it.

Challenger applied to the state to become an Air Reserve Squadron in the Illinois National Guard. The state rejected their request because it did not permit African Americans to serve in the National Guard. Undaunted, Challenger did not give up and pursued their efforts.

Eventually Illinois chartered Challenger as a Military Order of Guard, Aviation Squadron (MOG) and allowed Challenger to display the MOG insignia on one of their airplanes.

Although it was a symbolic gesture, this was the first African American aviation squadron designated by a governmental body. It gave the members status similar to the state militia. Cornelius Coffey and John Robinson both became Lt. Colonels.[616]

1935   Willa Brown Graduates Aviation University

Willa Brown had been a Gary school teacher and Chicago social worker with an MBA from Northwestern University, when she met John Robinson in 1934 and became interested in aviation.

Brown enrolled in the Curtiss-Wright Aviation University program for African Americans taught by Robinson and Cornelius Coffey. Brown graduated with her Mechanic's Certificate in 1935, a year after Janet Harmon Bragg, and became active in Challenger Air Pilots Assn. [617]

1935/01/02   Lewis Holy Name School of Aeronautics Begins

In 1932, the Archdiocese of Chicago started the Holy Name Institute in
Lockport as a high school for disadvantaged boys. The school was officially
incorporated on October 2, 1934, as the Lewis Holy Name Technical
School, honoring Frank J. Lewis.

The school quickly developed an emphasis on aviation courses and a
few months later, on January 2, 1935, it was renamed the Lewis Holy Name
School of Aeronautics. A funding shortage forced a temporary closing in
1936, but the school reopened a year later.[618]

1935/01/12–13   Amelia Earhart Flies Solo from Hawaii

Amelia Earhart became the first person to make a solo flight from
Honolulu to Oakland in 18 hr. and 15 min.[619]

1935/02/22   Airship *Macon* Crashes

The Navy's rigid airship *Macon* crashed in the Pacific off California. This
crash, which followed that of the *Macon*'s sister ship the *Akron* in 1933,
ended U.S. military interest in lighter-than-air vehicles.[620]

1935/04   Robinson Arrives in Ethiopia

Throughout the 1930s, war clouds loomed in Europe. Insignificant to most
of the country, Ethiopia was a big concern in the U.S. African American
community. Haile Selassie ruled the proud Empire of Ethiopia, the last
independent African nation. Ethiopia's small military stood alone against
the Italian fascists who wanted to be like other European nations and have
a colony in Africa.

The Challenger Air Pilots Assn. held air shows and dinners to raise
money and supplies to support Ethiopians in their struggle. At least seven
Challengers volunteered to fly for Ethiopia, but the U.S. neutrality policy
prevented it. The threat to Ethiopia particularly upset John Robinson who
somehow got around the policy and moved to Ethiopia in April 1935 to
participate personally in the fight.

Robinson received a commission in the Imperial Ethiopian Air Force
and began giving flight lessons and conducting other training activities.
Impressed with Robinson's abilities, Emperor Selassie promoted Robinson
to Colonel and made him the Commander of the Ethiopian Air Force,
which consisted of about 25 planes.

Ethiopia put up a valiant but doomed fight against Italy and fell to the Fascists in May 1936. Robinson returned home and received a hero's welcome in black communities around the country. The newspapers gave him the nickname "Brown Condor." [621]

Robinson's war record and widespread publicity forced some Americans to reconsider the abilities of black people. That, along with his prior visit to Tuskegee, resulted in Robinson being considered the "Father of the Tuskegee Airmen."[622]

1935/08/30–09/02   Howard Sweeps National Air Races

Chicago designer and builder Benny Howard swept the 1935 National Air Races held in Cleveland. Howard and his partner Gordon Israel flew *Mr. Mulligan* (DGA-6) to victory in the Bendix Race from Santa Monica to Cleveland. *Mr. Mulligan* was able to make the trip nonstop for the first time in race history. It beat Roscoe Turner's faster Wedell-Williams 44 by only 23 sec. because Turner's plane required a fuel stop.

Mr. Mulligan was later flown by Harold Neumann to win the Thompson Trophy. Flying another Howard plane, *Mike* (DGA-4), Neumann also won three heats of the Greve Race, giving him permanent possession of the Greve Trophy.[623]

1935/09/02   Dickinson Flies West

Charles "Pop" Dickinson died of a heart attack on September 2, 1935, at age 77. Although he did little actual flying himself, Dickinson was instrumental in developing aviation in Chicago. A charter member of the Aero Club of Illinois, Dickinson helped organize and sponsor the Air Shows of 1911 and 1912. His generous nature led him to support many aviators, especially youth breaking into the field. Dickinson purchased the land and outfitted Ashburn Field for both the ACI and general public. He also started two airlines, although neither was successful.

Two of Dickinson's closest friends, Ervin Ballough and Al Sporrer, spread his ashes out of a plane over Lake Michigan.[624]

1935/11/12–14   Airway Traffic Control Conference

The Bureau of Air Commerce convened a meeting of all key participants in aviation to address problems with airway traffic control. It was generally agreed that it would be best for the bureau to establish a control system but funding restrictions prohibited that from happening. Instead, the airline cooperated via an Interairline Air Traffic Agreement.

On December 1, an Air Traffic Control Center went operational in Newark, staffed and funded by a consortium of airlines. It provided pilots information about weather and other planes in the area.[625]

1935/12/17   Douglas Introduces DC-3 Sleeper

On the anniversary of the Kitty Hawk flight, December 17, 1935, Douglas Aircraft Corp. announced the DC-3, which was to become the mainstay of commercial aviation for decades.

Following Boeing's 1933 introduction of the 247, the first modern commercial airplane, United received exclusive deliveries for at least a year. The competition did not rest idly, waiting for the 247 to become available. TWA's president Jack Frye put out specifications for a competitive aircraft. Douglas responded producing the DC-2, which went into service with TWA on May 18, 1934, and American soon after. Roughly comparable to the 247, the DC-2 kept both TWA and American in the game.[626]

American Airlines wasn't entirely satisfied with the DC-2 design. American had introduced sleeper service on their Curtiss Condors, which were then woefully obsolete. American's president, C.R. Smith had an extended phone call with Donald Douglas detailing a wish list of improvements to the DC-2.

In June 1936, American received the first Douglas Sleeper Transport (DST), a variation of the DC-3 that was delivered a few month later. The DST had 14 seats that transformed into sleeping berths. The passenger configuration, called the DC-3, had 21seats.

Both configurations could fly at over 190 mph. The DC-3's range was double the Boeing 247's and needed only three fuel stops to fly across the country. Safety was excellent with the ability to fly across the Rockies on one engine.

With a passenger load usually of 21, but which could be up to 28, double Boeing's 247, the DC-3 was an immediate success with the airlines.[627]

The DC-3 was the first economically viable airliner allowing airlines to turn a profit from passenger revenue without depending on government-paid air mail. Although United began adding some DC-3s to its fleet as early as November 1936, American's quick adoption of them helped them surge ahead of their competitor. By 1938, American's revenues were twice as much as United's which was still heavily invested in the Boeing plane.

During the war, a DC-3 variation became the C-47. By the time production ended, Douglas had produced 10,655 planes in military and commercial configurations. After the war, many C-47s were converted for civilian use by scheduled and non-scheduled airlines, charter services, corporate executive use, freight operations, and more.[628]

1936   Airline Travel Record

For the first time, U.S. airlines flew more than a million passengers.[629]

1936/01/03   Air Transport Association Formed

Representatives of the airlines met in Chicago and formed a trade group, the Air Transport Assn. of America.

The ATA was headquartered on LaSalle St. in Chicago until 1942, when it moved to Washington, DC, to improve access to lawmakers, although it continued to maintain a regional office in Chicago. In December 2011 the ATA changed its name to Airlines for America (A4A).[630]

1936/05/14   Hughes Sets Cross Country Record

Howard Hughes set a record flying his modified Northrop Gamma from Chicago Municipal to Burbank in 8 hr., 10 min., and 25 sec. The flight set several records and was a factor in Hughes receiving both the American Harmon Trophy and the International Harmon Trophy.[631]

1936/05/31   TWA Airliner Makes Forced Landing Near Municipal

On May 31, 1936 shortly after 9 p.m., TWA Flight 1409 was on approach with one engine out in gusty winds. The DC-2 from Newark made a forced landing about a half mile from Municipal near 61st St. and Kilbourn Ave. The plane struck a tree and a house, totally destroying the plane. Fortunately, there were no injuries either on the ground or in the plane.[632]

1936/07/06   Federal Air Traffic Control Begins

The Bureau of Air Commerce assumed control of air traffic at Chicago, Newark, and Cleveland. Since the previous December, this function had been performed by a consortium of airlines.[633]

1936/08/15   Instrument Flying Regulations Take Effect

New rules for instrument flight took effect on August 15, 1936, requiring pilots to have an Instrument Rating, file a flight plan, and fly in a plane equipped with a two-way radio.[634]

1936/08/17   Chicago Girl's Club Flying Club Airshow
As part of the 1936 Air and Water Show, the Chicago Girls Flying Club held an airshow on the lakefront.[635]

1936/09   Robinson Opens National Air College
In 1936, after his return from volunteering in the Ethiopian war effort, John Robinson began work on his plan to open an aviation school. By September, funds had been raised and the Illinois Dept. of Commerce chartered the John C. Robinson National Air College and School of Automotive Engineering. It was probably the first black-owned and operated flight school to receive a state charter.

Robinson and others from the Challenger Air Pilots Assn. were the instructors. Harlem Airport was the base for all flight training. Ground school for pilots as well as mechanics was conducted in buildings provided by Mrs. Anne Malone, President of Poro College, a Chicago music school. She met Robinson at a banquet upon his return from Ethiopia and was impressed with his achievements and plans for the school.[636]

1936/09   Howard Crashes in Bendix Race
Benny Howard and his wife Maxine, or Mike as she preferred, flew *Mr. Mulligan* (DGA-6) in the 1936 Bendix Race from New York to Los Angeles.

Mr. Mulligan had won the Bendix Race the previous year and was one of the favorites to win again. While flying over New Mexico, a propeller came off the plane. The jolt caused Benny to black out for a few moments, but Mike was able to keep the plane upright. Together they maintained enough control to crash land in a clearing between some mountains.

The plane was totaled and both Benny and Mike were injured. Benny lost one leg and both Mike's legs were severely injured requiring months of hospitalization.[637]

1936/09/04   Women Win the Bendix Trophy Race
For the first time, two women, Blanche Noyes and Louise Thaden, beat a field almost wholly made up of men to win the Bendix Trophy Race from New York to Los Angeles.[638]

1936/12/31   Merrill Meigs Chairs Illinois Aero Commission
Merrill C. Meigs, became Chairman of the Illinois Aeronautics Commission on December 31, 1936.

The publisher of the *Chicago Herald and Examiner*, Meigs had been inspired by Lindbergh's transatlantic flight and had gotten his own pilot's license by the end of 1927. He flew often and used his newspaper to promote Chicago as an aviation center.

In the 1930s as Chairman of the Chicago Aero Commission, Meigs guided the development of Municipal Field. Both in his role with the Aero Commission and through his newspaper, Meigs emphasized the importance of airports in close proximity to the downtown area to eliminate time wasted commuting to the airport.

During WWII, Meigs worked as the aviation expert for the Office of Production Management in Washington. To facilitate his travels, he acquired a Howard DGA-15P.

Following the war, Meigs returned to the Chicago Aero Commission. In December 1948, Chicago opened a downtown airport on Northerly Island. The following year, the Commission renamed all three Chicago airports, designating the one on Northerly Island as Meigs Field.[639]

1937   Ford Sells Lansing Airport

By 1937, Ford Motor Co. had abandoned its aviation sideline to focus on automobiles. Ford's airport in Lansing was still an all-direction airport with no runways. After Ford sold it, and it became known as Chicago-Hammond Airport, and later Lansing Airport.[640]

1937   Tufts-Edgecumbe Starts at Pal-Waukee

In 1937, Al Tufts and George Edgecumbe started a Piper distributorship with associated services, such as charter, instruction, and maintenance. Both were Mt. Prospect residents, so they chose nearby Pal-Waukee as their base.[641]

In the 1940s, Tufts-Edgecumbe operated out of Ravenswood Airport, either in addition to or instead of Pal-Waukee. In 1940, Edgecumbe won Piper's top sales award for selling 117 airplanes.[642]

In 1942, Al Tufts began a Civilian Pilot Training Program giving elementary flight training for the military. At the end of the eight-week program students had completed 35 hours of flying and were able to perform basic maneuvers. Students simultaneously took ground school at either Lake Forest College or Loyola University. About 70% of each class of around a hundred students successfully completed the training.[643]

1937   Kling Wins Thompson Trophy

A farm boy from the Joliet area, Rudy Kling won the 1937 Thompson Trophy at the National Air Races in Cleveland.

Kling and his brother ran an auto repair shop when they got caught up with the excitement of Lindbergh's flight. Kling studied aerial navigation at night and hung around airports. At Wilhelmi Airport, south of Joliet, he became friends with Art Chester, who taught him to fly. Chester also instilled a love of air racing in Kling.

Kling rebuilt a Folkert SK-3 that he named *Jupiter, the Pride of Lemont,* which he entered in the NAR.[644]

1937/01/01   Howard Aircraft Is Born

Benjamin "Benny" Howard worked at a Curtiss factory in Texas, where he learned about aircraft design. On the side, he built a plane for a bootlegger, who called it a "Damn Good Airplane." Howard applied the DGA[a] identifier throughout his career.[645]

Howard moved to Chicago, where he flew for United out of Municipal. With his partner Gordon Israel, Howard continued designing and building planes, primarily for racing. Howard competed in the 1930 National Air Races (NAR) in Chicago without much success but set a speed record at the 1932 NAR in Cleveland.[646]

After sweeping the big three air races at the 1935 NAR in Cleveland, Howard used the winnings to kickstart his aircraft business and purchased Mattie Laird's old factory on 65th St., two blocks south of Municipal. On January 1, 1937, the Howard Aircraft Corp. came to life.[647]

The DGA-7, known as *Flanigan*, was based on *Mr. Mulligan* but had a smaller engine and longer wingspan making it more suitable for normal cross-country flying. The DGA-9, DGA-11, and DGA-12 were all variations on the same airframe with differing powerplants and other small details.[648]

In the 1930s, Howard's commercial planes found a niche with Hollywood and society people. The DGA-11, which cost $16,500 in 1930, boasted a luxury cabin and a top speed in excess of 200 mph.[649] Actor Wallace Beery, an accomplished pilot, had a fleet of Howards, including a DGA-8, DGA-9, and DGA-11, and he appeared in print ads for Howard

---

a   With the exception of the DGA-18, all of Benny Howard's DGA airplanes were single-engine, high-wing, closed-cabin monoplanes. The twin-engine, twin-tail executive Howard 500, produced in the 1960s, was made by Howard Aero of San Antonio, TX, and had no relation to Benny Howard or the Howard Aircraft Corp.

Aircraft. The CAA owned four Howards used to transport investigators to crash sites.[650]

In 1939, their top-of-the-line plane, the DGA-15, had a price tag just under $20,000 and was available with one of three engines.[651] In addition to society types, major corporations purchased the DGA-15. Among those were Shell Oil and Pure Oil, which each bought two, as well as Texaco, Humble Oil, Chicago and Southern Airways, and du Pont.[652]

1937/01/26   Pilot from 108th Squadron Saves Lives in Flood

In 1936, the 108th Aero Squadron from Municipal Field was restructured as the 108th Observation Squadron. It was attached directly to the Illinois National Guard without its previous association with the 33rd Aviation Division.

When extensive floods hit southern Illinois in January 1937, the 108th was called to assist. Winter storms created treacherous flying conditions. Despite the weather, the Squadron flew a variety of missions[a]: providing surveillance of levees, taking photos of affected areas, and dropping food and medicine to stranded people and fodder to livestock.

On January 26, weather conditions were so bad that all aircraft were grounded. Nevertheless, Capt. Wilson V. Newhall convinced his superiors that the situation was so grave that it warranted the risk of his life and plane.

Newhall spotted a levee being breached and radioed a warning to the ground in time to evacuate the area. Because of his flight, no lives were lost. For his heroic action Capt. Newhall was awarded the Illinois State Distinguished Service Medal (one of only three ever awarded). Newhall was later promoted to Maj. General and became the first Chief of Staff of the Illinois Air National Guard.[653]

1937/03/01   Fagg Becomes Head of Air Commerce Bureau

Chicagoan Fred D. Fagg Jr. succeeded Eugene Vidal as Director of the Air Commerce Bureau. After serving in WWI as a lieutenant in the 92nd Aero Squadron, Fagg graduated law school at Northwestern University.

In 1929, he participated in the Cook County study of airport safety. In September 1933, Governor Horner appointed Fagg as Chairman of the Illinois Aeronautics Commission, a position he held through 1936.

---

a   Hill states that the squadron flew open-cockpit O-30s. However, the only record of an O-30 is a single prototype XO-30 built by Curtiss. Other versions of the 108th's history indicate they started flying the closed-cockpit Douglas O-38 biplanes in 1935.

In 1930, he founded the Institute of Air Law at Northwestern and became director of the school's *Journal of Air Law*. Fagg served as a consultant to the Air Commerce Bureau before becoming director on March 1, 1937. He was the driving force behind the release of the Civil Air Regulations, a consolidation and revision of aviation regulations.[654]

1937/04/26   Air Assault on Guernica

German air forces crushed the Spanish city of Guernica on April 26, 1937, supporting the government of Generalissimo Franco during the Spanish Civil War. In a test of their air-assault tactics, the Luftwaffe's four-hour bombing campaign razed the city, killing as many as 1,600 civilians. The carnage inspired the painting *Guernica* by Pablo Picasso, which he completed only two months later.[655]

1937/05/06   Hindenburg Explosion

The Zeppelin *Hindenburg* exploded in flames while landing at Lakehurst, NJ.[656]

1937/07/02   Earhart Goes Missing

Amelia Earhart and Fred Noonan's Lockheed Electra never arrived at a mid-Pacific stop at Howland Island on her around-the-world trip.[657]

1937/08/28   Naval Air Squadron Moves to Curtiss-Reynolds

The U.S. Navy's aviation squadron, which had outgrown the facilities at Great Lakes, relocated to Curtiss-Reynolds Field in early 1937. The Navy rented the north half of Hangar One and invested an additional $120,000 in improving the facilities to accommodate more men and faster planes. On August 28, 1937, the Navy commissioned the new base that housed 18 planes, 20 officers and 120 cadets.[658]

1937/11/01   Civil Air Regulations (CAR)

The myriad of separate rules and regulations from the Air Commerce Bureau were gathered and organized into the Civil Air Regulations.[659]

1938   Piper Cub is Born

In 1938, Piper Aircraft Corp. introduced the popular J-3 Cub, which became one of the world's most popular airplanes. Over 19,000 were produced between 1938 and 1947 for both military and civilian use. The military versions, which featured a skylight and rear windows for improved visibility, were designated O-59 and L-4 (before/after April 1942) in the Army and NE in the Navy. For a time, the name Cub became a generic term among the general public for all small airplanes no matter the manufacturer or model.

The J-3 is an outgrowth of the E-2 designed and introduced by Taylor Aircraft in Bradford, PA. Investor William T. Piper bought controlling interest in the company in 1930 but Piper retained both the Taylor Aircraft name and Clarence Gilbert Taylor as President and designer.

Taylor continued enhancing and improving the plane over the years. While Taylor was on sick leave, Piper implemented some changes by designer Walter Jamouneau as the J-2. Upon his return, Taylor was furious about the decision, and he and Piper parted ways in December 1935 with Taylor subsequently starting the Taylorcraft Aircraft Co.

Fire destroyed the Taylor factory in Bradford in 1937. In 1938, Piper opened a new factory in Lock Haven, PA, where the renamed Piper Aircraft Corp. started producing the upgraded J-3 Cub.[660]

1938   First Female Helicopter Pilot

In 1938, German Hanna Reitsch flew the Focke-Wulf Fw-61 (later called the Focke-Achegelis Fa-61), the world's first successful helicopter. A distinguished aviator, Reitsch also flew a variety of gliders, bombers, dive bombers, fighters, and the Me-163 rocket plane. She was also the only person of either gender to fly a V-1 rocket.[661]

1938   Cornelius Coffey and Willa Brown Form Aviation School

Willa Brown may have been romantically involved with John Robinson before he volunteered with the Ethiopian airforce in April 1935. During Robinson's absence, Brown developed a relationship with Cornelius Coffey and the couple married in 1937.[662]

Robinson and Coffey parted ways professionally in 1937. In addition to whatever personal conflicts existed over the marriage, there were disputes about operating the business. A major issue was Robinson's refusal to obtain a Transport Pilot's License. Coffey felt that Robinson's flight instruction, cargo, and commuter flights without the license jeopardized their charter.[663]

In 1938, Coffey started the Coffey School of Aeronautics at Harlem Airport. It was the first federally certified flight school owned by an African American.[a] Willa Brown, who received her Commercial License that year, was

---

[a]   Launius dates the school opening in 1935, but the discrepancy might be when the school became certified.

Coffey's partner in the school, assisting in both the business and aviation areas. Other Challenger members also taught flying and mechanics.[664]

Although the students were predominantly African American, Coffey was known for accepting all races and genders. One estimate stated that 10% of his students were white and 10% female.[665]

1938   United Flights at Curtiss-Reynolds

As a convenience to North Shore residents, United Air Lines started offering flights between Curtiss-Reynolds and New York, with intermediate stops at Cleveland and Philadelphia.[666]

1938   Burris Field Gets New Life

In 1938, Frederic Stripe turned over the position as airport manager of Burris Field to Wayne Carpenter, who also worked there as a mechanic.

Carpenter worked to revitalize the airport by lowering rates and sponsoring a new Economy Flying Club. By 1949, there were four unpaved runways, the longest of which was 2,500 ft. In the 1950s, a new club, the Brewster Flying Club, was named after Irene Brewster, who was Carpenter's assistant and handled many of the operational details at the airport.

In 1954, a Civil Air Patrol squadron was formed at Waukegan (Burris). On July 18th, they held a public event with an air show featuring the Cole Brothers Flying Circus, food, drink, and dancing.[667]

1938/01/26   First ILS Airliner Landing

The first landing of a scheduled airliner using the Instrument Landing System (ILS) was made by a Boeing 247 at Pittsburgh.[668]

1938/05/15–21   Air Mail Week

For an entire week in May 1938, the U.S. celebrated the 20th anniversary of Air Mail Service. Special flights and observances were conducted all around the country, publicizing the service as the wave of tomorrow.[669]

Grover C Nash, a member of Challenger Air Pilots Assn., made a flight from Mattoon, IL, to Chicago, becoming the first African American pilot commissioned to fly air mail.[670]

Pal-Waukee's unique celebration consisted of special delivery to and from Arlington Heights. A plane from Pal-Waukee dropped mail bags at Arlington Park Race Track. Then, letters from local residents addressed to destinations around the nation were collected at the race track and delivered to Pal-Waukee Pony-Express style using a three-horse relay.[671]

Another flight during that week was made by an autogyro that landed on the Chicago Main Post Office building spanning the Congress Expressway.[672]

1938/08/22   CAA Created

The Civil Aeronautic Act, signed into law on June 23, 1938, created the Civil Aeronautics Authority to regulate air transportation, replacing the existing Air Commerce Bureau. The new Authority had regulatory powers governing air mail and airline fares and rates, air navigation and traffic, and airports.[673]

1938/10/18   Bauhaus Comes to Chicago

The former head of the Bauhaus School of Design, Ludwig Mies van der Rohe, emigrated to Chicago where he joined the faculty of the Armour Institute of Technology.

The German school had revolutionized the appearance of the contemporary world introducing a modern, no-frills design approach not only to architecture, but also to furniture and other household objects. With the rise of the Nazis, the Bauhaus faculty left Germany.

From his new Chicago home, Mies introduced the International Style of architecture characterized by simple glass and steel walls. Mies, along with Frank Lloyd Wright, continued Chicago's dominant role at the heart of architecture in the last half of the 20th century.[674]

1939   American Airlines Headquarters Leaves Chicago

C.R. Smith, American Airlines CEO, moved the company's headquarters, departing Chicago for New York.[675]

1939   United Airlines Develops Static Discharger

To reduce radio interference caused by static buildup on an airplane, United Air Lines developed the static discharger, small metal strips attached to the trailing edge of wings and tail.[676]

1939   Turgeon Takes Over Sky Harbor

The lavish Sky Harbor Airport, opened on the eve of the Great Depression, suffered greatly from the poor economy. Despite a few bright spots, such as the Hunter Brothers endurance flight and the American Legion's Air Meet, the luxury airport was essentially abandoned and fell into disrepair.

In 1939, Bill Turgeon and some associates purchased Sky Harbor. They demolished the beautiful but decrepit terminal building with the Patrushka Club and started the Turgeon Flying School in a smaller, functional building.

In the early 1940s as the war approached, the Navy began training pilots at Sky Harbor and the airport added a second hangar. Sky Harbor also became home to an Aviation Country Club, like Pal-Waukee and other airports.[677]

1939   Al Tufts Passes

Only two years after forming Tufts-Edgecumbe, Al Tufts died unexpectedly in 1939. His friend and business partner, George Edgecumbe, continued to associate Tufts' name with the company until it disbanded in August 1991.[678]

1939   Washington Park Airport Breaks Away

In 1939, a group of seven pilots, dissatisfied with the facilities at Chicago Heights Airport, secured 160 acres in Homewood on 187th St. between Halsted and Center streets, calling it Washington Park Airport.

The group constructed two hangars and several grass runways that were 125 ft. wide. Limestone outlined the edges of the runways for improved daytime visibility. Kerosene smudge pots did the same at night.

Washington Park Airport became a busy place, serving transient pilots from around the area. The airport provided a shuttle service, transporting pilots and passengers to and from the Washington Park Race Track, as well as to a nearby auto track and dog track.[679]

In September 1942, the airport began training military service pilots who performed vital noncombat activities such as towing targets, ferrying planes, and flying cargo.

Later, two fires substantially damaged the airport. The first, on the night of August 5, 1947, was started by lightning and destroyed more than 15 planes as well as airport records and pilot logs. On February 7, 1950, workmen sparked another fire that destroyed more planes. The airport closed in the 1960s.[680]

1939/04/01   Zero Goes First

The famous Japanese Zero made its first flight. The Mitsubishi A6M, Allied code name "Zeke," entered combat in China in July 1940.[681]

1939/03/02   Suicide Jones Sets Parachute Altitude Record

After several failed attempts, African American aviator and parachutist William "Suicide" Jones established the official record for Delayed Parachute Jump on March 2, 1939, at Chicago Municipal Airport. Wearing a face mask and fur-lined outfit for protection, his plane climbed for over three hours before reaching an altitude where the air temperature was –45°. Jones jumped out the plane and deployed his chute at 800 ft. for a successful landing. The official barograph established the jump record of 24,468 ft.

For years, Jones, a member of the Challenger Air Pilots Assn., had thrilled crowds with parachute jumps from 10,000 ft. and higher. Not content, Jones wanted to push the boundaries and establish the record for a Delayed Parachute Jump.

Jones made his first attempt on August 28, 1938 at Dixie Airport, but for unknown reasons his jump was not recorded.[682]

His next attempt on September 1, 1938, was at Markham Airport in Harvey. Jones jumped from 29,400 ft. and opened his chute at 2,400 ft. before landing, setting a new recored. Later, the record was classified as "unofficial" because his instruments were not properly sealed.[683]

A third attempt on November 28, 1938 when Jones again jumped from 29–30,000 ft. where the temperature was –25°. He deployed his chute at 2,500 ft. However, Jones was not attired for the extreme temperature and was unconscious from exposure when he landed in an empty field at 167th St. and Wood St.[684]

1939/05/08   Challenger Goes to Washington

During 1939, Chicago-based Challenger Air Pilots Assn. was reorganizing itself in 1939 into a national group called the National Airmen Assn. of America (NAAA). Some members made a goodwill tour to promote the planned new organization and a national conference to be held in Chicago later in the year. The tour included a stop in Washington, DC, to lobby to allow Negros in the Army Air Corps and other defense efforts.

Two Challenger pilots, Dale White and Chauncey Spencer were to make the journey. They departed Harlem Airport in an old Lincoln-Page biplane they named *Old Faithful*. The well-worn plane was very basic with no lights or brakes. The only instruments were oil and speed gauges.

Not unexpectedly, their cross-country trip was fraught with problems. After a brief mechanical delay in Auburn IN, they continued to Sherwood, OH, where the engine stopped. They made an emergency landing in a corn field, where they diagnosed a broken crankshaft. Cornelius Coffey brought a new one from Chicago and installed it on the plane.

After several days, they departed Sherwood for Pittsburgh. Without lights on the plane, as dark approached they landed at the Morgantown, WV, airport. Ground personnel were less than welcoming of the two black pilots. They strongly urged White and Spencer to buy some gas and move on.

With no choice but to fly, White and Spencer took off again. They spotted an airport beacon and then an airliner heading toward Pittsburgh. The followed the big plane and landed in Pittsburgh.

But all was not well. Upon landing, they were informed they had violated numerous CAA regulations, including failing to maintain proper distance from the airliner. The CAA grounded them pending a hearing. Fortunately, Robert L. Vann, the publisher of the *Pittsburgh Courier*, successfully pleaded their case. The two made it to Washington with only one additional, minor mechanical problem.

In Washington, the Chicago pilots met with Edgar Brown, the president of the Negro Federal Workers Employees Union who would become the lobbyist for the NAAA. Brown took White and Spencer to visit several congressmen, including Rep. Everett Dirksen of Illinois. Dirksen later introduced an amendment to the Civil Aeronautics bill prohibiting discrimination in the benefits of the Act.

The group also met with other Illinois Congressmen, including Sen. James M. Slattery and Rep. Arthur Mitchell. Mitchell was the only black Congressman of the period and the first elected from Illinois.

Between their formal meetings, the group had a chance encounter in the halls with Sen. Harry Truman of Missouri. As a member of the Military Affairs Committee, Truman was influential on all bills that pertained to the military and associated programs, such as the CPTP. Truman was very receptive as White and Spencer related their story and explained the desire of the black community to be accepted into the military.

Truman was so impressed with the pair that he made arrangements to see their airplane. After looking at *Old Faithful* and asking questions about their flight, Truman politely refused a ride. Truman was quoted as telling the pair, "If you had the guts to fly this plane from Chicago to Washington, then I have the guts to see that you get what you ask for."

Later that summer, Congress, spurred by Sen. Truman and Rep. Dirksen, authorized the CPTP program with specific inclusion for African American training. Years later as President, Harry Truman finally desegregated the military.[685]

1939/05/15   Founding of AOPA

The Aircraft Owners and Pilots Assn. (AOPA) was founded to look out for the interest of general aviation.[686]

1939/06/27   CPTP Signed into Law

President Roosevelt established the Civil Pilot Training Program on June 27, 1939. The program provided money to colleges and flying schools to train additional pilots in anticipation of looming hostilities.

As a result of the meeting with Chauncey Spencer and Dale White of the Challenger Air Pilots Assn., Sen. Everett Dirksen amended the Act to specify that "none of the benefits of training or programs shall be denied on account of race, creed, or color."[687]

1939/08   Chicago Girls Flying Club Show at Pal-Waukee

In August 1939, the Chicago Girls Flying Club thrilled 20,000 spectators at Pal-Waukee Air Port with their eighth annual air show. Ten flyers competed in events including a cross-country race making a round trip between Pal-Waukee and Naperville. Other events involved faux-bomb dropping and spot landing competitions.

One novelty race started when the pilots got in their planes, flew around the airport and landed. Then they ran 100 yards where they ate a hamburger and drank a soda before running back to their planes for another flight around the field.[688]

1939/08/16   Challengers Go National

The National Airmen Assn. of America (NAAA), was formally formed in Chicago on August 16, 1939.

The National Airmen Assn. (NAA), as the group was commonly called, was an outgrowth of the Challenger Air Pilots Assn., a Chicago organization of African American men and women pilots and aircraft mechanics. Early in 1939, *Chicago Defender* editor Enoch Waters, a pilot and member of Challenger, had suggested the group widen its perspective to encompass the whole country rather than just Chicago. Before it's official formation, the group reached out to African American pilots across the country to create a broad base of members.

Cornelius Coffey, Willa Brown, and Enoch Waters were the NAA's primary leaders. The *Chicago Defender* provided office space to the new organization.

The same month that it formed, the NAAA held its first national conference in Chicago, drawing hundreds of black aviators from around the country. Much publicity for the NAAA came through the *Chicago Defender*, which had a national reach. Also, during their cross-country trip to and from

Washington, DC the previous May, Challenger members Dale White and
Chauncey Spencer promoted the new organization at stops along the way. By
1940, the NAAA had branches in most major cities outside the South.[689]

1939/08/27   First Turbojet Flies

In Germany, Ernst Heinkel developed the first flying turbojet aircraft,
the He-178.[690]

1939/09/01   WWII Begins as Germany Invades Poland

Germany applied the lessons they learned at Guernica, Spain, as they
launched a blitzkrieg against Poland. For the first time in history, air
assaults were an essential, rather than an ancillary, element of combat.[691]

1939/10/14   Coffey School Approved for CPTP

As soon as there was talk about establishing a Civilian Pilot Training
Program, Willa Brown and Cornelius Coffey lobbied government officials
including Senators Harry Truman (MO) and Everett Dirksen (IL) to ensure
the Coffey School's participation.

Their efforts paid off. Less than six months after the CPTP started,
Coffey School of Aeronautics was formally approved as part of the CPTP.
Coffey taught flying and mechanics.

Using her teaching experience, Brown conducted ground school at
Chicago's Wendell Phillips High School. Brown's MBA made her perfect for
handling the administrative end of the business. Also, being qualified in
both flying and mechanics, Brown could fill in as needed. The Federal
government recognized Brown's talent and in 1940 made her the
Coordinator for the entire Chicago Unit of the CPTP.

The Coffey School was the only black CPTP school not affiliated with a
university. The Curtiss-Wright Aeronautics University along with the Coffey
School made Chicago the only city in the U.S. with two CPTP schools
accepting African Americans.

The CPTP program at Coffey School had trained more than 500 pilots
by the end of the war. Many went on to become Tuskegee Airmen and later
the first black commercial airline pilots in the country.[692]

1939/11/30   Eisenhower Gets Private License

While on staff for Gen. Douglas McArthur, in the Philippines, Lt. Col.
Dwight Eisenhower learned to fly and soloed in 1938. The following year he
earned his Private Pilot's License at Fort Lewis, WA, but was not considered

a military pilot. Although he did not keep his license current, Eisenhower became the first President[a] to have received a pilot's license.[693]

1939/12/02   New York City Opens an Airport

New York Municipal Airport, previously known as the Glenn H. Curtiss Airport, opened for commercial traffic on December 2, 1939. New York City had made major improvements to accommodate commercial traffic. In 1947, the airport was renamed LaGuardia Field.[694]

---

a   Both Presidents George H.W. Bush and George W. Bush were military pilots.

1940–1944

1940   First Chicago TV Station

John Balaban, who owned a chain of Chicago luxury theaters, started the first television station in Illinois, WBKB.[695]

1940   Chicago Handles a Quarter of U.S. Passengers

Of the 2.8 million passengers that boarded airplanes in the U.S. in 1940, slightly over 25% of them (704,846) boarded in Chicago.[696]

1940   United Introduces Two-Tier Fares

Attempting to expand the passenger market, United created a two-tier price structure for air travel on its San Francisco to Los Angeles route. Tickets for flights on the older Boeing 247s were substantially cheaper than on the newer DC-3s ($13.90 vs. $18.90). United only kept the fare structure for a couple of years. After WWII, several airlines began experimenting with multiple fare levels.[697]

1940   Navy Purchases Curtiss-Reynolds Field

In early 1940, the Navy purchased Curtiss-Reynolds Field and all facilities including Hangar One for $530,000. The price represented the economic hardship of the airfield which cost $3 million initially and in which the owners had invested considerably more since the 1929 opening. The Navy renamed the airport Glenview Naval Air Station.[698]

1940/02/23   First Black Woman Gets License Through CPTP

In Baltimore, Dorothy Layne McIntyre was the first African American woman to receive her pilot's license through the Civilian Pilot Training Program on February 23, 1940. She applied to become a member of the Women's Airforce Service Pilots, but was denied because of her race.[699]

1940/05/13   First Helicopter With Tail Rotor

The Sikorsky VS-300 made it first flight in Stratford, CT on May 13, 1940. It was the first helicopter to use a tail rotor to counter the rotation of the main rotor.[700]

1940/06/30   CAA Is Divided Into Two Organizations

On June 3, 1940, the Civil Aviation Authority was reorganized into the Civil
Aeronautics Administration in the Dept. of Commerce and the independent
Civil Aeronautics Board. [701]

1940/07/03   Northrup Tests Flying Wing

Northrop Corp. began flight tests on the N1M on July 3, 1940. The
Northrup test plane consisted of a wing without a traditional fuselage.[702]

1940/07/08   Pressurized Airliner Enters Service

TWA began flying the Boeing 307 Stratoliner, the first airliner with a
pressurized cabin. Pressurization allowed the airline to fly higher to avoid
storms and turbulence at lower altitudes.[703]

1940/12/04   United Flight 21 Crashes Near Municipal

A DC-3, United Airlines Flight 21, which originated at La Guardia, crashed
as it was approaching Chicago Municipal the evening of December 4, 1940.

The pilot had made one go-around to clear ice from the windshield. On
final approach during the second pass, the plane stalled at an altitude of
160 ft., crashing a half-mile from the airport. The plane struck a house at
6350 S. Keating Ave. There were no injuries on the ground, but all three of
the crew and seven of the thirteen passengers died in the crash. The CAB
determined icing was the main cause of the crash but a contributing factor
was the pilot's selection of the short NW-SE runway.[704]

1941   Willie Howell Starts Airport

In 1941, Willis "Willie" Howell opened a small airport in what was then
Blue Island (later Crestwood). Howell bought a 137-acre parcel at Cicero
Ave. and Rt. 83[a] for $18,000. Over the years, the airport grew from one to
three turf and crushed gravel runways. By 1971, two of those runways were
paved.[705]

1941   Navy Acquires St. Charles Airport

In the 1920s, St. Charles Airport (currently DuPage Airport) opened with
turf runways serving pilots of DuPage and Kane Counties. In 1941, the
Navy took over the airport and paved two of the runways.[706]

---

a   The location has also been listed as Cicero and Cal Sag Road or Cicero and 127th Street.

1941/02   108th Squadron Mobilized for War

With the buildup to the war, the 108th Observation Squadron stationed at Municipal Field began doing live-fire exercises. The unit was equipped with North American O-47s. The low-winged monoplane had a three-man crew and was armed with one forward-facing and one rear-facing 30-caliber machine guns.

In February 1941, the Army Air Corps mobilized the 108th to active duty, where the squadron spent three months towing targets at Fort Sheridan.

The squadron was stationed in Michigan, Tennessee, and Louisiana before being shipped overseas. The squadron was initially scheduled to move to Iceland for submarine patrols over the North Atlantic. However their O-47s were unsuitable for cold climates, and the following January they were deployed instead to protect the Panama Canal.[707]

1941/03   Black Aviators Trained at Rantoul

The Army Air Corps had refused to accept African Americans into service until they were confronted with outstanding proficiency scores. Reluctantly, they admitted blacks into the 99th Pursuit Squadron. Since the Tuskegee Institute's flight program was not yet operational, the Air Corps assigned training for nonflying mechanics, armorers, weather forecasters, and supply clerks to Chanute Field. Chanute provided segregated housing, educational, and recreational facilities for the recruits.[708]

1941/05/15   First British Jet Flies

The Gloster E28/39, Whittle, began flight testing, becoming the first British jet in the air. The groundbreaking turbine engine was designed by RAF officer, Frank Whittle.[709]

1941/06/16   Washington National Airport Opens

Washington National Airport opened in the nation's capitol, on June 16, 1941. The airport's newness and location made it immediately popular. In the first six months of operation, more than 300,000 passengers went through the airport plus more than 2 million spectators visited to see what it was all about.[710]

1941/06/30   Municipal Rededicated Without Railroad

With war on the horizon, Municipal Airport took on military significance. However, tracks of the Chicago and Western Indiana Railroad (also known as the Belt Line) bisected the airport and severely hindered air operations. The railroad had a perpetual lease and was reluctant to move its tracks.

The railroad experienced pressure from a number of sources. The military appealed to their patriotic responsibility. The city threatened to tear out the railroad's tracks elsewhere around the city where they crossed streets without authorization. Finally, Congress passed special legislation forcing the railroad to relocate the tracks. Eventually the Belt Line relented and agreed to move their tracks north of 55th St., away from the airport.[a]

On May 1, 1941, a ceremony marked the beginning of track removal from Municipal Airport. The ceremony featured Mayor Ed Kelly, Airport Manager John Casey, and a host of other city officials and railroad executives. Once the tracks were gone, the airport paved over the rail bed, making it into runway 9L/27R.

On June 30, 1941, 350,000 people turned out for a rededication ceremony at the start of operations of the enhanced airport. With the exception of Hale School, Muni finally had full control of the airport property.[711]

WWII changed the nature of air travel. Leisurely trips, such as by rail, were a luxury. Time became a precious commodity. Many people urgently needed to arrive at their destinations as quickly as possible and were willing to put up with the expense and discomfort of flying in order to reduce transit time. At the center of the industrial heartland, Municipal's traffic grew rapidly as businessmen and government officials rushed to meetings for the war effort. [712]

1941/07   Final Laird Airplane Produced

The E.M. Laird Airplane Co. was forced to shut its doors in July 1941. The Great Depression had limited money spent by air racers on newer, better-performing planes. Increasingly air mail and airlines required a greater quantity of planes than could be produced by a custom shop such as Liard's. Likewise, Laird's lack of production capability meant he was unable to secure any military contracts.[713]

Matty Laird became President of LaPorte Corp., a subsidiary of Metal Door and Trim in LaPorte, IN, which had received some aircraft subcontracts. Laird moved to the Indiana community and worked tirelessly through the war, producing subassemblies for B-24, B-25, SBD, C-46, PBM and other aircraft.

---

a   Scamehorn (p. 174) states the relocation occurred in 1934. Young (p. 182) claims that
     Chicago and the railroad reached agreement about the relocation in 1937.

After the war, Laird retired from full-time aviation involvement, but he continued as a consultant for LaPorte Corp. and managed Ashburn Field until it closed in 1951. When he retired, Laird moved south, spending time in Florida and North Carolina. [714]

1941/11/01   CAA Operates Control Towers

Reliable air transportation was vital to the war effort, and the CAA took over operation of all air traffic control, both towers and routes, on November 1, 1941.

Prior to WWII, air traffic control towers at airports were the responsibility of the airport owner. Control by the CAA provided more consistent and secure operations.

Municipal, like other large airports, had a staff that used radios to communicate with pilots. Previously, this was all coordinated by the airport and paid for by the City of Chicago.

Following the war, the CAA began returning operation of the air traffic control system to local authorities. Inconsistency quickly became apparent and in 1947, Congress began appropriating funds for the CAA to resume operation of control towers.[715]

1941/12/01   Illinois CAP Squadrons Started

A week before Pearl Harbor, on December 1, 1941, the Civil Air Patrol organized the first groups in Illinois. Group 611-1 created its first three squadrons in Illinois at Sky Harbor, Machesny Field, and Pal-Waukee. On December 8, Jack Vilas was named the state Wing Commander.

The Civil Air Patrol was created to utilize civilian equipment and personnel to supplement the military. CAP units in the Chicago area performed tasks such as search and rescue, courier service, and target towing. It also made planes available to transport people around the region for bond drives and defense-related business. By March 1, 1942, the CAP had organized nine groups organized in Illinois with 1,880 members, 35% of the pilots in the state.[716]

1941/12/01   U.S. Planes and Pilots Required to Be Certificated

Until this time, there had been a patchwork of Federal and local regulations determined by involvement in interstate commerce and other factors. As part of security measures in anticipation of an upcoming war, as of December 1, 1941, the government required Federal licensing and certification of both pilots and planes.[717]

1941/12/07   Pearl Harbor Attack Brings Restrictions

Following the Japanese attack, the U.S. placed severe restrictions on aviation. For several weeks, all small airports were closed. In order to reopen, airports needed to have a 24-hour manager on duty plus an armed guard at night. Planes at unguarded airports needed the wings and propellers removed. All pilot licenses were reissued after CAA clearance and included the pilot's picture as well as fingerprints. New requirements provided that departure clearance required a physical check of the pilot and plane by the airport manager.[718]

1942   Glenview Naval Air Station Construction Program

With U.S. entry into WWII, in 1942 the Navy undertook a crash $12.5-million construction program at Glenview Naval Air Station. In 121 working days, they laid 1.5 million square yards of concrete making two 200 ft.-wide runways, one 6,500 ft. long, the other 5,000 ft.

Additional new facilities included barracks, a mess hall, fire station, gymnasium, hospital, and chapel along with associated streets, sidewalks, streetlights and more. Operations expanded even while the construction was in progress. Cadet training requirements increased to 100 hours. The base housed 350 aircraft and 5,000 personnel. [719]

1942   Navy Builds Drones in DeKalb

In 1942, the U.S. Navy initiated a secret project in DeKalb. Interstate Aircraft and Engineering Corp., the maker of the two-seat high-wing Cadet, had a contract to build a wooden airplane. They acquired the Arlington Furniture Co., which had a factory with the largest furniture assembly line in the country. The Navy also acquired land nearby and constructed a hangar and runways on a secure airfield which was known as Interstate Airport.

The newly constructed factory and airfield built and tested an unmanned drone, the TDR-1. The twin-engine plane had a cockpit that was used during testing but empty during actual missions. The drone had a television camera and radio that enabled the drone to be controlled from another airplane. Each one carried a two-thousand-pound bomb. Nearly 200 Interstate drones saw service in the South Pacific.[720]

1942   Lewis School Goes Navy

Lewis Holy Name School of Aeronautics had added flight training and similar aviation courses during the buildup prior to WWII. In 1942, the high school closed and the Navy took over the facilities. The Navy used Lewis to train flight instructors who would go on to train recruits.

In 1944, the Navy departed and civilian classes resumed in the fall of 1944. The archdiocese reorganized the school to include a junior college as well as the high school. Under the GI Bill, returning servicemen filled its programs, which were changing from technical into a traditional arts and sciences curriculum.

By 1949, Lewis had dropped the high school and begun admitting women to its junior college. The school began awarding Bachelor's degrees in 1952 under its new name, Lewis College of Science and Technology.

To this day, Lewis has continued a strong aviation program that includes specialties in flight, maintenance, air traffic control, and administration. [721]

1942   Huge Hotel Becomes Barracks

The lavish Stevens Hotel (currently the Chicago Hilton) did not weather the Depression well and went bankrupt in the late 1930s. In 1942, the U.S. Army purchased the Stevens Hotel for $6 million, down substantially from its $30 million construction price. The Army Air Corps used the hotel as a radio training center and barracks, housing 10,000 air cadets. [722]

1942   Howard Aircraft War Production

The Depression hit Howard Aircraft hard and while they still sold a few planes, there was no demand for new designs. In 1941, Benny Howard sold the company.

By the beginning of WWII, about 80 Howard aircraft had been built. The military commandeered the civilian Howards, converting them into air ambulances and officer transport planes designated the UC-70. During the war, Howard built 525 DGA-15s for the Navy as the NH-1 instrument trainer, the GH-1 and GH-3 utility transports, and the GH-2 Nightingale air ambulance.[723]

Howard was the only Illinois factory, other than Douglas, during the war that produced complete aircraft for the military during the war.[724]

Production outgrew the factory at Municipal, so Howard Aircraft built another factory in West Chicago across the street from the St. Charles Airport (now the DuPage Airport). The company produced a new design, the DGA-18 (also called the DGA-125), with a low wing and open cockpit that was used for the Civilian Pilot Training Program. Howard also received a license from Fairchild to build PT-23s.

Even before the war ended, the government began phasing out military contracts and the Howard plant closed in 1944.[725]

1942/01/13   108th Squadron Goes to Panama

A year after being mobilized, the 108th Observation Squadron became the first National Guard aviation unit to serve overseas in WWII, when it received orders for Howard Field in Panama. Although still designated an Observation Squadron, the unit defended the Canal Zone with a variety of A-18s, B-18s, L-4s, O-47s, O-49s, P-36s, and P-39s.

In June 1943, the observation squadron was redesignated the 108th Reconnaissance Squadron. However, the tide of the war had turned and the Panama Canal was no longer threatened. In November 1943, the 108th was officially disbanded and its personnel reassigned to other units.[726]

1942/02/20   Butch O'Hare Becomes Ace

Annapolis graduate and Naval aviator Lt. Edward Henry "Butch" O'Hare served in an F4F Wildcat squadron on the USS *Lexington*. O'Hare was under the command of Lt. Commander John Thatch, developer of the "Thatch Weave" aerial tactic.

While in route on February 20, 1942, to disrupt Japanese shipping, the *Lexington* was spotted by a Japanese scout plane. Other Wildcats dispatched the first wave of bombers headed for the *Lexington*. When a second wave of bombers was spotted, O'Hare and five other Wildcats went up to intercept.

Except for O'Hare and his wingman, the other Wildcats were out of position to reach the nine incoming bombers. When they engaged, his wingman's guns jammed but O'Hare didn't hesitate to attack alone and downed five of the nine attackers. Not only did O'Hare become an ace in a single engagement, he became the Navy's first ace. By the time he was out of ammunition, the rest of his squadron was in position and finished off the remaining bombers.

O'Hare's heroism was credited with saving the *Lexington*. He was promoted to Lt. Commander and awarded the Medal of Honor, the Navy's first in WWII. As a national hero, O'Hare spent time stateside going on bond tours and boosting morale.

Returning to combat, O'Hare flew an F6F Hellcat off the USS *Enterprise*. On November 26, 1943, O'Hare embarked on two firsts for the Navy: a night combat mission and a mission combining two Hellcats with a TBF Avenger, which was large enough to carry radar. O'Hare's group launched

to stop incoming Japanese bombers and his plane went down during the
ensuing firefight. His aircraft was never found.[727]

1942/02/25   LA Defends Against Air Raid

Following the bombing of Pearl Harbor, tensions ran high in the Los
Angeles area because of the concentration of aircraft manufacturers, Navy
and other military centers. In late December 1941, a Japanese submarine
sank one ship and damaged another off the L.A. coast. Just a few days
earlier, another Japanese submarine shelled a nearby offshore oil field.

In the early morning hours of February 25, 1942, three newly installed
radar stations picked up an unidentified blip heading for L.A. At 2:25 a.m.,
air raid warnings went off. Over a 40-mile stretch from Santa Monica to
Long Beach, anti-aircraft batteries began firing at suspected targets.

By the time the All Clear sounded at 7:21 a.m., more than 1,400
anti-aircraft shells and countless rounds of smaller arms fire lit the night
sky over L.A.

In the end, officials concluded it was a false alarm. The blip was never
absolutely identified but was probably a weather balloon.[728]

1942/03/07   First Integrated CAP Squadron

The Illinois Wing of the CAP organized the first desegregated squadron in
the nation, accepting African American and Caucasian members at Harlem
Airport on March 7, 1942.

Cornelius Coffey was named Commander of the unit and Willa Brown
became the Squadron Adjutant, becoming the first black commander and
black female officer respectively. Most of the personnel were associated
with the National Airmen's Association or the Coffey School of Aeronautics,
which was a feeder school for Tuskegee Institute.[729]

1942/06/09   Douglas Expands Its Factory

On June 9, 1942, Douglas Aircraft announced that its factory at Municipal
was at capacity and they needed a larger facility. Douglas chose a 1,347-
acre plot in Orchard Place, IL, west of Bensenville. By the end of June,
construction started, and the factory began producing aircraft before the
end of the year.

Douglas chose the location because three rail lines provided easy access
to the site. The $20 million factory would eventually employ more than
15,000 workers, most from the surrounding area. Because of wartime steel
restrictions, the main assembly building, with more than 2 million sq. ft. of

floor space, was primarily constructed of wood making it the largest all-wood factory in the world. The first of 655 C-54s rolled off the assembly line on July 30, 1943.[730]

1942/08/01   Carrier Qualifications Begin at GNAS

On August 1, 1942, the Carrier Qualification Training Unit began operations at Glenview Naval Air Station under command of the Naval Air Station.

Two coal-burning side-wheel excursion ships, the *Seeandbee* and the *Greater Buffalo* had their superstructures replaced by a simulated carrier deck and were renamed the USS *Wolverine* and USS *Sable* respectively. By war's end, the two ships qualified over 15,000 pilots and handled 135,000 landings with a loss of only 200 aircraft. The Navy decommissioned the two carriers on November 7, 1945, and ultimately sold them for scrap.

Glenview also trained aircarrier deck crews. A full-size carrier deck was constructed inside Hangar One so deck crews could train and qualify throughout the year.[731]

1942/09   Prosperi Airport Opens

Ed Prosperi opened a small airport in September 1942 on Harlem Ave. about five miles north of Lincoln Highway (US-30) near Tinley Park. Propseri Airport started with a single grass field on which pilots could land or takeoff in any direction. By 1951, it had three unpaved runways.[732]

1942/09   Navy Opens Landing Field in Libertyville

The Navy established a landing field in Libertyville in September 1942. Originally called Allendale, it was soon renamed Libertyville Naval Outlying Landing Field (NOLF).

The NOLFs, also called satellite fields, were used by Glenview Naval Air Station (GNAS) to distribute training flights. By using multiple NOLFs simultaneously, GNAS could provide more practice for many more pilots than if they only used the Air Station's runways.

Like other NOLFs, Libertyville was originally built with grass runways, but it was the only NOLF to have them replaced by four concrete runways. Libertyville was also the only NOLF with an additional fifth runway made of wood in the dimensions of a carrier deck complete with catapult and arresting gear. It allowed pilots to practice prior to actual carrier landings.[733]

1942/10   Chicagoland Airport Takes Root

The Navy leased a 185-acre field in October 1942, near the intersection of Milwaukee Ave. (US 45) and Half Day Rd. (IL 22). The land was originally in the Village of Half Day but later became a part of Lincolnshire.

Half Day Landing Field was one of the outlying practice fields used by the Glenview Naval Air Station. The Navy continued using Half Day until shortly after the war, closing it in late 1945 or early 1946 when it was purchased to become Chicagoland Airport.[734]

1942/10/01   First U.S. Jet Plane Tested

A Bell XP-59A Airacomet made the first flight of an American jet aircraft at Muroc Army Airfield.[a] Two GE I-A turbine engines were developed based on Frank Whittle's design patented in 1930.[735]

1942/12/02   First Nuclear Reaction

In Chicago Pile No. 1, located at the University of Chicago under the football stadium Stagg Field, Enrico Fermi achieved the first controlled release of atomic energy. Scientists with briefcases handcuffed to their wrists regularly traveled through Chicago Municipal on B-17s to work on the project.[736]

1942/12/07   CPTP Becomes WTS

The CAA redesignated the Civilian Pilot Training Program into the War Training Service on the first anniversary of the attack on Pearl Harbor. The new name reflected changes in the program that had been made to more closely align with the needs of the Army and Navy. By the time the program ended in 1944, about 300,000 pilots had been trained.[737]

1943   Fish Hassell Back in the Arctic

In August 1928, Bruce "Fish" Hassell attempted the first Great Circle Route to Sweden but ran short on fuel and landed on a Greenland icecap.[738]

During WWII, the Army recalled Hassell to active duty to utilize his Great Circle expertise. Around 1943, Col. Hassell was assigned to construct an air base, Blue West One, on the southern tip of Greenland as a stopping point to ferry planes to Europe. Later, Hassell received responsibility for the entire Crystal I route ferrying aircraft into the European theater.

a   Now Edwards Air Force Base.

Following the war, Hassell was in charge of building a base at Thule, Greenland, the most northerly of U.S. bases. Working as a civilian contractor, he helped build the Distant Early Warning (DEW) System throughout the Arctic.[739]

1943   Glenview Officially Renamed

On January 1, 1943, the Navy base at Curtiss-Reynolds Field was officially renamed Naval Air Station Glenview (NASG) although it was commonly called Glenview Naval Air Station (GNAS). During the war 9,000 cadets received flight training, including 2.25 million takeoffs and landings and 787,000 daytime and 27,000 nighttime flight hours.[740] Glenview was considered one of the three most important Naval Air Stations during the war.[741]

1943   Rockford Establishes Airport Authority

The privately-owned Machesney Airport had served Rockford since the middle of the 1920s. In the early 1930s, Rockford voters rejected a proposal to purchase Machesney Airport and operate it as a municipally-owned facility.[742]

Attitudes changed during the following decade. In 1943, voters approved the establishment of the Greater Rockford Airport Authority. However, that law was found unconstitutional, but revised legislation was enacted in 1945.[743]

1943   Bragg Tries to Serve in the War

African American Janet Bragg was both a skilled nurse and aviator. She received her Private Pilot License in 1934 and flew many hours in her own planes.

In 1943[a] she applied to become a Women's Air Service Pilot and went for an interview with an assistant to Jacqueline Cochran, the head of the WASP program. Upon seeing the color of Bragg's skin, the assistant sent her away without an interview. Shortly thereafter, Bragg received a formal letter from Cochran rejecting her because of her race.

Bragg then applied to be a nurse for the military, but again was rejected because the "colored quota" was already full.

Next, Bragg went to Tuskegee's Civilian Pilot Training Program to obtain her Commercial License. She completed the course but flew her checkride with an Alabama pilot who refused to license a "colored girl."

a   Some sources place these events in 1942.

Later in 1943, she returned to Chicago, where she passed her checkride at Pal-Waukee Air Port.[744]

1943   Brown is First Black Woman with Both Pilot and Mechanic Licenses

Like Janet Bragg, Willa Brown tried to enter the Women's Air Service Pilot program only to be denied due to her race. In 1943, Brown earned her Mechanic License, making her the first black woman to have both a Commercial Pilot License and a Mechanic License.[745]

1943/01/11   First President to Fly

President Franklin Roosevelt became the first U.S. President to fly while in office. After taking off in Pan Am's Dixie Clipper from Miami on Jan. 11, Roosevelt arrived on Jan. 14 in Casablanca for a summit of Allied Leaders.[746]

1943/05/04   Virginia Rabung Solos

After a few hours of instruction at Rubinkam Airport, Virginia Rabung completed her training and soloed at Stinson Airport along Route 66 in McCook, IL. She went on to get her Private and Commercial Licenses and an Instrument Rating.

For Rabung, flying was the easy part—getting to the airport was hard. She didn't know how to drive and took extended bus trips from her residence in Chicago to the suburban airports where she could afford lessons.

Rabung went on to a long career as only an amateur aviator since flying professionally was regarded as "man's work." In October 1953, she purchased a 1946 Cessna 140 which she flew for the next 40 years in numerous long and challenging cross-country flights.[747]

1943/05/20   B-24 Crashes Near Municipal

While approaching Chicago Municipal Airport for a landing, a B-24 Liberator crashed into a natural gas storage tank killing all twelve soldiers on board. Flying conditions were poor with light rain, light fog, light smoke, and a 500 ft. ceiling with .75 mi. visibility.[748]

1943/07   Goggin Starts Douglas Flying Club

Jim Goggin, who worked at the Douglas plant, started the Douglas Flying Club in July, 1943, for Douglas employees. The club flew out of American Airport in Park Ridge.

Goggin had experience with a previous flying club and knew how to effectively run a club. The club grew quickly and by September 1944, operated four planes. The club became a model for other corporate flying clubs around the area.

Eventually, other area flying clubs merged with the Douglas Club. An influx of people from Magnaflux, Western Electric, Motorola, and the Arlington Flying Club swelled the ranks of the club. Goggin renamed the group Associated Flying Club of America to more accurately reflect the nature of the group.

With 300 members flying seven planes, the traffic was too much for little American Airport, so Goggin moved the AFCA to the larger Pal-Waukee. About half the AFCA's members were women.[749]

1943/08   George H.W. Bush Carrier Qualifications

Future President, then Ensign George H.W. Bush, was stationed at Glenview Naval Air Station for three days, during which he qualified for carrier landings on the USS *Sable*.[750]

1943/08/05   WASP Created

Two predecessor organizations merged into the Women Airforce Service Pilots. Jackie Cochran became the director of these women who ferried airplanes and did other technically non-dangerous flights. Before the program ended in December 1944, WASPs flew over 60 million miles with only 38 fatalities.[751]

1943/08/31   Orchard Place Becomes an Airport

Douglas Aircraft Corp. had outgrown its factory at Municipal Airport and was unable to handle the contract for their new four-engine transport, the C-54 Skymaster.

Douglas found a suitable location for an additional factory at Orchard Place in Park Ridge. They also built an airport, Douglas Field with four runways. Steel scarcity meant the runways did not have reinforcing rods. Runways consisted of 10 inches of concrete over 15 inches of stone.[752]

1944   POWs Arrive at Arlington Heights Airport

During World War II, Arlington Heights Auxiliary Field, with three runways, was one of the best equipped of the Navy's Outlying Landing Fields for the Glenview Naval Air Station. The airport was located on the south side of Central Rd. one mile west of Arlington Heights Rd., near Kirchhoff Rd.

Starting in 1944, the airport became a Prisoner of War camp. At its peak, it housed 200 German POWs, mostly from Rommel's Afrika Corps. Following the war, the Arlington Heights Field was one of three satellite fields that remained in operation.[753]

1944   Norden Bombsights from Chicago

Chicago's Victor Adding Machine Co. became the only company other than Norden itself to produce the Norden bombsight. During WWII, Victor's bombsight contracts totaled over $50 million.[754]

1944/04/25   Army's First Helicopter Rescues

Using the Sikorsky R-4, the Army made its first use of helicopters to rescue downed pilots in Burma.[755]

1944/06   Me 262 Goes Into Production

In Germany, Willy Messerschmitt's aircraft, the Me 262, became the first production jet in June 1944. Although only a small number became operational, it was credited with 427 kills of Allied aircraft.[756]

1944/06   First Woman Controller at Municipal

Born and raised in Mendota, IL, Ruth Van Etten trained as a Women's Air Service Pilot in June 1944, but by that time the Army was no longer accepting WASPs. Van Etten came to Chicago, where she became the first female air traffic controller, working in the tower at Chicago Municipal.[757]

1944/06/13   First Buzz Bomb Strikes

The first of 3500 V-1 Buzz Bombs struck the London area. Recognizable by the distinctive on-and-off buzzing of their pulsejet engines, the V-1 traveled about 350 mph at around 3,000 ft., making them susceptible to interceptors, anti-aircraft guns, and barrage balloons. Roughly a third were destroyed before reaching their targets.[758]

1944/07/16 WAC Recruiting at Pal-Waukee

Pal-Waukee's Civil Air Patrol squadron sponsored an air show to encourage girls to apply for the Woman' Army Corps. The Sunday afternoon event included displays of army and CAP aircraft, parachute drops, and music.[759]

1944/07/18   Fire Destroys Douglas Admin Building

A fire in the early hours of Tuesday morning July 18, 1944, destroyed the wooden administration building at the Douglas Aircraft Corp.'s new suburban factory. Damage was valued at $1.5 million but did not interfere with aircraft production. By the end of the week, temporary offices were set up around Des Plaines and surrounding suburbs and plans were underway to construct a fireproof replacement office within two months.[760]

1944/09/03–10   DuPage Recruiting Drive

Civil Air Patrol squadron 611-2 at Elmhurst Airport conducted a week-long recruiting drive starting September 3, 1944. During the week, CAP planes dropped leaflets on surrounding towns with 1,000 or more people. On Sunday, September 10, an afternoon program demonstrated flight maneuvers, including formation flying, mock bombings, and message pickup. Boys and girls aged 15–17 were given information on the Air Corps Enlisted Reserves, CAP, and Women's Army Corps programs.[761]

1944/09/08   First V-2 Strikes London

On September 8, 1944, the first of more than a thousand German V-2 rockets fell on London. In addition to the physical destruction they caused, the V-2s induced great terror since unlike the V-1, the V-2 was essentially undetectable and unstoppable until impact.[762]

1944/10   First Publication of *Statistical Handbook of Civil Aviation*

The CAA produced the first edition of the *Statistical Handbook of Civil Aviation*.[763]

1944/11/01–12/07   Chicago Defines International Cooperation

Representatives of 52 countries attended the International Civil Aviation Conference to establish guidelines for global air traffic. With the war still underway, the Axis powers had no voice in the conference. The Soviet Union chose not to participate preferring to develop their own internal network and regulations.

During the month-long meeting between November 1 and December 7, 1944, representatives agreed upon the rules for international air travel as formulated in the Convention on International Civil Aviation, also known as the Chicago Convention. To ensure uniform standards and practices for operations and safety, the Convention created the regulatory body, the International Civil Aviation Organization (ICAO)[a].[764]

1944/11/22   IL Court Rerverses Airport Act

On November 11, 1944, the Illinois Supreme Court overturned the Illinois County Airport Act of 1943[765]. The Act enabled counties and municipalities with a population of less than one million to establish an airport authority to control and finance airports. Chicago, by virtue of its population, was excuded from the law because it already possessed this authority.

The Sangamon County Attorney challenged the Springfield Airport Authority. The Court found numerous objections to the Act including the ability of a municipality to create another entity (the airport authority) that has taxing powers. The Court also challenged whether tax funds would be used for private parties, such as the airlines, rather than strictly public use. Finally, the Court also envisioned conflicts with overlapping airport authorities under other Illinois law, such as the Park Airport Act.[766]

1944/11/28   National Airport Plan

The CAA submitted the National Airport Plan to Congress on November 28, 1944. The plan envisioned a postwar America as a nation on wings. Among other things, the plan proposed spending $1.25 billion to construct more than 3,000 new airports and improve hundreds of other one. The plan envisioned a high level of cooperation between federal, state, and local governments in the same way they cooperated on the much more costly highway program.[767]

1944/12   Ester Noffke Comes to Chicago

After being deactivated from the Women's Airforce Service Corp, Ester Noffke came to Pal-Waukee. After a brief stint with Tufts-Edgecumbe Aviation, Noffke met George Priester and became a stalwart of Priester Aviation for decades.[768]

1944/12/15   Pal-Waukee Santa Flies Gifts to Kids

The Prospect Heights Lions Club sponsored a Community Christmas Party on Friday afternoon, December 15, 1944. Santa Al Tufts and his helper George Edgecumbe with skis on their plane flew gifts from Pal-Waukee to a nearby snow-covered recreation field where the party took place.[769]

a   ICAO replaced its predecessor International Commission for Air Navigation (ICAN).

1945–1949

1945   Delta Gains First Chicago Access
Delta Airlines obtained its first Chicago access with a route to Cincinnati.[770]

1945   Priester Aviation Started
George Priester established Priester Aviation at Pal-Waukee Air Port, providing basic and advanced training. Priester acquired a Link Trainer to provide instrument training.[771]

1945/04/12   Truman Becomes President
Harry Truman took the oath of office following the sudden death of FDR. [772]

1945/04/19   Airlines Reorganize IATA
At a meeting in Havana, Cuba, 41 airlines from 25 nations created the International Air Transport Assn. (IATA). This voluntary organization was formed to prevent unethical methods of controlling rates and schedules. The new IATA replaced the previous IATA (International Air Traffic Assn.) which was formed in 1919 in The Hague.[773]

1945/06/17   Field's Sells Ercoupes
Marshall Field's announced it would become the first department store in the country to sell airplanes starting in the fall of 1946. In a deal with Park Aircraft Sales and Service, Oliver L. Parks operated a flight facility at Pal-Waukee selling and servicing Ercoupe airplanes. Parks and Field's offered Ercoupe for sale in Field's State St. store in the sporting goods department on the first floor.

The Ercoupe was designed to be the vanguard of a post-war surge in the popularity of flying. Priced under $3,000, the Ercoupe had interconnected ailerons and rudder, which eliminated the need for rudder pedals and was claimed to make the plane spinproof. A yoke replaced the stick making it more familiar for automobile drivers. The announcement claimed that "many persons have learned to fly the plane in five hours."[774]

1945/06/21   108th Squadron Reconstituted with Illinois Guard

After being the first Guard unit to serve overseas in WWII, the 108th Reconnaissance Squadron had been officially disbanded in November 1943.

After the war, on June 21, 1945, the squadron was reconstituted as the 108th Bombardment Squadron (Light) as part of the Illinois Air National Guard. It was briefly stationed at Douglas/Orchard Field before returning to its previous home at Municipal Airport.

In November 1946, the 108th became part of the 56th Fighter Wing of the Illinois National Guard. The Wing included three squadrons stationed at Springfield, Peoria, and Municipal Field. The Wing's headquarters were at Muni along with the 108th Squadron.

The Wing went through a number of reorganizations as its mission changed with military requirements becoming consecutively the 66th Fighter Wing (February 1947), the 126th Composite Wing (November 1950), and the 126th Bombardment Wing (Light) (May 1951). During this period, the squadron flew a variety of planes, including P-51 Mustangs and the Douglas B-26 Invaders, depending on its current mission.[775]

1945/07/05   Pan Am Monopoly Broken

Prior to WWII, Pan American Airways was the exclusive international carrier for the U.S. However, war demands exceeded Pan Am's capacity, so other carriers also began delivering supplies down the Atlantic coast of South America. TWA made nearly 10,000 trips to Europe with its four-engine Boeing 307 Stratoliner.[776]

On July 5, 1945, CAB awarded the first non-wartime overseas route to an airline other than Pan American, breaking its monopoly. Additional routes were given to TWA and American Export Airlines (later the American Overseas Airlines), which had flown internationally as part of the war effort.[777]

1945/07/28   Empire State Building Hit By Plane

A B-25 flying in heavy fog flew into the Empire State Building. The crash killed eleven in the building as well as the B-25's crew of three.[778]

1945/08/06   Atomic Bomb Dropped

The B-29 *Enola Gay* drops the Little Boy atomic bomb on Hiroshima, ushering in the nuclear age.[779]

1945/09   Air Scout Squadron Formed at Pal-Waukee

A branch of the Boy Scouts of America established a squadron of Air Scouts at Pal-Waukee Air Port. The program, for boys age 15 and above, provided preflight training. Those who completed training were then able to join the Civilian Pilot Training Program (CPTP).[780]

1945/09/19   Three B-29s Land at Municipal

Three B-29s were modified in an attempt to set the world distance record with a nonstop flight from Japan to Washington, DC. On September 18, 1945, the planes, each commanded by a general, including Curtis LeMay, who took off from Hokkaido, Japan's northern island on the 6,500-mi. journey. Stronger than expected headwinds hindered their progress, forcing them to refuel in Chicago before continuing to Washington, DC.[781]

1945/10   Wartime Travel Restrictions Lifted

A month after V-J Day, federal restrictions imposed on transportation were removed and civilian air travel took off. In the U.S., 6.7 million passengers flew in 1945, and nearly doubled to 12.5 million the following year.[782]

1946   Brown Runs for Congress

Pioneering Chicago aviator Willa Brown, who had already broken many color and gender barriers, broke another one in 1946 when she became the first African American woman to run for Congress. Although she lost three times, she remained politically active for the rest of her life.[783]

1946   Chicago Heights Airport Sold

August "Auggie" Maross owned a small airport in Chicago Heights. In 1946, Maross sold the airport to Walt Thielman, who named it Chicago Heights Airport. Originally opened in 1927 as Legion Field, the airport was known for a while as Ashland Airport.

Prior to WWII, the airport was busy and needed to expand. However, it was surrounded by a golf course that prevented expansion. Following the war, the area south of Chicago grew rapidly with commercial and residential development, constraining the airport.

Thielman's time at the airport was limited. In 1947, he sold Chicago Heights Airport to developers. Thielman moved his operations to Governor's Airpark, also in Chicago Heights.[784]

1946   Elgin Airport Sold

After the war, the Navy disposed of its satellite fields. The Elgin Airport
Corp., headed by George Edgecumbe,[a] sought permission from the state to
reactivate the Elgin field. Neighbors objected complaining about potential
noise and safety hazards, but the state granted permission. The new operators built an office and a Quonset hut that became a repair shop.

In 1949, a helicopter air mail shuttle served Elgin and nine other
communities, carrying mail to the main Chicago Post Office.

Edgecumbe relocated his Piper distributorship from Elmhurst Airport
to Elgin in 1956–1957. He installed landing lights and erected a number
of T-hangars.[785]

1946   Chicagoland Airport Blossoms

In the middle of 1946, A.W. "Art" Schelter and some investors bought Half
Day Field, one of Glenview's satellite fields in the Village of Half Day, now
Vernon Hills, IL.

Anticipating a post-war surge in civilian flying, they named it
Chicagoland Airport and built hangars for storage and maintenance. The
airport had an air mail beacon and featured a circular gas pump area which
was more convenient than the traditional layout requiring planes to line up
and wait for fuel.

Schelter also operated a Piper dealership and flight school. Three
propeller shops were also located on the field.[786]

1946   German Planes at Orchard Field

As the war wound down, military contracts dried up and Douglas closed the
Orchard Place factory. Orchard Field continued to be used primarily for the
air reserves and National Guard.

In 1946, the Army based the 803rd Special Depot at Orchard Field. The
unit housed and studied captured Axis aircraft, including the German jet
fighter Messerschmitt Me-262 and the Japanese night fighter Nakajima
C6N1-S Saiun. The depot closed in 1948 and the aircraft were dispersed.[787]

1946   Lloyd Creates Sky Haven

Richard "Dick" Lloyd II started the little 75-acre Sky Haven Airport in 1946
along Wolf Rd. north of Grand Ave. The airport was on unincorporated land

---

a   The same year, George Edgecumbe moved his Piper Distributorship from Pal-Waukee to
      Elmhurst Airport.

between Bensenville and Schiller Park, IL, about five miles from Douglas Field. In February 1950, Sky Haven was raided by sheriff's police, who confiscated a slot machine.[788]

1946   Navy Sells Interstate Airport to DeKalb

In 1946, the Navy sold Interstate Airport, which had been used for manufacturing and testing the unmanned TDR-1 drone, to the city of DeKalb, IL.

The city created the DeKalb Municipal Airport and made Willard Rue "Pete" Taylor the Airport Manager. Under Taylor's supervision, over several decades, DeKalb airport developed with new runways, lighting and instrument landing equipment, and other facilities. DeKalb became an O'Hare reliever airport with executive and cargo flights in addition to a lot of general aviation activity.[789]

1946   DuPage Acquires St. Charles Airport

No longer needed for the war effort, in 1946, the Navy gave the St. Charles Airport to DuPage County.

The first Midway Airlines initiated shuttle service between St. Charles Airport and Midway in June 1952. Starting in 1955, Chicago Airways included St. Charles as part of its service to Midway, Milwaukee, and Rockford. The air taxi services ended around 1958, as O'Hare's activity grew.[790]

1946   John Dacy Gets Started

Growing up on a farm outside of Harvard, IL, John Dacy learned to fly an OX-5 Pheasant in 1933. He made a grass runway in a field and started an airplane repair business. Later, Dacy served as a crew chief on a B-24 in Italy in WWII.

Returning from the war, Dacy revived his airport and the state licensed it as a commercial airport in 1946, the same year he married Elsie Reese. John expanded Dacy Airport, giving it three turf runways. Elsie assisted in running the airport and also flew aerobatic performances.

Dacy also restarted his repair business. He specialized in restoring and rebuilding vintage biplanes and their radial engines and had a special affinity for Stearmans.

1946   C&S Moves HQ to Chicago

Since the end of WWII, Chicago and Southern Air Lines had greatly expanded its routes around the Midwest and South and added several

Caribbean destinations. In 1946, C&S relocated its corporate headquarters from Memphis to Chicago, intending to rent office space in the Loop. However, its precarious financial position forced them to cancel plans after learning about Chicago's prices, and they moved into additional hangar space at Municipal instead.[791]

1946/01/26   P-80 Sets Speed Record

America's newest jet fighter, the P-80, traveled from Los Angeles to New York in 4 hr. and 13 min., a new speed record.[792]

1946/02/05   Municipal Goes International

TWA's Constellation L-049 *The Star of Paris* initiated transatlantic service between Chicago Municipal and Orly Airport in Paris. On May 3, TWA also started service to London.

After the war, activity at Chicago Municipal changed substantially. Not only were there more flights, but planes were larger, many with four engines. In 1940, more than 700,000 passengers passed through Municipal. That number had grown to more than 2.6 million in 1946.[793] Pan American no longer had a monopoly on international flights.

The limited range of planes used by TWA and other transatlantic carriers required at least two intermediate stops in Gander Bay, Newfoundland and Shannon, Ireland.[794]

1946/02/26   Rockford Airport Receives Camp Grant

On February 26, 1946, President Truman signed the deed transferring 1,600 acres of Camp Grant to the Greater Rockford Airport Authority.[795] The airport was located on 39th Ave. and bounded by the Rock River on the west and the Kishwaukee River on the south.

The GRAA constructed three runways in a triangular arrangement. The old Camp Grant Officers Ballroom was moved to a new location and remodeled into a terminal building.[796]

1946/03/15   CAA Selects Oklahoma City

On March 15, 1946, the CAA chose Will Rogers Field at Oklahoma City as the site for its new training and administration center.[797]

1946/03/22   Chicago Purchases Orchard Field

With Chicago Municipal Airport nearing capacity, the City of Chicago studied alternatives to find a location for an airport that could accommodate existing larger planes and those anticipated in the future.ᵃ Keeping the airport within the city limits was also a major goal. Douglas Field or Orchard Place looked promising. Already 50% larger than Municipal (1081 vs. 640 acres), both of its runways were more than 5,500 ft., exceeding Municipal's longest runway.

On March 22, 1946, Chicago acquired Orchard Field from the War Assets Administration. The city received the land and a single hangar, while the military retained the old Douglas factory and related buildings. The military also retained rights to 25% of the airport's operating capacity. While larger than Municipal, Orchard Field, as it stood, would not be sufficient in the future. The city quickly acquired more land, expanding its size to 7,700 acres.

Once again, a railroad ran through a major Chicago airport. This time, the city negotiated with the Chicago and North Western Railway to relocate a spur right from the start. Nevertheless, the final footprint of the airport was bounded on the west by the Chicago and North Western Railway and on the east by the Soo Line. Just south of the boundary were the large Bensenville Freight Yards, operated by the Chicago, Milwaukee, St. Paul and Pacific Railroad.

In October 1946, a cargo plane became the first commercial flight to land at the as yet unnamed airport.[798]

1946/04   *Airman's Guide* First Published

The CAA started publishing the *Airman's Guide* on a biweekly basis. It consolidated pilot information from three previous publications.[799]

1946/05/01   Parks Aircraft Takes Ownership of Pal-Waukee

For unspecified reasons, Owen Jones sold Pal-Waukee on May 1, 1946, to his tenant Oliver Parks for an undisclosed sum. The 92-acre airport had three gravel runways up to 2,600 ft. Two hangars holding up to 25 planes each, an administration building, and two other office buildings were included in the purchase.

Oliver L. Parks, the founder of Parks Air College in East St. Louis, expanded his aviation enterprises after WWII. He opened Ercoupe sales and service centers at several Midwest locations, including Pal-Waukee,

a   Other locations considered were the Clearing neighborhood south of Midway and the Belt Line rail yards, Lake Calumet, building an island in the lake similar to but much larger than Northerly Island, building dikes in the lake and constructing the airport on dried lakebed.

intending to capitalize on an anticipated post-war surge of many people wanting to have their own planes.

At the time of the sale, the largest tenant was Tufts-Edgecombe, the Piper distributor, which offered flight instruction, charter service, leased hangar space, and performed aircraft maintenance. Also at the airport were Jim Goggin's Associated Flying Club and George Priester's flying school.[800]

The Parks operation quickly developed a reputation as being unfriendly toward those he considered competitors. By the end of 1946, Tufts-Edgecumbe relocated its entire operation to Elmhurst Airport. Priester also relocated his flight services to Elmhurst but left some ground school training at Pal-Waukee.[801]

1946/05/08   First Helicopter Certificated

The Bell 47 became the first helicopter to receive a CAA Type Certificate that permitted mass production for the civilian market.[802]

1946/05/13   Federal Airport Act Signed

The Federal Airport Act, sponsored by Sen. Pat McCarran (NV) and Rep. Clarence F. Lea (CA), was signed by President Truman on May 13, 1946.

The Airport Act was the first peacetime program providing financial aid to promote America's airport development without being connected to either the military or work relief (WPA). The emphasis was on smaller airports in anticipation of a postwar boom of private pilots.

The Act authorized appropriations of $500 million for the 48 states plus another $20 million for the territories of Alaska and Hawaii, to be spent over the next seven years.[803]

1946/07/02   TWA Flight 456 Crashes After Takeoff

After a 9 a.m. takeoff from Municipal on July 2, 1946, TWA Flight 456, a DC-3, experienced engine failure during its initial climb. The first engine ceased operation at 600 ft., followed shortly by the second. After hitting a telephone pole, the plane came to stop on a railroad track. There were no injuries either in the plane or on the ground. The engine failure was attributed to fuel starvation from an unknown cause.[804]

1946/07/21   Carrier Jet Landing

The Navy's experimental XFD-1 Phantom became the first American jet to land on an aircraft carrier on July 21, 1946. Earlier, a British de Havilland

DH.100 Sea Vampire had completed a carrier landing and takeoff on
December 3, 1945.[805]

1946/08/02   Congress Authorizes Air Museum

Congress authorized the creation of a National Air Museum as part of the
Smithsonian Institution[a].[806]

1946/08/15   CAA Begins Charging Fees for Services

The CAA began charging fees for selected services, such as registering
planes and certifying school and repair centers.[807]

1946/10   Rock Falls Airport Begins

In 1946, Whiteside County voters established an Airport Authority to own
and operate an airport. The existing Sterling Airport was not suitable for
their vision, and they selected a site two miles south of Rock Falls.

However, the County did not have funds for an airport. Instead, Darryl
Wolfe and Kenneth Paul "Kenny" Zimmerman used their own funds to
open the Rock Falls Airport in October 1946.

Two years later, Wolfe dropped out, leaving Zimmerman as sole owner
and operator. An Army Air Corps veteran, Zimmerman provided a wide
range of services, from charter flights to crop spraying. His Piper dealership provided flight instruction as well as aircraft sales and maintenance.[808]

1947   VOR Experimentally Implemented

Another wartime technology, Very high frequency Omnidirectional Radio
Range (VOR) navigation was implemented experimentally between Chicago
and New York.[809]

1947   Moline Sells Airport to MAA

In 1947, Rock Island County voters created the Metropolitan Airport
Authority (MAA), which then purchased Moline Airport from the City of
Moline. The MAA consisted of seven townships in Rock Island County. Over
the years, the MAA developed and improved the airport, which today is one
of the busiest in the State.[810]

a   In 1976, the name was changed to National Air and Space Museum, recognizing inclusion of
the space program in the collection.

1947   Navy Leases Arlington Heights Airport

In 1947, the Navy disposed of the Arlington Heights Airport by leasing it to Illinois Aircraft Services and Sales Co., a Luscombe dealership, instead of the Village of Arlington Heights.

Maurice "Mo" Fishman operated the dealership and became airport manager. Flight lessons were free for veterans under the GI Bill and very inexpensive for civilians. The plane, a Luscombe Silvaire, sold for under $2,500 at a time when a Chevrolet Fleetmaster cost $1,450.

Supplementing the aviation income, the airport rented out the former barracks as apartments and devoted part of the unused land to a trailer park. The Forest View School was also located on airport grounds.[811]

1947   ATE Starts Flying at Municipal

I.H. "Monte" Montgomery started a flight school, Aviation Training Enterprises, in 1947 at Chicago Municipal. ATE was a pioneering training facility providing instrument instruction for civilians to fly in Instrument Meteorological Conditions. It claimed to be the first to use civilian flight simulators.

ATE continued operating under its own banner until 1980 when it merged with American Flyers out of Fort Worth. It continued training using the American Flyers name at its Texas headquarters.[812]

1947/04/03   Ground Controlled Approach Tested

Chicago Municipal and Washington National were the first civilian airports to perform in-service testing of Ground Controlled Radar. Initially developed by the military, the radar allowed controllers to work with pilots to improve landing safety.[813]

1947/04/04   Chicago Convention Goes Into Effect

The International Civil Aviation Organization (ICAO) became operational on April 4, 1947. ICAO is the organization that regulates international aviation under the 1944 Convention on International Civil Aviation known as the "Chicago Convention."[814]

1947/07/25   National Security Act Approved

On July 25, 1947, President Truman approved the National Security Act of 1947, which created the cabinet-level Dept. of Defense.

The Act totally reorganized the U.S. military command structure into a single organization[a] that included both the Army and the Navy. The Marine Corps was permanently affixed to the Navy and prohibited from becoming a part of the Army. The Army Air Corps became an independent branch of service, the Air Force, on September 18 of that year.

The Act also created the Central Intelligence Agency and the National Security Council.[815]

1947/10/01   CTA Is Formed

The Chicago Transit Authority was formed to take over operations of all "L" trains and streetcars from various private transportation companies.[816]

1947/10/01   F-86 Breaks Sound Barrier

Flying the prototype XF-86, George "Wheaties" Welch unofficially broke the sound barrier during a dive on October 1, 1947.[817]

1947/10/11   World Meteorological Organization Established

Common standards for meteorological reporting and communication were established by agreement of 42 nations at a meeting in Washington, DC, on October 11, 1947. In 1951, the World Meteorological Organization became a part of the United Nations.[818]

1947/10/14   Yeager Breaks Sound Barrier

A few days after the F-86 unofficially broke the sound barrier, on October 14, 1947, Chuck Yeager broke it officially in level flight in the Bell X-1.[819]

1947/11   Sanger Airport Opens

Sanger Field opened in November 1947 when two brothers, Paul and Al Sanger, bought 53 acres in Monee, IL, and built a 2,400 ft. E-W grass runway. The Illinois Dept. of Transportation, Div. of Aeronautics issued a Restricted Landing Area (RLA) permit by November 1947.

In the mid-1960s, Sanger expanded with the purchase of another 80 acres. The brothers lengthened and paved the runways and, in June 1968, it became a Commercial Airport. Sanger Airport went out of business sometime after 2002 and the facilities, including the runways, sat unused.[820]

a   Previously, the War Department and the Navy Department were both cabinet-level organizations with totally separate command structures.

1947/11/02   Spruce Goose Flies

Howard Hughes made a short, straight, singular flight of the flying boat HK-1. Also known as the H-4 Hercules, the all-wood, eight-engine plane remains the largest[a] aircraft ever flown.[821]

1947/12/17   B-47's First Flight

America's first swept-wing jet bomber, Boeing's XB-47 made its first flight. When it went into production, it became the first mass-produced swept-wing airplane. The B-47's general design, with swept wings and pylon-mounted engines, became the Boeing standard for large military and commercial aircraft and was adopted by other companies worldwide.[822]

1948   Coach Service Begins

Capital Airlines introduced the first coach service on Chicago-LaGuardia flights. The dedicated DC-4 coach flight departed at 1 a.m. (a red-eye flight) and cost $26, as opposed to $44 on regular flights.[823]

1948   Chanute Changes Its Name

Following the creation of the U.S. Air Force, the Rantoul field was renamed Chanute Air Force Base in 1948. It remained a vital training center for aircraft mechanics through the Vietnam War and beyond. Starting in the 1960s, Chanute became a prime training center for missile operations including the Minuteman ICBM.[824]

1948   Movie Shot at Municipal

Jimmy Stewart starred in the 1948 movie *You Gotta Be Happy* and appeared in scenes shot in front of Monarch Aviation Hangar at Municipal.[825]

1948   Thomas Mitchell Takes Over Sky-Line

The Sky-Line Airport started in Addison, IL[b] around 1946 at the intersection of Fullerton Ave. and Rt. 53. By 1948, the airport had been renamed Mitchell Field[c] by its new owner, K. Thomas Mitchell.[826]

---

a   The Spruce Goose has the largest by wingspan (320 ft.) compared to the Anatov 225 Mriya (290 ft.). It is also taller with a height of 79 ft. vs. 59.5 ft. However, the Anatov is substantially longer (275.5 ft. vs. 218.5 ft.).
b   Some sources place the location in Lombard.
c   Mitchell Field in Addison, IL was named after its owner. Milwaukee's Mitchell Field was named after Gen. Billy Mitchell.

1948/01   Burke's Master Plan for O'Hare

In January 1948, architect and design consultant Ralph H. Burke unveiled the *Master Plan of the Chicago Orchard (Douglas) Airport*. Burke had previously done a lot of work for Chicago, including the State Stree subway, Meigs Field, and Grant Park underground lot (the largest underground lot at the time).

Burke's original master plan placed the terminal complex in the center surrounded by ten or twelve runways in a spiral or pinwheel pattern, to enable safe operations with any wind direction. An access road from Mannheim Road would tunnel under a runway and several taxiways to the terminal. His plan also included subway access to the "L" system and a new northwest expressway to downtown.

The terminal would have two levels, the upper one for passengers and the lower one for service and support. Burke's unique design specified a central terminal that would contain a number of arms, each with split fingers. Planes would load and unload passengers from numerous gates placed along these extensions. Burke's diagram also showed "loading bridges" that would swing out from the gate to the airplane, similar to today's jetways.

A distributed fuel system was another of Burke's unique concepts. Most large airports had a fuel farm in a remote corner of the airport. Fuel trucks would fill at the large storage tanks and then deliver fuel to planes on the ramp. Instead, Burke's plan ran underground pipes from the fuel farm directly to the gates. Pump trucks would transfer the fuel directly from the pipes into the planes' tanks. The plan eliminated the time-consuming and costly commute of fuel trucks to and from the tank farm.

Three problems confronted Burkes's master plan. First, new jets required runways of more than 11,000 ft. while Burke's runways were limited to about 8,500 ft. The airport's existing footprint wouldn't allow long enough runways without substantial land acquisition. Second, the airport would generate only minimal revenue for Chicago until all the construction was complete and major commercial operations began. Under Burke's plan, it would be a long time before that could happen. Third, and perhaps most important, was that Municipal would reach its capacity long before the complex facility would become operational.

After Burke's death in 1956, the city partially abandoned his master plan. Burke's star-shaped terminal in the center of the airport was replaced by a U-shaped terminal arrangement on a side of the property with ample room for long runways. However, both the arm-and-finger gate design and an underground fuel system were not only incorporated in the city's new master plan, but became standard in airports worldwide.[827]

1948/01/30   Orville Wright Dies

Orville Wright died in Dayton on January 30, 1948, at age 76.[828]

1948/03/10   Delta Flight Crashes at Municipal

On March 10, 1948, Delta Air Lines Flight 705 departed Chicago Municipal after a two-hour delay. Before reaching an altitude of 200 ft., the DC-4 suddenly went into a near vertical climb causing it to stall. It crashed into a field north of the airport and burst into flames. There was one survivor, but twelve others on board died in the crash.[829]

The NTSB did not identify a definite cause of the crash but suspected the elevator locking mechanism. Intended to keep the plane secure from wind gusts when on the ground, some DC-4s had a foot pedal to engage the locking mechanism and speculation was that the lock was inadvertently engaged during a critical time.[830]

1948/03/20   Municipal's Cloud Room Opens

On March 20, 1948, the luxurious Cloud Room Restaurant opened on the second level of Chicago Municipal's new terminal. Marshall Field and Co. paid $90,000 to build out the 3,600-sq. ft. space and spent an additional $260,000 to equip it. A formal gala held the night before the official opening featured Mayor Martin Kennelly.[831]

Municipal's new terminal building was designed by Paul Gerhardt Jr., who had also designed the airport's first terminal. The new $470,000 building was something of a throwback to classical structures. The circular central rotunda was fluted and resembled a short, wide classical column. Above the main floor was a second, smaller layer. The still smaller circle for the Control Tower perched on top made the structure resemble a wedding cake. A 300-car garage provided parking for airport visitors.

The new terminal was a boon to travelers. During WWII, the high volume of traffic and the low priority of maintenance made conditions at the original terminal deplorable. An extensive building program in 1947–1948 addressed these conditions.[832]

The Cloud Room was the second of the terminal's two restaurants. On the first level, the Blue and Gold snack shop, also operated by Marshall

Field, offered a convenient place to get coffee and sandwiches.[833] In an era when air travel was a luxury for the privileged few, the Cloud Room provided an elegant setting for dinner or drinks with a fabulous view of the airport.[834] Celebrities of all kinds who passed through Municipal often spent time relaxing in the Cloud Room.[835]

1948/06/24   Berlin Blockade Begins

On June 24, 1948, the Soviet Union blocked all rail and road access to Berlin cutting the Western half of the city off from all supplies. The allies, led by the U.S., provided supplies by air, primarily using C-47s (DC-3s) and C-54s (DC-4s), until the blockade was lifted on May 12, 1949. The airlift, however, continued until September 30 of that year.[836]

1948/09/10–12   Chicagoland Air Show

Chicagoland Airport held the first major airshow in years on September 10–12, 1948. One of the featured acts was the Cole Brothers' Flying Circus.

Duane Cole, a veteran air show performer, later recalled being impressed by a parachute jump by Willie "Suicide" Jones:

> It was made by a black man who did trapeze acts on his way down and closed his act by hanging by his knees until about fifty feet above the ground. From there he made a recovery to land on his feet. I will never forget Willie "Suicide" Jones.[837]

1948/11/22   Wright Flyer Arrives at Smithsonian

On November 22, 1948, after a bitter feud between Orville Wright and the Smithsonian Institution, the Wright Flyer I arrived at the Smithsonian.

Orville had refused to display the Flyer at the Smithsonian because Secretary Charles Walcott, a close friend of his predecessor Samuel Langley, gave Langley credit for making the first powered flight and downplayed Wright's achievements. Wright was indignant and refused to let the Smithsonian put the Wright Flyer on display, and in 1925 sent it to the Science Museum in London.

In 1942, a new Secretary of the Smithsonian, Charles Abbott, reversed Walcott's position, publishing a list of Langley's shortcomings. Abbott's statement also declared unequivocally that the Wright brothers made the first powered flight. After several years of correspondence, the Wright Flyer returned to the U.S. Sadly, Orville Wright died earlier that year (January 30) and did not live to see the Flyer receive the recognition it deserved.[838]

1948/12/10   Northerly Island Airport Dedicated

The Grand Opening of Northerly Island Airport took place on December 10, 1948. Over 100 planes from around the area flew in for the celebration. Stuart Symington, then Secretary of the Air Force, gave the dedicatory remarks.

Plans for the lakefront airport had been circulating after successful flight operations at Northerly Island during the Century of Progress. For various reasons, the project was delayed until 1946. Once the project had begun, it was realized Northerly Island needed to be enlarged to accommodate the airport, further delaying construction.[839]

1949   Airport Opens in Gary

Paul and Nick Jankovich started Calumet Aviation and opened an airport in Merrillville near 61st Ave. and Broadway. Their sister handled administrative matters. In 1949, the Jankoviches leased land west of their original airport from the City of Gary and started the the Gary Municipal Airport.[840]

1949/02/01   Nation's First Planned Suburb

In October, 1946, developer Philip Klutznik announced plans for a new self-governing community. The plan envisioned 5,000 homes, extensive parks, outdoor shopping plaza and extensive municipal services.

On February 1, 1949, Park Forest, IL, incorporated as a village. Park Forest received national attention and grew quickly with returning servicemen using the GI Bill. The design became a model community for middle class families with children.[841]

1949/07/01   Chicago Airports Get New Names

Chicago officially renamed its three airports on July 1, 1949. Chicago Municipal Field became Midway Airport in honor of the Battle of Midway and the military pilots stationed here during the war. Orchard Place was renamed O'Hare after Navy ace Edward "Butch" O'Hare. Lakefront Field, or Northerly Island Airport, was renamed Meigs Field, honoring Chicago publisher and aviation advocate Charles C. Meigs.[842]

1949/07/04   National Air Fair at O'Hare

Several days after the city changed Orchard Field's name to O'Hare, the newly-formed U.S. Air Force brought the National Air Fair to the airport. On the Fourth of July, 1949, 145,000 people braved 102° heat for the exhibition.

A squadron of B-26s gave a precision bombing demonstration. Helicopters flew exhibition flights. A formation of B-36s included twelve aircraft. Fighter flights included the F-80 and the F-86. Static aircraft displays included the B-29 *Enola Gay*. One hangar exhibited captured German aircraft. Mobile displays on tractor-trailer trucks showed various engines and other aviation-related equipment.[843]

1949/07/31   First Communications Between Plane and ARTCC

Starting with the Chicago Air Route Traffic Control Center (ARTCC), the CAA inaugurated direct radiotelephone communications with aircraft. The expanded communications service was rolled out to all ARTCCs by 1955.[844]

1949/08/29   Helicopter Shuttle Begins in Chicago

Helicopter Air Service of Chicago (HAS) began operations on August 29, 1949, becoming the nation's second helicopter mail service. Based at Midway, the copters flew between the roof of the Chicago Main Post Office building at Canal and Van Buren streets and 43 small suburban heliports. HAS's Bell Model 47 helicopters (the kind seen on *M.A.S.H.*) had a bubble cockpit and carried up to 500 pounds of mail and small packages.

By June 1951, HAS's ten pilots and six helicopters had flown more than 567,000 mi. carrying 4.5 million pounds of mail. With some helicopters making two or three trips each day, they made more than 200,000 land-ings—19,720 on the roof of the main Chicago Post Office—without an accident.[845] HAS's charter only permitted it to fly mail and they had to turn down requests to pick up motorists stranded in a snowstorm or people stranded on the roof of a building by a broken elevator.[846]

1949/09/23   USSR Explodes Atomic Bomb

The Soviet Union became the second nation to have operational nuclear weapons on September 23, 1949.[847]

1949/12/18   TWA Crashes Midway Fence on Landing

Shortly after midnight on December 18, 1949, TWA Flight 154 departed San Francisco for New York with an intermediate stop at Midway. At about 7 a.m., as the flight approached Midway, air traffic control informed the L-049 Constellation that there would be a delay before landing.

Around 8 a.m., Midway reported a 300 ft. ceiling and 1.5 mi. visibility with moderate fog and smoke and controllers cleared the plane to make an Instrument Landing System (ILS) approach. The captain decided to abandon the instrument approach and made a visual approach instead. The plane set down approximately 3,200 ft. past the approach end of the runway, with less than half the runway remaining. The speeding plane tore through a fence before striking a billboard 875 ft. past the end of the runway.

Fortunately, all 31 people on board lived to tell about the accident, which was attributed to pilot error for excessive landing speed.[848]

1950–1954

1950   The Galts Open an Airport

Arthur T. Galt and his wife Vera opened an airport in the midst of McHenry County cornfields near Woodstock, IL, in 1950. In the 1960s Galt built hangars and a 3,000 ft. asphalt runway.

Galt Airport became a gathering place not just for aviators but for the community as well. The Galts maintained walking trails, a fire pit, and a stocked fishing pond for casual visitors and also built a concert stage and held music concerts.[849] The airport was the venue for the celebration of the 40th anniversary of Woodstock in August 2009.[850] In 1995, author Laurence Gonzales penned the novel *One Zero Charlie* using the airport as a back-drop for his characters.[851]

1950   National Guard Departs Rubinkam

The Illinois Air National Guard had a unit Aeroncas stationed at Rubinkam Airport in Markham, IL. In 1950, the Guard moved the unit from Rubinkam to Lansing Airport.[852]

Shortly before WWII, Markham had two adjacent airports: Dixie Airport and Rubinkam Airport, both located along 167th St. Henry Rubinkam started his airport at 167th St. and California Ave.; across a drainage ditch, Dixie Airport was located at 167th St. and Dixie Highway. A bridge over the ditch allowed planes to taxi from one airport to the other.

For a while, Dixie seemed to be more active than Rubinkam. Willie Howell had a hangar at Dixie before starting Howell Airport. Likewise, Ed Prosperi flew out of Dixie before he opened Prosperi Airport. Following the war, Dixie was absorbed into Rubinkam Airport. Eventually, Henry Rubinkam sold the airport to Izzie Langenderfer.

1950   State Approves Starved Rock Airport

In 1950, the State of Illinois issued a permit to operate a landing strip on Plum Island in the Illinois River just across from Starved Rock State Park.

By the early 1960s, the field had a 3,100 ft. turf runway and a cable car to transport people to and from the state park. An ad offered airplane rides for $2.00 and cable car rides for $0.25, but the cable car was free to those arriving by plane. The landing field closed about 1979.[853]

1950   Moody Starts Wood Dale Airport

Moody Aviation started its own airport. Wood Dale Airport in 1950, at the intersection of Rt. 83 and Thorndale Ave. in Wood Dale, IL.

Before moving to Wood Dale, Moody Aviation, started by Paul Robinson, operated at Elmhurst Airport. Robinson, a Baptist minister and a flight instructor, saw the need for a flight school for those entering the mission field. Robinson shared his vision with his alma mater, Moody Bible Institute on Clark St. in Chicago. Together they formed a flight school that focused on training bush pilots and developing techniques useful delivering people and supplies in remote areas.

While Moody was the primary user of Wood Dale, it was not the only one. The Chicago Glider Club and a number of other pilots also conducted operations there.

A decade later, O'Hare's expansion was hurting Wood Dale. Flights to and from the airport had to stay under 1,500 ft. to stay out of O'Hare's airspace but higher than 1,000 ft. above the area residences. Frustrated with the situation, Moody moved its flight school to Tennessee and sold the airport land to developers.[854]

1950/05/09   CAA Contracts for DME

The CAA issued its largest contract to date for over $4.2 million to set up 450 Distance Measuring Equipment (DME) ground stations.[855]

1950/05/13   TWA Changes Name but Not Acronym

On May 13, 1950, TWA formally changed its name from Transcontinental and Western Airways (TWA) to Trans World Airlines, retaining the TWA acronym.[856]

1950/06/23   Northwest 2501 Disappears over Lake

Northwest Airlines Flight 2501 was in route from New York to Seattle on June 23, 1950, with 58 passengers and crew. Flying at about 3,500 ft., the flight ran into storms over Lake Michigan and wasn't heard from again. The plane's log book and other wreckage were found floating in the water but there was not enough on which to base an investigation.[857]

1950/06/25   North Korea Invades South Korea

North Korean military forces invaded South Korea. President Truman ordered the newly formed Air Force to assist the South Koreans. This was the start of U.S. military involvement in the country. The conflict saw the first wide-spread use of jets in combat.[858]

1950/06/30   Meigs Renaming Dedication

On June 30, 1950, Chicago held a ceremony to dedicate the newly renamed Meigs Field.

Formerly known as the Northerly Island Airport, the field was named after Merrill C. Meigs, the publisher of the *Chicago Herald and Examiner* who had served as head of both the Chicago Aero Commission and the Illinois Aeronautics Commission.

Special guests to the dedication ceremony were about 2,000 Flying Farmers, who arrived from 30 states in 890 planes at Chicago area airports.[859]

1950/09/26   Rockford Gets Commercial Flights

Commercial service began on September 26, 1950 when Mid-Continent Airlines started its Rockford to Chicago Midway service.

The following year, on May 16, Ozark Airlines commenced flights between St. Louis and Rockford. Ozark also established Rockford as a major maintenance facility for its DC-3s.[860]

1950/10/15   First VOR Airways Go Operational

The first VOR airways were put into commission on October 15, 1950, providing aircraft with improved in-flight navigation capabilities.[861]

1951   Plane Passenger-Miles Exceed Train

For the first time in history, planes exceeded trains in the number of passenger-miles traveled: 10,679,281,000 plane vs. 10,224,718,000 train in 1951.[862]

1951   DME Testing

In order to determine the efficacy of Distance Measuring Equipment, the Chicago to New York airway was equipped with nine DME ground stations in 1951.[863]

1951   ACI Fades Away

The Aero Club of Illinois, which had ignited Chicago's aviation fire in 1910 and fanned the flames during the first crucial decades of the 20th century, faded into the background and ceased operation in 1951. Ashburn Field, having operated since 1916 as one of Chicago's earliest and busiest airports,

operated for several years as a private airport with restricted landings
before finally being sold to developers. [864]

1951   Jim Goggin Leaves Pal-Waukee

In 1951, prominent Pal-Waukee aviator Jim Goggin decided to relocate to
Whiteman Field near Los Angeles. Goggin took several planes with him and
sold his remaining business to his instructors. Vic Jacobs purchased the
flight school.

Sally Duncan Strempel took over the Associated Flying Club of America
(AFCA). Strempel had a varied background that included barnstorming
around the Midwest, being an air traffic controller in Kansas City, MO, and
working as the airport manager in Racine, WI.

Goggin had hired Strempel as a flight instructor for the Douglas Flying
Club while still at American Airport. She followed Goggin to Pal-Waukee as
the club expanded into the Associated Flying Club of America. Besides
instructing, Strempel was active in organizing social events such as dances
for the AFCA. In addition to building camaraderie, these events helped raise
money to meet expenses.

Strempel changed the club's name to Sally's Flying School, which was
a more accurate reflection of her organization. Sally's husband, Erwin
"Erv" Strempel, a police officer,[a] was also active in the flight school performing many maintenance functions and other tasks.

Originally, Sally's operated in what had been the AFCA's clubhouse,
a converted barracks on Palatine Road. The school moved into a Quonset
hut near the end of 24 left, the short runway known as the "Cub runway."
A distinctive red band around the fuselage identified Sally's fleet of
yellow Cubs.

Sally's Flying School operated at Pal-Waukee, training thousands of
pilots until Strempel retired in 1966. [865]

1951/01/04   Monarch Non-Sked Crashes on Takeoff at Midway

Monarch Flight 1090, a non-scheduled (non-sked) airliner, crashed on
takeoff from Midway on the afternoon of January 4, 1952. The converted
C-46 Commando carrying 45 passengers with a crew of three was bound
for Newark.

The plane was overloaded by 1,100 pounds and the pilot incorrectly
configured the plane for takeoff using insufficient manifold and RPM. As

a   Sources say Erv Strempel served either with the Des Plaines or the Park Ridge Police
    Department.

soon as the gear retracted, the co-pilot noticed the situation and gave full power, but not in time. The plane struck some parked aircraft, went through a fence and came down about a half-mile west near 58th St. and Massassoit Ave. The plane burned but all 48 people were evacuated safely.[866]

1951/04/01   108th Squadron Activated for Korea

During the buildup for the Korean War, the 126th Bombardment Wing, including the Chicago-based 108th Bombardment Squadron,was activated on April 1, 1951. As part of the Tactical Air Command, the unit arrived in France at the Bordeaux-Merignac Air Base that November. Later they were assigned to Laon Air Base as part of the 12th Air Force. The 126th Wing flew their B-26s in maneuvers and other training missions until May 1953, when they returned to the Illinois Air National Guard.[867]

1951/05/29   First Solo Nonstop Polar Flight

Departing Norway, a P-51C flew nonstop over the North Pole to Alaska.[868]

1951/05/31   New York's Roosevelt Field Closed

After 40 years of operation, New York's Roosevelt Field ceased operations on May 31, 1951. During its life, the field was the base for Amelia Earhart, Richard Byrd, and Clarence Chamberlin, not to mention being the origination of Lindbergh's transatlantic flight.[869]

1951/06/29   Original Midway Air Lines Begins Operation

On June 29, 1951 the original Midway Air Lines[a] began operations offering North Shore passengers commuter service from Sky Harbor to Midway eliminating the lengthy drive. Later that year, the airline added flights to Meigs Field and DuPage Airport. Midway billed itself as the "World's Shortest Airline" and adorned its planes with a kangaroo logo.

Flying only during daylight, by 1955 Midway Air Lines had 15 daily scheduled round-trips making the 17-minute flight between Sky Harbor to Midway. An interchange agreement with United Airlines allowed them to book passengers through onto United flights. More than 2,000 passengers flew Midway Air Lines each month.

Increased use of O'Hare caused the demise for Midway's commuter service. North Shore passengers found the drive to O'Hare much shorter and easier than the trip to Midway Airport. By 1958, Midway's air taxi service ceased.[870]

a   No relation to either of the two more recent Midway Air Lines that offered jet service.

1951/09/16   Peninsular Engine Loss on Takeoff

Pensinular Air Transport Flight 108 was making a flight from Midway to Miami on the morning of September 16, 1951. During its flight from Miami the previous day, the converted C-46 had experienced intermittent problems with the left engine. Butler Aviation at Midway had worked on the engine and corrected the problem.

Flight 108 carried 49 passengers with a crew of four and was nearly 2,000 pounds overweight. The plane took off at a speed just over 100 mph when an engine faltered and failed. The overloaded plane was unable to climb on a single engine. The captain spotted an open area and made an emergency gear-up landing near 61st St. and Archer Rd. The impact was so great it tore both engines from their mounts. All 53 people on board survived the accident.[871]

1952/04/01   CAA Changes Alphabet

On April 1, 1952, the CAA replaced the previous Able-Baker-Charlie phonetic alphabet with the International Civil Aviation Organization (ICAO) standard Alpha-Bravo-Charlie.[872]

Three months later, on July 1, the CAA also switched to "knots" and "nautical miles," conforming to the military measurement of speed and distance.[873]

1952/05   First Jet Passenger Service

British Overseas Airways Corp. (BOAC) introduced the first jet passenger service, using the de Havilland Comet. The Comet carried 38 passengers at 490 mph.

The Comet got off to a rough start. After three crashes in two years, the entire fleet was grounded.[874]

1953   Sterling Airport Closes

After the Rock Falls Airport opened in 1946, activity at the nearby Sterling Airport slowly diminished. Eventually, Vic Jacoby closed Sterling Airport in 1953.[875]

1953   Chicago and Southern Air Lines Merges with Delta

Chicago and Southern Air Lines and Delta Air Lines merged in 1953. The new company operated for two years as Delta C&S before becoming simply Delta Air Lines.[876]

1953/02   Airline Service Begins at Gary

Lake Central Airlines started airline service to Gary Municipal Airport in February 1953. Lake Central offered 15-minute flights to Midway with service to Indianapolis, Pittsburgh, and Lima, OH.

Lake Central was the first of numerous airlines that served Gary for short periods until 1975, when commercial air service to Gary ceased for years.[877]

1953/04/10   SAGE System Proceeds

The Air Force decided to proceed with the advanced radar defense system developed by MIT's Lincoln Labs. SAGE (Semi-Automatic Ground Environment) coordinated multiple radar inputs and sent intercept coordinates to fighters.[878]

1953/07/03   Chicago Women Compete in Cross-Country Race

Two Chicago women, Virginia Rabung and Helen O'Hara departed Lawrence, MA, on July 3, 1953, destined for Long Beach, competing in the 7th All Women's Air Race organized by the 99s.

Since neither woman could afford the expenses of such a long trip, Rabung convinced her employer to sponsor their entry. The International Minerals and Chemical Corp. had just introduced a food flavoring spice called Ac'cent. Their plane bore a large sign advertising the product and at each of the 13 intermediate stops along the way, the women gave media interviews promoting the product.

Prior to the race, the women flew a Cessna 120, owned by O'Hara and her husband, Jerry, from Chicago to the race's Massachusetts starting point. The two-seat Cessna 120 had an 85 hp engine that needed to be hand propped to start. There was no autopilot, so one of the women had hands on the controls the entire trip.

Following the race, they returned to Chicago by going north to San Francisco and then east, enabling them to make publicity stops in a whole new set of cities.[879]

1953/11/27   Meigs Field Loses Its AAA Defense

The Army announced on November 27, 1953, that the 45th Anti-Aircraft Artillery Brigade would leave its current site at the north end of Meigs Field. A combination of factors forced the relocation of the 120-millimeter guns. Their position in line with Meigs runway was becoming an issue as traffic at the airport increased. Also the Army was deemphasizing the role of artillery for air defense as the new Nike missiles became available.[880]

1953/12/01   Playboy Goes to Press

Chicago native Hugh Hefner spent $200 to publish the first issue of *Playboy*. The magazine was followed by the creation of a series of Playboy Clubs around the country. Hefner resided in and controlled his company from the Playboy Mansion on North State Pkwy. In 1965, Playboy purchased the old Palmolive building on Lake Shore Dr., including the Lindbergh beacon, to be the corporate headquarters. For better or worse, the Playboy empire changed the image of sexual relationships in our culture.[881]

1954   First Omni Navigation Stations in Chicago Area

Chicago Heights and Naperville were the sites of the first two installations of the new Omni navigation radio transmitters.[882]

1954   First Nike Missiles Installed in the Chicago Area

Starting in early 1954, the first Nike-Ajax missile complex in the Chicago area opened at the old Libertyville Naval Outlying Landing Field. The Army operated two sites (C-92 and C-94) at the northeast and northwest corners of the field. Although the runways remained at the missile site, they were officially closed.

Later the same year, the government canceled the lease with Illinois Aircraft Sales and Service for the Arlington Heights Airport to make it part of Chicago's air defense system. The Arlington Heights site contained both a missile launch facility (C-80) and a radar control Direction Center (C-80DC). Unlike the Libertyville site, the landing strip remained in operation.[883]

The Libertyville Nike batteries were deactivated in 1963. The location was considered as a site for the Sentinel Missiles in the late 1960s.[884]

1954   108th Relocates to O'Hare

Following its service overseas during the Korean Conflict, the 126th Bombardment Wing, including its associated 126th Bombardment Group and 108th Bombardment Squadron returned to Midway as part of the Illinois National Guard in January 1953. The following year, the Wing, Group, and Squadron's designation was changed from "Bombardment" to "Fighter-Bomber" flying P-51 Mustangs.

Less than a year later, in 1954, the 126th Fighter-Bomber Group and the 108th Fighter-Bomber Squadron moved to O'Hare while the 126th

Fighter-Bomber Wing remained at Midway. In July 1955, the old Mustangs were replaced by newer F-84F Thunderstreak jets, which were again upgraded to F-86L Sabres two years later.[885]

1954/03/26   Robinson Killed in Crash

John Robinson, founder of the Challenger Air Pilots Assn. and major figure in Ethiopian aviation, died in a plane crash in Ethiopia on March 26, 1954.

After a ground-breaking career as an African American pilot and mechanic in Chicago, Robinson fought in Ethiopia against the Italian Fascists in 1935–1936 and became commander of the Ethiopian Air Force. After the end of the war, Robinson returned to Ethiopia. After helping to rebuild their air force, he stayed to create the first airline in Ethiopia.

In February 2015, the U.S. Embassy in Addis Ababa dedicated the Embassy Reading Garden in honor of Col. John Robinson.[886]

1954/06/29   B-52 Enters Service

The Boeing B-52 Stratofortress entered service with the U.S. Air Force on June 29, 1954. It remains in service after more than 60 years, becoming one of the longest-used aircraft in the U.S. arsenal. [887]

1954/08/23   C-130 Becomes Airborne

The C-130 Hercules took its first flight on August 23, 1954. The Lockheed cargo was in production for more than half a century and remains in service at the time of this writing.[888]

1955–1959

1955   Mixed Class (First and Coach) Cabins Introduced

TWA introduced the first flights offering Sky Coach Service on its L-049 Constellations in Chicago. Sky Coach seats were priced lower than other seats on the same flight. Until this time, airlines had offered economy service only on separate flights.[889]

1955   First Forest Fire Extinguished by Airplane

The first recorded instance of a forest fire being extinguished using water sprayed from a plane took place in the state of Washington in 1955.[890]

1955   Chicagoland Gets Passenger Service

Starting in 1955, Chicago Airways added Chicagoland Airport as a stop on its route between Midway and Mitchell Field in Milwaukee. Three flights a day used the airport's turf runways for the 20-minute flight to and from Midway. Chicago Airways stopped service in 1958, about the time one of the airport's turf runways was paved.

Also in the late 1950s, the original Northbrook VHF Omni Directional Beacon was located by Chicagoland Airport. In the early 1970s, the beacon was relocated to Libertyville.[891]

1955   Meigs Field Extends Runway

In 1955, Chicago's lakefront airport, Meigs Field, extended its sole runway from 2,800 ft. to 3,500 ft.[892]

1955/02/11   Comet Airworthiness Certificate Withdrawn

Following two crashes of the Comet in the previous year, a British Court of Inquiry determined the cause to be metal fatigue and withdrew the Comet's airworthiness certificate. Because of the delay, American manufacturers had an opportunity to catch up in passenger jet development.[893]

1955/04/15   First McDonald's Restaurant Opens

Arlington Heights businessman Raymond Kroc opened the first franchised McDonald's Restaurant in Des Plaines on April 15, 1954.

Kroc, a restaurant supply salesman, had visited customers Dick and Mack McDonald in their popular San Bernandino burger place. He was impressed with their Speedee Service System. The brothers weren't interested in expanding but in 1954, Kroc and the McDonald brothers inked a deal for Kroc to franchise their restaurant around the country. Kroc later bought out the brothers (in 1961). Today the chain currently has tens of thousands of restaurants in dozens of countries.[894]

1955/04/20   Richard J. Daley First Elected Mayor

Richard J. Daley was sworn in for the first of six terms as Mayor of Chicago on April 20, 1955. He served 21 years before his death on December 20, 1976.[895]

1955/04/28   Whirly-Girls Formed

Thirteen female helicopter pilots from the U.S., France, and Germany started the Whirly-Girls International to share information about rotary wing flying. Jean Ross Howard Phelan became the first president. The organization did much to promote the medical use of helicopters and the establishment of hospital heliports.[896]

1955/05/05   DEW Line Approved

The U.S. and Canada agreed to implement a line of radar stations in northern Canada, the Distant Early Warning (DEW) Line.[897]

1955/06/13   Rabung Reaches Havana

Having been hooked on cross-country flying with the 7th All Women's Air Race from Massachusetts to California, Virginia Rabung joined the first All Women's International Trans-Ocean Air Race. The race departed from Washington, DC, and arrived in Havana, Cuba, on June 13, 1955.

For this trip, Rabung flew her own Cessna 140, which had a metal fuselage and fabric wings. Her 140 had a hand-propped 85 hp engine and no automated flight controls. This trip was sponsored by Dictaphone Corp. in exchange for publicity meets.

Rabung flew solo the entire cross-country trip without a copilot to assist with navigation.The challenging part of this race was the 90-mi. segment over open water between Key West and Havana.[a] Navigation was by Low Frequency Radio Range (also called Four-Course Range) using one of the first segments installed in 1928.

a   Today, most pilots won't fly a single-engine plane over open water out of the sight of land.

The following year, Rabung participated in the race a second time. The second year's route began in Hamilton, ONT, and ended in Varadero, Cuba.[898]

1955/07/17   Braniff Flight 560 Crashes at Midway

On Sunday July 17, 1955, Braniff Flight 560 from Dallas to Chicago via Kansas City was in its descent when it struck a sign at 55th St. and Central Ave. Debris from the sign struck a passing car before the plane slammed through the airport fence, rupturing the gas tank and bursting into flame. There were 22 fatalities and another 21 people injured.

The twin-engine Convair CV-340 was making its approach under Instrument Flight Rules for runway 13R. On an otherwise clear day, Midway was obscured by fog and haze with limited (half mile) visibility.[899]

1955/07/26   First Turboprop Enters U.S. Service

Capital Airlines put the first turboprop, a Vickers V-701 Viscount, in service on the Chicago to Washington route.[900]

1955/08/05   Crash at Midway Without Injuries

A couple of weeks after the Braniff flight crashed through the fence at Midway, on August 5, 1955, Northwest Orient Flight 410 had a similar incident, also in the vicinity of 55th St. and Central Ave. Arriving from Minneapolis-St. Paul, the Boeing 377 Stratocruiser touched down but failed to stop until it crashed through the fence at the end of the runway and came to rest on Central Ave. All 60 passengers and 8 crew members survived.[901]

1955/10   Skymotive Opens at O'Hare

In October 1955, Skymotive Terminal opened becoming the first aviation facility in the country designed exclusively for business aviation.

Skymotive had been started by former Air Force General John P. "Jock" Henebry in 1947. Henebry completed 280 missions in WWII and commanded the Korean Airlift from 1950–1952.

For many years, Henebry had run a small repair shop, Skymotive, which was the only civilian facility at O'Hare. As business aviation boomed after the Korean War, Henebry raised $750,000 for a new facility.

Henebry got a 20-year lease for 2.5 acres around his existing shop, which was adjacent to O'Hare's new terminal and close to the runways. This was unique at commercial airports where hangars for non-airlines were usually located in a remote corner.

The new Skymotive hangar was huge (125 x 400 ft.), with all the latest features including huge, powered doors and radiant heat. In addition to plane storage, the hangar contained complete maintenance and repair facilities. A luxurious terminal area provided executives with an area to relax, with a conference room for meetings. Upstairs offered a spacious, private area for flight crews.[902]

1955/10/29   O'Hare Opens to Passengers

Passenger service at O'Hare Airport began on October 29, 1955. That year, not coincidentally, was also when the major airlines began ordering jets.

By the middle of the following year, O'Hare consisted of a small, two-level terminal with sixteen gates, a control tower, four intersecting runways and parking for 1,400 cars. At first, O'Hare handled only jets with most other flights continuing to use Midway. The first year, only 471,000 passengers passed through O'Hare, about 20% of Midway's volume.[903]

1955/11/22   Hale School Relocated

On November 22, 1955, the Board of Education moved the Nathan Hale School from 63rd St. and Central Ave. to a new building farther west from Midway Airport.

The original school building, nestled in a corner of the square mile used by Midway, was built when the airport was smaller and the planes were fewer and quieter. After the war, the frequency of flights increased, as did the size of the planes. When the four-engine airliners revved their engines prior to taking off, the school's windows and furnishings rattled. Talking and concentrating was impossible. Even though the two closest runways (4L/22R and 4R/22L) were closed during school hours, constant aircraft noise made teaching difficult.

Shortly after the school settled in its new location, the old building was demolished and the land was used by the airport.[904]

1956   Chess Begins Recording

Brothers Leonard and Phil Chess, who sought to give blues music wider distribution, started Chess Records. Chess used several locations on the South Side, the most notable of which was 2120 S. Michigan Avenue.

For a decade between 1956 and 1965, Chess recorded and released some of the greatest musicians in the world. Blues artists included Willie Dixon, Howlin' Wolf, Muddy Waters, Etta James, and others. Early rockers such as Bo Diddley and Chuck Berry got their start at Chess. The Rolling Stones had three recording sessions that included their 1964 instrumental song "2120 South Michigan Ave."[905]

1956   Cessna Introduces the 172

Cessna introduced the four-place 172 Skyhawk. It became the longest produced and most popular general aviation airplane.[906]

1956   United Introduces Baggage Conveyors

In 1956, United became the first airline to use a conveyor system at Midway and other major airports to handle passenger baggage.[907]

1956   Toll Road Disrupts Gary Airport

In 1956, the Indiana Toll Road constructed a highway directly in the flight path of a runway at Gary Airport.The airport sued to block the toll road and recover over $3 million in future revenue lost because flights would be disrupted.[908]

The state court did not grant an injunction but provided about $164,000 in financial compensation to the airport. However, the Indiana Supreme Court reversed the decision. An appeal to the U.S. Supreme Court was denied in a split decision saying it was a state matter.[909]

1956   Waukegan Port Authority Takes Over Airports

In 1956, the Waukegan Port Authority took over responsibility for area airports. The Authority continued operating the existing Burris Field and constructed the new Waukegan Memorial Airport a few miles away.[910]

1956   Whiteside County Buys Airport

Ten years after Whiteside County established an Airport Authority, it finally got an airport. Initially the Airport Authority lacked funds to start an airport, so private individuals stepped up and started the Rock Falls Airport at the site selected by the Airport Authority. Air Corps veteran Kenny Zimmerman operated and developed the airport. Illini Airlines offered service from Rock Falls to Chicago, Rockford, and Madison starting in 1955.

In 1956, with funds in hand, Whiteside County purchased the airport from Zimmerman. The Airport Authority operated Rock Falls Airport as a public airport and added land expanding its footprint. The Authority renamed the airport Whiteside County Airport.

With public ownership and the increased size and level of activity, the airport qualified for state assistance. Whiteside built a 3,000 ft. N-S runway and by 1957 added runway lighting. In 1962, Ozark Airlines began service to Whiteside.[911]

1956   Selig Embarks on Aviation Endeavors

As a kid, Nicholas "Nick" Selig would drive from his Elmhurst home to Pal-Waukee to watch the airplanes. Nick's future wife, Suzette, also had an early fascination with flying. While she was still in high school, she soloed at Pal-Waukee before she was old enough to get a driver's license. Living near the Lake, it required determination for her to get to the airport, since her parents didn't drive.

Selig joined the Army, where he serviced aircraft through the Korean War. After the war, he worked for B&M Aircraft at Elmhurst Airport until it closed in 1956. Selig realized that his military experience was insufficient for the commercial world.

In 1957, Selig used some of his GI Bill funds, to get his Aircraft and Engine certificate, but at the time jobs were in short supply for those without experience. After working as a machinist for several years, in 1959, Selig went to Pal-Waukee to pursue his pilot's license. During his first lesson, he learned Priester Aviation was looking for a mechanic. While working as a mechanic at Priester, Selig completed his Private License, then went on to earn his Commercial, Instrument and Multi-engine Licenses. He started flying charter flights for Priester in addition to working as a mechanic.

Selig had a long career as both pilot and mechanic and is one of a few individuals to receive both the Wright Brothers Master Pilot Award and the Charles Taylor Master Mechanic Award.[912]

1956/03   Chicago Annexes O'Hare

Although Chicago owned the land O'Hare sat on, it was not officially a part of the city until March 1956, when the City of Chicago annexed the land, as well as a small corridor to connect it with the nearest part of the city. Rosemont granted the land to connect the airport in an exchange for a 45-in. water main to bring Lake Michigan drinking water to Rosemont.[913]

1956/06/30   Grand Canyon Crash

At about 10 a.m. on June 30, 1956, United Flight 718, a DC-7, collided with TWA Flight 2, an L-1049 Super Constellation, over 20,000 ft. above the Grand Canyon.

Both planes left Los Angeles around the same time flying under Visual Flight Rules (VFR). The United flight was headed to Chicago and the TWA flight was bound for Kansas City. They were flying in uncontrolled airspace, and both pilots diverted over the Grand Canyon to give passengers a spectacular view. The wreckage was at the bottom of the Grand Canyon making recovery of the 128 victims and the accident investigation extremely difficult.[a]

Subsequent investigations, including Congressional hearings, revealed the fact that despite great increases in commercial air traffic, the Air Traffic Control system had not kept pace with the growth. The aftermath of this crash resulted in changes in air space and air traffic control including increased use of Instrument Flight Rules (IFR) by air carriers.[914]

1956/08/15   First Pal-Waukee Rattlesnake Hunt

The first rattlesnake hunt was organized in Wheeling on August 15, 1956, in the Forest Preserve across Milwaukee Ave. from Pal-Waukee. The rattlesnake population had grown significantly, with some area residents being bitten.[915]

1956/08/20   Chicago Helicopters Carry Passengers

After five years of operating a mail-only service, the Helicopter Air Service (HAS) of Chicago got a charter to allow passenger service[916] and was reorganized into Chicago Helicopter Airways as a passenger-carrying airline on August 20, 1956. The new shuttle service began flying Sikorsky S-55 helicopters between Midway, O'Hare, and Meigs.

Later, they upgraded their fleet to the newer Sikorsky S-58 copters that could carry 12 passengers and added Gary and Winnetka as destinations. Flights departed on the hour from Midway to Meigs and then O'Hare. Flights left O'Hare on the half-hour back to Meigs and Midway. Ticket prices were roughly comparable to cab fare. With a fleet of eight helicopters making more than 150 flights daily, CHA became the world's largest helicopter service. It carried more than 300,000 passengers in 1960.[917]

The idea was supported by Mayor Richard J. Daley and some aldermen. However, the original Midway Air Lines (with the Kangaroo logo) argued the added competition would destroy their commuter shuttle, which had just begun operating in the black. They pointed out that HAS survived

---

a   The nephew of a passenger on the DC-7, Mike Nelson, has written a marvelously descriptive historical account of the crash, *We Are Going In.*

because of an annual half million dollar federal subsidy to fly mail, giving it an unfair advantage.[918]

1956/08/30   VORTAC Navigation Approved

After years of acrimonious debate about whether to use the military TACAN or the civil VOR system, the Air Coordinating Committee recommended a combination of both, implemented as VORTAC.[919]

1956/09/01   Harlem Airport Closes

On Sept 1, 1956, Fred Schumacher reluctantly closed Harlem Airport, which gave way to a strip mall and a development of 1,000 houses. Fred and Eleanor Schumacher and one of their pilots, Wilbur Bohl, moved their operation to Lansing Airport.[920]

1956/12/31   Elmhurst Airport Closes

Elmhurst Airport closed on December 31, 1956, when the property owners failed to renew the lease.[921] Increased traffic and flight restrictions from O'Hare made Elmhurst less appealing to those flying small planes and the proximity to O'Hare made the land very attractive to developers.[922]

1957/05/03   Kankakee Airport Authority Commences Operation

On May 3, 1957, Kankakee County created the Kankakee Valley Airport Authority to create and operate the Greater Kankakee Airport. The KVAA taxing district included the City of Kankakee and the Villages of Bradley and Bourbonnais.[923]

The small Kankakee Airport on Route 115 southwest of Kankakee, IL had served the area around Kankakee for years with its two turf runways.[924]

In 1962, the KVAA opened Greater Kankakee Airport three miles south of the City of Kankakee. The new airport had two asphalt runways, the longest nearly 6,000 ft.[925]

The original Kankake Airport continues operating today as a privately-owned public use facility and is often referred to as "Lesser Kankakee Airport" to distinguish it from its newer, larger cousin.[926]

1957/07/06   High Speed Weather Teletypewriters

The CAA announced an upgrade of its weather network with new high-speed teletypewriters capable of 100 words per minute.[927]

1957/07/12   Midway Gets Flooded

Starting on Friday, July 12 1957, a record 6.24 in. of rain fell on Chicago flooding many streets, underpasses, subway segments, and countless buildings. Midway was isolated without power and communications lines. Access roads were flooded and 2 ft. of water covered the runways, stranding 5,000 people in the partially flooded terminal building. Some hangars had up to 7 ft. of water in their basements. It took 36 hr. before the cleanup efforts could begin.[928]

1957/08/05   FDR Required on Certain Flights

The CAB issued a requirement on August 5, 1957, that larger commercial planes install a Flight Data Recorder (FDR). As years progressed, the CAB expanded the scope of planes subject to the requirement.[929]

1957/10/04   Sputnik Orbits the Earth

On October 10, 1957, the Soviet Union launched Sputnik, the first artificial satellite into earth orbit, triggering a space race between the two superpowers.[930]

1957/10/20   Boeing 707 First Flies

The Boeing 707 made its first flight on October 20, 1957.[931]

1958   Northwest Tollway Opens

A new stretch of the Northwest Tollway (I-90) opened between Chicago and Rockford, easing and speeding automobile transportation between the two cities.

The highway that had been envisioned in Ralph Burke's 1948 Airport Master Plan also made an impact on air traffic. The easier drive into O'Hare gave a slight boost to its business, but at a significant expense to Rockford Airport. In June 1962, the Peoria-Rockford Bus Co. began shuttle service between O'Hare and Rockford Airports, drawing more passengers away from the smaller airport.[932]

1958   Frasca Aviation Launched

In 1958, Rudy Frasca formed Frasca Aviation and built his first flight simulator in his garage. He continued making simulators using mechanical computers at various locations before moving into a permanent factory in Champaign.

Growing up in central Illinois, Frasca had developed an early interest in aviation and took flying lessons when he was 14. Frasca joined the Navy in 1949 and was stationed at Glenview Naval Air Station as a flight instructor using the Link Trainer. He realized there could be a better way to teach instrument flight skills.

After leaving the Navy, Frasca attended the University of Illinois, where he majored in Aviation Psychology. There he developed an interest in flight simulation. He believed he could produce a product superior to those available at the time, so he launched his company.

In the late 1970s Frasca made a technological leap, using electronic analog computers instead of mechanical ones. Digital technology gradually replaced analog and by 1983, Frasca simulators used PC-based systems.[933]

1958/01/31   First U.S. Satellite Launch

After a series of failed attempts, the U.S. successfully launched the Explorer I satellite into earth orbit.[934]

1958/06/15   GMT Adopted for Aviation

On June 15, 1958, the CAA adopted Greenwich Mean Time (Zulu Time) for all air traffic control operations.[935]

1958/06/21   Chicago Streetcars Roll into History

After dropping off its last passenger, the last green-and-cream streetcar headed for the garage on June 21, 1958, never to carry passengers again. From a single horse-drawn trolley nearly a century earlier, the Chicago streetcar system had grown into the largest in the nation.[936]

1958/08/08   First International Flight at O'Hare

Former air racer Harold Neumann was at the controls of the first international flight to land at O'Hare. The TWA L-1649A Super Starliner arrived nonstop from Paris.[937]

1958/08/23   Federal Aviation Act of 1958

On August 23, 1958, President Eisenhower signed the Federal Aviation Act of 1958, a sweeping reorganization of aviation replacing all existing regulations since the Air Commerce Act of 1926. The Act reorganized all aviation-related supervisory and regulatory functions from various agencies into two independent organizations the Civil Aeronautics Board and the Federal Aviation Agency.[938]

1958/10/01   NASA Created

The Space Act signed by President Eisenhower in July created the National Aeronautics and Space Administration, resolving debate about whether the space program would be under civilian or military control.[939]

1958/10/26   Boeing 707 Enters Service

The Boeing 707 was certificated on September 23, 1958.[940] About a month later, on October 26, Pan American put the 707 into transatlantic service.

The 707 was an outgrowth of Boeing's 367-80 or Dash 80. The Dash 80 and subsequent large Boing aircraft followed the basic overall design Boeing first used in the B-47. The KC-135 Stratotanker, also based on the Dash 80, started service earlier with the USAF in June 1957.[941]

1959   EAA Brings Convention and Fly-Ins to Rockford

Beginning in 1959 the Experimental Aircraft Assn. (EAA) held its annual convention and fly-ins at Rockford.

The previous year's opening of the Northwest Tollway made it much easier for attendees to drive there. At Rockford's first fly-in , the EAA drew 35,000 people and nearly 500 aircraft. During the week, the control tower handled almost 4,000 flight operations.[942]

1959/01/03   U.S. Adds the Biggest State

On January 3, 1959, Alaska became the 49th state in the United States. Alaska was first state added since Oklahoma in 1911.[943]

1959/01/25   Nonstop Transcontinental Air Service

American Airlines inaugurated nonstop flights between Los Angeles and New York using its new 707s.[944]

1959/02/03   The Day the Music Died in a Plane Crash

After finishing a concert in Clear Lake, IA, Buddy Holly chartered a plane to fly to Moorhead, MN, the next stop on their tour. Buddy Holly, Richie Valens, and Jiles Perry Richardson (the Big Bopper) boarded a V-tail Bonanza in Mason City for the flight to Fargo, ND, adjacent to Moorhead.

At about 1 a.m., they departed in light snow and deteriorating VFR conditions. The plane went only about six miles before it crashed in a cornfield, killing all on board. The wreckage wasn't discovered until the next morning.

The investigation lay blame for the crash on the pilot. Although he had passed his written exam and logged 52 hours of instrument time, he had not passed his checkride nor received his instrument rating. A contributing factor was that his training had been done using a conventional artificial horizon, but the Bonanza had an older Sperry F3 attitude gyroscope, which displayed pitch attitude, the opposite of an artificial horizon.[945]

1959/02/20   Avro Arrow Project Canceled

Abruptly on February 20, 1959, the Canadian Prime Minister announced the immediate cancellation of the project. Shortly thereafter, orders were given to destroy and scrap everything related to the Arrow project, including the prototypes.

The CF-105 Arrow was a high-performance delta-wing interceptor developed by Avro Canada. Five prototypes had flown 66 hours of test flights with an official top speed of 1.96 Mach (unofficially, it exceeded Mach 2).[946]

1959/03/15   American Airlines Cargo Crashes into Tower

Shortly after midnight, American Airlines Flight 2815 collided with a 96 ft. tall steel tower and crashed in a railway yard near 70th St. and Cicero Ave. during takeoff from Midway. There were no fatalities on the cargo flight, a Convair 240 that originated at La Guardia. The pilot was making his second ILS-approach at the time of the crash. The cause of the accident was determined to be the pilot's inattention to his instruments and failure to maintain altitude.[947]

1959/06/08   X-15 Makes First Flight

NASA began high altitude research flights with its two X-15 aircraft. The flights continued until the X-15s were retired in 1969.[948]

1959/07/26   Queen Elizabeth II Visits Chicago

The first reigning British monarch to visit Chicago, Queen Elizabeth II, with her husband Prince Phillip, arrived for a one-day visit on July 6, 1959. Recognizing the opening of the St. Lawrence Seaway, the Queen sailed down the Seaway in the royal yacht *Britannia* and docked in front of Buckingham Fountain in an area that has since been known as the Queen's Landing.[949]

1959/08   First Chicago Air and Water Show

The Chicago Park District sponsored the Lake Shore Park Air and Water Show starting a tradition that has endured for more than a half a century. Al Benedict organized the one-day event with a budget of only $88. A barge in Lake Michigan was the base for a diving exhibition, water skiers, and a water ballet. A Coast Guard HUS-1G Seahorse helicopter from Glenview conducted a rescue demo.[950]

1959/08/21   Hawaii Becomes a State

Hawaii becomes is admitted as the 50th of the United States. Statehood was a boon for tourism and United Airlines capitalized on its routes to Honolulu. In addition to traditional advertising about its Hawaiian connection, United undertook some groundbreaking product placement advertising, such as sponsoring the Tiki Room at Disneyland in Anaheim and featuring a United jet in Elvis Presley's movie *Blue Hawaii.*

1959/10   O'Hare's First Runway Expansion Program

With jet operations coming soon, O'Hare began the first of many runway improvement programs. Runway 14R/32L had been originally built of asphalt. In October 1959, it was rebuilt in concrete and lengthened to 11,600 ft. to handle jet airliners. Construction was complete by June of 1960.[951]

1959/11/24   TWA Cargo Plane Crashes in West Lawn

Loaded with cargo, TWA Flight 595 took off from Midway for Los Angeles about 5:30 in the morning of November 24, 1959. Shortly after taking off, the pilot notified the tower that the number two engine of the Lockheed L-1049 Super Constellation had a fire and was shut down.

While circling back for an emergency landing, the plane banked more than 45 degrees and sank rapidly. The crew quickly leveled out and tried to climb but not in time. The Constellation crashed into the West Lawn residential area at 64th St. and Kilpatrick Ave. The plane's path destroyed seven houses, three garages, and an eight-unit apartment building. Besides the three-man crew, nine people on the ground were killed and another ten were injured.[952]

1959   Midway Traffic Peaks

Traffic at Midway reached its zenith with 431,400 flights and 10,040,353 passengers, retaining the crown as the world's busiest airport.[953]

1960–1964

1960/11/18   McCormick Place Opens

Chicago had long been a destination for conventions and trade shows with its International Amphitheater, Chicago Coliseum, and the Chicago Stadium. However, some large events were outgrowing their existing venues.

Despite opposition from those supporting Burnham's plan to preserve an open lakefront for recreational purposes, McCormick Place opened a lakefront building in November 1960.[954]

1960/03/15   FAA Establishes Age-60 Rule

An FAA regulation took effect on March 15, 1960, that prohibited pilots over the age of 60 from operating large aircraft on air carrier routes.[955]

1960/03/17   Northwest Flight 710 Loses Wing Over Indiana

On March 17, 1960, Northwest Orient Flight 710, made a brief stop at Midway before departing for Miami. Over Indiana, the L-188C Electra suddenly disintegrated in flight and plunged into a farm near Cannelton, IN, killing all 66 people on board. Subsequent investigation revealed a problem with Electras in which a flutter in the outboard engine nacelles resulted in the sudden separation of the right wing from the rest of the airplane.[956]

1960/05/01   U-2 Spy Plane Shot Down

A U-2 flying a photo reconnaissance mission over the Soviet Union was shot down and pilot Gary Powers was captured.[957]

1960/07/27   CHA Helicopter Crash

A Sikorsky S-58C operated by Chicago Helicopter Airways was making a routine 15-minute commute between Midway and O'Hare on July 27, 1960. At about 1,500 ft., the copter came apart in mid-air and crashed into Forest Home Cemetery, in Forest Park, IL, becoming the first crash of a commercial helicopter service flight in the country. All 13 people on board died.

The day after the crash, a rotor blade was found in a tree more than a half-mile from the crash site. The subsequent investigation revealed the blade, which had more than 3,000 hours in service, failed due to metal fatigue. The resulting gyrations from an unbalanced rotor severely stressed the copter causing the tail cone and rotor to break off.[958]

1960/09/08   FAA Adopts Glide Path Lights

The FAA adopted a British-developed system of glide path landing lights. This external system was installed at airports and required no additional equipment in planes.[959]

1960/09/26   Nixon-Kennedy Debate

The first televised presidential debate between Richard Nixon and John F. Kennedy took place in Chicago, changing political campaigns forever.[960]

1960/10/15   FAA Tests Controlling Air Traffic by Area Rather Than Route

Chicago and Indianapolis were selected for the FAA's Operation Pathfinder program. Airspace between 24,000 ft. and 35,000 ft. around the cities was under positive control of Air Traffic Control Centers. Planes in that airspace were required to be equipped with a radio and transponder and to operate under instrument flight rules (IFR).[961]

1960/11/05   Expressway to O'Hare Complete

The final segments of the Northwest Tollway (later called the Kennedy Expressway) were completed, greatly simplifying travel from downtown Chicago to O'Hare.[962]

1961   Tallman Returns to California

California native Frank Tallman operated a business at Chicagoland Airport in what is now Lincolnshire. Tallman also began collecting pre-war and other vintage airplanes. In 1961 he moved his business back to California, where he partnered with Paul Mantz to form Tallmantz Aviation to serve the movie industry. They did stunt flying in films as well as providing period planes for background scenes.

Tallman learned to fly as a teenager and lived in Chicago prior to WWII. He was a civilian instructor for military pilots until he became a Navy pilot. After the war, he remained in Chicago serving in the reserves while running his business at Chicagoland Airport, where he began restoring vintage aircraft.[963]

1961   United Shifts Headquarters

In 1961, United moved their headquarters out of Midway Airport to an area near O'Hare in Elk Grove Township. With the shift in operations from Midway to O'Hare, United wanted its headquarters location to be more accessible to O'Hare.[964]

1961   Scotty O'Carroll Flies West

The founder of Monarch Aviation and a mainstay at Municipal/Midway for many years, Scotty O'Carroll, died of a stroke while vacationing out of state. As the plane carrying his casket landed at Midway, the tower dimmed the runway lights in his honor.[965]

1961/04/12   First Man in Space

The first man to go into space was Soviet cosmonaut Yuri Gagarin, who made a single orbit before safely returning.[966]

1961/05   Rabung Conquors Bermuda Triangle

Having flown her Cessna 140 to Cuba twice, flying over open ocean had become "old hat" for Virginia Rabung. In May 1961, she participated in the 11th All Women's International Air Race from Florida to five separate islands in the Bahamas. This trip featured a 180-mi. over-water segment, double the one to Cuba. There were no incidents in the race for Rabung or any of the competitors.[967]

1961/05/01   First U.S. Hijacking

The first airline hijacking in the U.S. took place on May 1, 1961, when a plane in route to Key West was diverted to Havana. The incident started a rash of hijackings, resulting in increasing security measures.[968]

1961/05/05   First American in Space

Alan Shepard became the first American in space when he rode a Mercury-Redstone rocket in a suborbital flight.[969]

1961/05/25   Illinois Certifies Roselle Airfield

On May 25, 1961 an Illinois Safety inspector certified that the Roselle Airfield[a] was safe to become operational, and it officially opened in

a   Roselle Field dates back to the war years, but is not to be confused with Schaumburg Field, one of the Glenview Naval Air Station's satellite airfields located at Barrington and Schaumburg roads.

mid-July. Roselle Airfield was the product of Leonard Boeske who, in 1959, purchased and expanded an existing airport on Irving Park Rd. near Rodenburg Rd. in unincorporated Cook and DuPage counties in what would become Schaumburg, IL. By 1963, Roselle Airfield had two FBOs.[970]

1961/06/01   United Acquires Capital

On June 1, 1961, United Air Lines completed the acquisition and merger with Capital Airlines. The combination of the second and fifth largest airlines made United the largest in the U.S.

Capital, which had been headquartered in Washington, DC, was an innovative airline that served destinations throughout the Northeast and Midwest. In 1948, it pioneered the introduction of coach fares on separate flights. In the mid-1950s, it introduced the turboprop Vickers Viscounts on routes from Chicago to both New York and Washington. However, by the late 1950s, Capital had been struggling financially.

Acquisition of Capital provided a double benefit for United. In addition to the fleet of modern Viscounts, Capital provide United with access to Florida routes.[971]

1961/07   108th Squadron Gets New Home and New Missions

In July 1961, the 126th Wing underwent major mission change, becoming an Air Refueling Wing as did units under its command, including the 108th Squadron.

The Wing received the first KC-97 Stratofreighters. It was the first Air National Guard (ANG) unit to fly an air refueling mission. Two years later, in 1963, they were the first ANG to refuel the USAF Thunderbirds.

Starting in 1966 and over the next decade, various units of the 126th had rotating assignments in Europe, refueling planes as they moved to and from Southeast Asia. In 1976, the 126th got rid of the propeller-driven KC-97s, replacing them with KC-135 Stratotankers.[972]

1961/08   First Appropriations for SST

Congress made the first appropriation to develop, by 1970–71, a commercial Super Sonic Transport that would travel at Mach 3.[973]

1961/08   Two New O'Hare Terminals Open

All the additional activity, as airlines shifted operations to O'Hare, put a tremendous load on the single, small terminal, so the airport engaged Stanislav Gladych to design two new terminals. The terminal design adhered to Mies van der Rohe's principle that "less is more." Gladych designed two long rectangular terminals connected by walkways.

The airport side of each terminal had arms and split fingers holding gates, as in Ralph Burke's original plan for O'Hare. The beauty of Gladych's plan was that additional terminals could be added to the chain without disrupting activity in the existing ones.[974]

When Gladych's two new terminals opened in August 1961, it took a 4,200 ft. hike to move between the most distant gates.[975]

1961/09/01   TWA Flight 529 Crashes in Clarendon Hills

Shortly after taking off from Midway on September 1, 1961, TWA Flight 529 crashed into a Clarendon Hills cornfield, killing all 78 on board.

According to the CAB, the accident was caused when a bolt fell out of the Lockheed L-049's elevator boost mechanism for an unknown reason. However, TWA contended the bolt was sheared off during impact with the ground.[976]

1961/09/17   Northwest Flight 706 Loses Control

On September 17, 1961, Northwest Orient Flight 706 made a stop at O'Hare on its way from Minneapolis to Fort Lauderdale. Shortly after takeoff, the L-188C Electra went into a very steep right bank and struck the ground, cartwheeling over its nose. All 37 people were killed. The cause was determined to be improper maintenance procedures on the aileron boost assembly.[977]

1962   Commercial Flights Shift to O'Hare

Although commercial flights to O'Hare started in 1955, the airlines didn't abandon Midway until 1962. In less than a year, scheduled flights at Midway fell from more than 1,000 per day to zero. Within just a few years, Midway's passengers dropped from more than 10 million to only 417,544 annually (fewer than the number of flights in 1959).[978]

1962/02/20   Glenn Orbits the Earth

John Glenn made the first American orbital flight on Feb 20, 1962. A Mercury-Atlas rocket boosted Glenn into space, where he made three orbits before splashing down in the North Atlantic four hours later.[979]

1962/03/05   Robert Taylor Homes Welcomes Residents

With high hopes to provide high quality affordable housing, the Chicago
Housing Authority (CHA) opened the Robert Taylor Homes on March 5,
1962. The 28 high-rise buildings in Robert Taylor Homes contained 4,400
housing units and was the first of many high-density housing projects
developed by the CHA.

It didn't take long before the poor construction and minimal maintenance of the buildings started to become evident. The high population
density with a corresponding lack of public services—including police
protection—made CHA housing a national disgrace. In 1995, the CHA
began the demolition of its high-rises.[980]

1962/03/23   First U.S. Twin Jet Executive Plane Certificated

North American's Sabreliner (Model 265), the first twin turbojet executive
airplane designed and manufactured in the U.S., was certificated on
March 23, 1962.[981]

1962/07/30   Ravenswood Airport Closes

Tiny Ravenswood Airport closed to the public on July 30, 1962, after being
at its Touhy Ave. location since 1928. O'Hare's rapid growth overwhelmed
the small general-aviation airport. Flying into or out of Ravenswood
required two-way radio contact and an altitude of less than 400 ft.

However, the owners, Abe and Shirley Marmel, continued their maintenance operation at Ravenswood. They were working in a hangar on May 25,
1979, when American Flight 191 lost an engine and crashed into their
former airport. Ravenswood closed completely after the incident.[982]

1962/08/05   Chicago Air and Water Show Features Thunderbirds

For the first time, the Chicago Air and Water Show featured one of the
military's aerial demonstration teams, the Thunderbirds flying their F-100
Super Sabres. The Army's Golden Knights parachute team also made their
first appearance parachuting from their DHC-2 Beavers.

Since then, one of the military aerial demonstration teams, such as the
USAF Thunderbirds or Navy Blue Angels, has been a big part of the Air and
Water Show.[983]

1962/10/22   Kennedy Blockades Cuba

During a TV address to the nation, President Kennedy announced a blockade of Cuba because of Soviet missiles based there.[984]

1962/11/17   Dulles Airport Opens

After years of discussion about Congressional appropriations, site selection, organizational battles, and other issues, Dulles International Airport finally opened. Usage was slow at first with only a little more than 110,000 flight operations in fiscal year 1964.[985]

1962/12/05   Lenny Bruce Arrested for Obscenity

While performing at the Gate of the Horn's midnight show, 37-year old Lenny Bruce was arrested by Chicago Police in the middle of his act. Charged with obscenity, Bruce was tried in absentia. After one hour of deliberation, an all-Catholic jury found Bruce guilty and a Catholic judge sentenced him to one year in prison in March 1963. In July 1964, the Illinois Supreme Court reversed the conviction.[986]

1962/12/15   Simultaneous Landings on Parallel Runways

For the first time, the FAA authorized simultaneous landings on parallel runways, to relieve periods of peak congestion at O'Hare. Both planes had to operate under IFR and were vectored in to parallel ILS systems.[987]

1963   O'Hare Becomes Busiest Airport

With the addition of United flights, the last airline to shift operations in 1962, O'Hare first earned the designation of the "world's busiest airport" in 1963.[988]

1963   Rochelle Gets an Airport

LaVerne Schultz owned a factory in Rochelle on Highway 251 and had built a grass runway beside it in the mid 1940s. In 1963, Schultz donated his 27-acre airport to the City of Rochelle. Over the next couple of decades, the city improved Rochelle Airport paving and expanding the runways.[989]

1963/02/09   First Flight of 727

The Boeing 727 made its maiden flight on February 9, 1963. The popular airliner entered service almost exactly a year later.[990]

1963/03   New Restaurant in O'Hare's Rotunda

To break the design monotony of O'Hare's two rectangular airport terminals, Gertrude Kerbis of CF Murphy and Associates designed the Rotunda Building, a $6 million circular rotunda joining them.

Completed in early 1963, the Rotunda Building had a large, open, two-story atrium capped by a shallow dome, with two floating staircases leading to the balcony. Large windows provided excellent views of the airport.

As the crossroads between terminals, the Rotunda provided a range of food service options, all operated by Carson, Pirie, Scott & Co. Nearly a thousand people could be served at a cafeteria, coffee shop, pancake house, and two cocktail lounges. The lower level housed an employee cafeteria as well as operational facilities. A single kitchen served about 8 million meals and 6 million barrels of beer each year through the 17 food-service facilities in the Rotunda.

Upstairs on the second level, the Seven Continents restaurant opened for business in March 1963. Similar to the much-acclaimed Cloud Room at Midway, the elegant Seven Continents restaurant offered fine food accompanied by a wide assortment of imported wines. Recognizing the international mix of O'Hare passengers, each member of the waitstaff was expected to speak three languages. Floor-to-ceiling windows provided the 450 diners with a fabulous view of the tarmac.

Today numerous food-service facilities are spread throughout all the terminals on the other side of security screening. The Rotunda's central food-service facilities are long-closed and the building is currently used as office space for O'Hare operations.[991]

1963/03/23   Kennedy Rededicates O'Hare International Airport

Fourteen years after the airport's opening with the National Air Fair and eight years after commercial passengers began arriving, O'Hare was finally ready for its rededication on March 23, 1963. Mayor Richard J. Daley pulled out all the stops and brought in President Kennedy for the ceremony.[992]

1963/03/28   Supreme Court Allows Black Airline Pilots

African American Marlon Green sued Continental Airlines for discrimination in hiring and in 1963, the Supreme Court ruled that Continental was guilty. Continental hired Green as a pilot in 1965 and he flew for them until 1978. Following the Supreme Court's finding, in 1964, American Airlines became the first major airline to hire a black pilot, David Harris.[993]

1963/06/16   First Woman in Space

Valentina Tereshkova, a Russian cosmonaut, became the first woman to go into space on June 16, 1963.[994]

1963/10/07   Learjet Takes to the Sky

The Learjet 23 made its first flight on October 7, 1963. The first customer delivery, made a year later, started a wave of jet aircraft for nonmilitary, noncommercial use.[995]

1963/11/22   JFK Assassinated

While people may not agree on who or how many people were involved, nobody disputes the fact that the President of the United States was killed with a gunshot to the head while visiting Dallas, TX. Following confirmation of President Kennedy's death, Vice President Lyndon Johnson quickly took the oath of office to assure continuity of government.[996]

1963/12   Schaumburg Annexes Roselle Airfield

The Village of Schaumburg annexed Roselle Airfield in December 1963. In 1965, the airfield constructed a terminal.[997]

1964/03/16   Maintenance Personnel Shortage

An FAA study revealed a severe shortage of aircraft maintenance personnel because younger mechanics as well as those entering the field found much better job opportunities in the missile and space sector. [998]

1964/04/17   Solo Around-the-World Flight by a Woman

Landing at Ohio's Port Columbus Airport on April 17, 1964, Geraldine "Jerrie" Mock completed the first solo flight around the world by a woman. Departing on March 19, the flight took her 29 days, 11 hr., and 59 min. to make the 23,103 mi. trip.[999]

1964/04/24   FAA Crashes Planes

The FAA and Flight Safety Foundation undertook an extensive study to reduce post-impact fatalities by examining data from crashes. Without leaving the ground, they deliberately crashed a DC-7 in April and an L-1649 Starliner in September, 1964. The following year, they conducted emergency evacuation tests using the Starliner's fuselage.[1000]

1964/05/19   King Air Certificated

The Beech King Air became the first business class twin-engine turboprop to receive FAA approval on May 19, 1964.[1001]

1964/06/26   Cockpit Voice Recorders Required

On June 26, 1964, the FAA began requiring the use of Cockpit Voice Recorders (CVR) in certain commercial aircraft. As with the 1957 implementation of Flight Data Recorders, the requirements began with larger planes of large carriers and worked their way down to smaller planes over the following years.[1002]

The mandate for CVRs resulted from the efforts of U.S. Representative Roman Pucinski, who served the Illinois 11th District (the area around O'Hare) from 1959 to 1973. Pucinski's crusade began his first year in the House and the bill was passed three years later. The FAA formally recognized his contribution, awarding him the Silver Medal of Distinguished Service on December 18, 1998.

Pucinski's dedication to aviation was rooted in his service during WWII. He served under Gen. Jimmy Doolittle as the lead bombardier for the Tokyo raid. As a pilot, he flew 49 combat missions and was awarded both the Distinguished Flying Cross and the Air Medal with Clusters.[1003]

1964/07/21   Pan Am Installs Inertial Navigation Systems

On July 21, 1964, Pan American began the installation of Inertial Navigation Systems on its entire fleet. The system was entirely internal, with no reliance on external navigation aids or magnetic compass readings. It was most useful over areas such as oceans where electronic navigation aids don't exist and over polar regions where magnetic readings are unreliable.[1004]

1964/08/10   Gulf of Tonkin Resolution

In response to a questionable attack on Navy warships earlier in August 1964, Congress jointly passed the Gulf of Tonkin Resolution on August 10, 1964, authorizing intervention in the Vietnam conflict. The resolution became the basis for increasingly extensive involvement in successive years.[1005]

1964/09/05   The Beatles Perform at the Amphitheater

Greeted by a crowd of 5,000 when they landed at Midway, the Beatles gave an earth-shaking performance at the International Amphitheater.[1006]

Although all the major airlines had been using O'Hare since 1962, the overwhelming crowds drawn to other airports by the Beatles caused Chicago officials to have them fly into Midway rather than risk disruption at O'Hare.[1007]

Besides introducing a new musical style, the Beatles round-the-world jet tour paved the way for performers to reach global audiences.[1008]

1964/10/06   First Helicopters IFR Approved

On October 6, 1964, two versions of the Sikorsky S-61 helicopter were certificated for instrument flight (IFR).[1009]

1964/10/16   First Chinese Nuclear Test

The Chinese became a nuclear power with their first test of a nuclear weapon on October 16, 1964.[1010]

1964/12/08   First Automated Landing

A French Caravelle operated by United Airlines made the first computer automated landing at Dulles on December 8, 1964.[1011]

1964/12/10   AIM First Published

On December 10, 1964, the first edition of the *Airmen's Information Manual* (AIM) was published consolidating information from three previous FAA publications. In July 1995, the AIM's title was changed to *Aeronautical Information Manual.*[1012]

1964/12/21   First Test Flight of the F-111

The F-111 Aardvark, which became the first production swing-wing airplane, made its first flight on December 21, 1964. The variable-sweep wing concept had been around since before WWII but only became feasible as technology developed.[1013]

1964/12/31   Complete FAR Is Published

Completing a process of consolidation and streamlining aviation regulations begun in August 1961, on December 31, 1964, the FAA published the complete version of the *Federal Aviation Regulations.*[1014]

1965–1969

1965   Feris Buys Taylorcraft

In 1965, Chicago aviator Charles Feris purchased Taylorcraft Aviation Corp. which was then in bankruptcy. Feris had started the Hinsdale Airport in the 1940s. Located near the intersection of Routes 66 and 83, in what is now Willowbrook, IL, Hinsdale had developed into a thriving little airport.[1015]

1965   Old Waukegan Airport Replaced

Wayne Carpenter, who had operated Waukegan Airport (the old Burris Field) since 1938, continued as airport manager until 1965, when the airport was sold. The Waukegan Port Authority replaced the aging facility with the new Waukegan Memorial Airport about two miles northeast. [1016]

1965/07   EAA Gets Breezy

Carl Unger took the EAA Fly-In at Rockford by storm with his RLU-1 Breezy. Designed and built by Unger and two fellow pilots, Charles Roloff and Robert Liposky, the Breezy consisted of the wing of a Piper PA-12 above a welded steel frame with a pusher engine and three seats. The Breezy embodied the joy of low-and-slow with the wind-in-your-face flying.

Over the years, Unger and his associates gave more than 7,000 free rides at the EAA gatherings in Rockford and Oshkosh, WI, as well as anywhere they went. The original Breezy is now housed at the EAA Museum in Oshkosh, but hundreds of Breezy's made from kits are flying around the country.[1017]

1965/07/23   First Surface-to-Air Missile Kill in Vietnam

On July 23, 1965, an American F-4C Phantom II in Vietnam became the first aircraft shot down by a Soviet missile fired from a ground launcher.[1018]

1965/08/16   United Flight 389 Crashes Into Lake

On the night of August 16, 1965, United Flight 389 from LaGuardia crashed into Lake Michigan east of Lake Forest as it was descending for a landing at Midway. All 30 people on the flight died in the crash.

The Boeing 727 had been in service less than two months with fewer than 150 cycles (takeoffs and landings) and no mechanical issues. The Flight Data Recorder was found but was inoperable. No official cause was determined for the crash. The predominant theory of the crash[a] was that the style of altimeter used in the plane was easily misread, causing the crew to incorrectly determine their altitude.[1019]

1965/11/09   New York City Blacks Out

An overloaded switch at a generating plant failed during the evening rush hour on November 9, 1965. The failure cascaded until 80,000 sq. mi. around New York City were without electricity for 13 hours. Both LaGuardia and Kennedy Airports were forced to shut down.[1020]

1965/12/31   Chicago Helicopter Airways Shuts Down

In the early 1960s, as major airlines moved all their operations to O'Hare, fewer people needed a shuttle to Midway. Chicago Helicopter Airways sold off its larger, more costly helicopters and reduced service.

Nationally, helicopter shuttles, including CHA, operated on Federal subsidies. In April 1965, the government ended subsidies for copter shuttle services in New York, Los Angeles, and Chicago. Without the outside money, CHA was unable to continue operations and closed its doors on December 31, 1965.[1021]

1966   Patterson Leaves United

Pat Patterson retired as head of United in 1966. At the time, United was the largest carrier in the free world, second in size only to Aeroflot in the Soviet Union. During his 30 years with United, Patterson led the transition from air mail to passenger service to jets.

Patterson began United's journey into the jet age in 1955 with an order of Douglas DC-8s, which were still under development. The DC-8 matched United's requirements better than the Boeing 707, which was a year further along in its development. Before the long-range DC-8s were delivered, in 1961, United placed French Caravelles in service on medium-range routes, including the vital Chicago to LaGuardia one. The last piston-engine airliner was retired from United's service in 1970.[1022]

1966   Sally Strempel Retires

In 1966, Sally Strempel retired and closed Sally's Flying School. During her career, Strempel flew more than 17,000 hours without an accident and

a   Another source indicated that a contributing factor may have been the new type of Fowler flaps that required more power during approach. When the power was pulled back as normal, the plane lost lift and fell from the sky.

trained more than 3,000 pilots. As the first woman FAA flight examiner in Illinois, she flight tested nearly 1,500 students.[1023]

1966   Prosperi Airport Closes

Prosperi Airport near Tinley Park, IL, closed in 1966 so a cloverleaf for I-80 could be built. There were reports of Ed Prosperi threatening state employees who arrived to shut the airport down.[1024]

1966   New Aurora Municipal Airport Opens

The current Aurora Municipal Airport opened in 1966, with three paved runways up to 6,500 ft. in length.[1025]

Peter Julius had owned and managed the first Aurora Airport. In the 1950s, Julius transferred ownership of a portion of airport property to the City of Aurora. In the late 1950s, I-88 was built through a part of the airport; however, both Julius and Aurora received buyouts. The money received by Aurora was sufficient for the city to construct another airport about ten miles away in Sugar Grove.

1966/01/07   SR-71 Enters Service

The stealthy reconnaissance aircraft capable of flying at Mach 3, the SR-71 Blackbird entered service on January 7, 1966.[1026]

1966/08/11   Beatles Arrive at O'Hare

On the last of their three trips to Chicago, the Beatles arrived at O'Hare rather than Midway. By this time the city knew what to expect with the crowds, which had been diminishing. The group's novelty was wearing off and they were becoming somewhat controversial. While in Chicago, the group held a press conference apologizing for John Lennon's remark that the Beatles were more popular than Jesus.[1027]

1966/09/09   Bird Committee Formed

The Federal government formed an interagency committee on September 9, 1966, to study the interaction between birds and airplanes. The committee consisted of representatives from FAA, NASA, CAB, Dept. of the Interior, Dept. of HEW, and the three branches of the armed forces.[1028]

1966/09/09   O'Hare Sets Flight Record

On September 9, 1966, O'Hare became the first airport to handle more than 2,000 flight operations in a single day.[1029]

1966/10/15   Johnson Creates Dept. of Transportation

President Johnson created the Dept. of Transportation on October 15, 1966, consolidating 31 separate agencies into a single cabinet-level department.[1030]

1967   Cardinal Born at Campbell

Two American Airlines Mechanics, Gary Campbell and Jim Tahaney, quit their day jobs in 1967 to form Cardinal Aviation Services at Campbell Airport. Cardinal provided flight lessons and aircraft service.

Campbell, near Grayslake, IL, is the only public-use airport in Lake County other than Waukegan. It was started in the 1950s and its name has no relation to Gary Campbell.[1031]

1967   St. Germains Buy Hinsdale Airport

Charles Feris, owner of Hinsdale Airport, purchased the bankrupt Taylorcraft Aviation Corp. in 1965. Unfortunately, Feris didn't fare much better than the previous Taylorcraft owners. In 1967, he sold the airport to support his struggling aircraft company.

Two long-time tenants, William and Wilma St. Germain, purchased Hinsdale Airport in Willowbrook, IL from Ferris. They owned one of the largest Piper dealerships in the area, with a flight school operating 30 airplanes. The St. Germains retained Feris as the Airport Manager.[1032]

1967/01/16   McCormick Place Burns

About six years after it opened, Chicago's new convention facility, McCormick Place, burned to the ground on January 16, 1967. Like a phoenix, a newer, more modern McCormick Place rose from the ashes and opened in 1971. Since then, several buildings have been added to the complex, allowing it to maintain its standing as one of the largest, most complete convention venues in the world.[1033]

1967/01/26   First Major Chicago Blizzard

An unusually warm January with highs in the sixties was suddenly shattered by a blizzard with thunderstorms on January 26, 1967. The storm lasted 29 hr., officially dumping 23 in. of snow (16.4 in. on January 26 alone) with wind speeds exceeding 50 mph. As the city was recovering, two additional storms on February 1st and then on the 5th dropped another foot of snow.[1034]

1967/04/01   FAA Gets a "Promotion"

A new cabinet-level Dept. of Transportation (DOT) began operation on
April 1, 1967, with Alan S. Boyd, previously the Chairman of the CAB,
becoming the first Secretary of Transportation.

DOT is the result of President Johnson's decision to consolidate various
Federal agencies involved in transportation into single department. As part
of the change, the Federal Aviation *Agency* became the Federal Aviation
Administration with added powers and responsibilities. The new DOT also
established the National Transportation Safety Board (NTSB) to investigate
accidents involving all modes of commercial transportation.[1035]

1967/04/09   Boeing 737's First Flight

Boeing's short-haul 737 made its first flight on April 9, 1967. The FAA
gave it a type-rating certificate in December and it entered service in
February 1968.[1036]

1967/04/23   First Person Dies During Space Flight

During the landing of his Soyuz I spacecraft, Cosmonaut Vladimir Komarov
became the first person confirmed to have died during a space mission.[1037]

1967/04/29   Pal-Waukee Gets Control Tower

Pal-Waukee Airport became a safer airport when it dedicated an air traffic
control tower on April 29, 1967. The tower came as a result of lengthy
negotiations between George Priester and the FAA.

Priester argued that because of Pal-Waukee's volume of air traffic and
proximity to O'Hare, "Pilots were playing Russian roulette in the air."
However, building a tower would be counter the FAA's policy to only
provide control towers at public, not private, airports. At the time, the FAA
had only constructed two towers at private airports: Burbank, CA, and
Redbird Field in Dallas

Eventually the two parties reached an agreement. The airport bore
about $100,000 in construction costs for the 65-ft. orange-and-white-
striped tower and the associated infrastructure. The FAA invested $15,000
in radio and electronic equipment and would staff the tower from 6 a.m. to
10 p.m. daily.[1038]

A year after the dedication of the tower, an Instrument Landing System
(ILS) system was installed, enabling airplanes to land in marginal weather
conditions which became increasingly important with the increase in
business jet traffic at the airport.[1039]

1967/07/07   Chicago Woman Retraces Earhart's Flight

Ann Holtgren Pellegreno, a Chicago native, successfully followed Amelia
Earhart's route around the world. She departed Oakland on July 9, 1967,
and returned on July 7.

Accompanying Pellegreno on the flight was Lee Koepke, owner and
restorer of the Lockheed 10A Electra, the same model flown by Earhart.
William R. Payne was the co-pilot and William L. Polhemus was navigator
for the trip.

On the 30th anniversary of Earhart's disappearance, the crew dropped a
wreath over Howland Island. In 1971, Pellegreno published her experiences
in *World Flight: The Earhart Trail*.[1040]

1967/10/03   Riverview Sold to Developers

Airports weren't the only institutions gobbled up by developers. During its
63 years of operation, Riverview Amusement Park had become a Chicago
institution. During the 1967 season, 1.7 million patrons visited Riverview,
almost as many as attended Chicago baseball home games that year. On
October 3, Riverview owners announced that developers had purchased the
park and would be turning it into a shopping center.[1041]

1967/10/19   Gulfstream II Receives Type Certificate

The Grumman Gulfstream II received its type certificate on October 19,
1967. The airplane was the first in a dynasty of twin-engine long-range,
luxury corporate jets.[a] Only a few months after its introduction, on May 5,
1968, the G-II made a nonstop transatlantic flight, ushering in a new level
of bizjet acceptance.[1042]

1968   New Lenox Airport Opens

The New Lenox Airport opened at the southeast corners of W. Laraway and
Schmul roads in 1968.[1043]

1968   Developer Buys Sky Harbor

In 1968, the developer Arthur Rubloff bought Sky Harbor from Bill
Turgeon with the intention of creating an "air-industrial park." Rubloff's
concept was to develop an industrial park for companies operating their
own airplanes.[1044]

---

a   The Gulfstream I used turbo-prop engines rather than turbojet.

1968   Rock Valley Trains Mechanics

Rock Valley College, a community college in Rockford, began offering an Airframe and Powerplant Certification for aircraft mechanics in 1968. In 1970, Rock Valley was given a hangar at the Greater Rockford Airport and has conducted its program there ever since.[1045]

1968/07/20   Special Olympics at Soldier Field

The first U.S. Special Olympics competition kicked off at Soldier Field on July 20, 1968. The brainchild of Eunice Kennedy Shriver, the 1968 Special Olympics was a joint project of the Kennedy Foundation and the Chicago Park District. Anne McGlone Burke,[a] then a physical education teacher with the Park District, brought the event from concept to reality. The first Special Olympics provided those with intellectual disabilities an opportunity to compete in front of a supportive audience. Over 1,000 entrants from 26 states participated in the First Special Olympics.[1046]

1968/08/26–29   Democratic Convention Spawns Riots

At the Chicago International Amphitheater, the Democratic National Convention nominated Hubert Humphrey as their candidate for President. Starting a week before the Convention, various groups converged on Chicago to demonstrate against the Vietnam War, for Civil Rights, and for freedom of expression.

Determined to present a positive image of Chicago, Mayor Richard J. Daley did everything he could to quash the demonstrations. His efforts backfired. Nightly protests were splashed across the national news as police violently broke up the demonstrations with billy clubs and tear gas. There were even scuffles on the floor of the convention itself. Eventually National Guard troops were called up forming a line separating the two opposing sides.

The following year, in order to recover the image of the city, Chicago brought charges against eight people it claimed were responsible for organizing the violence. The "Trial of the Chicago Seven"[b] made the situation worse. Several defendants acted out, making a mockery of the proceedings, while the federal judge made repeated rulings against the defense that many legal experts found questionable. Outside the courtroom, there were regular demonstrations against the proceedings. As with

a   Anne Burke, wife of Chicago alderman Edward Burke, has since become a Justice on the Illinois Supreme Court.
b   One defendant, Bobby Seale, was removed from the courtroom to be tried separately.

the convention, national news gave nightly updates about the proceedings both inside and outside the courtroom.

Following the conclusion of the trial, all convictions were either dismissed by higher courts or dropped by the government.[1047]

1968/12/27 North Central Flight 458 Encounters Wake Turbulence

While landing at O'Hare on December 27, 1972, North Central Flight 458, a Convair 580, encountered wake turbulence from the previously departing jet, causing the pilot to lose control. The left wing broke off when it struck the ground and the remainder of the plane crashed into a Braniff hangar, killing 28 of the 45 people on the plane and another person in the hangar.[1048]

1968/12/31 Maiden Flight of Tu-144

The world's first supersonic transport, the Tupolev Tu-144, made its first flight on December 31, 1968. On May 2, 1970, it became the first airliner to exceed Mach 2.[1049]

1969 EAA Flies Out of Rockford

By 1966, the EAA's annual fly-ins were stretching Rockford's resources and hospitality. Over half a million people attended with nearly 6,500 airplanes. The 1969 event was EAA's last appearance in Rockford as the EAA selected Oshkosh, WI, as its new location for its permanent offices, museum, and annual convention with the air show.[1050]

1969 UAL Is Hatched

In 1969 United created a holding corporation, UAL, Inc., to operate United and other subsidiaries. In 1974, the air carrier changed its name to United Airlines, combining the two previously separate words.[1051]

1969/01 Increased Hijackings

During January 1969, eight airliners were hijacked to Havana. Increased security measures included developing a profile of potential hijackers to be employed by air carriers.[1052]

1969/03/01 Glenview Gets Coast Guard Helicopters

A Coast Guard Air Station with two Sikorsky HH-52A helicopters became operational at Glenview Naval Air Station on March 1, 1969. During its tenure at Glenview, the unit flew 2,815 search and rescue missions covering the southern part of Lake Michigan and saving 501 lives.[1053]

1969/03/02   Concorde's Maiden Flight

A prototype of the supersonic transport Concorde, jointly developed by England and France, made its maiden flight on March 2, 1969, in Toulouse. A British prototype took to the skies on April 2. [1054]

1969/04/01   Harrier Enters Service

On April 1, 1969, the British Harrier becomes the first VTOL airplane to enter military service.[1055]

1969/05/20   CHA Gets Its Second Wind

After ceasing operations at the end of 1965, Chicago Helicopter Airways experienced a brief resurgence, resuming shuttle service on May 20, 1969. Its fleet of Bell JetRangers flew ten flights daily between Midway, O'Hare, and Meigs. The revival was short-lived and CHA ended operations permanently on July 15, 1975.[1056]

1969/06/01   FAA Throttles O'Hare

O'Hare had become a bottleneck for the nation's air transportation system, forcing the FAA to control activity. On June 1, 1969, the FAA implemented the High Density Rule to relieve congestion at O'Hare and four of the other busiest U.S. airports. The FAA Rule established quotas limiting the number of IFR flights between 6 a.m. and midnight.

O'Hare's popularity had consistently exceeded expectations. Projections in 1947 were that in 1970 O'Hare would handle 500,000 flights with 22 million passengers. When 1970 arrived, it had exceeded the projection by more than 25% handling 641,390 flights and 29.7 million passengers.[1057] The new 1962 Master Plan estimated that in 1980 there would be 533,000 aircraft movements. O'Hare achieved that number only four years later, in 1966.

In addition to the upswing in passenger service, as airlines shifted service from Midway, O'Hare's cargo operations also rapidly expanded in the 1960s. Both United Airlines and Emery Freight Forwarding built massive cargo terminals on the west side of the airport.

Under the new FAA controls, only 135 IFR flights were permitted each hour: 115 for air carriers and supplementals, 10 for scheduled air taxis, 10 for general aviation. Arriving IFR flights were required to make advance reservations prior to takeoff to obtain their time slot for arrival. As the overall level of air traffic ebbed and flowed, the FAA would adjust the number of flights permitted and the hours during which the rule was in effect.[1058]

1969/07/20   Humans Walk on the Moon

Apollo 11 brought the first humans to the moon. Astronauts Neil
Armstrong and Buzz Aldrin took the lunar module to the surface while
Michael Collins remained in orbit around the moon.[1059]

1969/08/09–10   Chicago Air & Water Show Changes Things Up

For the second and final time, the 1969 Chicago Air and Water show
performed in two venues. On Saturday August 8, the show was at Rainbow
Beach (75th–78th streets) then on Sunday August 9, it was at Lake Front
Park as usual.

    Instead of the Thunderbirds or Blue Angels, the Naval Reserve's Air
Barons did a comparable performance in their A-4 Skyhawks. Other acts
included a Navy underwater demolition team and a trapeze performer
suspended from a helicopter.[1060]

1969/12/17   Anniversary London to Australia Flight

Commemorating the 50th anniversary of the first flight from London to
Australia, a group of private planes recreated the flight along a similar 12,000
mi. route, competing for more than $100,000 in prize money. Race rules
allowed for gas stops but prohibited overnight stays during the journey.

    Two pilots from Pal-Waukee entered, flying their Twin Comanche.
Bruce R. Anderson of Lake Forest was a professional pilot for a local
company and William Dart from Melbourne was co-owner of an Australian
aviation company. However, a complete list of the competitors did not show
the Pal-Waukee team as one of the 77 entries that took off from Gatwick.[1061]

1969/12/04   Tokyo Convention Takes Effect

In 1963, an agreement on handling hijackings, called the Tokyo
Convention, was drafted by a committee of the International Civil Aviation
Organization (ICAO. When the U.S. became the 12th signatory, the
required minimum number of nations was reached and the Tokyo
Convention went into effect.[1062]

1970–1974

1970   New Illinois Constitution
After more than a century, the State of Illinois adopted a new constitution.[1063]

1970/01/22   Boeing 747 Goes into Service
The first wide-body jetliner, the 747, made its initial flight on February 9, 1969. It entered service with Pan American, flying from New York to London on January 22, 1970.[1064]

1970/02/06   Nixon Flies into Schaumburg
On his way to dedicate a water treatment plant, President Nixon flew Marine One into Roselle Airfield in Schaumburg.[1065]

1970/05/21   Nixon Signs New Aviation Funding Bill
On May 21, 1970, President Nixon signed the Airport and Airways Development Act, establishing the Airport and Airways Trust Fund.

Following the extraordinary growth of airports in the 1960s, the Trust Fund provided a dedicated source of money to fund airport and air traffic control development projects, instead of drawing from the general fund. The Trust Fund was supported by taxes and fees on airplane tickets, aviation fuel, air cargo, and aircraft registration.[1066]

1970/06/25   FAA Introduces TCAs
Effective June 25, 1970, the FAA established Terminal Control Areas to control flight operations around the nation's busiest terminals. Air Traffic Controllers would manage aircraft movements in widening circles around the airport in a pattern that resembled an "inverted wedding cake."

The TCA in Atlanta became operational on the day the rule became effective. Less than a month later, on July 23, Chicago became the second airport with an operational TCA.[1067]

1970/10/28   Sky Marshall Service Created
Sky Marshalls became a permanent security force for commercial passenger flights. The Transportation Dept. and Treasury Dept. concurred they should be trained by the Bureau of Customs.[1068]

1970/12/31   First Non-Fatal Year

For the first time, there were no passenger or crew fatalities on domestic, scheduled airlines for the entire calendar year. Only two people died on international flights, and one person was killed in a propeller accident on the ground.[1069]

1971   Hilton Opens Hotel at O'Hare

A substantial portion of the 37 million passengers who moved through O'Hare each year were business people bound for Chicago. To accommodate the needs of the business traveler, Hilton Hotels opened a 10-story facility on O'Hare property. Not only were their rooms for overnight passengers but also a large business center with meeting and conference rooms as well as the Hilton Athletic Club.[1070]

1971/03   SST Bombs in Congress

After having made the first appropriation for a supersonic transport in August 1961, then making numerous intermediate decisions to proceed with the next level of the program development, Congress finally pulled the plug, draining the financial funding for the project.[1071]

1971/03/18   Major O'Hare Traffic Disruption

On March 18, 1971, O'Hare experienced a major disruption as two minor accidents and a snowstorm[a] temporarily closed two of the ten runways. More than 680 arriving flights were delayed for up to 90 minutes, and hundreds of other planes were held on the ground in other cities.[1072]

1971/05/03   New O'Hare Control Tower Dedicated

To handle the increased O'Hare traffic, the airport dedicated a new 225 ft. control tower on May 3, 1971. One of the tallest control towers in the world, it was by far the most sophisticated and the first location using the FAA's new ARTS III radar traffic system. Up to 33 controllers with 15 radar scopes could work traffic on the seven runways and numerous taxiways.

In 1971, O'Hare's travelers totaled 37.6 million, nearly four times Midway's peak year and 12 million more than the second busiest airport.[1073]

---

a   Although Young and Branigan both mention a snowstorm, the Weather Underground archive shows snowfall as 0.00 in. for the 18th as well as for the days before and after.

1971/05/26   Cessna Reaches 100K
On May 26, 1971, Cessna built its 100,000th airplane.[1074]

1971/06/18   Southwest Airlines Starts
The first of the no-frills airlines, Southwest Airlines started operations in Texas on June 18, 1972. [1075]

1971/07/30   Stockyard Closes
After processing millions of animals over its 106 years of operation, the Union Stockyard & Transit Co. closed for good on July 30, 1971.[1076]

1971/09/08   Hague or Hijacking Convention Approved
On September 8, 1971, the Senate approved the Convention for the Suppression of Unlawful Seizure of Aircraft, developed under the auspices of the International Civil Aviation Organization (ICAO). Also known as The Hague or Hijacking Convention, the agreement defined treatment of hijackers by destination countries.[1077]

1971/09/26   Concorde Crosses Atlantic
On September 26, 1971, the supersonic Concorde made its first commercial supersonic crossing of the Atlantic.[1078]

1972   O'Hare Gets People-Mover System
With more than 37 million passengers moving through O'Hare every year, getting people around proved a major problem. In 1972, the airport tasked C.F. Murphy and Associates with finding a solution. The result was a network of six underground pedestrian tunnels, some with moving sidewalks, to connect the terminals, parking garage, and hotel.[1079]

1972   Brown on FAA Board
The FAA appointed Willa Brown Chappel to the Women's Advisory Board in 1972, "in recognition of her contributions to aviation in the United States as a pilot, instructor, and activist."[1080]

1972/02   Cessna Citation Certificated
In February 1972, the FAA certificated the first model of one the most popular business jets, the Cessna Model 500 Citation I.[1081]

1972/03   Bombs on Planes Trigger New Security

In less than a week, three airliners on the ground around the world were discovered to contain bombs. This triggered increased security measures and the FAA announced new requirements in February 1972, to improve screening passengers and baggage. Additional measures included the increased use of bomb-sniffing dogs and funding to research improved techniques to detect weapons and explosives.[1082]

1972/10/28   First Airbus Flight

The first Airbus airplane, the A300, made its first flight on October 28, 1972, from Toulouse-Blagnac International Airport. By the middle of 1974, the A300 had been certificated in France, Germany, and the U.S. Ten years after the official launch, the plane had more than 25% of the market share (by dollars), enabling Airbus to develop subsequent aircraft. [1083]

1972/12/05   Mandatory Baggage Screening

A continued rash of hijackings resulted in the FAA issuing an emergency order on December 5, 1972, that air carriers inspect all carry-on baggage. Previous rulings only mandated inspections of passengers who fit a certain profile.[1084]

1972/12/08   United Flight Crash Creates Conspiracy Theory

On December 8, 1972, a United 737, Flight 553, departed Washington-National for Midway with 55 passengers and a crew of 6. During its approach into Midway, the pilot failed to reduce speed sufficiently to maintain safe distance from an Aero Commander in front of it, causing the controller to direct Flight 553 to execute a missed approach.

The United crew attempted to go around, but the plane stalled instead. Less than two miles from the runway, the 737 struck trees and rooftops along 71st St. before crashing into a bungalow on W. 70th Place. The plane's crew of 3 and 40 of the 55 passengers were killed. On the ground, five houses were destroyed and two people killed.

The investigation was particularly meticulous for several reasons. First the plane's Flight Data Recorder (FDR) had mechanical problems and was nonfunctional. Second, the flight contained several high-profile passengers including Illinois Congressman George W. Collins and CBS correspondent Michele Clark, one of the first African American network correspondents.

However, it was another passenger, Dorothy Hunt, wife of Howard Hunt, who became the center of a conspiracy theory. Dorothy Hunt's purse contained $10,000 in cash and her husband was a former CIA officer indicted for his role in the break-in at the Democratic offices in Watergate.

In this post-Watergate period, speculation about a coverup was rampant. Some theorized that Mrs. Hunt was traveling to buy off witnesses and was stopped by those who wanted the investigation to continue. Others speculated that the CIA sabotaged the flight either to prevent Mrs. Hunt from revealing what she knew or to derail any efforts by Collins and/or Clark to pursue the investigation.

In the end, the NTSB found no evidence of any foul play. Data from O'Hare's Automated Terminal Radar Services (ATRS-III) filled in much of what was missing from the FDR. The NTSB found the captain failed to retract the spoilers when he executed the go-around, which subsequently caused the plane to stall.[1085]

1972/12/20 O'Hare Runway Incursion Results in Crash

With dense fog covering O'Hare on December 20, 1972, Delta Airlines Flight 954, a Convair CV-880 taxied across a runway into the path of a DC-9, North Central's Flight 575, as it was taking off. Poor visibility from the fog hampered rescue efforts, Nevertheless all but 10 of the 138 people on both planes escaped. The cause of the accident was identified as poor communication between the tower controller and the crew of the Convair.[1086]

1973 Hinsdale Airport Closes

Developers acquired Hinsdale Airport from owners William and Wilma St. Germain in 1973. Soon after, the Village of Willowbrook annexed the land.[1087]

1973/01 First Woman on a Flight Crew

Emily Howell, hired by Frontier Airlines, became the first woman in recent history to become a member of a flight crew for a commercial air carrier.[1088]

1973/01/31 Sky Harbor Closes

Real estate developer Arthur Rubloff had purchased Sky Harbor Airport in 1968, for the purpose of creating an "air-industrial park" for companies operating their own aircraft. While the industrial park thrived, there was little interest from companies that owned airplanes. By the time Sky Harbor closed the airport on January 31, 1973, the surrounding industrial park had impinged on the airport, reducing its size. One of the two paved runways had already been closed for several years.[1089]

1973/02/19   First Illinois Governor to Go to Jail

Otto Kerner, who resigned as Governor to become a judge, was convicted
of multiple charges, including fraud, bribery, and tax evasion on February
19, 1973.

Kerner became the first Illinois governor in recent history to be
convicted and spend time in prison. His conviction was followed by Governors Dan Walker (August 5, 1987), George Ryan (April 17, 2006), and Rod
Blagojevich (December 9, 2008), who all spent time behind bars. Of course,
Kerner didn't invent corruption in the state. After Governor Joel Matteson
left office in 1857, he was convicted of defrauding the state and forced to
repay approximately a quarter of a million dollars.

Simarly, criminal problems aren't limited to governors in the state.
Other officials are also capable of being convicted. U.S. Representative and
Speaker of the House Dennis Hastert was sentenced for sexual abuse in
2016. U.S. Representatives Dan Rostenkowski and Mel Reynolds both left
office in 1995 before serving time in prison. Misusing campaign funds
resulted in Representative Jesse Jackson, Jr., going to prison.

Attorney General William Scott served time for tax fraud in the 1980s
and State Auditor Orville Hodge pled guilty to embezzlement in the 1950s.
Although he never saw the inside of a courtroom, Illinois Secretary of State
Paul Powell had stashed about $800,000 in shoeboxes that weren't discov-
ered until after his death in 1970.[1090]

1973/04   Last Beacon Decommissioned

The FAA announced that the final airway beacon, located near Palm Beach,
CA, was decommissioned in April 1973. At its peak in 1946, the airway
system contained 2112 beacon lights.[1091]

1973/05/03   Sears Tower Becomes World's Tallest Building

The topping-off ceremony was held for the second Sears Tower, which
became the tallest building in the world. At 1450 ft., the 108-story building
remained the tallest in the world until 1998, when the Petronas Towers
were completed in Malaysia.

In 1974, Sears vacated the original Sears Tower, a 14-story building in
the Holman Square neighborhood constructed in 1906.[1092]

1973/10/06   Arab Oil Embargo

In the Middle East, a fierce war erupted between Israel and its neighbors. Oil-exporting Arab nations began an embargo against the U.S. and countries they considered supporters of Israel. In Europe and the U.S., oil and gas prices skyrocketed. The transportation industry, including air travel, was extremely hard hit.

The oil embargo's higher gas prices resulted in a host of changes by airlines to reduce the financial impact. Planned flight speeds, altitudes, and routes were modified to optimize fuel efficiency.[1093]

1973/11/20   Aviation Fuel Conservation Plan Takes Effect

In response to the Arab Oil Embargo, the FAA implemented new "flow control" procedures to reduce oil consumption by the airlines.

Provisions of their new plan included modified gate holding procedures, to reduce time spent with engines running; reducing the number of engines used while taxiing; changing flight procedures to optimize cruising speed, altitude, and routing; and revising traffic flow to reduce time in holding pattern.[1094]

1974   Fox Valley Airport Authority Created

To prevent expansion of DuPage Airport, the surrounding communities created the Fox Valley Airport Authority. After a long court battle and two trips to the Illinois legislature for special legislation, the issue was finally resolved in the Airport's favor in 1990.[1095]

1974   Machesney Airport Becomes a Mall

Fred Machesney finally sold his Rockford airport in 1974. Owned and operated by Machesney from 1927 to 1974, Machesney Airport had the distinction of being the oldest, privately-owned, continuously-operated-by-one-owner airport in the nation. The developers converted the old airport into Machesney Park Mall, named in his honor.[1096] During his career, Machesney flew 77,330 hours and more than 7,633,000 miles.[1097]

1974   Mitchell Field Becomes an Interstate

Mitchell Field[a] in Addison, IL, closed in 1974 to make way for I-355. Owned by K.T. Mitchell the airport, located along Rt. 53, had a 3,000 ft. bituminous runway.[1098]

---

a   This is unrelated to the Mitchell Field in Milwaukee.

1974/01/01   No U.S. Hijackings in 1973

Following increased security measures, no U.S. airlines were hijacked during 1973.[1099]

1974/08/09   President Nixon Resigns

President Richard Nixon, facing imminent impeachment on obstruction and other charges, became the first U.S. President to resign the office on August 9, 1974. His successor, President Gerald Ford, pardoned Nixon, sparing him further prosecution for his crimes.[1100]

1975–1979

1975   Manufacturer's Aircraft Association Dissolved

The Manufacturer's Aircraft Association was dissolved and the pool of aviation patents it held distributed under terms of a consent decree challenging the organization under the Sherman Antitrust Act.[1101]

1976   Prospect Heights Incorporates

The informal arrangement of the Prospect Heights Improvement Association, created in 1938, finally incorporated as the City of Prospect Heights.[1102]

1976   Lansing Acquires Airport

The Village of Lansing acquired the Lansing Airport in 1976.[1103]

1976/01/21   Concorde Starts Service

Two Concordes took off simultaneously on January 21, 1976, inaugurating service by the new SST. A British Airways flight departed London for Bahrain and an Air France plane left Paris for Rio de Janerio.[1104]

1976/03/18   Postage Stamp Commemorates Commercial Aviation

In recognition of the 50th anniversary of commercial aviation (the Contract Air Mail system), on March 18, 1976, the U.S. Postal Service issued a commemorative stamp showing two airplanes that were backbones of the early system. The foreground shows a Laird Swallow and the background a Ford 2-AT Pullman, Stout's single-engine predecessor to the Tri-Motor.[1105]

1976/04/06   First Contract Air Mail Flight Reenacted

UAL planned a major celebration to commemorate the 50th anniversary of both United Air Lines and the U.S. Air Mail Service. As part of the commemoration, on April 6, 1976, Chicago-area native Buck Hilbert recreated the first Contract Air Mail flight of Varney Air Lines, flying a 1927 OX-5 Swallow.

Hilbert, a United Airlines captain, flew from Pasco, WA, to Boise, ID, the initial leg of the Seattle-Chicago route (CAM-5).[1106] The evening after the commemorative flight, Hilbert was honored at a banquet, along with the original Varney pilot, Leon D. Cuddeback.

Hilbert grew up in Chicago idolizing Matty Laird. In high school, Hilbert hung around airports and soloed in 1941. He flew B-17s in WWII and was recalled for the Korean War.

Several years before making the CAM flight, Hilbert had discovered an old Swallow and, with the help of several friends, spent two years restoring it. In the summer of 1976, Hilbert took the Swallow on a 40-city tour. While visiting Atlanta, Hilbert reunited with his old friends Matty and Elsie Laird, treating them both to a ride in the Swallow.[1107]

1976/08/06 B-25 Crashes into Houses by Midway

During takeoff on a training flight on August 6, 1976, War Aero Inc.'s[a] converted B-25 experienced engine failure and subsequent fire. It crashed in a residential area, destroying two houses and two garages and damaging nine additional houses. Both crew members and a woman on the ground died during the crash.[1108]

1976/10/15 Standardized PIREPS Implemented

An existing informal system of relaying weather reports was replaced nationwide by a standardized Pilot Report (PIREP) that was distributed through both civilian and military networks.[1109]

1976/12/20 Mayor Richard J. Daley Dies

After winning an unprecedented sixth term, Mayor Richard J. Daley's lengthy career as an Illinois politician came to an end when he suffered a heart attack on December 20, 1976. Richard J. Daley was the longest-serving Chicago Mayor at the time, with 21 years in office.[1110]

1977 Gary Airport Becomes Municipally Owned

The City of Gary purchased Gary Airport facilities from the Jankovich brothers in 1977. The city took over operation of the airport, which quickly became a political pawn.

During the term of Mayor Hatcher (1968–1987), the city changed the name to Richard G. Hatcher Gary Regional Airport. In 1987, Hatcher's successor, Thomas Barnes, removed Hatcher's name from the airport and his appointees from the airport board.

Throughout this time, many airport records were missing or misfiled, resulting both in legal action and the FAA withholding grant money. By the

---

a   Some sources claim the owner was Air Chicago Freight but according to Warbird Registry, Air Chicago Freight owned the plane from 1974–75, when it sold it to War Aero.

end of the decade, the airport reached a low point, without a director, operating airline, or federal funds.[1111]

1977   Bessie Coleman Aviator's Club Formed

To honor Bessie Coleman, a group of Chicago women aviators formed the Bessie Coleman Aviator's Club in 1977. The extent of the Bessie Coleman Aviator's Club activity is unknown.[1112]

1977/02/04   Deadly "L" Crash

A rush hour "L" train rounding the curve at Lake and Wabash slammed into a stopped train on February 4, 1977. Eleven people were killed and more than 180 were injured.[1113]

1977/07/30   Rain Drenches O'Hare

Torrential rain on June 30, 1977, brought operations at O'Hare to a stand-still. Thunderstorms trapped 300 planes on the ground. At the time this was about a quarter of the civil aircraft in service, essentially disrupting flights coast-to-coast for several days.[1114]

1977/08/31   New Altitude Record Set

On August 31, 1977, a MiG-25 established a new altitude record for non-rocket powered aircraft when it reached 123,534 ft.[1115]

1978   Army Copters Move to Glenview

In 1978, an Army Flight Detachment from Fort Sheridan moved its Huey helicopters into a hangar at Glenview Naval Air Station. The Flight Detachment provided transportation for various activities based at Fort Sheridan, including the Recruiting Command and the Corps of Engineers.[1116]

1978/08/11   Vulcan Crashes Near Glenview

During a practice flight before the 1978 Air and Water Show portion of the Lakefront Festival, an RAF Vulcan B Mk. 2 crashed near the staging area at Glenview Naval Air Station on August 11, 1978.[a] The four-engine Hawker-Siddeley bomber made a low-level, low-power run then pulled up to do a wingover, resulting in a stall.[b] The pilot was able to guide the plane to avoid residential areas and crashed in a landfill. All four crew members died in the fiery crash.[1117]

a   Some sources place the crash on Saturday, August 12th.
b   Another rumor claimed the plane received Jet-A fuel instead of the required Jet-B, causing a substantial power loss during climb out.

1978/09/30   Chicagoland Airport Closes

Chicagoland Airport closed after the Village of Lincolnshire denied Art Schelter's improvement plan. The state made an effort to save Chicagoland through public ownership, but none of the local governments would take on the task. The airport closed on September 30, 1978.[1118]

1978/10/24   Airline Deregulation Act of 1978 Signed

President Jimmy Carter signed the Airline Deregulation Act on October 24, 1978. Prior to deregulation, the CAB considered interstate airline travel to be a public utility and controlled the fares, routes and schedules. The CAB's rational for this was twofold. First, that routes not become so overcrowded with carriers that they would be unable to operate profitably. Second, they ensured that air service would be available in some smaller areas where service may not be economically feasible.

Air carriers had to get approval from the CAB to change flight times and fares, as well as to add or drop destinations. Frequently, it took years for the CAB to rule on a request. Sometimes the CAB would drop a request without resolution simply because it was "too old." Airlines would appeal some CAB rulings in court, but this added to the delay in getting a decision.

The airlines always resented this process. Airlines contended that they needed to be more nimble with their schedules and that the marketplace was the best way to control profitability.

The Deregulation Act gave airlines more direct control of their operations with little CAB involvement. Airlines could add or drop destinations and flights at will and reduce fares by up to 70%. Over the next several years, the CAB's authority was gradually reduced and the CAB was scheduled to shut down in January 1985.

Prior to deregulation, airlines competed on service since fares were set by the CAB. After deregulation, service became secondary to fare competition. Some larger air carriers, such as Pan American, were unable to function in such an environment.

Without the CAB's route coordination, competing airlines scheduled flights between the busiest destinations at the busiest times. The new schedules exacerbated rush hour congestion at the major airports. Similarly, airlines dropped direct service to many smaller cities and adopted the hub-and-spoke system of routing.

Airline competition became fierce. Many established airlines went bankrupt or were acquired by the larger carriers. New air carriers emerged to capitalize on profitable markets with fewer destinations, without attempting to provide service to the entire nation. Often these startups were financially feasible by acquiring aircraft and flight crews from older carriers that had gone out of business. Their feasibility, and companies themselves, often vanished as conditions in the market changed.

Deregulation also put a strain on airports. Some airports were practically abandoned while others were straining at the seams with many flights wanting to load and depart simultaneously. The hub-and-spoke system added pressure on both airports and passengers. Some studies showed approximately 70% of passengers at hub airports were transferring planes. Not only passengers but baggage needed to move from one airplane to another in a limited time period.

As the nation's only dual-hub airport, serving both American and United, O'Hare was hit hardest by increased congestion. The airport's terminal space had grown so that passengers were faced with a mile and a half trek between the most distant gates.[1119]

1978/12/29   FAA Begins Naming Approach Fixes After Aviators

An FAA program began renaming approach fixes after aviation pioneers. The first fix to be renamed was the Laird fix at the intersection of airways Victor 7 and Victor 172. Named for Matty Laird, the fix near the Lake Michigan shore is the transition from center control to approach control for O'Hare.[1120]

1979/01/13–14   Second Major Chicago Blizzard

What started as an exceptionally warm November 1978 turned into the infamous "Blizzard of 1979." A modest 6 in. of snow fell November 26–27, but unusually cold weather kept the snow on the ground for 100 days.[1121]

A major storm New Year's Eve and Day dumped another 9–12 in. on the Chicago area. The first day of the storm, O'Hare's operations were down to 25% of normal. On New Year's Day, they reached 50% before returning to normal the next day.

Two weeks later, O'Hare was operating normally but Chicago was still recovering from the previous storm. Weather forecasters projected a mere 2–4 in. of snow for January 13. When the storm actually arrived, it snowed continuously for 38 hours, dumping 21 in. of snow. Accompanying winds of nearly 40 mph made the situation worse by imparing visibility and drifting.

Airport ground crews were unable to keep up with the snow even on a single runway. On runway 14R, a third of the lights failed. O'Hare was completely shut down for 96 hours, with no planes going in or out. The impact cascaded across the country, and it took more than a week before schedules returned to normal.[1122]

1979/04/03   Jane Byrne Becomes Mayor in Chicago.

Jane Byrne became the first woman in Chicago to be elected Mayor. Her victory in the general election followed her stunning defeat of incumbent Michael Bilandic in the Democratic primary. The recent blizzard that paralyzed the city was a major campaign issue.[1123]

1979/05/25   DC-10 Crashes at O'Hare

On May 25, 1979, an American Airlines DC-10, Flight 191, crashed in a field during takeoff from O'Hare when it literally lost an engine. The crash killed 274, making it the worst air disaster in U.S. history. Analysis of the crash identified incorrect maintenance procedures as the cause for the left engine and pylon separating from the wing.[1124]

1979/10/04–06   Grant Park Mass

During his first visit to the U.S., Pope John Paul II spent October 4–6, 1979, in Chicago. While here, the pontiff celebrated Mass in Grant Park, with an estimated 1.5 million people attending.[1125]

1979/11/12   Midway Revitalized

The second Midway Airlines operation began on November 12, 1979,[a] when the airline's three DC-9s began service to Cleveland, Detroit, and Kansas City. Midway Airlines was based in Chicago operating out of Midway Airport, which had languished nearly unused since the airlines moved to O'Hare in 1962.

Midway Airlines was a product of the post-deregulation era, although it was actually formed on August 6, 1976, two years before the passage of the Airline Deregulation Act. Investor Kenneth Carlson and others controlled the company and named Gordon Linkon, formerly from Frontier Airlines, as President.

---

a   Other sources place the date November 1.

Midway Airport proved an ideal base, since the City of Chicago happily provided the airline with great rates to promote use of the airport. Thanks to cutbacks throughout the aviation industry, Midway Airlines was able to take advantage of bargain-priced used airplanes and experienced crews that were let go by the other airlines.

Within two years, by 1981, the fleet had grown to 13 DC-9s and the company made a profit of $9 million.[1126]

1980–1984

1980   Byrne Proposes World's Fair

In 1980, Mayor Jane Byrne proposed bringing another World's Fair to Chicago in 1992. Had her plans been realized, Meigs Field would have been replaced by exhibit areas.[1127]

1980   FAA Gives Coffey a Fix

In 1979, the FAA began recognizing dominant aviation individuals by naming navigation waypoints after them. In 1980, the FAA established the "Cofey Fix"[a] near Lake Calumet leading into Midway after Cornelius Coffey.

Recognizing a lifetime of aviation achievements, the FAA also awarded him with the Charles Taylor Master Mechanic Award.

Coffey continued flying until 1992 when he was 89. He continued a little longer as a mechanic and reported doing annual inspections into the following year.[1128]

1980   Frasca Buys Illini Airport

In 1980, Rudy Frasca, of Frasca Aviation, purchased Illini Airport in Urbana and renamed it Frasca Field.

From the early 1950s, Illini Airport had been a thriving aviation center in the Champaign area, operated by Louis Dyson and Harold Haynes.[1129] Business at Illini Airport had faded by 1980, when Dyson sold it to Frasca.

Frasca Aviation produced flight simulators for everything from small general aviation planes like the Cessna 172 up to commercial aircraft, including the Boeing 737. As Frasca's technology developed, his customer base grew and the company changed its name to Frasca International. In 1990, Frasca outgrew its factory in Champaign and built a new larger manufacturing facility adjacent to Frasca Field.

A warbird enthusiast, Rudy Frasca established a nonprofit corporation to keep warbirds operational, making them available to the public through museums and air shows. The collection, which is still around today, includes a fully restored P-40 Warhawk, F4F Wildcat, British Spitfire, and a rare Italian Fiat G.46. Airworthy replicas include a Japanese Zero and German Focke-Wulf Fw-190.[1130]

a   His name was shortened to five letters to conform with the FAA naming standard.

1980   Meigs Field Traffic Peaks

Passenger traffic at Meigs Field peaked in 1980, when it served 468,933 passengers. Traffic was boosted by a State of Illinois shuttle to Springfield, as well as commuter airlines. Following the peak, traffic began a slow decline over the following years.[1131]

Due to its location, Meigs was often a challenging airport. Rapidly changing weather, unpredictable wind shifts, a slippery or obscured runway, spatial disorientation, and birdstrikes were all potential challenges for pilots.[1132]

1980/05/18   Mt. Saint Helens Erupts

The volcanic eruption of Mt. Saint Helens in Washington left 61 people dead or missing, destroyed 100 sq. mi. of timber, and generated a widespread ash cloud that disrupted air travel in parts of the Northwest.[1133]

1981/01/20   Reagan Becomes President

Born in Tampico and raised in Dixon, IL, Ronald Reagan left Illinois for the Golden State where he had a career as an actor. He became interested in politics and left acting to become a two-term governor of California. Then on January 20, 1981, Reagan took the oath of office and became the U.S. president.[1134]

1981/08/03   PATCO ATC Strike

The biggest aviation labor event happened on August 3, 1981 when 12,500 of the 15,000 controllers belonging to the Professional Air Traffic Controllers Organization (PATCO) went on strike nationwide, which is not legal and for federal employees and punishable by fine and/or a jail sentence.

At O'Hare 250 flights were canceled the first day of the strike. Nationwide, flight cancellations cost the airlines $30 million per day.

President Ronald Reagan moved swiftly to curtail the strike. On August 5, he firied striking controllers, who ignored the order to return to work. Air traffic control was hampered as towers operated with supervisors, nonstriking controllers, and military controllers. The controllers were aided by other aviation professionals, who assisted with administrative tasks that did not directly control air traffic.

The FAA moved as quickly as it could to replace the fired workers and in October, it contracted with Oklahoma University to train replacement controllers. Also in October, the Federal Labor Relations Board (FLRB) decertified PATCO as representative for the controllers.

It took months and even years for the system to completely return to normal as the new controllers were integrated into the system. During that time there were no disasters and the system continued operating.[1135]

1982   Chicago Buys Midway Airport

In 1982, the City of Chicago finally purchased the square mile of land occupied by Midway Airport from the Chicago Board of Education, which had leased the land to the City since 1925.[1136]

1982   New O'Hare Master Plan for Expansion

To address rapidly increasing congestion, O'Hare embarked on a new $2 billion master plan in 1982.

O'Hare greatly expanded Terminal 3 and added a new concourse (L) for Delta Air Lines. More people-mover systems throughout the terminal complex eased lengthy walks between gates. New facilities were provided for commuter airlines as well as general and business aviation users.

The cargo area in the southwest portion of the field was improved and expanded. For the airlines, new construction provided maintenance, field kitchen, and other support facilities.[1137]

1982/03/19   Tanker Explodes Over McHenry County

On March 19, 1982, an Illinois Air National Guard KC-135 tanker exploded in mid-air over Greenwood, IL, barely missing an elementary school. An Air Force investigation determined the probable cause was a spark of unknown origin causing an explosion in one of the fuel tanks.[1138]

1982/07/02   Lawn-Chair Larry's Flight

In Long Beach, CA, Larry Walters made a 45-min. flight reaching an altitude of 16,000 ft. in a lawn chair attached to numerous helium balloons. When landing, Walters crashed into high-voltage power lines, but plastic tethers kept him from being electrocuted. His adventure cost him a $1,500 fine from the FAA for breaking numerous laws and endangering other people.[1139]

1982/09/03   Reagan Increases Aviation Taxes

To generate money for the Airport and Airways Trust Fund, administered as part of the Airport Improvement Program, President Reagan increased or added taxes on aviation services on September 3, 1982. Additional funds came from an increase in the passenger ticket tax and GA gasoline tax, as well as imposing taxes on aviation jet fuel, air cargo, and international departures.[1140]

1982/09/30   Around-the-World Helicopter Flight

The first flight around the world in a helicopter ended successfully in Dallas on September 30, 1982. H. Ross Perot Jr. and Jay Coburn flew their Bell 206L-1 JetRanger III on a trip lasting 29 days, 3 hr., and 8 min.[1141]

1983/04/12   Washington Becomes Mayor

In a three-way race, on April 14, 1983, Chicago elected Harold Washington the city's first African American Mayor. His term was cut short on November 25, 1987, when he suffered a massive heart attack while working at his desk in City Hall.[1142]

1983/05/01   New Cuba Hijacking

After an extended lull, a new wave of hijackings began on May 1, 1983, when a passenger hijacked a flight to Havana. A new set of increased airport security measures put in place to deal with hijackings lowered the rate until, in 1985 and 1986, there were no hijackings in the U.S.[1143]

1983/05/23   First Transatlantic GPS

A Sabreliner executive jet made the first civilian transatlantic flight relying solely on GPS navigation.[1144]

1983/10/11   Air Illinois Crash

On October 11, 1983, a turboprop Hawker Siddeley 748, Air Illinois Flight 710, crashed near Pinckneyville, IL, killing ten people. The flight departed Meigs Field for Carbondale via Springfield.

The crash was attributed to the pilot's decision to continue the flight after both generators stopped producing electrical power. Following the crash, the FAA increased inspection efforts at all commuter and air charter airlines and Air Illinois specifically. As a result of this crash, Air Illinois filed for bankruptcy in April 1984.[1145]

1983/11/01   Elgin Airport Closes

Although George Edgecumbe operated Elgin Airport, he didn't own the land. The land's owners decided to develop a shopping center and business park on the property and closed the airport on November 1, 1983.[1146]

1983/12/31   New Computers for FAA

On December 31, 1983, the FAA installed the first of its new IBM 4341 and, later, the more powerful IBM 3083 computers. The new computers replaced old IBM 9020 computers first installed in July, 1967. The 9020 was a complex of multiple IBM System/360 Model 50 and 65 computers specifically designed for the FAA. The new systems used at least some software unchanged from the 9020, running in 360-emulation mode.[1147]

1984/09/03   Blue Line Arrives at O'Hare

The CTA connected O'Hare to the "L" system in 1984. The Milwaukee Line, or the West-Northwest Route,[a] was extended along the median of the I-90/94 Kennedy Expressway from the existing Jefferson Park station. A new station below the parking lot near Terminal 2 gave airline passengers access to downtown in 30 minutes, and from there throughout the Chicago area.[1148]

1984/12/01   FAA Crashes Another Plane

Twenty years after the FAA's first crash experiment, they joined with NASA to conduct another Controlled Impact Demonstration at Edwards Air Force Base. Instead of creating an impact without leaving the ground, this time the FAA crashed a remotely piloted Boeing 720 into the test site.[1149]

1984/12/31   CAB Dissolved

Pursuant to the 1978 Airline Deregulation Act, the Civil Aviation Board ceased operation. The few CAB functions that were not abolished under the Deregulation Act were transferred to the Dept. of Transportation.[1150]

a   This became the Blue Line in 1993 when the CTA assigned color names to its various lines.

1985–1989

1985   O'Hare Puts International Passengers in Garage

In 1985, O'Hare moved international passengers and customs from the original Terminal 1 to a new Terminal 4 located in the lower level of a parking garage as a stop-gap location during construction of a new International terminal.

Airlines, passengers, and customs officers immediately felt the limitations of the makeshift facilities. Probably the biggest inconvenience was that the terminal had no direct access to gates. Passengers boarded buses at the terminal to be driven onto the ramp to board planes.[1151]

1985/02/08   PAPI Standardized

The FAA standardized on the Precision Approach Position Indicator (PAPI), a series of lights that visually indicate to pilots how much they were above or below the glideslope. This change followed a period in which the FAA also allowed the older, less-precise Visual Approach Slope Indicator (VASI) to be installed at some airports.[1152]

1985/10/22   Concorde Serves Rockford

British Airways made two nonstop flights between London and the Greater Rockford Airport on October 22 and 30, 1985. The flights were originally destined for O'Hare, but were relocated because of noise considerations.[1153]

1986/01/26   Da Bears Take Da Bowl

The Chicago Bears, coached by Mike Ditka, smashed the New England Patriots 46–10 in Super Bowl XX on January 26, 1986, in the Louisiana Superdome.[1154]

1986/01/28   *Challenger* Explodes

NASA's space shuttle *Challenger* exploded shortly after liftoff, killing all seven astronauts on board. All shuttle flights were suspended for more than two years, and the U.S. space program suffered a severe setback.[1155]

1986/09/08   First Oprah Show Broadcast

After hosting the WLS *A.M. Chicago* show for several years, Oprah Winfrey appeared for the first time on her own show, the *Oprah Winfrey Show*, which was broadcast from the WLS studios. Oprah quickly became the most popular TV talk show in the country. In 1989, she opened her own Harpo Studios in the West Loop, providing a much-needed boost for the neighborhood.[1156]

1986/12/14–23   Around the World Without Refueling

Dick Rutan and Jeana Yeager became the first pilots to circle the globe without refueling. Their plane, *Voyager*, was designed by Dick's brother Burt Rutan.

Rutan and Yeager took off from Edwards Air Force Base on December 14, 1986. *Voyager* carried 1,200 gallons of fuel in its 111 ft.-long wing. Only 8 gallons remained when it landed back at Edwards nine days later.[1157]

1986/12/26   Prospect Heights & Wheeling Purchase Pal-Waukee

At a ceremony on December 26, 1986, George Priester and Esther Noffke transferred ownership of Pal-Waukee Airport to Wheeling Village President Sheila Schultz and Prospect Heights Mayor John Gilligan.[1158]

As private airports around the country closed, the planes they served were forced to move to the larger commercial airports. Aviation officials became concerned the trend would interfere with rapidly increasing airline traffic creating delays. After much deliberation, officials made a concerted effort to preserve the smaller, general-aviation airports through public ownership.

This problem was particularly acute in the Chicago area where many airports, such as Sky Harbor, had already been sold to developers. Officials viewed Pal-Waukee as an important airport to keep operational. The IL Div. of Aeronautics, with the support of the FAA, sought a solution to preserve Pal-Waukee as a publically owned airport.

Various acquisition studies had begun starting in 1977. By the middle of the 1980s, the City of Prospect Heights and the Village of Wheeling were in serious negotiations. In addition to the financial terms, the two municipalities needed an agreement on how to govern and operate the airport.

In 1986, all parties reached an agreement and the Priesters sold Pal-Waukee for $22 million.[a] An Intergovernmental Agreement between the

a   Young (p. 195) put the price tag at $40 million and stated the entire amount was paid by the Federal and state governments.

two municipalities became the basis for operating the airport, to be called Palwaukee Municipal Airport. At the time of the purchase, there were 430 resident aircraft operating from five runways in three directions.

1987   O'Hare's New Terminal 1 Opens

As soon as international operations moved into the temporary Terminal 4, O'Hare demolished the original Terminal 1.

Noted architect Helmut Jahn designed a spectacular "Terminal for Tomorrow" exclusively for United Airlines. Jahn broke with the trend of providing bare-bones minimalist space and designed a modern-looking structure that opened in 1987. The terminal was built with green-tinted glass walls and a curved glass ceiling supported by exposed steel I-beams.

Two long concourses (B and C) held more than 40 gates with many able to handle 747s and other jumbo jets. The C-concourse was out in the middle of the tarmac more than 800 feet from the B-concourse, where all passengers arrived and checked in. Jahn connected the two concourses by an underground passageway with moving sidewalks. Rather than a maze-like passage of plain concrete walls, Jahn covered the walls with backlit color panels of varying hues. On the reflective ceiling, an undulating neon sculpture by Michael Hayden pulsed with lights of different colors. William Kraft composed an original music score to fill the air rather than the typical nondescript background music.[1159]

1987/04/30   UAL Becomes Allegis

Caught up in the diversification trend, on April 30, 1987, UAL Inc. changed its name to Allegis Corp., attempting to rebrand itself and shed its aviation association. UAL had begun investing in nonairline travel businesses, purchasing Hilton Hotels and Hertz Car Rental and embarking on a joint credit card venture.

The diversification moves were not popular with many on Wall Street, who felt the subsidiaries had more value separately than together. Takeover rumors were rampant and at least one takeover attempt had to be averted. Likewise the employees, represented by several unions, were furious at the cost cutting they endured in order to facilitate the diversification purchases.

With trouble on all fronts, the company reversed course. A little more than a year after the name change, on May 26, 1988, Allegis returned to UAL Corp. Striving to return to its core business, UAL divested itself of all the nonairline companies.[1160]

1987/05/21   Lindbergh's Replica Lands in Paris

Verne Jobst, a United Airlines captain, landed a replica of the *Spirit of St. Louis* at Le Bourget Airport in Paris 60 years to the day after Lindbergh's arrival on May 21, 1927.

The EAA sponsored the construction of a Ryan monoplane replica in 1977 to commemorate the 50th anniversary of the Atlantic crossing. That year, Jobst took the replica around the country, recreating Lindbergh's victory tour. By the time the replica was retired in 1988, it had visited over 200 cities and logged over 1,300 hr. Unlike Lindbergh, the replica was shipped rather than flown across the Atlantic.[1161]

1987/07/18–19   Air & Water Show Relocates

In July 1987, the Chicago Air and Water Show left its original venue at Lake Shore Park/Oak Street Beach, performing its demonstrations instead at Lincoln Park/North Avenue Beach, north of the old location.

The main factor was the "air show box" defined by the FAA as the area in which planes are allowed to perform. The box must be parallel to the audience at a distance determined safe for the specifications of the performing aircraft. The other inviolate rule of air shows is that performing planes never fly toward the audience. The Lake Shore Park area mostly met those criteria, except for Navy Pier. Flying parallel to the park, the planes would fly directly toward Navy Pier, which contained spectators as well as thousands of people working and shopping. In the FAA's opinion, that was not the safest configuration.

Another reason for the move was that Streeterville residents were increasingly upset at the growing size of the crowd invading their area. Not that the residents of Lincoln Park were much more welcoming. They felt the area was already sufficiently crowded on summer weekends without adding a million additional people. However, the safety of the venue prevailed and the air show relocated.[1162]

1987/09   Rockford Dedicates New Terminal

The introduction of commercial jet service in the 1970s had returned passengers to the languishing Rockford Airport.

The Greater Rockford Airport Association adopted an expansion in 1978 that included building a new terminal. They engaged Larson-Darby Architects to design a modern 50,000 sq.-ft. terminal that included jetways and a fine dining restaurant. Construction of the $4.9 million terminal began in 1986 and it was dedicated in September 1987.[1163]

1988/02/08   FAA Retires Earhart's Aircraft Number

The FAA officially retired, or "permanently reserved," the aircraft registration number, N16020, on the Lockheed Electra flown by Amelia Earhart on her ill-fated flight.[1164]

1988/04/23   Limited Flight Smoking Ban

A smoking ban took effect on all scheduled domestic flights of less than two hours. Smoking is still acceptable on international and long domestic flights as well as on non-scheduled flights.[1165]

1988/04/28   First A320 Enters Service

The first Airbus A320 entered service with Air France. The A320 was the first fly-by-wire airliner in operation.[1166]

1988/05/08   Telephone Fire Impedes Flights

Illinois Bell Telephone had a fire at one of their switching centers that severely limited communications between O'Hare, Midway, and the Aurora Center. The entire country experienced flight delays during the 56-hr outage.[1167]

1988/06/14   Beech Starship Certificated

The FAA issued a type certificate to the first major airplane constructed entirely of composites. The twin-turboprop canard Starship was designed in part by Burt Rutan's company, Scaled Composites.[1168]

1988/06/26   *Greater Rockford* Dedicated in Museum

After being recovered from a glacier in Greeenland, *The Greater Rockford* was restored and dedicated at the Midway Village Museum in Rockford on June 26, 1988.

In August 1928, *The Greater Rockford*, a modified Stinson Detroiter, had departed Rockford's Machesney Field for Sweden. Fish Hassell and co-pilot Shorty Cramer planned the trip to follow the economical and efficient Great Circle Route.

Unfortunately, they ran short on fuel over Greenland. Hassell made the first landing on an icecap, leaving the plane undamaged. Hassell and Cramer hiked for two weeks before being rescued. They returned to the U.S. but abandoned their plane.[1169]

In 1968, an effort was made to recover *The Greater Rockford*. The plane was in good condition, with some damage caused when the wind blew it

over long after it had been abandoned. Recovering the plane was a complicated process involving the U.S. military and the Danish government, but it
eventually returned to the States.

Hassell was in Rockford to welcome the plane home, but it hadn't been
restored at the time of his death on September 12, 1974 at age 81. Restoration was considerable, mostly due to damage inflicted while transporting
the plane.[1170]

1988/08   Herb Hunter Becomes Voice of Air & Water Show

Following years of service with both United Airlines and the Illinois Air
National Guard, Herb Hunter became the voice of the Chicago Air and
Water Show in August 1988.

Hunter's popularity as an air show announcer soared due to his vast
flying experience and close relationship with air show performers. He
provided listeners with interesting information about the pilots, the planes,
and the maneuvers. His treasure chest of knowledge allowed him to fill
"dead time" with fascinating anecdotes.

Upon graduating college in 1971, Hunter enlisted in the U.S. Air Force,
where he flew KC-135s until 1977, when he transferred to the Air National
Guard. By the time he retired from the Guard in 1992, he was a Lt. Col.
with 5,000 hr. in the KC-135. Hunter had flown combat operations in SE
Asia, Vietnam, and Operation Desert Storm.

In addition to his time with the National Guard, Hunter flew for United
Airlines starting in 1978. During his career with United, he flew nearly
every Boeing model in their fleet nationally and internationally.

Hunter's first appearance at the CAWS was in 1979 as the pilot of an
Illinois Air National Guard KC-135. In 1981 and 1982, he was the Air
National Guard's Supervisor of Flying for the air show. For the next five
years, Hunter was the Guard's announcer for the 9-minute performance of
the KC-135 and the 183rd Tactical Fighter Wing.

Starting in 1988, Hunter became the voice of the CAWS, announcing
the entire event, not just the Air National Guard acts. He became a part-
time air show announcer, appearing at events nationwide. Hunter's vocal
abilities also made him a very capable singer of the national anthem.[1171]

1988/08/08   Wrigley Gets Lights

After years of fighting with community groups, artificial lights illuminated
the first night game at Wrigley Field on August 8, 1988.[1172]

1988/08/28   German Air Show Disaster

An air show at Ramstein Air Base in Germany became a disaster scene when three Italian jets collided in mid-air. About 50 of the 300,000 people in attendance were killed as the fiery wreckage reached the viewing area.[1173]

1988/10/03   O'Hare Arrivals Reduced

The number of arrivals at O'Hare was reduced from 96 to 80 per hour. The FAA cited increased congestion and ATC operational errors as the reason for the indefinite reduction.[1174]

1988/12/21   Bomb Destroys Pan Am Flight

A bomb placed in the luggage compartment of Pan American Flight 103, a 747, exploded near Lockerbie, Scotland on December 21, 1988. By January 3, the FAA implemented the first of a series of new security measures to prevent guns and explosives on planes.[1175]

1988/12/27   U.S. Territorial Limits Expanded

In the final days of his term of office, President Reagan signed a proclamation expanding the U.S. territorial limits from 3 to 12 nautical miles. The FAA adjusted airspace rules to accommodate the new limits. [1176]

1989/02/06   Samuel Skinner Becomes Secretary of Transportation

President George H.W. Bush appointed Samuel Skinner to head the Dept. of Transportation. Born in Chicago, Skinner graduated DePaul Law School.

After eight years working for IBM, Skinner entered public service in a variety of positions for several administrations prior to going to the DOT. Following his service, he returned to Chicago serving in various executive and advisory roles. A pilot himself, Skinner frequented Palwaukee Airport during many of his trips.[1177]

1989/04   Emery Starts Regular Rockford Service

Cargo operations, always a substantial part of Rockford's operations, increased greatly in April 1989, when Emery Worldwide began regular service to Rockford Airport. While Emery flew regular cargo flights to Rockford, they did not establish a permanent facility.[1178]

1989/04/24   Chicago Gets Daley Version 2

Following in his father's footsteps, Richard M. Daley, the son of Richard J. Daley, was inaugurated Mayor of the City of Chicago on April 24, 1989, his 47th birthday. Richard M. surpassed his father's record by serving 22 years in office, one year longer than his father.[1179]

1989/05/31   Howell Relocates

Bill Howell, the son of Willie Howell, who founded the Howell Airport in Blue Island, closed the airport on May 31, 1989. Howell sold the 137-acre lot to developers for $12 million. The airport's last day was a festival, as thousands of people turned out to say farewell. The last plane out was Bill Howell in his 1942 Stearman.[1180]

Taking off from his closed airport, Howell flew to New Lenox Airport in unincorporated Will County, which became his new base of operation. New Lennox Airport had started in 1968, and in 1983, Howell obtained a financial interest in it. After he relocated there, the airport was often referred to as the Howell/New Lenox Airport. [1181]

By 1993, Howell was looking for another buyer. He had added new hangars and his property tax had tripled from $36,000 to $140,000, making it impossible for him to continue operations.[1182]

1989/06/07   Eastern Airlines Shuttle Sold

New Yorker Donald Trump purchased Eastern Airlines shuttle service between Boston, New York, and Washington, DC, renaming it Trump Airlines.[1183]

1989/08/31   Recreational Pilot License

The FAA created a new level of licensing, the Recreational License, that was designed for those flying near their home airports with limited air traffic control interaction.[1184]

1990–1994

1990   Courts Finally Resolve DuPage Airport Dispute

In 1990, after nearly 20 years, the courts resolved a dispute between DuPage Airport and the surrounding communities over airport expansion.

By the 1970s, DuPage's location made it seem ideal as a major reliever airport for O'Hare. However, its short 4,000 ft. runway and lack of instrument approaches prohibited this. DuPage County sought to extend the runway and add instrumentation, but the airport's location on the Kane County border required Kane County's approval to extend it.

Kane County and nearby municipalities fought any expansion, and in 1974 created the Fox Valley Airport Authority under the auspices of the Municipal Airport Authorities Act. After a court battle, the FVAA had assumed control of the airport from DuPage County. Making DuPage a reliever airport was a state and even a national priority, but the FVAA steadfastly refused any expansion.

The Illinois legislature intervened in 1985 with legislation that authorized the DuPage County Board to appoint a majority of the members to the FVAA, but the newly constituted Airport Authority was still unable to agree on expansion plans for several years.

In 1987, the Illinois legislature intervened again, creating the DuPage Airport Authority, not only giving it total control of the airport but also the authority to issue bonds and levy a property tax to pay off the bonds. Naturally, those opposed to expansion challenged the new Authority in court. Finally, in 1990, the courts settled the matter in favor of the DuPage Airport Authority.[1185]

1990/03/06   SR-71 Sets Speed Record

After flying coast-to-coast in 68 min., the SR-71 Blackbird arrived at Dulles before being retired to the Air and Space Museum.[1186]

1990/09/30   Last Game at Comiskey

Comiskey Park had served as the home for the White Sox since June 1, 1910. Then on September 30, 1990, the Sox played their final game at the old Comiskey Park. The following season, the new Comiskey Park opened across the street and the old stadium site was turned into a parking lot.[1187]

1991   Airborne Constructs Cargo Facility at Rockford

In 1991, Airborne Express (later acquired by DHL Global) built a 26,000 sq.-ft. cargo facility. While Emery Worldwide had regular cargo operations at Rockford for several years, it had not previously had a permanent facility.[1188]

1991/07/04   Rochelle Airport Honors a Vet

On July 4, 1991, the Greater Rochelle Municipal Airport changed its name to Koritz Field to honor Maj. Thomas F. Koritz.

Koritz learned to fly at Rochelle in March 1969. Later, in the Air Force, Maj. Koritz was one of only five flight surgeons who were also pilots. While flying a combat mission in Operation Desert Storm in Iraq the night of January 17, 1991, enemy fire downed his F-15E over Basra. His body was not immediately recovered. On the Fourth of July, 1991, Rochelle renamed the airport to honor Maj. Koritz. He remained missing in action until 2002, when his body was finally recovered.[1189]

1991/08   George Edgecumbe Retires

After 61 years in aviation, George Edgecumbe retired in August 1991. Edgecumbe had started flying an OX-5 American Eagle[a] in 1930. In 1937 he and Al Tufts formed the Piper Distributorship, Tufts-Edgecumbe first at Pal-Waukee, then at Elmhurst Airport, and finally at Elgin Airport. Tufts-Edgecumbe also operated facilities in Green Bay, WI, and Land O'Lakes, WI, on the Wisconsin-Michigan border.[1190]

1991/11/13   Second Midway Airline Folds

After starting operations in 1979, the second Midway Airways enjoyed a period of success in both service and profits from its Midway Airport base. In 1982 the airline board replaced President Gordon Linkon with Arthur Bass of Federal Express.

Bass saw the need to expand and in 1984 acquired bankrupt Air Florida, giving Midway access to Caribbean destinations, which it operated as Midway Express. Bass also experimented with a single-class service for business passengers called Midway Metrolink, which was very unprofitable and shut down in 1985.

After Midway lost money for two years, Bass's presidency came to an abrupt end when, in February 1985, he was replaced by David Hinson.

a   An open-cockpit biplane, the American Eagle was popular in the 1920s. It was powered either by the OX-5 or a Kinner 5-cylinder engine. Obviously, there is no relation with American Airlines' current regional brand.

Hinson continued an expansion program but in a different direction, starting Midway Connection as a feeder carrier from smaller cities in Illinois, Indiana, Michigan, and Wisconsin.

In June 1989, Midway purchased the Philadelphia hub of Eastern Airlines, which was in bankruptcy. In addition to gates and more airplanes, the acquisition added Toronto and Montreal as destinations.

Midway Airlines reached its zenith in 1989, when it flew 10.1 billion passenger-kilometers. On a single day, it had more than 115 flights arriving at Midway Airport from 25 cities plus another 75 Midway Connection flights from 17 more cities.

All the expansion had accumulated a substantial debt burden. Unfortunately, things went downhill very quickly. With the Gulf War, oil prices spiked, tipping Midway Airlines over the edge. It negotiated a buyout with Northwest Airlines, but it fell through. Midway ceased operations on November 13, 1991, and its assets were liquidated. David Hinson later became the head of the FAA.[1191]

1991/12/04   Pan American World Airways Makes Final Flight

After 64 years, Pan Am's final flight landed at Miami on December 4, 1991. The pioneering U.S. international air carrier suffered deep losses due to airline deregulation and an economic recession.[1192]

1992/04/13   Chicago Basements Flood

On April 13, 1992, millions of gallons of water from the Chicago River poured through the damaged wall of a freight tunnel. The water flooded the large network of tunnels and from there, into basements of buildings throughout the Loop.[1193]

1992/06   Midway Remembers the Battle

In June 1992, on the 50th anniversary of the Battle of Midway, the decisive battle was commemorated by an air show at Midway Airport featuring vintage military and civilian planes. The Union League Club also donated a major statue, *America*, by sculptor Gary Weisman, although the statue itself wasn't unveiled until May 13, 1993.[1194]

1992/10/15   United 727 Lands at Meigs Field

A lightly loaded 727 destined for the Museum of Science and Industry landed at Meigs Field on October 15, 1992. The plane was placed on a barge and moved to the museum, where it became a permanent exhibit.[1195]

1993   O'Hare Completes 1982 Modernization Plan

More than a decade after work began on the O'Hare Modernization Plan of 1982, the last two improvements became operational

A brand new International Terminal, Terminal 5, opened with 21 gates and full customs services. The old Terminal 4, which had been built in a parking lot and required that passengers be bussed to and from planes, was closed and demolished.

A new light rail system, the Airport Transit System, improved movement over greater distances than the existing people-mover systems. The elevated system had stops at the three domestic terminals, the new international terminal, and a remote parking lot.[1196]

1993   DeKalb Airport Changes Name

In 1993, the City of DeKalb renamed its airport the DeKalb Taylor Municipal Airport to honor Pete Taylor for his dedication to the airport.

Willard Rue "Pete" Taylor became interested in aviation in the 1930s. Following WWII, Taylor operated a flight school near DeKalb, first on Kenslinger Rd. and then on Crego Rd.

During WWII, the Navy built an airport for Interstate Aircraft and Engineering to construct and test TDR-1 unmanned drones. Following the war, DeKalb acquired the airport and made Taylor the manager of the new DeKalb Airport.

Besides running the airport and a Piper Dealership, Taylor brought the airport into the age of executive travel. Taylor installed new runways, lighting, and instrument landing equipment, transforming the small airport into an O'Hare reliever.[1197]

1993/07/02   Mississippi River Floods

On July 2, 1993, major flooding along the Mississippi River disrupted aviation as an Automated Flight Service Station, 36 GA airports, and two FAA control towers were closed. In response, the FAA activated a temporary control tower for St. Louis.[1198]

1993/09/30   Chanute Air Force Base Closes

With reductions following the end of the Cold War, in 1988 Chanute Air Force Base was designated for closing and was finally decommissioned on September 30, 1993.

Most of the base was repurposed. A portion of the facilities and many of the aircraft became the core of the Chanute Air Museum. The collection contained about 40 aircraft, primarily ones that had been used as part of Chanute's mission to train mechanics to service personnel. Many aircraft were prototypes or very early production models. The museum also displayed a number of missiles, including a portion of a Minuteman silo and control facility. Most of the collection was housed inside the main hangar, but about a dozen of the larger planes were kept outside, exposed to the elements.[1199]

Other base facilities were used by various National Guard units and light industry.[1200] The airfield itself remains active today as a civilian airport, the Rantoul National Aviation Center or Frank Elliot Field.[1201]

1993/10/31   Orange Line Goes to Midway

On October 31, 1993, the CTA extended the "L" rail system with the Orange Line becoming operational from the Loop to Midway Airport. The $500 million project to connect Midway Airport was built primarily using existing right-of-ways unused by freight railroads.[1202]

1993/11   Midway Airlines Third Iteration

Two years after the second Midway Airlines shuttered its operations, in November 1993, the third Midway Airlines was reborn out of the ashes.

Jet Express had been flying into Midway Airport from Atlantic City since 1985 and had witnessed the growth and decline of the earlier Midway. After the second Midway Airline foundered, Jet Express purchased the Midway name.

The new Midway Airlines took off flying Fokker 100s, initially offering service from Chicago to Dallas, Denver, and New York. Most employees were veterans of the second Midway, including its President, Kenneth Carlson, a founder of the earlier incarnation.

However, their business model was not producing profits, and in July 1994, Chicagoan Sam Zell purchased 90% of the company. Zell replaced the executive staff and moved the base of operations from Midway Airport to Raleigh-Durham, NC.[a]

Midway Airlines abandoned the no-frills model and attempted to provide some amenities but at a lower fare. Again, for a while, Midway expanded rapidly, this time by adding flights rather than acquisition. Stretching beyond the regional image, Midway had flights from Raleigh-Durham to Los Angeles and San Jose. They also added feeder routes as the Midway Connection, but this time through two regional carriers, rather

a   The new company maintained that "Midway Airlines" was still an appropriate name since Raleigh-Durham was "midway" between the North and the South.

than adding their own routes. At its peak, Midway had 200 daily flights operating out of Raleigh-Durham. The company went public on the NASDAQ exchange in November 1997.

As with the second Midway Airlines, the end came quickly. Starting in 2000, the tech slump greatly reduced business travel for the Raleigh-Durham research community. The airline filed for Chapter 11 on August 13, 2001, with immediate layoffs and scaled back operations. A month later, the 9/11 terrorist attacks depressed all air travel. Midway continued on-and-off operations, at the same time, reaching out to various suitors and investors, but closed for good on October 30, 2003.[1203]

1993/12/08   NAFTA Signed

Following negotiations begun by President George H.W. Bush between the U.S., Canada, and Mexico, the North American Free Trade Agreement (NAFTA) was ratified by both houses of Congress and signed by President Clinton.[1204]

1993/12/22   White Rule Ends in South Africa

Following centuries of white-only rule and policies of strict racial separation, the South African Parliament voted itself out of existence on December 22, 1993.[1205]

1994   UPS Opens Major Facility at Rockford

Rockford had been a cargo hub for more than five years when, in 1994, United Parcel Service moved it into a whole new category. UPS opened a new sorting center with more than 500,000 sq. ft., nearly 20 times the size of the Airbourne facility, and with sufficient ramp space to accommodate 15 planes.[1206]

1994   Schaumburg Purchases Airport

In 1994, the owners put Schaumburg Airpark, previously called Roselle Airfield, up for sale.

The FAA, fearing the trend of general aviation airports being sold to developers, urged the Village of Schaumburg to purchase the airport. The village agreed and purchased the airport with subsidies from both the state and federal governments, renaming it Schaumburg Municipal Airport.[1207]

Northwest Flyers became the airport's Fixed Base Operator (FBO) in 1985 and continues in that role into 2018.

1994/01/17   LA Earthquake

A 6.6-level earthquake struck Los Angeles, knocking glass out of the LAX control tower. After closing the airport briefly, operations resumed from the damaged tower until a temporary tower could be put in service.[1208]

1994/07/12   United Employees Take Ownership

On July 12, 1994, UAL became an employee-owned company with 55% of stock in employee hands. Two unions, the pilots and machinists, owned a bulk of the shares and got two seats on the board of directors. The decision made United the largest employee-owned company in the U.S.

UAL's diversification in the 1980s proved to be a disaster, resulting in extreme cost-cutting measures on its core airline business. By the 1990s, UAL had reversed course, but financial conditions continued to stress the company as a whole, especially the employees. Employee ownership was seen as a solution to the problem. [1209]

1994/10/31   American Eagle Crashes in Roselawn, IN

While in a holding pattern for O'Hare on Halloween (October 31, 1994), a Simmons Airlines, flying as American Eagle Flight 4184, accumulated ice on its wings. Ice changed airflow over the ailerons, causing the French-built turboprop ATR-72 to roll and crash near Roselawn, IN. All 68 on board perished.[1210]

1995-1999

1995 Chicago-Gary Airport Compact Signed

In 1995, Gary and Chicago signed the Chicago-Gary Airport Compact. Under the arrangement, Chicago provided more operating money to the Gary Airport than it had received from the state of Indiana. Once again, the airport changed its name, this time to the Gary/Chicago International Airport.

In the 1990s, there was widespread talk of creating a third airport in the Chicago area. Suburban and downstate communities looked to locations such as Peotone, IL, and Chicago investigated a site around Lake Calumet, but those plans fizzled. Instead, Chicago pursued the joint arrangement with Gary.[1211]

1995/06/07 Boeing 777 Enters Service

United Airlines placed the Boeing 777 into service between Washington and London. The 777 was the first large airliner designed entirely on computer instead of paper.[1212]

1995/09/09 GNAS Decommissioned

A formal closure ceremony on September 9, 1995, officially shuttered Glenview Naval Air Station. At the time, the base had five runways, including a recently rebuilt 8,000 ft. one. The Coast Guard Air Station relocated to Traverse City, MI.

With a reduction in military tensions following the end of the Cold War, the Navy's Base Realignment and Closure committee identified GNAS for closure in April 1993. The land and buildings were turned over to the Village of Glenview, which cleared most of the area. Over 1 million cu. yd. of concrete and 108 military buildings were removed from the base and replaced by a variety of houses, townhomes, a golf course, movie theater, shops, and restaurants.[1213]

One former hangar continues to serve as a 32,000 sq.-ft. training facility as part of the Northeastern Illinois Public Safety Training Academy (NIPSTA).[1214]

1996/09/30   Meigs Field First Closes

Chicago's lakefront airport was shut down on September 30, 1996, as part
of Mayor Richard M. Daley's plan to create a park on Northerly Island.
Governor Jim Edgar strongly opposed the idea, and the two reached a
compromise resulting in Meigs Field being reopened on January 6, 1997.[1215]

1996/10/30   G-IV Crashes During Palwaukee Takeoff

Taking off in a gusty crosswind on October 30, 1996, a Gulfstream IV struck
a drainage ditch at Palwaukee during takeoff, then bounced over the airport
fence and Hintz Rd. before crashing in a field near an apartment complex.
All four people on board were killed.

The plane was owned by Alberto-Culver but was being flown for Aon
Insurance by an Aon pilot with a co-pilot from Alberto-Culver. A year-
and-a-half investigation by the NTSB spread the responsibility to both
companies as well as the airport for the location of the ditch.

Court actions spread over the next decade, with a number of suits being
settled out of court and several going to trial. At long last, the final suit was
settled on September 4, 2008.[1216]

1997   United Forms Star Alliance

United joined with four other airlines (Air Canada, Lufthansa, Scandinavian
Airlines System [SAS], and Thai Airways) to form a global cooperative. Star
Alliance members cooperated in ticketing, passenger and freight transfer,
rewards programs, and maintenance support. As of 2017, more than 25
airlines were part of Star Alliance.[1217]

1997/02/06   First Advanced Explosive Detection Equipment

O'Hare, along with the New York City airports, was the first to receive the
most advanced explosive detection equipment, the CTX 5000 SP.[1218]

1997/06/04   Monarch Air Service Says Farewell

After serving Municipal/Midway for 65 years, Monarch Air Service was sold
to Signature Flight Support, an international chain of FBOs. [1219]

1997/08/01   Boeing-McDonnell Merger Complete

Boeing Co. and McDonnell Douglas Corp. formally merged on August 1,
1997. The combined companies, operating under the Boeing name,
controlled two-thirds of the world aviation market.[1220]

1998/02   Meigs Field Receives Instrument Approach

In February 1998, Meigs Field established an instrument approach proce-
dure. Given the lakefront's weather, the instrument approach was a major
improvement for pilots.[1221]

1998/06/14   Chicago Bulls Repeat the Three-Peat

The Chicago Bulls won their sixth NBA championship of the decade on
June 14, 1998.[1222]

1998/05/19   Final Early Bird Flies West

The Early Birds of Aviation, a group of aviation pioneers, dissolved upon
the death of the final member, George D. Grundy, Jr., on May 19, 1998, at
the age of 99.[1223]

1999   Bange Wins Emmy for Skydiving

In 1999, journalist Jackie Bange won a regional Emmy Award for
Best Feature Reporting for a piece she did on preparations for a large
formation skydive.

   Bange was an anchor and reporter at WGN TV with an active interest in
skydiving. The skydive featured in the report was one in 1996, in which
Bange was one of 246 skydivers who linked together to form the largest
formation to that time.

   By 2017, Bange had made more than 1,800 jumps from an assortment
of aircraft including a C-130, B-24, Ford Tri-Motor, Boeing 727, a biplane
flying inverted, and a Bell JetRanger helicopter.[1224]

1999/07/31   108th Squadron Leaves Chicago

On July 31, 1999, the 108th Refueling Squadron departed Chicago for good
when it transferred downstate to Scott Air Force Base. The military eliminated the last of its facilities at O'Hare because of constant conflicts with
commercial operations.

   In December 1990, the 108th Refueling Squadron had been activated as
part of the U.S. response to the 1990–1991 Gulf Crisis and participated in
Operation Desert Storm. When the mission was accomplished, the squadron returned to O'Hare for a short time. From its new home at Scott AFB,
the 108th continues supporting the USAF, participating in Operation
Enduring Freedom and Operation Iraqi Freedom as well as other short-
term assignments to the present day.[1225]

2000–2004

2000   Ceiling Zero at Old Sky Harbor

Although the Sky Harbor Airport had been closed for more than 25 years, one of the art deco hangars survived and had been repurposed several times. Around 2000, an upscale or "swank" restaurant called Ceiling Zero opened. It experienced a flash period of popularity before closing.[1226]

2000/01/01   Y2K Arrives

The calendar rolled over to 2000 with only minor computer glitches. To avoid Y2K problems, the FAA hired foreign nationals to do program coding with incomplete background checks.[1227]

2000/06/02   Smoking Prohibited on All Flights

The Dept. of Transportation issued a rule prohibiting smoking on all scheduled flights.[1228]

2000/06/26   DaVinci's Parachute Tested

For more than five centuries, scientists and engineers debated whether or a parachute sketched by Leonardo da Vinci would function. On June 26, 2000, the debate was settled in South Africa when Adrian Nicholas proved the parachute's functionality. The British record-holding parachutist used a device that duplicated da Vinci's design as closely as possible. Nicholas made a 7,000-ft. descent, also wearing a modern parachute as backup and accompanied by two other parachutists for safety.[1229]

2000/07/22   Air France Concorde Crashes

A Concorde operated by Air France Flight 4590 crashed on takeoff from Charles de Gaulle Airport in Paris when its engines ingested a piece of debris on the runway from a previous Continental flight. All on board the plane were killed, as well as four people in the hotel into which the plane crashed.[1230]

2001/02/21   First Test Firing of Missile from UAV

A new era of aerial warfare was achieved on February 21, 2001, when an RQ-1 Predator fired an AGM114 Hellfire missile on a test range. The

Predator was first used in combat in December 2001, when it attacked
targets in Afghanistan as part of the U.S. response to the 9/11 attacks.[1231]

2001/03/07   Newest Terminal at Midway

Midway Airport opened a new state-of-the-art terminal on March 7, 2001.
Following deregulation, the new breed of regional and low-cost airlines
reenergized Midway, and in 1998 it surpassed its previous passenger record.

A new 900,000 sq.-ft. terminal was constructed to accommodate the
increased traffic. In June 2004, Midway completed the Terminal Construc-
ton Project with the addition of fourteen new gates. The following December, a new parking garage opened to accommodate 6,300 vehicles.[1232]

2001/03/11–04/07   London to Sydney Air Race Revisited

As part of Australia's Centenary of Federation celebrations, Australia
sponsored a re-creation of the original 1919 air race from London to
Sydney. A total of 38 entries from 9 countries started the race, flying a
wide variety of aircraft including a Piper Cub, Robinson R44 helicopter, a
Shrike Commander, and an assortment of contemporary single and
twin-engine planes.[1233]

One plane, an amphibian named *Miss Nancy,* was entered by a Chicago
team. The 1954 Grumman HU-16 Albatross was purchased and totally
refurbished by Lyle Campbell, a Chicagoan living in Scottsdale, AZ. The
co-pilot was Lyle's son, Scott, a Chicago area resident. Another pilot (Lonny
McClung), a mechanical engineer (Frank Wilkins), and a photojournalist
(Samaruddin Stewart) rounded out the team.[1234]

They departed Falcon Field in Mesa, AZ, on February 11th and flew
across the Atlantic to arrive at Biggin Hill Airport in London well before
the start of the air race. On March 11, 2001, the Albatross and other entrants embarked on the 28-leg, 12,000 mi. journey to Sydney arriving 28
days later on April 7.[1235]

When they arrived, the Campbells didn't exactly fly under the Sydney
Bridge, but they did land the Albatross outside of the harbor, then taxied
under the bridge into the harbor where they spent a half-hour looking at
the sights, including the Sydney Opera House.[1236]

After participating in the Centenary celebrations and doing a little
R&R, the team began their return to the U.S. on April 12. Their flight
island-hopped across the Pacific to Peru, then north until they arrived back
in Mesa on April 23.[1237]

2001/05/01   Boeing Headquarters Comes to Chicago

Boeing selected Chicago over Dallas and Denver for their new corporate headquarters. Reasons for selection included Chicago's strong business environment and its broad cultural diversity.[1238]

2001/08/17   Signature Buys Priester FBO

Signature Flight Support announced the purchase of Priester's FBO at Palwaukee on August 17, 2001, taking over Priester Aviation's fueling and other services. Signature also received more than 450,000 sq. ft. of hangar space. Priester retained its charter and other aviation services. At the time of the sale, the FAA listed Palwaukee as the 25th busiest airport in the nation. With more than 50 FBOs worldwide, Signature already operated FBOs at the other major Chicago airports including O'Hare, Midway, and Meigs.[1239]

2001/09/11   Terrorists Attack U.S.

Following terrorist attacks on New York and Washington, DC, all U.S. aviation was grounded for several days. Subsequently, the FAA implemented new security measures at all airports.[1240]

2001/09/27   President Bush Speaks at O'Hare

In a major speech at O'Hare on September 27, 2001, President George W. Bush announced provisions to increase aviation security in response to the 9/11 attacks. He expanded the air marshal program and established for airlines to secure cockpits. Bush also worked with Congress to put airport screening and security under Federal jurisdiction.[1241]

2001/11/19   TSA Created

On November 19, President Bush signed the Aviation and Transportation Security Act into law, which, among other things, created the Transportation Security Administration (TSA).

Initially part of the Dept. of Transportation, the TSA was transferred to the Dept. of Homeland Security after the passage of the Homeland Security Act in 2002.[1242]

2002   Commercial Air Service Resumes at Gary

In 2002, Pan American Airways[a] became the first commercial carrier to operate at Gary Airport since 1975. As during the 1950s-1970s, commercial

a   This Pan Am was a low-cost carrier that purchased the name and logo from the bankrupt major carrier but had no other connection with the prior enterprise.

carriers started and stopped service frequently. In August 2013, Allegiant Air ceased operations to Gary. As of 2017, there is no commercial service at the airport.[1243]

2002   O'Hare Gets Funds for New Runways

In 2002, President George W. Bush and Congress allocated funds to construct two new runways at O'Hare to relieve congestion. The funding struck a major blow to opponents of any expansion of the airport.

Around the end of the 20th century, O'Hare's future was hotly contested. Political leaders, primarily Republican, from the communities surrounding O'Hare as well as counties downstate resented the fact that Chicago, primarily Democratic, had control of O'Hare and its revenue. Most political leaders outside the City of Chicago vehemently opposed any expansion to O'Hare.

Instead, O'Hare opponents proposed construction of a new South Suburban Airport in Peotone, with the hopes that the new airport would gradually siphon off much of O'Hare's traffic.

The fight wasn't limited to within the state or adjacent states. O'Hare had a pivotal role as an aviation crossroads. Its ability to disrupt air travel nationwide made O'Hare's future a national issue which was resolved by Congress and President Bush.[1244]

2002/07/04   Balloon Flies Around the World

On July 4, 2002, Steve Fossett became the first person to circumnavigate the globe in a hot air balloon.

This was Fossett's sixth attempt at the record. The *Spirit of Freedom* departed Western Australia and landed in Queensland, Australia, 15 days later on July 19.

Fossett, who had a successful career on the Chicago Board of Trade and the Chicago Options Exchange, was an adventurer at heart. Fossett challenged himself often, establishing world records by sail, balloon, and plane. The FAI recognized 91 world records by Fossett and the World Sailing Speed Record Council recognized another 23 records. Fossett was also active in mountain climbing and cross-country skiing.[1245]

2002/12/09   United Files for Bankruptcy

After defaulting on loans a few days earlier, on December 9, 2002, United filed for bankruptcy protection under Chapter 11. At the time, it was the sixth largest bankruptcy in the country and remains the largest in airline history.

United was caught up in a perfect storm of events that led to disaster. The lingering financial effects of UAL's diversification efforts continued to haunt the company. The 1978 Deregulation Act took its toll on major airlines: Pan American and Eastern both went out of business. TWA filed for bankruptcy three times, and US Airways filed for bankruptcy as well.

After the terrorist attacks of September 11, 2001, many people avoided air travel, making the situation worse. United hung on longer than the others but could not hold out forever.

Following the longest and costliest airline restructuring to that time, United emerged from bankruptcy on February 1, 2006. During that period, United shed 460 planes (about 20% of the fleet) and 58,000 employees (about 30% of the workforce). Other changes included renegotiating labor contracts with the unions, charging passengers for meals, and shifting about a third of their capacity to a low-cost carrier. Overall, United reduced annual expenditures by more than $7 billion.[1246]

2003   Chicago Aviation History Revival

In 2003, David Young, transportation editor of the *Chicago Tribune* published his volume, *Chicago Aviation: An Illustrated Hisory*. Young's comprehensive work has become the backbone of the study of Chicago aviation history, providing a fascinating description of the aviators, airports, and aviation activities from the earliest days.[1247]

That same year, Christopher Lynch published *Chicago's Midway Airport: The First Seventy-Five Years*, the first of his three books on the subject. Lynch's book, filled with photographs and personal stories, resonated with many pilots and aviation enthusiasts who flew into or lived around Midway and other Chicago airports.[1248]

2003/02/01   Space Shuttle *Columbia* Breaks Up

During reentry, the Space Shuttle *Columbia* disintegrated in the sky over Texas. All seven astronauts died.[1249]

2003/03/31   Meigs Field Destroyed

Mayor Richard M. Daley ordered equipment from the City of Chicago to destroy Meigs Field's runway during the night of March 31, 2003. Owners of more than a dozen aircraft parked at Meigs were kept away from their planes for several days and were unable to remove them for even longer.

For years there had been disagreements between the City of Chicago, FAA, State of Illinois, and aviation users over threats to close Meigs Field.

The first proposal came in 1972, when Mayor Richard J. Daley proposed closing Meigs Field. However, Daley changed his position when the FAA threatened to cut off funds.

Next, in 1980, Mayor Byrne pursued plans to hold another World's Fair in Chicago. The proposed lakefront location replaced Meigs Field with exhibit areas.[1250]

Things were relatively quiet for about a decade, but in 1994, the city again made noises about closing Meigs. By the end of 1994, the Illinois legislature passed a bill to keep the airport open under state control and the city backed down.

In September 1996, the Chicago Dept. of Aviation and the Park District actually closed Meigs Field. The airport had become a bargaining chip between the State of Illinois and the City of Chicago. The State wanted Meigs open for the convenience of Springfield shuttle flights. The city wanted an expansion of O'Hare instead of efforts to build a third major airport. Governor Edgar and Mayor Richard M. Daley reached a compromise to keep Meigs open under Chicago control for at least five years. In exchange, Chicago was given approval to construct a third east-west runway at O'Hare.

Like his father, Mayor Richard M. Daley had opposed Meigs Field for years. Claiming the 9/11 attack demonstrated the threat of airplanes to urban areas, he ordered the airport destroyed.

So in the middle of the night on March 31, 2003, Daley had the police escort construction equipment that dug a series of giant Xs in the runway. Despite the small size of Meigs Field, the surprise airport destruction received national attention.[1251]

2003/07/31   New Pilot License Format

As part of ongoing security enhancements, the FAA announced a new physical format for Pilot Licenses. Instead of the previous paper licenses, the new credit-card style licenses included a hologram and other security features on composite media.[1252]

2003/09/08   National Air Tour in Lansing

As part of the re-creation of the Ford National Air Tours, a contingent of about two dozen planes arrived at Lansing Airport, Ford's original Chicago area hub.[1253]

2003/09/20–21   Wright Redux Makes a Flight

In September 2003, as part of activities to recognize the 100th anniversary of the Wright Brother's first flight, a group in the Chicago area constructed and flew a replica of the Wright 1903 Flyer.

The effort had sprung from a high school project around 2000, in which a student built a small model based on Wright's 1900 glider. The student's father learned that Wright's original Flyer was destroyed in a crash and that there had never been an air-worthy replica built. The father gathered a group of Glen Ellyn people to form the nonprofit Wright Redux Association with the goal of flying a replica 1903 Flyer by the 100th anniversary of the Wright's first flight, December 17.

The project attracted partners, including the Museum of Science and Industry, National Geographic Television, and the History Channel. Miller Woodworking in Glen Ellyn constructed the body. Packer Engineering in Naperville built a replica of the original Charles Taylor engine. Thirty other companies and many individuals contributed time, money, and materials to complete the project.

Final assembly was done at Clow International Airport in Bolingbrook. The replica was named the *Spirit of Glen Ellyn*. The FAA certificated the Flyer in the Experimental category, assigning it the tail number N203WF.

The replica made its first flight using a contemporary engine on April 27, 2003, when it flew 136 feet before making a perfect landing. The *Spirit of Glen Ellyn* made two more flights on August 3rd and was on display at the Chicago Air and Water Show on August 17th.

On September 7th, a replica of the original engine was mounted to the plane. An official 100th anniversary celebration held September 20–21 at the Museum of Science and Industry included activities for children and an exhibit by the Tuskegee Airmen. Unfortunately, the wind was uncooperative. The Wrights had relied upon the 26 mph wind at Kill Devil Hills to get the original glider into the air. After numerous unsuccessful tries in several directions, the *Spirit of Glen Ellyn* was placed on display in the MSI rotunda.[1254]

2003/12   Wood Founds the Warbird Heritage Foundation

Paul Wood and others founded the nonprofit Warbird Heritage Foundation (WHF) to promote public interest in historic military aircraft. After a successful career as a founder and director of a leading private equity firm, Wood took an interest in military aviation and now manages the affairs of WHF.

Located at the Waukegan Regional Airport, WHF restores antique military aircraft to flying condition whenever possible. The collection contains more than a dozen aircraft from WWI, WWII, Korea, and Vietnam, including everything from a L-3 Grasshopper and a N2S-3 Stearman to a T-33 Shooting Star, an F-86 Sabre, and an A-4B Skyhawk. The only replica in the collection is of an WWI Nieuport.

Wood and other WFH pilots fly planes from the collection at air shows nationwide, including the EAA AirVenture in Oshkosh and the annual Wings Over Waukegan (Northern Illinois Airshow). Wood also does formation flying as part of the U.S. Navy Legacy Flight program and performs with The Hoppers, an L-39 Albatross demonstration team.[1255]

2004   Bolingbrook Acquires Clow Airport

In 2004, the Village of Bolingbrook acquired the Clow Airport and developed it into an international airport.

The airport began in the 1950s when Oliver Boyd Clow traded a tractor for an airplane and learned to fly. Clow developed a Restricted Landing Area (RLA) north of two nearby RLAs, one owned by Richard and Mary Alice Lambert on Washington St. (now Weber Rd.) and the other off Rt. 66 known as the Plainfield-George Airport.

Clow's airport drew activity from the surrounding area. Starting in the 1960s, a very active glider club made Clow its home. In the 1990s, half of the property was sold to developers, while the rest remained an airport.

Each year, Clow hosts the Cavalcade of Planes, giving the public an opportunity to have a close-up view of aviation. Clow is also home to the Illinois Aviation Museum.[1256]

2004/01/21   O'Hare Flight Delays Targeted

Flight delays at O'Hare rippled through the nation and became the focus of the FAA and DOT. On January 21, 2004, they reached an agreement with American and United to reduce flight operations during peak hours by 5%. By June the reduction was increased to 7.5%. Most of these reductions were accomplished by rescheduling flights to less busy times.

Congestion continued, and in August, under threat of FAA directives, both American and United made more severe adjustments to their schedules including canceling some flights altogether. Other airlines with less of a presence at O'Hare also adjusted their schedules to reduce peak congestion.[1257]

2004/01/27   NextGen Announced

Transportation Secretary Norman Mineta announced the Next Generation of air traffic control during an address to the Aero Club of Washington. Based on state-of-the-art technology, the NextGen system would prevent gridlock, reduce congestion, improve efficiency, and increase security for the entire aviation community.[1258]

2004/04   Chicago Midway Historians Formed

Publication of books by Christopher Lynch and David Young spurred interest in the history of Midway Airport and aviation around Chicago. A core group of people crystalized and formed the Midway Historians in April 2004.

The group meets informally and maintains an online presence, exchanging information and encouraging each other to discover and preserve aviation history. Several current and past aviation authors including Christopher Lynch, David Kent, and the late Nicholas Selig, as well as many nonpublished aviation historians are active in the group. This book is the result of inspiration and support of Midway Historians.[1259]

2004/06/21   First Manned Civilian Space Flight

SpaceShipOne, created by Burt Rutan's Scaled Composites, made a suborbital flight reaching an altitude of 62 mi. before landing in the Mojave Desert. Mike Melville piloted the spacecraft on the first flight and again on September 29. On October 4, the craft made another trip, piloted by Brian Binnie winning the X-Prize of $10 million for Scaled Composites.[1260]

2004/07/16   Millennium Park Opens

Four years late and millions over budget ($475 final vs. $150 planned), Chicago welcomed the new millennium with the fabulous Millennium Park. The project began in 1997 with the goal of replacing the unsightly Illinois Central Railroad yard. Starting on July 16, 2004, the three-day dedication celebration was attended by 300,000 people.

Almost immediately, Millennium Park became popular with tourists as well as locals. Its major features include the *Cloudgate* sculpture (affectionately known as the Bean), the Pritzker Pavilion for concerts, and the water-spouting Crown Fountain.[1261]

2004/09/01   FAA Gets Sporty

In order to accommodate less-expensive, recreational flying, the FAA established new provisions for small aircraft. Light Sport Aircraft (LSA) are limited to two passengers, a gross weight of 1,320 pounds, and a maximum speed of 120 knots.

Less training is required to obtain a Sport Pilot License than a Private Pilot License. However, sport pilots are limited to noncommercial flight carrying a single passenger during daytime VFR conditions and outside of congested airspace.[1262]

2005–2009

2005/02/05   Teterboro Challenger Takeoff Failure

On February 5, 2005, a CL-600 Challenger, operated by Platinum Jet Management, was unable to take off at Teterboro Airport, crashing through a fence and crossing a six-lane highway before slamming into a building. There were no fatalities, but four people were seriously injured and another ten sustained minor injuries.

The NTSB report concluded the plane was unable to rotate because it was overweight and the center of gravity was forward of the specified limit.

Subsequent investigation revealed a multitude of problems at Platinum. Records were falsified and it turned out that not all flight crews were qualified to operate the equipment they flew, including the Challenger's pilot and the flight attendant, a Miami dancer who was unable to operate the airplane's door. To take advantage of cheap fuel prices, pilots were expected to take on as much as possible, ignoring the airplane's weight limitations. The excessive fuel load contributed to the Challenger's failure to launch.

Three people pled guilty to a variety of criminal charges, including one of Platinum's pilots, Francis Viera, who was sentenced to six months in prison, six months of home confinement and three years of supervision for conspiracy to defraud and obstruction of the investigation.

The two brothers who started and owned Platinum Jet also stood trial and were convicted. Michael Brassington, the President and Chief Pilot, was convicted of endangering the safety of an aircraft and eight additional charges and was sentenced to 30 months in prison. His younger brother Paul Brassington, Platinum's VP, received an 18 month prison term for conspiracy to commit wire fraud.[1263]

2005/08/29   Hurricane Katrina

Hurricane Katrina made landfall, causing widespread destruction along the Gulf Coast. Airports throughout the region were closed, some for as long as two weeks. The main airport in New Orleans opened for relief flights on September 1, but could only handle a maximum of nine VFR flights an hour.[1264]

2005/10/26   Sox Sweep Houston

The Chicago White Sox swept the Houston Astros to win the World Series on October 26, 2005.[1265]

2005/12/08   Southwest 737 Overruns Runway

Southwest Airlines Flight 1248 arrived at Midway during a snowstorm on December 8, 2005. When the 737 landed on runway 31C, the pilot did not use the plane's thrust reversers. Eight inches of snow had fallen on the ground. Although the runway was clear, it was wet and the plane's braking was not sufficient to stop on the runway.

The nose gear collapsed as the plane left the runway and skidded through a fence and into an intersection at 55th St. and Central Ave. Everyone on the plane was uninjured. However, the plane struck three cars and twelve people were rushed to area hospitals. Only one person, a six-year-old boy, did not survive. This was the first fatality for Southwest in its 35-year history.[1266]

As a result of this accident, Midway became the first airport in the Chicago area to install an Engineered Materials Arresting System (EMAS) in 2006. Installed at both ends of the four main runways, EMAS consists of concrete blocks that are designed to collapse under heavy weight. EMAS can bring an airliner to a halt in just a few yards.[1267]

2006/04   Signature Opens New Terminal at Palwaukee

Signature Flight Support opened a new 10,000 sq.-ft. executive terminal at Palwaukee Airport.[1268]

2006/08/05   Developers Get Second Howell Airport

On August 5, 2006, the Howell/New Lenox Airport closed, becoming the second Howell facility to give way to developers.[1269]

2006/10/17   Palwaukee Gets New Name

Palwaukee Airport became Chicago Executive Airport on October 17, 2006. The airport selected the new name, with the approval of its owners the City of Prospect Heights and the Village of Wheeling, because the name was more reflective of the airport's role in the national air system.[1270]

2007   Bult Field Is Built

In 2007, businessman James Bult purchased the land of the then-shuttered Sanger Field on Kedzie Ave. in Monee, south of Chicago. Bult constructed a modern airport for general and corporate aviation. The new airport had a 5,000 ft. runway with hangars and a terminal on 288 acres.[1271]

2007   Chicago Rockford Gets Current Name

Since the year 2000, the Greater Rockford Airport had gone through a number of name changes. In the early 2000s, Rockford sought a closer association with Chicago in the minds of passengers. Accordingly, it changed its name to the Northwest Chicagoland Regional Airport at Rockford.

To reflect its status as an official U.S. Port of Entry in 2004, the airport underwent another name change to the Chicago/Rockford International Airport. Finally, in 2007, they removed the slash between the two city names, becoming the current Chicago Rockford International Airport.[1272]

2007/05   John Dacy Passes the Torch

Before his passing in May 2007, John Dacy had passed on the flying bug to his offspring. Four of his five children are pilots and three earn their living by flying.[1273]

John's oldest son, Dave Dacy, soloed at his parents' airport in an Aeronca Champ when he was 16. Before he was 20, he was learning aerobatics in a Stearman, aided by his mother Elsie. Dave began performing aerobatics professionally and later formed Dacy Airshows, which booked him and other performers for air shows around the country.[1274]

Another son, Phil, also learned to fly under his father's instruction and became thoroughly involved in aviation. He became a captain flying for Priester Aviation's charter flights out of Chicago Executive Airport. During the air show season, he is an announcer for the family business, Dacy Airshows. Other times, he can be found at Dacy Airport where he runs the flight school and maintenance operations.[1275]

Like her two aviator brothers, Susan Dacy, the only daughter of John and Elsie, lives and breathes aviation. Growing up working at the airport, she worked both in the office and on the flight line, taking care of planes. Susan learned to fly from her parents and soloed in a Piper Cub when she was just sixteen. Susan bought and restored a Stearman that she continues to fly. Eventually, she flew for American Airlines where she became a captain, flying 777s internationally.

When not flying the big jets, Susan flies one of her two Stearmans. As a regular performer with Dacy Airshows, Susan does aerobatics in the Stearman she affectionately calls *Big Red*. While there are many female performers on the air show circuit, very few perform in open-cockpit biplanes as Susan does.[1276]

2008/05/24   Oldest ATP Pilot Licensed

Chicagoan Howard Levinson, a month shy of his 84th birthday, became the most senior pilot to receive his initial Airline Transport Pilot License on May 24, 2008. He pursued the ATP, the license required to fly for the airlines, because it was the only fixed-wing license or rating that he didn't have.

Born in 1923, Levinson decided to fly a decade later when he saw the *Graf Zeppelin* fly over his house as it circled the city, escorted by two Army pursuit planes. After joining the Army and learning to fly, he took command of a B-24 with its crew of 10 flying photo-reconnaissance missions in the South Pacific at age 21 with a total of only 322 flight hours.

Following the war, Levinson continued serving with the 2471st Air Force Reserve Combat Training Center at O'Hare. On the Fourth of July, 1949, he piloted a C-46 in formation as part of the National Air Fair held at O'Hare.

Although he pursued a nonaviation career, as a civilian Levinson continued to fly actively in a wide variety of aircraft and in 2009, was inducted into the Illinois Aviation Hall of Fame.[1277]

2008/06/16   O'Hare Flight Caps Lifted

Peak period operational limits at O'Hare, established in 2004 to reduce congestion, were eliminated. However, all air carriers were required to provide the FAA their schedules six months in advance.[1278]

2008/07/18   O'Hare EMAS Is Used

An Engineered Materials Arresting System (EMAS) that had been installed at O'Hare stopped Mexicana Airlines Flight MX802, an Airbus A320 with 145 on board. The plane overran runway 22L in rainy, gusty weather but did not reach the airport fence, and no one was injured.[1279]

2009/01/15   Sully Lands on the Hudson

Shortly after takeoff from LaGuardia Airport, US Airways 1549 encountered a flock of Canada Geese and lost both engines. Unable to reach an airport,

Capt. Chesley "Sully" Sullenberger and First Officer Jeffrey Skiles made a controlled landing of their Airbus A320 in the middle of the Hudson River. All on board survived with only minor injuries.[1280]

2009/01/20   Barack Obama Inaugurated

Illinois Senator Barack Obama was inaugurated the 44th President of the U.S., becoming the first African American to hold that office.[1281]

2010–2014

2010/06/09   Blackhawks Become a Powerhouse

For the first time since 1961, the Chicago Blackhawks won the Stanley Cup
on June 9, 2010. Thanks to the combo of Jonathan Toews and Patrick Kane,
the Hawks brought the Cup to Chicago again in 2013 and 2015.[1282]

2010/10/01   United and Continental Airlines Merge

After emerging from bankruptcy in 2006, United searched for merger
partners. In early 2010, they reached an agreement with Continental
Airlines subject to approval by both company's shareholders, the SEC, and
the EU. On October 1, 2010, UAL Corp. acquired Continental Airlines and
was renamed United Continental Holdings Inc.

The new airline was an amalgam of parts of both predecessor airlines.
Continental operated under its own name briefly but adopted United as
the brand while the new United logo was based on Continental's design.
Corporate staffs were similarly combined, operating out of United's
headquarters but incorporating a large portion of Continental executives
and organization.[1283]

2011/02/25   iPad Approved for Flight

On February 25, 2011, after extensive testing, the FAA approved the use of
the Apple iPad as an electronic flight bag for all phases of flight.[1284]

2011/06/13   *Liberty Belle* Burns in Aurora

Aurora Municipal Airport hosted activities to commemorate the 67th
anniversary of D-Day. *Liberty Belle*, a B-17 operated by Liberty Foundation
of Tulsa, was a highlight of the event, providing people the chance to walk
through and/or ride in the historic bomber.

Over the weekend, mechanics identified and repaired a small fuel leak
in one of the tanks. Monday, June 13, the *Liberty Belle* departed Aurora
with seven crew and passengers. Immediately they detected an acrid smell
and began to return to the airport.

The pilot of a companion T-6 Texan, spotted flames on the B-17s wing
and alerted the pilot. In less than two minutes, *Liberty Belle's* crew identi-

fied a suitable cornfield and made an emergency landing with no damage to the plane other than the fire. Everyone on the plane exited safely.

The Aurora Tower contacted the Aurora Fire Dept., which arrived on the scene quickly. Recent rains had left the field muddy, and following their long-standing policy, the fire crew decided that since everybody was safe, they would not risk life or equipment to save property. Flames rapidly engulfed *Liberty Belle,* badly damaging the historic airplane.[1285]

By the following May, restoration efforts were already underway.[1286]

2011/12/01   FAA Explores New Jet Fuel

The FAA issued contracts on December 1, 2011, for research into alternative, environmentally friendly, sustainable jet fuel that would work with existing engines. Out of the eight contracts, two were for Chicago-area companies: Honeywell HOP in Des Plaines and LanzaTech of Roselle.[1287]

2012/04/30   Delta Airlines Buys Refinery

On April 30, 2012, in order to decrease its fuel costs, Delta Airlines purchased the Trainer, PA, refinery from ConocoPhillips.[1288]

2012/05/25   Commercial Spacecraft Docks at ISS

The SpaceX Falcon 9 became the first commercial spacecraft to dock with the International Space Station on May 25, 2012.[1289]

2012/06/18   New Standards for Space Travel

On June 18, 2012, the FAA and NASA agreed to coordinate commercial space travel, whether governmental or commercial, from low-earth orbit to the ISS.[1290]

2013   Selig Publishes First Book

In 2013, aviation historian Nick Selig published *Lost Airports of Chicago,* an extremely readable book about Chicago airports that no longer exist, as well as the colorful pilots who used them.

Selig had a long, successful aviation career as both a pilot and a mechanic. He was one of the few people to receive both the Wright Brothers Master Pilot Award and the Charles Taylor Master Mechanic Award from the FAA. Selig and his wife Suzette were active both in the EAA and its Vintage Aircraft Association as well as in a host of other local and national aviation organizations. Selig's companion book, *Forgotten Chicago Airfields* was released in 2014.[1291]

2013   Galt Airport Gets New Life

Little Galt Airport, opened in 1956 by Arthur and Vera Galt, languished for years before going into foreclosure. Claude and Diane Sonday, who had been users of Galt for more than three decades, bought the airport in 2013 with the intent to revitalize it while preserving its friendly character. They immediately undertook maintenance that had been neglected during the long foreclosure and made many additional improvements. Their efforts were recognized in 2014, when the IL Div. of Aeronautics recognized Galt as the Privately-Owned Airport of the Year.[1292]

2013/03/01   Federal Budget Sequestration

On March 1, 2013, the first fiscal austerity measures took effect with across-the-board, with some exceptions, spending reductions.[1293]

2013/03/14   Scientists Find God

Physicists at CERN announced on March 14, 2013, that they had analyzed data indicating that a Higgs boson had been generated by the Large Hadron Collider. The Higgs boson had been postulated since the mid-1960s as an elementary particle essential to the makeup of all matter, hence references by the popular press to it as the "God particle."[1294]

2013/06/19   FBI Acknowledges Drone Use

In testimony before the Senate Judiciary Committee on June 19, 2013, the FBI Director acknowledged the use of drones to conduct surveillance.[1295]

2013/07/23   United Moves to Willis

After fifty years in the suburban wilderness of Elk Grove Village, IL, United's headquarters returned to the City of Chicago. United Continental Holdings finalized the move into Willis Tower (former Sears Tower) on July 23, 2013, when over 4,000 employees took occupancy of about 25% of the building with offices covering 830,000 sq. ft.[1296]

2013/08/22   Paul Poberzny Dies

Paul Poberzny, the founder of EAA and strong proponent of homebuilt aircraft, died at the age 91 on August 22, 2013.[1297]

2013/10/17   O'Hare Modernization Begins

On October 17, 2013, O'Hare placed in service its new 10,800-ft. runway, 10C/28C,which is able to handle the largest airliners in operation. The runway was the first part of a $9 million O'Hare Modernization Plan.[1298]

2013/10/25   United Delays Produce Fines

On July 13, 2012, thunderstorms raked the Chicago area. During the storms, United left 939 passengers stranded on the tarmac in 13 planes for over three hours each. Passengers were held on one plane 4 hr. 17 min. Two planes, operated by United Express, had inoperable lavatories.

On October 25, 2013, the Dept. of Transportation levied a record $1.1 million fine, the largest in history, against United for the tarmac delays. The fine was only a fraction of the $27,500 per passenger that the legislation authorized (in excess of $25 million).

Only $185,000 of the fine actually went to the nearly 1,000 passengers restrained by United. The bulk, $475,000, was paid to the government and another $440,000 was used by United itself to purchase and operate better equipment.[1299]

2014   Midway Replaces EMAS

In 2006, Midway became the first airport in the Chicago area to install the Engineered Materials Arresting System at the end of four runways. In 2014, it undertook a two-year project to replace the original EMAS with an improved green EMAS system.[1300]

2014/01   Waukegan Goes "National"

The Waukegan Port Authority changed the name of Waukegan Regional Airport to Waukegan National Airport in January 2014.

2014/04/30   LA Control Center Delay

A computer problem at the Los Angeles Air Route Traffic Control Center (ARTCC) caused a one-hour ground stop and disrupted hundreds of flights throughout southern California. The problem was a result of the recent modernization of en route center's computer system, which misinterpreted a U-2 flying at 60,000 ft. as flying below 10,000 ft. When the computer attempted to eliminate conflicts with the fast-moving U-2, it tried to reroute so many flights that the system overloaded.[1301]

2014/05/13   Elgin TRACON Fire

A burning electric motor produced sufficient smoke to force the evacuation of the Elgin TRACON that controled the approaches to Chicago airports. During the four-hour outage, more than 1,000 flights were canceled at O'Hare and Midway.[1302]

2014/07/01   State Buys Bult Field

On July 1, 2014, the State of Illinois spent $34 million to purchase Bult Field which was intended to become the core of its South Suburban Airport. Bult was a privately-owned airport with a 5,000-ft. runway. The same year, the state acquired an additional 3,314 acres at a cost of $42 million.[1303]

Currently the IL Div. of Aeronautics owns and operates Bult Field.[1304]

2014/09/25   Aurora Control Center Fire

At 6 a.m. on September 25, 2014, a fire in the basement telecom room of the Air Route Traffic Control Center (ARTCC) in Aurora, IL, disrupted air traffic in Chicago and, as a result, across the country. Traffic normally controlled by the center was rerouted to avoid the area, and flights that couldn't be rerouted were handled by other centers. Between the destruction of the fire and the water used to strike the fire, the entire communications system needed to be dried out or replaced. Other centers covered the Chicago area for nearly a month until the Aurora Center became operational again on October 13.[1305]

2015–2018

2015/08/16   Two Parachutists Collide

During a joint performance at the Chicago Air and Water Show, 13 sky-divers from the Army Golden Knights and Navy Leap Frogs linked hands in a bomb burst maneuver.

When they broke the circle, a Navy and an Army jumper collided in mid-air, apparently knocking Sgt. 1st Class Corey Hood unconscious. As his chute descended, he struck an apartment building and fell to the ground. He survived the crash and underwent surgery but later succumbed to his injuries.[1306]

2015/10/31   Chanute Air Museum Closes

Although an excellent museum, Chanute Air Museum was unable to generate sufficient visitors and contributors to continue operating. During the year prior to closing, the museum lost $500,000 (utilities alone were $350,000).

The Village of Rantoul, IL, had been providing financial support to the museum, but when other tenants of the building moved out, the village lost income from their rent and was unable to continue its support. The museum was forced to shutter its doors at the end of October 2015.

The Air Force, which still owned the museum's aircraft, was able to relocate most of the collection to other museums. Sadly, some planes were too large to move or in such poor condition that they were scrapped.[1307]

2016/1/07   Another Record Fine for United

On January 7, 2016, the DOT again gave United the distinction of receiving the largest fine in aviation history, $2.75 million.

Just two months after receiving a record-setting $1.1 million fine on October 25, 2013, for stranding passengers on the tarmac, United did it again. Starting in December 2013, United had a series of additional incidents in which planes were left on the tarmac for more than three hours. In addition, United was cited for a pattern of failing to provide passengers with disabilities adequate assistance at a number of major airports, including O'Hare.

These dubious achievements earned United the distinction of an even larger fine, setting another record. As with the previous fine, United was able to use much of the money internally to make operational improvements rather than compensating those who actually suffered the damages.[1308]

2016/01/26   Chicago Executive Uses EMAS

During 2014 and 2015, Chicago Executive Airport installed Engineered Materials Arresting System (EMAS) at both ends of the main runway, 16-34.

In the early hours of January 26, 2016, a Falcon 20 landing from the north overran the runway and was headed for the fence separating the runway from Palatine Rd. Shortly before going through the fence, the Falcon encountered the newly-installed EMAS and came to an immediate halt long before reaching the road. Neither of the pilots on board were injured and the airplane suffered only minor damage.[1309]

2016/02/19   Downey's Final Departure

Charles "Chuck" Downey, a Chicago aviator and aviation historian, died on February 19, 2016.

Born in Connecticut, Downey trained at Glenview Naval Air Station where, at age 18, he became the youngest naval aviator[a] in WWII. In 1944, he flew an SB2C Helldiver from the USS *Ticonderoga*. On one mission, he assisted in sinking a Japanese cruiser and was awarded the Distinguished Flying Cross.

After the war, Downey returned to Chicago, where he flew for several airlines including American and Midway. He resided in an air park in Poplar Grove, where he was a founder and long-time advisor to the Wheels and Wings Museum. Downey was inducted into the Illinois Aviation Hall of Fame in 1995.[1310]

2016/11/03   World Does NOT End

Following a thrilling baseball game in which the Chicago Cubs won the seventh game of the World Series, the world continued without ending. There were no weather reports about record low temperatures in the netherworld.

---

a   George H.W. Bush had claimed that distinction, but he and Downey met in February 2014 and determined that Downey was actually 11 days younger than Bush when he earned his wings shortly before his 19th birthday.

2017/08/28   AOPA File Complaint About Waukegan

The Aircraft Owner's and Pilot's Assn. (AOPA) filed an FAA Part 13 complaint against Waukegan National Airport and four others around the country. The AOPA complaint alleged egregious pricing practices for transient aircraft that resulted in impeding public use of the airport.

As a result, Waukegan Port Authority began providing a ramp area where transient aircraft can park overnight.[1311]

2017/10/18   Geneseo Couple Circles Globe

John and Carla Edwards of Genesseo, IL, landed at Moline after flying their TBM-900 around the world. They began their journey in Anchorage, AK, with five other planes on August 22. For the most part, the trip was uneventful. The exception came in Russia, where they were detained by security officers for six hours for a violation of Russian air space. They completed the 62-day trip covering 27,000 nautical miles in 115 flight hours.[1312]

2018/03/28   Major ORD Upgrade Approved

On March 28, 2018, the City of Chicago and airlines operating at O'Hare signed a lease agreement, the O'Hare 21 Plan (for 21st Century), which included major redevelopment and expansion at O'Hare. American, Delta, Spirit, and United all participated in the signing ceremony. The $8.5 billion project, expected to be paid for by the airlines using no tax dollars and planned for completion by 2026, is the largest airport construction program in U.S. history.

A Terminal Action Plan is the heart of O'Hare 21, increasing the number of gates 25%, from 180 to 220. Terminal 2 would be replaced and include a satellite terminal connected by an underground tunnel. The new Terminal 2 would become the international gateway. Terminal 5 would be significantly extended and both Terminals 1 and 3 would be refreshed and expanded.

Infrastructure modifications designed to reduce passenger wait times include improved self check-in facilities and updated security screening measures. A new baggage handling infrastructure would also improve the passenger experience. Less obvious but also vital are repairs to runways, taxiways, and other airport infrastructure.[1313]

2018/06/14   City Approves High-Speed Rail to O'Hare

The City of Chicago approved a proposal by Elon Musk's The Boring Co. to construct an underground high-speed rail system from Chicago's Loop to

O'Hare. Musk proposed to complete the project at no cost to the city as a demonstration of his new, yet unproven, boring and transport technology.

Musk's planned system will originate at Block 37 on Randolph St. in an unused underground facility that Mayor Richard M. Daley had constructed as a transfer point for the Blue and Red lines of the "L." It would travel nonstop to a station in the new International Terminal 2.

The Boring Co.'s equipment is designed to bore 14 ft. diameter holes, about half the size of other boring equipment. This necessitates the use of smaller vehicles and Musk's design specifies 16-passenger pods that will make the 18-mi. trip at speeds of up to 150 mph in about 12 min. for $25. The current Blue Line takes 45 min. to reach downtown for only $5. The small size of Musk's pods limits the system to 2,000 passengers in each direction per day.[1314]

2018/07/30   Midway Food Court

Midway Airport opened a modern new food court in Concourse A on July 30, 2018. The 6,300 sq. ft. area replaces several temporary food services in place during construction for over a year. The food court is only one phase in a major upgrade at Midway that includes an 80,000-sq.-ft. security pavilion and a pedestrian walkway over Cicero Ave.[1315]

20??/??   Wheel of Aviation Life Keeps on Spinning[a]

For nearly a century and a quarter, aviation in Chicago has changed and evolved. New planes are introduced. Airports come and go (more disappear than are formed). The corporate landscape continuously changes as companies are formed, expand, get acquired, reorganize, and go bankrupt. The latest trends either become commonplace or fade into oblivion. O'Hare continues to expand. Barring nuclear holocaust, comet strikes, or biological catastrophe, these changes won't stop. We should embrace them.

The purpose of history is not to look back, yearning for something lost. Rather it is to examine the past to understand how we got to this point in our lives. When reviewing history, we learn that things today aren't all that different—only the names and details have changed. We've survived the past and can continue surviving into the future. But it's not just about surviving. By learning from the past, we can make better, more informed choices and give ourselves a better future full of Blue Skies.

---

a   Note: This is an editorial opinion of the author.

My Village
(Acknowledgments)

When my wife, JoAnn, first saw my Acknowledgments, she said "There you go again, running on and on." A voracious reader, she pointed out that, in most books, this section is a few sentences or, at most, a couple pages long. I guess I need much more help than other authors, because I'm indebted to a lot of people.

That fact that this book exists is directly because of Chris Lynch, an aviation historian, author, and friend. Chris has written three books (and counting) about Midway Airport and is one of the driving forces behind the Midway Historians group. He has encouraged and supported my efforts in many ways. You could consider him my role model or coach.

Actually, "nag" is a more accurate description. For years, every time I spoke with Chris, he'd tell me, "There's a book inside you, and I want to read it. So, get it written." Well, this one's for you, Chris. Thanks.

The fact that I was able to convert a multitude of incoherent thoughts into an organized stream of words on paper is the result of J.R. Salzer, my mentor. For nearly forty years, JR has been a trusted friend and teacher. A gifted scriptwriter and instructional designer, JR has patiently worked with me in a variety of settings. I rarely write anything more than an email without asking JR to do a quick edit. It is impossible to adequately express my gratitude to him.

I began to entertain the thoughts about writing on Chicago's aviation history several years before I actually embarked on the project. Gerry and Janet Souter had recently published a book on the Chicago Air and Water Show. Out of the blue, I emailed Gerry expressing my interest in writing. He met with me for over two hours, selflessly sharing his extensive writing experience and giving me guidelines to improve my writing and to become involved with Chicago's writing community. I'm sure he doesn't recall the encounter, but I continue to draw on the wisdom he shared that day.

Once I dove into writing, I thrashed around for the direction I wanted to go. I harangued countless friends and colleagues, foisting on them various versions of preliminary outlines and rudimentary manuscripts. Thankfully, they took the time to listen to my thoughts and responded with honesty, often brutal, and helped forge my vague ideas into the tangible product you see today.

There are far too many people to thank them all individually, but I'm grateful to those in the following groups from whom I sought advice.

- Aviation Exploration Base (Oshkosh)
- Aviation Explorer Post #9 (Chicago Executive Airport)
- Chicago Area Business Aviation Association (CABAA)
- Chicago Executive Pilots Association-CEPA (formerly Palwaukee Airport Pilots Association [PAPA])
- Chicago Executive Young Eagles
- Chicago Writers Association
- EAA Chapter 414—Lake County (Waukegan)
- Illinois Aviation Hall of Fame banquet attendees
- Leading Edge Flying Club (Chicago Executive Airport)
- Midway Historians
- Ninety-Nines—Chicago Area Chapter
- O'Hare Airport Watch
- Our Saviour's Lutheran Church (Arlington Heights)
- Silver Wings—Chicago Chapter

As the manuscript neared completion, I knew I needed some serious fact checking to ensure that I hadn't made some technical mistakes during the writing. I solicited assistance from multiple people of diverse aviation backgrounds. Each of them plowed through several hundred pages of dense, unedited text, reading it carefully to ensure the technical details were correct, uncovering errors that would have been embarrassing had they gotten into print.

Maj. Jim Griggs, CAP, was formerly the Vice Commander of the CAP's Illinois Wing and currently is the Palwaukee Squadron Historian. An avid historian, Jim made valuable contributions as well as clarifying areas that were incorrect.

Charles Heftman, retired after a career with the FAA, was most recently a controller at the Air Traffic Control Center in Aurora. Chuck is also a pilot and an advisor of the Aviation Explorer Post at Chicago Executive Airport.

Jim Hull is a pilot, homebuilder, and aircraft restorer. Jim has been President of EAA Chapter 414 and spearheaded the project rescuing an F-111 Aardvark from Chanute Museum when it closed. Under Jim's leadership, the plane was relocated to Waukegan Airport, where it was restored and put on display.

Howard Levinson commanded a B-24 in the South Pacific during World War II. After the war, he continued flying and received every license and rating the FAA offers pilots of fixed-wing aircraft. Howard became the oldest person, at age 83, to receive an ATP (Airline Transport Pilot) license.

John Meneely is an aviation enthusiast and plane spotter. Originally from Ireland, John's comprehensive knowledge of airplanes and aviation spans the Atlantic.

Madeleine Monaco is a flight instructor and a vocal proponent of general aviation. Madeleine has served as an officer in the Ninety-Nines and on the board of the Illinois Aviation Hall of Fame. She was a co-founder of the Palwaukee Airport Pilots Assn. (PAPA) and has been active in the Young Eagles program.

Aviation Chicago Timeline is not only the first book I've written, but it's also my initial foray into publishing and required a new set of skills. I am indebted to two people who assisted me early in the process. Sharon Woodhouse (conspirecreative.com) and Anthony Paustian (adpaustian.com) provided insights and directions about this new world I was entering.

Eventually, I assembled a top-notch team to prepare my manuscript for production. Cynthia Clampitt is not only an amazing editor but also a very talented writer with works published in several genres. Besides polishing my words and turning them into something worthy of being printed, Cynthia took me under her wing. She put me in contact with other production people, gave me invaluable tips on marketing, and helped me network with the extensive Chicago writing community. I am forever indebted.

Molly (or M, as she prefers) Hurley of Teknigram Graphics (teknigram. com) has that rare combination of visual creativity and technical talent required of graphic designers in today's computer-based world. She is one of the few artists I know with the temperament to tackle long and intense verbal content. M created the book's cover along with the splendid original artwork that adorns the timeline. Her design of the book's interior made dense, black pages of text far less intimidating.

Working closely with M was Linda Shew Wolf, who did the actual typesetting and oversaw the final proofreading. Another multifaceted talent, Linda owns and operates both Network Publishing Partners and Network Typesetting (networktype.com) providing a broad range of services from editing to design and typesetting. Linda didn't function as a mechanical typesetter but as an active participant of the creative team determined to make this book the best quality possible based on the words I gave them.

Alexandra Uth (loomisandlyman.com) served as the final quality control person for the book. Originally intended as a proofreader, Alexandra was so much more. Her wide range of skills enabled her to be the final proofreader, typesetting inspector, and fact checker. She alerted me to several errors that had slipped past my technical reviewers. Her participation improved the book in countless ways readers would only notice by her absence.

Finally, I must acknowledge my incredible wife, JoAnn, who is responsible for my life as I know it. As my link to the real world for the past 40 years, she keeps me in touch with reality instead of being totally absorbed by this book or whatever project I've been working on. JoAnn has stood with me through several major career changes, each of which had a far less than certain outcome. She is a truly remarkable woman who has transformed my life in many more ways than she realizes and has enabled me to write this book.

ABOUT THE AUTHOR

Michael Haupt is a widely
recognized aviation historian and
lifelong aviation enthusiast.

Michael moved to Chicago in
1980 and wholeheartedly adopted
the city, becoming engrossed in its fascinating history. Nearing the end of
his career working with IBM large-system mainframe computers, he
rekindled his interest in aviation. Michael became deeply involved in
organizations that focus on all aspects of aviation and aviation history, as
well as those that celebrate Chicago's remarkable history.

As part of a community-liaison group associated with Palwaukee
Airport, Michael became the airport's unofficial historian. His research
about Palwaukee resulted in a presentation that he has given many times
to various aviation and community organizations, including a forum at
EAA's AirVenture in Oshkosh.

Determined to give youth a chance to pursue an early interest in
aviation, Michael volunteers with youth aviation groups, including Aviation
Explorer Post #9 and Young Eagles, both at Chicago Executive Airport
(formerly Palwaukee), as well as at the annual Aviation Exploration Base
held during AirVenture. In addition, Michael nominated Chicago aviation
pioneer Edward Bayard Heath to the Illinois Aviation Hall of Fame and
made a presentation about Heath at the group's Induction Banquet.

Aviation Chicago Timeline is Michael's first book addressing his twin
passions for Chicago and aviation. His insatiable curiosity and research
have uncovered fascinating events that are in many cases barely remembered today. His meticulous attention to detail and copious references
enable readers to satisfy their own curiosity. Michael formed Aviation
Chicago Press to publish this work as well as future non-fiction titles by
himself and other authors.

BIBLIOGRAPHY

How to use this bibliography:

Tag as shown in Endnotes *(Type of Publication)*   **Title of Resource**
List of articles within this resource and URL as applicable

126-ARW *(Online)*   **126th Air Refueling Wing**
126th Air Refueling Wing; U.S. Air Force
1. 126th ARW Chronological Wing History; updated March 28, 2011; accessed 8/26/2018
2. History of the 126th Air Refueling Wing; updated September 26, 2008; accessed 8/26/2018

20C_AvMag *(Online)*   **20th Century Aviation Magazine**
1. Edward "Eddie" Stinson; accessed 2/24/2018 (unavailable 8/22/2018) http://20thcenturyaviationmagazine.com/jr-hafer-2/x-notable-people/edward-eddie-stinson/

456_Interceptor *(Online)*   **456th Fighter Interceptor Squadron**
1. Aviation Corporation (AVCO); updated February 10, 2014; accessed 4/8/2017 http://www.456fis.org/CONVAIR_AVCO.htm

99s *(Online)*   **Ninety-Nines**
1. Our History; accessed 6/27/2017 https://www.ninety-nines.org/our-history.htm
2. Ruth Law—Queen of the Air: Challenging Stereotypes and Inspiring a Nation; by Billie Holladay Skelley; accessed 2/17/2018 https://www.ninety-nines.org/ruth-law.htm

A

A4A *(Online)*   **Airlines for America**
1. About Us—History; accessed 7/23/2017 http://airlines.org/about-us/history/

AARegistry *(Online)*   **African American Registry**
1. Cornelius Coffey Pioneered Aviation; accessed 12/6/2017 http://www.aaregistry.org/historic_events/view/cornelius-coffey-pioneered-aviation-0

2. Janet Bragg—Nurse, Aviator and Businesswoman; accessed 4/5/2017
   http://www.aaregistry.org/historic_events/view/janet-bragg-nurse-aviator-
   and-businesswoman

ABC7_Chicago *(Online)*   **ABC-7 News Chicago**
1. Chicago City Council approves $8.5B O'Hare expansion project; by Craig
   Wall; updated March 28, 2018; accessed 6/20/2018
   http://abc7chicago.com/travel/chicago-city-council-approves-$85b-ohare-
   expansion-project/3273774/

AcePilots *(Online)*   **Ace Pilots**
1. Lt. Cdr. Edward "Butch" O'Hare: First U.S. Navy Ace, Medal of Honor
   Recipient; by Stephen Sherman; updated July 2, 2011; accessed 7/21/2017
   http://acepilots.com/usn_ohare.html
2. Wiley Post; by Stephen Sherman; updated June 27, 2011; accessed 2/26/2018
   http://acepilots.com/post.html

ActiveHist *(Online)*   **Active History—Canada**
1. Marjorie Stinson, the Flying Schoolmarm; by Liz Millward; updated
   February 29, 2016; accessed 2/24/2018
   http://activehistory.ca/2016/02/marjorie-stinson-the-flying-schoolmarm/

AerialAge *(Periodical)*   ***Aerial Age***
Aerial Age; Chicago: Aerial Age Publishing
1. Gay Paddocks for Cicero Field; by John G. DeLong; June 1912, p. 11

AerialAgeW *(Periodical)*   ***Aerial Age Weekly***
Aerial Age Weekly; New York
1. Chicago Air Service Reserve Officers Organized; February 20, 1922 p. 560
2. Cicero Notes: Chicago Has Big Week; August 2, 1915, p. 474
3. New Interests Paid Curtiss $5,000,000 in Cash; January 24, 1916, Vol. 2
4. Floyd Smith Life Pack Co. (advertisement); August 23, 1920 p. 818

Aero *(Periodical)*   ***Aero***
Aero: America's Aviation Weekly; St. Louis: Aero Publications
1. America Now Has Forty Flying Fields; updated April 6, 1912, p. 1–6
2. Chicago; August 12, 1911, p. 412, Vol. 2, No. 19
3. Chicago International Meet Begins Saturday; August 12, 1911, p. 405–406.
   Vol. 2, No. 19
4. Designs High-Speed Plane; August 5, 1911, p. 395, Vol. 2, No. 18
5. Greatest Meet Ever Held Ends Happily; August 26, 1911 p. 453–459, 463,
   468, Vol. 2, No. 21
6. International Aviation Cup Defender Design, by E.R. Armstrong, February
   24, 1912, p. 417, Vol. 3, No. 21
7. Making Aero History at Grant Park; August 19, 1911 p 425–432, 443, 445,
   Vol. 2, No. 20
8. Many Entries Promise Success of Chicago Meet; August 5, 1911, p. 387,
   Vol. 2, No. 18
9. Preparing for Big Meet; August 5, 1911, p. 395, Vol. 2, No. 18

Aerodacious *(Online)*   **Aerodacious**
Aerodacious; Washington DC
1. Contract Air Mail Flights: CAM-9; updated January 20, 2008; accessed 4/17/2017
    http://www.aerodacious.com/ccCAM009.HTM
2. US Airport Dedication Covers—Illinois; accessed 4/10/2017
    http://www.aerodacious.com/DED-IL.HTM

AeroDigest *(Periodical)*   ***Aero Digest***
1. Bellanca "Blue Streak" Tandem; November, 1930, p. 72

Aerofiles *(Online)*   **Aerofiles**
Aerofiles: A Century of American Aviation; by K.O. Eckland
1. Fantastically Flighty Gray Goose; accessed 8/15/2017
    http://www.aerofiles.com/graygoose.html
2. Partridge-Keller; accessed 4/17/2017
    http://aerofiles.com/_pa.html
3. Taylor, Taylor-Young, Taylorcraft; updated February 1, 2008; accessed 6/2/2018
    http://www.aerofiles.com/_taylor.html
4. Waco; accessed 11/7/2017
    http://www.aerofiles.com/_waco.html

AeroHydro *(Periodical)*   ***Aero and Hydro***
Aero and Hydro: E. Percy Noel, ed.; multiple locations
1. Cicero Meet Begins Thursday Afternoon; September 14, 1912, p. 519
2. Demonstrating and Selling Aeroplanes and Air Boats (advertisement by Lillie Aviation); April 19, 1913, p. 64. Vol. VI, No. 3
3. First Hydro Aero Meet Is Held Successfully; September 28, 1912, p. 557
4. Flies Nearly Four Hours With Passenger; November 9, 1912, p. 97, Vol. 5, No. 6
5. Model Meet, Aero Club of Illinois, Cicero Field; July 13, 1912, p. 343, Vol. 4, No. 15
6. More Cicero Pilots; July 20, 1912, p. 363, Vol. 4, No. 16
7. New Corporations; August 12, 1911, p. 407
8. Roster of American Aviation Pilots; April 19, 1913, p. 38, Vol. 6, No. 3
9. Seven Entered in Aero and Hydro Cruise; April 19, 1913, p. 34–34: Vol. 6, No. 3
10. Somerville Fliers (advertisement); April 19, 1913, p. 51, Vol. 6, No. 3
11. Wing Collapse Blamed for Lillie's Death; September 20, 1913, p. 463

Aeronautics *(Periodical)*   ***Aeronautics***
Aeronautics: For Sportsman, Business Man and Pilot; Chicago: Aeronautical Publications, Inc.
1. Continued Leadership after 27 Years of Success; Greer College (Advertisement), September 1929, p. 77, accessed 9/30/2017
    https://books.google.com/books?id=d5MrNJNkZ88C&printsec=frontcover#v=onepage&q&f=true

2. Danger that Lurks in a Frozen Stick Is Eliminated (advertisement); July, 1929, p. 44–45
3. Floyd Smith Life Pack Co. (advertisement); August 23, 1920, p. 818
4. JW Curzon Starts Aero School; August, 1910, p. 67
5. News in General: Incorporations; November 1910, p. 175.
6. Who's Who in American Aeronautics; August 21, 1922, Vol. 13

AeroNews *(Online)* **Aero News Network**
1. EMAS System Installed at Chicago's Midway; updated November 27, 2006; accessed 7/13/2017
   http://www.aero-news.net/index.cfm?do=main.textpost&id=c4c3d38d-2955-4a11-8748-26033a13b504

AFMag *(Periodical)* **Air Force Magazine**
Air Force Magazine; Arlington, VA: Air Force Association
1. Air Mail Fiasco; John T. Correll; March, 2008, p. 60–65; accessed 8/15/2018
   http://www.airforcemag.com/MagazineArchive/Documents/2008/March%202008/0308airmail.pdf

AINOnline *(Online)* **Aviation News International**
1. EMAS Saves Falcon 20 at Chicago Executive; by Robert F. Mark; updated January 26, 2016; accessed 8/18/2017
   http://www.ainonline.com/aviation-news/business-aviation/2016-01-28/emas-saves-falcon-20-chicago-executive

Air Classics *(Periodical)* **Air Classics**
1. King of the Fords; August-September 1965

Air_Transportation *(Periodical)* **Air Transportation**
Air Transportation; East Stroudsburg, PA
1. Announcing Chicago Aero Sales Corp.; June 15, 1929, p. 81
2. Col. Paul Henderson: The Air Mail's Big Brother; by Harry A. Bliss; June 1, 1929, p. 107
3. Greer School of Aviation Gets Chicago Waco Agency; June 22, 1929, p. 22, Vol. 8, No. 4
4. Weekly News Letter: American Air Transport Assn.; July 29, 1929, p. 38.

Air_Travel *(Periodical)* **Air Travel News**
Air Travel News; Detroit
1. International Civil Aeronautics Conference Called by President Coolidge; February, 1929, p. 5–6

Aircraft *(Periodical)* **Aircraft**
Aircraft; New York: Lawson Publishing Co.
1. General News; Ada Gibson; October 1910, p. 261

AirNav *(Online)* **AirNav**
AirNav: the pilot's window into a world of aviation information
1. KIKK—Greater Kankakee Airport; accessed 1/15/2018
   https://www.airnav.com/airport/IKK
2. KTIP: Rantoul National Aviation Center Airport-Frank Elliott Field; accessed 8/27/2017

Airport_Council *(Online)*   **Airports Council International**
1. Developments in Technology Arrestor Beds—EMASMAX; by Mark Slimko; presented at ACI World Safety Seminar; Beijing, November 18–19, 2008; accessed http://www.aci.aero/Media/aci/file/2008%20Events/Safety%20Seminar%20 2008/Speakers/day%202/Mark%20Slimko,%20Arrestor%20Beds.pdf

AirPigz *(Online)*   **AirPigz**
AirPigz: Hog Wild About Anything that Flies; by Matt Clupper
1. Jimmy Doolittle, the Curtiss R3C-2 and the Schneider Trophy Air Race (1925); updated May 7, 2012; accessed 4/12/2018 http://airpigz.com/blog/2012/5/7/jimmy-doolittle-the-curtiss-r3c-2-and-the-schneider-trophy-a.html

Airport_Data *(Online)*   **Airport Data**
1. Kankakee Airport (3KK) Information; updated December 12, 2013; accessed 11/23/2017 http://www.airport-data.com/airport/3KK

AirportJour *(Online)*   **Airport Journals**
Airport Journals: Serving the General Aviation Community with Creativity, Passion and Focus
1. Chicago Executive Airport—Big Changes for a Growing Airport; by Pete Tobin; updated December 1, 2016; accessed 8/22/2018 http://airportjournals.com/chicago-executive-airport-big-changes-for-a-growing-airport/

AirRace *(Online)*   **Air Race**
Air Race; by Society of Air Racing Historians
1. 1935 NAR; accessed 5/21/2017 http://www.airrace.com/1935NAR.htm
2. Bendix Trophy; accessed 2/13/2018. http://www.air-racing-history.com/Between%20the%20wars(2).htm
3. Thompson Trophy; accessed 2/15/2018 http://www.air-racing-history.com/Thompson%20Trophy.htm

AirRacingHistory *(Online)*   **Air Racing History**
1. Harold Johnson; accessed 4/3/2017 http://www.air-racing-history.com/PILOTS/Harold%20Johnson.htm

Airships *(Online)*   **Airships**
1. Graf Zeppelin History; accessed 4/11/2017 http://www.airships.net/lz127-graf-zeppelin/history/
2. Worst Airship Disaster in History: USS Akron; by Dan Grossman; updated April 4, 2013; accessed 10/14/2017 http://www.airships.net/blog/worst-airship-disaster-history-uss-akron/

AirSpace *(Periodical)*   ***Air & Space Magazine***
Air and Space Magazine; Smithsonian Institution, Washington DC
1. Flying Success: For an entire week in 1938 the country celebrated air mail; by Rebecca Maksel; September 2008

2. Last Words of Otto Lilienthal; Tony Reichardt; Air Space Magazine, August, 10, 2016.
3. Other Harlem: In 1930s Chicago, at the corner of 87th St and Harlem Ave, Cornelius Coffey made aviation history; by Giles Lamberton; March 2010.
4. Out in the Breezy; by Jason Paur; January 2008

Airways *(Periodical)* ***Airways Magazine***
1. Fascinating History Chicago's O'Hare International Airport: 1920–1960; April 7, 2014
2. Fascinating History Chicago's O'Hare International Airport: 1960–2000; April 14, 2014

Alaspa, 2010 *(Book)*
Chicago Disasters; Atglen PA: Schiffer Publishing, 2010

Albion_MI *(Online)* **Historic Albion Michigan**
1. Palwaukee Airport (Illinois) Featured on Lithuanian Banknote; by Frank Passic; accessed 10/1/2017
http://www.albionmich.com/history/histor_notebook/MM0303.shtml

Almond, 2002 *(Book)*
Story of Flight; Peter Almond; NY: Barnes and Noble Books, 2002

ALPA *(Online)* **Air Line Pilots Assn. (ALPA)**
1. ALPA History; accessed 5/10/2017
http://www.alpa.org/about-alpa/our-history

Am_Aeronaut *(Periodical)* ***American Aeronaut & Aerostatist***
American Aeronaut and Aerostatist; St Louis: Greely Printery
1. Chicago's Aeronautique Meet; January, 1908, p. 34, Vol. 1, No. 3
2. Chicago's Great Meet; May 1908, p. 161–164, Vol. 1, No. 7

AmFlyers *(Online)* **American Flyers**
1. History of American Flyers; accessed 7/18/2017
http://americanflyers.com/about/history/

AMAHist *(Online)* **American Model Assn. History Project**
Model Aircraft—American Model Association History Project
1. History of the Illinois Model Aero Club; updated January 2017; accessed 4/18/2017
https://www.modelaircraft.org/files/illinoismodelaeroclub.pdf

ANG_Hist *(Online)* **Air National Guard History**
Air National Guard, ANG History Office
1. Chronological History of the Air National Guard and Its Antecedents; updated December 30, 2013; accessed 7/31/2017
http://www.ang.af.mil/Portals/77/documents/history/01--ANG%20CHRON%20JAN%201908-2013--20141218.pdf?ver=2017-01-11-143817-627

AOPA *(Online)* **Aircraft Owners and Pilots Assn.**
1. AOPA Files Official Complaints Over FBO Fees; updated August 28, 2017; accessed 1/31/2018

https://www.aopa.org/news-and-media/all-news/2017/august/28/aopa-files-
official-complaints-over-fbo-fees

2. FAA Issues Guidance on FBO Pricing; updated December 28, 2017;
   accessed 1/31/2018
   https://www.aopa.org/news-and-media/all-news/2017/december/08/
   faa-issues-guidance-on-fbo-pricing

ArlHts_Herald *(Periodical)*   ***Arlington Heights Herald***
Arlington Heights Herald; Paddock Publications
1. $1,500,000 fire at Douglas; July 21, 1944, p. 1, col. 6
2. Air show Sunday at Pal-Waukee to recruit WACs; July 14, 1944, p. 1, col. 2
3. Big Airport in Northern County; November 23, 1928, p. 1 col. 3
4. Discarded scrap from Blimp hangar goes to Maine high; June 12, 1942,
   Sect. 2, p. 1, col. 8
5. Palwaukee Host to 54 Army Planes; May 22, 1931, p. 1, col. 8
6. To Bring Second "Blimp" to Airport; To Enlarge Hangar; March 3, 1933, p. 1

Around_Pattern *(Online)*   **Around the Pattern**
Around the Pattern: Ramblings about flying for fun and profit; by Tracy Rhodes
1. Not Your Average DC-3; updated October 30, 2009; accessed 7/23/2017
   https://aroundthepattern.com/sport-flying/not-your-average-dc-3/

Arrowheads, 1980 *(Book)*
Avro Arrow: The Story of the Avro Arrow From Its Evolution to Its Extinction;
by The Arrowheads; Erin, Ontario: Boston Mills Press, 1980

AWST *(Periodical)*   ***Aviation Week and Space Technology***
1. Airlines Move to Meet Regulatory Shifts; November 6, 1978, p. 36

AvBusinessJour *(Periodical)*   ***Aviation Business Journal***
1. Falsification: A Deadly Sin; by Lindsey McFarren; 4th Quarter 2011

AvFoundAm *(Online)*   **Aviation Foundation of America|**
1. National Air Tour of 2003; accessed 4/24/2017
   http://www.nationalairtour.org/

AvGeekery *(Online)*   **AvGeekery**
AvGeekery: Aviation News and Stories by Professional Avgeeks
1. Early History of ALPA, the Air Line Pilots Association and the First Airline
   Strike; by JP Santiago; accessed 5/10/2017
   http://www.avgeekery.com/early-history-alpa-air-line-pilots-association-
   first-airline-strike/

Aviation *(Periodical)*   ***Aviation***
Aviation; New York
1. Aeronautical Chamber of Commerce Organized; January 2, 1922, Vol. 12,
   No. 1
2. Chicago's Aviation Meet; September, 1911, Vol. 2, No. 7
3. Registering Civil Aircraft; February 6, 1922, p. 159–161, Vol. 12, No. 6
4. Underwriters' Laboratories and Aviation; A.R. Small; January 3, 1921 p.
   20–21, Vol. 10, No. 1

AviationLofts *(Online)*   **Aviation Lofts**
1. 1338–1340 S Michigan Ave., Rich History; accessed 4/7/2017 (unavailable 8/21/2018)
    http://aviationlofts.com/building-history/

AvSafeNet *(Online)*   **Aviation Safety Network**
Aviation Safety Network; by Flight Safety Foundation
1. 11 August 1978; accessed 7/19/2017
    http://aviation-safety.net/wikibase/wiki.php?id=22819
2. 19 June 2008; updated May 26, 2017; accessed 10/11/2017
    https://aviation-safety.net/wikibase/wiki.php?id=21776
3. Friday, 1 December 1961; accessed 7/12/2017
    https://aviation-safety.net/database/record.php?id=19610901-0
4. Friday, 5 August 1955; accessed 1/26/2018
    https://aviation-safety.net/database/record.php?id=19550805-1
5. Friday 8 December 1972; accessed 12/23/2017
    https://aviation-safety.net/database/record.php?id=19721208-1
6. Monday 31 October 1994; accessed 11/23/2017
    https://aviation-safety.net/database/record.php?id=19941031-1
7. Sunday, 15 March 1959; accessed 12/23/2017
    https://aviation-safety.net/database/record.php?id=19590315-1
8. Sunday, 16 September 1951; accessed 9/16/2016
    https://aviation-safety.net/database/record.php?id=19510916-0
9. Sunday, 17 July 1955; accessed 11/29/2017
    https://aviation-safety.net/database/record.php?id=19550717-0
10. Sunday, 17 September 1961; accessed 7/12/2017
    https://aviation-safety.net/database/record.php?id=19610917-3
11. Sunday, 18 December 1949; accessed 7/13/2017
    https://aviation-safety.net/database/record.php?id=19491218-1
12. Sunday, 31 May 1936; accessed 12/24/2017
    https://aviation-safety.net/database/record.php?id=19360531-0
13. Thursday, 17 March 1960; accessed 7/12/2017
    https://aviation-safety.net/database/record.php?id=19600317-0
14. Thursday, 4 January 1951; accessed 12/23/2017
    https://aviation-safety.net/database/record.php?id=19510104-0
16. Thursday, 8 December 2005; accessed 12/30/2017.
    https://aviation-safety.net/database/record.php?id=20051208-0
17. Tuesday, 2 July 1940; accessed 12/23/2017
    https://aviation-safety.net/database/record.php?id=19460702-0
18. Tuesday, 24 November 1959; accessed 7/13/2017
    https://aviation-safety.net/database/record.php?id=19591124-0
19. Wednesday, 10 March 1948; accessed 7/12/2017
    https://aviation-safety.net/database/record.php?id=19480310-1
20. Wednesday, 30 October 1996; accessed 10/11/2017.
    https://aviation-safety.net/database/record.php?id=19961030-0
21. Wednesday, 4 December 1940; accessed 12/23/2017
    https://aviation-safety.net/database/record.php?id=19401204-0

AvStop *(Online)* **AvStop**
AvStop: Aviation Online Magazine;
1. Air Commerce Act of 1926; accessed 2/19/2018
   http://avstop.com/History/needregulations/act1926.htm
2. Air Mail Act of 1930; accessed 5/16/2017
   http://avstop.com/history/needregulations/act1930.htm
3. Airmail Act of 1934; accessed 2/19/2018
   http://avstop.com/History/needregulations/act1934.htm

AvWeek *(Online)* **Aviation Week Network**
1. Law That Changed Airline Industry Beyond Recognition (1978); by Madhu
   Unnikrishnan; updated January 4, 2015; accessed 8/28/2018
   http://aviationweek.com/blog/law-changed-airline-industry-beyond-
   recognition-1978
2. Signature Acquires Monarch Air Service at Midway; updated July 1, 1997;
   accessed 11/29/2017
   http://aviationweek.com/awin/signature-acquires-monarch-air-service-
   midway

AYB *(Book)* **Aircraft Year Book**
Aircraft Year Book; multiple publishers and locations
1. *Aircraft Yearbook for 1920*
2. *Aircraft Yearbook for 1921*
3. *Aircraft Yearbook for 1929*
4. *Aircraft Yearbook for 1930*

B

BAE_Sys *(Online)* **BAE Systems**
1. Gloster E.28/39: Britain's first aircraft that demonstrated the potential of
   Whittle's innovative jet engine design; accessed 8/23/2018
   https://www.baesystems.com/en/heritage/gloster-e-28-39

Balloon_Britain *(Online)* **Balloons Over Britain**
1. First Successful Around the World Solo Attempt; accessed 2/9/2018
   https://www.balloonsoverbritain.co.uk/around-the-world-flights-first-suc-
   cessful-solo

Bednarek *(Book)*
America's Airports: Airfield Development, 1918–1947 (Centennial of Flight
Series); by Janet R. Daly Bednarek; College Station TX: Texas A&M University
Press, 2001

Beyond_B&W *(Online)* **Beyond Black & White**
1. Black Women's History: Chicago Airwomen Behind Tuskegee Airmen; by
   Stanley Sotomillo; updated February 16, 2016; accessed 1/31/2018
   http://www.beyondblackwhite.com/black-womens-history-chicago-
   airwomen-behind-tuskegee-airmen/

Bilstein, 1994 *(Book)*
Flight in America: From the Wrights to the Astronauts; Baltimore : Johns Hopkins University Press, 1994

Blackman, 2017 *(Book)*
This Used to Be Chicago; Joni Hirsch Blackman; St. Louis: Reedy Press,

BlackPast *(Online)*   **Black Past**
1. Brown, Willa B (1906–1992); by Edmond Davis; accessed 4/7/2017
   http://www.blackpast.org/aah/brown-willa-b-1906-1992
2. Coffey, Cornelius R (1903–1994); accessed 4/7/2017
   http://www.blackpast.org/aah/coffey-cornelius-r-1903-1994
3. DuSable, Jean Baptiste Point (1745–1818); Wilson Edward Reed; accessed 5/12/2018
   http://www.blackpast.org/aah/dusable-jean-baptiste-point-1745-1818

Blaze *(Online)*   **The Blaze**
1. Another Day, Another Claim by Scientists That They've Found the 'God Particle' (Again); Liz Klimas; updated March 14, 2013; accessed 3/23/2018
   https://www.theblaze.com/stories/2013/03/14/another-day-another-claim-by-scientists-that-theyve-found-the-god-particle-again

BluesHeaven *(Online)*   **Blues Heaven**
Willie Dixon's Blues Heaven Foundation; Chicago
1. Historic Chess Records; accessed 1/12/2018
   http://www.bluesheaven.com/historic-chess-studios.html

BobBeagle *(Online)*   **Bob the Beagle Pup**
1. Air Race; accessed 7/14/2017
   http://www.bobthebeagle.co.uk/air-race-2/

Boeing *(Online)*   **Boeing Aircraft**
1. Boeing History Chronology; accessed 11/1/2017
   http://www.boeing.com/resources/boeingdotcom/history/pdf/Boeing_Chronology.pdf
2. DC-3 Commercial Transport; accessed 7/23/2017
   http://www.boeing.com/history/products/dc-3.page

Borgeson *(Book)*
Errett Loban Cord: His empire, his motorcars; by Griffith Borgeson; Automobile Quarterly Publications, 1985

BournemouthEcho *(Periodical)*   ***Bournemouth Daily Echo***
Daily Echo; Bournemouth UK
1. Charles Rolls and the tragic Dorset plane crash that ended the aviation pioneer's life; Jade Grassby; October 1, 2016

Branigan *(Book)*
History of Chicago's O'Hare Airport; Charleston SC: History Press, 2011

Britannica *(Online)*   **Encyclopedia Britannica**
1. Aircraft Carrier; accessed 3/15/2018
   https://www.britannica.com/technology/aircraft-carrier

BultField *(Online)*   **Bult Field**
1. Bult Field: Future Site of the South Suburban Airport; accessed 8/27.2017
    http://www.bultfield.com/

BurbankBeat *(Online)*   **Burbank Beat**
The Burbank Beat—the unofficial website of Burbank, Illinois
1. Midway Mishaps: A Brief History of Area Plane Crashes; updated November
    18, 2014; accessed 12/23/2017
    http://www.burbankbeat.net/news/midway-mishaps-a-brief-history-of-area-
    plane-crashes

Burke *(Book)*
Master Plan for Chicago Orchard (Douglas) Airport; Ralph H. Burke;
Chicago; 1948

Bus_Insider *(Online)*   **Business Insider**
1. First Catapult Launch of a Plane from an Aircraft Carrier Took Place 100
    Years Ago Today; by Jeremy Bender; updated November 5, 2015; accessed
    3/17/2018
    http://www.businessinsider.com/the-first-catapult-launch-of-a-plane-from-
    an-aircraft-carrier-took-place-100-years-ago-today-2015-11

C

C&S *(Book)*
Open the Throttle: The Story of Chicago & Southern Airlines; Chicago and
Southern Air Lines, 1950

CAF_Memb *(Periodical)*   **CAF Member Magazine**
CAF Member Magazine; Chicago Architecture Foundation
1. 125 Years of the L; by Patrick Miner; Summer 2017, p.6–7

CAP_Gold *(Online)*   **CAP Gold Medal**
1. Willa Brown; by Brenda Reed; updated June 2, 2014; accessed 1/31/2018
    http://www.capgoldmedal.com/blog/gold_medal_journey_blog/?willa_
    brown&show=entry&blogID=1262#.WnII3VjxFEY

CentFlight *(Online)*   **Centennial of Flight**
U.S. Centennial of Flight Commission
1. Aerial Refueling; by Duane A. Day; accessed 05/28/2018
    https://www.centennialofflight.net/essay/Evolution_of_Technology/
    refueling/Tech22.htm
2. American Airlines; accessed 4/8/2017
    http://www.centennialofflight.net/essay/Commercial_Aviation/American/
    Tran15.htm
3. Glenn Curtiss and the Wright Patent Battles; accessed 4/12/2017
    http://www.centennialofflight.net/essay/Wright_Bros/Patent_Battles/
    WR12.htm

4. Italo Balbo; accessed 1/31/2018
http://www.century-of-flight.net/Aviation%20history/pathfinders/
Italo%20Balboa.htm
5. Metal Plane; accessed 03/18.2018
https://www.centennialofflight.net/essay/Evolution_of_Technology/
metal_plane/Tech15G2.htm
6. National Advisory Committee on Aeronautics; accessed 4/29/2018
https://www.centennialofflight.net/essay/Evolution_of_Technology/NACA/
Tech1.htm
7. WACO Aircraft Corporation; accessed 11/7/2017
http://www.centennialofflight.net/essay/GENERAL_AVIATION/WACO/
GA3.htm

CentProg *(Book)*
Official Guide: Book of the Fair 1933; Chicago: A Century of Progress, 1933

Chambanamoms *(Online)*   **Chambamoms**
Chambamoms; The top online resource for families in the Champaign-
Urbana area
1. Chanute Air Museum Closing Its Doors; by Kelly Youngblood; updated
October 26, 2015; accessed 8/27/2017
http://www.chambanamoms.com/2015/10/26/chanute-air-museum-
closing-its-doors/

Chanute, 1894 *(Book)*
Proceedings of the Third International Conference on Aerial Navigation;
Octave Chanute, ed.; New York: American Railroad and Engineer Journal,
1894; accessed 6/5/2017
https://books.google.com/books?id=adE-AQAAMAAJ&pg=PA6&lpg=
PA6&dq#v=onepage&q&f=false

Chanute, 1894, 1997 *(Book)*
Progress of Flying Machines; Octave Chanute, ed.; reprint, Minneola NY:
Dover Publications, 1894, 1997; accessed 6/5/2017
http://invention.psychology.msstate.edu/i/Chanute/library/Prog_Contents.html

ChicagoL *(Online)*
1. Blue Line; accessed 8/6/2017
https://www.chicago-l.org/operations/lines/blue.html
2. CTA Reinvents Itself: The "L" Heads Into the 21st Century; accessed
1/23/2018
https://www.chicago-l.org/history/CTA4.html

Chicagology *(Online)*   **Chicagology**
1. 1910 Union Stock Yards Fire; accessed 10/17/2017
https://chicagology.com/notorious-chicago/stockyardfire/
2. 1920-Taxi Wars; accessed 8/20/2017
https://chicagology.com/notorious-chicago/1920taxiwars/
3. Aviation Carnival; accessed 8/20/2017
https://chicagology.com/transportation/1910aviationcarnival/

4. Aeronautical Center Intro—Chicago's Aviation Pioneers; accessed 2/1/2018
   https://chicagology.com/transportation/flyingcapital/
5. Aeronautical Center Part 1—Octave Chanute, the Father of Aviation; accessed 2/1/2018
   https://chicagology.com/transportation/chanute/
6. Aeronautical Center Part 2—Aero Club of Illinois; accessed 2/2/2018
   https://chicagology.com/transportation/aeroclubillinois/
7. Aeronautical Center Part 3—First Flights Over Chicago; accessed 2/2/2018
   https://chicagology.com/transportation/firstaeroplanechicago/
8. Aeronautical Center Part 4—Chicago to Springfield Race; accessed 2/2/2018
   https://chicagology.com/transportation/1910chicagospringfield/
9. From Chicago to Berlin and Back in "Untin' Bowler"; accessed 8/2/2018
   https://chicagology.com/newspapers/chicagotribune/untinbowlerberlin/

ChiDeptAv *(Online)*   **Chicago Department of Aviation**
Fly Chicago; Chicago Dept. of Aviation
1. Mayor Emmanuel and Airline Sign Historic $8.5 Billion Agreement to Transform Chicago O'Hare Intrernational Terminal; updated 3/28/2018; accessed 6/20/2018
   https://www.flychicago.com/sites/ohare21/newsroom/Pages/article.aspx?newsid=4
2. Midway History; accessed 6/11/2018
   https://www.flychicago.com/business/CDA/Pages/Midway.aspx
3. O'Hare History; accessed 1/25/2018
   http://www.flychicago.com/business/CDA/Pages/OHare.aspx

ChiHist *(Online)*   **Chicago History**
Chicago History; by Chicago Historical Society
1. Descriptive inventory for the Aero Club of Illinois records, 1909–1951;
   http://digitalcollection.chicagohistory.org/cdm/ref/collection/p16029coll6/id/500

ChiMod *(Online)*   **Chicago Modern Blog**
Chicago Modern: More Modern than Mies; by Nate Lielasus
1. "Jet Set" Modern in Chicago: The Rotunda; updated January 29, 2012; accessed 10/3/2017
   https://chicagomodern.wordpress.com/2012/01/29/chicagos-jet-set-modern/

ChiOutSculpt *(Online)*   **Chicago Outdoor Sculptures**
Chicago Outdoor Sculptures; by Jyoti; on Blogspot
1. Balbo Monument; updated September 1, 2008; accessed 7/6/2017
   http://chicago-outdoor-sculptures.blogspot.com/2009/04/balbo-monument.html

ChiPubLib *(Online)*   **Chicago Public Library**
1. Mayor Jane Byrne Biography; accessed 10/19/2017
   https://www.chipublib.org/mayor-jane-byrne-biography/
2. Mayor Richard J. Daley Biography; accessed 7/19/2017
   https://www.chipublib.org/mayor-richard-j-daley-biography/

Citylab *(Online)*   **Citylab**
Citylab: Committed to telling the story of the world's cities: how they work, the challenges they face and the solutions they need. By Atlantic Monthly Group
1. Craziest Thing About Elon Musk's 'Express Loop' Is the Price; by Laura Bliss; updated June 15, 2018; accessed 6/20/2018
    https://www.citylab.com/transportation/2018/06/for-1-billion-elon-musks-tunnel-to-ohare-would-be-a-miracle/562841/

CNN *(Online)*   **CNN—Cable News Network**
1. Army skydiver dies after airshow accident; by Ralph Ellis; updated August 17, 2015; accessed 11/30/2017
    http://www.cnn.com/2015/08/16/us/skydiver-death/index.html
2. The day politics and TV changed forever; accessed 7/15/2017
    http://www.cnn.com/2016/02/29/politics/jfk-nixon-debate/index.html

Coachbuilt *(Online)*   **Coach Built**
Coachbuilt: Encyclopedia of Coachbuilders & Coachbuilding
1. Bill Stout—William Bushnell Stout (b. 1880–d. 1956), accessed 11/25/2017
    http://www.coachbuilt.com/des/s/stout/stout.htm

Cole, 1997 *(Book)*
Airport Memories ... more than 1400 airports in a lifetime; by Duane Cole; Milwaukee: Ken Cook Co., 1997

Coleman_Official *(Online)*   **Official Website of Bessie Coleman**
By the Bessie Coleman Family
1. Biography of Bessie Coleman; by Thelma Rudd; accessed 10/3/2017
    http://www.bessiecoleman.org/bio-bessie-coleman.php

Comics_Comic *(Online)*   **The Comic's Comic**
1. Comedians in Courthouses: Getting Cuffed: Lenny Bruce and George Carlin, December 1962; by Sean L. McCarthy; updated March 25, 2014; accessed 9/29/2017
    http://thecomicscomic.com/2014/03/25/comedians-in-courthouses-getting-cuffed-lenny-bruce-and-george-carlin-december-1962/

Connecting_Windy_City *(Online)*   **Connecting Windy City**
Connecting Windy City; by Jim Bartholomew
1. Chicago: A look back at June 9, 1942; by Jim Bartholomew; updated June 9, 2012; accessed 11/18/2017
    http://www.connectingthewindycity.com/2012/06/chicago-look-back-at-june-9-1942.html
2. January 18, 1945—Agreement Is Reached on Midway Airport Terminal; updated January 18, 2016; accessed 1/23/2018
    http://www.connectingthewindycity.com/2016/01/january-18-1945-agreement-is-reached-on.html
3. June 30, 1950—The Lake Front Airport Gets a Name; updated June 30, 2016; accessed 1/18/2018
    http://www.connectingthewindycity.com/2016/06/june-30-1950-lake-front-airport-gets.html

4. March 20, 1948—Cloud Room Opened at Chicago Airport; updated March 20, 2016; accessed 1/23/2018
    http://www.connectingthewindycity.com/2016/03/march-20-1948-cloud-room-opened-at.html
5. November 15, 1931, Chicago Airport; by Jim Bartholomew; updated 11/15/2016; accessed 11/17/2017.
    http://www.connectingthewindycity.com/2016/11/november-15-1931-chicago-airport-is.html
6. November 27, 1953, Meigs Loses Its Big Guns; updated November 27, 2016; accessed 1/23/2018
    http://www.connectingthewindycity.com/2016/11/november-27-1953-meigs-loses-its-big.html

CookCty_Herald *(Periodical)* ***Cook County Herald***
Cook County Herald; Paddock Publications
1. Air Stunts to Feature This Year's Fair; September 3, 1926, p. 1, col. 3
2. Firebug Sets Blaze at the Palwaukee Port; July 1, 1930, p. 8 col. 3
3. Night Flying Introduced at Pal-Waukee—A New Airport; August 5, 1930, p. 5 col. 5
4. Only Five Local Air Fields O.K.'d; November 19, 1929, p. 1, col. 8
5. Pony Express Carries Air Letters to Pal-Waukee; Planes Drop Mail for Arlington Race Track; May 20, 1938, p. 1, col 6–8
6. Races; Stunt Flying; Fireworks—Everything at Exposition; September 3, 1926, p. 1, col. 6

Crains_Chi *(Periodical)* ***Crain's Chicago Business***
1. See details of the O'Hare expansion plan; by Joe Pletz; March 9, 2018
2. Take a look at the sleek new food court at Midway Airport; updated July 27, 2018

Crouch, 1989 *(Book)*
Dream of Wings: Americans and the Airplane 1875–1905; Tom D. Crouch; Washington DC: Smithsonian Institution Press, 1989

Culver, 1986 *(Book)*
Tailspins: A Story of Early Aviation Days; Santa Fe, NM: Sunstone Press, 1986

CurbedChi *(Online)* **Curbed Chicago**
Curbed Chicago; by Vox Media
1. Elon Musk's Borning Company wins contract to build O'Hare Express; by Jay Koziarz; updated June 14, 2018; accessed 6/20/2018
    https://chicago.curbed.com/2018/6/14/17463294/elon-musk-ohare-express-boring-company-wins-bid

D

DacyAirp *(Online)* **Dacy Airport**
1. Airport History; accessed 11/10/2017
    http://www.dacyairport.com/history.html

Daily_Banner *(Periodical)* ***Daily Banner***
Daily Banner; Greencastle IN
1. Commission Sued; July 4, 1956, p. 1

Daily_Herald *(Periodical)* ***Daily Herald***
Daily Herald; Paddock Publications
1. Florida company to buy Palwaukee aviation firm; by Fred Woodhams; August 17, 2001
2. How the Chicago Defender became a national voice for black Americans; February 11, 2017, p. 17
3. Pioneer Aviator—Sally Strempel; September 10, 1984, Sect. 2, p. 1 col. 1
4. Queen Elizabeth praises Royal Air Force on centenary; April 2, 2018, p. 2
5. Suburban pilot ready to soar at Chicago Air and Water Show; by Scott Morgan; August 19, 2016.
6. Wheeling, Prospect Heights fete purchase of Pal-Waukee; January 3, 1987, p. 1 col. 1

Daily_Southtown *(Periodical)* ***Daily Southtown***
Daily Southtown; Tribune Publishing Co.; Chicago
1. Robbins Gave African-Americans Access to the Skies; by Matt McCall; February 10, 2017

Daniel, 2000 *(Book)*
20th Century Day by Day; by Clifton Daniel; Dorling-Kindersly Books, 2000

DefMediaNet *(Online)* **Defense Media Network**
1. B-17 Crash Highlights the Debate Over Flying Warbirds; by Robert F. Dorr; updated June 17, 2011; accessed 1/26/2018
https://www.defensemedianetwork.com/stories/b-17-crash-highlights-the-debate-over-flying-warbirds/

Disciples_Flight *(Online)* **Disciples of Flight**
Octave Chanute's Contributions Had a Far-Reaching Impact on Aviation; Anders Clark; Disciples of Flight, updated June 22, 2016; accessed 2/1/2018
https://disciplesofflight.com/octave-chanute/

DMarfield *(Online)* **D. Marfield**
Davis-Monthan Aviation Field Register; by D. Marfield
1. Hunter Brothers: Albert, John, Kenneth and Walter; accessed 4/7/2017
http://dmairfield.com/people/hunter_bros/
2. Hunter Brothers of Sparta Illinois; by Robert H. Hayes; accessed 4/7/2017
http://dmairfield.com/people/hunter_bros/20100522_RobertHayes_Hunter_Brothers.pdf

DNAInfo *(Online)* **DNA Info**
DNA Info; Chicago Neighborhood News
1. How Is Chicago Connected to O'Hare?; by Justin Breen; updated February 13, 2016; accessed 8/10/2017
https://www.dnainfo.com/chicago/20160128/ohare/how-is-chicago-connected-ohare-this-tiny-strip-surrounded-by-suburbs

Doherty, 1970 *(Unpublished)*
Origin and Development of Chicago-O'Hare International Airport; Richard
Paul Doherty, Ph.D. dissertation; Muncie IN: Ball State University, 1970;
accessed 6/20/2018
https://www.library.northwestern.edu/documents/libraries-collections/
origin-development.pdf

DOT *(Online)*   **Dept. of Transportation**
1. United Fined for Violating Airline Disability and Tarmac Delay Rules;
    accessed 7/13/2017; unavailable 6/20/2018
    https://www.transportation.gov/briefing-room/united-fined-violating-
    airline-disability-tarmac-delay-rules

DuPage_Reg *(Periodical)*   ***DuPage County Register***
1. Quick Blaze Takes Planes and Hangar; December 26, 1930

E

EAA *(Online)*   **EAA**
EAA—Experimental Aircraft Assn.; Oshkosh, WI
1. 1964 Roloff/Unger RLU-1 Breezy—N59Y; accessed 3/14/2018
    https://www.eaa.org/en/eaa-museum/museum-collection/aircraft-
    collection-folder/1964-roloff-unger-rlu-1-breezy---n59y
2. Early Years; accessed 8/18/2018
    https://www.eaa.org/en/airventure/about-eaa-airventure-oshkosh/history/
    the-early-years-of-eaa-fly-in
3. History; accessed 8/18/2018
    https://www.eaa.org/en/eaa/about-eaa/eaa-history
4. Notable Dates and Milestones; accessed 8/18/2018
    https://www.eaa.org/en/eaa/about-eaa/eaa-history/eaa-notable-dates-and-
    milestones
5. Spirit of St. Louis Replica; accessed 2/13/2018
    https://www.eaa.org/en/eaa-museum/museum-collection/aircraft-
    collection-folder/spirit-of-st-louis-replica

EarlyAv *(Online)*   **Early Aviators**
Early Aviators; Early Birds of Aviation
1. Bert R.J. Hassell; accessed 11/4/2017
    http://www.earlyaviators.com/ehassell.htm
2. Billy Robinson 1884–1916; accessed 11/8/2017
    http://www.earlyaviators.com/erobbill.htm
3. Charles Dickinson 1858–1935; accessed 4/15/2017
    http://www.earlyaviators.com/edickins.htm
4. George Weaver; accessed 11/7/2017
    http://www.earlyaviators.com/eweaver.htm
5. Hillary Beachey 1885–1964; accessed 8/6/2017
    http://earlyaviators.com/ebeachey.htm

6. History of the Early Birds of Aviation; accessed 11/12/2017
    http://earlyaviators.com/ehistory.htm
7. James Floyd Smith 1884–1956; accessed 11/8/2017
    http://www.earlyaviators.com/esmithfl.htm
8. Logan A "Jack" Vilas 1891–1976; accessed: 4/27/2017
    http://www.earlyaviators.com/evilas.htm
9. Marjorie Stinson; accessed 2/24/2018
    http://www.earlyaviators.com/estinmar.htm
10. Max Lillie (1881–1913); accessed 8/15/2017
    http://earlyaviators.com/elillie.htm
11. Otto Brodie; accessed 10/3/2017
    http://www.earlyaviators.com/ebrodot1.htm
12. Parker Dresser Cramer; accessed 11/7/2017.
    http://www.earlyaviators.com/ecramer.htm
13. Rudolph William Schroeder 1886–1952; accessed 4/24/2017
    http://www.earlyaviators.com/eschroed.htm
14. St. Croix Johnstone 1893–1911; accessed 2/13/2018
    http://www.earlyaviators.com/ejohncroi.htm
15. Walter R. Brookins (1889–1953); accessed 8/20/2017
    http://www.earlyaviators.com/ebrookin.htm

EbonyJr *(Periodical)*   **Ebony Jr**
Ebony Jr.; Johnson Publishing Co., Chicago
1. Willie Jones the Wing-Walker; by Mary C. Lewis; March 1982

Edwards, 2003 *(Book)*
Chicago: City of Flight (Images of America); Jim and Wynette Edwards;
Charleston SC: Arcadia Publishing, 2003

Edwards, 2009 *(Book)*
*Orville's Aviators: Outstanding Alumni of the Wright Flying School 1910–
1916*; John Carver Edwards; Jefferson NC: McFarland Publishing, 2009

ElginHist *(Online)*   **Elgin History**
1. Landmarks Gone—The Airport; accessed 1/8/2017
    http://www.elginhistory.com/dgb/ch12.htm

Elmhurst_Hist *(Online)*   **Elmhurst History Museum**
1. Elmhurst Airport; updated 1999; accessed 12/2/2017
    https://www.elmhurst.org/DocumentCenter/Home/View/254

EngIngenuity *(Online)*   **Engines of Ingenuity**
Engines of Our Ingenuity—University of Houston
1. No. 2438—Phoebie Omlie and her Monocoupe; by John H. Lienhard;
    accessed 1/26/2018
    https://www.uh.edu/engines/epi2438.htm

Eventful *(Online)*   **Eventful**
1. Crystal Lake: Woodstock Tribute Galt Airport 40th Anniversary; updated
    August 14, 2009; accessed 8/27/2017

http://eventful.com/crystallake/events/woodstock-tributegalt-airport-40-
year-annivers-/E0-001-023032143-5

Examiner *(Periodical)* ***Chicago Examiner***
Chicago Examiner; Chicago
1. Atwood Soars 286 Miles from St. Louis to Chicago at Speed of Express
    Train; August 15, 1911

F

FAAChron *(Online)* **FAA Chronology**
1. FAA Historical Chronology 1926–1996; accessed 4/7/2017
    https://www.faa.gov/about/history/chronolog_history/
2. FAA Historical Chronology 1997–2016; accessed 4/22/2017
    https://www.faa.gov/about/history/media/final_1997_2016_chronology.pdf

FAAFact *(Online)* **FAA Fact Sheet**
1. Engineered Material Arresting System (EMAS); updated 8/5/2017;
    accessed 10/11/2017
    https://www.faa.gov/news/fact_sheets/news_story.cfm?newsId=13754

FAA_GANews *(Periodical)* ***FAA General Aviation News***
1. Waterfront Airports: Lessons to be learned from Meigs Field; November-
    December 1981

FAALearned *(Online)* **FAA Lessons Learned**
FAA Lessons Learned from Civil Aviation Accidents
1. Southwest Airlines Flight 1248; accessed 10/11/2017
    http://lessonslearned.faa.gov/ll_main.cfm?TabID=3&LLID=56

FAAMilestones *(Online)* **FAA Milestones**
1. William P. MacCracken, Jr.: America's First Federal Regulator for Aviation;
    accessed 4/22/2017
    https://www.faa.gov/about/history/milestones/media/The_First_Federal_
    Regulator_for_Aviation.pdf

FAAPeople *(Online)* **FAA People**
1. Louis Hopewell Ba/uer and the First Federal Aviation Medical Examiners;
    accessed 4/22/2017
    https://www.faa.gov/about/history/people/

FAATimL *(Online)* **FAA Timeline**
FAA History Timeline; accessed 4/28/2017
https://www.faa.gov/about/history/timeline/

Famous_Trials *(Online)* **Famous Trials**
Famous Trials; Univ. of Missouri School of Law
1. Lenny Bruce; by Douglas O. Linder; accessed 9/29/2017
    http://www.famous-trials.com/lennybruce/557-biography

FirstLanding *(Online)* **First Landings**
1. Why Fly Sport: A BriefHistory of the Sport Pilot Rating; accessed 5/16/2018
   http://www.firstlandings.com/why-fly-sport-a-brief-history-of-the-sport-pilot-rating/

FirstWW *(Online)* **First World War**
1. Who's Who—Reed Landis; accessed 2/16/2018
   http://www.firstworldwar.com/bio/landis.htm

FlightBlog *(Online)* **Flight Blog**
Flight Blog; by Aviation Oil Outlet
1. US President Pilots; by Sara Simonovich; updated February 20, 2017;
   accessed 10/14/2017
   http://theflightblog.com/us-president-pilots/

FlightJour *(Periodical)* **Flight Journal**
Flight Journal; Palm Coast FL
1. Teddy's Excellent Adventure; John Lockwood; October 2015, p. 66

FL_Times *(Periodical)* **Florida Times Union**
Florida Times Union; Jacksonville FL
1. Men Flew Northward to Fame and Fate; December 6, 1998

FlyGirls *(Online)* **Fly Girls**
1. Janet Harmon Bragg; updated February 23, 2016; accessed 1/30/2018
   https://flygirlstheseries.com/blogpage/2016/2/22/janet-harmon-bragg

Flying *(Periodical)* **Flying**
Flying magazine; multiple publishers and locations
1. Airport Closed: Tax Collectors Are Stealing Away Some of Our Best Airports; by Robert B. Parke; February 2, 1979, p. 59f
2. Early Birds; by Patricia Trenner; September 1977, p. 93
3. Operators Sell Flying; December 1951, p. 61
4. Pioneeering the Business Air Base: Skymotive; by C.L. Hamilton; October, 1956 p. 38f
5. Ready for Tomorrow; by Cecile Hamilton; June 1961, p. 44f
6. Return of the Rockford; November 1970, p. 52
7. War Workers Flying Club; by Lawrence Keil; April 1945, p. 26f

Flying [old] *(Periodical)* **Flying**
Flying; Flying Association Inc.; New York (not related to current *Flying* magazine)
1. National Aeroplane Fund Shows Wonderful Accomplishments; November 1916, p 407–410, accessed 4/7/2018
   https://books.google.com/books?id=uT08AQAAMAAJ&pg=PA407&lpg=PA407&dq=national+aeroplane+fund&source=bl&ots=m0htCySaao&sig=bn57wmXQwmF5qhvxnph9IEaXmwA&hl=en&sa=X&ved=0ahUKEwiQiP6p7NbTAhXs7YMKHWbJAqIQ6AEILTAB#v=onepage&q=national%20aeroplane%20fund&f=false

FlyMachines *(Online)*   **Flying Machines**
Flying Machines; by Carroll Gray
1. Octave Alexandre Chanute & Augustus Moore Herring; accessed 2/1/2018
    http://www.flyingmachines.org/chan.html

FlyRFD *(Online)*   **Fly Rockford**
Fly RFD; by Chicago Rockford International Airport
1. Decades Photo Display; updated 2006; accessed 10/2/2017
    http://flyrfd.com/wp-content/uploads/2015/08/DisplayBoards06.pdf

Ford_Cty_Record *(Periodical)*   ***Ford County Record***
1. Chanute Air Museum closing in Rantoul; by Dave Hinton; April 23, 2015

Forden, et al., 2003 *(Book)*
Ford Air Tours 1925–1931; by Lesley Forden and Gregory Herrick; New
Brightton, MN: Aviation Foundation of America, 2003 (Edition in Connection
with Revival Tour)

ForestPres *(Online)*   **Forest Preserve District of Cook County**
Early History of the Forest Preserve District of Cook County, 1869–1922; by
Ralph C. Thornton; accessed 7/3/2017
http://fpdcc.com/about/history/

ForgottenChi *(Online)*   **Forgotten Chicago**
Forgotten Chicago; by Patrick Steffes
1. Uncovering Forgotten Chicago Through Research and Events; accessed
    8/9/2017
    http://forgottenchicago.com/features/uncovering-fc/

Franzosenbusch *(Online)*   **Franzosenbusch Heritage Project**
Wilfred Anthony (Tony) Yackey; accessed 06/11/2017, unavailable 8/18/2018
(see fhproject.org)
http://www.franzosenbuschheritagesociety.org/Histories/Maywood/Wilfred
%20Yackey.htm

FrascaInt *(Online)*   **Frasca International**
Frasca International; Urbana IL
1. Frasca History; accessed 10/15/2017
    http://www.frasca.com/frasca-history/

Freeman *(Online)*   **Abandoned & Little Known Airfields**
Abandoned & Little Known Airfields; by Paul Freeman
1. Illinois-Chicago Central Area; updated December 3, 2016; accessed
    4/11/2017
    http://www.airfields-freeman.com/IL/Airfields_IL_Chicago_C.htm
2. Illinois-Chicago Northern Area; updated March 28, 2017; accessed
    5/12/2017
    http://www.airfields-freeman.com/IL/Airfields_IL_Chicago_N.htm
3. Illinois-Chicago Northwestern Area; updated April 30, 2017; accessed
    10/28/2017
    http://www.airfields-freeman.com/IL/Airfields_IL_Chicago_NW.htm

4. Illinois-Chicago Southern Area; updated March 20, 2017; accessed 6/21/2017
http://www.airfields-freeman.com/IL/Airfields_IL_Chicago_S.htm
5. Illinois-Chicago Western Area; updated June 11, 2017; accessed 7/3/2017
http://www.airfields-freeman.com/IL/Airfields_IL_Chicago_W.htm#aeroclub
6. Illinois-Northern Area; updated June 11, 2017; accessed 8/26/2017
http://www.airfields-freeman.com/IL/Airfields_IL_N.htm

FriendsofMeigs *(Online)*   **Friends of Meigs**
1. History of Northerly Island and Meigs Field; accessed June 2, 2017
http://www.friendsofmeigs.org/html/history/meigs_history.htm

FSHArchives *(Online)*   **Forest Service History Archives**
FSH Archives.- Forest Service History—Peeling Back the Bark,
1. First Aerial Fire Patrol Took Flight; by Jamie Lewis; updated June 29, 2011; accessed 4/27/2017
https://fhsarchives.wordpress.com/2011/06/29/june-29-1915-first-aerial-fire-patrol-took-flight/

FundUniv *(Online)*   **Funding Universe**
1. Midway Airlines Corporation History; accessed 8/8/2017
http://www.fundinguniverse.com/company-histories/midway-airlines-corporation-history/

G

Galt *(Online)*   **Galt Airport**
1. Galt Airport; accessed 8/27/2017

GaltSale *(Online)*   **Galt Airport Sale—Wordpress**
1. Galt Airport Sale; accessed 8/27/2017
https://galtairportsale.wordpress.com/

Ganz, 2012 *(Book)*
1933 World's Fair: A Century of Progress; Cheryl R. Ganz; Champaign IL: University of Illinois Press, 2012

Gapers_Block *(Online)*   **Gaper's Block**
1. Italo Balbo and Chicago's Forgotten Gift from Fascist Italy; by Alice Maggio; updated April 15, 2004; accessed 1/31/2018
http://gapersblock.com/airbags/archives/italo_balbo_and_chicagos_forgotten_gift_from_fascist_italy/

Gardner, 1922 *(Book)*
Who's Who in American Aeronautics; New York: Gardner, Moffat Co., 1922, p. 66

Garvey, et al., 2002 *(Book)*
Age of Flight: A History of America's Pioneering Airline (United); by William Garvey and David Fisher; Greensboro NC: Pace Communications, 2002

GenDisasters *(Online)*   **Gen Disasters**
Genealogy Disasters: Events that Touched Our Ancestors' Lives
1. Glenview IL—Sightseeing Plane Crash, June 1933; by Stu Beitler; accessed 12/28/2017
    https://www.gendisasters.com/illinois/12481/glenview-il-sightseeing-plane-crash-june-1933

Geneseo_History *(Other)*   **Geneseo History Museum**
1. Harold Neumann Exhibit; visited 8/22/2017

Gen_Winnebago *(Online)*   **Genealogy-Winnebago Cty, IL**
Genealogy Trails History Group—Winnebago County IL
1. Fred Machesney: Proprietor of the Rockford Airport; accessed 2/19/2018
    http://genealogytrails.com/ill/winnebago/fredmachesney.htm

Glines, 2000 *(Book)*
First Flight Around The World; by Carroll V. Glines and Stan Cohen; Missoula MT: Pictorial Histories Publishing, 2000

GNAS *(Book)*
U.S. Naval Air Station—Glenview: The Final Salute: Base Closure Magazine; 1995

Gonzales, 1995 *(Book)*
One Zero Charlie: Adventures in Grassroots Aviation; by Lawrence Gonzales; New York: Simon & Schuster, 1995

Google_Patent *(Online)*   **Google Patent**
Parachute US 1340423 A; accessed 11/8/2017
https://www.google.com/patents/US1340423

Gordon, 2008 *(Book)*
Naked Airport: A Cultural History of the World's Most Revolutionary Structure; by Alastair Gordon; Chicago: University of Chicago Press, 2008

Graf, et al., 2000 *(Book)*
Chicago's Monuments, Markers and Memorials: Images of America; John Graf and Steve Skorpad; Charleston SC: Arcadia, 2002

Griggs *(Unpublished)*
Major Jim Griggs, CAP
1. Illinois CAP Timeline v1.0; unpublished memo; May 20, 2018

Grinnell_Lib *(Online)*   **Drake Community Library**
Grinnell Library, Drake Community Library
1. Story of Billy Robinson; accessed 5/19/2018
    http://www.grinnell.lib.ia.us/files/images/archive%20pages/Robinson Story.pdf

Grossman 2004 *(Book)*
Encyclopedia of Chicago; James R. Grossman, Ann Dunkin Keating, Janice L. Reiff (editors); Chicago: University of Chicago Press, 2004

Guardian *(Periodical)*   ***The Guardian***
1. Skydiver proves Da Vinci chute works; by Julia Hartley-Brewer; June 27, 2000

Gubert, et al., 2001 *(Book)*
Distinguished African Americans in Aviation and Space Science; by Betty Kaplan Gubert, Miriam Sawyer, and Caroline M. Fannin; Westport CT: Greenwood Press, 2001

H

Hangar 1 *(Online)*   **Hangar One**
Hangar One; Hangar One Foundation; Glenview IL
1. Glenview Hangar One—History; updated July 11, 2003; accessed 7/11/2017

Hanson, 2011 *(Book)*
Rantoul and Chanute Air Force Base Images of America; Charleston SC: Arcadia Publishing, 2011

Hardesty, 2008 *(Book)*
Black Wings: Courageous Stories or African Americans in Aviation and Space; New York: Harper Collins Publishers, 2008

Harris *(Online)*   **Richard Harris blog**
iWichita; server by Hubris Communications
1. Flying the Beam: LF/MF Four-Course Radio Ranges; by Richard Harris; updated 2014, Draft 5G; accessed 7/3/2017
   http://home.iwichita.com/rh1/hold/av/stories/avionics/radiorange.htm

Harvard_Main *(Periodical)*   ***Harvard Main Line***
Harvard Main Line; Harvard IL
1. Dacy Airport soars through history, stays in family; Zach Wrublewski; December 1, 2010
2. Stunt Pilot Dave Dacy Still Thrills After 25 Years; by Marjie Reed; November 2, 2011

Haynes, 1995 *(Book)*
Flying Field: The Monmouth Flying Club; by James Haynes; Bushnell IL: Robins Nest Company, 1995

HeathCo *(Other)*   **Heath Aircraft Co**
Heath Aircraft Co., Chicago; sales brochures from EAA Collection
1. Parasol—A Safe and Efficient Light Plane at a Price Within Your Reach; pre-1928
2. Reasons Why You Should Buy or Build the Heath Super Parasol; post-1928

Heftman *(Interview)*
Charles Heftman; retired FAA Air Traffic Control Center controller; interview by author 2/5/2018

Hill, 2013 *(Book)*
   Little Known Story of the Land Called Clearing; Robert Milton Hill; reprint—
   Lulu.com 2013

Historic_Hotels *(Online)*   **Historic Hotels**
   1. Hilton Chicago; accessed 10/15/2017
       http://www.historichotels.org/hotels-resorts/hilton-chicago/history.php

History *(Online)*   **History.com**
   1. First Day of Work at the Motorola Corporation; accessed 2/17/2018
       http://www.history.com/this-day-in-history/first-day-of-work-at-the-
       galvin-manufacturing-corporation
   2. Haymarket Square Riot; accessed 3/18/2018
       https://www.history.com/topics/haymarket-riot
   3. Russian Revolution; accessed 2/15/2018
       http://www.history.com/topics/russian-revolution

History_Net *(Online)*   **History Net**
   1. Bert R.J. "Fish" Hassell and Parker D. "Shorty" Cramer: Pilots of the
       Remarkable Rockford-to-Stockholm Flight; updated June 12, 2006;
       accessed 11/04/2017.\
       http://www.historynet.com/bert-rj-fish-hassell-and-parker-d-shorty-
       cramer-pilots-of-a-remarkable-rockford-to-stockholm-flight.htm

HistWings *(Online)*   **Historic Wings**
   1. First Aerial Refueling; updated November 12, 2012; accessed 5/22/2018
       http://fly.historicwings.com/2012/11/first-aerial-refueling/

Homan, et al., 2001 *(Book)*
   Black Knights: The Story of the Tuskegee Airmen; by Lynn M. Homan and
   Thomas Reilly; Gretna, LA: Pelican Publishing, 2001

Hopkins, 1982 *(Book)*
   Flying the Line: The First Half Century of the Air Line Pilots Association; by
   George E. Hopkins; Washington D.C.: Air Line Pilots Assn. International, 1982

HouseRep *(Online)*   **U.S. House of Representatives**
   1. Representative Arthur Mitchell of Illinois and the Supreme Court (April
       28, 1941); accessed 4/30/2018
       http://history.house.gov/Historical-Highlights/1901-1950/Representative-
       Arthur-Mitchell-of-Illinois-successfully-argued-a-segregation-case-before-
       the-Supreme-Court/

Howard, 1998 *(Book)*
   Wilbur and Orville: A Biography of the Wright Brothers; Fred Howard;
   Mineola NY: Dover Publications, 1998

HowardAir *(Online)*   **Howard Aircraft**
   1. Benny Howard; by Donald Douglas Sr.; updated December 8, 1970;
       accessed 5/31/2017
       http://www.howardaircraft.org/history/110-benny-howard

2. Howard DGA-8 and DGA-11; by Leslie Sargent; accessed 5/31/2017
   http://www.howardaircraft.org/aircraft/113-howard-dga-8-and-dga-11
3. Howard DGA-15; accessed 5/31/2017
   http://www.howardaircraft.org/aircraft/116-howard-dga-15

Hudson, 2004 *(Book)*
Chicago Skyscrapers in Vintage Postcards: Postcard History Series; by Leslie
A. Hudson; Charleston SC: Arcadia Publishing

I

IA-HOF *(Online)*   **Iowa Hall of Fame**
Flying Museum—Iowa Aviation Museum
1. Iowa Aviation Hall of Fame; accessed 11/9/2017
   http://flyingmuseum.com/hall-of-fame/

IATA *(Online)*   **International Air Transport Assn**
1. Founding of IATA; accessed 7/3/2017
   http://www.iata.org/about/Pages/history.aspx

IL_DeptAero *(Online)*   **Illinois Dept. of Aeronautics**
1. Illinois Airports Recognized by IDOT's Division of Aeronautics for Outstanding Service; Press Release; updated May 14, 2014; accessed 9/8/2018
   http://www.idot.illinois.gov/Assets/uploads/files/About-IDOT/News/
   Press-Releases/051414%20IDOT%202014%20Aero%20Awards%20
   Press%20Release.pdf

IL_GA *(Online)*   **Illinois General Assembly**
1. (620 ILCS 45) County Airport Law of 1943; accessed 7/13/2018
   http://www.ilga.gov/legislation/ilcs/ilcs3.asp?ActID=1811&ChapterID=48

IL_Glory_Days *(Online)*   **Illinois High School Glory Days**
1. Lewis Lockport Holy Name Institute "Flyers"; accessed 1/19/2018
   http://www.illinoishsIglorydays.com/id630.html

IL-HOF-Pgm *(Other)*   **Illinois Aviation Hall of Fame Program**
1. 1997 Induction Banquet Program

IL_SupCt *(Online)*   **Illinois Supreme Court**
1. People ex rel. Greening v. Bartholf et al. (No. 27863), 58 N.E.2d. 172, 388
   Ill. 445.- November 22, 1944; accessed 7/13/2018
   https://case-law.vlex.com/vid/58-n-2d-172-614154194

IndHistS *(Online)*   **Indiana Historical Society**
Air Mail Pioneers by Indiana Historical Society
1. Smash Up Kid: Fort Wayne Aviator Art Smith; Racher Sherwood Roberts,
   updated 1998; accessed 4/11/2017.
   http://www.airmailpioneers.org/content/Pilots/AartSmith.htm

Inter-Ocean *(Periodical)   Chicago Inter-Ocean*
Clubs to Meet Here: Local Organization Issues Call for Convention; *Chicago Inter-Ocean;* Chicago, February 2, 1908, p. 19

J

JAAER *(Periodical)*   **Jour. Of Aviation/Aerospace Education**
Journal of Aviation/Aerospace Education; Embry-Riddle Aviation University
1. Aircraft Accident Investigation That Never Was; by Tim Brady; Winter, 2014, accessed 2/19/2018
   https://commons.erau.edu/cgi/viewcontent.cgi?article=1610&context=jaaer

Jackson, 1982 *(Book)*
Flying the Mail; Alexamdria VA: Time-Life Books, 1982

Jalopnik *(Online)*   **Jalopnik**
Jalopnik: a news and opinion about cars, the automotive industry, racing, transportation, airplanes, technology, motorcycles and much more
1. World's First Multi-Engine Plane Had a Ridiculous Open Balcony; by Jason Torchinksy; updated February 5, 2012; accessed 4/4/2017
   http://jalopnik.com/the-worlds-first-multi-engine-plane-had-a-ridiculous-o-1516398280

Johnson, 2004 *(Book)*
Rockford 1920 and Beyond—Postcard History Series; Charleston, SC: Arcadia Publishing, 2004

K

Kaieteur *(Online)*   **Kaieteur News**
1. Luxury Jet Crash in US ... Brassington Brothers Jailed; updated September 21, 2011; accessed 4/29/2017
   http://www.kaieteurnewsonline.com/2011/09/21/luxury-jet-crash-in-us%E2%80%A6brassington-brothers-jailed/

Kane, 1996 *(Book)*
Air Transportation; Dubuque IA: Kendall/Hunt Publishing, 1996, 12th edition

Kasmar, M.K. *(Book)*
First Lessons in Flight; M.K. Kasmar; Chicago: American Aeronautical Society, 1909

Kent *(Book)*
Midway Airport: Images of Aviation; Charleston SC: Arcadia Publishing, 2012

Kobler, 1993 *(Book)*
Ardent Spirits: The Rise and Fall of Prohibition; Lebanon, IN: Da Capo Press (reprint edition), 1993

Koontz, 2011 *(Book)*
Pioneer Mechanics in Aviation; Giacinta Bradley Koontz; Prescott AZ: Running Iron Publications, 2011

Krist, 2012 *(Book)*
City of Scoundrels; New York: Random House, 2012

L

Lakeland_Times *(Periodical)*   **Lakeland Times**
Lakeland Times; Minocqua WI
1. Arlene Edgecumbe: Found her home in the skies; by Joyce Laabs; August 7, 2009

Landis *(Book)*
Business Future of Aviation; Chicago: Chicago Daily News, 1920

Launius *(Online)*   **Roger Launius's Blog**
1. Katherine Stinson and the Early Age of Flight in America; updated December 16, 2016; accessed 4/18/2017 https://launiusr.wordpress.com/2016/12/16/katherine-stinson-and-the-early-age-of-flight-in-america/
2. Willa Brown: Out from the Shadows of Aeronautical History; updated December 19, 2014; accessed 12/7/2017 https://launiusr.wordpress.com/2014/12/19/willa-brown-out-from-the-shadows-of-aeronautical-history/

Lawson, 1939 *(Book)*
Lawson: Aircraft Industry Builder; Alfred W. Lawson; Detroit: Humanity Publishing Company, 1932

Legal_Info *(Online)*   **Legal Information**
Legal Information Institute; Cornell University
1. 379 U.S. 487 (85 S.Ct. 493, 13 L.Ed.2d 439); Nick JANKOVICH and Paul Jankovich, Co-Partners, doing business as Calumet Aviation Company, Petitioners, v. INDIANA TOLL ROAD COMMISSION; January 18, 1965; accessed 12/2/2017 https://www.law.cornell.edu/supremecourt/text/379/487

Lest_We_Forget *(Periodical)*   **Lest We Forget**
Lest We Forget; LWF Publications; Trotwood OH
1. National Airmen Association of America ... before the Tuskegee Airmen; by Bennie J. McRae Jr.; July 1995, Vol. 3, No. 3

Levinson *(Interview)*
Howard Levinson; aviator and WWII B-24 commander in South Pacific; interview by author 6/14/2018

Lewis, 2007 *(Book)*
It Was an Airport Before It Was an Airport; by Richard Lewis; Pontiac IL: Johnson Press, 2007

LewisU *(Online)*   **Lewis University**
1. About Us: History; accessed 10/15/2017
   http://www.lewisu.edu/welcome/history.htm
2. About Us: Timeline; accessed 1/19/2018
   http://www.lewisu.edu/welcome/timeline.htm

LincBeach *(Online)*   **Lincoln Beachey**
Lincoln Beachey; by Carroll Gray
1. *Cicero Flying Field: Origin, Operation, Obscurity and Legacy—1891 to 1916*; updated 2013; accessed 5/5/2017
   http://www.lincolnbeachey.com/cicart.html
2. Lincoln Beachey: A Brief Biography; updated 2006; accessed 8/7/2017
   http://www.lincolnbeachey.com/lbbio.html

Lituanus *(Periodical)*   ***Lituanus***
Lituanus; Lithuanian Students Assn.
1. Two Fliers: Darius and Giernas; by K. Skrupskelis; September 1958

LivHistIL *(Online)*   **Living History of Illinois**
Living History of Illinois; by Digital Research Library of Illinois History
1. *Timeline of Illinois History*; accessed 5/6/2017
   http://livinghistoryofillinois.com/pdf_files/Timeline%20of%20Illinois%20History.pdf

LOC_Memory *(Online)*   **Library of Congress Memory**
1. Octave Chanute and His Photos of the Wright Experiments at the Kill Devil Hills; accessed 2/1/2018
   http://memory.loc.gov/master/ipo/qcdata/qcdata/wrightold/wb005.html

Longyard, 1994 *(Book)*
Who's Who in Aviation History; William H. Longyard; Novato CA: Presidio Press, 1994

Lougheed, 1909 *(Book)*
Vehicles of the Air: A Popular Exposition of Modern Aeronautics with Working Drawings; Victor Lougheed; Chicago: Reilly and Britton Co., 1909

Lougheed, 1912 *(Book)*
Aeroplane Designing for Amateurs: A Plain Treatment of the Basic Principles of Flight Engineering; Victor Lougheed; Chicago: Reilly and Britton Co., 1912

LWReedy *(Online)*   **L.W. Reedy Blog**
1. Elmhurst's Place in Airport History; updated February 24, 2015; accessed 12/2/2017
   https://lwreedy.wordpress.com/2015/02/24/elmhursts-place-in-airport-history/

Lynch, 2003 *(Book)*
Chicago's Midway Airport: The First Seventy-Five Years; by Christopher Lynch; Chicago: Lake Claremont Press, 2003

M

MALTA *(Online)* **Maltivation**
M.A.L.T.A (Motivation and Learning Through Aviation), Hayward CA
1. Bessie Coleman: African American Aviatrix; accessed 7/7/2017
    http://maltaviation.org/pdf/BessieColemanAviatrix.pdf
2. Saga of Willie "Suicide" Jones; accessed 4/6/2017
    http://www.maltaviation.org/pdf/The%20Saga%20of%20Willie%20Jones.pdf
3. Willa Brown: Aviatrix; accessed 7/7/2017
    http://maltaviation.org/pdf/Willa%20Brown%20Aviatrix.pdf

Maguire *(Book)*
Chicago Then and Now; by Kathleen Maguire; London: Salamander Books Ltd., 2015

Mashable *(Online)* **Mashable**
1. Aug 28, 1929, Graf Zeppelin Over Chicago; by Chris Wild; updated November 29, 2014; accessed 4/11/2017
    http://mashable.com/2014/11/29/graf-zeppelin-airship/#6UIQg1snBkq7

Maurer, 1967 *(Book)*
Aviation in the US Army 1919–1939; Washington DC: US Government Printing Office, 1967

McBriarty, 2013 *(Book)*
Chicago River Bridges; Patrick T. McBriarty; Urbana, IL: University of Illinois Press, 2013

McDonaldHist *(Online)* **McDonald's Restaurants**
1. About Us-History; accessed 5/4/2018
    http://corporate.mcdonalds.com/corpmcd/about-us/history.html

McIntyre, et al., 1987 *(Book)*
Wheeling Through the Years: An Oral History of Wheeling, An Illinois Village; by Barbara K. McIntyre and Robert McIntyre, eds.; Wheeling IL: Whitehall Company, 1987

MDWHist *(Online)* **Midway Historians**
1. Midway Airport Audios and Videos; accessed 8/10/2017
    http://www.midwayhistorians.com/Audio-Video.html
2. Welcome to Midway Airport; accessed 4/17/2017
    http://midwayhistorians.com/

Meetup_NEPilots *(Online)* **Meetup: Northeast Pilots Group**
1. Restoring the Liberty Belle B-17; by Chuck Bugard; updated May 18, 2018; accessed 1/6/2018
    https://www.meetup.com/NEPilotsGroup/messages/boards/thread/23431802

Meigs_Family *(Online)* **Meigs Family History & Genealogy**
1. Meigs—The Man Who Loved to Fly; accessed 10/3/2017
    http://www.meigs.org/merrill1289.htm

MHUGL *(Online)*   **Military History**
Military History of the Upper Great Lakes; by Michigan Technical University
1.   Thomas Koritz—Koritz Field; by David Eychaner; updated October 19,
     2016; accessed 11/2/2017
     http://ss.sites.mtu.edu/mhugl/2016/10/19/thomas-koritz-koritz-field/

Midw_Flyer *(Periodical)*   ***Midwest Flyer***
Quad Cities International Airport ... A Quick Look Back in History; March 22,
2013

Miller, 1996 *(Book)*
City of the Century: The Epic of Chicago and the Making of America; Donald
M. Miller; New York: Simon & Schuster, 1996

Militarian *(Online)*   **Militarian**
Militarian: Military History Forum
1.   Reed Landis; updated March 26, 2009; accessed 2/16/2018
     http://www.militarian.com/threads/reed-landis.7174/

Mlinaric, 2018 *(Book)*
Secret Chicago: A Guide to the Weird, Wonderful and Obscure; Jessica
Mlinaric; St. Louis: Reedy Press, 2018

MHomanSq *(Online)*   **Homan Square Foundation**
Original Sears Tower; Homan Square Foundation; accessed 1/12/2018
http://www.homansquare.org/history/original-sears-tower

MNHist *(Periodical)*   ***Minnesota History***
Shooting Star: Aviator Jimmie Ward of Crookston; Steven R. Hoffbeck;
Minnesota History Winter, 1995

ModMech *(Periodical)*   ***Modern Mechanax***
1.   Twenty-Three Days in the Air; October 1930

Monaco *(Interview)*
Madeleine Monaco; cofounder of Palwaukee Airport Pilots Assn. (PAPA);
interview by author July 19, 2018

Monash *(Online)*   **Monash University—Australia**
Hargrave—The Pioneers; produced by Archive Pandora, Australian National
Library, Canberra
1.   Chauncy (Chance) Milton Vought; accessed 10/10/2017
     http://www.ctie.monash.edu.au/hargrave/vought.html
2.   Katherine (1891–1977) and Marjorie (1899–1975) Stinson; updated March
     25, 2005; accessed 7/13/2018
     http://www.ctie.monash.edu.au/hargrave/stinson_bio.html

Morgan, et al., 2010 *(Book)*
*Rings of Supersonic Steel: Introduction & Site Guifde to the Air Defenses of
the US Army 1950–1979*; by Mark L. Morgan and Mark A. Berhow; Hole in the
Head Press, 2010.

Moscrop, et al., 2008 *(Book)*
100 Greatest Women in Aviation; Liz Moscrop & Rampal Sanjay; Essex, UK: Aerocomm Ltd., 2008

MSStateEdu *(Online)*   **Mississippi State Univ.**
O & W Flying Machine; Mississippi State University, source date 1903; accessed: 4/7/2017
http://invention.psychology.msstate.edu/i/Wrights/WrightUSPatent/WrightPatent.html

MtProsHerald *(Periodical)*   *Mt. Prospect Herald*
Mt. Prospect Herald; Paddock Publications
1. Air Scouts squadrons formed in Mt. Prospect; November 2, 1945
2. Civilian pilot trng. progtram outlines; by A.C. Tufts; July 3, 1942, Sect. 2 p. 2 col. 2
3. Santa to arrive by air this Friday afternoon; December 15, 1944, p. 3 col 1
4. Train army pilots at Pal-Waukee; December 3, 1942, p. 1 col. 7

MWAirmail *(Periodical)*   *Midwest Airmail*
1. Ira Biffle—He Also Flew the Mail; updated 3/27/2016; accessed 5/9/2017.4 https://midwestairmail.wordpress.com/tag/ira-biffle/

N

NASA *(Online)*   **National Aeronautics & Space Administration**
1. Dr. Robert H. Goddard, American Rocketry Pioneer; updated December 15, 2016; accessed 4/12/2017.
    https://www.nasa.gov/centers/goddard/about/history/dr_goddard.html
2. NACA-NASA Aero Contributions Timeline 1915–2015; accessed 4/29/2018
    https://www.nasa.gov/sites/default/files/atoms/files/naca-nasa-aero-contributions-timeline.pdf

NASM *(Online)*   **National Air & Space Museum**
1. Floyd Smith Collection; accessed 11/8/2017
    https://airandspace.si.edu/collection-objects/floyd-smith-collection
2. J.W. Smith Collection; accessed 5/18/2018
    https://airandspace.si.edu/collection-objects/jw-smith-collection-2001-0011
3. Wall of Honor: Cornelius Robinson Coffey; accessed 12/7/2017
    https://airandspace.si.edu/support/wall-of-honor/cornelious-robinson-coffey
4. Women in Aviation Janet Bragg; by D. Cochrane and P. Ramirez; accessed
    https://airandspace.si.edu/explore-and-learn/topics/women-in-aviation/bragg.cfm
5. World's First Scheduled Airline; accessed 4/21/2018
    https://airandspace.si.edu/exhibitions/america-by-air/online/early_years/early_years01.cfm
6. Wright-Smithsonian Feud; accessed 5/19/2017
    https://airandspace.si.edu/exhibitions/wright-brothers/online/icon/feud.cfm

NatArcPrologue *(Periodical)* **Prologue**
Prologue; National Archive; Washington DC
1. International Civil Aeronautics Conference of 1928; by Charles F. Downs II; Winter 2003, Vol. 35, No. 4

NatAvHOF *(Online)* **National Aviation Hall of Fame**
National Aviation Hall of Fame; Dayton OH;
1. Our Enshrinees; accessed 6/1/2017
http://www.nationalaviation.org/our-enshrinees/

NatWACO_Club *(Online)* **National WACO Club**
1. History of WACO Aircraft; accessed 2/28/2018
http://www.nationalwacoclub.com/waco-aircraft/waco-company/

NBC *(Online)* **NBC News**
1. United Airlines finally flies out of bankruptcy; by Associated Press; updated 2/2/2006; accessed 10/4/2017
http://www.nbcnews.com/id/11126203/ns/business-us_business/t/united-airlines-finally-flies-out-bankruptcy/#.WdZeh1uPJEY.

NBCChicago *(Online)* **NBC News Chicago**
1. 80 Years Later, Plane Bombing Remains a Mystery; by Phil Rogers; updated October 7, 2013; accessed 12/28/2017
https://www.nbcchicago.com/news/local/80-Years-Later-Plane-Bombing-Remains-A-Mystery-226840081.html

Nelson, 2012 *(Book)*
We Are Going In: The Story of the Grand Canyon Disaster; Bloomington IN: AuthorHouse, 2012

Neumann, 1940s *(Unpublished)*
Corn Plow to Cockpit: Early Life Story of Harold E. Neumann as told to Charles A. Fordyce; edited by Sandra S. Pobanz; unpublished circa 1940s

NIPSTA *(Online)* **Northeastern Illinois Public Safety Training Academy**
1. NIPSTA Campus Map; accessed 11/25/2017
http://www.nipsta.org/about/documents/NIPSTACampusMap2009.pdf

NIU-Lib *(Online)* **Northern Illinois Univ. Library**
1. Octave Chanute, The Chicago Connection and the Birth of Aviation; by Roger D. Launius; Northern Illinois University Library; accessed 2/1/2018
http://www.lib.niu.edu/2001/iht810114.html

NJer *(Online)* **New Jersey Local News**
1. Platinum Jet charter pilot pleads guilty to illegal flights following Teterboro Airport crash scrutiny; by Ted Sherman; September 28, 2010; accessed 4/29/2017
http://www.nj.com/news/index.ssf/2010/09/pilo_who_worked_for_jet_charte.html

NPS *(Online)*   **National Park Service**
1. Indiana Dunes National Lakeshore—House of Tomorrow; updated April 10, 2015; accessed 12/28/2017
    https://www.nps.gov/indu/learn/historyculture/house-of-tomorrow.htm

NRHP *(Online)*   **National Register of Historic Places**
National Register of Historic Places—National Park Service
1. Curtiss Wright Aeronautical University Building; updated 10/16/2013; accessed 4/19/2018
    https://www.nps.gov/nr/feature/places/pdfs/13000827.pdf

NWA_Hist *(Periodical)*   ***Northwest Airlines History Center***
Reflections; Minneapolis: NWA History Centre
Remembering David L. Behncke; by Bob Johnson; Summer, 2012, Vol. 10, No. 3

NW_Herald *(Periodical)*   ***Northwest Herald***
Northwest Herald; Paddock Publications
1. Elroy Edward Hilbert (obituary); August 19, 2016
2. Founder of Dacy Airport dies after lifetime of flight; by Jenn Wient; May 17, 2007
3. New owners, same feel for Galt Airport; by Kevin P. Craver; August 15, 2013

NWQtr *(Periodical)*   ***Northwest Quarterly***
Northwest Quarterly; Rockford IL; Hughes Media Group
1. Youngest Naval Aviator of WWII; Robert Randall Ryder; Spring-Summer 2016

NWU-TransLib *(Online)*   **NW Univ. Transportation Library**
Northwestern University—Transportation Library; Evanston IL
1. Ralph H. Burke: Early Innovator of Chicago O'Hare International Airport; accessed June 15, 2018
    https://www.library.northwestern.edu/libraries-collections/transportation/collection/o-hare-at-50/research-materials/ralph-h-burke.html

NYTimes *(Periodical)*   ***New York Times***
1. Chicago Mayor Bulldozes a Small Downtown Airport; by John W. Fountain; April 1, 2013
2. Miss Stinson Makes New Flying Record; May 24, 2018

O

Oak_Parker *(Periodical)*   ***Oak Parker***
Oak Parker; Oak Park, IL
Number of Atlas employees attended the funeral; August 8, 1924, p. 27

P

Pacyga, 2009 *(Book)*
Chicago: A Biography; Dominic A. Pacyga, Chicago: University of Chicago Press, 2009

Pal_Ent *(Periodical)*   ***Palatine Enterprise***
Palatine Enterprise; Paddock Publishing
1. Air Circus to be Additional Fair Feature; August 6, 1926, p. 1, col. 4
2. Largest Air Port in the Chicago Dist; March 22, 1929, p. 4, col. 4
3 Pal-Waukee Station Opens June 1st; May 28, 1926, p. 9, col. 5

PandoraArc *(Online)*   **Pandora Archive**
Pandora Web Archive; by National Library of Australia and Partners
1. London to Sydney Air Race Entrants—London to Sydney Air Race 2001; updated April 10, 2001; accessed 7/7/2017
2. http://pandora.nla.gov.au/nph-wb/20010409130000/http://www.airrace.com.au/entrants.htm

Peek, 2003 *(Book)*
The Heath Story; Chet Peek; Norman, OK: Three Peaks Publishing, 2003

Pellegreno, 1971 *(Book)*
World Flight: The Earhart Trail; by Anne Hultgren Pellegreno; Ames IA: Iowa State University Press, 1971

PilotFriend *(Online)*   ***Pilot Friend***
1. Stinson Aircraft; accessed 2/24/2018.
   http://www.pilotfriend.com/acft_manu/Stinson%20Aircraft.htm

PioneerPrs *(Periodical)*   ***Pioneeer Press***
1. New terminal serves Palwaukee workers; by Casey Moffitt; April 6, 2006
2. Priester sells Palwaukee operation; by Casey Moffitt; August 30, 2001, p. 5, 11
3. Roman Pucinski earns recognition from FAA; by Mila Nolan; January 21, 1999

Plumbe, et al., 1922 *(Book)*
Chicago Daily News Year Book and Almanac for 1922; by George Edward Plumbe, James Lanagland and Claude Othello Pike; Chicago: Chicago Daily News, 1922, Vol. 38

Poetry *(Periodical)*   ***Poetry***
1. Chicago; by Carl Sandburg; March, 1914

PopAviation *(Periodical)*   ***Popular Aviation***
Popular Aviation; Popular Aviation Publishing Co., Chicago
1. And now—In Chicago (advertisement); December 1928, p. 95.
2. Aviation Products Company (advertisement); May 1936, p. 375

PopMech *(Periodical)*   **Popular Mechanics**
1. Beachey flying Brookes Biplane at Chicago with both hands off the controls (advertisement); September 1912, ad section p. 167

PopScience *(Periodical)*   ***Popular Science***
1. Pig That Came in the Air Mail; June 1920, p. 43

Post, 2000 *(Book)*
Shoestring to the Stars: The Life Story of E.M. "Matty" Laird; Joan Laird Post; Bloomington IN: 1st Books Library, 2000

PostalMus *(Online)*   **Postal Museum**
Postal Museum—Smithsonian Institution
1. Airmail Creates an Industry: Lipsner vs. Praeger; accessed 2/19/2018
   https://postalmuseum.si.edu/airmail/airmail/foundation/airmail_
   foundation_lipsnerpraeger_long.html
2. 1934 Airmail Scandal; by Nancy A. Pope; updated March 2009; accessed
   2/19/2018
   https://postalmuseum.si.edu/collections/object-spotlight/1934-airmail-
   scandal.html

Pridmore, et al., 2005 *(Book)*
Chicago Architecture and Design; New York: Harry N. Abrams Inc., 2005

ProAirshow *(Online)*   **Pro Airshow**
1. Airshow Announcer Herb Hunter; accessed 7/8/2017
   http://www.proairshow.com/Herb%20Hunter.htm

Q

QCAirport *(Online)*   **Quad City Airport**
History—Quad City International Airport; Quad City Airport; accessed
1/26/2018
http://www.qcairport.com/history.html

QCOnline *(Periodical)*   ***Quad Cities Online***
Dispatch and Rock Island Argus; Moline, IL
1. Aviation pioneers paved way for Q-C airport; by Marlene Gantt; updated,
   January 16, 2016; accessed 10/29/2017
   http://www.qconline.com/opinion/columnists/marlene_gantt/aviation-
   pioneers-paved-way-for-q-c-airport/article_bef0aaf2-7cf3-5b00-8da8-
   ee1208997408.htm
2. Geneseo couple pilots their own plane in trip around the world; by Claudia
   Loucks; November 6, 2017; accessed 4/27/2018
   http://qconline.com/news/local/geneseo-couple-pilots-their-own-plane-in-
   trip-around-the/article_420d6fa6-c0c1-5876-a049-891035cadb09.html
3. Pioneers Saw Future in an Empty Field; by Marlene Gantt; July 20, 2012;
   accessed 10/29/2017
   http://www.qconline.com/editorials/pioneers-saw-future-in-empty-field/
   article_4f251778-ec0c-502a-9dfa-ae97609a7983.html

R

Rabung, 2009 *(Book)*
Virginia, Where do you keep the parachute?; by Virginia Rabung; Mundelein
IL: self-published

Relevance *(Periodical)*   ***Relevance***
Relevance: Quarterly Journal of the Great War Society; Stanford CA
1. US Aircraft Production: Success or Scandal; by Paul Hare; Summer, 1996, Vol. 5, No. 3; accessed 11/7/2017
http://www.worldwar1.com/tgws/relairprod.htm

Reuters *(Online)*   **Reuters News**
1. Chicago O'Hare $8.5 billion expansion plan approved by city council; by Alana Wise; updated March 28, 2018; accessed 6/20/2018.
https://www.reuters.com/article/us-chicago-airport/chicago-ohare-8-5-billion-expansion-plan-approved-by-city-council-idUSKBN1H43EZ
2. United Air Fined $2.75 million over treatment of disabled, tarmac delays; updated January 7, 2016; accessed 6/20/2018
https://www.reuters.com/article/us-ual-fine/united-air-fined-2-75-million-over-treatment-of-disabled-tarmac-delays-idUSKBN0UL2ML20160107

Roach, 2014 *(Book)*
Wright Company: From Invention to Industry; Edward J. Roach; Athens OH: Ohio University Press, 2014

RochelleAirp *(Online)*   **Rochelle Airport**
1. Rochelle Municipal Airport—Koritz Field; accessed 1/27/2018
http://flyrpj.com/

Rockford_Reminisce *(Online)*   **Rockford Reminisce**
1. Bert Hassell & The Greater Rockford; accessed 11/7/2017
http://www.rockfordreminisce.com/bert-hassell-and-the-greater-rockford/

Rock_Valley *(Online)*   **Rock Valley College**
1. Aircraft Maintenance Technology; accessed 10/2/2017
https://www.rockvalleycollege.edu/Courses/Programs/Aviation/index.cfm

Rose_Parrakeet *(Online)*   **Rose Parrakeet**
Rose Parrakeet Aeroplane Pilots Club; by Don Gilmore
1. Curious History; by Barry Taylor; updated June 12, 2009; accessed 2/22/2018
http://www.roseparrakeet.org/curious.html
2. Jennings W. "Jack" Rose; updated June 12, 2009; accessed 2/22/2018
http://www.roseparrakeet.org/jack_rose.html
3. Rose Aeroplane & Motor Co.; updated June 15, 2009; accessed 2/22/ 2018
http://www.roseparrakeet.org/rose_parrakeet.html
4. Rose Parrakeet Aeroplane History 1929–Present; updated June 28, 2009; accessed 2/22/2018
http://www.roseparrakeet.org/history.html
5. Welcome to the Rose Parrakeet Aeroplane Home Page; updated April 2, 2010; accessed 2/22/2018
http://www.roseparrakeet.org/

Ros_Reg *(Periodical)*   ***Roselle Register***
1. Leaflets from air to open recruit drive; August 11, 1944, p. 1, col. 2

RRStar *(Periodical)*   ***Rockford Register Star***
1. Charles Downey 1924–2016, obituary; February 28, 2016
2. Chuck Downey, Youngest WWII Naval Pilot and Poplar Grove Resident, Dies; Adam Poulisse; February 21, 2016
3. Our View: How Rockford Lost EAA Fly-In to Oshkosh; by Editorial Board; February 19, 2015

RunwaySafe *(Online)*   **Runway Safe**
1. Chicago Midway; accessed 7/13/2017
   http://runwaysafe.com/our-product/cases/chicago-midway/

RuudLeeuw *(Online)*   **Ruud Leeuw**
1. Airlines Remembered: Midway Airlines 2; accessed 8/8/2017; unavailable 9/7/2018
   http://www.ruudleeuw.com/rem-midway2.htmA

S

Samaruddin, 2002 *(Book)*
Adventure Continues: London to Sydney Air Race 2001; by Steward Samaruddin; Seattle: Peanut Butter Publishing, 2002

Scamehorn, 2000 *(Book)*
Balloons to Jets: A Century of Aviation in Illinois 1855–1955; Howard L. Scamehorn; Carbondale IL: Southern Illinois University Press, 2000

Schultz, et al., 2001 *(Book)*
Women Building Chicago 1790–1990; by Rima Lunin Schultz & Adele Hast, ed.; Bloomington IN: University of Indiana Press, 2001

Schwieterman, 2014 *(Book)*
Terminal Town; by Joseph P. Schwieterman; Lake Forest IL: Lake Forest College Press, 2014

Scott, 1998 *(Book)*
Double V: The Civil Rights Struggle of the Tuskegee Airmen; Lawrence P. Scott and William M. Womack, Sr.; East Lansing MI: Michigan State University Press, 1998

Selig, 2013 *(Book)*
Lost Airports of Chicago; by Nicholas C. Selig; Charleston SC: History Press, 2013

Selig, 2014 *(Book)*
Forgotten Chicago Airfields; by Nicholas C. Selig; Charleston SC: History Press, 2014

Shrenk, 2007 *(Book)*
Building a Century of Progress: Architecture of Chicago's 1933–34 World's Fair; Minneapolis: University of Minnesota Press, 2007

SilvWings-IL *(Periodical)*   **Silver Wings—IL**
Silver Wings Fraternity—Illinois Chapter Newsletter; Orland Park IL
1. Silver Wings Greets Fall with a "Bange"; Fall, 2017, p. 1

Simanaitas *(Online)*   **Simanaitas Says**
1. Italo Balbo's Chicago Visit; updated August 17, 2013; accessed 1/31/2018
    https://simanaitissays.com/2013/08/17/italo-balbos-chicago-visit/

Skydive_Wiki *(Online)*   **Skydiving Wiki**
Skydiving Wiki—Skydiving Museum and Hall of Fame
1. 1919: Smith Aerial Life Pack; by Pat Works; updated February 5, 2015;
    accessed 10/4/2017
    http://works-words.com/NSM-WIKI/WP/wordpress/wiki/skydiving/early-
    history/history/1919-smith-aerial-life-pack/

SlideShare *(Online)*   **Slide Share**
1. Welcome to the Greater Kankakee Airport (PowerPoint); by Bevis Acevedo,
    Greater Kankakee Airport Authority; updated November 18, 2014; accessed
    9/2/2018
    https://www.slideserve.com/bevis-acevedo/welcome-to-the-greater-
    kankakee-airport

Smithsonian *(Periodical)*   *Smithsonian Magazine*
Smithsonian Magazine; Smithsonian Institution, Washington DC
1. Early History of the Parachute; by Jimmy Stamp; March 7, 2013; accessed
    11/8/2017
2. Great Los Angeles Air Raid Terrified Citizens—Even Though No Bombs
    Were Dropped; by Lorraine Boissoneault; January 2018

Somers, 2003 *(Book)*
Lake Michigan's Aircraft Carriers: Images of America; by Paul M. Somers;
Charleston SC: Arcadia Publishing, 2003

Souter, 2010 *(Book)*
Chicago Air and Water Show: A History of Wings Above the Waves; Gerry and
Janet Souter; Charleston SC: History Press, 2010.

Speedway *(Online)*   **First Super Speedway**
Rheims Air Show 1909; First Super Speedway—Mark Dill Enterprises;
accessed 6/2/2017
http://www.firstsuperspeedway.com/articles/rheims-air-show-1909

Spenser, 2009 *(Book)*
Airplane: How Ideas Gave Us Wings; Jay Spenser; New York: HarperCollins, 2009

StandardAero *(Online)*   **StandardAero Corp**
StandardAero Corp.; Scottsdale, AZ
1. About StandardAero; accessed 3/18/2018
    http://www.standardaero.com/AboutUs.aspx

StanfordDaily *(Periodical)*   *Stanford Daily*
Stanford Daily; Stanford, CA

1. Airmen Thrill Chicago Crowd—600 Planes Participate as Army Stages Review; May 22, 1931, p. 1, col. 5

Straipsniai *(Online)* **Straipsniai**
Straipsniai.It: Independent and Informative Portal; Vilnius, Lithuania
1. Lithuanian Pilots: Steponas Darius and Stasys Giernas; accessed 10/17/2017 http://old.straipsniai.lt/en/Aviation/page/7729

Strawfoot *(Online)* **The Strawfoot**
The Strawfoot; by Keith Muchowski
1. Remembering Victor Carlstrom's Flight; updated May 26, 2016; accessed 2/17/2018 https://thestrawfoot.com/2016/05/26/remembering-victor-carlstroms-flight/

Stein, 1985 *(Book)*
Flight of the Vin Fiz; E.P. Stein; New York: Arbor House, 1985

Stoff, 2000 *(Book)*
Transatlantic Flight: Picture History, 1873–1939; by Joshua Stoff; Mineola NY: Dover Publications, 2000

SunTimes *(Periodical)* ***Chicago Sun Times***
1. How Pucinski won fight for cockpit recorders; by Steve Neal; September 11, 1998

SunTimesMG, 2018 *(Book)*
Illinois 200: Two Centuries of State History Through the Pages of the Sun Times; Chicago: Sun Times Media Group, 2018

Swanson, et al., 1997 *(Book)*
Chicago Days: 150 Defining Moments in the Life of a Great City; Stevenson Swanson, ed.; Wheaton IL: Cantigny First Division Foundation, 1997

Sweeting, 2015 *(Book)*
United States Army Aviators' Equipment, 1917–1945; Jefferson, N: McFarland & Company, 2015, https://books.google.com/books?id=oi-vBwAAQBAJ&pg=PA126&lpg=PA126&dq=floyd+smith+aerial+equipment&source=bl&ots=ofTssp3UlP&sig=RdhdvcJ_POpxuE38N6zxQiNT2Pg&hl=en&sa=X&ved=0ahUKEwjnzvD3gdrWAhVpxoMKHXksB38Q6AEITDAI#v=onepage&q=floyd%20smith%20aerial%20equipm

T

Tadias *(Online)* **Tadias**
Tadias; by Adam Saunders for the Ethiopian-American community; New York
1. African American Pilot Col. John Robertson (Brown Condor) to be Honored in Ethiopia; updated May 1, 2015; accessed 2/4/2018 http://www.tadias.com/05/01/2015/african-american-pilot-col-john-robinson-the-brown-condor-honored-in-ethiopia/

Tails_Time *(Online)*   **Tails Through Time**
Tails Through Time; blog by J.P. Santiago; Dallas/Fort Worth TX
1. Four-Course Radio Range: Birth of Modern Federal Airway System;
    updated August 5, 2015; accessed 1/18/2018
    http://www.tailsthroughtime.com/2015/08/the-four-course-radio-range-
    birth-of.html

Thelen *(Online)*   **Ed Thelen**
Ed Thelen's Nike Missile Web Site
1. Low-Frequency Radio Ranges; by Tom Johnson; updated June 7, 2010;
    accessed 1/18/2018
    http://ed-thelen.org/TJohnson-LFRDF.html

ThisDayAviation *(Online)*   **This Day in Aviation**
1. De Havilland DH 100 Sea Vampire Mk. 10., 3 December 1945; by Brian R.
    Swopes; updated December 3, 2017; accessed 5/3/2018
    https://www.thisdayinaviation.com/tag/de-havilland-dh-100-sea-vampire-
    mk-10/
2. Louise Thaden Wins Bendix Troply; 4 September 1936; by Brian R.
    Swopes; updated September 4, 2017; accessed 2/13/2018
    https://www.thisdayinaviation.com/3-september-1936/
3. Ruth Law Oliver, 19 November 2016; by Brian R. Swopes; updated Novem-
    ber 19, 2017; accessed 6/26/2018
    https://www.thisdayinaviation.com/tag/ruth-law-oliver/

Thomas, 1927 *(Book)*
European Skyways: The Story of a Tour of Europe by Airplane; by Lowell
Thomas; New York: Houghton Mifflin Co., 1927

Thornton, undated *(Unpublished)*
Barnstorming the Airshows, Etc.; by Roy Thornton; unpublished and undated
manuscript in Geneseo History Museum

Time *(Periodical)*   **Time: The Weekly Newsmagazine**
1. Man of the Year; January 2, 1928, Vol. 11, No. 1, cover

Tribune *(Periodical)*   ***Chicago Tribune***
Chicago Tribune; Chicago: Tribune Publishing
2. 10 Girl Flyers Thrill 20,000 at Aerial Show; August 21, 1939 p. 11
3. 145,000 See Opening of National Air Fair; July 4, 1949, p. 72.
4. 145,000 Watch Thrill Jammed Air Force Show; by Wayne Thomis; July 4,
    1949, p. 3
5. 22 Killed in Midway Crash: Incoming Plane Clips Sign in Fog and Falls;
    July 18, 1955, p. 1
6. 30th anniversary of Chicago's worst winter on record: 1978–1979; by Tom
    Skilling; November 30, 2008
7. 4 Are Killed in Palwaukee Jet Crash; by Dennis O'Brien and Gary Wash-
    burn; October 31, 1996

8. Airport Owner Takes Flight, Progress Moves In; by Steve Kerch; April 16, 1989
9. Airports Wary as Land Takes Off; by David Ibata; July 16, 1993
10. Army parachutist dies after Chicago Air & Water Show accident; by Patrick M. O'Connell, Deanese Williams-Harris, Dawn Rhodes; August 17, 2015
11. Aviator Janet Harmon Bragg, 86; by Paul Sloan; April 4, 1993
12. Aviation Notes; June 27, 1929, p. 15
13. Aviator's Wife Tries Suicide; June 28, 1913, p. 3
14. Beatles Invade Chicago; by Stephan Benzkofer; July 31, 2011
15. Chicago taps Elon Musks The Borning Company to build high-speed transit tunnels that would tie Loop with O'Hare; by Bill Ruthheart & John Byrnel; June 14, 2018
16. Chicago Team Entered in Air Race in Britain; by Wayne Thomas; November 29, 1969, sect. 1b, p. 18 col. 8
17. Chicago Will Be Assured of Aeroplane Races: Glenn H. Curtiss Meet Will Be Held at Hawthorne Park July 2,3,4; June 18, 1910, p. 7, col. 5
18. Cockpit crusader Pucinski honored; by Jon Hilkevitch; December 19, 1998
19. Copter Line Is Purchased by Syndicate; April 30, 1955, Business Sect. p. 5
20. David Young & Henry Wood: Military jet crashes near suburb; March 20, 1982, p. 1
21. Death Leap Seen by 75,000; July 5, 1933, p. 1
22. Dedicate Sky Harbor, Airport De Luxe; July 27, 1929, p. 15 col. 3
23. Disclose Sale of Pal-Waukee Port to Lesee; March 17, 1946
24. Early Years at Chicago's Midway Airport; May 31, 2013
25. Field's to Sell Light Planes, It's Announced; June 18, 1945, p. 15
26. Find Copter Lost Rotor, Fell Apart; by Wayne Thomas; July 29, 1960, p. 1–2, col. 1
27. Flashback: How Midway Airport took off; by Ron Grossman; December 17, 2017, p. 21
28. Gary/Chicago International Airport sputtered for decades, now poised for growth; by Carole Carlson; June 19, 2015
29. H.N. Atwood Flies into Chicago from St. Louis; August 15, 1911 p. 1 col. 7, Vol. 70, No. 194M.
30. Hugh Sexton, 120,000 Fans Thrill to Air Race Spectacle; July 5, 1933, p. 1
31. In the 1950s, 2 horrific Midway crashes stunned Chicago; by Stephan Benzkofer; December 9, 2012
32. Inflating the Captive Balloon; June 7, 1893 p. 3;
33. John A. Casey Once Airports Manager, Dies; May 11, 1969, sect. 4, p, 22 col. 3
34. John Dacy 1915–2007: Avid Flier Founded His Own Airport; Megan Graydon; May 18, 2007
35. Just Plane Folks: The Dacy Family Is at Home in the Air; by Steve Stanek; October 10, 1999.
36. Last Words to O'Hare: 'No Control'; by Wayne Thomis; September 18, 1961, p. 1
37. Litigation ends in 1996 Palwaukee Municipal Airport crash that killed 4 people; by Jeff Long; September 4, 2003

38. Little Airport That Could; by Ted Saylor; January 8, 1997
39. Looking Back at an Aviation Pioneer's Hall-of-Fame Career; by Jim Mueller; September 3, 2000
40. Lost the Balloon: Wind Wrecks the Captive Airship at Jackson Park; July 10, 1893, p.1
41. Max Lillie Killed by Fall; September 16, 1913, p 5
42. Mayor Favors Use of Copters as Taxi Service; June 21, 1955, p. 22
43. McCormick Flies in New Airboat; July 28, 1913, p.2
44. Meigs, the Man Who Loved to Fly; by Charles Leroux; October 20, 1996
45. Men Who Fly Helicopter Air Mail in Chicago; by Wayne Thomis; July 12, 1951, p. 3 col. 2
46. Midway Field Crews Fight Mire and Water; July 14, 1957, p. 1–2
47. Moody Puts Aviation on a Religious Plane; by Steve Kloehn; July 28, 1997
48. N.U. Professor Named to Head US Air Bureau; March 2, 1937
49. Noted Harlem Airport Will Close Today; by Wayne Thomis; September 1, 1956, p. 14
50. Owen B. Jones, Society Aviator, Sued by Wife; May 20, 1930, p. 2
51. Owen Barton Jones Is Recovering from Plane Crash Injuries; March 29, 1928, p. 27 col. 1
52. People in Jam Cry 'SOS' for an 'Eggbeater'; November 30, 1952, part 3
53. Pioneer Pilot Sally Strempel; by Kenan Heise; October 7, 1987
54. Planes to Bring Cargo from Detroit; April 4, 1925
55. Queen Elizabeth II's 14-hour visit to Chicago: Hour by Hour; September 9, 2015
56. Ruth Cavell Van Etten Osgood; March 25, 2012
57. Speed Holman Killed in Stunt at Air Races; May 17, 1931, p. 1, col. 7
58. State acquires Will County airfield in step toward new large airport; by Jon Hilkevitch; July 1, 2014
59. Story of the Dedication of O'Hare International Airport: The Story Behind the Pictures; March 14, 2013
60. United completes HQ move into Willis Tower; by Gregory; Karp; July 23, 2013
61. Wright airplane replication plane takes off; by Ted Gregory; June 18, 2002

Trimble *(Book)*
Admiral William A. Moffett: Architect of Naval Aviation; by William F. Beck; Annapolis MD: Naval Institute Press, 2007

Tucker, 2012 *(Book)*
Father of the Tuskegee Airmen, John C. Robinson; by Philip Thomas Tucker; Dulles VA: Potomac Books, 2012

U

UAL *(Online)*   **United Airlines**
1. Star Alliance Air Travel Rewards; accessed 8/14/2017
   https://www.united.com/web/en-US/content/mileageplus/awards/travel/starairawards.aspx

UCLA_LawTech *(Periodical)*   ***UCLA Journal of Law and Technology***
UCLA Journal of Law and Technology;- Los Angeles
  1. Progress in the Aircraft Industry and the Role of Patent Pools; by Dustin Szakalski, Spring 2011, Vol. 15; accessed 4/18/2017 http://www.lawtechjournal.com/articles/2011/01_110402_szakalski.pdf

UPI *(Online)*   **UPI Archive**
  1. Lindbergh's Historic Flight Commemorated; updated May 21, 1987; accessed 2/13/2018 https://www.upi.com/Archives/1987/05/21/Lindberghs-historic-flight-commemorated/6458548568000/

US_Air_Services *(Periodical)*   ***U.S. Air Services***
U.S. Air Services; Air Service Publishing Co., Washington DC
  1. Parker Cramer; September 1931, p. 37.

USAFMuseum *(Online)*   **National Museum of U.S. Air Force**
  1. First Air-to-Air Refueling; accessed 5/28/2018 http://www.nationalmuseum.af.mil/Visit/Museum-Exhibits/Fact-Sheets/Display/Article/197385/first-air-to-air-refueling/

USAF_Units *(Online)*   **USAF Unit History**
USAF Unit History.- USAF Orders of Battle
  1. 108th Air Refueling Squadron; accessed 9/30/2017 http://usafunithistory.com/PDF/0100/101-124/108%20AIR%20REFUELING%20SQ.pdf

USA_Today *(Periodical)*   ***USA Today***
  1. DOT hits United with record fine for long tarmac delays; by Bart Jansen; October 25, 2013.
  2. Timeline of United Airlines' Bankruptcy; by Associated Press; February 1, 2006; accessed 10/4/2017 https://usatoday30.usatoday.com/travel/flights/2006-02-01-united-timeline_x.htm

V

Vil_Maches *(Online)*   **Village of Machesney Park**
  1. Machesney "Rockford" Airport; accessed 10/1/2017 http://machesneypark.org/home/about-us/machesney-rockford-airport/

Vil_Schaumburg *(Online)*   **Village of Schaumburg**
  1. Airport—Airport History; accessed 1/28/2018 http://www.villageofschaumburg.com/depts/transport/airport/default.htm

VintageAir *(Online)*   **Vintage Air Photos**
  1. Tin Goose for Grey Goose; by Alan Radecki; updated January 29, 2015; accessed 8/25/2017 http://vintageairphotos.blogspot.com/2015/01/tin-goose-for-gray-goose.html

VintageAirplane *(Periodical)*   ***Vintage Airplane***
Vintage Airplane; EAA Antiques/Classics Div.; Hales Corners WI
1. Greater Rockford; by Henry G. Frautschy; April 1997, Vol. 25, No. 4
2. Howard Story—Part 1; by Nick Rezich; June 1974 p. 10–14: Vol. 2, No. 6
3. Howard Story—Part 2; by Nick Rezich; July 1974, cover, p. 4–12: Vol. 6, No. 7
4. Silver Eagle: Biography of E.M. "Matty" Laird (part 1); by Robert G. Elliott and Ed Escailon; July, 1976, p. 15–22, Vol. 4, No. 7
5. Silver Eagle: Biography of E.M. "Matty" Laird (part 2); by Robert G. Elliott and Ed Escailon; August 1976: Vol. 4, No. 8
6. Uptown Swallow; by Edward D. Williams; June 1976, Vol. 4, No. 6

VoughtOrg *(Online)*   **Vought Heritage**
1. Chance Milton Vought—Founder; accessed 10/10/2017
   http://www.vought.org/peoplaces/html/bcmv.html
2. McCormick-Romme Cycloplane—Umbrella Plane; accessed 5/7/2017
   http://www.vought.org/products/html/romme.html

W

Waco_Trib_Herald *(Periodical)*   ***Waco Tribune Herald***
Waco Tribune Herald; Waco TX
1. Pioneer aviators trained WWI pilots at Rich Field; Terri Jo Ryan; January 1, 2009

Wallis, 1990 *(Book)*
Route 66: The Mother Road; by Michael Wallis; New York: St. Martin's Press, 1990

WarbirdAlley *(Online)*   **Warbird Alley**
1. Octave Chanute Aerospace Museum: A Final Look; updated September 2015; accessed 9/30/2017
   http://www.warbirdalley.com/articles/chanute.htm

WarbirdReg *(Online)*   **Warbird Registry**
1. B-25 Mitchell / 44-30737; accessed 6/18/2018
   http://www.warbirdregistry.org/b25registry/b25-4430737.html

Watters, 1951 *(Book)*
Illinois in the Second World War Vol. I: Operation Home Front; Springfield: Illinois State Historical Library, 1951

Watters, 1952 *(Book)*
Illinois in the Second World War Vol. II: The Production Front; Springfield: Illinois State Historical Library, 1952

Waymarking *(Online)*   **Waymarking**
1. Battle of Midway—50 Years; updated June 15, 2011; accessed 6/11/2018
   http://www.waymarking.com/waymarks/WMBR5R_Battle_of_Midway_50_Years_Chicago_IL

WBEZ *(Online)*   **WBEZ 91.5 Chicago**
1. Long List of Illinois politicians convicted of corruption; by Associated Press; updated December 7, 2011; accessed 3/9/2018
    https://www.wbez.org/shows/wbez-blogs/long-list-of-illinois-politicians-convicted-for-corruption/86da77fb-c3e4-4d08-adb2-f1c42110afe8

Wheeling_Herald *(Periodical)*   *Wheeling Herald*
Wheeling Herald; Paddock Publications
1. Jet Landings May Be Softer—Guidance Systems May Help Reduce Noise; December 13, 1968, p. 1 col. 1
2. Set Pal-Waukee Dedication—6 Story Tower is Under FAA; May 5, 1967, p. 1, col. 1

WHF *(Online)*   **Warbird Heritage Foundation**
Warbird Heritage Foundation; Waukegan IL
1. Foundation Staff; accessed 8/15/2017
    http://warbirdheritagefoundation.org/WHF_1150_0000_Staff.html
2. Warbird Heritage Foundation; updated August 3, 2017; accessed 8/15/2017
    http://warbirdheritagefoundation.org/index.php

WhirlyGirls *(Online)*   **Whirly Girls**
1. Whirly Girls History; accessed 4/29/2017
    https://www.whirlygirls.org/history/

WhitesideCtyAirp *(Online)*   **Whiteside County Airport**
Whiteside County Airport
1. Hall of Fame; accessed 10/12/2017
    https://www.whitesidecountyairport.org/hall-of-fame
2. History of the Whiteside County Airport; accessed 11/12/2017
    https://www.whitesidecountyairport.org/history

Wikipedia *(Online)*   **English Wikipedia**
1. 108th Air Refueling Squadron; accessed 7/31/2017.
    https://en.wikipedia.org/wiki/108th_Air_Refueling_Squadron
2. 1906 World Series; accessed 8/24/2017
    https://en.wikipedia.org/wiki/1906_World_Series
3. 1933 United Airlines Boeing 247 mid-air explosion; accessed 12/28/2017
    https://en.wikipedia.org/wiki/1933_United_Airlines_Boeing_247_mid-air_explosion
4. 1945 Japan-Washington Flight; accessed 10/14/2017
    https://en.wikipedia.org/wiki/1945_Japan%E2%80%93Washington_flight
5. 1956 Grand Canyon mid-air collision; accessed 7/6/2017
    https://en.wikipedia.org/wiki/1956_Grand_Canyon_mid-air_collision
6. 1960 U-2 incident; accessed 7/15/2017
    https://en.wikipedia.org/wiki/1960_U-2_incident
7. 1967 Chicago Blizzard; accessed 4/3/2017
    https://en.wikipedia.org/wiki/1967_Chicago_blizzard
8. 1968 Special Olympics Summer World Games; accessed 4/6/2018.
    https://en.wikipedia.org/wiki/1968_Special_Olympics_Summer_World_Games

9. 1972 Chicago-O'Hare runway collision; accessed 7/12/2017
   https://en.wikipedia.org/wiki/1972_Chicago%E2%80%93O%27Hare_
   runway_collision
10. 1979 Chicago Blizzard; accessed 4/3/2017
   https://en.wikipedia.org/wiki/1979_Chicago_blizzard
11. 8-track tape; accessed 2/17/2018
   https://en.wikipedia.org/wiki/8-track_tape
12. Accidents and incidents involving the Consolidated B-24 Liberator;
   accessed 7/13/2017
   https://en.wikipedia.org/wiki/Accidents_and_incidents_involving_the_
   Consolidated_B-24_Liberator
13. Aero Club of America; accessed 6/2/2018
   https://en.wikipedia.org/wiki/Aero_Club_of_America
14. Air France Flight 4590; accessed 4/28/2017
   https://en.wikipedia.org/wiki/Air_France_Flight_4590
15. Air Illinois; accessed 4/22/2017.
   https://en.wikipedia.org/wiki/Air_Illinois
16. Air Mail Scandal; accessed 2/19/2018
   https://en.wikipedia.org/wiki/Air_Mail_scandal
17. Airbus A300; accessed 5/9/2018
   https://en.wikipedia.org/wiki/Airbus_A300
18. Airco DH-4; accessed 4/11/2017
   https://en.wikipedia.org/wiki/Airco_DH.4
19. Airline Deregulation Act
   https://en.wikipedia.org/wiki/Airline_Deregulation_Act
20. Allan Lockheed; access 4/11/2017
   https://en.wikipedia.org/wiki/Allan_Lockheed
21. Alaska; accessed 8/26/2018
   https://en.wikipedia.org/wiki/Alaska
22. Amelia Earhart; accessed 4/28/2018
   https://en.wikipedia.org/wiki/Amelia_Earhart
23. American Airlines Flight 191; accessed 7/13/2017
   https://en.wikipedia.org/wiki/American_Airlines_Flight_191
24. American Eagle A-129; accessed 7/15/2018
   https://en.wikipedia.org/wiki/American_Eagle_A-129
25. American Eagle Flight 4184; accessed 7/12/2017
   https://en.wikipedia.org/wiki/American_Eagle_Flight_4184
26. Ann Pellegreno; accessed 4/10/2017
   https://en.wikipedia.org/wiki/Ann_Pellegreno
27. Archie League; accessed 4/28/2017
   https://en.wikipedia.org/wiki/Archie_League
28. Aviation Transportation and Security Act; accessed 6/19/2018
   https://en.wikipedia.org/wiki/Aviation_and_Transportation_Security_Act
29. Avro Vulcan; accessed 7/19/2017
   https://en.wikipedia.org/wiki/Avro_Vulcan

30. Ben Howard (aviator); accessed 5/21/2017
https://en.wikipedia.org/wiki/Ben_Howard_(aviator)
31. Bendix Trophy; accessed 2/13/2018
https://en.wikipedia.org/wiki/Bendix_Trophy
32. Berlin Blockade; accessed 5/19/2017
https://en.wikipedia.org/wiki/Berlin_Blockade
33. Bessie Raiche; accessed 4/1/2017
https://en.wikipedia.org/wiki/Bessie_Raiche
34. Bill Lear; accessed 5/20/2017
https://en.wikipedia.org/wiki/Bill_Lear
35. Billy Robinson (aviator); accessed 11/8/2017
https://en.wikipedia.org/wiki/Billy_Robinson_(aviator)
36. Blanche Scott; accessed 5/17/2018
https://en.wikipedia.org/wiki/Blanche_Scott
37. Boeing 247; accessed 7/22/2017
https://en.wikipedia.org/wiki/Boeing_247
38. Bombing of Guernica; accessed 6/10/2018
https://en.wikipedia.org/wiki/Bombing_of_Guernica
39. C.R. Smith; accessed 6/6/2017
https://en.wikipedia.org/wiki/C._R._Smith
40. Capital Airlines; accessed 8/2/2017
https://en.wikipedia.org/wiki/Capital_Airlines
41. Carl Sandburg; accessed 4/28/2018
https://en.wikipedia.org/wiki/Carl_Sandburg
42. Century of Progress Architectural District; accessed 12/28/2017
https://en.wikipedia.org/wiki/Century_of_Progress_Architectural_District
43. Cessna 172; accessed 4/27/2017
https://en.wikipedia.org/wiki/Cessna_172
44. Chanute Air Force Base; accessed 5/5/2017
https://en.wikipedia.org/wiki/Chanute_Air_Force_Base
45. Charles W. "Speed" Holman; accessed 2/10/2018
https://en.wikipedia.org/wiki/Charles_W._%22Speed%22_Holman
46. Chicago and Southern Air Lines; accessed 8/2/2017
https://en.wikipedia.org/wiki/Chicago_and_Southern_Air_Lines
47. Chicago Rockford International Airport; accessed 10/20/2017
https://en.wikipedia.org/wiki/Chicago_Rockford_International_Airport
48. Clow International Airport; accessed 7/21/2017
https://en.wikipedia.org/wiki/Bolingbrook%27s_Clow_International_Airport
49. Curtiss T-32 Condor II; accessed 4/23/2018
https://en.wikipedia.org/wiki/Curtiss_T-32_Condor_II
50. Curtiss-Wright; accessed 5/14/2017
https://en.wikipedia.org/wiki/Curtiss-Wright
51. Douglas DC-2; accessed 3/4/2018
https://en.wikipedia.org/wiki/Douglas_DC-2
52. Douglas World Cruisers; accessed 5/29/2018
https://en.wikipedia.org/wiki/Douglas_World_Cruiser

53. Economy Class; accessed 4/18/2017
https://en.wikipedia.org/wiki/Economy_class
54. Edward O'Hare; accessed 6/12/2018
https://en.wikipedia.org/wiki/Edward_O%27Hare
55. E.M. Laird Airplane Company; accessed 6/22/2017
https://en.wikipedia.org/wiki/E._M._Laird_Airplane_Company
56. Eighteenth Amendment to the United States Constitution; accessed 9/17/2017
https://en.wikipedia.org/wiki/Eighteenth_Amendment_to_the_United_States_Constitution
57. Farnum Fish; accessed 5/16/2017
https://en.wikipedia.org/wiki/Farnum_Fish
58. First Inauguration of Barack Obama; accessed 11/29/2017
https://en.wikipedia.org/wiki/First_inauguration_of_Barack_Obama
59. Ford Air Transport Service; accessed 5/15/2017
https://en.wikipedia.org/wiki/Ford_Air_Transport_Service
60. Frank Lloyd Wright; accessed 8/22/2017
https://en.wikipedia.org/wiki/Frank_Lloyd_Wright
61. Frank Tallman; accessed 4/13/2017
https://en.wikipedia.org/wiki/Frank_Tallman
62. Frasca Field; accessed 10/15/2017
https://en.wikipedia.org/wiki/Frasca_Field
63. Frasca International; accessed 10/15/2017
https://en.wikipedia.org/wiki/Frasca_International
64. Gordon Bennett Cup—Ballooning; accessed 4/10/2017
https://en.wikipedia.org/wiki/Gordon_Bennett_Cup_(ballooning)
65. Gordon Bennett Trophy (Aeroplanes); accessed 4/25/2017
https://en.wikipedia.org/wiki/Gordon_Bennett_Trophy_(aeroplanes)
66. Gulf of Tonkin Resolution; accessed 7/15/2017
https://en.wikipedia.org/wiki/Gulf_of_Tonkin_Resolution
67. Harriet Quimby; accessed 5/15/2018
https://en.wikipedia.org/wiki/Harriet_Quimby
68. Harry Atwood; accessed 7/10/2017
https://en.wikipedia.org/wiki/Harry_Atwood
69. Helen Richey; accessed 6/18/2018
https://en.wikipedia.org/wiki/Helen_Richey
70. Hilton Chicago; accessed 10/15/2017
https://en.wikipedia.org/wiki/Hilton_Chicago
71. History of United Airlines; accessed 10/4/2017
https://en.wikipedia.org/wiki/History_of_United_Airlines
72. Howard Aircraft Corporation; accessed 5/31/2017
https://en.wikipedia.org/wiki/Howard_Aircraft_Corporation
73. IBM 9020; accessed 4/22/2017
https://en.wikipedia.org/wiki/IBM_9020
74. Interstate 90 in Illinois; accessed 10/2/2017
https://en.wikipedia.org/wiki/Interstate_90_in_Illinois

75. Interstate TDR; accessed 2/25/2018
https://en.wikipedia.org/wiki/Interstate_TDR
76. James Gordon Bennett Jr. accessed 8/3/2018
https://en.wikipedia.org/wiki/James_Gordon_Bennett_Jr.
77. Jane's All the Worlds Aircraft; accessed 4/11/2017
https://en.wikipedia.org/wiki/Jane%27s_All_the_World%27s_Aircraft
78. John Robinson; accessed 4/5/2017
https://en.wikipedia.org/wiki/John_Robinson_(aviator)
79. Kankakee Airport; accessed 11/23/2017
https://en.wikipedia.org/wiki/Kankakee_Airport
80. Land Speed Record; accessed 4/25/2017
https://en.wikipedia.org/wiki/Land_speed_record#1898.E2.80.931965_.28wheel-driven.29
81. Lansing Municipal Airport; accessed 5/31/2018
https://en.wikipedia.org/wiki/Lansing_Municipal_Airport
82. Lituanica; accessed 10/17/2017
https://en.wikipedia.org/wiki/Lituanica
83. Long-Count Fight; accessed 7/7/2017
https://en.wikipedia.org/wiki/The_Long_Count_Fight
84. Marjorie Stinson; accessed 2/24/2018
https://en.wikipedia.org/wiki/Marjorie_Stinson
85. Marlon Green; accessed 4/16/2017
https://en.wikipedia.org/wiki/Marlon_Green
86. Marshall Fields; accessed 12/20/2017
https://en.wikipedia.org/wiki/Marshall_Field%27s
87. Mercury-Atlas 6; accessed 5/7/2018
https://en.wikipedia.org/wiki/Mercury-Atlas_6
88. Midway Airlines (1976–1991); accessed 8/8/2017
https://en.wikipedia.org/wiki/Midway_Airlines_(1976%E2%80%931991)
89. Midway International Airport; accessed 8/1/2017
https://en.wikipedia.org/wiki/Midway_International_Airport
90. Midway Airlines (1993–2003); accessed 8/8/2017
https://en.wikipedia.org/wiki/Midway_Airlines_(1993%E2%80%932003)
91. Millennium Park; accessed 12/18/2017
https://en.wikipedia.org/wiki/Millennium_Park
92. Montgolfier Brothers; accessed 4/3/2017
https://en.wikipedia.org/wiki/Montgolfier_brothers
93. National Air Transport; accessed 5/16/2017.
https://en.wikipedia.org/wiki/National_Air_Transport
94. Naval Air Station Glenview; accessed 11/25/2017
https://en.wikipedia.org/wiki/Naval_Air_Station_Glenview
95. Norman Prince; accessed 4/4/2017
https://en.wikipedia.org/wiki/Norman_Prince
96. North American Free Trade Agreement; accessed 11/29/2017
https://en.wikipedia.org/wiki/North_American_Free_Trade_Agreement

97. North Central Airlines Flight 458; accessed 7/12/2017
https://en.wikipedia.org/wiki/North_Central_Airlines_Flight_458
98. Northwest Orient Flight 710; accessed 7/12/2017
https://en.wikipedia.org/wiki/Northwest_Orient_Airlines_Flight_710
99. Oakley G Kelly; accessed 04/28/2017
https://en.wikipedia.org/wiki/Oakley_G._Kelly
100. Orange Line (CTA); accessed 11/29/2017
https://en.wikipedia.org/wiki/Orange_Line_(CTA)
101. Phoebe Omlie; accessed 1/26/2018
https://en.wikipedia.org/wiki/Phoebe_Omlie
102. Piper Aircraft; accessed 6/2/2018
https://en.wikipedia.org/wiki/Piper_Aircraft
103. Piper J-3 Cub; accessed 6/3/2018
https://en.wikipedia.org/wiki/Piper_J-3_Cub
104. Professional Air Traffic Controllers Organization (1968); accessed 8/14/2017
https://en.wikipedia.org/wiki/Professional_Air_Traffic_Controllers_
Organization_(1968)
105. Quad City International Airport; accessed 10/29/2017
https://en.wikipedia.org/wiki/Quad_City_International_Airport
106. Reed G. Landis; accessed 2/16/2018
https://en.wikipedia.org/wiki/Reed_G._Landis
107. Richard J. Daley; accessed 3/22/2018
https://en.wikipedia.org/wiki/Richard_J._Daley
108. Richard M. Daley; accessed 3/22/2018
https://en.wikipedia.org/wiki/Richard_M._Daley
109. Riverview Park (Chicago); accessed 4/22/2017
https://en.wikipedia.org/wiki/Riverview_Park_(Chicago)
110. Roman Pucinski; accessed 3/23/2018
https://en.wikipedia.org/wiki/Roman_Pucinski
111. Schaumburg Regional Airport; accessed 1/27/2018
https://en.wikipedia.org/wiki/Schaumburg_Regional_Airport
112. Schneider Trophy; accessed 4/27/2017
https://en.wikipedia.org/wiki/Schneider_Trophy
113. Sikorsky—Ilya Muromets; accessed 4/2/2017
https://en.wikipedia.org/wiki/Sikorsky_Ilya_Muromets
114. Southwest Airlines Flight 1248; accessed 7/13/2017;
https://en.wikipedia.org/wiki/Southwest_Airlines_Flight_1248
115. Special Olympics; accessed 6/19/2018
https://en.wikipedia.org/wiki/Special_Olympics
116. Standard Aero Corporation (c. 1911); accessed 3/18/2018
https://en.wikipedia.org/wiki/Standard_Aero_Corporation_(c.1911)
117. Steve Fossett; accessed 10/3/2017.
https://en.wikipedia.org/wiki/Steve_Fossett
118. Stout Air Services; accessed 5/3/2017
https://en.wikipedia.org/wiki/Stout_Air_Services

119. Taylor Cub; accessed 4/20/2018
https://en.wikipedia.org/wiki/Taylor_Cub
120. Taylor J-2; accessed 4/20/2018
https://en.wikipedia.org/wiki/Taylor_J-2
121. Thatch Weave; accessed 7/21/2017
https://en.wikipedia.org/wiki/Thach_Weave
122. The Day the Music Died; accessed 7/7/2017
https://en.wikipedia.org/wiki/The_Day_the_Music_Died
123. Thompson Trophy; accessed 5/15/2017
https://en.wikipedia.org/wiki/Thompson_Trophy
124. Tiny Broadwick; accessed 5/13/2017
https://en.wikipedia.org/wiki/Tiny_Broadwick
125. Transportation Security Administration; accessed 6/19/2018
https://en.wikipedia.org/wiki/Transportation_Security_Administration
126. Union Stock Yards; accessed 5/7/2017
https://en.wikipedia.org/wiki/Union_Stock_Yards
127. United Aircraft and Transport Corporation; accessed 8/26/2017
https://en.wikipedia.org/wiki/United_Aircraft_and_Transport_Corporation
128. United Airlines Flight 553; accessed 7/12/2017
https://en.wikipedia.org/wiki/United_Airlines_Flight_553
129. United States Budget Sequestration in 2013; accessed 5/5/2017
https://en.wikipedia.org/wiki/United_States_budget_sequestration_
in_2013
130. V-1 Flying Bomb; accessed 5/19/2017
https://en.wikipedia.org/wiki/V-1_flying_bomb
131. Variable-Sweep Wing; accessed 4/28/2017
https://en.wikipedia.org/wiki/Variable-sweep_wing
132. Volstead Act; accessed 9/17/2017
https://en.wikipedia.org/wiki/Volstead_Act
133. Walter Brookins; accessed 8/20/2017
https://en.wikipedia.org/wiki/Walter_Brookins
134. Waukegan National Airport; accessed 1/28/2018
https://en.wikipedia.org/wiki/Waukegan_National_Airport
135. Wiley Post; 4/12/2017
https://en.wikipedia.org/wiki/Wiley_Post
136. Wilfred Yackey; accessed 5/10/2017.
https://en.wikipedia.org/wiki/Wilfred_Yackey
137. Willa Brown; accessed 1/31/2018
https://en.wikipedia.org/wiki/Willa_Brown
138. William Bushnell Stout; accessed 4/18/2017
https://en.wikipedia.org/wiki/William_Bushnell_Stout
139. Willis Tower; accessed 5/7/2017
https://en.wikipedia.org/wiki/Willis_Tower
140. World War I; accessed 8/24/2017
https://en.wikipedia.org/wiki/World_War_I

Wikisource *(Online)*   **Wikisource**
Wikisource; hosted by Wikimedia Foundation
1. Aircraft Accident Report: United Airlines Flight 389 (1967); by NTSB;
    December 19, 1967; accessed 11/23/2017

Wikispaces *(Online)*   **Wikispaces**
1. Elmhurst Airport; by Maggie K; accessed 12/07/2017
    https://elmhurst.wikispaces.com/%E2%80%A2Elmhurst++Airport

Winchester, 2013 *(Book)*
Chronology of Aviation: The Ultimate History of a Century of Powered Flight;
Jim Winchester, New York: Metro Books, 2013

Woman_Pilot *(Periodical)*   ***Woman Pilot***
Woman Pilot; Aviatrix Publishing, Lake Forest, IL
1. Aviation Pioneer Phoebie Fairgrave Omlie; by Janet Sherman; updated
    March 29, 2008; accessed 1/26/2018
    http://womanpilot.co;m/?p=13

WorldHist *(Online)*   **World History Biz**
1. Helicopter Air Services (HAS): United States (1949–1956); updated May 23,
    2015; accessed 7/25/2017
    http://www.worldhistory.biz/contemporary-history/72657-helicopter-
    air-services-has-united-states-1949-1956.html

WrightBrosOrg *(Online)*   **Wright Brothers Org**
Tale of Vin Fiz; Wright Brothers Aeroplane Co. virtual museum; accessed
3/26/2018
http://www.wright-brothers.org/History_Wing/History_of_the_Airplane/
Doers_and_Dreamers/Cal_Rodgers/Tale_of_Vin_Fiz/Tale_of_Vin_Fiz.htm

WrightBrosUSA *(Online)*   **Wright Brothers USA**
Wright Brothers' Historical Timeline; Wright Brothers USA; accessed 8/10/2017
http://thewrightbrothersusa.com/one-of-worlds-greatest-stories/wright-
brothers-historical-timeline/

WrightCol *(Online)*   **Wright State Univ.—Dayton**
President Taft Presents Medals to Wright Brothers 1909; Lisa Rickey updated
February 16, 2015; Wright State University, Dayton OH; accessed 5/15/2017
https://www.libraries.wright.edu/community/outofthebox/2015/02/16/
president-taft-presents-medals-to-wright-brothers-1909/

Wright_Redux *(Online)*   **Wright Redux**
1. Wright Redux Association; accessed 12/31/2017
    http://chuckclendenin.com/wrightredux/

Wright_Stories *(Online)*   **Wright Stories**
The Wright Stories run by Dr. Richard Stimson
1. Story of the Vin Fiz; accessed 3/25/2018
    http://wrightstories.com/the-story-of-the-vin-fiz/

Y

Yanul *(Online)*   **Thomas Yanul**
1. Lawrence Lewis Aeroplane Co.; accessed 8/10/2017
    http://www.thomasyanul.com/grl.html

Young, 2003 *(Book)*
Chicago Aviation: An Illustrated History; David M. Young; DeKalbIL: Northern
Illinois University Press, 2003

ENDNOTES

How to use these endnotes:
#. (Resource ID as listed in Bibliography) Specific article names and page numbers as applicable

Introduction
1. (Chicagology) "Intro—Chicago's Aviation Pioneers"
2. (Aeronautics, 1929) September 1929, "AD: Continued Leadership after 27 Years of Success"

Pre-1900
3. (Wikipedia, 2017) "Montgolfier Brothers"
4. (Pacyga, 2009) p. 12–13; (BlackPast) "DuSable, Jean Baptiste Point (1745–1818)"
5. (SunTimesMG, 2018) p. 5
6. (Swanson, et al., 1997) p. 9
7. (Grossman, et al., 2004) p. 225 "Chicago Tribune"; (Swanson, et al., 1997) p. 18–19
8. (Grossman, et al., 2004) p. 406–407 "Illinois & Michigan Canal"; (Swanson, et al., 1997) p. 12–13
9. (Miller, 1996) p. 93–95; (Swanson, et al., 1997) p. 14–15
10. (Spenser, 2009) p. 4–11
11. (Scamehorn, 2000) p. 5–8
12. (Miller, 1996) p. 124–126; (SunTimesMG, 2018) p. 7; (Swanson, et al., 1997) p. 20–21
13. (Winchester, 2013) p. 13
14. (Swanson, et al., 1997) p. 28–29
15. (Wikipedia) "Frank Lloyd Wright"
16. (SunTimesMG, 2018) p. 26
17. (Miller, 1996) p. 143–171; (Swanson, et al., 1997) p. 36–39
18. (Miller, 1996) p. 245–246; (Swanson, et al., 1997) p. 40
19. (History) "Haymarket Square Riot"; (Swanson, et al., 1997) p. 48–49
20. (Doherty, 1970) p. 10
21. (SunTimesMG, 2018) p. 31; (Swanson, et al., 1997) p. 56–57
22. (LivHistIL) "A Timeline of Illinois History"
23. (Crouch, 1989) p. 77; (Chanute, 1894); (Chanute, 1894, 1997)
24. (Wikipedia) "Marshall Field's"; (Blackman, 2017) p. 86–87
25. (Swanson, et al., 1997) p. 64–65; (CAF_Mag, 2017)
26. (Miller, 1996) p. 528
27. (Grossman, et al., 2004) p. 898–902, "World's Columbian Exposition"
28. (Tribune, 1893) June 7, 1893 p. 3 "Inflating the Captive Balloon"; (Souter, et al., 2010) p. 17; (Tribune, 1893) July 10, 1893, p. 1, "Lost the Balloon"

29. (Edwards, 2003) p. 10
30. (Swanson, et al., 1997) p. 72
31. (Scamehorn, 2000) p. 22–25; (Crouch, 1989) p. 77, 84; (Swanson, et al., 1997) p. 42–43; (LincBeach, 2013) "1893—The International Conference on Aerial Navigation"; (Disciples_Flight, 2016) June 22, 2016 "Octave Chanute's Contributions Had a Far-Reaching Impact on Aviation"; (NIU-Lib) "Octave Chanute, The Chicago Connection and the Birth of Aviation; (Chanute, 1894), (Chanute, 1894, 1997)
32. (Crouch, 1989) p. 56–60, 149–156
33. (Crouch, 1989) p. 196–199; (FlyMachines) "Octave Alexandre Chanute & Augustus Moore Herring"; (Swanson, et al., 1997) p. 74
34. (Crouch, 1989) p. 162, 164, 166–169; (AirSpace, 2016) Aug. 10, 2016, "Last Words of Otto Lilienthal"
35. (CAF_Mag, 2017)
36. (Blackman, 2017) p. 22–23
37. (Winchester, 2013) p. 15–18
38. (Blackman, 2017) p. 74–75
39. (Winchester, 2013) p. 55–56

1900–1904
40. (Swanson, et al., 1997) p. 76–77; (Grossman, et al., 2004) p. 730, "Sanitary and Ship Canal"
41. (Crouch, 1989) p. 235–238
42. (Howard, 1998) p. 69–73; (LincBeach, 2013) "1900 & 1901—Chanute and Wilbur Wright"
43. (McBriarty, 2013) p. 265–269; (Graf, et al., 2002) p. 93
44. (Young, 2003) p. 11–12
45. (MSStateEdu, 1903) "Patent for 'O & W Flying Machine'"
46. (Crouch, 1989) p. 300–305
47. (LivHistIL) "A Timeline of Illinois History"; (SunTimesMG, 2018) p. 9; (Swanson, et al., 1997) p. 82–83
48. (Wikipedia) "Riverview Park (Chicago)"

1905–1909
49. (Wikipedia) "Aero Club of America"
50. (Howard, 1998) p. 163–170
51. (Daily_Herald, 2018) February 11, 2018, "How the Chicago Defender became a national voice for black Americans"; (Swanson, et al., 1997) p. 84
52. (HomanSq) "Original Sears Tower"; (Blackman, 2017) p. 168; (Mlinaric, 2018) p. 4–5
53. (Blackman, 2017) p. 50
54. (SunTimesMG, 2018) p. 46
55. (MSStateEdu, 1903) "Patent for 'O & W Flying Machine'"
56. (Wikipedia) "1906 World Series"
57. (Spenser, 2009) p. 44–46
58. (Winchester, 2013) p. 32–33
59. (Young, 2003) p. 11–13; (LincBeach, 2013) "Balloons, Airships, Knabenshue & Wild"; (Crouch, 1983) p. 531–534; (Souter, et al., 2010) p. 17
60. (Winchester, 2013) p. 25
61. (WrightBrosUSA) 1907, February 8
62. (Winchester, 2013) p. 31–32

63.   (Inter-Ocean, 1908) February 2, 1908, "Clubs to Meet Here: Local Organization Issues Call for Convention"
64.   (Am_Aeronaut, 1908) January 1908, "Chicago's Aeronautique Meet"; (Am_Aeronaut, 1908) May 1908, "Chicago's Great Meet"
65.   (Young, 2003) p. 11–13; (LincBeach, 2013) "Balloons, Airships, Knabenshue & Wild"; (Crouch, 1983) p. 531–534; (Am_Aeronaut, 1908) May 1908, "Chicago's Great Meet"
66.   (Winchester, 2013) p. 25, 30; (Spenser, 2009) p. 142–147
67.   (WrightBrosUSA) 1909, August 18 and August 19; (CentFlight) "Glenn Curtiss and the Wright Patent Battles"
68.   (Winchester, 2013) p. 25
69.   (Scamehorn, 2000) p. 42–46, 69; (Young, 2003) p. 72
70.   (Aero, 1911) August 5, 1911 "Designs High-Speed Plane"
71.   (Wikipedia) "Jane All the World's Aircraft"
72.   (Aeronautics, 1910) "JW Curzon Starts Aero School"; (Scamehorn, 2000) p. 52, 67; (Aircraft, 1910) September, 1910, p. 261, "General News"; (Kasmar, 1909)
73.   (Young, 2003) p. 63–64; (Lougheed, 1909)
74.   (MNHist, 1995) Winter 1995, "Shooting Star: Aviator Jimmie Ward of Crookston"
75.   (WrightCol, 2015) "President Taft Presents Medals to Wright Brothers 1909"
76.   (WrightBrosUSA) 1909, June 26; (Shulman, 2002) p. 147
77.   (Grossman, et al., 2004) p. 191 "Burnham Plan"; (Swanson, et al., 1997) p. 94–95
78.   (Spenser, 2009) p. 48–49; (Winchester, 2013) p. 33–35
79.   (Spenser, 2009) p. 49–51; (Winchester, 2013) p. 33–35
80.   (Speedway) "Rheims Air Show 1909"; (Winchester, 2013) p. 29, 31; (Wikipedia) "James Gordon Bennett, Jr."
81.   (Hill, 2013) p. 209; (LincBeach, 2013) "1909 & 1910—Glenn H. Curtiss & the Aero Club of Illinois"; (Young, 2003) p. 40–41; (Scamehorn, 2000) p. 50
82.   (Young, 2003) p. 12–13
83.   (Roach, 2014) p. 19
84.   (WrightBrosUSA) 1908, November 30; 1909 May 13 and November 22
85.   (Hill, 2013) p. 210–211, 219–220; (Young, 2003) p. 63, 72, 74–75; (LincBeach, 2013) "1911—Two Great Events"; (Chicagology) "Intro—Chicago's Aviation Pioneers"; (Koontz, 2011) p. 52–58; (EarlyAv) "Rudolph William Schroeder; 1886–1952; (Post, 2000) p. 46

1910–1914

86.   (Almond, 2002) p. 11
87.   (Wikipedia) "Quad City International Airport"; (QCAirport) "History—Quad City International Airport"
88.   (WhitesideCtyAirp) "History of the Whiteside County Airport"
89.   (Aeronautics, 1910) August, 1910, p. 67, "JW Curzon Starts Aero School"; (Scamehorn, 2000) p. 52, 67; (Young, 2003) p. 72; (Aircraft, 1910) October, 1910, p. 261, "General News"; (Kasmar, 1909)
90.   (Scamehorn, 2000) p. 67–68; (AeroHydro, 1913) April 19, 1913, "Somerville Fliers (ad)"
91.   (Winchester, 2013) p. 29
92.   (Scamehorn, 2000) p. 53; (Chicagology) "Part 2—Aero Club of Illinois"
93.   (BournemouthEcho, 2016) October 1, 2016, "Charles Rolls and the tragic Dorset plane crash that ended the aviation pioneer's life"; (Almond, 2002) p. 68–69
94.   (Tribune, 1910) June 18, 1910, p. 7, "Chicago Will Be Assured of Aeroplane Races: Glenn H. Curtiss Meet Will Be Held at Hawthorne Park July 2,3,4"; (LincBeach,

2013) "1909 & 1910—Glenn H. Curtiss & the Aero Club of Illinois"; (Scamehorn, 2000) p. 59, 78–79

95.   (Scamehorn, 2000) p. 59
96.   (Peek, 2003) p. 1–3
97.   (Wikipedia) "Bessica Raiche"; (Scamehorn, 2000) p. 72; (Hill, 2013) p. 218; (Wikipedia) "Blanche Scott"
98.   (Chicagology) "Intro—Chicago's Aviation Pioneers"
99.   (Examiner, 1910) "Brookins Soars Over Loop"; (Edwards, 2003) p. 20; (Chicagology) "1910 Aviation Carnival"; (Chicagology) "Part 3—First Flights Over Chicago"
100.   (Young, 2003) p. 41; (Chicagology) "Part 4—Chicago to Springfield Race"
101.   (EarlyAv) "Walter R. Brookins (1889–1953)"; (Wikipedia) "Walter Brookins"
102.   (LincBeach, 2013) "1909 & 1910—Glenn H. Curtiss & the Aero Club of Illinois"; (Scamehorn, 2000) p. 59, 77–79; (Young, 2003) p. 41–42
103.   (FlightJour, 2015) October 2015 p. 66, "Teddy's Excellent Adventure"
104.   (LOC_Memory) "Octave Chanute and His Photos Of the Wright Experiments at the Kill Devil Hills"
105.   (Howard, 1998) p. 337–345
106.   (Chicagology) "Part 1—Octave Chanute, the Father of Aviation"
107.   (Spenser, 2009) p. 214–215; (Winchester, 2013) p. 32; (Britannica) "Aircraft Carrier"
108.   (AeroHydro, 1913) April 19, 1913, p. 38, "Roster of American Aviation Pilots"
109.   (Chicagology) "1910 Union Stock Yards Fire"
110.   (Peek, 2003) p. 3–4; (Scamehorn, 2000) p. 69; (Young, 2003) p. 72, 126
111.   (Young, 2003) p. 75
112.   (Hill, 2013) p. 210
113.   (Young, 2003) p. 72
114.   (LincBeach, 2013) "1911—Two Great Events"
115.   (Young, 2003) p. 42–45; (Aviation, 1911) September 1911, "Chicago Aviation Meet"; (Lawson, 1932) p. 92–93
116.   (Edwards, 2003) p. 49; (Young, 2003) p. 73–75
117.   (LincBeach, 2013) "1911—Two Great Events"
118.   (Young, 2003) p. 40; (LincBeach, 2013) "Opening Day"
119.   (Scamehorn, 2000) p. 66–67; (EarlyAv) "Billy Robinson 1884–1916"
120.   (Scamehorn, 2000) p. 63–65; (IndHistS, 1998) "Smash Up Kid: Fort Wayne Aviator Art Smith"
121.   (Edwards, 2003) p. 49; (LincBeach, 2013) "Opening Day"; (Chicagology) "Part 2—Aero Club of Illinois"
122.   (LincBeach, 2013) "1911—Two Great Events," "Opening Day"; (Young, 2003) p. 73–75
123.   (LincBeach, 2013) "Legacy"; (Young, 2003) p. 73–75
124.   (Young, 2003) p. 63, 72, 74–75; (MNHist, 1995) "Shooting Star: Aviator Jimmie Ward of Crookston"; (Wikipedia) "Allan Lockheed"
125.   (Aeronautics, 1910) November 1910, "News in General: Incorporations"
126.   (AeroHydro, 1911) August 12, 1911, "New Corporations"
127.   (AeroHydro, 1912); July 13, 1912, p. 351
128.   (Hill, 2013) p. 213, 218; (Wikipedia) "Standard Aero Corporation"; (StandardAero) "About StandardAero"
129.   (Winchester, 2013) p. 31–33; (Scott, 2011) p. 57, 65–66; (Wikipedia) "Harriet Quimby"
130.   (Young, et al., 1981) p. 33

131. (Aero, 1911) August 12, 1911, "Chicago"; (Stein, 1985) p. 133–134; (Aero, 1911) August 5, 2011

132. (Aero, 1911) August 19, 1911, "Making Aero History at Grant Park"; (Scamehorn, 2000) p. 82–83

133. (Aero, 1911) August 5, 1911, "Preparing for Big Meet"; (Aero, 1911) August 12, 1911 "Chicago International Meet Begins Saturday"; (Hill, 2013) p. 210

134. (Young, 2003) p. 42–52

135. (EarlyAv) "Hillary Beachey 1885–1964": (LincBeach, 2013) "1914—Beachy & Royalties"; (LincBeach, 2006) Lincoln Beachey: A Brief Biography"; (Longyard, 1994) p. 18–19; (Aero, 1911) August 19, 1911 "Making Aero History at Grant Park"; (Stein, 1985) p. 140–141

136. (Souter, et al., 2010) p. 20–22; (Tribune, 1913) "Aviator's Wife Tries Suicide"; (MNHist, 1995) Winter 1995, "Shooting Star: Aviator Jimmie Ward of Crookston"

137. (Examiner, 1911) August 15, 1911, "Atwood Soars 286 Miles from St. Louis to Chicago at Speed of Express Train"; (Tribune, 1911) August 15, 1911 "H.N. Atwood Flies into Chicago from St. Louis"

138. (Wikipedia) "Harry Atwood"

139. (Young, 2003) p. 46–51

140. (Aero, 1911) August 26, 1911, "Greatest Meet Ever Held Ends Happily"

141. (Aero, 1911) August 26, 1911, "Greatest Meet Ever Held Ends Happily"; (Scamehorn, 2000) p. 81–83; (Young, 2003) p. 47–50; (EarlyAv) "St. Croix Johnstone 1893–1911"

142. (Aero, 1911) August 26, 1911, "Greatest Meet Ever Held Ends Happily"; (AeroHydro, 1912) November 9, 1912 "Flies Nearly Four Hours With Passenger"

143. (Aero, 1911) August 26, 1911, "Greatest Meet Ever Held Ends Happily"; (AeroHydro, 1912) November 9, 1912 "Flies Nearly Four Hours With Passenger"

144. (Aero, 1911) August 26, 1911, "Greatest Meet Ever Held Ends Happily"; (Souter, et al., 2010) p. 27

145. (Aero, 1911) August 26, 1911, "Greatest Meet Ever Held Ends Happily"

146. (LincBeach, 2013) "Opening Day"; (Young, 2003) p. 58–59; (LincBeach, 2013) "1911—Two Great Events"

147. (Young, 2003) p. 62

148. (LincBeach, 2013) "Opening Day"; (Young, 2003) p. 58–59; (LincBeach, 2013) "1911—Two Great Events"

149. (LincBeach, 2013) "Opening Day"

150. (Scamehorn, 2000) p. 93–94

151. (Stein, 1985) p. 174–176; (Wright_Stories) "Story of the Vin Fiz"; (WrightBrosOrg) "Tale of Vin Fiz"; (Wikipedia) "Vin Fiz Flyer"

152. (Winchester, 2013) p. 31

153. (Almond, 2002) p. 86

154. (Wikipedia) "Bessica Raiche"

155. (Wikipedia) "William Bushnell Stout"

156. (Coachbuilt, 2014) "Bill Stout—William Bushnell Stout"

157. (EarlyAV) "Charles Dickinson 1858–1935"

158. (LincBeach, 2013) "Opening Day"

159. (Peek, 2003) p. 3–4; (Scamehorn, 2000) p. 69; (Young, 2003) p. 72, 126

160. (Winchester, 2013) p. 33

161. (AMAHist, 2017)

162. (AMAHist, 2017); (Young, 2003) p. 81; (Coachbuilt, 2014) "Bill Stout—William Bushnell Stout"

163. (EarlyAV) "Charles Dickinson 1858–1935"

164. (Scamehorn, 2000) p. 145–146; (Koontz, 2011) p. 59–62; (AMAHist, 2017); (Young, 2003) p. 81; (Coachbuilt, 2014) "Bill Stout—William Bushnell Stout"

165. (Scamehorn, 2000) p. 70; (Edwards, 2009) p. 49–50; (Young, 2003) p. 56–57; (EarlyAv) "Max Lillie"

166. (Winchester, 2013) p. 31–33; (Wikipedia) "Harriet Quimby"

167. (LincBeach, 2013) "1912—Busy, Exciting, Disappointing and Deadly"

168. (Chicagology) "Part 2—Aero Club of Illinois"

169. (LincBeach, 2013) "1912–Busy, Exciting, Disappointing and Deadly"; (Scamehorn, 2000) p. 72, 95–96; (Wikipedia) "Farnum Fish"

170. (Winchester, 2013) p. 33

171. (LincBeach, 2013) "1912–Busy, Exciting, Disappointing & Deadly"

172. (Young, 2003) p. 105; (LincBeach, 2013) "1912–Busy, Exciting, Disappointing & Deadly"

173. (Monash) "Chauncy (Chance) Milton Vought"; (Scamehorn, 2000) p. 70; (VoughtOrg) "Chance Milton Vought—Founder"; (LincBeach, 2013) "1912–Busy, Exciting, Disappointing & Deadly"; (VoughtOrg) "McCormick-Romme Cycloplane—Umbrella Plane"

174. (NASM) "J.W. Smith Collection"; (Aero, 1912) April 6, 1912, "America Now Has Forty Flying Fields"; (LincBeach, 2013) "1912–Busy, Exciting, Disappointing & Deadly"

175. (Aero, 1912) April 6, 1912, "America Now Has Forty Flying Fields"; (LincBeach, 2013) "1912–Busy, Exciting, Disappointing & Deadly"; (AerialAge, 1912) June 1912, "Gay Paddocks for Cicero Field"

176. (Aero, 1912) April 6, 1912, "America Now Has Forty Flying Fields"; (LincBeach, 2013) "1912–Busy, Exciting, Disappointing & Deadly"; (Scamehorn, 2000) p. 54; (PopMech, 1912) September 1912, "Ad: Hillary Beachey flying Brookes Biplane at Chicago with both hands off the controls"

177. (Kinney, 2017) p. 30; (Scamehorn, 2000) p. 54–55

178. (Aero, 1912) April 6, 1912, "America Now Has Forty Flying Fields"; (LincBeach, 2013) "1912–Busy, Exciting, Disappointing & Deadly"

179. (LincBeach, 2013) "1912–Busy, Exciting, Disappointing & Deadly"

180. (LincBeach, 2013) "1912–Busy, Exciting, Disappointing and Deadly" & "Opening Day"; (Aero, 1912) April 6, 1912, "America Now Has Forty Flying Fields"; (AerialAge, 1912) June 1912, "Gay Paddocks for Cicero Field"

181. (Scamehorn, 2000) p. 72; (AeroHydro, 1912) July 20, 1912 "More Cicero Pilots"; (Chicagology) "Part 2—Aero Club of Illinois"; (Koontz, 2011) p. 47–52; (Moscrop, et al., 2008) p. 26–27; (Lanius, 2016) "Katherine Stinson and the Early Age of Flight in America"

182. (AeroHydro, 1912) July 13, 1912 "Model Meet, Aero Club of Illinois, Cicero Field"; (Young, 2003) p. 81

183. (Young, 2003) p. 76–77

184. (Hill, 2013) p. 213–217

185. (Young, 2003) p. 59, p. 77–78; (Aero, 1912) February 24, 1912 "International Aviation Cup Defender Design"; (Scamehorn, 2000) p. 87–88

186. (Wikipedia); "Gordon Bennett Trophy (Aeroplanes)"

187. (Wikipedia); "Land Speed Record"

188. (Young, 2003) p. 79–81; (Scamehorn, 2000) p. 88–92; (AeroHydro, 1912) September 14, 1912, "Cicero Meet Begins Thursday Afternoon"; (AeroHydro, 1912) September 28, 1912, "First Hydro Aero Meet Is Held Successfully"

189. (Scamehorn, 2000) p. 92

190. (Aerodacious) "US Airport Dedication Covers—Illinois"

191.   (AeroHydro, 1913) April 19, 1913, p. 64 "Ad: Demonstrating and Selling Aeroplanes and Air Boats"
192.   (Wikipedia) "Tiny Broadwick"; (LincBeach, 2013) "1912–Busy, Exciting, Disappointing & Deadly"
193.   (NatAvHOF) "Knabenshue, A. Roy"
194.   (Aerofiles) "Partridge-Keller"; (Scamehorn, 2000) p. 68–69; (Young, 2003) p. 84; 95; (Monash, 2005) Katherine and Marjorie Stinson"
195.   (Yanul) "Lawrence Lewis Aeroplane Co."
196.   (Hill, 2013) p. 288
197.   (LincBeach, 2013) "1913—Flying Boats"
198.   (Wikipedia) "Schneider Trophy"
199.   (Hill, 2013) p. 218; (LincBeach, 2013) "1912–Busy, Exciting, Disappointing & Deadly"; (EarlyAV) "Otto Brodie"
200.   (Tribune, 1913) July 28, 1913, "McCormick Flies in New Airboat"; (Stein, 1985) p. 132
201.   (EarlyAv) "Logan A. "Jack" Vilas 1891–1976"; (Young, 2003) p. 82
202.   (LincBeach, 2013) "1913—Flying Boats"; (AeroHydro, 1913) April 19, 1913 "Seven Entered in Aero and Hydro Cruise"; (Young, 2003) p. 57, 81–82
203.   (Almond, 2002) p. 81; (AYB, 1921) p. 282
204.   (Post, 2000) p. 13–19, 21–27; (Young, 2003) p. 126–127; (LincBeach, 2013) "1913—Flying Boats"; (VintageAirplane, 1976) July 1976, "Silver Eagle: Biography of E.M. "Matty" Laird (part 1)"
205.   (Tribune, 1913) p. 5; "Max Lillie Killed by Fall"; (AeroHydro, 1913) September 20, 1913, "Wing Collapse Blamed for Lillie's Death"; (Scamehorn, 2000) p. 70; (Edwards, 2009) p. 49–50; (Young, 2003) p. 56–57; (EarlyAv) "Max Lillie"; (LincBeach, 2013) "1913—Flying Boats"
206.   (Wikipedia) "Lincoln Highway"
207.   (Jalopnik, 2012) "World's First Multi-Engine Plane Had a Ridiculous Open Balcony"; (Winchester, 2013) p. 48; (Wikipedia) "Sikorsky—Ilya Muromets"
208.   (Blackman, 2017) p. 64–65
209.   (EarlyAv) "George Weaver"; (Post, 2000) p. 121
210.   (Waco_Trib_Herald, 2009) "Pioneer aviators trained WW I pilots at Rich Field"
211.   (Aerofiles) "Waco"; (CentFlight) "WACO Aircraft Corporation"
212.   (NASM) "World's First Scheduled Airline"; (Young, 2003) p. 119; (FAATimL) January 1, 2014
213.   (Bilstein, 1994) p. 26–28
214.   (Roach, 2014) p. 98
215.   (Young, 2003) p. 119; (Chicagology) "Part 3—First Flights Over Chicago" "
216.   (Young, 2003) p. 83
217.   (Chicagology) "Part 3—First Flights Over Chicago"
218.   (Wikipedia) "World War I"; (Swanson, et al., 1997) p. 103
219.   (Wikipedia) "Marjorie Stinson"
220.   (Hargrave) "Katherine (1891–1977) & Marjorie (1896–1975) Stinson"; (ActiveHist_ Canada, 2016) "Marjorie Stinson, the Flying Schoolmarm"; (EarlyAv) "Marjorie Stinson"
221.   (LincBeach, 2013) "1914—Beachey & Royalties"; (Grinnell_Lib) "Story of Billy Robinson"; (EarlyAv) "Billy Robinson 1884–1916"; (IA-HOF) "William 'Billy' C. Robinson, Sr."; (Wikipedia) "Billy Robinson (aviator)"
222.   (ForestPres) "Early History of the Forest Preserve District of Cook County, 1869–1922"
223.   (Winchester, 2013) p. 41, 43

1915–1919

224. (Scamehorn, 2000) p. 53
225. (Flying, 1916) November 1916, p. 406–410; "National Aeroplane Fund Shows Wonderful Accomplishments"
226. (Young, 2003) p. 87
227. (Wikipedia) "Norman Prince"; (Young, 2003) p. 59,78, 87–88
228. (CentFlight) "National Advisory Committee on Aeronautics"
229. (Young, 2003) p. 83; (IndHistS, 1998) "Smash Up Kid: Fort Wayne Aviator Art Smith"
230. (Rockford_Reminisce) "Bert Hassell & The Greater Rockford"; (EarlyAv) "Bert R.J. Hassell"
231. (FSHArchives, 2011) "June 29, 1915—First Aerial Fire Patrol Took Flight"
232. (Somers, 2003) p. 60; (GNAS, 1995) p. 2; (Swanson, et al., 1997) p. 104–105
233. (LincBeach, 2013) "1915—The End Draws Near"; (Young, 2003) p. 83–84; (Chicagology) "Part 2—Aero Club of Illinois"; (Moscrop, et al., 2008) p. 26–27
234. (Young, 2003) p. 84, 95
235. (AerialAgeW, 1915) "Cicero Notes: Chicago Has a Big Week"
236. (Post, 2000) p. 27–33; (VintageAirplane, 1976); July 1976, "Silver Eagle: Biography of E.M. "Matty" Laird (part 1)"
237. (Roach, 2014) p. 169
238. (Bus_Insider, 2015) "First Catapult Launch of a Plane from an Aircraft Carrier Took Place 100 Years Ago Today"
239. (Krist, 2012) p. 98–99; (Poetry, 1914) March 1914, "Chicago by Carl Sandburg"; (Wikipedia) "Carl Sandburg"
240. (Wikipedia) "Amelia Earhart"
241. (AerialAgeW, 1916) "New Interests Paid Curtiss $5,000,000 in Cash"
242. (LincBeach, 2013) "1915—The End Draws Near"; (Young, 2003) p. 83–84
243. (Hill, 2013) p. 288; (Young, 2003) p. 95
244. (LincBeach, 2013) "Obscurity"; (Chicagology) "Part 2—Aero Club of Illinois"; (LincBeach, 2013) "1915—The End Draws Near"; (Young, 2003) p. 83–84
245. (Winchester, 2013) p. 45
246. (Scamehorn, 2000) p. 114–115
247. (Grossman, et al., 2004) p. 561, "Navy Pier {Douglas Bukowski}"; (Blackman, 2017) p. 106–107
248. (WrightBrosUSA) 1916, August 7
249. (Wikipedia) "Norman Prince"
250. (Chicagology) "Part 2—Aero Club of Illinois"
251. (Young, 2003) p. 88–89; (Chicagology) "Part 2—Aero Club of Illinois"
252. (Scamehorn, 2000) p. 99–100; (Young, 2003) p. 105, 108; (Strawfoot, 2016)
253. (Post, 2000) p. 44–45
254. (99s) "Ruth Law—Queen of the Air: Challenging Stereotypes and Inspiring a Nation"; (ThisDayAviation, 2017) "November 19, 1916, Ruth Law Oliver"; (Scamehorn, 2000) p. 100
255. (Post, 2000) p. 38–40; (Moscrop, et al., 2008) p. 26–27
256. (Lewis, 2007) p. 7–31
257. (History) "Russian Revolution"
258. (Scamehorn, 2000) p. 113–114; (Swanson, et al., 1997) p. 108–110
259. (Relevance, 1996) Summer 1996, "US Aircraft Production: Success or Scandal"
260. (Boeing) "Boeing History Chronology: 1917, May 9"
261. (Trimble, 2007) p. 54–60; (Scamehorn, 2000) p. 125–127; (Young, 2003) p. 93

262. (UCLA_LawTech, 2011) Spring 2011, "Progress in the Aircraft Industry and the Role of Patent Pools"
263. (Young, 2003) p. 88–91, 185; (Wikipedia) "Chanute Air Force Base"; (Hill, 2013) p. 285; (Chicagology) "Part 2—Aero Club of Illinois
264. (Almond, 2002) p. 112–113; (Somers, 2003) p. 9
265. (Peek, 2003) p. 6–7, 13–20
266. (Winchester, 2013) p. 49; (Wikipedia) "Airco DH-4"
267. (Daily_Herald, 2018) April 2, 2018, p. 2, "Queen Elizabeth praises Royal Air Force on centenary"
268. (Winchester, 2013) p. 51–52
269. (Young, 2003) p. 91–93; (Hanson, 2011) p. 9; (FirstWW) "Who's Who—Reed Landis"; (Wikipedia) "Reed G. Landis"; (Scamehorn, 2000) p. 199
270. (Winchester, 2013) p. 53
271. (Culver, 1986) p. 24
272. (NYTimes, 1918) May 24, 1918, "Miss Stinson Makes New Flying Record"; (Young, 2003) p. 66
273. (Scamehorn, 2000) p. 103–105; (Young, 2003) p. 108–112; (JAAER, 2014) Winter 2014, "Aircraft Accident Investigation that Never Was"
274. (Smithsonian, 2013) March 07, 2013, "Early History of the Parachute"; (NASM) "Floyd Smith Collection"
275. (Sweeting, 2015) p. 126; (Skydive_Wiki, 2015) "1919: Smith Aerial Life Pack"; (AerialAgeW, 1920) "August 23, 1920, "AD: Floyd Smith Aerial Life Pack Co."; (Smithsonian, 2013) March 07, 2013, "Early History of the Parachute"; (NASM) "Floyd Smith Collection"; (EarlyAv) "James Floyd Smith 1884–1956"; (Google_Patent) "Parachute US 1340423 A"
276. (VintageAirplane, 1976) July 1976; (Post, 2000) p. 46–58
277. (Jackson, 1982) 29–34; (Young, 2003) p. 108–110
278. (Wikipedia) "World War I"
279. (Jackson, 1982) p. 34; (Young, 2003) p. 110; (JAAER, 2014) Winter 2014, "Aircraft Accident Investigation that Never Was"; (PostalMus) "Airmail Creates an Industry: Lipsner vs. Praeger"
280. (LivHistIL) "A Timeline of Illinois History"
281. (IATA) "Founding of IATA"
282. (AYB, 1920) p. 312
283. (Haynes, 1995) p. 1–3
284. (VintageAirplane, 1976) July 1976, "Silver Eagle: Biography of E.M. "Matty" Laird (part 1)"; (Post, 2000) p. 57–63, 116
285. (Krist, 2012) p. 30
286. (Young, 2003) p. 108
287. (Young, 2003) p. 109
288. (AYB, 1921) p. 22–33
289. (Almond, 2002) p. 126–27
290. (Young, 2003) p. 102–103
291. (NWA_Hist, 2012) Summer 2012, "Remembering David L. Behncke"; (Young, 2003) p. 101–103
292. (Young, 2003) p. 17–21, 95, 139–140; (Krist, 2012) p. 2–19; (Edwards, 2003) p. 28–29
293. (Young, 2003) p. 104
294. (Maurer, 1967) p. 25–27
295. (Young, 2003) p. 60
296. (Roach, 2014) p. 173

297. (Aviation, 1922) February 6, 1922; "Registering Civil Aircraft"
298. (Kane, 1996) p. 12–2
299. (Samaruddin, 2002) p. 12–15

1920–1924
300. (AYB, 1921) p. 107, 119, 180–182
301. (Wikipedia) "Eighteenth Amendment to the United States Constitution"
302. (Wikipedia) "Volstead Act"
303. (Kobler, 1993) p. 268; (Swanson, et al., 1997) p. 114–117
304. (Young, 2003) p. 96–97, 101–103; (Jackson, 1982) p. 70f; (AYB, 1921) p. 16 "Commercial Aircraft Operating Companies in the United States and Canada"
305. (AYB, 1921) p. 63
306. (NASA, 2015)
307. (Chicagology) "1920 Taxi Wars"
308. (Winchester, 2013) p. 57
309. (Scamehorn, 2000) p. 196–197
310. (Aviation, 1922) February 6, 1922, p. 159–161, "Registering Civil Aircraft"; (Aviation, 1921) January 3, 1921, p. 20–21; (AYB, 1921) p. 273–275; (VintageAirplane, 1976) July 1976, "Silver Eagle: Biography of E.M. 'Matty' Laird (part 1)"
311. (Koontz, 2011) p. 52–58; (EarlyAv) "Rudolph William Schroeder: 1886–1952"
312. (Young, 2003) p. 101–103
313. (Young, 2003) p. 111
314. (Aeronautics, 1922) August 21, 1922, "Who's Who in American Aeronautics"; (Scamehorn, 2000) p. 137, 172; (Young, 2003) p. 103–104
315. (MALTA) "Bessie Coleman: African American Aviatrix"; (Schultz, et al., 2001) p. 178–180, "Coleman, Bessie"; (Hardesty, 2008) p. 4–17; (Coleman_Official) "Biography of Bessie Coleman"
316. (Winchester, 2013) p. 57
317. (Plumbe, et al., 1922) p. 497
318. (HistWings, 2012) "First Aerial Refueling"
319. (FAAChron, 1926+) January 29, 1929
320. (Young, 2003) p. 113
321. (Scamehorn, 2000) p. 172–173; (Selig, 2013) p. 41–46
322. (Peek, 2003) p. 6–8
323. (Aviation, 1922) January 22, 1922, p. 5; "Aeronautical Chamber of Commerce Organized"
324. (AerialAgeW, 1922) February 20, 1922 p. 560, "Chicago Air Service Reserve Officers Organized"
325. (Kent, 2012) p. 9; (Young, 2003) p. 113; (Scamehorn, 2000) p. 170; (Hill, 2013) p. 220, 285
326. (Scamehorn, 2000) p. 141; (CentFlight) "Metal Plane"
327. (QCOnline, 2012) "Pioneers Saw Future in an Empty Field"; (QCOnline, 2016) "Aviation pioneers paved way for Q-C airport"
328. (Midw_Flyer, 2013) "Quad Cities International Airport ... A Quick Look Back in History"
329. (Franzanobusch) "Wilfred Anthony (Tony) Yackey"; (Wikipedia) "Wilfred Yackey"; (Scamehorn, 2000) p. 170–171; (Young, 2003) p. 103
330. (Wikispaces) "Elmhurst Airport"; (LWReedy) "Elmhurst's Place in Airport History"
331. (Young, 2003) p. 101–103; (Edwards, 2003) 41, 43–45
332. (Wikipedia) "Oakley G Kelly"

333.   (CentFlight) "Aerial Refueling"; (USAFMuseum) "First Air-to-Air Refueling"
334.   (Young, 2003) p. 60–62
335.   (Young, 2003) p. 60–63, 114
336.   (Gordon, 2008) p. 22–23
337.   (Post, 2000) p. 123
338.   (Young, 2003) p. 128–129
339.   (VintageAirplane, 1976) July 1976, "Silver Eagle: Biography of E.M. "Matty" Laird (part 1)"
340.   (Post, 2000) p. 121, 123; (NatWACO_Club) "History of WACO Aircraft"
341.   (Post, 2000) p. 90, 125–129; (Young, 2003) p. 113, 128–131; (Edwards, 2003) p. 74; (Wikipedia) "E.M. Laird Airplane Company"
342.   (Scamehorn, 2000) p. 137, 172; (Young, 2003) p. 103–104
343.   (Tribune, 1993) July 16, 1993, "Airports Wary as Land Takes Off"; (Selig, 2013) p. 92–95
344.   (Post, 2000) p. 90, 125–137, 139–147, 163–166; (Young, 2003) p. 113, 128–131; (Edwards, 2003) p. 74; (Wikipedia) "E.M. Laird Airplane Company"; (Aerofiles) "Laird, Laird-Swallow, Laird-Turner"
345.   (Young, 2003) p. 115
346.   (Aerofiles) "Waco"; (CentFlight) "WACO Aircraft Corporation"; (NatWACO_Club) "History of WACO Aircraft"; (EarlyAv) "George Weaver"; (Post, 2000) p. 130; (Oak_Parker, 1924) August 8, 1924, p. 27, "Number of Atlas employees attended the funeral"
347.   (Glines, et al., 2000); (Post, 2000) p. 130–131; (Wikipedia) "Douglas World Cruisers"

1925–1929

348.   (Scamehorn, 2000) p. 172; (Selig, 2013) p. 76
349.   (Freeman, 2017) "Northern Chicago: Sky Harbor"
350.   (Scamehorn, 2000) p. 172
351.   (Scamehorn, 2000) p. 137, 172; (Young, 2003) p. 103–104; (Selig, 2014) p. 72
352.   (FAAChron, 1926+) February 22, 1925
353.   (Young, 2003) p. 115–116, 123–124; (FAAChron, 1926+) June 3, 1926
354.   (Young, 2003) p. 101–103; (Edwards, 2003) 41, 43–45
355.   (Tribune, 1925) April 4, 1925, p. 1, "Planes to Bring Cargo from Detroit"; (Young, 2003) p. 115; (Hill, 2013) p. 220, 285–286; 394; (Kent, 2012) p. 9; (Scamehorn, 2000) p. 173
356.   (Young, 2003) p. 113–115; (Wikipedia) "Ford Air Transport Service"; (Selig, 2014) p. 54–58, 73
357.   (Garvey, et al., 2002) p. 45; (Scamehorn, 2000) p. 145; (Wikipedia) "National Air Transport"
358.   (Air_Transportation, 1929) *Air Transportation* June 1, 1929 "Col. Paul Henderson, Air Mail's Big Brother"; (Young, 2003) p. 120–121; (Scamehorn, 2000) p. 145
359.   (Wikipedia) "Ford National Reliability Air Tour"; (Forden, et al., 2003)
360.   (AirPigz, 2012) May 7, 2012, "Jimmy Doolittle, the Curtiss R3C-2 and the Schneider Trophy Air Race (1925)"; (Winchester, 2013) p. 61
361.   (Young, 2003) p. 103
362.   (Selig, 2013) p. 125–128; (ElginHist) "Landmarks Gone—The Airport"
363.   (Kane, 1996) p. 5–4; (Young, 2003) p. 116
364.   (NASA, 2016) "Dr. Robert H. Goddard, American Rocketry Pioneer"
365.   (Scamehorn, 2000) p. 140, 144–145; (Edwards, 2003) p. 41–43; (Young, 2003) p. 113

366. (MALTA) "Bessie Coleman: African American Aviatrix"; (Schultz, et al., 2001) p. 178–180, "Coleman, Bessie"; (Hardesty, 2008) p. 4–17

367. (Lynch, 2003) p. 53; (Tribune, 2017) December 17, 2017, p. 1, "Flashback: How Midway Airport took off"

368. (Young, 2003) p. 115; (Hill, 2013) p. 220, 285–286; 394; (Scamehorn, 2000) p. 173; (Swanson, et al., 1997) p. 132

369. (Wikipedia) "National Air Transport"

370. (Air_Transportation, 1929) *Air Transportation* June 1, 1929 "Col. Paul Henderson, Air Mail's Big Brother"; (Young, 2003) p. 122, 162; (Wikipedia) "National Air Transport"

371. (FAAMilestones) "William p. MacCracken, Jr.: America's First Federal Regulator for Aviation"; (Young, 2003) p. 113; (Gordon, 2008) p. 22; (Scamehorn, 2000) p. 238–239

372. (Pal_Ent, 1926) "Pal-Waukee Station Opens June 1st"; (McIntyre, et al., 1987) p. 143–144

373. (Pal_Ent, 1926) "Pal-Waukee Station Opens June 1st"

374. (Young, 2003) p. 62, 103, 120; (Scamehorn, 2000) p. 146; (LincBeach, 2013) "Legacy"; (NWA_Hist, 2012) "Remembering David L. Behncke"; (Aerodacious, 2008) "Contract Air Mail Routes: CAM-9"

375. (Winchester, 2013) p. 61

376. (FAAChron, 1926+) August 11, 1926; (FAAMilestones) "William p. MacCracken, Jr.: America's First Federal Regulator for Aviation"; (AvStop) "Air Commerce Act of 1926"

377. (Peek, 2003) p. 31–46

378. (Pal_Ent, 1926) August 6, 1926, "Air Circus to be Additional Fair Feature"; (CookCty_Herald, 1926) September 3, 1926, "Air Stunts to Feature This Year's Fair" (and) "Races; Stunt Flying; Fireworks—Everything at Exposition"

379. (Jackson, 1982) p. 148

380. (FAAChron, 1926+) December 7, 1926

381. (FAAChron, 1926+) March 22, 1927; (FAAMilestones) "William p. MacCracken, Jr."; (Scamehorn, 2000) p. 139

382. (Gordon, 2008) p. 13–21, 24–25; (Thomas, 1927)

383. (Wallis, 1990)

384. (Young, 2003) p. 62; (Wikipedia) "Charles W. 'Speed' Holman"

385. (Harris, 2014) "Flying the Beam: LF/MF Four-Course Radio Ranges"; (Thelen, 2010) "Low-Frequency Radio Ranges"; (Tails_Time, 2015) "Four-Course Radio Range: Birth of Modern Federal Airway System"

386. (Freeman, 2017) "Northern Chicago: Burris Field / (Original) Waukegan Field"

387. (WhitesideCtyAirp) "History of the Whiteside County Airport"; (WhitesideCtyAirp) "Hall of Fame: Vern Jacoby"

388. (Selig, 2014) p. 17–20; (Scamehorn, 2000) p. 140

389. (Tribune, 1969) "John A. Casey Once Airports Manager, Dies"; (Hill, 2013) p. 347, 384; (Scamehorn, 2000) p. 174; (Edwards, 2003) p. 52

390. (Tribune, 2000) September 3, 2000, "Looking Back at an Aviation Pioneer's Hall-of-Fame Career"

391. (Selig, 2013) p. 51–56; (Selig, 2014) p. 73, 107

392. (Boeing) "Boeing History Chronology: 1927, January 28," "June 30," "July 1"

393. (Wikipedia) "Lansing Municipal Airport"

394. (Peek, 2003) p. 47–62; (Young, 2003) p. 126; (HeathCo, pre-1928) "Parasol—A Safe and Efficient Light Plane at a Price Within Your Reach"; (HeathCo, post-1928) "Reasons Why You Should Buy or Build the Heath Super Parasol"

395. (Peek, 2003) p. 61–65
396. (Peek, 2003) p. 26–30
397. (FAAPeople) "Louis Hopewell Bauer and the First Federal Aviation Medical Examiners"; (AYB, 1930) p. 548
398. (FAAChron, 1926+) March 22, 1927
399. (FAAChron, 1926+) April 6, 1927; (FAAMilestones) "William p. MacCracken, Jr."
400. (Historic_Hotels) "Hilton Chicago"; (Wikipedia) "Hilton Chicago"
401. (Scamehorn, 2000) p. 206
402. (FAAChron, 1926+) June 30, 1927
403. (FAAChron, 1926+) July, 1, 1927
404. (ANG_Hist, 2013) "January 1937," "January 1942"; (Hill, 2013) p. 384–388; (USAF_Units) "108th Air Refueling Squadron"; (Wikipedia) "108th Air Refueling Squadron"
405. (Scamehorn, 2000) p. 148; (FAAChron, 1926+) July, 1, 1927; (Aerodacious) "US Airport Dedication Covers—Illinois"
406. (MWAirmail, 2016) "Ira Biffle—He Also Flew the Mail"; (Hill, 2013) p. 286
407. (NWA_Hist, 2012) Summer 2012, "Remembering David L. Behncke"; (Young, 2003) p. 62, 103; (Scamehorn, 2000) p. 146
408. (Vil_Maches) "Machesney 'Rockford' Airport"; (Scamehorn, 2000) p. 178; (Gen_Winnebago) "Fred Machesney: Proprietor of the Rockford Airport"
409. (Scamehorn, 2000) p. 151; (Young, 2003) p. 162
410. (Gordon, 2008) p. 24–25; (Lynch, 2003) p. 55, 58
411. (Wikipedia) "Quad City International Airport"
412. (Wikipedia) "Long Count Fight"
413. (FAAChron, 1926+) October 10, 1927
414. (Wikipedia) "Wilfred Yackey"; (Scamehorn, 2000) p. 170–171; (Young, 2003) p. 103
415. (Hill, 2013) p. 286; (Young, 2003) p. 116; (Scamehorn, 2000) p. 173; (Lynch, 2003) p. 56; (Tribune, 2017) December 17, 2017, p. 21; "Flashback: How Midway Airport took off"
416. (Freeman, 2016) "Central Chicago: Checkerboard Field / Maywood Airmail Field / Hines Field"
417. (Hill, 2013) p. 286; (Young, 2003) p. 116; (Scamehorn, 2000) p. 173; (Lynch, 2003) p. 56; (Tribune, 2017) December 17, 2017, p. 21; "Flashback: How Midway Airport took off"
418. (Young, 2003) p. 57–58, 180
419. (Scamehorn, 2000) p. 148–149; (CentFlight) "American Airlines"
420. (EngIngenuity) "No. 2438—Phoebie Omlie and her Monocoupe"; (Woman_Pilot, 2008) "Aviation Pioneer Phoebie Fairgrave Omlie"; (Wikipedia) "Phoebie Omlie"; (FAAChron, 1926+) June 30, 1927
421. (McIntyre, et al., 1987) p. 142
422. (Freeman, 2017) "Northern Chicago: Ravenswood Airport"; (CookCty_Herald, 1929) November 19, 1929, "Only Five Local Air Fields O.K.'D"
423. (Edwards, 2003) p. 34; (AYB, 1929) p. 58; (AYB, 1930) p. 271; (AeroDigest, 1930) November 1930, p. 72, "Bellanca 'Blue Streak' Tandem"
424. (AYB, 1930) p. 211
425. (Peek, 2003) p. 11, 39
426. (Young, 2003) p. 119; (Wikipedia) "Stout Air Services"
427. (Scamehorn, 2000) p. 172–173; (Selig, 2013) p. 41
428. (FAAChron, 1926+) January 31, 1928
429. (Time, 1928) January 2, 1928, cover

430. (Tribune, 1931) May 18, 1931, "Speed Holman Killed in Stunt at Air Races"; (NWA_Hist, 2012) Summer 2012, "Remembering David L. Behncke"
431. (Thelen, 2010) "Low-Frequency Radio Ranges"; (Tails_Time, 2015) "Four-Course Radio Range: Birth of Modern Federal Airway System"; (FAAChron, 1926+) 1928; (FAAMilestones) "William p. MacCracken, Jr.: America's First Federal Regulator for Aviation"; (Harris, 2014) "Flying the Beam: LF/MF Four-Course Radio Ranges"
432. (Gordon, 2008) p. 59
433. (FAAChron, 1926+) May 1, 1928
434. (FAAChron, 1926+) May 16, 1928
435. (Scamehorn, 2000) p. 226–229
436. (FAAChron, 1926+) June 30, 1928
437. (FAAChron, 1926+) July 1, 1928
438. (History_Net, 2006) "Bert R.J. 'Fish' Hassell and Parker D. 'Shorty' Cramer: Pilots of a Remarkable Rockford-to-Stockholm Flight"; (Stoff, 2000) p. 50; (Johnson, 2004) p. 69; (FL_Times, 1998) December 6, 1998, "Men Flew Northward to Fame and Fate"; (EarlyAv) "Parker Dresser Cramer"
439. (Wikipedia) "Bill Lear"; (History) "First Day of Work at the Motorola Corporation"; (Hangar1, 2002); (Wikipedia) "8-track tape"
440. (ArlHts_Herald, 1928) November 23, 1928, "Big Airport in Northern Cook County"; (McIntyre, et al., 1987) p. 144
441. (Tribune, 1930) May 20, 1930, "Owen B. Jones, Society Aviator, Sued by Wife"; (Tribune, 1928) March 29, 1928, "Owen Barton Jones Is Recovering From Plane Crash Injuries"
442. (Pal_Ent, 1929) March 22, 1929, "Largest Air Port in the Chicago Dist"; (AYB, 1930) p. 211
443. (PopAviation, 1928) December, 1928, p. 95, "AD: And Now—In Chicago"
444. (456_Interceptor, 2014) "Aviation Corporation (AVCO)"
445. (AYB, 1929) p. 181–187
446. (FAAChron, 1926+) December 12–14, 1928; (Air_Travel, 1929) February, 1926, p. 5–6, "International Civil Aeronautics Conference Called by President Coolidge"; (AYB, 1929) p. 181–187; (NatArcPrologue, 2003) Winter 2003, "International Civil Aeronautics Conference of 1928"
447. (EarlyAv) "History of the Early Birds of Aviation"; (Flying, 1977) September 1977, "Early Birds"; (Wikipedia) "Early Birds of Aviation"
448. (Lynch, 2003) p. 57; (Young, 2003) p. 180–181; (Kent, 2012) p. 12–13
449. (Gordon, 2008) p. 26
450. (CookCty_Herald, 1929) November 19, 1929, "Only Five Local Air Fields O.K.'D"
451. (NRHP, 2013) "Curtiss Wright Aeronautical University Building"; (AviationLofts, 2014) 1338–1340 S Michigan Ave, "Rich History"
452. (Selig, 2013) p. 125–128, (ElginHist) "Landmarks Gone—The Airport"
453. (Wikispaces) "Elmhurst Airport"; (LWReedy) "Elmhurst's Place in Airport History"; (Selig, 2014) p. 7
454. (AYB, 1930) p. 211, 618; (Aeronautics, 1929) p. 44–45, "AD: Danger that Lurks in a Frozen Stick Is Eliminated"; (Pal_Ent, 1929) March 22, 1929, "Largest Air Port in the Chicago Dist"; (ArlHts_Herald, 1928) November 23, 1928, "Big Airport in Northern Cook County"; (CookCty_Herald, 1929) November 19, 1929, "Only Five Local Air Fields O.K.'D"; (CookCty_Herald, 1930) August 5, 1930, "Night Flying Introduced at Pal-Waukee—A New Airport"; (Selig, 2014) p. 98–104; (McIntyre, et al., 1987) p. 144
455. (Aeronautics, 1929) September 1929, "AD: Continued Leadership after 27 Years of Success"

456. (Freeman, 2016) "Central Chicago: Eagle Flying Field / Elmhurst Airport"; (Selig, 2014) p. 8–9; (Elmhurst_Hist, 1999) "Elmhurst Airport"
457. (Air_Transportation, 1929) June 22, 1929, p 22, "Greer School of Aviation Gets Chicago Waco Agency"; (Air_Transportation, 1929) June 15, 1929, p. 81, "Announcing Chicago Aero Sales Corp."
458. (Wikipedia) "Archie League"
459. (FAAMilestones) "William p. MacCracken, Jr.: America's First Federal Regulator for Aviation"
460. (Garvey, et al., 2002) p. 50; (Young, 2003) p. 122–123; (Wikipedia) "United Aircraft and Transport Corporation"
461. (LivHistIL) "A Timeline of Illinois History"; (Swanson, et al., 1997) p. 134–135
462. (CentFlight) "American Airlines"; (456_Interceptor, 2014) "Aviation Corporation"; (Scamehorn, 2000) p. 151–152; (Young, 2003) p. 162
463. (FAAChron, 1926+) June 1929
464. (NRHP, 2013) "Curtiss Wright Aeronautical University Building"
465. (Schwieterman, 2014) p. 244–245; (Selig, 2013) p. 74–78; (Tribune, 1929) June 27, 1929, "Dedicate Sky Harbor, Airport De Luxe"
466. (Tribune, 1929) June 27, 1929, "Dedicate Sky Harbor, Airport De Luxe"; (Freeman, 2017) "Northern Chicago: Sky Harbor Airport"; (Edwards, 2003) p. 59
467. (Freeman, 2017) "Northern Chicago: Sky Harbor"
468. (ForgottenChi) "Forgotten Chicago"
469. (Tribune, 1929) June 27, 1929, "Dedicate Sky Harbor, Airport De Luxe"; (Edwards, 2001) p. 103
470. (CookCty_Herald, 1929) November 19, 1929, "Only Five Local Air Fields O.K.'D"
471. (AYB, 1930) p. 65, 612
472. (Aerofiles) "Fantastically Flighty Gray Goose"; (VintageAir, 2015) "Tin Goose for Gray Goose"
473. (LincBeach, 2013) "1914—Beachey & Royalties"
474. (Tribune, 1929) June 27, 1929, "Aviation Notes"; (Freeman, 2017) "Northern Chicago: Curtiss-Reynolds Field / Glenview NAS / CGAF Chicago"
475. (AYB, 1930) p. 134, 477; (Chicagology) "From Chicago to Berlin and Back in the 'Untin' Bowler"; (US_Air_Services, 1931) September 1931, "Parker Cramer"; (EarlyAv) "Parker Dresser Cramer"
476. (456_Interceptor, 2014) "Aviation Corporation (AVCO)"
477. (Gordon, 2008) p. 31; (FAAChron, 1926+) July 7, 1929
478. (FAAChron, 1926+) June 17, 1929
479. (Air_Transportation, 1929) July 29, 1929, p. 38, "Weekly News Letter: American Air Transport Assn."
480. (Wikipedia) "Curtiss-Wright"
481. (Mashable) "Graf Zeppelin Over Chicago"; (Edwards, 2003) p. 30; (FAAChron, 1926+) August 8–29, 1929
482. (FAAChron, 1926+) September 24, 1929
483. (Gordon, 2008) p. 30
484. (Schwieterman, 2014) p. 244–245
485. (Gordon, 2008) p. 28
486. (Freeman, 2017) "Northern Chicago Area: Curtiss-Reynolds Field / Glenview NAS / CGAF Chicago"; (Schwieterman, 2014) p. 244–245; (Scamehorn, 2000) p. 197–198; (AYB, 1930) p. 211, 217
487. (Gordon, 2008) p. 29, 91–92; (Swanson, et al., 1997) p. 136–137
488. (99s) "Our History"

489. (FAATimL) November 28, 1929
490. (FAATimL) December 2, 1929

1930–1934
491. (FAAChron, 1926+) Calendar year 1930
492. (Young, 2003) p. 119
493. (Lynch, 2003) p. 59
494. (Tribune, 2017) December 17, 2017, "Flashback: How Midway Airport Took Off"
495. (Blackman, 2017) p. 140; (Maguire, 2015) p. 9
496. (Rose_Parrakeet, 2010) "Welcome to the Rose Parrakeet Aeroplane Home Page";
     (Rose_Parrakeet, 2009) "Rose Parrakeet Aeroplane History 1929–Present"; (Rose_
     Parrakeet, 2009) "Jennings W. 'Jack' Rose"; (Rose_Parrakeet, 2009) "Rose
     Aeroplane & Motor Co."; (Rose_Parrakeet, 2009) "Curious History"
497. (FAAChron, 1926+) January 16, 1930
498. (CentFlight) "American Airlines"; (Scamehorn, 2000) p. 151–152
499. (Scamehorn, 2000) p. 178–179; (Johnson, 2004) p. 69–70; (Lewis, 2007) p. 33
500. (FAAChron, 1926+) March 26, 1930
501. (Garvey, et al., 2002) p. 50; (Young, 2003) p. 122–123; (Wikipedia) "National Air
     Transport"
502. (AvStop) "Air Mail Act of 1930"; (Young, 2003) p. 123–125; (FAAChron, 1926+)
     October 1, 1929
503. (Scott, et al., 1998) p. 43–45; (AirSpace, 2010) March 2010, "Other Harlem: In
     1930s Chicago, at the corner of 87th St and Harlem Ave, Cornelius Coffey made
     aviation history"; (Daily_Southtown, 2017) February 10, 2017, "Robbins Gave
     African-Americans Access to the Skies"
504. (Koontz, 2011) p. 115–118
505. (WhitesideCtyAirp) "History of the Whiteside County Airport"; (WhitesideCtyAirp)
     "Hall of Fame: Vern Jacoby"
506. (Garvey, et al., 2002) p. 62–64
507. (FAAChron, 1926+) May 15, 1930
508. (Kent, 2012) p. 15; (Wikipedia) "Stout Air Services"
509. (Young, 2003) p. 119; (Wikipedia) "Stout Air Services"
510. (CookCty_Herald, 1930) July 1, 1930, "Firebug Sets Blaze at the Palwaukee Port";
     (DuPage_Reg, 1930) December 26, 1930, "Quick Blaze Takes Planes and Hangar"
511. (Freeman, 2017) Northwestern Chicago: Elgin Airport; (ElginHist) "Landmarks
     Gone—The Airport"; (Selig, 2013) p. 125–128
512. (DMarfield, 2010) "Hunter Brothers of Sparta Illinois"; (DMarfield, HB) "Hunter
     Brothers: Albert, John, Kenneth and Walter"; (ModMech, 1930) October 1930,
     "Twenty-Three Days in the Air"; (Edwards, 2003) p. 26
513. (Hangar1, 2002); (Scamehorn, 2000) p. 215; (Freeman, 2017) "Northern Chicago
     Area: Curtiss-Reynolds Field / Glenview NAS / CGAF Chicago"
514. (Scamehorn, 2000) p. 217; (Wikipedia) "Thompson Trophy"
515. (FAAChron, 1926+) September 10, 1930; (Aerofiles, 2008) "Taylor, Taylor-Young,
     Taylorcraft"; (Wikipedia) "Taylor Cub"; (Wikipedia) "Taylor J-2"; (Wikipedia) "Piper
     Aircraft"
516. (Young, 2003) p. 62–63
517. (FAAChron, 1926+) October 25, 1930
518. (Scamehorn, 2000) p. 152–153, 225; (FAAChron, 1926+) October 25, 1930
519. (DuPage_Reg, 1930) December 26, 1930, "Quick Blaze Takes Planes and Hangar";
     (Selig, 2014) p. 98

520. (Daily_Southtown, 2017) February 10, 2017, "Robbins Gave African-Americans Access to the Skies"; (Scott, et al., 1998) p. 44–46; (AirSpace, 2010) March, 2010, "Other Harlem: In 1930s Chicago, at the corner of 87th St and Harlem Ave, Cornelius Coffey made aviation history"; (Koontz, 2011) p. 115–118

521. (Daily_Southtown, 2017) February 10, 2017, "Robbins Gave African-Americans Access to the Skies"; (Scott, et al., 1998) p. 44–46; (AirSpace, 2010) March, 2010, "Other Harlem: In 1930s Chicago, at the corner of 87th St and Harlem Ave, Cornelius Coffey made aviation history"; (Koontz, 2011) p. 115–118

522. (Borgeson, 1985) p. 124–125; (Scamehorn, 2000) p. 151–152; (Wikipedia) "Errett Lobban Cord"

523. (Airships, 2013) "Worst Airship Disaster in History: USS Akron"

524. (FAAChron, 1926+) April 29, 1931

525. (Scamehorn, 2000) p. 152–153, 225

526. (Tribune, 1931) May 18, 1931, "Speed Holman Killed in Stunt at Air Races"; (Hill, 2013) p. 343

527. (StanfordDaily, 1931) May 22, 1931, "Airman Thrill Chicago Crowd—600 Planes Participate as Army Stages Review"; (ArlHts_Herald, 1931) May 22, 1931, "Palwaukee Host to 54 Army Planes"

528. (Young, 2003) p. 142–143; (FAAChron, 1926+) March 31, 1931

529. (FAAChron, 1926+) June 23–July 1, 1931

530. (Garvey, et al., 2002) p. 50–52; (Scamehorn, 2000) p. 151

531. (AvGeekery, 2016) "The Early History of ALPA, the Air Line Pilots Association and the First Airline Strike"; (Young, 2003) p. 103; (FAAChron, 1926+) July 27, 1931; (Scamehorn, 2000) p. 151–152

532. (ALPA) "ALPA History"

533. (Young, 2003) p. 91–93

534. (PopScience, 1920) June 1920, "Pig that Came in the Air Mail"

535. (Militarian, 2009) "Reed Landis"

536. (Gardner, 1922) p. 66; (Landis, 1920)

537. (Young, 2003) p. 91–93; (Scamehorn, 2000) p. 201

538. (SunTimesMG, 2018) p. 40; (Swanson, et al., 1997) p. 140

539. (Branigan, 2011) p. 54–57; (Wikipedia) "Edward J. O'Hare"

540. (Connecting_Windy_City, 2016) "November 15, 1931, Chicago Airport"; (Lynch, 2003) p. 69, 78; (Young, 2003) p. 181; (Edwards, 2003) p. 52

541. (Blackman, 2017) p. 24–25

542. (AvGeekery, 2016) "Early History of ALPA, the Air Line Pilots Association and the First Airline Strike"; (Borgeson, 1985) p. 124–129; (Hopkins, 1982) p. 43–53; (Scamehorn, 2000) p. 152

543. (CentFlight) "American Airlines"; (456_Interceptor, 2014) "Aviation Corporation (AVCO)"; (Scamehorn, 2000) p. 151–152; (Young, 2003) p. 162

544. (Koontz, 2011) p. 116

545. (Lynch, 2003) p. 60–62, 80–83, 110

546. (ArlHts_Herald, 1933) March 3, 1933, "To Bring Second 'Blimp' to Airport; To Enlarge Hangar"; (McIntyre, et al., 1987) p. 145

547. (ArlHts_Herald, 1942) June 12, 1942, "Discarded scrap from Blimp hangar goes to Maine high"

548. (Gubert, et al., 2001) p. 91

549. (Freeman, 2017) "Northern Chicago: Greer Airport /Park Ridge Airport / River Road Airport"

550. (IL-HOF-Pgm, 1997) "Harold S. Johnson"; (AirClassics, 1965) August–September 1965, "King of the Fords"; (AirRacingHistory) "Harold Johnson"

551. (Young, 2003) p. 66–67; (Scamehorn, 2000) p. 71; (20C_AvMag) "Edward 'Eddie' Stinson"; (PilotFriend) "Stinson Aircraft"
552. (Post, 2000) p. 39, 54
553. (Young, 2003) p. 114
554. (20C_AvMag) "Edward 'Eddie' Stinson"; (PilotFriend) "Stinson Aircraft"
555. (Winchester, 2013) p. 65
556. (Lynch, 2003) p. 74–75; (Young, 2003) p. 142–145
557. (Scamehorn, 2000) p. 214–215
558. (Lynch, 2003) p. 78
559. (AARegistry) "Janet Bragg, nurse, aviator and businesswoman"; (FlyGirls, 2016) "Janet Harmon Bragg"; (Tribune, 1993) April 13, 1993, "Aviator Janet Harmon Bragg, 86"; (NASM) "Women in Aviation Janet Bragg"
560. (Koontz, 2011) p. 116; (Scott, et al., 1998) p. 45–46; (Hardesty, 2008) p. 34–35; (Hill, 2013) p. 384, 414; (Freeman, 2017) "Western Chicago: Harlem Airport"; (AirSpace, 2010) March, 2010, "Other Harlem: In 1930s Chicago, at the corner of 87th St and Harlem Ave, Cornelius Coffey made aviation history"; (Daily_Southtown, 2017) February 10, 2017, "Robbins Gave African-Americans Access to the Skies"
561. (Selig, 2014) p. 84–87; (Freeman, 2017) "Northern Chicago: Ravenswood Airport"
562. (DacyAirp) "Airport History"; (Harvard_Main, 2010) December 1, 2010, "Dacy Airport soars through history, stays in family"; (NW_Herald, 2007) May 17, 2007, "Founder of Dacy Airport dies after lifetime of flight; (Tribune, 2007) May 18, 2007, "John Dacy 1915–2007: Avid Flier Founded His Own Airport"
563. (Dacy_Airshow) "Dacy Airshows"; (Harvard_Main, 2010) December 1, 2010, "Dacy Airport soars through history, stays in family"
564. (Scamehorn, 2000) p. 172–173; (Selig, 2013) p. 41–46
565. (Young, 2003) p. 163; (Wikipedia) "Boeing 247"; (Ganz, 2012) p. 139
566. (Around_Pattern, 2009) "Not Your Average DC-3"; (Grossman, et al., 2004) p. 124–126, "Century of Progress Exposition"; (Swanson, et al., 1997) p. 146–149
567. (Ganz, 2012) p. 138–140; (Hill, 2013) p. 342
568. (Hill, 2013) p. 346; (Lynch, 2003) p. 69, 78; (Young, 2003) p. 181; (Edwards, 2003) p. 52
569. (Freeman, 2016) "Central Chicago: Meigs Field"; (FriendsofMeigs) "History of Meigs"
570. (AYB, 1929) p. 106
571. (ArlHts_Herald, 1933) March 3, 1933, "To Bring Second 'Blimp' to Airport; To Enlarge Hangar"; (McIntyre, et al., 1987) p. 145
572. (CentProg, 1933) p. 174
573. (Freeman, 2016) "Central Chicago: Meigs Field"; (FriendsofMeigs) "History of Meigs"
574. (ElginHist) "Landmarks Gone—The Airport"; (Selig, 2013) p. 125–128; (Freeman, 2017) Northwestern Chicago: Elgin Airport
575. (Tribune, 1933) June 12, 1933, "Blazing Plane Kills Nine"; (GenDisasters) "Glenview IL—Sightseeing Plane Crash, June 1933"; (Finding, 1995) p. 128
576. (Scamehorn, 2000) p. 218–219; (Hill, 2013) p. 341–343; (Edwards, 2003) p. 36; (Neumann, Circa 1940s, 2011) p. 86; (ForestPres, undated) p. 9
577. (Neumann, Circa 1940s, 2011) p. 86
578. (Selig, 2014) p. 56
579. (Homan, et al., 2001) p. 262
580. (Scamehorn, 2000) p. 218–219; (Hill, 2013) p. 341–343; (Edwards, 2003) p. 36; (Neumann, Circa 1940s, 2011) p. 86; (ForestPres, undated) p. 9

581. (Hill, 2013) p. 342; (Tribune, 1933) July 5, 1933 p. 1, "Hugh Sexton, 120,000 Fans Thrill to Air Race Spectacle"
582. (Tribune, 1933) July 5, 1933 p. 1, "Death Leap Seen by 75,000"
583. (Simanaitas, 2013) August 17, 2013, "Italo Balbo's Chicago Visit"; (CentFlight) "Italo Balbo"
584. (Jyoti, 2008) "Grant Park: Balbo Monument"; (Graf, et al., 2002) p. 15; (Gapers_Block, 2004) April 15, 2004, "Italo Balbo and Chicago's Forgotten Gift from Fascist Italy"
585. (Straipsniai) "Lithuanian Pilots: Steponas Darius and Stasys Giernas"; (Lituanus, 1958) "Two Fliers: Darius and Giernas"; (Albion_MI) "Palwaukee Airport (Illinois) Featured on Lithuanian Banknote"; (Wikipedia) "Lituanica"
586. (Wikipedia) "Wiley Post"; (AcePilots, 2011) "Wiley Post"
587. (Scamehorn, 2000) p. 219–221
588. (Hangar1, 2002)
589. (Scamehorn, 2000) p. 219–221
590. (Wikipedia) "Gordon Bennett Cup (Ballooning)"
591. (NBCChicago, 2013) "80 Years Later, Plane Bombing Remains a Mystery"; (Wikipedia) "1933 United Airlines Boeing 247 mid-air explosion"
592. (Schwieterman, 2014) p. 244–245
593. (Airships) "Graf Zeppelin History"
594. (Airships) "Graf Zeppelin History"; (Schwieterman, 2014) p. 244–245
595. (Gubert, et al., 2001) p. 179–182; (MALTA) "Saga of Willie 'Suicide' Jones"; (EbonyJr, 1982) March 1982, p. 22, "Willie Jones the Wing-Walker"
596. (Young, 2003) p. 124–125, 162, 166–167; (Garvey, et al., 2002) p. 50–58; (Scamehorn, 2000) p. 150–151, 155–156
597. (Young, 2003) p. 124–125, 141, 164; (FAAChron, 1926+) February 9, 1934; (Scamehorn, 2000) p. 154–155; (FAAMilestones) "William p. MacCracken, Jr."; (PostalMus, 2009) "1934 Airmail Scandal"; (Wikipedia) "Air Mail Scandal"
598. (Wikipedia) "C.R. Smith"; (Young, 2003) p. 162–166; (456_Interceptor, 2014)
599. (Young, 2003) p. 162
600. (Young, 2003) p. 125; (Garvey, et al., 2002) p. 55–58
601. (Young, 2003) p. 103
602. (Scott, et al., 1998) p. 46–48; (AirSpace, 2010) March, 2010, "Other Harlem: In 1930s Chicago, at the corner of 87th St and Harlem Ave, Cornelius Coffey made aviation history"
603. (C&S, 1950); (Young, 2003) p. 172–175; (Wikipedia) "Chicago and Southern Air Lines"; (Scamehorn, 2000) p. 157; (Edwards, 2003) p. 62–63
604. (FAAChron, 1926+) June 12, 1934; (AvStop) "Airmail Act of 1934"
605. (Scamehorn, 2000) p. 155
606. (FAAChron, 1926+) July 1, 1934
607. (Daniel, et al., 2000) p. 434; (Wikipedia) "Curtiss T-32 Condor II"
608. (AFMag, 2008) March 2008, "Air Mail Fiasco"; (FAAChron, 1926+) July 18, 1934
609. (Young, 2003) p. 124–125, 162; (Garvey, et al., 2002) p. 50–52; (Scamehorn, 2000) p. 150–151, 155–156
610. (Wikipedia) "Wiley Post"; (AcePilots, 2011) "Wiley Post"
611. (Wikipedia) "Helen Richey"

1935–1939
612. (Pridmore, et al., 2005) p. 146–149; (Shrenk, 2007) p. 159–167; (NPS, 2015) "House of Tomorrow at Indiana Dunes"; (Wikipedia) "Century of Progress Architectural District"

613. (Midw_Flyer, 2013) "Quad Cities International Airport: A Quick Look Back in History"; (Wikipedia) "Quad City International Airport"
614. (Hill, 2013) p. 348, 372; (Wikipedia) "Midway International Airport"
615. (Hill, 2013) p. 332–338
616. (Scott, et al., 1998) p. 49
617. (Beyond_B&W, 2016) February 16, 2016, "Black Women's History: Chicago Airwomen Behind Tuskegee Airmen"
618. (IL_Glory_Days) "Lewis Lockport Holy Name Institute 'Flyers'"; (LewisU) "About Us—History"; (LewisU) "About Us—Timeline"; (Selig, 2014) p. 49
619. (FAAChron, 1926+) January 12–13, 1935
620. (FAAChron, 1926+) February 22, 1935
621. (Scott, et al., 1998) p. 49–55, 64–68; (Wikipedia) "John Robinson (aviator)"; (Hardesty, 2008) p. 31–34
622. (Tucker, 2012)
623. (AirRace) "1935 NAR"; (Geneseo_History) Harold Neumann Exhibit; (Wikipedia) "Bendix Trophy"
624. (Young, 2003) p. 62–63
625. (FAAChron, 1926+) November 12–14, 1935
626. (Around_Pattern, 2009) "Not Your Average DC-3"; (Wikipedia) "Douglas DC-2"
627. (Boeing) "DC-3 Commercial Transport"
628. (Winchester, 2013) p. 66–67, 69; (Young, 2003) p. 131, 164; (Edwards, 2003) p. 65
629. (FAAChron, 1926+) Calendar year 1936
630. (FAAChron, 1926+) January 3, 1936; (A4A) "About Us—History"
631. (Kent, 2012) p. 26
632. (Tribune, 2012) December 9, 2012, "In the 1950s 2 horrific Midway crashes stunned Chicago"; (Tribune, 2017) December 17, 2017, "Flashback: How Midway Airport took off"; (AvSafeNet, 2017) Sunday, 31 May 1936
633. (FAAChron, 1926+) July 6, 1936
634. (FAAChron, 1926+) August 15, 1936
635. (Souter, et al., 2010) p. 37
636. (Scott, et al., 1998) p. 67–70
637. (VintageAirplane, 1974) June 1974, p. 10–14, "Howard Story—Part 1"; (AirRace) "Bendix Trophy"
638. (FAATimL) September 4, 1936; (ThisDay_Aviation, 2017) 4 September 1936
639. (Meigs_Family) "Meigs—The Man Who Loved to Fly"; (Scamehorn, 2000) p. 228, 243; (VintageAirplane, 1974) July 1974, cov, p. 4–12, "Howard Story—Part 2"; (Tribune, 1996) October 20, 1996, "Meigs, the Man Who Loved to Fly"
640. (Selig, 2014) p. 54–58
641. (Tribune, 1946) March 17, 1946, "Disclose Sale of Pal-Waukee Port to Lesee"; (Lakeland_Times, 2009) "Arlene Edgecumbe: Found her home in the skies"
642. (Selig, 2014) p. 84–85
643. (MtProsHerald, 1942) July 3, 1942, "Civilian pilot trng. program outlined by A.C. Tufts"; (MtProsHerald, 1942) "Train army pilots at Pal-Waukee"
644. (Selig, 2013) p. 92–95; (AirRace) "Thompson Trophy"
645. (Wikipedia) "Ben Howard (aviator)"
646. (Scamehorn, 2000) p. 217, 219
647. (VintageAirplane, 1974) June 1974, p. 10–14, "Howard Story—Part 1"
648. (HowardAir) "Howard DGA-8 and DGA-11"
649. (Wikipedia) "Howard Aircraft Corp."
650. (Edwards, 2003) p. 87–96
651. (HowardAir) "Howard DGA-15"

652. (VintageAirplane, 1974) July 1974, cov, p. 4–12, "Howard Story—Part 2"
653. (Hill, 2013) p. 385
654. (Scamehorn, 2000) p. 242–243; (Tribune, 1937) March 2, 1937, "N.U. Professor Named to Head US Air Bureau"; (FAAChron, 1926+) February 28, 1937; (CookCty_ Herald, 1929) November 19, 1929, "Only Five Local Air Fields O.K.'D"
655. (Almond, 2002) p. 17, 196–197; (Wikipedia) "Bombing of Guernica"
656. (Winchester, 2013) p. 69–71
657. (Winchester, 2013) p. 71
658. (GNAS, 1995); (Hangar1, 2002); (Freeman, 2017) "Northern Chicago: Curtiss-Reynolds Field / Glenview NAS / CGAF Chicago"; (Souter, et al., 2010) p. 39–40
659. (FAAChron, 1926+) November 1, 1937
660. (Aerofiles, 2008) "Taylor, Taylor-Young, Taylorcraft"; (Aerofiles, 2008) "Piper"; (Wikipedia) "Taylor J-2"; (Wikipedia) "Piper Aircraft"; (Wikipedia) "Piper J-3 Cub"
661. (WhirlyGirls) "Whirly Girls History"
662. (Koontz, 2011) p. 89–90, 117; (BlackPast) "Brown, Willa B (1906–1992)"
663. (Scott, et al., 1998) p. 68–69, 85
664. (BlackPast) "Coffey, Cornelius R. (1903–1994)"; (Koontz, 2011) p. 89–90, 117; (Launius, 2014) "Willa Brown: Out from the Shadows of Aeronautical History"; (BlackPast) "Brown, Willa B. (1906–1992)"
665. (BlackPast) "Coffey, Cornelius R. (1903–1994)"; (Koontz, 2011) p. 89–90, 115–115; (Launius, 2014) "Willa Brown: Out from the Shadows of Aeronautical History"; (AirSpace, 2010) March 2010, "Other Harlem: In 1930s Chicago, at the corner of 87th St and Harlem Ave, Cornelius Coffey made aviation history"
666. (Hangar1, 2002)
667. (Freeman, 2017) "Northern Chicago: Burris Field / (Original) Waukegan Field"
668. (Winchester, 2013) p. 71
669. (AirSpace, 2008) September 2008, "Flying Success: For an entire week in 1938 the country celebrated air mail"
670. (Scott, et al., 1998) p. 85
671. (CookCty_Herald, 1938) May 20, 1938, "Pony Express Carries Air Letters to Pal-Waukee; Planes Drop Mail for Arlington Race Track"
672. (AirSpace, 2008) September 2008, "Flying Success: For an entire week in 1938, the country celebrated airmail"
673. (FAAChron, 1926+) August 22, 1938
674. (Swanson, et al., 1997) p. 158–159
675. (Young, 2003) p. 162–163
676. (Garvey, et al., 2002) p. 198
677. (Freeman, 2017) "Northern Chicago: Sky Harbor Airport"; (Selig, 2014) p. 102
678. (Lakeland_Times, 2009) "Arlene Edgecumbe: Found her home in the skies"
679. (Selig, 2014) p. 107–112
680. (Selig, 2014) p. 107–112
681. (Winchester, 2013) p. 75, 82–83
682. (Hardesty, 2008) p. 41
683. (Scott, et al., 1998) p. 85
684. (Gubert, et al., 2001) p. 179–182; (MALTA) "Saga of Willie 'Suicide' Jones"; (EbonyJr, 1982) March 1982, "Willie Jones the Wing-Walker"
685. (Lest_We_Forget, 1995) July 1995, "National Airmen Association of America before the Tuskegee Airmen"; (Scott, et al., 1998) p. 91–93; (AirSpace, 2010) March 2010, "Other Harlem: In 1930s Chicago, at the corner of 87th St and Harlem Ave, Cornelius Coffey made aviation history"; (HouseRep) "Representative Arthur Mitchell of Illinois and the Supreme Court"

686. (FAAChron, 1926+) May 15, 1939
687. (FAAChron, 1926+) June 27, 1939
688. (Tribune, 1939) August 21, 1939, "10 Girl Flyers Thrill 20,000 at Aerial Show"
689. (Lest_We_Forget, 1995) July 1995, "National Airmen Association of America before the Tuskegee Airmen"; (AirSpace, 2010) March 2010, "Other Harlem: In 1930s Chicago, at the corner of 87th St and Harlem Ave, Cornelius Coffey made aviation history"; (Scott, et al., 1998) p. 61–64, 68, 91; (Hardesty, 2008) p. 35–39
690. (Winchester, 2013) p. 77
691. (Almond, 2002) p. 17–18
692. (BlackPast) "Brown, Willa B (1906–1992)"; (MALTA) "Willa Brown: Aviatrix"; (Scott, et al., 1998) p. 97–98; (Beyond_B&W, 2016) "Black Women's History: The Chicago Airwomen Behind the Tuskegee Airmen"; (Koontz, 2011) p. 115–118
693. (FlightBlog, 2017) "US President Pilots"
694. (FAAChron, 1926+) December 2, 1939

1940–1944
695. (LivHistIL) "A Timeline of Illinois History"
696. (Young, 2003) p. 160–161
697. (Wikipedia) "Economy Class"; (Young, 2003) p. 167–168
698. (GNAS, 1995); (Hangar1, 2002); (Freeman, 2017) "Northern Chicago: Curtiss-Reynolds Field / Glenview NAS / CGAF Chicago"; (Souter, et al., 2010) p. 39–40
699. (FAATimL) February 23, 1940
700. (Winchester, 2013) p. 79
701. (FAAChron, 1926+) June 30, 1940
702. (Winchester, 2013) p. 79
703. (Winchester, 2013) p. 83
704. (Tribune, 2012) December 9, 2016, "In the 1950s 2 horrific Midway crashes stunned Chicago"; (AvSafeNet) Wednesday, 4 December 1940; (Young, 2003) p. 148, 221; (Kent, 2012) p. 37
705. (Freeman, 2017) "Southern Chicago: Howell Airport (1st Location); (Tribune, 1989) "Airport Owner Takes Flight, Progress Moves In"
706. (Schwieterman, 2014) p. 242–243
707. (ANG_Hist, 2013) "January 1937," "January 1942"; (Hill, 2013) p. 384–388; (Wikipedia) "108th Air Refueling Squadron"
708. (Scott, et al., 1998) p. 150–155; (Wikipedia) "Chanute Air Force Base"
709. (Winchester, 2013) p. 83; (BAE_Sys) "Gloster E.28/39: Britain's first aircraft that demonstrated the potential of Whittle's innovative jet engine design"
710. (FAAChron, 1926+) June 16, 1941
711. (Lynch, 2003) p. 84–92; (Kent, 2012) p. 35–39; (Hill, 2013) p. 347–348, 379; (Tribune, 2017) December 17, 2017, "Flashback: How Midway Airport took off"
712. (Hill, 2013) p. 380
713. (Post, 2000) p. 168; (Young, 2003) p. 128–131; (VintageAirplane, 1976) August 1976, "Silver Eagle: Biography of E.M. "Matty" Laird (part 2)"
714. (Post, 2000) p. 93–94, 167–169
715. (FAAChron, 1926+) November 1, 1941; (Young, 2003) p. 182
716. (Griggs, 2018) "Illinois CAP Timeline" unpublished
717. (FAAChron, 1926+) December 12, 1941
718. (Selig, 2013) p. 11,16, 27–28, 114–115
719. (GNAS, 1995); (Hangar1, 2002); (Freeman, 2017) "Northern Chicago: Curtiss-Reynolds Field / Glenview NAS / CGAF Chicago"; (Souter, et al., 2010) p. 39–40; (Somers, 2003)

720. (Selig, 2014) p. 21–25
721. (LewisU) "About Us—History"; (LewisU) "About Us—Timeline"; (Selig, 2014) p. 49
722. (Historic_Hotels) "Hilton Chicago"; (Hudson, 2004) p. 13; (Wikipedia) "Hilton Chicago"
723. (HowardAir) "Howard DGA-15"; (Wikipedia) "Howard Aircraft Corporation"; (Edwards, 2003) p. 84–85
724. (Watters, 1952) p. 93
725. (VintageAirplane, 1974) July 1974, cov, p. 4–12, "Howard Story—Part 2"; (HowardAir, 1970) "Benny Howard"
726. (ANG_Hist, 2013) "January 1937," "January 1942"; (Hill, 2013) p. 384–388; (Wikipedia) "108th Air Refueling Squadron"
727. (AcePilots, 2011) "Lt. Cdr. Edward 'Butch' O'Hare"; (Branigan, 2011) p. 53–61; (Wikipedia) "Thatch Weave"; (Wikipedia) "Edward O'Hare"
728. (Smithsonian, 2018) January 2018, "Great Los Angeles Air Raid Terrified Citizens—Even Though No Bombs Were Dropped"
729. (Griggs, 2018) "Illinois CAP Timeline" unpublished; (CAP_Gold_Medal, 2014) "Willa Brown"; (Beyond_B&W, 2016) "Black Women's History: Chicago Airwomen Behind Tuskegee Airmen"; (Launius, 2014) "Willa Brown: Out from the Shadows of Aeronautical History"; (NASM) "Cornelius Robinson Coffey"
730. (Connecting_Windy_City, 2012) June 9, 2012, "Chicago: A look back at June 9, 1942"; (Edwards, 2003) p. 54, 81, 86; (Lynch, 2003) p. 92, 106; (Doherty, 1970) p. 27–28, 33
731. (Somers, 2003) p. 39–40, 59–60, 81–83,113–114; (GNAS, 1995); (Hangar1, 2002); (Freeman, 2017) "Northern Chicago: Curtiss-Reynolds Field / Glenview NAS / CGAF Chicago"
732. (Selig, 2013) p. 57–60; (Freeman, 2017) "Southern Chicago: Prosperi Airport"
733. (Freeman, 2017) "Northwestern Chicago Area: Allendale Field / Libertyville NOLF / Libertyville Airport (Vernon Hills, IL)"; (Somers, 2003) p. 81–82; (Selig, 2013) p. 120
734. (Freeman, 2017) "Northwestern Chicago Area: Half Day NOLF / Chicagoland Airport"
735. (FAAChron, 1926+) October 1, 1942
736. (Young, 2003) p. 92; (Swanson, et al., 1997) p. 163
737. (FAAChron, 1926+) December 2, 1942
738. (History_Net, 2006) "Bert R.J. 'Fish' Hassell and Parker D. 'Shorty' Cramer: Pilots of the Remarkable Rockford-to-Stockholm Flight."; (EarlyAv) "Parker Dresser Cramer"
739. (VintageAirplane, 1997) April 1997, p. 17, "The Greater Rockford"
740. (GNAS, 1995); (Hangar1, 2002); (Freeman, 2017) "Northern Chicago: Curtiss-Reynolds Field / Glenview NAS / CGAF Chicago"; (Souter, et al., 2010) p. 39–40
741. (Schwieterman, 2014) p. 244–245
742. (Scamehorn, 2000) p. 178–179
743. (Vil_Maches) "Machesney 'Rockford' Airport"
744. (AARegistry) "Janet Bragg, nurse, aviator and businesswoman"; (FlyGirls, 2016) "Janet Harmon Bragg"; (Tribune, 1993) April 13, 1993, "Aviator Janet Harmon Bragg, 86"
745. (Wikipedia) "Willa Brown"; (Koontz, 2011) 89–92, 117
746. (FAAChron, 1926+) January 11, 1943
747. (Selig, 2014) p. 56; (Rabung, 2009) p. 1–3

748. (Young, 2003) p. 182; (Kent, 2012) p. 41, 45; (Wikipedia) "Accidents and incidents

involving the Consolidated B-24 Liberator"
749. (Flying, 1945) April 1946, p. 26, "War Workers Flying Club"; (Selig, 2013) p. 80–81
750. (GNAS, 1995) p. 12; (Hangar1, 2002); (Somers, 2003) p. 83
751. (FAAChron, 1926+) August 5, 1943
752. (Connecting_Windy_City, 2012) June 9, 2012, "Chicago: A look back at June 9, 1942"; (Edwards, 2003) p. 54, 81, 86; (Lynch, 2003) p. 92, 106; (Young, 2003) p. 92
753. (Selig, 2014) p. 10–14
754. (Watters, 1952) p. 95
755. (Winchester, 2013) p. 89
756. (Winchester, 2013) p. 95; (Almond, 2002) p. 21
757. (Kent, 2012) p. 47; (Tribune, 2012) "Ruth Cavell Van Etten Osgood"
758. (Wikipedia) "V-1 Flying Bomb"
759. (ArlHts_Herald, 1944) July 14, 1944, "Air show Sunday at Pal-Waukee to recruit WACs"
760. (ArlHts_Herald, 1944) July 21, 1944, "$1,500,000 fire at Douglas"
761. (Ros_Reg, 1944) August 11, 1944, "Leaflets from air to open recruit drive"
762. (Winchester, 2013) p. 91
763. (FAAChron, 1926+) October 1944
764. (FAAChron, 1926+) November 1—December 7, 1944; (Gordon, 2008) p. 135; (Young, 2003) p. 182–183
765. (IL_GA) County Airport Act of 1943
766. (Doherty, 1970) p. 48–49; (IL_SupCt, 1944) People ex rel. Greening v. Bartholf et al. (No. 27863)
767. (FAAChron, 1926+) November 28, 1944; (Gordon, 2008) p. 146–147
768. (McIntyre, et al., 1987) p. 145
769. (MtProsHerald, 1944) December 15, 1944, "Santa to arrive by air this Friday afternoon"

1945–1949

770. (Young, 2003) p. 175
771. (McIntyre, et al., 1987) p. 146
772. (Daniel, et al., 2000) p. 588
773. (FAAChron, 1926+) April 19, 1945
774. (Tribune, 1945) June 18, 1945, "Field's To Sell Light Planes, It's Announced"
775. (ANG_Hist, 2013) "January 1937," "January 1942"; (Hill, 2013) p. 384–388; (Wikipedia) "108th Air Refueling Squadron"
776. (Gordon, 2008) p. 134–135
777. (Scamehorn, 2000) p. 160
778. (FAAChron, 1926+) July 28, 1945
779. (Winchester, 2013) p. 95
780. (MtPros_Hearald, 1945) November 2, 1945, "Air Scouts squadrons formed in Mt. Prospect"
781. (Wikipedia) "1945 Japan-Washington Flight"
782. (Gordon, 2008) p. 142
783. (BlackPast) "Brown, Willa B (1906–1992)"
784. (Selig, 2013) p. 51–56, 64–65; (Selig, 2014) p. 73, 107
785. (ElginHist) "Landmarks Gone—The Airport"
786. (Selig, 2013) p. 117–120
787. (Young, 2003) p. 185
788. (Selig, 2013) p. 31–37
789. (Selig, 2014) p. 21–25; (Wikipedia) "Interstate TDR"

790.	(Schwieterman, 2014) p. 242–243
791.	(C&S, 1950); (Young, 2003) p. 172–175; (Wikipedia) "Chicago and Southern Air Lines"; (Scamehorn, 2000) p. 157; (Edwards, 2003) p. 62–63
792.	(Winchester, 2013) p. 99
793.	(Young, 2003) p. 184
794.	(Kent, 2012) p. 42; (Lynch, 2003) p. 106
795.	(FlyRFD, 2006) "Decades Photo Display: 1940s"
796.	(Lewis, 2007) p. 35–37; (Johnson, 2004) p. 71
797.	(FAAChron, 1926+) May 15, 1946
798.	(Airways, 2014) April 7, 2014, "Fascinating History Chicago's O'Hare International Airport: 1920–1960"; (Young, 2003) p. 188–189; (Lynch, 2003) p. 106; (Edwards, 2003) p. 54; (Doherty, 1970) p. 40
799.	(FAAChron, 1926+) April 1946
800.	(Tribune, 1946) March 17, 1946, "Disclose Sale of Pal-Waukee Port to Lesee"
801.	(McIntyre, et al., 1987) p. 146–147
802.	(FAAChron, 1926+) May 8, 1946
803.	(FAAChron, 1926+) May 13, 1946; (Bednarek, 2001) p. 170
804.	(AvSafeNet) Tuesday, 2 July 1940
805.	(Winchester, 2013) p. 99; (ThisDayAviation, 2016) 3 December 1945, "de Havilland DH 100 Sea Vampire Mk. 10"
806.	(FAAChron, 1926+) August 2, 1946
807.	(FAAChron, 1926+) August 15, 1946
808.	(WhitesideCtyAirp) "History of the Whiteside County Airport"; (WhitesideCtyAirp) "Hall of Fame: Kenneth (Kenny) Paul Zimmerman"
809.	(FAAChron, 1926+) Calendar year 1947
810.	(Midw_Flyer, 2013) "Quad Cities International Airport: A Quick Look Back in History"; (Wikipedia) "Quad City International Airport"
811.	(Selig, 2014) p. 10–14
812.	(AmFlyers) "History of American Flyers"; (Selig, 2013) p. 51
813.	(FAAChron, 1926+) April 3, 1947
814.	(FAAChron, 1926+) April 4, 1947
815.	(FAAChron, 1926+) July 25, 1947; (Wikipedia) "National Security Act of 1947"
816.	(CAF_Mag, 2017) Summer 2017, "125 Years of the L"
817.	(Winchester, 2013) p. 99
818.	(FAAChron, 1926+) October 11, 1947
819.	(Winchester, 2013) p. 98–99
820.	(Selig, 2013) p. 61–68
821.	(Spenser, 2009) p. 247; (Winchester, 2013) p. 99
822.	(Winchester, 2013) p. 101; (Spenser, 2009) p. 132
823.	(Wikipedia) "Economy Class"
824.	(Young, 2003) p. 89–91, 185; (Wikipedia) "Chanute Air Force Base"
825.	(Kent, 2012) p. 50
826.	(Selig, 2013) p. 21
827.	(Burke, 1948); (Young, 2003) p. 187–189; (Airways, 2014) April 7, 2014, "Fascinating History Chicago's O'Hare International Airport: 1920–1960"; (Branigan, 2011) p. 52; (NWU-TransLib) "Ralph H. Burke: Early Innovator of Chicago O'Hare International Airport"
828.	(Winchester, 2013) p. 101
829.	(Tribune, 2012) December 9, 2012, "In the 1950s 2 horrific Midway crashes stunned Chicago"
830.	(Young, 2003) p. 151, 221–222; (AvSafeNet) "Wednesday, 10 March 1948"

831. (Connecting_Windy_City, 2016) "March 20, 1948—Cloud Room Opened at Chicago Airport"
832. (Lynch, 2003) p. 124–127; (Gordon, 2008) p. 162; (Kent, 2012) p. 56–57; (Connecting_Windy_City, 2016) "January 18, 1945—Agreement Is Reached on Midway Airport Terminal"
833. (MDWHist) "Midway Airport Audios and Videos"; (Lynch, 2003) p. 130–131
834. (Lynch, 2003) p. 124–129
835. (Lynch, 2012)
836. (FAAChron, 1926+) June 24, 1948; (Wikipedia) "Berlin Blockade"
837. (Cole, 1997) p. 38; (Gubert, et al., 2001) p. 182
838. (NASM) "Wright-Smithsonian Feud" (Wikipedia) "Wright Flyer"
839. (Freeman, 2016) "Central Chicago: Meigs Field"; (FriendsofMeigs) "History of Northerly Island and Meigs"
840. (Tribune, 2015) June 16, 2015, "Gary/Chicago International Airport sputtered for decades, now poised for growth"
841. (Grossman, et al., 2004) "Park Forest"; (Swanson, et al., 1997) p. 166–167
842. (Lynch, 2003) p. 126
843. (Grandstaff, 1997) p. 199; (Tribune, 1949) July 4, 1949, p. 72, "145,000 See Opening of National Air Fair"; (Tribune, 1949) July 4, 1949 p. 3, "145,000 Watch Thrill Jammed Air Force Show"; (Branigan, 2011) p. 62
844. (FAATimL) July 31, 1949
845. (Tribune, 1951) July 12, 1951, "Men Who Fly Helicopter Air Mail in Chicago"; (WorldHist, 2015) "Helicopter Air Services (HAS): United States (1949–1956)"; (Young, 2003) p. 170
846. (Tribune, 1952) November 30, 1952, "People in Jam Cry 'SOS' for an 'Eggbeater'"
847. (Winchester, 2013) p. 101
848. (Kent, 2012) p. 61–62; (AvSafeNet) "Sunday, 18 December 1949, 08:17"

1950–1954
849. (Galt)
850. (Eventful, 2009) "Crystal Lake: Woodstock Tribute Galt Airport 40th Anniversary"
851. (Gonzales, 1995)
852. (Selig, 2013) p. 121–124; (Freeman, 2017) "Southern Chicago: Rubinkam Airport"; (Freeman, 2017) "Northern Chicago: Sky Harbor"
853. (Freeman) Northern Illinois: Starved Rock Airpark; (Selig, 2014) p. 73–74
854. (Tribune, 1997) July 28, 1997 "Moody Puts Aviation on a Religious Plane"; (Selig, 2014) p. 73, 114–118
855. (FAAChron, 1926+) May 9, 1950
856. (FAAChron, 1926+) July 13, 1930
857. (Young, 2003) p. 147, 222
858. (Daniel, et al., 2000) p. 680
859. (Connecting_Windy_City, 2016) "June 30, 1950—The Lake Front Airport Gets a Name"
860. (FlyRFD, 2006) "Decades Photo Display: 1950s & 1960s"
861. (FAAChron, 1926+) October 15, 1950
862. (FAAChron, 1926+) Calendar year 1951
863. (FAAChron, 1926+) Calendar year 1951
864. (ChiHist) "Descriptive inventory for the Aero Club of Illinois records, 1909–1951"; (Scamehorn, 2000) p. 170

865. (Daily_Herald) September 10, 1984, "Pioneer Aviator—Sally Strempel"; (Tribune,

1987) October 7, 1987, "Pioneer Pilot Sally Strempel"; (Selig, 2013) p. 79–82

866. (Tribune, 2012) December 9, 2016, "In the 1950s 2 horrific Midway crashes stunned Chicago"; (AvSafeNet) Thursday, 4 January 1951
867. (Hill, 2013) p. 391–392; (Wikipedia) "108th Air Refueling Squadron"
868. (Winchester, 2013) p. 103
869. (FAAChron, 1926+) May 31, 1951
870. (Schwieterman, 2014) p. 248–249
871. (Tribune, 2012) December 9, 2016, "In the 1950s 2 horrific Midway crashes stunned Chicago"; (AvSafeNet) Sunday, 16 September 1951
872. (FAAChron, 1926+) April 1, 1952
873. (FAAChron, 1926+) July 1, 1952
874. (Winchester, 2013) p. 108–109
875. (WhitesideCtyAirp) "History of the Whiteside County Airport"; (WhitesideCtyAirp) "Hall of Fame: Vern Jacoby"
876. (C&S, 1950); (Young, 2003) p. 172–175; (Wikipedia) "Chicago and Southern Air Lines"
877. (Schwieterman, 2014) p. 213
878. (FAAChron, 1926+) April 10, 1953
879. (Rabung, 2009) p. 13–26
880. (Connecting_Windy_City, 2016) "November 27, 1953—Meigs Loses Its Big Guns"
881. (Swanson, et al., 1997) p. 170–171
882. (Selig, 2013) p. 120
883. (Selig, 2014) p. 10–14; (Morgan, et al., 2010)
884. (Freeman, 2017) "Northwestern Chicago Area: Allendale Field / Libertyville NOLF / Libertyville Airport (Vernon Hills, IL)"; (Somers, 2003) p. 81, (126-ARW, 2008) "History of the 126th Air Refueling Wing"; (Selig, 2013) p. 120
885. (126-ARW, 2008) "History of the 126th Air Refueling Wing"; (126-ARW, 2011) "126th ARW Chronological Wing History"; (Hill, 2013) p. 391–392; (Wikipedia) "108th Air Refueling Squadron"
886. (Tadias, 2015) May 1, 2015, "African American Pilot Col. John Robertson (Brown Condor) to be Honored in Ethiopia"
887. (Winchester, 2013) p. 107
888. (Winchester, 2013) p. 107

1955–1959

889. (Kent, 2012) p. 75
890. (FAAChron, 1926+) Calendar year 1955
891. (Selig, 2013) p. 117–120; (Schwieterman, 2014) p. 240–241
892. (Freeman, 2016) "Central Chicago: Meigs Field"; (FriendsofMeigs) "History of Meigs"
893. (FAAChron, 1926+) February 11, 1955
894. (McDonaldHist) "About Us-History"; (LivHistIL) "A Timeline of Illinois History"; (Swanson, et al., 1997) p. 179
895. (Daniel, et al., 2000) p. 764, 1118; (SunTimesMG, 2018) p. 33; (Swanson, et al., 1997) p, 176–178
896. (WhirlyGirls)
897. (FAAChron, 1926+) May 5, 1955
898. (Rabung, 2009) p. 27–49
899. (Tribune, 1955) June 18, 1955, "22 Killed in Midway Crash: Incoming Plane Clips Sign in Fog and Falls"; (AvSafeNet) Sunday, 17 July 1955; (Kent, 2012) p. 72
900. (FAAChron, 1926+) July 26, 1955

901. (Tribune, 2012) December 9, 2016, "In the 1950s 2 horrific Midway crashes stunned Chicago"; (AvSafeNet) Friday, 5 August 1955
902. (Branigan, 2011) p. 66–67; (Flying, 1956) October, 1956, "Pioneering the Business Air Base: Skymotive"
903. (Branigan, 2011) p. 49–50, 65; (Young, 2003) p. 187–189; (Lynch, 2003) p. 126; (Swanson, et al., 1997) p, 180–181
904. (Kent, 2012) p. 64; (Hill, 2013) p. 396–398
905. (BluesHeaven) "Historic Chess Records"
906. (Wikipedia) "Cessna 172"
907. (Garvey, et al., 2002) p. 198
908. (Daily_Banner, 1956) July 4, 1956, "Commission Sued"
909. (Legal_Info, 1965) "379 U.S. 487 (85 S.Ct. 493, 13 L.Ed.2d 439); Nick JANKOVICH and Paul Jankovich, Co-Partners, doing business as Calumet Aviation Company, Petitioners, v. INDIANA TOLL ROAD COMMISSION"
910. (Freeman, 2017) "Northern Chicago: Burris Field / (Original) Waukegan Field"; (Wikipedia) "Waukegan National Airport"
911. (WhitesideCtyAirp) "History of the Whiteside County Airport"; (WhitesideCtyAirp) "Hall of Fame: Kenneth (Kenny) Paul Zimmerman"
912. (Selig, 2014) p. 31, 59–66, 88–89
913. (DNAInfo, 2016) "How Is Chicago Connected to O'Hare?"; (Grossman, et al., 2004) "O'Hare"
914. (FAAChron, 1926+) June 30, 1956; (Young, 2003) p. 144–145; (Wikipedia) "1956 Grand Canyon mid-air collision"; (Nelson, 2012)
915. (McIntyre, et al., 1987) p. 128
916. (Tribune, 1955) April 30, 1955, Business, p. 5, "Copter Line Is Purchased by Syndicate"; (WorldHist, 2015) "Helicopter Air Services (HAS): United States (1949–1956)"
917. (Young, 2003) p. 171–173; (Branigan, 2011) p. 99
918. (Tribune, 1955) June 21, 1955, p. 22, "Mayor Favors Use of Copters as Taxi Service"
919. (FAAChron, 1926+) August 30, 1956
920. (Tribune, 1956) September 1, 1956, "Noted Harlem Airport Will Close Today"
921. (Freeman, 2016) "Central Chicago: Eagle Flying Field / Elmhurst Airport"; (Selig, 2014) p. 8–9
922. (LWReedy) "Elmhurst's Place in Airport History"
923. (SlideShare, 2014) "Welcome to the Greater Kankakee Airport"
924. (Airport_Data, 2013) "Kankakee Airport (3KK) Information"; (Wikipedia) "Kankakee Airport"
925. (AirNav) "KIKK—Greater Kankakee Airport"
926. (Airport_Data, 2013) "Kankakee Airport (3KK) Information"; (Wikipedia) "Kankakee Airport"
927. (FAAChron, 1926+) July 6, 1957
928. (Kent, 2012) p. 78; (Tribune, 1957) July 14, 1957, p. 1–2, "Midway Field Crews Fight Mire and Water"
929. (FAAChron, 1926+) August 5, 1957
930. (Winchester, 2013) p. 111
931. (FAAChron, 1926+) October 20, 1957
932. (FlyRFD, 2006) "Decades Photo Display: 1960s"; (Wikipedia) "Interstate 90 in Illinois"; (Lewis, 2007) p. 56
933. (Wikipedia) "Frasca International"; (FrascaInt) "History"
934. (FAAChron, 1926+) January 31, 1958
935. (FAAChron, 1926+) June 15, 1958

936.   (Swanson, et al., 1997) p, 184
937.   (Kent, 2012) p. 76
938.   (FAAChron, 1926+) August 23, 1958
939.   (FAAChron, 1926+) October 1, 1958
940.   (FAAChron, 1926+) October 20, 1957
941.   (Winchester, 2013) p. 111–113
942.   (Lewis, 2007) p. 41, 56; (Wikipedia) "Interstate 90 in Illinois"; (EAA) "Notable
       Dates and Milestones"; (EAA) "Early Years"
943.   (Wikipedia) "Alaska"
944.   (Daniel, et al., 2000) p. 822
945.   (Wikipedia) "The Day the Music Died"
946.   (Arrowheads, 1980)
947.   (AvSafeNet) Sunday, 15 March 1959
948.   (FAAChron, 1926+) June 1, 1959
949.   (Tribune, 2015) September 9, 2015, "Queen Elizabeth II's 14-hour visit to Chicago:
       Hour by Hour"
950.   (Souter, et al., 2010) p. 44–47
951.   (Airways, 2014) April 7, 2014, "Fascinating History Chicago's O'Hare International
       Airport: 1920–1960"
952.   (Tribune, 2012) December 9, 2016, "In the 1950s 2 horrific Midway crashes
       stunned Chicago"; (AvSafeNet) Tuesday, 24 November 1959; (Kent, 2012) p. 96
953.   (Young, 2003) p. 189; (Edwards, 2003) p. 53; (Kent, 2012) p. 76

1960–1964

954.   (Swanson, et al., 1997) p. 191
955.   (FAAChron, 1926+) March 15, 1960
956.   (Young, 2003) p. 223; (Wikipedia) "Northwest Orient Flight 710"; (AvSafeNet)
       "Thursday, 17 March 1960, 15:25"
957.   (Wikipedia) "1960 U-2 incident"
958.   (Young, 2003) p. 150–151, 222–223; (Tribune, 1960) July 29, 1960, p. 1–2, "Find
       Copter Lost Rotor, Fell Apart"
959.   (FAAChron, 1926+) September 8, 1960
960.   (CNN) "The day politics and TV changed forever"; (Swanson, et al., 1997) p. 190
961.   (FAAChron, 1926+) October 15, 1960
962.   (Branigan, 2011) p. 71
963.   (Selig, 2013) p. 119; (Wikipedia) "Frank Tallman"
964.   (Young, 2003) p. 203
965.   (Lynch, 2003) p. 160
966.   (FAAChron, 1926+) April 12, 1961
967.   (Rabung, 2009) p. 77–83
968.   (FAAChron, 1926+) May 1, 1961
969.   (Winchester, 2013) p. 113
970.   (Selig, 2014) p. 33; (Wikipedia) "Schaumburg Regional Airport"
971.   (Young, 2003) p. 176–177; (Wikipedia) "Capital Airlines"
972.   (126-ARW, 2008) "History of the 126th Air Refueling Wing"; (126-ARW, 2011)
       "126th ARW Chronological Wing History"; (Hill, 2013) p. 390–393; (Wikipedia)
       "108th Air Refueling Squadron"
973.   (FAAChron, 1926+) August 1961
974.   (Gordon, 2008) p. 209–211
975.   (Branigan, 2011) p. 82
976.   (Young, 2003) p. 151, 223; (Kent, 2012) p. 108–110; (AvSafeNet) "Friday, 1

September 1961, 02:05"

977. (Young, 2003) p. 151, 223; (Tribune, 1961) September 18, 1961, "Last Words to O'Hare: 'No Control'"; (AvSafeNet) "Sunday, 17 September 1961, 08:57"

978. (Young, 2003) p. 171–173; (Tribune, 2017) December 17, 2017, "Flashback: How Midway Airport took off"; (Kent, 2012) p. 97–98

979. (Wikipedia) "Mercury-Atlas 6"

980. (Swanson, et al., 1997) p. 194–195

981. (FAAChron, 1926+) March 23, 1962

982. (Branigan, 2011) p. 129; (Selig, 2014) p. 83–87; (Freeman, 2017) "Northern Chicago: Ravenswood Airport"

983. (Souter, et al., 2010) p. 50

984. (FAAChron, 1926+) October 22, 1962

985. (FAAChron, 1926+) November 17, 1962

986. (Famous_Trials) "Lenny Bruce"; (Comics_Comic, 2014) "Comedians in Courthouses: Getting Cuffed: Lenny Bruce and George Carlin"

987. (FAAChron, 1926+) December 15, 1962

988. (Airways, 2014) April 7, 2014, "Fascinating History Chicago's O'Hare International Airport: 1920–1960"

989. (RochelleAirp) "Rochelle Municipal Airport—Koritz Field"

990. (FAAChron, 1926+) February 9, 1963

991. (Branigan, 2011) p. 85–90; (ChicagoMod, 2012) "'Jet Set' Modern in Chicago: The Rotunda"

992. (Airways, 2014) April 14, 2014, "Fascinating History Chicago's O'Hare International Airport: 1960–2000"; (Tribune, 2013) March 14, 2013, "The Story of the Dedication of O'Hare International Airport: The Story Behind the Pictures"; (Branigan, 2011) p. 90–91

993. (Wikipedia) "Marlon Green"

994. (Winchester, 2013) p. 117

995. (FAAChron, 1926+) October 7, 1963

996. (Daniel, et al., 2000) p. 906–909

997. (Selig, 2014) p. 33; (Wikipedia) "Schaumburg Regional Airport"

998. (FAAChron, 1926+) March 16, 1964

999. (FAAChron, 1926+) April 17, 1964

1000. (FAAChron, 1926+) April 24, 1964

1001. (FAAChron, 1926+) May 19, 1964

1002. (FAAChron, 1926+) June 26, 1964

1003. (SunTimes, 1998) September 11, 1998; (Tribune, 1998) December 19, 1998, "Cockpit crusader Pucinski honored"; (PioneerPrs, 1999) January 21, 1999, "Roman Pucinski earns recognition from FAA"; (Wikipedia) "Roman Pucinski"

1004. (FAAChron, 1926+) July 21, 1964

1005. (Wikipedia) "Gulf of Tonkin Resolution"

1006. (Tribune, 2011) July 31, 2011, "Beatles Invade Chicago"; (Tribune, 2013) May 31, 2013, "Early Years at Chicago's Midway Airport"

1007. (Branigan, 2011) p. 93

1008. (Gordon, 2008) p. 174; (Swanson, et al., 1997) p. 200

1009. (FAAChron, 1926+) October 6, 1964

1010. (Winchester, 2013) p. 119

1011. (FAAChron, 1926+) December 8, 1964

1012. (FAAChron, 1926+) December 10, 1964

1013. (Winchester, 2013) p. 119; (Wikipedia) "Variable-Sweep Wing"

1014. (FAAChron, 1926+) December 31, 1964

1965–1969

1015. (Selig, 2014) p. 49–53
1016. (Freeman, 2017) "Northern Chicago: Burris Field / (Original) Waukegan Field"
1017. (AirSpace, 2008) January 2008, "Out in the Breezy"; (EAA) "1964 Roloff/Unger RLU-1 Breezy"
1018. (Winchester, 2013) p. 121
1019. (Wikisource) "Aircraft Accident Report: United Airlines Flight 389"; (Wikipedia) "United Airlines Flight 389"; (Young, 2003) p. 147; (Heftman, 2018)
1020. (FAAChron, 1926+) November 9, 1965
1021. (Young, 2003) p. 170–173; (Tribune, 2017) December 17, 2017, "Flashback: How Midway Airport took off"; (Kent, 2012) p. 98
1022. (Young, 2003) p. 198–200
1023. (Daily_Herald) September 10, 1984, "Pioneer Aviator—Sally Strempel"; (Tribune, 1987) October 7, 1987, "Pioneer Pilot Sally Strempel"; (Selig, 2013) p. 79–82
1024. (Selig, 2013) p. 57–60; (Freeman, 2017) "Southern Chicago: Prosperi Airport"
1025. (Selig, 2014) p. 17–20; (Scamehorn, 2000) p. 140
1026. (Winchester, 2013) p. 121
1027. (Branigan, 2011) p. 93
1028. (FAAChron, 1926+) September 9, 1966
1029. (Branigan, 2011) p. 93
1030. (FAAChron, 1926+) October 15, 1966
1031. (Tribune, 1997) January 8, 1997, "Little Airport That Could"
1032. (Selig, 2014) p. 49–53
1033. (Swanson, et al., 1997) p. 191
1034. (Alaspa, 2010) p. 69–71; (Wikipedia) "1967 Chicago Blizzard"; (Swanson, et al., 1997) p. 204–205
1035. (FAAChron, 1926+) March 2, 1966; October 15, 1966; January 16, 1967; April 1, 1967
1036. (FAAChron, 1926+) April 9, 1967
1037. (Winchester, 2013) p. 123
1038. (Wheeling_Herald, 1967) May 5, 1967, "Set Pal-Waukee Dedication—6-Story Tower Is Under FAA"
1039. (Wheeling_Herald, 1968) December 13, 1968, "Jet Landings May Be Softer— Guidance Systems May Help Reduce Noise"
1040. (Wikipedia) "Ann Pellegreno"; (Pellegreno, 1971)
1041. (Swanson, et al., 1997) p. 209; (Wikipedia) "Riverview Park (Chicago)"
1042. (FAAChron, 1926+) October 19, 1967
1043. (Freeman, 2017) "Southern Chicago: New Lenox Airport / Howell Airport (2nd Location)"
1044. (Schwieterman, 2014) p. 248–249; (Freeman, 2017) "Northern Chicago: Sky Harbor Airport"
1045. (Rock_Valley) "Aircraft Maintenance Technology"; (Lewis, 2007) p. 92
1046. (Wikipedia) "1968 Special Olympics Summer World Games"; (Wikipedia) "Special Olympics"
1047. (Swanson, et al., 1997) p. 212–215; (SunTimesMG, 2018) p. 36
1048. (Young, 2003) p. 148, 223; (Wikipedia) "North Central Airlines Flight 458"
1049. (Winchester, 2013) p. 125

1050. (Lewis, 2007) p. 48; (RRStar, 2015) February 19, 2015, "Our View: How Rockford Lost EAA Fly-In to Oshkosh"; (EAA) "Notable Dates and Milestones"
1051. (Young, 2003) p. 162, 202

1052. (FAAChron, 1926+) Calendar year 1969
1053. (GNAS, 1995); (Hangar1, 2002); (Freeman, 2017) "Northern Chicago: Curtiss-Reynolds Field / Glenview NAS / CGAF Chicago"; (Schwieterman, 2014) p. 244–245
1054. (Winchester, 2013) p. 125
1055. (Winchester, 2013) p. 125
1056. (Young, 2003) p. 171–173
1057. (Young, 2003) p. 190
1058. (Airways, 2014) April 14, 2014 "Fascinating History Chicago's O'Hare International Airport: 1960–2000"; (FAAChron, 1926+) June 1, 1969; (Young, 2003) p. 190; (Branigan, 2011) p. 93–94, 106
1059. (FAAChron, 1926+) July 20, 1969
1060. (Souter, et al., 2010) p. 66–70
1061. (Tribune, 1969) November 29, 1969, "Chicago Team Entered in Air Race in Britain"; (BobBeagle) "Air Races"
1062. (FAAChron, 1926+) December 4, 1969

1970–1974

1063. (LivHistIL) "A Timeline of Illinois History"
1064. (Winchester, 2013) p. 127
1065. (Vil_Schaumburg) "Airport—Airport History"
1066. (FAAChron, 1926+) May 21, 1970
1067. (FAAChron, 1926+) June 25, 1970
1068. (FAAChron, 1926+) October 28, 1970
1069. (FAAChron, 1926+) December 31, 1970
1070. (Branigan, 2011) p. 104–105
1071. (FAAChron, 1926+) March 1971
1072. (Young, 2003) p. 193; (Branigan, 2011) p. 123–124
1073. (Branigan, 2011) p. 105
1074. (Winchester, 2013) p. 127
1075. (Winchester, 2013) p. 127
1076. (Wikipedia) "Union Stock Yards"
1077. (FAAChron, 1926+) September 9, 1971
1078. (Winchester, 2013) p. 129
1079. (Branigan, 2011) p. 104–105
1080. (BlackPast) "Brown, Willa B. (1906–1992)"
1081. (FAAChron, 1926+) July 1, 1971
1082. (FAAChron, 1926+) March 1972
1083. (Winchester, 2013) p. 129; (Wikipedia) "Airbus A300"
1084. (FAAChron, 1926+) December 5, 1972
1085. (Young, 2003) p. 148–150; (Kent, 2012) p. 116; (AvSafeNet) Friday 8 December 1972; (Wikipedia) "United Airlines Flight 553"; (Tribune, 2012) December 9, 2016, "In the 1950s 2 horrific Midway crashes stunned Chicago"
1086. (Young, 2003) p. 148, 224; (Wikipedia) "1972 Chicago-O'Hare runway collision"
1087. (Selig, 2014) p. 49–53
1088. (FAAChron, 1926+) January 1973
1089. (Schwieterman, 2014) p. 248–249; (Freeman, 2017) "Northern Chicago: Sky Harbor Airport"
1090. (SunTimesMG, 2018) p. 48–52; (WBEZ, 2011) "Long List of Illinois politicians convicted of corruption"
1091. (FAAChron, 1926+) April 1973
1092. (Wikipedia) "Willis Tower"; (Swanson, et al., 1997) p. 220–221
1093. (Daniel, et al., 2000) p. 1069–1075; (Young, 2003) p. 194

1094. (FAAChron, 1926+) November 20, 1973
1095. (Young, 2003) p. 197
1096. (Vil_Maches) "Machesney 'Rockford' Airport"; (Flying, 1961) p. 76, "Ready for Tomorrow"
1097. (Scamehorn, 2000) p. 178–179; (Johnson, 2004) p. 70
1098. (Freeman, 2016) "Central Chicago: Mitchell Field"
1099. (FAAChron, 1926+) January 1, 1974
1100. (Daniel, et al., 2000) p. 1082–1083; (Swanson, et al., 1997) p. 222

1974–1979
1101. (UCLA_LawTech, 2011)
1102. (Grossman, et al., 2004) p. 651, "Prospect Heights, IL"
1103. (Tribune, 1993) July 16, 1993, "Airports Wary as Land Takes Off"
1104. (FAAChron, 1926+) January 21, 1974
1105. (Post, 2000) p. 173
1106. (VintageAirplane, 1976) June 1976, "Uptown Swallow"
1107. (VintageAirplane, 1976) June 1976, "Uptown Swallow"; (Post, 2000) p. 173–176; (Selig, 2013) p. 13–16; (NW_Herald, 2016) "Obituary: Elroy Edward Hilbert"
1108. (BurbankBeat, 2014) "Midway Mishaps: A Brief History of Area Plane Crashes"; (Tribune, 2012) December 9, 2016, "In the 1950s 2 horirfic Midway crashes stunned Chicago"; (WarbirdReg) "B-25 Mitchell / 44–30737"
1109. (FAAChron, 1926+) October 15, 1976
1110. (ChiPubLib) "Mayor Richard J. Daley Biography"; (Wikipedia) "Richard J. Daley"
1111. (Tribune, 2015) June 16, 2015, "Gary/Chicago International Airport sputtered for decades, now poised for growth"
1112. (NatAvHOF) "Our Enshrinees—Bessie Coleman"
1113. (SunTimesMG, 2018) p. 12
1114. (Young, 2003) p. 193–194
1115. (Winchester, 2013) p. 133
1116. (Wikipedia) "Naval Air Station Glenview"
1117. (Wikipedia) "Avro Vulcan"; (AvSafeNet) "11 Aug 1978"
1118. (Flying, 1979) February 1979, "Airport Closed: Tax Collectors Are Stealing Away Some of Our Best Airports"; (Young, 2003) p. 195; (Selig, 2013) p. 120
1119. (AvWeek, 2015) "Law That Changed Airline Industry Beyond Recognition (1978)"; (AWST, 1978) November 6, 1978, "Airlines Move to Meet Regulatory Shifts"; (FAAChron, 1926+) October 24, 1978; (Gordon, 2008) p. 222, 245–247; (Branigan, 2011) p. 107; (Young, 2003) p. 204; (Wikipedia) "Airline Deregulation Act"
1120. (Post, 2000) p. 112. 176
1121. (Tribune, 2008) November 30, 2008, "30th anniversary of Chicago's worst winter on record: 1978–1979"
1122. (Branigan, 2011) p. 125; (Wikipedia) "1979 Chicago Blizzard"
1123. (ChiPubLib) "Mayor Jane Byrne Biography"; (Swanson, et al., 1997) p. 229
1124. (Young, 2003) p. 151–152, 224; (FAAChron, 1926+) May 25, 1979; (Wikipedia) "American Airlines Flight 191"; (Swanson, et al., 1997) p. 230–231
1125. (SunTimesMG, 2018) p. 38; (Swanson, et al., 1997) p. 233
1126. (Young, 2003) p. 207–209; (Wikipedia) "Midway Airlines (1976–1991)"; (FundUniv) "Midway Airlines Corporation History"; (FAAChron, 1926+) November 1, 1979

1980–1984
1127. (Freeman, 2016) "Central Chicago: Meigs Field"
1128. (BlackPast) "Coffey, Cornelius R. (1903–1994); (Hill, 2013) p. 414; (Koontz, 2011)

p. 118; (AARegistry) "Cornelius Coffey Pioneered Aviation"
1129. (Flying, 1951) December 1951, "Operators Sell Flying"
1130. (FrascaInt) "History"; (Wikipedia) "Frasca International"; (Wikipedia) "Frasca Field"
1131. (Freeman, 2016) "Central Chicago: Meigs Field"; (FriendsofMeigs) "History of Meigs"; (Young, 2003) p. 194–195; (Edwards, 2003) p. 60
1132. (FAA_GANews, 1981) November-December 1981, "Waterfront Airports: Lessons to be learned from Meigs Field"
1133. (FAAChron, 1926+) May 18, 1980
1134. (SunTimesMG, 2018) p. 27
1135. (FAAChron, 1926+) August 3, 1981; (Branigan, 2011) p. 132; (Young, 2003) p. 194; (Wikipedia) "Professional Air Traffic Controllers Organization (1968)"
1136. (Kent, 2012) p. 98
1137. (Branigan, 2011) p. 107–108; (Airways, 2014) April 14, 2014, "Fascinating History Chicago's O'Hare International Airport: 1960–2000"
1138. (Young, 2003) p. 224; (Tribune, 1982) "David Young & Henry Wood: Military jet crashes near suburb"
1139. (FAAChron, 1926+) July 2, 1982
1140. (FAAChron, 1926+) September 3, 1982
1141. (FAAChron, 1926+) September 30, 1982
1142. (Daniel, et al., 2000) p. 1219; (Swanson, et al., 1997) p. 236–237, 248
1143. (FAAChron, 1926+) May 1, 1983
1144. (FAAChron, 1926+) May 23, 1983
1145. (FAAChron, 1926+) October 11, 1983; (Wikipedia) "Air Illinois"
1146. (ElginHist) "Landmarks Gone—The Airport"
1147. (FAAChron, 1926+) December 21, 1983; (Wikipedia) "IBM 9020"
1148. (Young, 2003) p. 194; (ChicagoL) "Blue Line"
1149. (FAAChron, 1926+) December 1, 1984
1150. (FAAChron, 1926+) December 31, 1984

1985–1989

1151. (ChiDeptAv) "O'Hare History"; (TimeOut, 2009) December 1, 2009, "Why is there no terminal 4 at O'Hare Airport"
1152. (FAAChron, 1926+) February 8, 1985
1153. (Lewis, 2007) p. 98–99; (FlyRFD, 2006) "Decades Photo Display: 1980s"
1154. (SunTimesMG, 2018) p. 58; (Swanson, et al., 1997) p. 244–245; (Daniel, et al., 2000) p. 1274
1155. (FAAChron, 1926+) January 1, 1928
1156. (LivHistIL) "A Timeline of Illinois History"; (Blackman, 2017) p. 66–67
1157. (FAAChron, 1926+) December 14–23, 1986
1158. (Daily_Herald, 1987) January 3, 1987, "Wheeling, Prospect Heights fete purchase of Pal-Waukee"
1159. (Airways, 2014) April 14, 2014, "Fascinating History Chicago's O'Hare International Airport: 1960–2000"; (Gordon, 2008) p. 253
1160. (Young, 2003) p. 202–206; (Garvey, et al., 2002) p. 207–212
1161. (UPI, 1987) May 21, 1987, "Lindbergh's Historic Flight Commemorated"; (EAA) "Spirit of St. Louis Replica"
1162. (Souter, et al., 2010) p. 103–105, 109–111
1163. (FlyRFD, 2006) "Decades Photo Display: 1970s & 1980s"; (Lewis, 2007) p. 50–53
1164. (FAAChron, 1926+) February 8, 1988
1165. (FAAChron, 1926+) April 23, 1988

1166. (Winchester, 2013) p. 145
1167. (FAAChron, 1926+) May 8, 1988
1168. (FAAChron, 1926+) June 14, 1988
1169. (History_Net, 2006) "Bert R.J. 'Fish' Hassell and Parker D. 'Shorty' Cramer: Pilots of the Remarkable Rockford-to-Stockholm Flight."
1170. (VintageAirplane, 1997) April 1997, p. 17, "The Greater Rockford"; (History_Net, 2006) "Bert R.J. "Fish" Hassell and Parker D. "Shorty" Cramer: Pilots of the Remarkable Rockford-to-Stockholm Flight"; (Flying, 1970) November 1970, p. 52, "Return of the Rockford"
1171. (ProAirshow) "Airshow Announcer Herb Hunter"; (Souter, et al., 2010) p. 13–14
1172. (Swanson, et al., 1997) p. 249
1173. (Daniel, et al., 2000) p. 1317
1174. (FAAChron, 1926+) October 3, 1988
1175. (FAAChron, 1926+) December 21, 1988
1176. (FAAChron, 1926+) December 27, 1988
1177. (Wikipedia) "Samuel K. Skinner"; (M_Monaco, 2018)
1178. (Lewis, 2007) p. 94–97
1179. (Swanson, et al., 1997) p. 250–251; (Wikipedia) "Richard M. Daley"
1180. (Freeman, 2017) "Southern Chicago: Howell Airport (1st Location); (Tribune, 1989) "Airport Owner Takes Flight, Progress Moves In"
1181. (Freeman, 2017) "Southern Chicago: New Lenox Airport / Howell Airport (2nd Location); (Tribune, 1989) "Airport Owner Takes Flight, Progress Moves In"
1182. (Tribune, 1993) July 16, 1993, "Airports Wary as Land Takes Off"
1183. (FAAChron, 1926+) June 7, 1989
1184. (FAAChron, 1926+) August 31, 1989

1990–1994

1185. (Young, 2003) p. 197
1186. (FAAChron, 1926+) March 6, 1990
1187. (Swanson, et al., 1997) p. 253
1188. (Lewis, 2007) p. 94–97
1189. (MHUGL, 2016); (RochelleAirp) "Rochelle Municipal Airport—Koritz Field"
1190. (Lakeland_Times, 2009) "Arlene Edgecumbe: Found her home in the skies"; (Wikipedia) "American Eagle A-129"
1191. (Young, 2003) p. 207–209; (Wikipedia) "Midway Airlines (1976–1991)"; (FundUniv) "Midway Airlines Corporation History"
1192. (Daniel, et al., 2000) p. 1375
1193. (Alaspa, 2010) p. 72–77; (Swanson, et al., 1997) p. 256–257
1194. (Kent, 2012) p. 121; (Waymarking, 2011) "Battle of Midway-50 Years"
1195. (Freeman, 2016) "Central Chicago: Meigs Field"
1196. (Airways, 2014) April 14, 2014 "Fascinating History Chicago's O'Hare International Airport: 1960–2000"
1197. (Selig, 2014) p. 21–25
1198. (FAAChron, 1926+) July 2, 1993
1199. (WarbirdAlley, 2015) "Octave Chanute Aerospace Museum: A Final Look"
1200. (Young, 2003) p. 89–91, 185; (Wikipedia) "Chanute Air Force Base"
1201. (AirNav) "KTIP: Rantoul National Aviation Center Airport—Frank Elliott Field"
1202. (ChicagoL) "CTA Reinvents Itself: The 'L' Heads Into the 21st Century"; (Wikipedia) "Orange Line (CTA)"
1203. (FundUniv) "Midway Airlines Corporation History"; (RuudLeeuw) "Airlines Remembered: Midway Airlines 2"; (Wikipedia) "Midway Airlines (1993–2003)"
1204. (Wikipedia) "North American Free Trade Agreement"

1205. (Daniel, et al., 2000) p. 1401
1206. (Lewis, 2007) p. 94–97
1207. (Vil_Schaumburg) "Airport—Airport History"
1208. (FAAChron, 1926+) January 17, 1994
1209. (Young, 2003) p. 202–206; (Garvey, et al., 2002) p. 207–212; (FAAChron, 1926+) July 12, 1994
1210. (AvSafeNet) "Monday 31 October 1994"; (Young, 2003) p. 148, 224; (Wikipedia) "American Eagle Flight 4184"

1995–1999
1211. (Tribune, 2015) June 16, 2015, "Gary/Chicago International Airport sputtered for decades, now poised for growth"
1212. (Winchester, 2013) p. 149
1213. (GNAS, 1995); (Hangar1, 2002); (Freeman, 2017) "Northern Chicago: Curtiss-Reynolds Field / Glenview NAS / CGAF Chicago"; (Schwieterman, 2014) p. 244–245
1214. (NIPSTA) "NIPSTA Campus Map"
1215. (FAAChron, 1926+) September 30, 1996
1216. (AvSafeNet) Wednesday 30 October 1996; (Tribune, 1996) October 31, 1996, "4 Are Killed in Palwaukee Jet Crash"; (Tribune, 2003) September 9, 2003, "Litigation ends in 1996 Palwaukee Municipal Airport crash that killed 4 people"
1217. (Young, 2003) p. 215; (UAL) "Star Alliance Air Travel Rewards"
1218. (FAAChron, 1997+) February 6, 1997
1219. (Lynch, 2003) p. 183–189; (Av_Week, 1997) July 1, 1997, "Signature Acquires Monarch Air Service at Midway"
1220. (FAAChron, 1997+) August 1, 1997
1221. (Freeman, 2016) "Central Chicago: Meigs Field"; (FriendsofMeigs) "History of Meigs"; (Young, 2003) p. 194–195; (Edwards, 2003) p. 60
1222. (Grossman, et al., 2004) "Bulls"; (Swanson, et al., 1997) p. 262–265
1223. (EarlyAv) "History of the Early Birds of Aviation"
1224. (SilvWings-IL, 2017) "Silver Wings Greets Fall with a 'Bange'"
1225. (Hill, 2013) p. 390–393; (Wikipedia) "108th Air Refueling Squadron"

2000–2004
1226. (Selig, 2013) p. 74–78
1227. (FAAChron, 1997+) December 31, 1999, January 1, 2000
1228. (FAAChron, 1997+) June 02, 2000
1229. (Guardian, 2000) June 27, 2000, "Skydiver proves Da Vinci chute works"
1230. (Wikipedia) "Air France Flight 4590"
1231. (Winchester, 2013) p. 151
1232. (Lynch, 2003) p. 172, 178–179; (ChiDeptAv) "Midway History"; (Wikipedia) "Midway International Airport"
1233. (PandoraArc, 2001) "London to Sydney Air Race Entrants"; (Samaruddin, 2002) p. 12–13, 18–23
1234. (Samaruddin, 2002) p. 264–273
1235. (Samaruddin, 2002) p. 26–179
1236. (Samaruddin, 2002) p. 179–185
1237. (Samaruddin, 2002) p. 204–259
1238. (Young, 2003) p. 218; (Lynch, 2003) p. 172
1239. (Pioneer_Prs, 2001) August 30, 2001, "Priester sells Palwaukee operation"; (Daily_Herald, 2001) August 17, 2001, "Florida company to buy Palwaukee aviation firm"

1240. (Lynch, 2003) p. 172
1241. (FAAChron, 1997+) September 27, 2001
1242. (Wikipedia) "Aviation Transportation and Security Act"; (Wikipedia) "Transportation Security Administration"
1243. (Schwieterman, 2014) p. 214–215; (Tribune, 2015) June 16, 2015, "Gary/Chicago International Airport sputtered for decades, now poised for growth"
1244. (Young, 2003) p. 209–214
1245. (Balloon_Britain) "First Successful Around the World Solo Attempt"; (Wikipedia) "Steve Fossett"
1246. (NBC, 2006) "United Airlines finally flies out of bankruptcy"; (USA_Today, 2006) "Timeline of United Airlines' Bankruptcy"; (Young, 2003) p. 215–216
1247. (Young, 2003)
1248. (Lynch, 2003)
1249. (Winchester, 2013) p. 153
1250. (Freeman, 2016) "Central Chicago: Meigs Field"; (FriendsofMeigs) "History of Meigs"
1251. (NYTimes, 2003) April 1, 2003, "Chicago Mayor Bulldozes a Small Downtown Airport"; (Freeman, 2016) "Central Chicago: Meigs Field"; (FriendsofMeigs) "History of Meigs"; (Young, 2003) p. 194–195; (Edwards, 2003) p. 60
1252. (FAAChron, 1997+) July 31, 2003
1253. (AvFoundAm) "National Air Tour 2003"
1254. (Edwards, 2003) p. 107–126; (Wright_Redux, 2001) "Wright Redux Association"; (Tribune, 2002) June 18, 2002, "Wright airplane replication plane takes off"
1255. (WHF) "Foundation Staff"
1256. (Souter, et al., 2010) p. 26–30; (Wikipedia) "Clow International Airport"
1257. (FAAChron, 1997+) January 21, 2004
1258. (FAAChron, 1997+) January 27 2004
1259. (MDWHist) "Midway Airport Audios and Videos"; (MDWHist) "Welcome to Midway Airport"
1260. (FAAChron, 1997+) April 1, 2004
1261. (Blackman, 2017) p. 72–73; (Wikipedia) "Millennium Park"
1262. (FAAChron, 1997+) September 1, 2004; (FirstLanding) "Why Fly Sport: A History of the Sport Pilot Rating"; (EAA) "Light Sport Aircraft"

2005–2009

1263. (FAAChron, 1997+) February 2, 2005; (AvBusinessJour, 2011) 4th Quarter 2011, "Falsification: A Deadly Sin"; (NJer, 2010) "Platinum Jet charter pilot pleads guilty to illegal flights following Teterboro Airport crash scrutiny"; (Kaieteur, 2011) "Luxury Jet Crash in US … Brassington Brothers Jailed"
1264. (FAAChron, 1997+) August 29, 2005
1265. (SunTimesMG, 2018) p. 56
1266. (Kent, 2012) p. 124; (AvSafeNet) Thursday, 8 December 2005; (Wikipedia) "Southwest Airlines Flight 1248"; (FAALearned) "Southwest Airlines Flight 1248"
1267. (AeroNews, 2006) "EMAS System Installed at Chicago's Midway"; (FAAFact, 2017) "Engineered Material Arresting System (EMAS)"; (Airport_Council, November 18–19, 2008) "Developments in Technology Arrestor Beds—EMASMAX"
1268. (PioneerePrs, 2006) April 6, 2006 "New terminal serves Palwaukee workers"
1269. (Freeman, 2017) "Southern Chicago: New Lenox Airport / Howell Airport (2nd Location)
1270. (AirportJour, 2006) "Chicago Executive Airport—Big Changes for a Growing Airport"
1271. (Tribune, 2014) July 1, 2014 "State acquires Will County airfield in step toward new large airport"

1272. (Wikipedia) "Chicago Rockford International Airport"
1273. (NW_Herald, 2007) May 17, 2007, "Founder of Dacy Airport dies after lifetime of flight"; (Tribune, 2007) May 18, 2007, "John Dacy 1915–2007: Avid Flier Founded His Own Airport"
1274. (Harvard_Main, 2011) November 2, 2011, "Stunt Pilot Dave Dacy Still Thrills After 25 Years"; (Dacy_Airshow) "Dacy/Kazian Wingwalking"
1275. (Dacy_Airshow) "Phil Dacy—Airshow Announcer"
1276. (Tribune, 1999) October 10, 1999, "Just Plane Folks: The Dacy Family Is At Home in the Air"; (Daily_Herald, 2016) August 19, 2016, "Suburban pilot ready to soar at Chicago Air and Water Show"; (Dacy_Airshow) "Susan Dacy—'Big Red' "; (Harvard_Main, 2010) December 1, 2010, "Dacy Airport soars through history, stays in family"
1277. (Levinson, 2018) June 14, 2018, Interview by author
1278. (FAAChron, 1997+) June 16, 2008
1279. (AvSafeNet, 2017) 19-Jul-2008
1280. (FAAChron, 1997+) January 15, 2009
1281. (Wikipedia) "First Inauguration of Barack Obama"

2010–2014
1282. (SunTimesMG, 2018) p. 55
1283. (Wikipedia) "History of United Airlines"
1284. (FAAChron, 1997+) February 25, 2011
1285. (DefMediaNet, 2011) June 17, 2011, "B-17 Crash Highlights the Debate Over Flying Warbirds"
1286. (Meetup-NEPilots, 2012) May 18, 2012, "Restoring the Liberty Belle B-17"
1287. (FAAChron, 1997+) December 01, 2011
1288. (FAAChron, 1997+) April 30, 2011
1289. (FAAChron, 1997+) May 22, 2012
1290. (FAAChron, 1997+) June 18, 2012 June 7, 1989
1291. (Selig, 2013); (Selig, 2014)
1292. (GaltSale) "Galt Airport Sale"; (NW_Herald, 2013) August 15, 2014, "New owners, same feel for Galt Airport"; (ILDeptAero, 2014) May 14, 2014; "Illinois Airports Recognized by IDOT's Division of Aeronautics for Outstanding Service"
1293. (Wikipedia) "United States Budget Sequestration in 2013"
1294. (Blaze, 2013) March 14, 2013, "Another Day, Another Claim By Scientists That They've Found the 'God Particle' (Again)"
1295. (FAAChron, 1997+) June 6, 2013
1296. (Tribune, 2013) July 23, 2013, "United completes HQ move into Willis Tower"
1297. (FAAChron, 1997+) August 22, 2013
1298. (FAAChron, 1997+) October 17, 2013; October 15, 2015
1299. (USA_Today, 2013) October 25, 2013, "DOT hits United with record fine for long tarmac delays"; (FAAChron, 1997+) October 25, 2013
1300. (RunwaySafe)
1301. (FAAChron, 1997+) April 30, 2014
1302. (FAAChron, 1997+) May 13, 2014
1303. (Tribune, 2014) July 1, 2014, "State acquires Will County airfield in step toward new large airport"
1304. (BultField)
1305. (FAAChron, 1997+) September 24, 2014

2015–2018

1306. (Tribune, 2015) August 17, 2015, "Army parachutist dies after Chicago Air & Water Show accident"; (CNN, 2015) August 17, 2015, "Army skydiver dies after airshow accident"

1307. (Ford_Cty_Record, 2015) April 23, 2015, "Chanute Air Museum closing in Rantoul"; (Chambanamoms, 2015) "Chanute Air Museum Closing Its Doors"

1308. (DOT) "United Fined for Violating Airline Disability and Tarmac Delay Rules"; (Reuters, 2016) January 7, 2016, "United Air fined $2.75 million over treatment of disabled, tarmac delays"

1309. (AINOnline, 2016) "EMAS Saves Falcon 20 at Chicago Executive"

1310. (NWQtr, 2013) "Youngest Naval Aviator of WWII"; (RRStar, 2016) February 21, 2016, "Chuck Downey, youngest WWII naval pilot and Poplar Grove resident, dies"; (RRStar, 2016) February 28, 2016, "Charles Downey 1924–2016"

1311. (AOPA, 2017) August 28, 2017, "AOPA Files Official Complaints Over FBO Fees"; (AOPA, 2017) December 8, 2017, "FAA Issues Guidance on FBO Pricing"

1312. (QCOnline, 2017) November 6, 2017, "Geneseo couple pilots their own plane in trip around the world"

1313. (Reuters, 2018) March 28, 2018, "Chicago O'Hare $8.5 billion expansion plan approved by city council"; (ABC7_Chicago, 2018) March 28, 2018, "Chicago City Council approved $8.5B O'Hare expansion plan"; (Crains_Chi, 2018) March 9, 2018, "See details of the O'Hare expansion plan"; (ChiDeptAv, 2018) March 28, 2018, "Mayor Emmanuel and Airline Sign Historic $8.5 Billion Agreement"

1314. (Tribune, 2018) June 14, 2018, "Chicago Taps Elon Musk's The Boring Company"; (Citylab, 2018) June 15, 2018, "Craziest Thing About Elon Musk's 'Express Loop' Is the Price"; (CurbedChi, 2018) June 14, 2018, "Elon Musk's Boring Company Wins Contract to Build O'Hare Express"

1315. (Crains, 2018) July 27, 2018, "Take a look at the sleek new food court at Midway Airport"

INDEX

Associated Flying Club of America (AFCA),
192, 203, 217
astronauts/cosmonauts, 238, 244, 251,
256, 277, 299
Atlanta GA, 55, 115, 134, 266
Atlanta Hartsfield Airport, 257
Atlantic City NJ, 289
Atlas Educational Film Co., 87
Atwood, Harry, 33
Auburn IN, 174
Auburn MA, 92
Auditorium Building, 69
Aurora Airport (original), 100, 249
Aurora Aviation Co., 100
Aurora IL, 314
Aurora Municipal Airport, 249, 310
Austria-Hungary, 53, 63
autogyro, 122, 149, 172
Aviation and Transportation Security
Act, 297
aviation charts
airway strip map, 104
aviation class for women, 23
Aviation Corp. of Delaware (AVCO), 115,
121, 128, 140, 141, 154
Aviation Country Club, 119, 121, 173
Aviation Medical Examiner (AME), 103
aviation publications
Aerial Age, viii, 37
Aero and Hydro, 42
Airman's Guide, 202
*Airmen's/Aeronautical Information
Manual (AIM)*, 246
Business Future of Aviation, 139
*Chicago Aviation—An Illustrated
History*, ix
*Chicago's Midway Airport—First
Seventy-Five Years*, vi, ix, 299
Chirp, 116
Domestic Air News, 111
European Skyway, 98
Federal Aviation Regulations (FAR), 246
First Lessons in Aeronautics, viii, 16,
20, 23
Forgotten Chicago Airfields, ix, 121, 311
Jane's All the World's Aircraft, 16
Journal of Air Law, 169
Lost Airports of Chicago, ix, 311
*Master Plan of the Chicago Orchard
(Douglas) Airport*, 208
One Zero Charlie, 214
Popular Aviation, 102
*Proceedings of the Third International
Conference on Aerial Navigation*, 7

Progress on Flying Machines, 7, 25
Railroad and Engineering Journal,
5, 7
Statistical Handbook of Civil Aviation,
194
Vehicles of the Air, viii, 17, 23
We Are Going In, 229
World Flight—The Earhart Trail, 252
Aviation Training Enterprises, 205
Avondale Field, 31
Avro Canada aircraft
CF-105 Arrow, 234

B

B&M Aircraft, 228
Badger, William "Billy," 33
Bahrain, 265
Baker Commission, 156
Balaban, John, 179
Balbo, Italo, xi, 150
Baldwin aircraft, 33
Baldwin, Thomas Scott, 19
Balling, Charles, 109
balloons, 11, 27, 30, 274, 298
First International Aerial Race, 15
in Chicago, 2, 14
military, 3
Montgolfier, 1
World's Columbian Exposition, 6
Ballough, Ervin, 87, 99, 162
Baltimore MD, 45, 179
Bange, Jackie, 294
Barchard, Frank and Pete, 94, 95, 97,
114, 115
Barnes, Thomas, 266
barnstormers, viii, 27, 71, 80, 89, 94, 101,
106, 142
Bartlett, Robert, 159
Bass, Arthur, 286
Bates Aero Motor Co., 16
Bates, Carl S., 16, 38, 42
Battle of Midway, 211, 287
Bauer, Louis Hopewell, 103
Bauhaus School of Design, 172
Bazaar, KS, 137
Beachey, Lincoln, 15, 32, 33, 37, 45, 52,
56, 58
Beatles, 245, 246, 249
Beatty, George, 34
Beech aircraft
Model 35 Bonanza (V-tail), 233, 234
Model 65-90 King Air, 245

G

Stay in Touch

I trust you enjoyed reading *Aviation Chicago Timeline* and discovered many fascinating facts about aviation throughout Northern Illinois.

But wait! There's more!!
There are many other events that aren't included in this book. *That's where you come in.* My guess is that this isn't the first thing you've read on the subject and probably won't be the last.

You may already know, or may soon uncover, events that would be perfect in this book. Let me know about them. Go to the web page **aviation-chicago.com/timeline** to share your information, either with credit or anonymously.

Here is some of the information we're seeking:
- Corrections to the text if you find errors.
- Events of significance that aren't included.
- Elaborations on existing entries describing other people involved or interactions with other events.
- Additional details for existing entries such as full dates, specific locations or individuals involved.
- Resources including books and online sites pertaining to the subject that you think should be included.

Given the nature of book production, your additions may not be included right away. However, they will be acknowledged and included on the web site. Check it regularly to keep up with the latest information.

May your skies be blue and turbulence-free.

Aviation Chicago Timeline

Want More?

This book is available wherever you choose to shop. Bookstores and libraries may not have it in stock, but are able to order it. Likewise, be sure to check online sellers including Amazon.com and barnesandnoble.com.

You can also order it directly from **Aviation Chicago Press**. As a *bonus*, if you order directly from our site, you can have your books personalized. To order from the site, go to: **Aviation-Chicago.com/timeline/order**

You can also order by copying or scanning this form and sending it by mail to the address below, or email to: **orders@aviation-chicago.com**.

Quan.	Item	Price	Total
	Aviation Chicago Timeline (hardcover)	49.95	
	Aviation Chicago Timeline (softcover)	24.95	
	(Specify personalizations below.)	SubTotal	
		Tax 10%	
		TOTAL	

Shipping	
Name	
Street or PO Address	
Phone	
Address 2	
(Please print clearly.)	CITY STATE ZIP

Payment	
Credit Card Number	
Credit Card Info	
(Please print clearly.)	EX. DATE CVV ZIP

EMail: orders@aviation-chicago.com

Mail to: Aviation Chicago • 119 S. Emerson; Unit #272
Mt. Prospect, IL 60056

MICHAEL HAUPT